MEMOIRS

of the

Comte Alexandre de Tilly

MEMOIRS

OF THE

Comte Alexandre de Tilly

TRANSLATED BY

FRANÇOISE DELISLE

WITH AN INTRODUCTION BY

Havelock Ellis

WILDSIDE PRESS

MEMOIRS

of the

Comte Alexandre de Tilly

" *Y OU* will be surprised at the big packet I am sending with
this," wrote Stendhal on August 14, 1828, to his friend
in London, Sutton Sharpe, in a letter signed on this occasion,
with his love of pseudonyms, "William Crocodile"; "don't be
afraid. It is the most amusing book that has appeared in France
for a year past, the 'Mémoires de Tilly.' Tilly was the handsomest man of his time; he blew his brain out in 1812,[1] in
Brussels, to punish himself for having been robbed at play.
He had many women: nothing surprising in that. *But he loved
them.* That is why his book is so little in fashion at the mansions
in the suburbs of Paris. Unfortunately so handsome a man did
not know how to write and yet prided himself on being a man
of letters. He moralises and generalises on all occasions. By
reducing the three volumes to one we should have a delicious
book. I have written an article on Tilly, the first I have done
for eighteen months. But an English friend who translates my
articles fears to spoil his reputation by writing about such a
libertine book as Tilly's. Can you give my article to some literary journal in England? If you cannot, send it to Mr. Col-
bourne with the letter I enclose. If you could find an intelligent
publisher who has the same esteem that I have for this work,
which will have a great reputation in a year or two, I would
abridge the original and send it to him, arranged to form two
charming little octavo volumes."

One would be glad to find the article on Tilly's Memoirs
which Stendhal sent over to London. I have searched the maga-
zines with which he was in touch, the "Athenaeum" and "Col-
bourne's," but I have found no trace. Stendhal himself makes
no further reference to it in the later extant letters to Sutton
Sharpe and other English friends. Stendhal knew England and
was in touch with the literary world of London, where indeed
his genius was discovered half a century before it was clearly
discerned in France, and almost the first documented biography

---

[1] The correct date is 1816. See page 56.

of him was written by Paton, in 1874. It is but too probable, however, that English publishers shared the opinion of the English friend who refused to translate an article about such a libertine as Tilly.

Even in France Stendhal's prophecy of the swiftly approaching reputation of Tilly's Memoirs was not fulfilled. I happen to have known them myself for over thirty years, but they still seem to be among the least read and least commented memoirs of a century which is now so eagerly and so sympathetically studied. Barrière put an abridged version into his well-known series of eighteenth-century French memoirs, and Iwan Bloch, the scholarly and versatile sexologist, reprinted the early German edition. But until to-day Stendhal's desire to bring out an English edition has remained unfulfilled. It is a great satisfaction to me to be able to commemorate the centenary of that proposal, and the first publication of the work, by securing this English translation. It is true that neither I nor the translator has ventured to follow Stendhal's scheme of abridgment. We judge, indeed, that the English reader will prefer to have the book whole and select for himself the episodes which are "delicious."

Not only have the Memoirs of Tilly been neglected, but such attention as they have received has mostly been of an ambiguous kind. Tilly has been termed the typical roué of the eighteenth century, the embodiment in real life of Laclos's Valmont, and, since for a century and more after its publication "Les Liaisons Dangereuses" was vituperated and denounced, being only of recent years recognized for the great and significant achievement of art it is, this was not the way to draw favorable attention to the personality of Tilly. It may be noted that the comparison was not quite correct; unlike Valmont, Tilly was, as Jacques Morland has remarked, "a sentimental roué," who had fallen under the influence of Rousseau and was by his friends considered "romantic."

More than that: attacks were made on the authenticity of the Memoirs. To me it seems that careful reading alone furnishes sufficient evidence that they must be genuine. Indeed, a writer who possessed the skill and the knowledge to fake them would too obviously have here been wasting his talents. Many faked memoirs have been produced, most of them easy to see through, and few of them of any interest apart from their assumed authorship, for it is scarcely necessary to point out that faked memoirs are put forth as the work of people conspicuous in the public eye and not as of persons so little known generally as Tilly. Yet the frivolity with which some would-be acute critics have denied the authenticity of genuine memoirs remains astonishing. Lacroix, as is well known, attributed Casanova's memoirs to Stendhal. Maurice Tourneux in a work of repute, "Bibliographie de l'histoire de Paris pendant la Révolution," states that the authenticity of Tilly's Memoirs is "anything but certain." He adds, without giving the slightest evidence for the statement, that a part of the Memoirs would be due to Alphonse de Beauchamp, and his work would be finished by Auguste Coué, who was the author with Dittmer of the "Soirées de Neuilly," four plays published under the name of "M. de Fongeray." The climax to these reckless and random attributions is furnished by Dubosc, who suggested in " L'Intermédiaire des Checheurs" in 1918 that "M. de Fongeray" may well be Stendhal, since the portrait of him in the Soirées might easily be a caricature of Stendhal! Certainly it is a fine compliment to Stendhal that the Memoirs both of Casanova and of Tilly, so fine in their different kind yet so unlike, should each have been attributed to him. I may add, since I have examined the copy of the book in the British Museum (neglected and uncut for over a century), that there is no ground for saying that the sketch of "M. de Fongeray" resembles Stendhal.

It is scarcely necessary to show that Beauchamp and Coué, even if they could have secured the facts which we know to be accurately recorded in the Memoirs, give no evidence of possessing the qualities necessary to invent their varied and dramatic episodes; they showed nothing of that "certain impertinent grace" which, the historian Du Bled remarks, gives to these Memoirs so strange a savour and is at the same time so much in the tone of the real Tilly. Beauchamp had in 1824 (the year before Tilly's Memoirs first appeared in German) put forward, as anonymous editor, "Mémoires de Fouché," which led to an action in the law-courts and the declaration that they were not genuine. But Beauchamp wrote here of what he knew, and it is believed that he was working on real documents and notes of Fouché's. He was a writer of some ability, but his interests were in war and politics and police administration, while Coué was an insignificant collaborator in comedies of which we know little or nothing. It seems a fantastic notion that they possessed the inclination or the skill to write fictitious memoirs of Tilly—whose world was alien to them—for translation into German. Merely

to take the interviews narrated in the Memoirs with Laclos and
Restif de la Bretonne: to-day, with our present knowledge, we
regard the account of these meetings as absolutely convincing.
But in the early nineteenth century, when both Laclos and Restif
were neglected and contemned, it would have demanded the
insight of genius to invent them. It is difficult to guess what
motive they could possibly have had to expend so much skill,
if they really possessed it, in constructing the imaginary experiences of an undistinguished aristocrat of the court of Louis XVI,
who had died obscurely abroad by suicide, made no mark, and
long been forgotten. There seemed nothing for them to gain,
and it is not easy to see that they gained anything.

The further objection has been brought against the authen-
Nothing was heard of the Memoirs until they appeared in
1825, translated into German, in Berlin, which is where we
might expect them to appear since we know that Tilly had long
been settled in Berlin, there forming many relationships, but, it
seems, compelled to depart suddenly in 1807, leaving his papers
behind.

The further objection has been brought against the authenticity of the Memoirs that they reveal qualities not shown by
the earlier unquestioned volume by Tilly, the "Œuvres mêlées,"
mostly written in youth before the Revolution. This little volume
consists miscellaneously of verse and prose, *jeux d'esprit,* poetic
epistles, essays, and letters, of little or no importance, but all
fairly adequate to their usually trifling impulse and object, sufficiently vigorous in those of later date when the Revolution furnished motives of contempt or indignation. Tilly was here not less
skilful in writing than the Memoirs show him to be, for it may
be remarked that the Memoirs, with sentences that are awk-
wardly constructed and sometimes unduly prolonged, while excellently written for their purpose, do not reveal a master of
style. It is the vivacity and spontaneity of the narrative that
constitute its quality and its charm, so far as the personality
of the author is concerned. Beyond this, the Memoirs possess
a real impersonal value, independently of their authorship, as
a picture of the typical life of French aristocratic society of the
eighteenth century at its last expiring moment before the Revolution, for Tilly reveals, as Du Bled points out, "the germs of
an historian." This picture is all the more interesting because
at this distance of time we can often see deeper into the life
it presents than was possible for Tilly who moved on its surface,
and often failed to realise its real significance.

Even when we are convinced of the authenticity of the Memoirs it still has to be admitted that, outside them, Tilly remains a puzzling, mysterious, elusive figure. From his birth to his death the records we are entitled to expect we fail to find, and so remain in doubt. Of aristocratic family, occupying a place at court befitting his rank, and after his expulsion from France at the Revolution known in England and America and Germany, surrounded by friends, some of them distinguished, adored by women, of singularly attractive appearance and commonly known as "le beau Tilly," he seems to have left little mark, so far as easily accessible records extend, and we even search in vain for his portrait. By an unkind fate, such notices of him as we can discover are often unfavorable, even in a grossly calumnious degree, while his friends, though they seem to have been attached to him, left little record of their attachment.

To the Prince de Ligne, the most aristocratic and distinguished of these friends, he dedicated his Memoirs. They were in fairly close touch at the time Tilly wrote, and the Prince was enthusiastic over the Memoirs. He was a most acute, impartial, and unprejudiced observer, and his personal impressions whether of kings and emperors or of men of letters and art—Voltaire, Rousseau, Beaumarchais, Casanova, and the rest—are among the most illuminating we possess. We would gladly have his impressions of Tilly, whom he seems to have found so fascinating, but so far as I have searched he nowhere sets them down. There was, we divine, an element of instability in Tilly's temperament, a tendency to live in the present, shown even in the reckless generosity which helped to plunge him into debts and difficulties, and after 1792 a restless vagabondage was not incompatible with his constant longing to return to Paris. It is only thus, so far as I can see, that we may explain Tilly's abandonment of the manuscript of the Memoirs, with his correspondence and other papers, in Berlin when he fled from that city in 1807, though he lived for some nine years longer.

[II]

The doubts and obscurities enwrapping Tilly began, as I have said, at his birth, and even before. Concerning his family varying statements have been made. They were ancient and noble, belonging to Normandy and having their original château near Caen, but settled at Le Mans in Maine in the early eighteenth century. They seem to have claimed descent from an Umfroy, Sieur de Tilly, who accompanied William the Conqueror to England and became, it is said, castellan of Hastings. The Count Tilly famous in German history as a great soldier belonged to Tilly in Brabant, and is sometimes said to have been of the same family; he was in nearly all respects extremely unlike the Tilly we are here concerned with. There were various branches of the family. Our Tilly belonged to the Tilly-Prémarest branch, but a certain doubt surrounds this branch because, the author of the Memoirs tells us, his ancestors had failed to secure the proper registration of their titles of nobility. It was perhaps for this reason that another branch, that of Tilly-Blaru, which had become separate in the Middle Ages, refused to recognize the Tilly-Prémarest branch. There was even a duel over this dispute between our Count Alexander Tilly and Count Charles de Tilly-Blaru which, however, was followed by an amicable relationship. But another member of Charles's family, the Abbé de Tilly-Blaru, a pedantic genealogist, would admit no relationship with the "young intriguer," as he called Alexander.

Tilly's father was Jacques, Marquis (sometimes described as Chevalier) de Tilly, of the Royal Garde du Corps, and later senechal d'épée, or grand bailiff, of Beaumont-le-Vicomte in Maine. It may be noted that there were still ladies of the name of Tilly living at Le Mans under the Second Empire. The Chevalier de Tilly had married, as his first wife, in 1760, a noble lady of Le Mans, Anne-Suzanne Magdeleine le Bourdais de Chassillé; fifteen months later she died, a few days after giving birth to that worthless son—as so many have considered him—our hero, Jacques-Pierre Alexandre Comte de Tilly (though there is no exact agreement as to his baptismal names) generally known as Alexandre de Tilly. As the obscurities that hover over Tilly begin so early we are not surprised to learn that his act of baptism has not been found in the registers of Le Mans, but there now seems no doubt that he was born in the parish of the Crucifix on the 9th of August, 1761. For his childhood and youth we must rely on the Memoirs.

The most memorable period of Tilly's life is indeed his boyhood. It is as "a page of Marie Antoinette" that he is most usually referred to, and that period also, as he himself admits, before he had been spoilt by society and the world, was the time he looked back on with most satisfaction. Doubts have been raised even here. It is said that only young noblemen of unimpeachably high rank could be enrolled among the queen's twelve pages, and that Tilly's ancestry was open to doubt. It seems, however, to be ascertained that Tilly was really on the list of the queen's pages. His name is not mentioned by the Comte d'Hézecques, who was one of the royal pages, but he only arrived after Tilly had left, and was, moreover, one of the pages of the king's chamber, who were distinct from the queen's pages. It so happened that in the very same year, 1804, when Tilly was writing his Memoirs, d'Hézecques was writing his own reminiscences of the court, "Souvenirs d'un page," though they were not published until 1876 and then at once translated into English. d'Hézecques' book has nothing of the dashing brilliancy of Tilly's; he was an estimable man, who fought under the new banner of France when the revolutionary storms were passed and died in respectable old age. But he gives an interesting picture of Louis XVI's court with its rigid etiquette, and he describes the life of the royal pages.

So far as I have discovered, we first hear definitely of Tilly from an outside source when he was twenty-four. There was in those days a certain reverend father, Nepveu de la Manouillère, a canon of Le Mans cathedral, who kept a private chronicle in which he entered local events of the day, and set down frankly his opinion, sometimes highly unfavourable, of the most prominent people of the city and its neighbourhood. These Memoirs remained unknown until they were edited by the Abbé Esnault in 1877. They alone seem to demonstrate the authenticity of Tilly's Memoirs for they show that the writer of that work was familiar with the social life of Le Mans to a degree which would hardly be possible to an outsider half a century later. The canon knew all about the Tilly family, and held them (at all events on the male side) in low esteem. Under date March 15, 1785, he refers to our Tilly as "très mauvais sujet," and in prison for debt. On the following April 3, he records the death of Mme. de Chassillé, and continues: "M. de Tilly, aged twenty-four, who is quite mad [qui est un fou], has already been imprisoned for debt and is so still, but will shortly be released." It was a debt of 3,000 livres, we learn, long owing to M. de Saint-Victor and about to be paid by Mme. de Chassillé, who was rich, and left her property (34,000 livres) to be equally

divided between her three grandchildren, of whom Tilly was
one. Tilly himself avoids mentioning this imprisonment (and
his narrative, written many years later, cannot always be reconciled with the dates in the canon's contemporary chronicle)
though he acknowledges his recklessness in piling up debts.

"His father," the canon continues, "M. de Tilly, a widower,
and seneschal of Beaumont, from which office he deserves to
be driven out, is not worth much more and even less." I note,
however, that in 1782, M. de Tilly, I am not sure whether
it was the father or the son, was among sixty-six guests he invited to a great banquet; the canon enumerates the attractive
dishes at great length, and mentions that there was dancing till
three in the morning. The private judgments of the ecclesiastical
chronicler are harsh and unqualified, but it cannot be said that
they are seriously out of harmony with Tilly's own account of
himself and of his father. We need not, however, agree with
the opinion of Tilly's Memoirs added by Father Esnault in a
footnote, that "it is impossible for even the most benevolent
critic not to regret their publication." The canon has no more
to say about the Tilly family, but somewhat later (in April,
1786) he describes the sudden death of the Marquise de Broc.
She was, it appears, a woman of great beauty, grace, charm,
leading the gay social life of her time, and only twenty-eight
years of age. There was a report that she had been poisoned,
Father Esnault tells us, and it was noted that she died a few
hours after leaving a ball at which she had been offered refresh-
ments by "the Comte de T——." The calumnious suspicion was
absurd, apart from the fact that a post-mortem examination
showed that death was due to abdominal hæmorrhage, doubtless the result of pathological conditions. But it serves to show
that young Tilly's wild life was so notorious that some people
at Le Mans thought him capable of anything. Tilly himself,
it will be seen, writes at length of Madame de Broc, acknowledging that he was her lover, and giving an account of the
circumstances of her death which may well have been unknown
to the public.

That his usual avocations were innocent enough, however
frivolous, we may gather from the little volume in verse and
prose of "Œuvres mêlées du Comte Alexandre de Tilly," which
at this very period he had lately published in Paris and Amster-
dam. I have not been able to see this first edition, but I am
acquainted with the second much enlarged edition which Tilly

put forth in Berlin and Paris some twenty years later; and except for one or two pieces of fierce political invective the tone and character of the later issue remain fairly uniform. A modern critic has spoken of the mediocrity of this book when compared with the Memoirs so sparkling with wit. But I see no more contrast in this respect than we might anticipate. When writing the Memoirs Tilly found in the varied adventures of his own life the stimulus he needed to bring out his best literary qualities. In the earlier book he is simply concerned to play his part in the world of polite *belles-lettres* where the men of rank and leisure, French and English alike, commonly amused their more refined hours. If Tilly cannot here rival the wit and brilliance of Voltaire, or even many a lesser writer, he displays a characteristically spontaneous ease and skill fully adequate to the slight occasions which usually called forth such exercises.

The second edition of the "Œuvres mêlées" is preceded by an interesting dedicatory epistle to "Madame la comtesse d'An——," evidently Madame d'Angeviller, whom he introduces into the Memoirs. He says here, as a little later he also said in his Memoirs, that it was she who first encouraged him to cultivate poetry and letters. Tilly's association with Madame d'Angeviller (or Angivillers as it is sometimes spelt) was entirely to his credit. She was the wife of the inspector of royal buildings, the man to whom we owe the transformation of the Louvre into a gallery of pictures and sculpture, and he is said to have won her only after a courtship of twenty years. She is described by the Duc de Lévis as a rather grotesque figure, extremely small, and with nothing beautiful about her but her long hair. But beneath a rather ridiculous exterior, the duke tells us, she had a fine spirit, high intelligence, and an equably amiable temper. She united wit, animation, and sound judgement, so that one never grew tired of hearing her talk. "Nearly all the people who formed her social group," Lévis adds, "were persons of distinguished intelligence." At the Revolution her husband, who was a devoted royalist, fled from France, but she was favourable to the Revolution and remained behind. It seems hardly tactful on Tilly's part to dedicate this volume to Madame d'Angeviller, for his own fiercely anti-revolutionary sentiments come out strongly in many of his references to what he calls "the shame of our history and the scourge of humanity." Such invectives are scattered among poems to charming and aristocratic

ladies, written in the light, playful, and accomplished way which
a *bel esprit* of the age prided himself in achieving. There are
verses addressed to noblemen who were his friends; in one of
special interest, "To My Best Friend"—whom it may not be too
hazardous to assume to be himself—he deplores the friend's too
licentious life and resolves that he himself will renounce it, to
become so virtuous, and so devoted to his wife, if he ever has
one, that she will die of boredom. Such resolves, we learn to
know, were characteristic of Tilly but seldom lasted long.

There is a poem on the death of his friend the Marquis de
Senecterre, who died young and was much addicted to passing
amours, Tilly says, adding a poignant note of direct simplicity
as he refers to the ease with which people accept the death of
their friends. There is, again, a long discourse in verse on
Chamfort, "my dear Chamfort," of whom we hear more in
the Memoirs, as also of Rivarol, whom Tilly knew well. Several
of the items in this volume are dated from England, for which
at this period he had much admiration; thus in a fragment from
a letter to Madame de C., dated December, 1783, he speaks of
London as "one of the most beautiful towns of the world,"
being especially impressed by the vast and magnificent streets,
with (unlike Paris) pavements at the side for foot-passengers,
showing that this is a land where the people count for something; he notes, however, that the English do not form friendly
relationships so easily as the French; they give little and ask
little.

Two years later, again in England, he sends an invitation
in verse to a friend in France to come to London to see "a free
people loving virtue and law and maintaining them," where also
"the women are worthy of love for their grace, beautiful com-
plexions, and large eyes"; and he grows enthusiastic over "the
tragic Muse," Mrs. Siddons, with her magic voice, her eyes that
strike thunderbolts, her heart that seeks the heart, and with no
aid from cosmetics and plaster, or even powdered hair. It is
possible to find these and other little points of interest in the
"Œuvres mêlées," but it must be confessed that there would be
little occasion to consult them if they had not been written by
the author of the Memoirs.

From this period until 1792, when he was compelled to
leave France, it is on the Memoirs alone that we must rely for
the story of Tilly. They tell us all that for the most interesting
period of his life we need to ask, and they tell it with an inti-

macy, an impertinence, a recklessness in self-revelation, and an observational power mingled with keen insight, which impart to them the traits that render them imperishable, even though their literary style is careless, almost conversational (we can well believe that Tilly was brilliant in conversation), the style of the well-bred man of the world speaking among friends with whom few concealments are necessary.

It is mainly on the Memoirs that we must rely for Tilly's story; but I have come across one account of him in the first storms of the Revolution which must not be neglected, because it seems to stand alone even if it tells us little we could not guess. Tilly, as we know from the Memoirs, at this period fell in love with Amélie (now more usually and more correctly spelt Émilie) de Sainte-Amaranthe, one of the loveliest and most attractive victims of the Revolution, whose romantic story has often been told. Her mother—of ancient and noble family, remotely connected indeed with the English royal family—had led a rather adventurous life and at that time conducted a high-class and aristocratic gambling house in the Palais Royal. Amélie's beauty, charm, intelligence, and high spirit, to which all who knew her have testified, made a deep impression on Tilly, and his account of his experiences with her is one of the most moving and deeply felt episodes of the Memoirs.

It so happens that a society woman who moved in the Sainte-Amaranthe group, shortly before her death in old age, dictated her reminiscences of that family and their tragic fate. This Madame Amandine Rolland was the daughter of a distinguished financier and thus had known many notable persons of Louis XVI's court. She survived to 1852 though her reminiscences were only published in 1864 under the name of "La Famille Sainte-Amaranthe," par Madame A. R——. We are here concerned only with her references to Tilly. She speaks of "M. de Tilly's large black eyes constantly turned on Amélie, although his gaze and the flow of his language received no sign of encouragement from her." Madame Rolland—who says, in agreement with all other witnesses, that Amélie revealed an almost superhuman perfection of beauty in face and figure—then seeks to reproduce the words which Amélie's mother addressed to her:

M. de Tilly has certainly never been one of my preferred friends. I am not dazzled by his brilliant figure, and his mind, which is said to be so interesting, does not

amuse me in the least. His behaviour to Amélie does not
exactly give me the right to shut my door on him, and
yet I find at least ridiculous the effusive tenderness he
displays for her and talks about to a crowd of his friends.
One would say that it is with him a matter of pride and
pose. It brings back to me the part, even a thousandfold
more ridiculous, which he played some years before the
Revolution when he assumed a far too confident, sentimental tone in speaking to the Queen; his false confi-
dences might have led one to suppose some august
favours for the handsome page. Oh, what a *Cherubino
di amore*, M. de Tilly! Besides, could noble and delicate
passion be experienced by a man who consumes his youth
in deplorable liaisons with Miss Adeline and Miss Rosalie? You know, the little Antonio of *Richard Cœur de
Lion?* It is she who reigns now, and her bold tricks of
jealousy are really amusing. It is happily quite certain
that Amélie does not respond to M. de Tilly's sighs;
otherwise my poor child, on a simple suspicion, might be
the victim of a despair both ridiculous and alarming,
for the pretty Antonio, with her fair hair and gentle
face, when in a rage becomes, they say, a roaring tigress.
The end of such storms is, however, rather comical;
Rosalie pays him back by two infidelities for one, in
order, she says, to have the satisfaction of confessing
them to the lover-in-chief, and then it is his turn to rage.
But he remains more enslaved than ever in this pure and
worthy relationship. Lately he definitely announced his
intention to emigrate, but he stopped at Rosalie's little
house on the way. . . . Then [adds the author of these
reminiscences] Madame de Sainte-Amaranthe thanked
me for the interest I had shown in her long story, which,
she said, she might not have told to people with whom
she had been longer associated.

A little later, at dinner with the Sainte-Amaranthes, M. de
Morainville referred to Tilly's departure as certain. Madame
Rolland tells us:

I was opposite Amélie, and I looked at her; the delicious carnation of her cheek was not in the least heightened. Very certainly, M. de Tilly, the *émigré,* was for
her only one adorer less, and the crowd of them was too
large for her imagination to be thereby troubled. "And
what will become of Tilly's widows?" asked M. de

Monville, enjoying a slice of pineapple. "His widows?" replied M. de Morainville, laughing. "Perhaps Mlle. Adeline will think of him as she says, '*Il danse fort bien M. de la France*'; then she will redouble her seductions as she continues, '*Mais mon André, tu danses bien mieux à mon gré.*' As for Rosalie, oh, she is taking her despair seriously in honour of the fugitive! First of all she let all her splendid hair fall loose without care; then yesterday evening, they say, it was plaited by the handsome Amédée de K——, lately one of the Duc d'Orléans pages." "M. de Morainville," interrupted Madame de Sainte-Amaranthe, "you are too well versed in the histories of the green room; I bring the session to an end—" and she rose.

We cannot accept quite literally the old lady's gossip about events which happened as much as sixty years earlier, when she was little more than a girl; it is rather too detailed. It may even have been unconsciously refreshed by the perusal of Tilly's own Memoirs. But in the general drift and tone of her story Madame Rolland may be reliable. It is not sympathetic to Tilly, but, as the Memoirs show, in that respect it perhaps corresponds to Madame Sainte-Amaranthe's attitude towards him, nor is there any difficulty in believing that Amélie, whatever her relations with Tilly, refrained from making her mother her confidante, while her whole tragic story reveals a singular self-possession and presence of mind. There can, moreover, be little doubt that the narrative correctly presents the attitude of Tilly's social group. The eighteenth century may have been, as we are now commonly pleased to consider it, frivolous, but the eighteenth century itself was not over indulgent to frivolity. If the "roué" flourished, the name was that originally applied to the worst criminals. Even Tilly himself was a severe moralist.

The story of the Sainte-Amaranthes and their fellow victims of the Red Mass of the 29th Prairial, 1794, has been told many times, and it is widely agreed by historians that the profound impression it made, especially the fate of the noble and completely innocent Amélie, was responsible for the revulsion of feeling against Robespierre and his downfall; he slipped, it has been said, in the blood he had himself shed. The chapter on the Red Mass in the book on the Baron de Batz (translated into English), "A Gascon Royalist in Revolutionary Paris" by Lenôtre, the scholar who has studied so many of the social and personal aspects of the Revolution, presents what is probably a reliable account of this episode; he does not reject Tilly's story, though naturally not able to confirm its intimate details.

It is for his portraits that Tilly is most often cited by the select band of students to whom alone, until recently, his Memoirs have been known. He was on familiar terms with various prominent figures of the last days of the *ancien régime,* and they come in and out of his pages. But three portraits are specially notable, for they bring before us persons whom we still view with curiosity, and it has been possible to say of each that it realises that person more vividly than any other picture we possess. There is first Marie Antoinette, with whom Tilly was in daily touch during his early days of impressionable youth, so that he was able to describe her charm without either formality or extravagance. There is Restif de la Bretonne, whom we see here, from the outside, but with a fidelity we recognise as exact. The third is Laclos, and this is probably the most interesting of the three portraits, for it is the only real personal portrait we possess of the author of a novel which at length stands unchallenged as one of the masterpieces of literature; and there is, further, an amusing irony in the fact that Tilly, who is still fettered by the old-world notion that "Les Liaisons Dangereuses" was an outrage on morality, has sometimes himself been considered as the embodiment in real life of the accomplished seducer whom Laclos depicted, Valmont *en personne,* the typical eighteenth-century roué.

Looking at the Memoirs more broadly, we see in them a picture of the last stage of the eighteenth-century aristocratic society circling round the court, in its superficial brilliance, its light-hearted gaiety, the elegant corruption which still left those who moved in it with spirits high enough to mount even the scaffold with a jest. That is the society that Tilly presents and the society he himself embodied, alike in its dissoluteness and its wit and its high spirit, although it was his mixed good and bad fortune to escape the guillotine. Thus Tilly's Memoirs make an admirable companion work to Restif de la Bretonne's "Monsieur Nicholas," where we view with an even greater intimacy the same society from beneath and come in touch with those plebeian and lower-middle-class elements which were soon to become so prominent.

In the last chapters of the Memoirs we find Tilly in the full swift stream of the Revolution. Here perhaps he appears to

better advantage than at any other time of his life, even though
—or because—he was on the losing side. It was natural that
he should rally to the defence of the court and espouse the cause
of the royal persons with whom he had once been so closely
associated. He brought his facile wit and gay insolence to the
attack on the republicans, in the pages of "Les Actes des
Apôtres," which were then playing a prominent part on the literary side of the struggle. He wrote an open letter to the king
in which, with what has been held to be sound judgement, he
exhorted him to firmness and resolution. Among those whom he
attacked he evidently aroused strong resentment, and he believed, rightly or wrongly, that there were attempts to assassi-
nate him. To Condorcet, whom he regarded as a renegade, he
addressed an open letter of fierce vituperation, and he believed
that he, with Fabre d'Eglantine, had determined on his death.
Immediately afterwards he decided that he had better leave
France. He made his way slowly to the coast, paid a large sum to
be quietly and uncomfortably conveyed across the Channel in a
smuggler's boat, and the Memoirs end with his arrival in England. He never continued them, though twenty-four years more
of life remained to him and many strange adventures. But he was
probably wise. The most brilliant and attractive period of his life
was over; and, if in the Memoirs he must often crave our
indulgence, in the days that followed his discredit seems sometimes complete.

[III]

Tilly states at the end of his Memoirs that he landed in
England at Stockport, proceeded thence by a two hours' drive
to Dover, and therefrom to London. Various French writers
innocently repeat this statement without knowing that the only
English Stockport is at the opposite end of England from
Dover, and this statement in the Memoirs might seem a more
plausible argument against their authenticity than some other
little errors that have actually been brought forward. Tilly
merely claims to have landed at "Stockport" and may easily
have been mistaken in the name of the place, perhaps a port for
none but smugglers, unless we have here an error of transcrip-
tion as probably in the name of Mrs. Knouth, the landlady of
the British Hotel at Boulogne.

In London, Tilly was no stranger, having made prolonged

stays, two or three times before, and he had a good knowledge
of English literature; on some occasions, also, he had come into
contact with Burke and other distinguished people, even it
seems, the prince regent.

Many aristocratic French *émigrés*, including old friends of
Tilly, especially the Vicomte de Noailles, were already settled
in England, and on account of their rank and the sympathy felt
with their misfortunes were often able to mix in good society.
But they were naturally in reduced circumstances and compelled
to struggle with discomforts and difficulties. We do not know
how Tilly, so often in money troubles even at home, contrived
to live abroad. The German editor of his Memoirs, who had
many of Tilly's private papers before him, states that he was
everywhere treated with esteem and regard during his four
years' stay, but that it is a mystery on what he lived, though
he may have been engaged in some business with Noailles, "and
seems to have been fortunate at the gaming table and with
women." But among his papers was preserved a letter written by
the Comte de Vaudreuil—once so fascinating and influential a
figure at the French court—and this is worth quoting both for
Tilly's sake and for the light it throws on the existence of a noble
émigré. It was addressed to Tilly from Edinburgh on November
20, 1796, without signature but in Vaudreuil's handwriting:

> I will begin with myself and describe to you my
> situation. You know that for a long time Monsieur
> [that is the comte d'Artois, brother of Louis XVI,
> who later became Charles X] has wished us to come
> to him in Edinburgh. I have always sought to decline
> or at least to postpone this, on account of the length
> and difficulty of the journey, but Monsieur sent a brig
> to fetch us, and Madame de Vaudreuil and I had to
> decide on embarking. After a troublesome six-day voy-
> age with seasickness we at last arrived, extremely ex-
> hausted. Our lodgings alone cost us four pounds a
> month. One certainly lives here more cheaply than in
> London, but it is quite dear enough for people who
> have altogether only ten pounds a month to spend.
> Monsieur sends us daily two dishes from the castle
> to improve our slender meals. That, however, is all
> he does for us, or can do, for he is himself in a diffi-
> cult position. I own (but this is between ourselves)
> that I had counted on something more, but I have to
> accept things as they are, for the prince is not able

to pay his own household. I have to do my best with the ten pounds and do not know how I shall get on; my head whirls. How gladly would I come to London, but a seat in the coach costs ten guineas. It is sad. We live in the same island, my good Tilly, and cannot embrace each other; I had so much to say to you, and to confide. I have received a letter from Alphonse [his son]; he wants money. I am telling him of my sad position, and enclose the letter, to save postage.

We know little of Tilly's reception in English society. But we have definite information concerning his relations with two interesting women in London. The first was a lady not yet forgotten, Lady Elizabeth Craven, daughter of the Earl of Berkeley, married to Lord Craven at an early age and later to the Margrave of Anspach, while the King of Prussia raised her to the rank of Princess Berkeley. In her old age she wrote her own memoirs, and books have been written about her even in recent years. She was a woman of beauty and real charm as well as intelligence, but she was married at seventeen and had more than one lover afterwards in an almost public manner; so that though her second husband, the margrave, was a nephew of Frederick the Great, and she herself with the help of his immense wealth was able to maintain a little court of considerable magnificence in London at Brandenburg House, Hammersmith, her position was ambiguous, and while the prince regent visited her, George III and Queen Charlotte stayed away. Horace Walpole, who was at first on friendly terms with her, wrote in 1785 to Sir Horace Mann, the British minister at Florence, where Lady Craven then was: "She has, I fear, been *infinitamente* indiscreet, but what is that to you or me? She is very pretty, has parts, and is good-natured to the greatest degree; has not a grain of malice or mischief, and never has been an enemy but to herself." The famous Lauzun, who had also known her at a rather earlier period of her life, wrote of her that she was "a very pretty little woman, celebrated for her follies and her misfortunes," and added that "gentle, simple, and tender, it was impossible not to feel interest in her." At a later period she was certainly capable of being inordinately vain and arrogant. She married the Margrave in 1791, immediately after Lord Craven's death.

Tilly seems soon to have found entrance to the cosmopolitan gaieties of Hammersmith where we hear of him taking part in private theatricals, for the margravine wrote and performed numerous plays. She was now (in 1793), at forty-three years of age, still very attractive, and we are not surprised to hear of Tilly, though many years younger, making love to her. This episode is minimised by Broadley and Lewis Melville in their work, "The Beautiful Lady Craven," as "a mild flirtation." They quote, however, a letter of hers to Tilly which bears witness to stronger feelings, stating that it is "the only one which has escaped destruction," but not stating whence they derived it. Its original source is, no doubt, the German editor's supplement to Tilly's Memoirs; and here we find not one but four love-letters from the margravine to Tilly, with references to others, some in French, some in English. Nor do the English authors say anything of the story that Tilly had once at Hammersmith, presumably in a fit of jealous rage, struck the margravine with his riding whip. The German editor of 1825, who based himself on Tilly's own papers, knew nothing of this story. Its original source seems to be the French editor of 1828, who, after referring to Tilly's remark in the Memoirs in favour of a certain amount of violence in love, continues: "It has been notorious in London and Hamburg that the Comte de Tilly behaved in this manner with the Margravine of Anspach, and sometimes treated her with singular brutality in her park, using a horse-whip in the presence of witnesses."

Tilly certainly defended such conduct, as we know, referring to a distinguished lady (whether or not the Margravine) who after such an incident confided to a friend that now she felt assured her lover really loved her; and as we know besides that the Margrave placed the horses in the famous stables he owned at the disposition of his guests it is easy to account for the whip. Nietzsche also has advised that women should be approached with a whip, though we cannot imagine that gentle philosopher following his own advice. Tilly's moods of impulsive violence may be detected in his own pages, and the Margravine's letters show that he thought he had some grievances. We may not absolutely reject the story, and yet I much doubt it. I have not so far met with it in any contemporary record of the times. Horace Walpole, who frequently mentions the Margravine, and could not fail to have heard of such an extraordinary incident, says nothing about it, nor do the biographers of the Margravine. There is no reason to suppose the French editor was ever in London, and, if he was, most of the "notorious" stories he would hear about the Margravine of Anspach would be the silly gossip, inevitably aroused by so singular and conspicuous a figure, of which she frequently complains.

A few extracts may be given from the Margravine's letters to Tilly:

> How can you call me cruel? I cruel? And to you? I who cannot ever be unkind even to those whom I hate? You are joking, dearest! So far from putting anything in the way as regards your plans with D——— [of whom Tilly was jealous], I only wanted to warn you to be on your guard. As for the M. [the Margrave], he is mad against your nation, but especially against D.M———. But trust me to use my influence over him to secure my happiness. Never was I so necessary to the Margrave. His timid soul takes refuge in mine. When the people in the streets salute me and say "There she is!" he is delighted. . . . God is my witness that when I give up the pleasure of seeing you for a few weeks I give up what is dearest to me in the world; but it *must* be, for circumstances prevent. Your journey will give the final touch to my rights over the Margrave; all the others will seem to be in the wrong, and you the only one who has not deceived him. . . . I embrace you. Put a little cross somewhere in a corner of your letter and kiss it, and when I receive it I will kiss it too. Farewell, my dearest, my only friend. Love me well; take care of yourself, body and soul; that will prove that you want to make me happy. Kiss this place. [Here she has made a circle about the size of a florin.]

In the course of another letter she writes:

> The Margrave goes to Colney Chapel on Sunday and stays till the middle of the week. So I shall be quite free. If you come to me meanwhile, so that no one knows of it, choose one of two ways which I will indicate to you. Lord Thurlow [the lord chancellor and a friend of the Margravine's] will tell you of yesterday's doings with the Margrave. I press you to my troubled heart.

In a third letter she writes:

> My tears choke me. I do not think it wise to see you. You do not know *how* I love when I love. You

can only have a weak idea of it. Do not believe that I
will speak evil of you to the Margrave. Nor do I give
myself any trouble to deceive him—very unnecessary
trouble, for as soon as you are away I can do what I
like with him. I only avoid as much as possible to
speak of you to him for fear of betraying myself. My
heart is only fifteen, it jumps and beats if I but hear
your name. Then I blush and almost swoon. . . . I
am looking for a house in London, for myself alone,
and for all that my son needs. I will so arrange it
that you can come to me unobserved, by day or by
night. . . . But learn, dear friend, to beware of yourself even more than of your enemies. Have me as your
only friend.

In a further letter she writes:

It is a new torture for me, a deadly martyrdom,
to be so near you and not to see you. I am better today
but still far from recovery. I promise to be careful of
my health. Why are you silent about your own state?
Send me your Henri [Tilly's valet] that I may ask
him. I would like to see him if only because he has
seen you. Preserve all the strength of your soul to love
me as I deserve to be loved. And if ever your heart
changes be chivalrous enough to hide nothing from
me. I reckon on this and still more on my and your
tenderness. Both promise that you will never change.
At the present moment I am much troubled. Farewell.

There were other letters in French and in English, in some
of which she defends herself against Tilly's jealousy of D. who,
she says, had never been more than a friend. All these letters
date from 1793. They are interesting because they furnish evidence, independent of the Memoirs, that Tilly could arouse the
passionate love of a distinguished, cultured, and high-spirited
woman whose beauty, charm, and position brought so many men
to her feet. We do not know how the relationship ended. Tilly
put the letters in a packet on which he wrote "Marg. of Ans."
After his death this was found in Berlin among his other papers
by the first editor of the Memoirs. Perhaps it still lies neglected
somewhere.

There is nothing about Tilly in the Margravine's own
Memoirs, and we should not expect it, for they were written in

old age and with an anxious eye to her own reputation. So we do not know whether it was she who brought the relationship to an end or Tilly's volatile heart. However that may be, we soon find him in close relationship with another woman, this time French, and one in a very different position from the prodigal and magnificent Princess Berkeley.

Charlotte Marie Bobin, married to Dr. Arnould André Roberjot-Lartigues at Port-au-Prince in Santo Domingo, lived with her daughter, but apart from her husband, in London. Tilly seems to have become acquainted with her through the Prince de Poix, brother of his friend the Vicomte de Noailles and also acquainted with the Margravine. If it may seem characteristic of Tilly to be in the train of a woman of wealth and distinction like the Margravine, it is equally characteristic of him to expend a reckless and almost incredible generosity on a woman in misfortune and poverty. In her financial difficulties, which seem to have been largely due to careless extravagance, she repeatedly applied for help to the Prince and to Tilly. She must have made a deep impression on Tilly, for before the year 1795 was out he had advanced her over sixteen hundred pounds. Whence Tilly, an *émigré* and usually in debt, obtained this large sum is not clear; it is stated by his German editor that he sold or pawned rings, jewels, horses, books, and pistols to obtain money for Madame Lartigues. He very soon wanted the money back. In the same year 1795 he sent a demand to the lady's husband, who replied from Port-au-Prince on November 1, 1795, that it was owing to his wife's youthful frivolity and extravagant way of living that these debts were incurred, that the allowance he made her should amply suffice for her needs, and that the disturbed conditions in Santo Domingo prevented him from doing more.

Next year Tilly took the further step of forwarding to Dr. Lartigues an acknowledgment of the debt by Madame Lartigues, dated July 27, 1796, with a request for its acquittal. The document is as follows:

> I swear, affirm, and protest that this account of 1,649 pounds sterling in English money is exact in justice and truth, as is the eternal gratitude that I and my daughter owe to M. Alexandre de Tilly, who has saved me from perishing of hunger, illness, and misery on various occasions, as respectable witnesses can certify, in the intervals during which I received no

allowance (and when I was lost in debt), and especially during the past fourteen months when, with
heavy debts, I was receiving no allowance and was
abandoned by all my family, and obliged at last for
four months to seek the help granted by the English
government to the indigent, and that when all my
properties are bringing in a full return. I acknowledge,
I say, that the said sum of 1,649 pounds sterling, in
English money, is due to him in the most lawful manner, and that he, Alexandre de Tilly, is authorised before God and man to take by all means possible from
whatever I possess, and shall possess, and from whatever my husband possesses or shall possess, the repay-
ment of a debt so sacred.

It does not appear, however, that Dr. Lartigues recognised
this debt, and still less that he repaid the loan, for on December
3, 1801, Tilly, it is said, wrote with some bitterness from Berlin
to the lady, then in Bordeaux, reminding her of the acknowledgment just quoted. She replied on March 20, 1802, expressing
her gratitude to Tilly and describing her misfortunes since returning from Santo Domingo (then in a very disturbed state)
where she had apparently been to see her husband, of whom,
however, she makes no mention.

It was not, as you think, the deadly climate of San
Domingo [she writes in the course of this letter] from
which I have escaped, but the bloodthirsty fury of the
negroes. I have been in the midst of them for two
months, with my family and twenty-eight other whites,
in constant danger of being massacred. All this time I
could not change my linen or obtain food except such
as the more human of these inhuman creatures
allowed me, and that I gave nearly all to my children
and my father whose lives were dearer to me than my
own. After two months the monsters left us free, and
we had to wander through pathless woods, without
food or shoes or stockings, even robbed of my last
chemise, for nine miles, until we fortunately reached
Port-au-Prince. Here for three months I was dependent on the charity of Madame Leclerc [Napoleon's
sister, Pauline, then the young wife of Colonel Leclerc, captain-general of the French forces engaged in
suppressing the Negro revolt, and afterwards Princess
Borghese]. But when the French troops left the

island, I went across to New York and there for eight
months supported myself with difficulty by dressmak-
ing, until Heaven brought it about that my daughter
found the best of husbands, and I the noblest of sons-
in-law, who has taken care of me and my Alexander
[at this name, that of Tilly, the German editor "cannot repress a secret suspicion"]. Since returning to
Bordeaux, I have spent six months with him, though
his means are limited, and six months with my husband's relations. You may judge, therefore, whether it
is possible for me to fulfil my obligations otherwise
than by my feelings and words.

We know nothing further of Madame Lartigues.

In the summer of 1797 we find Tilly in Hamburg, whither
perhaps he went late in the previous year, possibly to escape
London creditors. It was one of the centres at which strangers
were then seeking refuge from the calamities of war, and as it
was at that moment also a chief continental port for English
vessels it was natural for Tilly to make his way there, even if
he was not drawn by the presence of his old friend Rivarol.

While living in Hamburg in July, 1797, Tilly wrote a letter,
partly in verse (published in the second edition of his "Œuvres
mêlées," to ask Rivarol for the loan of a copy of Rousseau's
"Nouvelle Héloïse," as he wishes to verify a quotation. He here
speaks of the novel as "that enchanting work which at twenty
we all know by heart and at forty forget [he was not himself
yet forty], where everything is false and empty and sophisti-
cated, yet where everything is true, thanks to the magic of its
style." In the course of the letter Tilly writes:

> I passed your door yesterday and was very pleased
> to find it hermetically closed. I followed the precept
> of him whose morals were so pure, who says, *"Pul-
> sate!"* and rejoiced that the *aperietur vobis* was not
> verified. I rejoiced to think that you were face to face
> with Posterity, at work for her and for yourself.
> You have conquered all difficulties, and all your rivals,
> since you have conquered idleness.

In his reply Rivarol writes:

> If I had guessed my good fortune yesterday my
> door would have been open; it will always be open

for you. I close it to bores and to those with whom
all time spent is wasted. Knock when you come again
twice only, and rather loud, at the downstairs door.
Come, if it suits you, just after dinner. It is well for
you to preach against idleness; you are yourself the
real culprit. Here, as in Paris, you waste your mind
and your facility on people with whom you ought at
your age to feel disgust, when you know them as well
as you do. You are always thirsting for empty pleasures, of which you ought to be weary. You have all
that is needed to impart the love of work. Believe me,
rest in work, it calls for you, and dissipation is no
longer worthy of you.

That was the wise and plain-spoken advice of a discerning
friend, even though Rivarol, who left so little to justify his
brilliant reputation, scarcely followed his own council. We may
be sure that the moralist in Tilly admitted its truth. Yet he never
outgrew the need for such advice and remained unchanged, save
for the worse, until his tragic death.

[IV]

Late in 1797 we suddenly find Tilly in the New World. It
is not, however, a matter for surprise. The gratitude felt in the
new American republic for the assistance derived from France
induced many distinguished *émigrés* to follow in the track of
La Fayette. Lauzun had gone to America. Friends and relatives
of Tilly's, including the Vicomte de Noailles (La Fayette's
brother-in-law) had already gone over. Perhaps Madame
Lartigues had stimulated the project. Whatever the motive,
Tilly appeared in New York and wrote to apprise Noailles of
his arrival. On November 2, Noailles writes in reply from Philadelphia: "Madame de Lartigues told me of your plan to come
to us. I took it for a fable as there is nothing *romantic* here.
But your letter of October 28 from New York tells me that
you have carried out your idea. I shall be pleased to see you
again, but I must confess to you that there could not be a more
unfavourable moment for undertaking any affairs here." It may
have been the presence of General Noailles (as he was always
called in America) which induced Tilly to proceed to Philadelphia. We do not know how he lived during the next twelve

months; we hear nothing of any mercantile affairs; as his German editor remarks, the goods that Tilly dealt in were hearts.

In 1799 we find Tilly settled in Philadelphia—we do not know how long he had been there—and in friendly touch with the Bingham family, to whom doubtless Noailles had introduced him. Now Philadelphia was at this time a centre of gaiety and splendour as well as temporarily the capital of the republic; and William Bingham—who had been born there in 1751 and died at Bath in England in 1804—was one of its chief citizens and still figures conspicuously in American biographical dictionaries. He was the wealthiest man in Philadelphia and once purchased two million acres in Maine. He was a senator and had even acted as president of the Senate. His wife was distinguished for her beauty and charm and the magnificent hospitality which her husband's position enabled her to exercise. His eldest daughter, Anne Louisa, had lately (1798) married an afterwards eminent Englishman, Alexander Baring, a financier and statesman (son of Sir Francis Baring, who has been termed "the first merchant in Europe of his time"), who later became the first Baron Ashburton and father by Anne Louisa of the second baron, whose wife, Lady Ashburton, well known as the friend of Carlyle, was sometimes an innocent cause of trouble in the Carlyle household.

We may now turn to the letters found among Tilly's papers by his German editor. We are not surprised to learn that he had quickly sought, and found, favour in the Bingham family, both with mother and daughter, that is, the second daughter, Maria Matilda, still a young girl. We soon find Maria writing little notes on gilt-edged satin paper to Tilly, who carefully preserved them. The first was a formal invitation written in correct French: "Mr. and Mrs. Bingham beg Monsieur le Comte de Tilly to do them the honour of dining with them *en famille* [this was underlined] next Sunday." The two notes that followed were in English: "Miss Bingham presents her compliments to Count Tilly. She takes the liberty of sending him some chocolate, having remarked yesterday, that he approved of it." In the next: "Miss Maria Matilda Bingham takes the liberty of offering Count Tilly some fruit just taken from the tree. She hopes it may prove acceptable to Count Tilly in his indisposition." There were no letters of a more intimate character, the reason being that in the subsequent proceedings they had to be returned to Maria's mother, so that there immediately follows a more alarming document:

This is to certify that on the 11 day of April in the year of our Lord, one thousand seven hundred and ninety-nine, James Alexander Count de Tilly was married to Maria Matilda Bingham. By me Thomas Jones, Minister of the Universal Church in Philadelphia, Pennsylvania.

(It may be noted that Tilly here for the only time used his first baptismal name.)

At this point we may leave for a moment the narrative of Tilly's matrimonial adventure, as set down in his German editor's supplement, to turn to American records. Here, I have discovered with interest, we may find some rather intimate details concerning Maria Matilda and her family. Philadelphia was at that time, as has already been remarked, a centre of luxury. The Duc de la Rochefoucauld-Liancourt said its luxury recalled that of Europe, with the difference that its women were more beautiful; it was indeed indisputably the leading American city in every respect. Its aristocratic society, surrounding what was at that time the seat of government, constituted the nearest approach to a court that the republic has ever tolerated. William Bingham and his father-in-law, Thomas Willing, were at the centre of this society, and his wife was its leader in fashion. Bingham was descended from a good English family long established in Philadelphia; at the age of eighteen he had already been appointed the British consul in Martinique, and his great wealth is said to have been obtained by trade speculation and the ownership of privateers. He founded the first American bank, and Thomas Willing, a wealthy merchant of great ability, was the president of the bank. The marriage of Willing's daughter to Bingham enabled the clan to constitute a ruling oligarchy in Philadelphian society, and the Binghams' mansion—a copy on a more splendid scale of Manchester House in London— became a great social centre; here Washington might often be found at tea.

Mrs. Bingham had moved in good society even before her marriage, and her sister had even been courted by Louis Philippe d'Orléans, afterwards King of France, but old Willing had forbidden the marriage. Anne, who married Bingham (twelve years her senior) at sixteen, was so beautiful that it was said she "might sit for the queen of Beauty." She certainly seems to have possessed great charm, intelligence, and social distinction, with nothing of either the democrat or the Puritan about her. She spent some years in London in the best English society, associating with the Duchess of Devonshire and other aristocrats, and was said to have brought back with her the bad habit of besprinkling her conversation with oaths and slightly risky anecdotes; but not a word has ever been uttered against her good name, and her husband was devoted to her.

It is in the "Life and Letters of H. G. Otis" that we obtain our only really intimate glimpse of Maria Matilda, and at the very moment of her unlucky matrimonial adventure with Tilly. Otis moved freely among this whole clan and writes familiarly to his wife about them—about Thomas Willing, whom he calls "Old Square Toes" on account of the old-fashioned boots he wore, about the charm and ultra-fashionable ways of Mrs. Bingham, and about Maria, only fifteen when she ran away with Tilly, but already, it seems, considered a little wild.

Any reader of the Memoirs will know enough of *le beau Tilly* to experience no surprise at his easy conquest of the beautiful and charming young Maria Matilda, who was certainly already surrounded by far more desirable suitors. But up to this moment Tilly's exploits in love and gallantry, however irresponsibly they have been conducted, have appeared the outcome of genuine attachment towards the objects by whom they are inspired and such as we might expect from a typical young French aristocrat of the late eighteenth century. But here we must evidently recognise designs of a less amiable sort.

The marriage caused profound consternation in the Bingham family directly it was known. It is clear that they had not suspected any matrimonial designs on Tilly's part. Whether or not they knew much of Tilly's reputation as a roué, and however friendly and hospitably disposed by his personal and social attractions, we soon discover that a marriage alliance with the French count was the last thing desired by this aristocratic clan who had already rejected an alliance with the future king of France. Unfortunately we cannot help thinking that Tilly himself had realised that beforehand. Tilly must be got rid of at once; and it soon appeared that the simplest and quickest way, and for a man of Bingham's wealth the easiest, was to buy him off. There is nothing to show that the young countess offered any opposition. It is remarkable that Tilly's friends did not desert him at this unpleasant crisis which he had himself brought about, and that even the Binghams, while determined to exclude him from the family at any price, do not appear hostile to him personally.

A committee was formed to settle the conditions of the separation, with three friends of Tilly's on one side and three friends of the Binghams on the other. On Tilly's side were Noailles (to whom the affair must have been painful if he was responsible for introducing Tilly), Guillaume Guéroult de Boisclairaux, a cousin of Tilly's on the paternal side, and Pierre Aupois, perhaps a business man, while on the other side were Mr. Thomas Willing, a Mr. Francis who also seems connected, and Alexander Baring, Maria's brother-in-law. A certain amount of discussion and arrangement of terms took place before the matter was settled to the satisfaction of both parties. Tilly agreed to the demand of the Binghams that he should at once and for ever renounce all association and communication with his wife, and Mr. Bingham agreed to the demands of Tilly as formulated in the following strange document, drawn up in French, which only too clearly reveals Tilly's motives in contracting this clandestine marriage:

I make the following demands:
1. Five thousand pounds sterling to pay my debts.
2. An annuity of five hundred pounds sterling, to be paid wherever I may wish, in any country, except the United States.
3. Due security that I shall not be disturbed in any manner whatsoever in connection with the circumstances of my marriage.
4. I demand that Mr. Baring shall write to me, or cause the statement to be made to me through General de Noailles, that he pushed me in a moment of agitation, on account of the condition of his wife. [This point is not cleared up by the context but it is noted that the condition was duly fulfilled through Noailles.] And never, on my honour, in this country or elsewhere, shall I trouble the peace of his family, or his own, even in the most remote manner.

These four articles being accepted and ratified under the responsibility of General de Noailles and Mr. T. Willing, I undertake to leave Philadelphia at once and America directly after.

I undertake on my part to give any security that may be imposed on me, as for example the loss of the annuity or a judgement against me for the sum allocated for payment of my debts, that I will never give any cause whatever for trouble to Mr. Bingham's family or the families of Mr. Willing and Mr. Francis. I will return the Comtesse de Tilly's letters to her mother, and if at any time it is considered that a divorce would contribute to her happiness, I will agree at the first demand and not ask a shilling of damages. I desire the signature of Mr. Bingham to these articles before two o'clock this afternoon, and before ten o'clock tomorrow morning the absolute fulfilment of these conditions, so that I may leave instantly a country where I have been too unfortunate.

Signed: *Philadelphia, the 10th. June, 1799.*

ALEX. DE TILLY.

Mr. Bingham at once signed and sent the following document (which is in English) :

Mr. Bingham has received the paper containing certain conditions offered on the part of Monsieur de Tilly—which under certain modifications, not substantially affecting the terms, he will agree to. The necessary Paper, to carry the same into operation, shall be prepared immediately, so that Monsieur de Tilly may leave town tomorrow morning.

WM. BINGHAM.

Monday morning.

In accordance with the contract Tilly left Philadelphia next morning, and sailed from New York to London in July, never to visit America again.

These details concerning the marriage, the separation that so swiftly followed, and the documents concerning the terms arranged, are all derived from Tilly's own papers, as left behind him in Berlin and first published by the German editor of the Memoirs. We can fortunately supplement them by the outside view which I have found in the "Life and Letters of H. G. Otis."

"It was a shocking and scandalous affair [we are here told by a friend of Otis, who remained anonymous] and created, at the time, prodigious sensation in our highest circles. De Tilly was ready, however, to be bought off. He was bribed to furnish evidence against himself, and the divorce was obtained by influence with the Legislature of Pennsylvania, whether by corruption I am not able to say." Otis himself, at the time, writes to his wife on January 18, 1800: "I just learn that a Bill for divorcing Maria Bingham has passed both Houses at Lancaster, where Mr. Bingham now is. She was, however, every day walking with her mother while the business was pending and in a dress which you would hardly believe it was possible for a lady to wear, at least at this season. A muslin robe and her chemise, and no other article of cloathing upon her body! I have been regaled with the sight of her whole legs for five minutes together, and do not know to what height the fashion will be carried. The particulars of her dress I hear from old Mrs. F——, who assures me that her chemise is fringed to look like a petticoat. However, she and the family are evidently dejected."

The divorce appears to have been really a declaration of nullity on the ground of Maria's age and the absence of parental consent. Mrs. Bingham's health had begun to fail at the beginning of 1800 after the birth of a child who did not survive, and the doctors advised a voyage to Madeira. The whole family went in the spring, but the divorce was obtained before they sailed.

In reviewing the peculiar circumstances of Tilly's marriage and separation, we cannot fail to note how rare a friend he possessed in Noailles, who seems to have been a man of high and honourable character. What Noailles thought of the transaction we may guess, and it is easy to do so when we read a letter he wrote to Tilly only a fortnight after he left. Tilly had made to him from New York the hardly tactful suggestion that he should marry one of his sons to the young countess after a divorce. Noailles replied with a cold and curt air of dignified pride which Tilly must have felt to be cutting: "I cherish the most tender regard for Maria, and the deepest reverence for Mrs. Bingham, but under no pretext would I agree that one of my children should become the son-in-law of Mr. Bingham; at no price in the world would I put a son of mine in the position of living by the favours of his father-in-law. You may make what use you please of this definite answer." (We know from other sources that each of the daughters had a marriage portion of one hundred thousand pounds.)

At the same time such seems to have been the personal fascination exerted by Tilly that not only Noailles, but even the Bingham family, retained amiable feelings towards him. One is inclined to think that, like the canon of Le Mans, but in a milder spirit, they regarded him as "quite mad."

Noailles wrote again from Philadelphia to Tilly, a letter which amid much concerning the state of France at the time contains some personal remarks:

> You wish me to deal frankly with you. You know that I have often done so, even to the point of brutality. So listen to me. The family has been considering two proposals. One was a judicial separation, the other a formal divorce. Mr. Bingham and his daughter are in favour of the divorce. This will not take a form offensive to you; the difference of age and your arts of seduction will be recognised. No Frenchman has ever felt offended by the accusation of sweet persuasiveness and irresistible fascination. . . . All through the summer [further on in the letters he adds] there have been many wooers round Maria. Her flight from the paternal home has been regarded as nothing more than a rash escapade. She has made much progress in intelligence and knowledge, as well as in accomplishments. Her first attempt to taste marriage has cost her so dearly that it will be hard to persuade her to make a second attempt. She possesses a rare gift for winning hearts. If she ever forms a new tie, it will be only as the result of a passion against which she has long struggled, and with the approval of her father, whose idol she is. Since your departure I have not heard your name once mentioned either in the Willing family or the Bingham family. I have communicated your letter to me in part to Mr. Bingham. He leaves you completely free to stay where you please. I should add that Mrs. Bingham cherishes sincere feelings towards you, and good wishes for your health and happiness. I unite my wishes to hers.

Maria later married her brother-in-law, Henry Baring. It seemed a promising union but ended unhappily at an early stage, for we are told by Otis's unnamed friend that Henry Baring, being himself unfaithful, threw his wife into dissipated society and then divorced her on account of an amour with a Captain Webster. She married for the third time the Marquis de Blaizel, a Frenchman in the Austrian army, and chamberlain of the Emperor. But again Maria was unhappy; the Marquis was a gambler and always in want of money which she could not supply, as Henry Baring had managed to secure the greater part of her fortune. "I knew her in Paris," writes Otis's friend, "then an old woman, but quite an amusing one. She had seen the world in many phases and had plenty of anecdotes which she told pleasantly. She was a very amiable, kind-hearted woman. She lived in rather an equivocal position in Paris. She was received at the Austrian ambassador's but not at the English Embassy." That is all I have been able to find out about the unfortunate Maria Matilda, and now it is unlikely we shall ever hear those anecdotes "she told pleasantly," perhaps sometimes about that early episode with Tilly, which alone was destined to preserve her name.

There is silence for a time. Then, in 1801, Tilly, evidently as extravagant as ever and even willing to sacrifice the future to the immediate present, conceived the idea of compounding his annuity by a lump sum of five thousand pounds down. He persuaded his friends Noailles and Guéroult de Boisclairaux to put the proposal before Bingham, who, however, preferred to stand by the original contract, bearing in mind, as he himself said, that he would not be able to rely on Tilly's conduct, especially as he had already, against his promise, written letters both to Maria and to her mother. After Bingham's death in 1804, however, Tilly renewed these attempts with the assistance of a lawyer, Barnett, and finally after much negotiation succeeded in 1805 and 1806 in obtaining a composition of the annuity from the representatives of the Bingham family.

That is the end of the most remarkable episode in Tilly's life, an episode unique even in his varied experience, and one which his most indulgent admirer can scarcely view with satisfaction.

[v]

In August, 1799, Tilly arrived back in London, and we find him applying at the Alien Office for a licence to remain in England. Now for the first time we have a little information concerning his personal appearance. Strangely enough, notwithstanding the admiration aroused by a man who was considered "one of the handsomest and best built men of his time," and his own interest in art and intercourse with painters, no authentic portrait of Tilly seems yet to have been traced. In the 1830 Jonquière edition of the Memoirs a "presumed portrait" of Tilly is reproduced; but as no information is given as to why and by whom this is "presumed," nor where the picture exists, there is no choice but to reject it. In the English passport of 1799, however, found among his papers by his German editor, Tilly is described as thirty-four (really thirty-eight) years of age, five feet five inches in height, and with black hair. But the rest of the description had been rendered illegible by Tilly. A later German passport among his papers gives further details: "Thirty-six years of age, of middle height, oval and rather pale face, black hair, large black eyes, regular nose."

Tilly soon changed his mind about staying in England. In September we find him applying to the English government, as well as to the Austrian and Danish ambassadors, for permission to go to Denmark and Germany. First he went to Hamburg, and during the next year or two he seems to have been at Leipzig or the neighbourhood, for he had his English and American letters addressed to a banker in that town.

Now began a new and happier period of Tilly's life. After a stay in Dresden, and then at Teplitz for the sake of the baths—for Tilly often suffered in health, and Teplitz was one of the most fashionable spas of the time—he came to Berlin. Frederick the Great, as we know, had set a fashion in Prussia for French culture, and an *émigré*, if of aristocratic birth, a soldier, a lover of *belles-lettres*, and accomplished in the social graces—all of which qualifications Tilly possessed—might expect in Berlin more than the mere friendly sympathy and occasional hospitality which was the most the *émigré* usually found in the cities of other lands. Even when we bear this in mind we are surprised at the high consideration and distinguished position which Tilly seems speedily to have secured in the court and the society of Berlin.

In 1801 the King of Prussia gave him an appointment as chamberlain at his court, while the Emperor Paul of Russia made him a Knight of Malta. This was probably in consequence of the intimate relations which Tilly formed with the Russian ambassador Baron von Krüdener and his wife, whose reputation has survived till to-day. Indeed both the royal family and the high nobility of Berlin seem to have treated Tilly in the most flattering manner, and his German editor found ample evidence of this in the letters left among his papers. Tilly addressed laudatory tributes in verse to the king and queen, with songs to be sung at court fêtes, was in touch with the whole royal family, and became an enthusiastic admirer of everything Prussian.

It seems, however, to have been the Baron and Baroness
von Krüdener with whom Tilly's relations were closest at this
time, and he was allowed to use their house as his own. An
account of them, found among his papers, helps to illustrate his
life at this time. It was written just after Krüdener's sudden
death in 1802, and Tilly describes his intellectual powers, the
wide extent of his outlook, his straightforwardness combined
with diplomatic skill and prudence, though his generous hospitality tended to go beyond the means at his disposal, so that the emperor he represented had to come to his aid.

> M. de Krüdener's death has much moved me
> [Tilly continues] though I saw less of him during the
> last six or eight months of his life, on account of ab-
> surd calumnies which had been brought to him, calum-
> nies which he sometimes accepted and sometimes re-
> jected. When I first arrived in Berlin he overwhelmed
> me with marks of interest that later turned to friend-
> ship, especially after he had ceased to see much of
> Rivarol, whom he had too much intelligence not to
> seek, but too much tact not at the same time to avoid,
> for his ministerial prudence could not sometimes but
> be alarmed by the political audacities with which that
> fine wit would amuse himself to embarrass the states-
> man. I was dining with him and a small party on the
> day when Rivarol was dying [April 13, 1801].
> Though then on distant terms with Rivarol I was none
> the less shocked by his death. I thought of that ex-
> traordinary conversational power now perishing, of
> the beautiful instrument which had given out such har-
> monious sounds and was now about to be broken, of
> that organisation so vast and so alive now reaching
> the annihilation of the grave. I had never hated him—
> I seemed to love him still.

After more in praise of Rivarol, Tilly passes without transition to speak of the baroness, who was without doubt the most
remarkable, and certainly the most famous (apart from Marie
Antoinette), of the numerous interesting and fascinating women
with whom Tilly came in close contact, though the period of
her fame belongs to a rather later date.

Julie de Wietinghoff was born in 1764 in Riga, of noble and
wealthy parentage, and was therefore a few years younger than
Tilly. Her father had brought her to Paris when she was nine

and introduced her to that advanced philosophical French society, to which he was himself attracted, dominated by Hel-
vétius, Diderot, d'Alembert, and Grimm, in which marriage was
regarded mainly as a convention enabling women to follow their
own inclinations in freedom. She was only eighteen when she
was married to Baron von Krüdener, then thirty-four and possessed of great wealth as well as social consideration. The young
baroness is described as full of grace and wit, with a most charming and expressive though not regularly beautiful face, light
brown hair that fell in ringlets on her shoulder, and calm blue
eyes that seemed, said Diderot, to penetrate alike the past and
the future. Krüdener took her to Venice where for some years
he was Russian minister; and two children were born of a union
which proved passionate and stormy and led in 1791 to a separation, though later when Tilly knew them the two had come
together again.

After returning for some years to her birthplace the baroness came in 1798 to Paris, formed an attachment with a young
Frenchman, and with him travelled widely through Europe. A
little later she published a novel in letters entitled "Valérie,"
the hero of which is tormented by a fatal passion for a married
woman and kills himself to escape his torments; it was founded
on the real history and fate of a secretary of legation of
Krüdener's who was hopelessly in love with the baroness. The
novel so well describes her own character and feelings, and
was written with so much sentimental energy, that it met with
wide success, which the baroness proceeded to Dresden and
Teplitz to enjoy, as well as to Berlin, where she was introduced
to the queen and admitted to the royal circle.

It was at this time that Tilly learned to know her, and they
entered into correspondence, partly through her daughter Sophie
as intermediary. Thus on July 3, 1801, she wrote him a long
letter from Teplitz, in French of curious orthography, which
characteristically brings out her traits as an early representative
of the romantic school.

> By some negligence of Sophie's [she wrote], who
> insisted on taking charge of one of my letters to you
> and adding a few words of her own, you have not
> received that letter, and I can see from here, monsieur
> le Comte, all the accusations which I seem to deserve.
> So I hasten to tell you that you are quite wrong if
> you dare to doubt the affectionate feelings and regards

of a family which is much devoted to you. The young
ladies have received your flowers and adorned themselves with them; they like to owe new graces to
you, for they well remember what charm you found in
them. Sophie especially would thank you for all those
charming bouquets and garlands. But her stupidity has
discouraged her, and as time passes I charge myself
with all the thanks and excuses, and the indulgence
I promise in your name, I am forbidden to write, for
my nerves are no joke. Will you not come and try
the waters here, for they are excellent? You will find
beautiful trees and beautiful mountains of which one
never grows tired. You will also find the Prince de
Ligne who is always cheerful—and a troop of German lords with ridiculous retinues which are always
amusing. And besides I hope you will find me and be
very pleased to see me, always good and frank for
my friends, always in open warfare against the Ger-
mans with thirty-two heraldic quarters, always loving
what is lovable, true, and simple—demanding nothing, living in my own way, on a very convenient reputation of eccentricity, because then one can do what
one likes and imitate the mountain scenery, which by
its diversity never wearies. But I must no longer try
your patience. Keep well and sometimes think of those
who are devoted to you and anxious to see you
again.

Tilly accepted the baroness's invitation, and went to Teplitz,
where he found the Prince de Ligne, with whom he was already
acquainted, though now their relations became closer. With the
baroness the relationship seems to have been one of congenial
friendship. Some passages may be extracted from the account
he wrote of her:

Baroness Krüdener was a woman of great intelligence, of many kinds and varieties of intelligence;
above all, she was what, had she been a man, would
have been called an original. She was in love with solitude, with unrestrained freedom, with the *dolce far
niente*. She was, however, fond of the fine arts, and
of French literature, and wrote a novel in that language; this described a relationship which had been
dear to herself, and, though it revealed no strong
imaginative power, had a tender melancholic strain.
The style shows too much mannerism and research,

but where it escapes these dangers it has freshness, maturity, and novelty. It is a wonderful book for a foreigner to write.

A harmony of tastes and opinions often brings us nearer than the inclination of the heart. It is thus simple and easy to explain that Madame Krüdener showed some interest in me. She should not perhaps have entered with so much warmth into my quarrel with M. de Rivarol, which was then occupying Berlin and dividing the public into two parties. But it is not for me to complain of the warmth with which she conducted my defence. M. Krüdener no doubt thought she showed unnecessary zeal.

Then Tilly proceeds to describe the difficulties and embarrassments that entered into his relations with Krüdener towards the end of the ambassador's life, and "the reserve which a man who lives in an attic feels that he must maintain with a man who still possesses a cook and a house." We are not told the cause of Krüdener's suspicions which—remembering what Tilly himself says of the Baron's shrewdness and judgement—possibly had more foundation than Tilly was willing to admit. And there was no further record of the Baroness found among his papers.

He could scarcely have foreseen the new and prominent part she was later to play in the world's affairs. She underwent a religious conversion, admitted, even publicly, the errors of her life, preached among the populace in a spirit midway between that of an English Methodist like Whitefield and a French mystic like Madame Guyon, and was thought by many to possess divine illumination. She foretold the approaching end of the world in a period of great political agitation when the fate of nations was in the balance, for a time found a disciple in Tsar Alexander himself, and became a figure of European significance. She went from country to country, lavishing her wealth on the poor, and preaching doctrines which were regarded as so revolutionary that she was constantly being expelled by the authorities; she finally died in the Crimea, after her influence had waned, in 1824. She had wandered far out of the orbit of Tilly.

[VI]

It is at this point in Tilly's career, that is to say during the first four years of his stay in Germany, that we begin to approach the author of these Memoirs directly, for here I am able to bring forward an entirely new contribution to the life of Tilly, the first indeed to be revealed from a source independent of his early editors. It thus possesses a definite value apart from its intrinsic interest, for it enables us to find indisputable proof of the statements made about Tilly by the original German editor who claimed to have access to his private papers, and it confirms the impressions which we gain from the Memoirs.

Tilly tells us, in the course of his narrative, of his duel in 1788 with his "cousin," Charles, Comte de Tilly-Blaru, a branch of the Tilly family which had become separate several centuries previously, and was disinclined to accept the claim of our Tilly's branch to belong to the family. Tilly fought the duel in support of this claim, which Tilly-Blaru thereupon agreed to recognise, and a permanent friendship was established, though the cousinship seems to be much more emphasised in the correspondence between them by our Tilly than by Tilly-Blaru. This gentleman, however, who was some ten years older, had much in common with the author of the Memoirs although he has left no record of himself in history. He was an ardent royalist and fought for Louis XVI; at the same time he occupied himself with *belles-lettres,* and was in correspondence with the Prince de Ligne and other distinguished persons. He found opportunity to return to Paris after the Revolution; but he remained an object of suspicion under every change of government and was watched by the police as a suspect, being once or twice ordered to leave Paris, though he seems to have disobeyed these orders. In consequence, a Tilly-Blaru dossier was constituted at the Paris Prefecture of Police, and this, being increased by the seizure of his letters and papers, at last included many hundreds of documents of the most various kinds.

I came on the track of this dossier through a reference in the "Intermédiaire des Chercheurs et des Curieux" for February 29, 1904, which stated that letters from Alexandre de Tilly were here to be found. It is a little troublesome to obtain access to the archives of the Paris prefecture of police, but this was achieved. With the skillful and scholarly aid of the Russian historian, M. Brian-Chaninov, who lives in Paris, I obtained all the information I desired concerning the letters of Alexandre de Tilly to Charles de Tilly-Blaru, twenty-three in number, dating from 1800 to 1803, and written sometimes from Leipzig, sometimes from Berlin, and once from Hamburg whither, it seems, Tilly occasionally had to go to claim money sent from England, probably his American annuity.

The letters are all in a friendly and even affectionate tone, although they are usually in response to incessant demands for favours—money, introductions to high personages able to confer situations, etc. For though our Tilly was still in exile, he was now in a superior position and able to exert influence. But incidentally we gain a number of little glimpses into Tilly's situation, tastes, and opinions, and from time to time also, we find Tilly playing his favourite part of mentor and moralist, though here addressing a man considerably older than himself and at least as well qualified to play the same part.

In 1800 Tilly is at Leipzig and writing with reference to a lady who is "the most intimate friend of the Duke of Weimar," but that is as near as Tilly ever brings us to Goethe. A little later he is in Berlin, ill, and regrets he cannot approach a great personage as requested. In July of the same year Tilly writes from Hamburg and fulminates against Bonaparte: "What do you think of Bonaparte, sitting republicanly on the most ancient throne in Europe and creating kings!" Two months later, from Leipzig, he regrets he cannot respond to the request for a loan: "At the moment I am in difficulties: I give you my word of honour." A week afterwards he is discussing the possibilities of returning to France: "God knows what I shall do, and if I can make up my mind to see once more my Lares." And later in the same letter: "Thank you again for all the sentiments you express, and also for all the compliments you pay to my Muse which, however, no longer has any voice."

In the same month he writes to ask news of Charles, and is pleased to hear of an improvement in his situation. He goes on to speak of old age and of the necessity for moderation in all things: "Here in Berlin there are many pleasures; I follow them in moderation, and the temperance prescribed to me in part by my ruined health and in part by the experience of a very full life, and that involuntary regret that always pursues me, far from our country, that I may perhaps never see again but shall ever bear in memory." Then follow letters mainly concerned with Charles's military career and his requests for intervention in his favour. In a letter of February, 1801, he seized on a remark of Charles, that he was a friend more than a relation, and observes: "That expression proves to me that you believe yourself convinced that I do not belong to the same house as

you." Several letters of little interest follow, one discussing the
recent death of Tsar Paul and the policy of his successor in
regard to the Order of Malta and the Grand Priory of Russia.

In August he writes of Bonaparte and considers that Charles
exaggerates his qualities. Later, in his letters, as in the Memoirs,
he becomes more enthusiastic about Bonaparte. In September
he writes from Leipzig: "I confess I have never advised you
to return to France." He proceeds to tell of his own position:
"I live at ease, which, however, is far from being a fortune,
with the calm of a happy insolence which never forsakes me on
necessary occasions, though in the ordinary course of life I am
apt to be melancholy. The fact is that, worn out by everything,
I no longer attach importance to anything, am surprised at
nothing, and flattered by nothing, but also allow myself to be
subjugated by nothing. The little Hollenshausen girl grants me
her amiability on credit, and a fine dance at little price. All that
has cost me three louis for fruits and hot water." In the same
letter he says: "My health, far from being good, has sent me
to these Neudorf waters, where the stay and the journey have
still further impaired my fortune." So he can send nothing to
Charles.

In November he writes a friendly letter from Berlin, and
next day he is writing again, this time about politics, with a
growing admiration for Bonaparte. Then there is a year's interval, and, meanwhile, Charles, who had apparently been previously at Weimar, has now returned to France, no doubt as a
result of that amnesty to the *émigrés* which specifically excepted
Tilly. But the return to Paris meant no peace for Tilly-Blaru;
his troubles with the government and the prefect of police began
almost at once, as his dossier shows, and increased as the years
passed. In September, 1802, Alexander writes to ask news of
Paris: "If you wish to give me a real pleasure, you will write
me a long letter, with a lively and unprejudiced picture of Paris,
of France and of her rulers, a picture of her government, her
amusements, her troubles, and her dangers." In another letter
of the same month he says: "My health is rather better, but I am
worn out by rheumatism, the result of my travels and indefinite
journeys." Towards the end of the year he writes appreciatively
of Charles's gift for verse (of which we know nothing), but
adds: "While I am on this subject, I will add something I have
on my mind: never write verses except for your mistress or your
pocket book!"

It will be seen that these letters have a real bearing on the life and career of Tilly—all the more valuable because they are the first letters of his to be brought to light—and it is instructive to find that they confirm the reliability of the German editor who—while careful, he tells us, to avoid quoting anything which would compromise Tilly-Blaru—gives numerous brief summaries of the very letters to which we now have our Tilly's replies. They are written from Weimar, Karlsruhe, etc., and most of the favours he begged seem to have come to nothing, but, the German editor states, Tilly had "in the noblest way" come to Tilly-Blaru's aid in October, 1800.

It may be worth while to quote at length a few of the letters in the Paris dossier. Thus Tilly writes from Leipzig on May 6, 1801:

> I have received your kind and polite assurances contained in your letter, my dear count, with regard to the interest which you take in what you call my successes; I received them with pleasure because I believe them, just as I believe in the loyalty of your disposition, and attach to your friendship a price which few people nowadays place on that noble sentiment.
>
> Even my enemies could scarcely grieve over the favours which fortune has occasionally shown me, since for long past, partly through the troubles, partly through the pleasures of a full and tumultuous life, my sensibilities are not easily moved. Believe me, I do not pretend to be a beau; in the autumn of my life, far from my country and my friends, I am not easily seducible, or easily impressed.
>
> However that may be, I am sensitive to the voice of your complaints, and the picture of your griefs causes me real grief. If we were talking together I could give you counsel by which I think you might profit; and if I can obtain the necessary light on the project, when I return from Hamburg (in a month's time), were we to pass twenty-four hours together, I could give you an idea which you might be able to utilise. I am only proposing what I think I could carry out, as I will try to prove to you.
>
> As regards the present, and my financial means, they are at zero, and I am going to Hamburg in a few days simply to negotiate a draft on England.
>
> Do not write until you hear from me, my dear

count. In the wandering life I am obliged to lead there
can be no fixity in our correspondence. And fixity is the
only foundation of prosperity and fortune.

In order to reply to your question as to the stability of Baron Krüdener's position in Berlin, it is
only necessary to refer to the gazette which tells us
that Emperor Alexander has confirmed him in his
post. And I may add that he has himself told me so;
he is a fine man, a man of wit and intelligence, and
with vast and varied knowledge. He is cold, buried
in affairs, and, I can see, has not much time to cultivate private correspondence.

Farewell, my dear count. I did not wish to leave
without talking to you, and repeating the assurance
of the real and tender friendship which devotes to
you for life your relative, Alexandre Comte de Tilly.

From Berlin, six months later, on November 11, Tilly writes:

It is long since I had a letter from you, my dear
count, and I have felt regret that our correspondence
was languishing: I hope that you received my last
letter; it was about the time of my arrival here, rather
more than a month ago.

I found an occasion to speak to Baron Krüdener
about your plan. "I am not allowed," he said, "to
send to my court one who is not actually attached to
the Emperor's service; but if the Comte de T.B. has
business calling him to Russia, and his only object is
to save the expenses of the journey he may come here,
and at the first departure of a special messenger he
will have a seat and travel at no expense." I made
clear that that was not the reason of your request, and
he repeated the expression of his regret. I am sorry
I can report nothing more satisfactory.

I am receiving letters from Paris. The sceptre of
B.C. [the Consul Bonaparte] is revealing itself and
gradually lengthening, and it will soon reach the pro-
portions of the late Charlemagne. His court is being
organised, and his throne will soon be surrounded by
almost the same courtiers as that of Louis XVI. But
the companions of his victories and his fortune will be
in the first rank, and the renegades from the monarchy will scarcely be seated even in the second row.

Courage and genius seldom reward servitude in the heart and timid inconstancy in the mind. For my own part, I surprise myself thinking that this extraordinary man deserves to restore the heritage of St. Louis, and such a thought is the false pretext of some and the holy excuse of others.

The good and celebrated Madame Lebrun is here; I offered her a bachelor dinner a few days ago, and was sufficiently inspired by her talent and fine productions to enter the field I had long abandoned, by addressing to her the following verses, which I send you because they have had much success here. [He quotes them, but they also appeared later in the second edition of his "œuvres mêlées"; Madame Lebrun is here compared with Titian, Correggio, Domenichino, and Albani.] Farewell, my dear count; happy are they who do nothing but make verses, who have a soul fresh enough to live in the fields with books and pencils! Far from the quarrels of jealousy, the blows of self-love, the machinations of envy and the fever of great social reunions, with a shepherd's pouch and a flute, shepherd's crook in hand, to wander on the banks of streams, in the green country! One needs also a shepherdess, not to mention a stomach. It is mine that throws me into this melancholy diatribe; I am having a serious quarrel with it, and would feel consoled by your affection. Assure him of it who is for you eternally a tender and sincere friend.

In January 1803 Tilly addressed from Berlin the last of his letters contained in this dossier:

A long time has elapsed since you heard of me, my dear count, and in spite of your wish for an answer you do not consider it my fault.

I had wished to tell you something satisfactory. I have neglected nothing to obtain that result, but unfortunately without success. First of all, I had to keep my room for a long time on account of the severe weather, though, even during my illness, I never lost sight of your interests. I will tell you my efforts and the issue:

To begin with your last proposition: it is only three days since I last made my court to the person

whose support you desire; I had the honour of dining
with him; he spoke to me with kindness, but it is not
in the midst of twenty-three to thirty people that one
can fittingly ask a favour. But I have cornered the
person who has most influence over him and best
knows what he feels and what he wishes. I will faithfully repeat the reply of this person, who deserves
consideration and is essentially good. "You will not
obtain, my dear count (I was told), what you ask;
any intervention of this kind is forbidden by *preliminary arrangements*. One could not ask, even for one's
brother, the smallest favour, and if one were to solicit
at Petersburg it would be without success. The imperial court grants nothing, and nothing is asked of it.
You would expose yourself," it was added, "to a definite refusal, which would do you neither harm nor
good, but would be painful to the giver."

To pass to the second hope which I had cherished
for you and have not yet abandoned, though its reali-
sation requires infinite care: I wrote to the one at
Munich on whom I counted for the service I wished to
render you, and the reply arrived only twenty-four
hours ago. It appears that the elector, so complacent
a few years ago in this matter, has to-day many more
officers than he needs, and rejects nearly every request; but that with very distinguished and long
service, and a good military reputation, there is very
little doubt that an advantageous position could be
obtained by an applicant *on the spot,* especially in
circumstances that I could arrange for you. But you
may imagine that I am far from proposing that you
should follow so uncertain a chance. Please believe
that even to obtain this poor response I have made
use of an influential person and exercised much care.
I am sorry that my genuine friendship for you has not
produced better results.

To console you, I would add that there is reason
to wager that a time will come (though I must not
speak more definitely) when I may be able to explore
the ground, and that you may assure yourself that we
shall have a better chance of success. If I were with
you, I could speak more clearly. The trouble is that
you are—and rightly—in a hurry.

I have myself endless troubles. My former father-
in-law is returning to America without completing the

affairs that I have a right to see terminated. [As we know, Bingham died at Bath without returning to America; the "affairs" left uncompleted were probably the composition of the annuity.] I no longer have any hope save in the Vicomte de Noailles, who is, in a way, the guarantor of my arrangements. M. de Poix wrote me last week that he is expected every day in Paris. Who has not his troubles?

I should like, my dear friend, to offer you consolation more prompt and direct; I repeat that if the horizon should clear I shall hasten to prepare the way for the reflections of its light to reach you. I embrace you tenderly.

That is the latest letter of Tilly's preserved in the Tilly-Blaru dossier, and the whole series shows him in no unamiable light, for it would scarcely seem that there were any motives of self-interest in his long-maintained anxiety to serve the interests of his unfortunate "cousin." We have here, not only a glimpse into Tilly's life and mind during his stay in Germany, but we are brought to the threshold of the Memoirs, for it was in this same year, 1803, that he began, at the age of forty-two, to write them.

[VII]

We do not clearly know how it was that at this moment Tilly conceived and carried out—we may be sure that in his impulsive temperament the execution swiftly followed the plan —the one great achievement which made him memorable. Various circumstances conspired to render the moment favourable. In spite of his endless troubles, this was a period of relative peace and comfort in Tilly's restless and agitated life, and he was enjoying an unusual degree of consideration. At the same time his days of adventure seemed over; he felt, as we have seen, that old age was approaching and that he must study to live moderately on account of his "ruined health"; his health never seems to have been robust, and, at all events after he left France, we frequently hear of indisposition or illness.

It may have been this need of a quieter life that turned his thoughts afresh to literature, and we know that at this time he was preparing for publication in Berlin the new and much enlarged edition of his "Œuvres mêlées." The feeling that the best part of his life was over—a feeling that might well be increased by the news that he had been definitely forbidden to return to France—may have furnished the impulse to set down in writing the record of that past life. The stimulating influence of Baroness Krüdener, with her literary and romantic tastes, possibly contributed to that impulse. And the Prince de Ligne, whom he had now been associating with—the dedicatee of the Memoirs—was perhaps the most decisive influence of all.

Tilly on his best side could not fail to be attracted to the Prince de Ligne. He was in personal touch with him, as was Tilly-Blaru, especially from about 1803 to 1806. They all belonged to the same aristocratic eighteenth-century world, the mingled world of courts and camps and salons and *belles-lettres,* the world of which the Prince de Ligne was the last and the supreme representative. The Revolution had driven him from France and his beautiful Belgian home; he was now living in Vienna and holding high position in the imperial army. He and Tilly frequently exchanged letters. The editor of the first German edition of the Memoirs, who claims to have had the prince's letters to Tilly in his hands, states that they are full of attachment, interest, and genuine friendship for Tilly, the highest admiration for his intellectual gifts, and a just judgement of his qualities and defects of heart and conduct, while he gives much excellent and sorely needed advice even on the most practical matters, such as money, literary style, and publishers—recommending to him a Dresden publisher with whom he had himself recently made an advantageous contract to issue a few volumes of what he modestly terms his "bêtises." Tilly showed his Memoirs to the prince, and the latter writes:

> I am most charmed to read you, and seem to hear you speaking, though I would much prefer to hear you, for then I could at the same time see you. Sad that we are separated by a sea of sand! If you ever feel inclined to emerge from it, come here and expiate in our salutary waters *delicta juventutis* and reward me for the feelings you have inspired.
>
> Nowadays [he adds with reference to the devastation of Europe by war as well as to his own love for gardening, for he had possessed in his Belgian home at Belœil the most famous of European gardens] one scarcely knows where to go when one only desires to see *ruins* in an English garden.

The Prince de Ligne was not only the last great figure of cosmopolitan significance in pre-revolutionary Europe but a most copious and facile writer, setting down fully for his own pleasure his impressions of himself and of the people he knew. "The careless and negligent ease of a man of quality," which Scott attributed to Byron's writings, was possessed in the highest degree by the Prince de Ligne. His style is the *ne plus ultra* of the aristocratic man of the world's familiar conversational tone, quiet, spontaneous, intimate but with a reserve of dignity, completely careless, abounding in flashes of insight but always tending to be too thin and too diffuse. It is hard to believe that it is written and not spoken. It is at the farthest remove from the more formal though also intimate style exemplified by, for instance, the Duc de Lauzun, another great and famous noble of the same period, in his Memoirs. Lauzun has an interesting narrative to tell, but there is always something bald, formal, and pedestrian in his telling of it. He is an inexpert writer, and by accident rather than by design he often omits necessary links in the narrative and desirable traits of description. So that we are always less interested than we feel we ought to be.

I would place Tilly as an analyst of manners between Lauzun and the Prince de Ligne, and above both. He has been regarded as personally an inferior sort of Lauzun, and in the life of courts and the adventures of gallantry he had much the same kind of story to tell. But Tilly's sense of life was more vivid, his interests were far wider, and notwithstanding all the defects of his own character he possessed a singular penetration into events and people, with a genuine literary power to transform his observations into words. Thus while his standpoint was like Lauzun's, he had much in common with the Prince de Ligne, though with the literary good sense to restrain the aristocratic conversational tone within more reasonable bounds, even while remaining careless and disorderly in style.

His manner of writing is sometimes peculiar, at moments a little difficult to follow; when riding his own high horse he is occasionally boring. But we are always carried on; we read to the end, even though the narrative is so broken. For Tilly is always vividly alive; at every moment he is all there, even though at the next moment his mood may have completely changed. And because he is so alive he draws us even though he may often at the same moment repel. It is by this balance of qualities—of historical significance with intimate personal

interest, of familiar conversational tone with literary instinct—
that Tilly's Memoirs, when we look back on them to-day,
possess unique value as a typical picture of the form and spirit
of the late French eighteenth century in its aristocratic aspects.
We can well understand the Prince de Ligne's admiration. "Since
the Memoirs of Louis XIV's time, and a few of those of the
Regent's," he wrote to Tilly, "the writers of such things have
been mere Versailles chair-porters. It is time that the last beautiful days of France should be in good hands." "Your collection," he is said to have written to Tilly again, "which I have
read with so much pleasure, is made for all ages and all countries, and is in no need of indulgence."

One would have thought that a work of which the most
competent of judges could speak so highly, and as we now see
so justly, would have been dealt with in the most reverently
careful spirit. Nothing of the kind! It has been left to chance.
Tilly wished it to be published after his death with, to prevent
offence, the omission of names. On his rather mysterious departure from Berlin in 1807, never to return, his private papers
and letters were left behind him, and we do not know in whose
hands he placed these Memoirs. For nine years after his death
they remained unknown, and his own name was almost forgotten. Then in 1825 to 1827 in Berlin appeared a German
translation in three volumes entitled "Memoiren des Grafen
Alexander von T——." The name of the translator and editor
was not given, and we do not know how he acquired the manuscript nor how he obtained access to the other papers of Tilly.
I have not seen this edition, but it was republished in Berlin in
1909, in Iwan Bloch's Sexualpsychologische Bibliothek, as "Die
Memoiren des Grafen von Tilly," edited by Feodor von Zobeltitz, who states in his preface that the original translator and
editor was Friedrich Wilhelm Bruckbräu (1729-1874), a Ba-
varian upper official in the Customs who found time from his
duties to write a number of books, verses, and rather loose
novels, historical or semi-historical books, and (three years after
his edition of Tilly) prose translations of Milton's "Paradise
Lost" and "Paradise Regained." In spite of these curiously miscellaneous literary avocations, he was certainly a good and careful translator with a wide knowledge of French literature and
history, which enabled him to supply valuable notes to his edition
of Tilly, while he was careful to give the words of the original
in a footnote when he could find no adequate German equivalent.

His supplement, moreover, describing the miscellaneous Tilly papers which came into his hands, is of great value for the light it throws on Tilly's life after 1792 when his own narrative ends. Our chief complaint against Bruckbräu remains that he fails to explain how these papers, as well as the manuscript of the Memoirs, came into his hands; and though he lived far into the nineteenth century he never seems to have made good this failure.

In 1828 appeared in Paris, also in three volumes, "Mémoires du Comte Alexandre de Tilly pour servir à l'Histoire des Mœurs de la Fin du 18e. Siècle," again without any editor's name. This is the standard edition of the Memoirs, extremely difficult to find nowadays, and it has served as the main foundation for the present translation. Here for the first time Tilly's name appears as author of the Memoirs, but the French editor's name still remains unknown. Like the German editor, he is competent and well acquainted with the history of Tilly's time, though he is able to add little of importance concerning Tilly himself, and what he does add is not always quite accurate. I conclude that he was the publisher of the work and must be added to the number of scholarly French publishers of the time, for as a supplement to one chapter he gives a "Note de l'Editeur" (regarding Mirabeau), stating that it is too long for a footnote; there is no publisher's name on the title page. We must assume that he had Tilly's original manuscript before him, though, like Bruckbräu, he gives no information as to how he obtained it. There can be no doubt that he also had the German edition, and his supplement concerning Tilly's later life follows, and somewhat amplifies, that of Bruckbräu.

But the anonymous French editor is not so reliable and conscientious as the German. The German, though a translator, is clearly anxious to present as nearly as possible what Tilly wrote. The Frenchman has no such anxiety; he wants to improve on Tilly. He adds alluring chapter headings; he omits sentences, even long passages, which do not seem to him interesting; he condenses, sometimes to the point of unintelligibility, and he has a trick of substituting more abstract expressions for Tilly's concrete statements ("I gave money to the woman who lighted me out" was in the German version, and surely in Tilly's words, "I placed money on the candlestick"; and for the description of a lady of title as "red as a fighting cock and sour as an unripe crabapple" we have in the French merely a reference to her acid disposition). More important are the constant transpositions. Tilly frequently digresses; he will break off an exciting love-adventure in the middle if a point of literary discussion suddenly occurs to him. These transpositions are so extensive and so numerous that it is not easy to compare the French edition with the German. They certainly, on the whole, render the narrative more easy to follow, and the order of the French version has in the present translation been accepted, though many of the omitted passages have been restored, as well as vigorous phrases which were toned down by the French editor.

Then there was a long period of silence. The "Mémoires de Tilly" could not fail to find readers in France, but Stendhal, who in so many other respects then stood alone, seems to have stood alone in his recognition of the significance of Tilly's Memoirs, and even he, as we have seen, proposed to abbreviate the work. So far as Tilly was known during the rest of the nineteenth century it was owing to the inclusion of an abridged version of the Memoirs under the title of "Souvenirs" in Vol. XXV (the first half of the volume being taken from Lauzun's Memoirs) of Barrière's Bibliotheque des Mémoires dealing with French history during the eighteenth century. Barrière attached no great value to "this awkward imitator of Lauzun," as he called him, and we cannot find fault with his moral disapprobation; he grudgingly admits the interest of the Memoirs, and remarks that, while they contain "some very strange episodes," they were not disputed when the book appeared so soon after Tilly's time. We may therefore accept them as furnishing an exact history of the manners of that age.

With the twentieth century a new era opened for Tilly's reputation. When his Memoirs first appeared the previous century was sinking from sight under a cloud of obloquy; it was not even seen that the nineteenth century itself, however magnificent, had its roots deep down in the eighteenth. With the coming of the twentieth century the reputation of the eighteenth began to grow clearer, and some of its representative figures no longer seemed to demand nothing more than moral indignation. If a halo could reverently be placed on the head of Casanova, hitherto objurgated when he was not shunned altogether, there was no longer any reason to despise Tilly. If the last century could accept the dictum that a man was a man "for a' that," the new century could take the further step of seeing that—in spite of all the still officially entrenched censors—a writer is a writer "for a' that."

So, in 1909, Iwan Bloch was able to place a reprint in two volumes of the earliest edition of Tilly's Memoirs at the head of his Sexualpsychologische Bibliothek, and the editor, Feodor von Zobeltitz, felt justified in making the highest claims for this "Song of songs of epicurean pessimism," as he calls it. He places it confidently above Casanova's Memoirs: "Tilly's Memoirs undoubtedly excel the Italian's in intimate charm and psychological delicacy, in stylistic form and artistic grace, above all in philosophic insight." That is, indeed, an extravagant and unjustifiable estimate; at none of these points is Tilly's superiority so clearly assured. Zobeltitz is on safer ground when he goes on to assert the value of Tilly's Memoirs as a picture of the court life, and especially the love life, of a man of the world of that age, of the rich and precious material here brought forward for the study of the women of the French rococo, of their special psychic constitution, of the spiritual refinements of the art of love in an age which largely devoted its literature to that matter, to the genial wantonness of society at that time, its extraordinary contrasts, its tumultuous progress to inevitable disaster. While Zobeltitz in the main follows the first German editor, he states that he has made some corrections and enlargements by comparison with the French edition, but, unfortunately, after the usual custom of Tilly's editors hereto, he neglects to give any precise indication of these changes.

In France the first French edition of 1828 has lately (1929) been reprinted in two pleasant volumes by the house of Jonquières, with an introduction and notes by M. Melchior-Bonnet, and some good portrait illustrations. But on examination this edition proves to be highly unsatisfactory. The text swarms with printer's errors and unintended omissions. The editor's notes are competent and his introduction most agreeably written, but he has added scarcely anything to the statements about Tilly brought by the French editor a century before; he has made no fresh examination of the text of the Memoirs and he seems to know nothing of the first German edition and of the problems raised by its variations, or of the doubts thrown on the authenticity of the whole work. The index, also, looks most elaborate and useful, but on examination its page references are found to be in the large majority completely inaccurate.

It is fully time that a competent French scholar arose to make a scientific study of this whole subject and to produce a really adequate edition of a work which increases in interest as the period it so vividly brings before us recedes into the past.

In Belgium M. Félicien Leuridant has brought a scholarly equip-
ment to bear on the life and work of the Prince de Ligne, and
Tilly is now beginning to be regarded as worthy of similar
careful study. In his "Livres du Second Rayon" (1926) a good
modern critic, Émile Henriot, well brings out the significance
of Tilly, viewed from the standpoint of to-day, as coming not
far short of the highest rank among annalists of the late eighteenth century, while some of the episodes of the Memoirs, as
Henriot well insists, are little masterpieces which might have
been written by Diderot.

It is not to be supposed that the most desirable edition of
Tilly's Memoirs could be produced in the version by which the
work is for the first time presented to the English reader. That
must be done by a French scholar working, so far as may be
possible, on the original French sources. Yet a considerable claim
may be made for the present edition. Not only is new material
here brought forward to elucidate Tilly's history, but here, for
the first time, an attempt, however imperfect, has been made
to compare the two original texts of the Memoirs, thus utilising
in some degree that primary German version, which, though a
translation, is evidently nearer in substance to what Tilly wrote
than the existing French text. So that, by combining many of
the features of the German and French texts, the present is in
some respects the best version of the Memoirs that has yet
appeared. It will, I believe, be seen by anyone who compares
the present version with the originals that it reproduces with
felicity not only the substance but the spirit and tone of the
Memoirs: the aristocratic nonchalance of the young nobleman
who had been Marie Antoinette's page, his gay impertinence,
the amusing solemnity of his misplaced moralisings, his literary
affectations, and the peculiar savour of his individual style with
its mingling of wayward impetuosity, stilted awkwardness, occasional seeming obscurity, yet really vivid and penetrating vital-
ity, and, piercing through, that sense of an approaching end
perhaps more tragic than the guillotine which, unlike so many of
his friends and associates, Tilly had escaped.

[VIII]

That end was now approaching and there is little more to
tell. Somewhere about 1803 Tilly had had a love experience—

his last so far as we know—which had a fatal termination and deeply affected him. He refers to it with genuine feeling in the Memoirs, which he was just then beginning to write. In this episode there seems to have been passion on both sides, but for some reason the lady committed suicide by drowning herself in the Spree. Bruckbräu describes how he found among Tilly's papers a small black-sealed packet with the inscription in the count's hand: "A memorial of great misfortune, of regret, and of eternal sorrow." It contained, together with various love favours and souvenirs, a farewell letter from Tilly's Clara— as she seems to have been named—written shortly before her death:

> I assure you, my dear Tilly, that it is from my own impulse, and by my own free will, that I write this to you; I swear that all that I have ever said to my beloved Tilly is true; I swear in God's name that I have never, never deceived, never betrayed him even in thought. If this oath is false, may God punish me in the most terrible way, by death, or the misfortunes of my worshipped Tilly. May He thrust me away without mercy when I appear before His judgement seat, and may the happiness of my children, now and there, be destroyed. These oaths also cover the future should I ever deceive you without having first acknowledged that I no longer love you. Then, Tilly, you may make this paper known and shame me before the whole world.

She goes on to reaffirm this oath even more emphatically, signing it C. E. P—— née St. —— from Berlin, December 13, 1803. She adds a postscript: "That story about the hair is also a puzzle to me; but all these sacred oaths are a warrant that it concerns no man that I know."

It seems to be suggested by this letter that the tragedy was caused by Tilly's unreasonable jealousy. That was evidently Bruckbräu's opinion, for he adds that thenceforward "a revenging Nemesis" pursued Tilly. The consideration with which he had been received and accepted in the highest circles of Berlin began to melt away, his credit lessened, his debts increased, creditors grew pressing. With Tilly's reckless and extravagant disposition the composition with Bingham's heirs which brought him a large lump sum and deprived him of an income was more a misfortune than a blessing. During 1806 he was making fruitless efforts to return to France. In the spring of 1807—at some date after April 30—he left Berlin, abruptly breaking off all relations with that city, and his German editor loses track of him and can tell us no more.

At an earlier point in his supplement, however, Bruckbräu had mentioned that Tilly was attempting through friends at the court of the Netherlands to obtain permission from the king to enter the country, hoping to settle in Brussels or the Hague, and thence perhaps be able to reach Paris; and he adds that Tilly is amongst a list of persons receiving the Cross of the Legion of Honour. But the abandonment in Berlin, not only of the Memoirs, but of his personal papers, letters, and treasured souvenirs, seems to indicate that his disappearance was sudden and due to an apprehension of immediate danger. The explanation may lie in the great victory of Jena, which at that time had placed Berlin at Napoleon's mercy. Tilly's Prussian protectors fled, and he was not himself acceptable to Napoleon. He may well have considered that the safest course lay in flight. The battle was fought in October, 1806, peace between France and Prussia not being arranged until July, 1807, some time after Tilly's disappearance from Berlin. It remains mysterious why Tilly never reclaimed these treasures during the remaining nine years of his life, and why he never made, so far as we know, any arrangements for their disposal. Bruckbräu, who only brought forward his translation after a further delay of nine years, gives no hint that he was acting in accordance with instructions received from Tilly. Possibly, during the later years of his life, Tilly had no means of returning to Berlin and no friends there to whom he could entrust a confidential mission.

From other sources it would appear that Tilly went to Brussels and only returned to France in 1814 after the Bourbon restoration, again, a little later, going back to Brussels, so that the longing for Paris which had gnawed at his heart for so many years proved but an empty satisfaction when at last he attained it.

It is not hard to understand. Tilly always belonged to the *ancien régime.* He remained at heart, what he still remains in popular repute—so far as he has any repute at all—the former page of Marie Antoinette. But the world he belonged to had vanished. It must have seemed an unrecognisable Paris, a melancholy Versailles, to which he at last came back. The people he had known had nothing in common with the new businesslike

bourgeois generation industriously building up another and
tamer society on the ground swept by the storms of the Revolution and disciplined by the rod of Napoleon.

Moreover, Tilly arrived home late. Most of the *émigrés*
had already returned, and made some kind of adaptation to
the new order. Tilly was not only late, he was inadaptable.
Even at the court of Marie Antoinette his conduct had called
for royal reproof. The "mad" Tilly of twenty years earlier was
now quite hopeless, and there was no longer the old spirit of
indulgence for madcap aristocrats, even among their own peers.
The worn-out man of the world who continued to lead a life of
pleasure and to show a lordly indifference to debts could only
be viewed with contempt in the practical nineteenth century.
It seems clear that during his last years Tilly had become disreputable. He no longer had any friends of repute. The friends
of old days either were dead or stood carefully aloof. The Prince
de Ligne, who had been so amiable, and so full of admiration
for the Memoirs of which he had accepted the dedication, was
indeed still alive though still in Austria. He wrote the most
interesting reminiscences we possess of Casanova. M. Félicien
Leuridant, who is the chief authority on the prince and is now
engaged in editing his correspondence, tells me that he has
nowhere found there even the mention of Tilly. And when by
his own hand Tilly died no one cared enough to record any
impressions of a man who now seems to us, with all his weaknesses and defects, so significant a figure.

Thus it is that a cloud still hangs over Tilly's end. We merely
hear a varying rumour. It is even a rumour which seems not to
have reached his first editor, nor the writer of the early and
rather inaccurate notice of Tilly, before the publication of the
Memoirs, in the Biographie Universelle, giving a date to
the suicide, which Stendhal also misdated. We find it first
brought forward by the French editor of 1828, who is likely to
have received a correct report, and until new documents are
discovered, it is his version of Tilly's end, since no friend came
forward to contradict it, which we must accept:

> He was seen in Paris in 1815, after the second
> Restoration; but he soon returned to Brussels. There,
> overcome by misery, he once more took to gambling,
> and that fatal passion having led him to commit an
> action which was intolerable to his naturally proud
> and independent spirit, he died by his own hand on

December 26, 1816, thus throwing off the burden of a life he could no longer support without dishonour. Such was the deplorable end of a man who by his intellectual and other brilliant qualities would have continued to be the ornament of society if he had known how to master his passions and to avoid the paths of vice.

HAVELOCK ELLIS

NOTE BY TRANSLATOR

The notes to this translation, given at the end of the book, are partly based on those in the German and French editions, and partly original. The translator wishes to acknowledge the valuable assistance she has received from Mr. Havelock Ellis in the preparation of these notes.

To the Prince

Charles-Joseph de Ligne [1]

General of Infantry
in the Service of His Majesty the Emperor of Austria.

Prince,

I present this work to you, not only because you have written much and are an excellent judge, but also because you are one of the men who have best seen Europe and best known France; consequently you have been loved there as much as anywhere, and people have found you delightful.

You have been famous in camps, courts, and drawing-rooms; I could add to this another kind of fame, but both your modesty and discretion would take fright were I to reveal secrets belonging to a sex you and I still revere to-day, though it is from afar we bring incense to its altars.

I should besides be offering you an embarrassing panegyric if I became too faithful an echo of your achievements in every field: the distinction of your life, the delicacy of your feelings, the kindness of your heart, the beauty and breadth of your intelligence cross my mind; yet you would not allow me to dwell on them; you may even reproach me for these few brilliant details.

I shall, then, limit myself to giving you my reasons for putting pen to paper.

It is my own story I write; having long since lost interest in my own cause, I shall speak of myself without petty vanity or false modesty, in fact as if I were writing the life of a stranger to whom I owe only the truth. Although my story is bestrewed with more out-of-the-way incidents than have happened to most people, I know too well the pitfalls in this sort of work to be under any illusion as to the drawbacks attached to it; so I long resisted the temptation to write it.

For, should one say little, one becomes insignificant, should one say everything, one is presumptuous; who knows even if

---

[1] See p. 497.

wounded pride will not tax one with deception and unfaithfulness?

As a matter of fact I am certain I should have thrown down
the pen, had there been only myself to speak of. I give my word
that, having no illusions left and having observed men and
events, I believe that this sketch of the manners of my century
which I want to offer to the public can be done in the manner
of a painter who has seen, analysed, and thought out the scheme
of a picture wherein he himself has an allotted place. Perhaps
some interest will be found in following him through half a
lifetime, so full as to appear to himself almost the whole course.

Whatever risk there is in speaking of oneself, I shall not
spare the readers what Pascal calls "the odious I." Here are
my reasons: this new production cannot be entirely without interest since men are made as they are, and the days we live
through are so distressing; but I am perfectly sure, that, by
the time it reaches publication whatever judgement may be
passed will no longer make any difference to me.

Besides, the book is much more the story of my period than
my own story, a matter of twenty-four years. On the other
hand, I do not think I am mistaken in believing that I have
memorised and observed, often at close quarters, better than
many people who have badly interpreted things and viewed them
from too far off, for they had no other means of information
than newspapers, legendary pamphlets, prejudices, or mutilated
and spiteful second-rate narratives; they imbibed opinions only
from backstairs sources and from lies, the diffusion of which
gave them secret pleasure. Others may have been more sincere,
but their style is often such as to disgust one with truth itself.

To you, Prince, I submit these considerations and motives.

The little I read you of these memoirs in Berlin, appeared
to win your approbation; you praised them with so much indulgence that I have not hesitated to bring them to a conclusion.

You know that only the truth is put down here in all that
concerns personal matters, and concerning other matters only
what I know to be true, or what I sincerely believe to be so.
I have seen and interpreted facts for myself; I have also sought
them from sources where they emerged in all their purity, or
else I have found the support of proved information through
eminent witnesses and unexceptionable authorities.

I have said nothing of what I did not know.

I have mentioned contemporary events with the impartiality

and calmness I should have brought to picture facts a thousand years distant, for indeed a thousand years have swept over us and we are already history.

History—that uncertain compilation of our transient apparition upon this globe of blood and mud! History—those pages which we can scarcely write when they are of our own time, though we long to bring forth the centuries in books packed with lies, long to unravel the mysteries of nature and the final secret of Him who created it! How can we attach importance to anything, since we were born yesterday, will die to-morrow, and are treading on a planet that will perish as well as we? But we write a few pages of our story, while all the pages of life are torn, while the big book of the universe will itself be obliterated, and there will only be infinite nothingness awaiting us.

How can one explain the attraction which prompts us to leave a name among wreckage and ruins? Does man love to dispute her spoils to Death, love to deposit some traces of himself, to hand down thoughts contemporaneous with his journey through life? He hopes that his writings will survive him a few days: he loves to contend with nothingness.

Such is the explanation of this book. It will at least have two main characteristics: truth and impartiality.

If there is about us any such thing as truth, I utter it here without reserve. Prince, I take pleasure in saying it again: my one object is truth. Rousseau declares: *Vitam impendere vero,* while I say: *Vitam—mortem.* For it means death to give oneself wholly to the public.

But this book will not be a libel against any one . . . unless it be against those people who are now beyond fearing libel and whose names belong to the realms of history or are claimed by public vengeance.

Prince, in offering you these first words, I shall not call them a preface, which is above me, nor an epistolary dedication, which is beneath you. They are simply the foreword to an account (the book could be so called) of my feelings, the events of my days, my mind's opinions and reflexions on my whole life.

Allow me to add the expression of my feelings of admiration, friendship, and tender esteem: the marks of my devotion.

Alexandre de Tilly.

CHAPTER I

Exegi monumentum. . . .

*It is meet that Truth should seek to impart a
useful lesson whenever a narrative is engaging
and varied: our century erects no defences of
modesty against the outspoken word, and leaves
one little credit for finding no subject unfit for
human ears.*

A STORMY life, extraordinary adventures, great misfortunes, frequent happiness at times leading to brilliant success, and coupled with these a decent memory, might raise any man above his ordinary station; and if, besides, he has travelled for over twelve years, explored a great part of Europe and the New World, and probed into all ranks of society and all conditions, one might believe him entitled to claim a right for his opinions with hope of converting thereto the fellow-men on behalf of whom he took the trouble of knocking about the world, fighting against odds and the elements, viewing things, observing and thinking. But I do not entertain the vain pretension of bringing enlightenment to any one in a century where every man believes himself in possession of sufficient education and wit to despise these qualities in others and to slander them.

I write for myself and for that small number of readers who think that nearly always a second-rate book offers material for a good one; I write to correct errors generally accepted as truth, to avenge some people whose memory has been maligned, and to establish facts; I am about to formulate things I am sure that I know, and which have only been talked about by people who did not know them; I write in short for those to whom the spectacle of human passions and the unravelling of the heart still present, even in our days, not only useful lessons, but pictures of the greatest interest.

If there are to be found in my narrative traces of a wounded and melancholy imagination, a rejection of all deceitful dreams tending to delude man through life, and the weariness and distastes of a heart worn old before its time, the reader may easily see that this is what must above all be found in such a story,

for I would not have allowed myself to write were I not dead
to the world before I have ceased to live. . . . But I forget
that a book like this needs no preface.

I was born in 1764,[1] in a provincial town renowned for the
beauty of its candles, which are famous all over France; I
might add that all good judges of cookery hold its chickens in
high esteem, so the reader will understand that I was born at
Le Mans, the old capital of the province of Maine. My family,
originating from Normandy, and one of the most ancient in this
province, had powerfully helped to bring it under our kings' rule.

My grandfather, a former state official, had retired early to
one of his estates, where he devoted his time to rural management and the upbringing of a fairly large family. His fortune
was middling as he was born a youngest son, and had besides
married a titled lady [2] with no other dowry than a pretty face.
He was a man of strict virtues, one of those honorable knights
of the days of chivalry. I knew him only at an advanced age.
I was then very young, and I am rather pleased with myself
for never having forgotten his patriarchal face, emblem of a
pure heart, and his serene inexhaustible mirth, the result of a
life wholly spent in the service of honour.

My father early entered on a military career, as did his two
brothers, who pursued that course to the end, while he abandoned it almost at the start. Thrown amongst all sorts of dissipations, he yet sufficiently kept his wits, while travelling through
the province of Maine, to appreciate my mother's beauty and
virtues as well as her fortune; he asked her hand and easily
obtained it from her family, who held honourable rank in this
province though of rather modern nobility. She had a brother
who had joined the mousquetaires and who, being called to
inherit what was then looked upon as a considerable fortune,
had vowed never to marry; he would most certainly have kept
his word if twenty years later, with a violence extremely to be
condemned, I had not more or less brought him to change his
resolve.

Blessed with an interesting face, an upright character, and a
cultivated mind (as I learned from all those who knew her) my
mother did not long see the hymeneal torch alight; before a
year was over, it gave place to funeral lamps burning by the
side of the coffin into which my birth had driven her; a mother's
death paid for my life—this stormy life which Fate has ever
since condemned to a few temporary pleasures, many lasting

sorrows, prolonged disturbances, ups and downs of fortune, and the injustice of exile.

A weakling, I was left to the care of Mme de C——,[3] my maternal grandmother, a woman of superior intelligence had not her natural and acquired gifts been obscured by a provincial religious zeal which I should call bigotry. I remember that she used to call Corneille and Racine corrupters of the soul; the first, she declared, "being a profane rhetorician and the second a charmer sent forth by the evil one, though, when won over by grace, he had died in a hair shirt. As for M. de Voltaire, my boy," she would add, "you should prefer death to his works." She spared nothing for my education but, as she spoiled me, she brought me up very badly.

The author of my days, in the meanwhile, ran through his fortune as well as mine, which was in his care, by plunging into costly pleasures. Born with tempestuous passions, middling wits, but a heart of more worth, he might have had some fine qualities had they not been tarnished by frightful fits of temper and a haughtiness that would justify a thoroughgoing revolution. I have never known a man to fall in love with such facility; his heart seemed to hold sap for ever renewed susceptibility. I have known him to have mistresses even at an advanced age; he always worshipped them and invariably left them. He must have brought in front of the Almighty Judge a soul full of the tenderest feelings; this soul is now in a safe harbor if, on leaving this earth, it gave itself to adoring God as utterly as it before had loved his creatures.

He never troubled much about my education. It did, however, occur to him that he might carry it out at home with more success; so he took me away. I was entrusted to valets and some sort of tutor, in many respects not unlike them. I hasten to put on record the other occasions when my father made it his duty to look after me, and, as they will prove the last instances of such care and reveal both his solicitude and severity as entirely out of place and harmful, I shall hurry through these, never to mention them again.

I was nine years of age when my father noticed that I was sensitive to the robust charms of a kind of housekeeper called Mme Rohu, whose caresses, arousing my desires, caused him to doubt my innocence. He wished to gain enlightenment and told the woman to give me encouragement. Out of sheer instinct, so I believe, I soon came to urge the woman to allow me, the following night, to enter the modest alcove where her charms reposed. Difficulties were raised on her side, meeting with increased desire on mine. The traitor having warned her master, he set out hunting on the morrow. No sooner was he gone than she gave me to understand that an opportunity as favourable as this would scarcely occur again. I became still more pressing, and she feigned to yield. Having gone to a secluded room that was to be the scene of my precocious felicity, I was on the point of being taught a lesson that I was scarcely in a position to act upon, when my father suddenly burst into the room by another door, the existence of which I did not even know. He piled pretended abuse upon my false accomplice and, armed with a riding whip, struck me severely without drawing from me a cry—so swift was my perception of a contrived treachery, which shocked both my pride and the generosity of my nature.

My spirits were hardly soothed when another incident, very soon after, rendered me indifferent to either threats or affection. My father possessed a handsome watch, which would be of little worth in our days; it disappeared from his room, and he dared to suspect me of having committed a base action. The servants protested their innocence, and mine was questioned. I was cross-examined, I scorned to reply; I was locked in my room, I refused all food; I was whipped, I showed only a cold and contemptuous anger that frightened him. I do not know how far this ordeal would have been carried, had not the wretched watch been found in the room of the valet who had stolen it. I asked that he should be forgiven; these were the last words I uttered until the time when I begged to be sent to a boarding-school or a college. I received satisfaction and went to the Collège de la Flèche, which was but the shadow of that once famous seminary where the Jesuits had taught their doctrine, erudition, and *belles-lettres,* but nevertheless was still an excellent school, I believe indeed one of the best in the world. I made rapid progress and laid there the foundations of my taste for study and the classic authors from whom the modern have stolen almost everything. Three years went by under the eyes of a man well worthy of being a guide to youth, teaching it whatever can be learned, and building up its strength in matters that do not come to one through learning. My father came only once to see me; he always travelled with his horses, whom he dearly loved; he scarcely spoke of anything else except of a fine carriage he had come near to smashing, at which he was greatly grieved.

I asked him for money to buy books; this he gave me, and it was not converted to any other use.

I dwell perhaps too long on the details of this period of life, which flows by so rapidly yet is remembered as long as one retains any traces of memory, though such recollections are rated by strangers as insipid selfishness only of interest to indulgent friends. But as youth is in my opinion a sample of the future life, and the inclinations and actions of the early years mark the course of the whole life, the attentive and observant reader will perhaps follow my first steps. Those whose imagination it hinders may skip this prelude.

I was thirteen years old and was completing my studies when one of my uncles obtained for me the post of page to the queen. I was torn from the seclusion of studies that gave me happiness and taken to my paternal grandmother, who, being jealous of my other grandmother, wanted to keep me with her and in her turn spoil me as much as she could before I started for Versailles.

In this soft leisure I suddenly fell in love with a fresh and discreet country girl, even more a novice than I was. Soon, being united by common sympathy, secrecy guided our early steps in love-making. The truth is that Suzette received the first tributes of one who since . . .[4] But we must not forestall— events will unfold themselves and each fall naturally in its place.

How easily does love betray itself! Our meetings were discovered; their secrecy was that of the secluded meadows, their shelter that of the woods; the sky and nature were always present. A witness saw what we wished to hide; he spoke, my grandmother learnt everything, and I was sent back to school, on this occasion to the Collège d'Alençon.

The reader will now be satisfied; in a more hurried narrative I will say nothing unnecessary; and there I am in a new school for six months before the date fixed for my going to Versailles. I went back to my studies with fervour; the vision of Suzette did not haunt me. An aunt came to see me whose kindness is for ever imprinted in my heart; she preached me a very pathetic sermon on the danger of attachments of a certain kind and the opprobrium meted out to seducers; she did not win me over entirely, but I appeared convinced and did not fall back into my sin—which was as much as was needed.

Some time later a complete new outfit was provided for me, and I was advised to kneel at the feet of a priest and pour out all my youthful pranks, wicked thoughts I was not sure I had

had, then purify myself of such pollution at the holy table. I do not repent having done so; I do not know whether religious observances, whatever they are, can be praise worthy of Him who is above our homage, but they cannot fail to interest Him in our weakness, which seeks to lean against the minor pillars of His throne and to partake of His infinite and unsearchable power.

Peaceful as to the intimate passions, rested as to health, shy to excess, and with a slight book learning, I found myself on the way to Versailles. The Marquis de V——," a relative of mine, who was also taking his son to be page to the queen, conducted me to his coach, and we were carried away towards the capital of France where the fate of nations has since hung in the balance.

CHAPTER II

Away with vain projects! No more petty schemes!
Come, follow my flight to the country of dreams;
To smiling Marly, to the pomp of Versailles,
Raised by Louis, Nature and Art, to the sky.
Here everything's great and Art shows no fear,
Armide's enchanted palace is here,
And the garden of Alcide, the glorious seat
Of a hero who seeks a noble retreat,
Yet accomplishing labours and vanquishing ill,
In his progress surrounded by miracles still.
                                        —DELILLE

*L*IKE a new Telemachus under the guidance of another
Mentor, I arrived at Versailles without meeting on the
way any Eucharis; the real ones live in Paris. I had believed
myself borne into fairyland, so I was surprised at nothing. It is
nearly always the fate of things we have admired in anticipation to fall far short of our dreams. By always hearing praises
of Versailles and its splendour, the varied and picturesque beauty
of its site, the magnificence of its palace, its park, gardens, and
statues, the lustre and glory around our king's throne, I had
been led to dream of impossibilities and to imagine works of
art which it is not given to men either to contemplate or to
attain.

What struck me most from the first was the immeasurable
distance from one man to another, and the suppleness of insolence, transforming itself instantaneously into submission: the
assiduous attention, the politeness, the mobility of countenance,
the uniformity of attitude, and the alternation of studied unconcern with factitious ardour.

These were things not learnt in books and no one had spoken
of them to a child of fourteen.

The King's presence left me unperturbed; his face did not
answer to what I had expected; it was simple and kindly, I
should have liked it strongly cast and majestic; his gaze was
that of a father resting on his children, I wished one could have
read in it: "If need be I could exert my will, command and

punish." Alas! as we all know to-day, righteous severity is a
cardinal virtue in a king, a virtue that preserves power.

The Queen was then in all her splendour.[1] I shall later speak
of her moral disposition. Although this work does not deal with
politics, I shall not avoid mentioning them, but I shall not seek
opportunities; besides I have no wish to anticipate. I shall speak
of the Queen whenever my personal story gives me occasion to;
I shall not speak of her as others have done; I shall tell what I
have myself seen and what I have known about her from unimpeachable authorities.

I shall tell what is not to be found about her in books made
up by writers too far removed from the real stage, or by
fanatics who hoped to exalt themselves by reviling great ones
thrown to earth, or again by scoundrels who have put into print
servants' gossip, which provincial people, and above all foreigners, greedily devour, taking it too often for the truth. I shall
draw a picture which I am sure will be in the likeness of this
unfortunate princess, whose sufferings have won over her former
enemies and presented her to posterity to claim the pity of the
least susceptible hearts. But I must reaffirm that this picture will
not appear of a piece; the reader will need to seek its essential
features scattered throughout these memoirs and take the
trouble to make them into a complete whole.

Marie Antoinette of Austria, Queen of France, always
treated with special kindness those who attended her person;
she was worshipped by her household: it was even from this
sphere of life that sprang the forces governing her, though
without special plan or scheme, for she never made any, save
to free herself from the exigencies and constraint of her rank,
the bearing and dignity of which she could assume when she
wished; but she more often did not wish.

I have heard many people speak of the beauty of this
princess. I must confess I have never entirely shared this opinion; but she had what on a throne counts for more than perfect
beauty—the face of a queen of France even at those moments
when she most tried to appear only a pretty woman. She had
eyes that were not beautiful but could reveal the whole range
of feeling; kindness or aversion could be depicted in her looks
more markedly than I have met them elsewhere. I am not sure
that her nose rightly belonged to her type of face. Her mouth
was decidedly unpleasant; the thick, protruding, and at times
drooping under lip has been pointed out as giving nobility and

distinction to her appearance; it could have been of use only to
portray anger and indignation, and this is not the usual look
on beauty's face. Her skin was admirable, her shoulders and
neck matched it; her bosom was rather too full, and her waist
might have been more elegant; but I have never met since with
arms and hands more beautiful. She had two distinctive gaits in
walking, one firm, rather hurried and always imposing, the other
more gentle and swinging, I should say almost caressing, yet
never prompting one to forget respect. No one has ever curt-
sied with so much grace, greeting ten people with a single inclination, and, by look and the pose of the head, giving each one his
due. . . . In short, just as one would offer a chair to any other
woman, for her one *nearly* always longed to bring forth a
throne.

As to the characteristic features of her disposition, I repeat
that I have no wish to give them any attention at present.
I shall mention only two, because they were very pronounced
and always recurred in both her private and public life: they are,
besides, the source of her mistakes and her misfortunes, unequalled and unparalleled in civilised countries. I have in mind
her distaste for the set rules surrounding royalty, more necessary in France than in any other land within my knowledge,
and her incurable prejudice (although as a rule she was by
nature rather uncertain and hesitant) in favour of, or against,
people who had been pointed out to her kind attention or her
hatred, or whom she had herself thoughtlessly marked out.

On my arrival she treated me as she did all the young boys
who were her pages, loading them with favours while displaying
a stately benevolence that could have been called maternal, as
she joined to it a dignified and warm-hearted politeness that rendered her, were it possible, more worthy of respect by adding
to the love one bore her.

I may be asked: "Did you observe all this at the time of
which you speak, and at an age so near to childhood?" To which
I answer: "Yes, for at fifteen I was worth more than I am
to-day; my wits, far less corrupted, were exceedingly clear."
But I shall not say much of wits, as I hold such powers in poor
esteem, not only in myself but also in others, when that is all
there is to boast of.

Besides, it is for those who will read these memoirs to judge
whether Nature has given me of this *drug*, nowaday in fairly
common use and nearly always fatal; whether it has endowed

me with some talent, which is quite another thing, or with warm-heartedness and strength, again two very different attributes, for they essentially belong to the kingdom of the soul.

The first year went by offering nothing worthy of notice. I observed life and endeavoured to collect my observations into some order which might one day guide me. But an inexhaustible leaning towards thoughtlessness in practical things imperilled a success that in theory seemed of fair promise. I made but moderate progress, though having masters of all descriptions, for I found little attraction in any task. My nature was handled in the wrong way and crushed under the imbecile mediocrity of a dominie who, goodness knows how, had been given the Saint Louis Cross at the age of twenty-two. He was always talking about it, yet never justified those who had bestowed it on him. The management of probationers during this first year was also in complete opposition to all my notions of fairness, and imbued me with aversion for a school that, in my opinion, offered more hindrance than advantage. Like every one else, I learned to ride, to dance, and to fence, but I failed even to reach mediocrity in mathematics and drawing. I never managed to know my German master's name and I remember that after three years he was still telling me that his name was Guérault de Palmfeld, while I was no further on than calling him M. Gérau. But on the other hand I succeeded, by myself, in learning Latin perfectly, as well as the technique of French verse, towards which I had an irresistible leaning, though I have since without the least attraction written many verses and now can read no poetry but the very best and never more than a hundred lines at a time.

During my second year, a staff officer whom I shall keep nameless was granted leave to take me to spend a week in Paris; he had been my father's friend and had met me in the palace at Versailles. To entrust me to such a mentor was far from wisdom at the best. He gave me a room in his house, where I met fairly good company as regards men but of the worst as to women. A very pretty mistress, who ruined him, since his income was not large, presided as hostess. As is the rule, she whole-heartedly detested her keeper. I threw her a few loving glances, to which she responded, giving me hope: she assured me I looked like a pretty girl of her acquaintance; I quickly proved to her that I was, so at least people used to say, only a pretty youth. My host noticed all this on the morrow (what does not jealousy observe?) and sought a duel with me. He was

made to feel how ridiculous this would be, and the episode was
submerged in floods of champagne, from which my wandering
wits drifted into the arms of a fragile nymph whose trade was
to sell pleasure and regrets. One of my friends, M. de Chillau,
having come up that day to Paris, I took him also to her; he met
there with the same misfortune.

On my return to Versailles I resumed my ordinary life; it
was difficult in the state I found myself through the siren who
had seduced me and punished me. I sought the advice of an
obscure quack, and my friend also had recourse to him; but his
disease becoming more serious than mine he thought he would
die. What it was so much in our interest to hide was discovered;
we were handed over to the doctors. I was quickly rid of my
trouble; but my friend's recovery was long and painful. I beg
the readers of both sexes to forgive me for the confession of
this none too honourable incident of my private life, but it had
a very direct influence upon my reputation as a page, and perhaps, in several respects, upon my whole future. I have promised
to tell everything and do not seek to exonerate myself. Let us
look naturally at the facts. A man holding an honourable rank
in society misleads by bad example and swift seduction a young
man of fifteen, who introduces to a friend—who begs him to
do so—the woman whose memory still charms his senses. They
have no suspicion of any danger, and both of them, as I have
said, find punishment in the fault itself. Dreading to confess the
misdemeanour to their superiors, and with due cause, they seek
help from strangers, are deceived in their hope, "and so this
horrible secret becomes known." [2] Let us see what will be the
consequences.

Rumours are spread abroad, even the Queen is told (for
there are veils for all kinds of narratives) that I went to Paris
under false pretences and abandoned myself to all the excesses
of an older man; that I fought a duel, became acquainted with
the whole prostitute world of Babylon, bringing back all its
corruption; that I *dragged* a friend, until then entirely faultless,
to a strumpet the disgrace of her sex; that I am the cause of
his misfortune; that his health is most likely to be forever lost;
that I hardened him in final impenitence by *dissuading* him from
making confession of his state and clandestinely thrusting him
into the hands of a shameless quack; that this proves a combina-
tion of debauchery, cunning, and vices of all kinds, symptoms
and seeds from which will come a *worthless fellow*. It is added

that I have received every punishment inflicted upon me with heedless scorn, but it is not said that it was because all the reproaches which I had not deserved went with the punishment, while I was really worthy of praise on one count, that of not having uttered a single word to betray a staff officer, for whom my complaints would have meant ludicrous dishonour, nor my accomplice, who shared half my faults as I had in no way enticed him.

Let those entrusted with the education of youth study their pupils' natures, weigh the delicacy and worth of their feelings, seek the right estimate of their affections, and, I would almost say, the slightness of their moral and physical organisation. Bear in mind that a first punishment, above all when in public, ought to be administered with moderation and discernment; that there are natures which must not be discouraged, for, unmoved by unjust and contemptuous treatment, they meet it with unconcern, and, rising superior to shame, leave it to those who have misjudged them.

A few months slipped away in this state of reprobation. What grieved me most was to read in the Queen's looks, whenever duty called me to her, the whole disfavour of her prejudiced mind. At last a rather remarkable opportunity arose to win back part of her esteem, and I seized it. I had scribbled three acts of a play in verse from one of Marmontel's tales. "Laurette or Virtue Crowned by Love" was the title of my play. Four candles giving me light, a glass of sugared water at my hand, and myself enthroned in an armchair, I had given a reading of my play to the dramatic Areopagus of Versailles. It had been accepted, and the author loaded with praises. These ladies and gentlemen assured me that I was giving new life to the muse of comedy, fallen into decay since Piron and Gresset. The Prince d'Hénin, a man not entirely devoid of wit though on one side rather stupid, was present at the reading and found my play "delightful," the character sketches " in the best of taste," and predicted that I was a young man of "great promise." "We have shaken off," he added, "those absurd and barbarous prejudices against a taste for fine literature; only blockheads without talent defame it in their helplessness and believe that to be of noble birth one should be downright ignorant and a fool. Persevere, monsieur, persevere; enter freely upon the career to which you are distinctly called. Francis I wrote verses. I would myself to-morrow write a comedy did I possess the gift; and if I were roused to it, I would take my part in the acting."

This poor lord was not entirely wrong, but, as might be seen, he had a mind that ran to excess. He has since been given a part in a great tragedy, the catastrophe of which was brought about by the revolutionary axe by means of which he perished, without really knowing to what party he belonged and what opinions he held. His conversation would sometimes mark him as a man of talent, but he would mar it by errors due to unsound judgement and a false philosophy. The Prince d'Hénin was of high birth but unceasingly displayed his pride and his gifts in a behaviour the exact opposite of his rank; he completely embodied the philanthropy of simpletons who love everyone because they care little for any one. He has, however, done and said things bearing witness to his energy and nobility. I may quote some repartees of his to support my assertions. The Comte d'Artois, under whom he was captain in the life guards, treating him bluntly one day, he replied: "Your lordship should bear in mind that if I am honoured by serving under you, I do you honour by being in your service." [3]

Another day when the Prince was joking, the count rather roughly pushed him on the head: "My head is here to answer for yours, my lord," said d'Hénin, "but not to be your plaything."

Once at Fontainebleau, going counter to the Queen's opinion, he spoke favourably of a play which turned out a complete failure: "Well, M. d'Hénin, *your* play has failed."

"Yes, madame, at court; that is why it will be a success in Paris."

This last repartee I myself heard; the other two I have from himself, and he was not acquainted with the low vice of lying. He was the patron, the friendly brother, and the king of the whole world of mountebanks, schemers, and courtesans, with whom he spent his time although he had a charge at court, and though, strangely enough, he could not put forth temperament as an excuse for his immoral life, for not only was he devoid of the commanding vigour that might have been his excuse, but he possessed all the weaknesses that irreparably condemned him.

This is a long digression on M. d'Hénin apropos of a comedy. . . . I really do not know why—or, rather, I do know: it is that I have never met so remarkable a nature, striking me by this odd mixture of reason and foolishness, nobility and prostitution, common sense and absurdity.

The Queen heard of my play; she expressed the wish to read

it. M. Campan,[4] her private secretary, who affected the importance of a spoiled subordinate but was worth more than his looks would warrant, was told to ask me for the manuscript. He had the kindness to tell me when the Queen had finished reading it. I went up to the palace. She honoured me by saying: "M. de Tilly, here is what belongs to you. I beg of you, I even enjoin you, if such means are necessary, not to have this comedy put on the stage."

And as I was seeking a reply she added:

"How can any one with your taste for poetry, and your facility in expressing virtuous sentiments, be guilty of such ill behaviour?"

Struck with grief, I could at first reply only with tears, but, composing myself, I swiftly represented to the Queen—though with caution and in general terms—the wretchedness of my position, the slanderous talk of a fool, the semblances that gave credit to it; and I dared ask her, in a voice slightly more assured, if at my age guilt was unforgivable when it had not impugned honour.

"You are right," she replied, looking straight at me, "and I believe M. de Pedreauville [5] to be a man of little competence. Let us forget all this. . . . Behave well and you will always find me on your side."

In the most gracious manner she dismissed me after adding some assurances of my return to her favour, which effectively remained mine until another incident . . . in which, though long after, she was certainly influenced by the ancient recollection.[6]

Checked in my first steps towards a dramatist's career, I quickly found consolation; impressions are seldom lasting at that age. However, I made bold to ask the Queen, some time later, if she persisted in the orders she had given me.

"Certainly. Does that surprise you?"

"Yes, madame. Is it so bad to put a play on the stage?"

"Bad, no: but it is not becoming. No man of birth, and at your age, should expose himself to public view."

"But your Majesty knows that the Cardinal de Bernis, M. de Boufflers, and even M. de Guibert—who surely is a man of the world and as good a colonel as any one in that post—have written and gone into print."

"You will oblige me by no longer giving the matter a thought."

I gave it thought, but kept silent.

Four years later Laurette was burnt through the mistake of a valet who wanted to light a candle: I saw her ashes and did not give them a tear.

Thus these early days went by, which leave such deep traces and yet fly away at so swift a pace.

My youth was about to meet with another trial where reason and honour carried the day over instinct.

M. de N——,[7] who was about to leave the pages for a cavalry regiment, argued with me that Mlle Allard was a very dignified tragic actress, and Mlle Arnould a dancer of note, through her remarkable agility. His mistake [8] was not of such a nature as to be taken seriously, besides he was older and more used to the world than I was; but we both lost our tempers to such an extreme that it was decided the quarrel had reached a point "Where outraged honour must be redeemed by blood." [9]

We fought with some desperation. I received a thrust of his sword in the upper part of the chest, for which I was twice bled; he escaped with a slight scratch at the throat. The Queen, in this affair, positively pronounced in my favour, above all on account of the disproportion in ages and vigour. Before engaging in this little encounter, I had had to face another one within myself, as nature, I believe, had not made me brave. I triumphed over nature, and ever since I have always found myself in the ranks of the brave.

This avowal is not troublesome to make, but it may give piquancy to the narrative of a man who has since had the misfortune to fight several very serious duels in which I believe I behaved with as much firmness as honour. I put to-day so small a price on life that in risking it I should no longer find any merit.

CHAPTER III

Non ego, te, meis
Chartis inornatam silebo
—HORACE, OD. IV. 9.

A WOMAN of thirty-six years of age, witty and still possessed of great beauty, must no doubt be carried beyond
her normal self by some powerful spell when she gives herself to
a presumptuous youth of sixteen. She is certainly betrayed by her
senses and impelled by a most mysterious call of the flesh when
she entrusts her fate and good name to such fragile hands.

The difference in ages and the fact that half the advances
must be made by her should prove sufficient to hold her back
and frighten her, but it is by an imperceptible progression and
through an impulse beyond reckoning, that a woman of fair
repute comes to such a folly; the more exalted the station the
swifter the fall.

For about a year I had not seen the Comtesse de ——,[1] a
lady of quality who came from a province next to mine and held
some office at court. One day she sent me tidings of her arrival
from her estate, and of how she had promised both my relatives
and other people interested in my welfare that she would see me.
Although she is no longer alive, I will not more clearly indicate
who is the subject of this chapter; she is dead, but her memory
lives in my heart, and I wish to revere it.

When I reached her home, she briefly stated the charge
entrusted to her; she added a few sentences as if interested in
me, some questions denoting the same interest, and becoming
aware of my eyes noting her charms (for she still possessed
many and was then at her dressing-table) she appeared thrown
into some confusion, and made me feel the same perturbation
I had caused her, which I had some trouble to hide. Her maids
received a scolding, and at last left the room after an everlasting toilet that went on for more than twenty minutes.

I felt myself blushing, and blushed the more. I was happy
to be there—yet wished to be far away. There followed a deep
silence which I was at a loss to explain, yet no strength was in

me to break it, had even my life been at stake. At last she
resumed our talk with a few broken words, and after a long
effort added with liveliness:

"You are prodigiously transformed since I saw you; greatly
improved. . . . You will be very handsome . . . you have the
most pleasing voice. . . . People have mentioned you to me as
a fine wit; I believe you to have a kindly heart; exercise some
control over your passions, and with your name you will go far,
and restore your house to its former standing."

I am not repeating this to-day out of conceit; the twenty-
three years which have elapsed since, and which are, one might
say, as so many centuries passing over France, bring back this
reminiscence more like a flattering dream that scarcely leaves an
imprint on awakening.

I give warning, once for all, that truth being the sole adornment of the story I write, and details the base of the whole, I
cannot suppress the latter. I certify that, as I set no importance
on anything, vanity appears to me the most futile of passions,
and the one to which my heart is to-day the least accessible.
Let this be stated, never to be mentioned again.

I thanked her without shyness or awkwardness, but with a
kind of bashfulness that added to the danger she ran by this
tête-à-tête, as if I felt she had for me an inclination I seemed to
catch a glimpse of, yet without clear comprehension, for such an
inclination fitted ill with the idea I had formed of her virtue.
This is what my eyes conveyed to her; she understood, and
was all the more agitated. A caller came in, and I availed myself
of this opportunity to steal away. I felt relieved, and so did
she, as I learned later from her, though it was no news to me.

The woman of whom I speak was in many respects a lady
of high rank. She had been married to a man who was not
worthy of her, the only things he could boast of being a title,
a fairly bad reputation, and a fortune once large but then so
shattered that it no longer deserved the appellation. Her own
restored his, and, what is still more precious, her good name
palliated the faults of a husband for whom she had no love;
she remained faithful to him despite the double temptation
always besetting her—I mean the fact of not loving her own
husband and being worshipped by the husbands of other women.
Finding herself a widow at an early age, she rejected all suitors
and repulsed all lovers, or rather the avowals with which they
threatened her; for it was difficult to go even that far with her,

and the most dauntless self-conceit was ill at ease at the task. She had reached the stage when one's reputation is made and the greatest dangers are passed. The men who claim success with women, or those who meet with it, seldom commit themselves for a lady of proved virtue, or risk damage to their pride against a rock marked by other wrecks. There no longer exists any danger for such a woman except in the attraction of ingenuous youth or the peril of sudden capture by a man of prodigious seductiveness, for fortunately women are few to whom the difference in sex and the privileges claimed by man prove a sufficient snare.

I recall having once asked a woman very famous for her charming face, why she had surrendered to a man I was sure she did not love, and who could boast of nothing to justify her choice. After having for long denied the fact, she replied: "I lived in a kind of solitude; *he was there, so was I;* I was seeing him every day and seeing no one but him."

Of all the answers which might inspire me with contempt this is the foremost. I should have much preferred her to say: "He was a man and I need one." But this kind of self-abandonment, of renunciation of honour (for such is honour for women, and fashion cannot alter), this carelessness, this apathetic surrender of the most precious of favours, this gift of one's person to a man who is not even found attractive, I do declare to be a monstrosity deserving of torture, a crime lowering one to the level of what is most abject in creation. Such is my belief, even if I must be suspected of being a ghost returned from another world, or if I find myself hissed by people of fashion. The woman who sells herself because of poverty has at least one excuse: she is asking alms through her charms. I pity her; I grant *my full indulgence* to the woman who errs through her strong temperament. During the wild days of my youth I should have said, *my full esteem.*

A few days after this call, I met someone who knew Mme de —— particularly well. I questioned him concerning her with as little awkwardness as I could. I was above all impatient to know if she had had lovers. She had never been suspected, he replied, either by people whose slanderous tongues seize upon everything, or by those women who blacken a good reputation to redeem their own. She had had a harder fight than many, being endowed with great sensitiveness, but her virtue, which was at first founded on principles, had ended as a habit.

So I can breathe, I said to myself; foolish self-conceit had led me astray; I had nothing to hope or fear. Going once more to see her, I was perfectly calm and showed in my bearing more assurance and reserve. As for her, it seemed that she had lost what I had gained; she looked as much embarrassed as she had been agitated on the first occasion; though she was somewhat paler; her interesting features seemed veiled by a shade of melancholy; she appeared to have suffered and to be displeased with herself; she composed her voice, yet it betrayed a longing to scold.

After some lifeless talk about Versailles, the Queen, my sports, my studies, and my coming entry into society, she asked me to leave her, for she had some urgent matter to write before taking it to Bellevue [2] on the following day.

Once in the street I decided not to come back in a hurry. Into what snares does not vanity make us fall, I exclaimed!

There was then at Versailles a charming actress who was good-natured, sang passably well in the manner of those days, and was endowed with a beautiful voice and a pretty face. She has since acted in Paris where I witnessed her death in the prime of life, yet most timely, for she had put on flesh which rendered her a shapeless mass; but she was now just what is required to compel love.

She had a mother who was very deaf but could see very well, and who, having been a great beauty, knew the wiles of lovers, the tricks played on tutors and mothers, both at the stage door and about town. She had conceived some queer notion of getting her daughter married, or at least of not allowing her any lover but one who would build her fortune. I was in no way eligible from her point of view, but I suited the heart of the young woman, and the reader knows the reply of a young girl just out of the convent school to whom a lover said: "What shall we do? Your mother is so much in your way!" "Win my favour," she answered, "and do not trouble about anything else."

It happened in this same way with us. Mlle Lescaut began by fixing our assignations at her window, her mother being present but never joining in the conversation and bearing a countenance so hostile and gloomy as to give little encouragement to sweethearts. Later, she invited me to come in (I refer to the daughter) and played delightfully on the harpsichord, or sang to her own accompaniment, during which I threw in the declaration of my love, or now and then called out "Bravo," or again clasped her knee as I pretended to beat time, but all wrongly no doubt.

So far there had been perfect openness in my method, much purity in my behaviour, a great deal of love subdued by even more common sense. But our unrelenting Argus lost patience even with so much virtue and innocence; she had, so at least I believe, warned that terrible master who had taken a dislike to me but who had left me at peace for some while. He had indeed been requested to do so by his superiors, while one of my uncles most emphatically enjoined him to; for, being convinced that this great man gratuitously sought to injure me since I was clever enough to perceive his lack of merit, my relative plainly warned him they might have a bone to pick together.

However this was, such an occasion was promising, and he seized it: the pedantic M. de Pedreauville put me under arrest with much ado, on the ground that I spent my time with actresses and tried to pervert those who followed the narrow path of virtue.

I was set free a few days later and made for the palace, feeling rather ashamed, but was reassured on seeing the Queen suppress a smile.

Next day brought me an invitation from Mme. de ———— to call at her home at seven that evening. She was alone and received me rather coldly, but this time without embarrassment. She hastened to tell me that my conduct was in no way edifying, that my relatives would be grieved at it, and that women of the theatre, even those of very good standing, are rather low class; she advised me, if ever I was in need of an attachment or of friendship with a woman, to bestow my affections in better quarters, to interest myself in a sensible and honest woman acquainted with people of standing, whose home would be a fit training school for perfect manners, good taste, and polite conversation. She did not say to me, "The lady is myself," but the emotion betrayed by her voice let it be inferred, so this time I remained convinced that she had said it. I threw myself at her knees. . . . My behaviour surprised her, she entreated me to get up. I told her that she had an undying right to my gratitude, that henceforth I wanted to look upon her as the most tender of sisters, a guardian angel, a goddess destined to bring me to more delicacy of feeling and to goodness . . . to shape me to whatever she might wish me to be, and that my heart, whose service I consecrated to her, she alone would now fill. My hands, I do not know how, found themselves in hers, which she let me cover with kisses and deluge with my tears; she was agitated with a terror that made her tremble like a leaf; literally, fear brushed away the rouge from her face.

I was still on my knees, and she, quite distracted, implored me to rise. "Think if one of my servants should come in!" she exclaimed. But as if in fear of having said too much she added: "However innocent our motives, there is no need to expose ourselves to slander. Come on Monday a little earlier, we will discuss your future . . . speak of your projects, and I shall fancy I am only busy with my own."

Some people were coming to supper; I took my leave the moment the gathering began.

I spent a very restless night, and scarcely grew calmer until the day she had appointed, which came at last. Her first words were: "If you wish to stay to supper, I have only two guests, who will arrive late and leave early." Anyone may judge my eagerness to accept, though I urged the indispensable condition that she should send one of her servants to report my stay; she asked leave for me, and it was granted.

She kept her word; spoke of nothing but the necessity of completing my education and studying by myself when once I should be in the army; she planned a course of studies that I more or less closely followed during the three or four years I specially devoted to obtaining whatever stock of knowledge I may have. She talked to me as a tender and enlightened mother would to a docile and heedful son.

The two guests came in after eight; they were in a way familiars of the house; I must give a picture of them. One was an army man of subordinate rank, some fifty years old, and wearing the cross of Saint Louis. He did not have the look of one precisely ill, but of a man who has no strength left to live. He appeared to know it and to care little. His eyes were dull, his voice weak and muffled; one could see that he was not bent through old age but broken before his time either by hardship or suffering. His style was not perfect in fashion, yet was not bad; he talked in a simple and concise way, and his manners, without being obsequious, denoted a man of discretion who had moved in the best society without belonging to it; yet at times he spoke in rather too peremptory a manner.

The young lady who came with him was his niece, a pretty

and fair girl of about twenty whom Nature had adorned with a thousand gifts more appealing than beauty. Her features were not perfect, but they offered, if I can express myself thus, a harmony between the blue eyes and the white teeth that won every heart when she smiled. She was built like a nymph and had the freshness of a rose, a supple and free waist, a voice as seductive as her gait, and one of the greatest attractions in her sex, ravishing arms and hands. I am forgetting another of her charms, at least for me: she was pale. I am not sure that a painter would have found her faultlessly pretty, but any susceptible man, rightly constituted, would have desired her for his mistress.

She was shy without losing countenance, but with that natural grace which cannot be learnt.

I fancy that La Bruyère has remarked that people who persistently look at each other and those who altogether abstain from looking, both bring to one's mind the same suspicion. Our eyes frequently met at first; then, for the remaining part of the evening, we never raised them to look at each other.

I shall never forget that the uncle, I do not know by what change in the conversation, brought in "Zémire and Azor."

He declared that it was a very moving play. I was of opinion that "Andromaque" or "Zaïre" [3] was even more so; but he firmly asserted that nothing could be more arresting than to see hideous ugliness in a woman overcoming aversion through the spell of her sweetness and goodness. He stuck to his opinion—though without heat—and then kept silent a very long while. Later, during supper, he proclaimed that the Duc de Vendôme had been a much greater military genius than the Maréchal de Turenne. I was enough in the know of these things to challenge this assertion, but he, slowly disjointing a chicken's wing, emphasized what he had said, and then dropped it saying "he had never eaten anything so tender." On rising from table he spoke of taking leave; his niece looked at him, and her eyes clearly said, "Already?" And he in loud tones replied, "Yes, mademoiselle." How I hated him then! However, we were still granted a few minutes, which he seized upon to announce that Europe was grossly ignorant compared with China. Ah, I came very near dispatching him to Peking, but I thought that the niece would be obliged to go as well! So I burst into laughter, to which his only reply was a deep bow and the words: "I am very pleased, sir, at having had the honour to make your acquaintance." Having said this in a solemn voice, he left with his niece.

"Now," asked my hostess, "what do you think of them?"

"Well," I replied, in all the falseness of my heart, "the young lady is neither handsome nor ugly, but it would be odious to me often to meet this gentleman who lives on paradoxes, repeats them, and then keeps silent."

"The young lady is neither handsome nor ugly! I am much vexed at this decision for either you lack taste or you have not sincerity. . . . You must look at her better another time."

I resorted to a compliment to hide my embarrassment: "One cannot look at another when you are present."

"Very good," she said. "But you are not taken by the uncle. You noticed that I kept silent. I wanted to leave you to talk freely; I was rather pleased with your first two replies, but the third was less fortunate, for to burst out laughing and shrug your shoulders is not polite, and then it is not an answer."

"But, madame," I replied, a little disturbed, "no such moonshine has ever been uttered."

"Then all the more easy to challenge," she went on, "and to show deference to old age and misfortune is always to be in the right. Do you know that at my expressed wish M. de Lorville wanted to put you to the test in matters of learning, ability, and patience? He will not have a good opinion of you in some of these. Besides he is not a man entirely devoid of merit; he has served in India, knows almost all Europe, and has even some refinement and culture. He was certainly handsome once, and has lived for close on ten years at my sister-in-law's estate. He is now, as he himself says, going to die at Montpellier, where the doctors are sending him to repair a health that is beyond repair. You know that my sister-in-law is not a model of what is most praiseworthy in the world; it has filled him with remorse that he should have devoted to her the last days of his life, and he does not know to whom he can entrust a niece he loves and who will only come into a very moderate fortune. I offered to take charge of her; I shall keep her with me until I can marry her off comfortably; she would scarcely be wise in relying upon her uncle, who is shortly leaving and whom she most likely will never see again."

I listened to this speech with a misgiving it was not even in my power to unravel. I could see that I should often have the opportunity of meeting this pretty girl and that I should fall in love with her; this was indeed a delight, but I felt I had begun to love another and that I would not wish, nor indeed be able, entirely to withdraw my heart from her: this was an anxiety. Then I began to think, without daring to stop at the idea, that I might love them both. This trend of thought was a sweet torture which did not completely seize hold of me until I was left to myself.

"Why, now," said Mme de ——, "are you plunged in such deep thoughts?"

"I was reflecting," I replied, calling a lie to my help, "that you speak of everything except yourself, and that instead of engaging me with your kind attentions you draw me into other people's stories—stories that leave me quite indifferent."

"Very well, let us cease this talk; it is already late; one of my men will see you home, sleep peacefully . . . have me a little in your thoughts," she added blushing. "This is only fair, as I have you often in mine."

She rang, a valet appeared, and I left.

The reader is apparently out of patience with my awkwardness; but have not beginners, in whatever way of life, a right to indulgence?

Next day, as I entered a theatre, an unprepossessing man, very simply clad, handed me a note and withdrew. This note deserves to be given, so I copy it:

Versailles, five in the morning

I was not satisfied with you last evening. The surest way to please is to be natural; this is the most dangerous weapon of seduction in a young man. A studied attitude wins little; everything partaking of treachery is repulsive . . . but perhaps I am mistaken. If so, that mistake proves my punishment. . . . If I am right, you do not deserve that I should make myself clearer. But what am I doing? This note is madness; do not torture your wits to guess at its meaning. It is a riddle of which you won't make sense, at least I hope not, and this is how it should be. *Bring me back this letter.* However insignificant it may be, I should be most disquieted should any other than you read it. One might suspect from it more than the artless interest here expressed. I am willing that you, dear young friend, should believe in my sincere friendship, but it would not be fit that outsiders should magnify this confession or abuse it.

P. S. On Thursday, about five in the evening, if
the weather continues fine, I shall come home through
the park. Be there and give me back this paper which
I have not the courage to destroy, though I am displeased at having written it.

This letter, which she pretended was not clear, greatly enlightened me. I saw that I had been much more *natural* than
she thought, as I had not been able to hide the impression Sophie
de Lorville had made on me; I saw that she was jealous. I de-
liberated a long time whether I ought to show I had understood
the letter, and I decided I would not, feeling convinced even then
that innocence, with a woman who is not vicious, is a surer
weapon than wit; besides I was thus sure to appear less guilty.

I was punctual at our meeting and with candour displayed
great surprise at the letter I had received. I thanked her gently
and tenderly for the kind attentions of which the note was a
warrant, but asked whether she would explain certain parts I
could not manage to understand.

Her face was crestfallen and altered, her walk slow, her
whole appearance burdened with melancholy.

"Mlle. de Lorville has gone to take her uncle as far as
Amiens," she told me. "She will spend a few days there with
one of her relatives. You are blushing; what will it be when you
see her again? I advise you not to carry out this idea; it would
not be a suitable match for you, and planning to seduce her
would be criminal and wild."

"Good heavens, madame," I exclaimed, "what strange plans
you attribute to me! I am so little prepared for what I hear that
I cannot find a word in answer."

"You will bear it in mind," she replied, "for here we are
at Mme de Tavenne's, to whom I owe a call," and wishing me
good-bye in a gentler voice, she parted from me.

What will all this lead to, I thought. I must see my way
out of this confusion. I believe—I am certain, that this woman
loves me. I cannot tell if my happiness depends on her, yet I
should find myself wretched if I gave her up. Of all the means
which my mind conjured for bringing about a favourable result,
I chose the stalest of all: I decided to pretend illness to arouse
her interest. In the novels made up by writers who profess to
know love and its storms amongst high society and the court,
I should perhaps have found some deceit in better taste, or some

more striking device. These great delineators of the hearts and
manners of polite society who furnish instruction to garrisons
and the provinces by propagating most faithfully their own notions of "fine manners" have reduced seduction to an exact and
fashionable system. Such great masters, I dare say, might have
suggested a more happy invention than that of feigned sickness,
which I own proved in me but poor ingenuity; but since this
contrivance, as slender as it was, succeeded marvellously, this
is my consolation for the mediocrity of my scheming.*

The object of so much attention sent daily to inform herself
of my state and entreated me earnestly to see her on my first
outing.

It is impossible to depict the agitation in which I found her
and the effect I produced upon her when I appeared. Forgetful
of all propriety, she held me long against her bosom, shedding
tears. All the caresses, all the passion I ventured to display she
returned with interest. After some embraces more prolonged
and a few moments of eloquent silence, I had enough common
sense to perceive that it only remained for me to attain complete bliss . . . and I found it: I found it without awkwardness on my side or resistance on hers.

After so swift a stroke, her tears, which had not ceased to
flow, were more abundant. I swore faithful love and discretion,
while imploring her to calm herself. "Ah," she said to me with
the most touching countenance, "it is not my fal' I regret! It is
not notoriety nor even disgrace I fear, but I grieve at having
seduced you, at having thrown myself in your arms and having
prepared for your senses, and perhaps your self-conceit, a triumph in which your heart does not share."

The reader easily guesses my answers, my protests and
oaths. We agreed that she should no longer receive me at her
home, but in rooms on the Avenue de Paris, that I should go
there on fixed days and hours, and that I should wear clothes
of some dull and unobtrusive colour, emblem of the mystery
which was to enshroud our love.

CHAPTER IV

*Love which survives storms and often thrives in
the midst of perfidy cannot always withstand the
calm of fidelity.*

NO obstacle came to thwart this attachment; neither jealousy nor anxiety rendered it more stimulating or more
bitter. There was too much quietness in our love. She, I believe,
found happiness therein while I only met pleasure.

The time of my entry into active life was approaching, and
I spent the six months preceding it under the protecting wing of
a loving mistress, at once an affectionate mother and a useful and
attentive friend. As not one indiscreet word ever escaped me
she loved me the more, for I rose in her esteem. My future
occupied her thoughts more than mine. She saw in anticipation
things of which I had no conception, and discovered pitfalls in
the way of life where youth could see only pleasant lanes strewn
with flowers.

The vision of Sophie sometimes pursued me, but having no
longer any occasion to meet her, and even thinking that unknowingly she had been the cause of Mme de ———'s resolve to
receive me seldom at home, I scarcely dared to utter her name.
At last chance served me better than either skill or foresight
could.

I suddenly developed a great liking for drawing, which led
to a very keen taste for pictures. All I have preserved of it is
that, though I am not a very distinguished connoisseur, I nevertheless know beautiful work from what is fair or bad.

There was then at Versailles a rather famous picture dealer,
an overt impostor, who might have chosen for his own the
Barber of Seville's motto: *Consilio manuque.* He painted portraits and gave lessons. This man of all trades also did quite
other things. Amongst other virtues he possessed a widespread
benevolence; being an accommodating philanthropist he had an
imperious need to oblige, above all if he gained thereby. Out of
love for humanity he has since thrown in his lot with the Revolution, which proved an ungrateful mistress. He died at the

guillotine though he had been one of the most zealous upholders
of the so-called safeguards for public safety. But, as there is no
question of this here, I must quickly pass over the accident that
a long while later deprived him of a head already set awry upon
his shoulders at the time I knew him.

He one day obligingly showed me the portraits and pictures
then in his possession. My surprise was only equalled by my joy
when amongst the former I found a face exactly similar to that
which so often occupied my thoughts. I hardly dared ask
M. Morand whose portrait this was, so much did I fear my
hopes might be deceived.

He at last replied to my question that the portrait was that
of one of his pupils. "I can give her that name," he went on,
"although she could already paint before I knew her, but I have
taught her the refined touch that provincial teachers never
impart. This portrait is hers and done by her. I have kept it to
infuse it with an elusive something she has missed, being, in a
way unable to catch it, for it partakes of her soul, and no mortal
can read his own. She lives with a lady of quality, who is her
guardian and is beautiful enough not to know jealousy, but who
yet keeps her in a sort of constraint and seclusion that, to say
the least, I find very strange. And so she seems to me steeped
in melancholy, which adds to the interest she inspires."

"You can paint indeed, M. Morand; but her name? her
name?"

"Ah, that is of no consequence—a provincial name! She is
called Mlle de Lorville, the daughter of one of those small
nobles who hunt often and badly, madden their curés and their
peasants, speak of wars in which they never served, of garrison
towns where they merely vegetated, and who live and will die
without having seen Paris or the court."

"So, you have seen the court, M. Morand?"

"More than that, sir, my profession led me on. I have lived
amongst the highest society, and at the same time in the midst
of the men of most consequence in their art."

"That is plain, M. Morand; but this young lady?"

"This young lady, sir, used sometimes to come here,
but—"

"What, M. Morand, Sophie—Mlle de Lorville comes
here? . . ."

"Ah, sir, so you know her! With what fire and what passion
you speak of her!"

"M. Morand, you will be greater than Michelangelo, Raphael, and Correggio put together if Sophie comes here and you inform me. Reckon on my everlasting gratitude, which will not stop at empty words. I am about to leave the School of Pages, to be set free—my own master. . . . Perhaps I may be of service to you, and you may rest assured—"

"Sir, do you believe me so vile as to consider self-interest? As I see no harm in bringing together two people who worship my art and who might win insight into the masterpieces of great artists by being, so to say, placed in presence of their genius, I will see what can be done; but this means some difficulties— truly, sir, numerous difficulties. She used often to come here in former days—she even sometimes came alone—now it is extremely rare; besides, I notice she is always accompanied by the oldest maid of the Comtesse de ——."

"That is Mlle Emery?"

"Precisely, sir. During my next lesson I shall find some pretence for getting her to visit here. . . . I shall advise her to come and examine my latest finds."

"Ah, M. Morand, you will be a god to me!"

"You gentlemen are all alike. Those who do you service and comply with your passions you call gods; but if they oppose you they are less than men."

"What gibberish, M. Morand! What redundant philosophical declamation, above all how unfair you are to me!"

This fellow had already a fragment of revolution in his head, and one day, like Minerva, it sprang up in arms from his brain.

I left him full of hope and of anxiety. All he had related strengthened my belief. Mme. de ——'s suspicions and mistrust were clearly proved to me. I accused her of such unfairness that, though it could not make her lose my devotion and my gratitude, it took away what love for her was left. This constraint in which Sophie lived, her sadness, which perhaps I exaggerated, won her my entire heart. I never gave M. Morand a moment's peace until he had fulfilled his promise; he kept it more easily than I had dared to hope and sent me word, some few days afterwards, that he was about to receive Sophie and her companion. I flew there.

"You have," I said to him, "a garden. Show it to the maid, show her everything, your flowers, your vegetables, and leave me a few minutes alone with your charming pupil; this is all

I ask of you. I shall emerge from the adjoining room as if by happy chance and promptly enough to detain the girl a few moments, of which I will take full advantage."

All went off as I wished, and I had the inexpressible happiness of being alone with Sophie, rejoicing at her surprise, her emotion, noticing she had not forgotten me and that she believed she had really touched me, though she feigned doubt.

The minutes were precious. With rapture I spoke to her of the swift attraction she had caused me to feel and of the sincere attachment which was going to bring either bliss or torment in my life.

"If all these beautiful things were true," she replied, "you would come more often to Mme de ——'s. I have been away for some time; on my return I ventured to remark that one no longer saw you. I was given to understand in a few words that your time was divided between your duties and your pleasures; that being on the eve of joining the army these duties were so increased that most likely you were better employed."

"How you were deceived! I have scarcely time to assure you to-day that not for one moment did you cease to be in my thoughts, and that my happiness will henceforth be measured by the amount of your forbearance. Give me proofs that I am not hateful to you by sometimes coming here. The owner of this establishment will serve my love, for I shall convince him of my sincerity; and if I cannot see you often enough, consent at least to receive the letters which M. Morand will hand over to you, and allow me to hope that replying to them will not be a painful task."

All this was said so quickly and with such passion that she replied only by agitation and blushes; we heard a noise and I hurriedly withdrew. When she was gone I thanked my zealous confidant with the earnest gratitude to which love lends such true accents, and in order that he should not regard his time as lost, I chose a rather poor picture, which he highly praised. It was Achilles disguised as a girl at Deïdameia's feet. I remarked to M. Morand that I wanted a handsome frame and that I should request him to store the picture for a while, as I knew not yet where to place it. The truth is that, generally speaking, a page has very little money and two months were still to elapse before I should more or less order my own life.

On coming back, I met one of my father's servants bringing tidings of his arrival at the Hôtel de Modène and an invita-

tion to dine with him. The master of the pages having raised
no objection at granting me leave, I followed my guide who,
on the way, informed me that Madame la Marquise had likewise arrived and showed great eagerness to make my acquaintance. My father, through a whim for which later he had too
much cause for repentance to deserve reproach, had thought fit
to marry again. This was a matter of indifference to me as my
fortune came from my mother's side, and, as he had begun to
squander it, the custody of it had been taken from him and
given over to a council of relatives.

He was still in the prime of life and, as is commonly said,
very well preserved; he had nevertheless been guilty of singular
folly in marrying a lady of aristocratic birth but little wealth,
who could easily have been his daughter.

My stepmother, who was by birth an Ameslon de Saint-Cher,
was a most striking brunette with one of those wanton counte-
nances one would like to declare ugly but which make as much
impression as a pretty one. The look of her eyes was near a
squint but, on giving it thought, one could see that this reflected
the conflict between the shamelessness of her disposition and the
modesty imposed upon her sex; such inward strife gave her this
cross-eyed and disorderly expression. Her rather thick nose,
and the vermilion lips of an unusual cut, uncovering neat though
not sparkling teeth, completed a face possessed of such mobility
that her incoherent talk could scarcely keep up with it. She was
fairly tall, well built, with a forest of hair and other feminine
charms a little too pronounced but not to the detriment of
beauty. Her voice was in turn caressing and sharp; her intelligence was limited, as I have since found; she was ill-behaved
but full of cunning, a heart perhaps not wicked, but weak enough
to present all the drawbacks of depravity.

My father was obviously exulting, and his passion flared the
more as he imagined me full of admiration. As for her, with a
dissembling look she begged my forgiveness for being my stepmother.

I remained lost in dreams, inattentive and coldly respectful.
My father told me that he intended buying a house in the Montmorency valley, to end his life there close to his old friends
the Marquis de Montmorency and the Commandeur de Champignolles. The Marquis did not rise above mediocrity, although
he bore a famous name, which had led him to the rank of lieutenant-general through no exertion of his own, but in the course

of a career disapproved of by his family, though the most distinguished men in the kingdom have entered it both before and
since. The Commander was a very decent man with no brains
whatsoever, who for a long time had been ruled over by an
old-fashioned and heavy Flemish woman. He would get drunk
every day, and invariably expressed surprise at it, for he always
took care to mix a few drops of water in each glass of champagne, which he swallowed in huge quantities. No one shared
his astonishment. My father assured me that the only purpose
of his visit to Versailles was to see me, and that he would leave
early on the morrow, not being able decently to stay longer as
Mme de Tilly was not yet presented at court.

We went to the play where Voltaire's "Tancrède" was
being acted. I recall that my father remarked: "Aménaide could
have cleared herself from the suspicion of treachery by one word
—she had only to speak that word." It surprised him M. de
Voltaire should have given so little semblance of truth to this
part of his tale, upon which my stepmother pointed out that the
pride of her sex and guilelessness were sufficient answer to this
charge. . . . She added that, besides, the play would have an
end. This explanation appeared to us much better than the other.

After supper I took leave of them. They went back to Paris
on the morrow, then a few days afterwards into the country,
from which they came back later to carry out the scheme of
establishment my father had conceived.

But let us come back to Mme de —— and her rival, who
now had none in my heart.

Captivating Sophie! Before I succeeded in writing you one
letter I tore up six. They all seemed cold and insignificant in
the light of this love so quickly born and now consuming me.
M. Morand undertook to deliver it; Sophie accepted it after
some protest, and with a positive refusal to send an answer.
Feeling I could face anything, I hastened in despair to Mme
de ——'s house at a time I felt sure the Countess had gone to
wait on Mesdames. I easily got access to Mlle de Lorville, and
in tones of the deepest grief implored her to respond to the
first real love I had ever experienced or, if she remained unrelenting, to instruct me without delay of a misfortune the consequences of which I dared not foresee.

If to-day I try to find reasons for the imperious sway of this
passion over me, I need to seek its roots in that mysterious
sympathy which wins the heart at first sight, above all in early

manhood, for then impressions sink deep and susceptibilities allow us no rest; then love is a burning fever that bears no semblance except in name to those prudent attachments of which we coolly weigh the motives, the course, and the social reactions when our withered souls have lost all illusions.

There was need to show Sophie the full extent of the passion which ruled over me, but to hide it from other eyes; need also of convincing Mme de ―― that my love for her had not altered, and such a task has always seemed to me, even when older, to be insuperable. On the eve of consecrating myself to another I had to make Mme de ―― believe that I still felt in subjection to her and found pleasure where only slavery and chains remained, the traces of which were then about to be obliterated.

I cannot carry pretence to that extent. . . . I have at times shown tenderness to a woman for whom I felt only desire. I have often assumed the jargon of feeling and displayed melancholy to palliate lust and enhance pleasure, but to swear to a woman who still holds our esteem the love with which we burn for another, to be moved while in her arms by the transports our heart conceals for her rival, to act to oneself this lie both of the spirit and the body, is but to deride the recipient of our supposed worship by making her a dupe and a victim, as well as renewing for oneself a torture similar to the one contrived by Mezentius.[1]

On the other hand I was grieved at the suffering Mme de ―― was about to incur; she already had vague premonitions of it. She complained of my coolness and my changed disposition, which I was unable to hide. I had imperfectly reassured her by blaming my health, which I declared shaky, but I had not succeeded in bringing consolation to a love only too ready to give credence, yet still more clear-sighted.

Meanwhile Sophie, distracted and frightened by my visit, my emotions, and my transports, promised to write to me; with much trepidation she gave me her word she would find means of sometimes meeting me. I urged her to feign renewed absorption in painting and not to make me die of grief (she believed this death possible and probable, just as I did) and I took leave of her, my heart more full of love than ever, since I carried away more hope.

M. Morand's house soon became the temple towards which my prayers went. Sophie often found opportunities for being

there. Contented with the sound of her voice and happy at her
response to my feelings, my love had not yet asked the final
surrender. But of what happiness does not one grow weary
when a greater is in store? I had the audacity to press her,
urging her to yield her full love at the cost of her innocence;
she resisted my outbursts of passion, was proof against scheming, tenderness, and persecution; some instinctive terror protected her as much as virtue itself.

Six weeks were spent in this struggle, during which I began
to feel disheartened. True grief was consuming me. I was much
altered in looks. Sophie's victory cost her even more, her charming face was still more changed, which in a woman is a serious loss.

I was soon to leave the School of Pages with an officer's
commission, and this fact rendered my wooing still more pressing. Having exhausted all possible arguments and enticements,
I offered her marriage, swearing with a warmth not devoid of
gloom that if she rejected this last proof of my worship, life
would hold for me no more glory, wealth, success, or purpose,
as I should renounce all such hopes in a world that had deceived
me before my time.

"Very well," she said in solemn tones, "I shall risk my own
happiness to make fast the full share of it you are born to meet
with in the life you enter, and where my tender wishes will follow
you—even when you have forgotten me. Swear no oaths," she
added, interrupting me. "You would not be such a danger for
me if at this moment you were not sincere; but it is not of
to-day I am afraid. I shall not accept your offer; such a marriage would seem void in the light of reason, honour, and the
law. I have no wish to close your career as soon as it opens.
Fate has not marked me out for the happiness of being united
to you by so sacred a bond; but neither was it fit I should be
your mistress. . . . Yet love lends beauty to all it touches;
and if in the future I must meet the trial of your unfairness,
the memory of such love will enliven my life and bring it consolation; so you will no more now meet with resistance than you
will later hear the voice of regret."

Virtue holds strange power over us; this is no idle fancy.
On the instant the turbulent desires that had consumed me were
quieted in my heart as if through magic, and Mlle de Lorville
became for me a sacrosanct divinity for whom I felt only reverence. The motives for injuring her were drained of life within

me; my one strength was in my reverence, and I was only weak in my powerlessness to lay violent hands upon her virtue.

With what sweet melancholy I went on my knees to Sophie, and rose up more worthy of her since I had not given her offence! And how eloquent was the silence with which she thanked me! How much more she loved me for my conduct and how much dearer she was to me! Love would be like some divine grace if it could but retain this inexpressible enchantment; it would be the noblest of all the fine emotions of the soul could it survive the loss of innocence, or could such innocence still be found at the remotest confines of bliss. But some traitorous spirit makes sport of us and leads our best feelings astray; our most praiseworthy resolutions are overthrown, madness sets us against ourselves and vanquishes by thus dividing us within our own hearts. It seems that man has been made to know goodness only the better to go towards evil, down a slope as slippery as his vices and stronger than his own disposition.

After so moving a scene my heart needed to retire within itself or, so to say, to express itself without indiscretion. I wrote to Sophie a letter which I now find rather romantic but which, on that account, then all the more fitted my position.

> Angel of consolation [I told her], you who are going to preside over my life and make it of invaluable price, were I worthy of you I should renounce you and then die. Such courage is beyond me; my only way is to accept your love and to respond to it by an everlasting worship. But since you did not surrender to me as most women would have done, neither do I wish to possess you as would any ordinary lover. . . . My Sophie! my friend forever! On Monday I shall be my own master. New days are rising for me. Say that you will make this dawn holy by the free gift of your most precious favour; that you will bring blessing upon my future through the omens of supreme bliss. Surrounded by such enchantment, protected by so powerful a spell, I shall enter upon life with a confidence that will help me to rise above myself. Ah, tell me that you wish all that I desire, and that you long to conform to my wishes! We shall go to a church . . . there, in the presence of Him who sees everything and allows only what meets His wishes, at the foot of His altar, there will be no need of His ministers to take Him as witness to our immutable

resolve to live and journey together upon this earth,
where He has not forbidden us some moments of
happiness. . . . Happiness and you, Sophie, are not
both these one and the same thing? . . . Dear loving
Sophie! I hope you will not see anything extravagant
in this note. . . . I love to believe that the impetuosity
of my passion reaches your soul, to kindle it and make
you feel at heart that the only madness would be to
renounce each other, the only crime and perjury our
separation.

I awaited her reply, I opened it. As she had written it almost
breathlessly it contained but a single word: "Yes."

This romantic plan was carried out. One very dark night
Sophie, taking every risk, availed herself of Mme de ——'s
absence from supper and joined me. We went to the church
of Saint Louis and there, alone together, celebrated the marriage ceremony to which so many people have since brought far
less significance and solemnity. I received the reward of this
deed at M. de Noailles's mansion, where the duke of that name
had lent me rooms. There I took the woman who, in justice to
myself and in homage to truth, I may say that at this moment
I regarded as my wife. Before midnight she was back at home,
before midnight she was irrevocably mine.

CHAPTER V

This devil, beauty, is compounded strangely.
It is a subtle point and hard to know,
Whether it has in it more active tempting
Or passive tempted. . . .
So soon it forces, and so soon it yields.

I DEEMED myself brave in confessing to Mme de —— that my heart was given to another. I abstained from mentioning any name, but I told her, what she knew better than myself, that love is a blind and imperious feeling, and that now, in spite of myself, it called me to another; that to deceive them both I considered to be a crime, though feelings exclusively depending on myself, such as gratitude, friendship, and a boundless devotion, would outlive those of a more fragile texture that it was not in my power to preserve everlastingly.

Although my previous behaviour had prepared Mme de —— for what she heard, surprise made her dumb.

To be left with such frank roughness would have proved a sad blow even to a courtesan, but though Mme de —— had surrendered herself with as much impropriety she was far from belonging to that type. My youth had seduced her virtue and now was chastising her; my frankness had misled her and now was her punishment. But, luckily, she followed the wrong scent, and instead of suspecting Mlle de Lorville she assumed that I had views the presumption and fatuity of which I did not entertain, and such that, even had I received the greatest provocation, I could not have been led to conceive.

"I am pleased at your frankness," she told me. "I praise you for being so honest, even though at my expense. May you be happy. Never dishonour the altar where you kindled your first ardours; I speak thus more for your sake than my own. Above all, beware of vanity, for it drags one into dangerous snares; likewise beware of pride, which would mislead you by means of perilous and deceitful illusions. Fair ladies and men of influence are possessed of a magic spell that makes us easily mistake the sort of interest they bestow upon us. This danger

is, as I repeat, prodigious, and the ridicule incurred even greater.
. . . I will say no more. . . . These are the last words of a
dying passion; may they be your guide and above all render you
cautious! Do not let us speak of the past; look upon my home
as yours; believe that my friendship still abides with you; keep
yours for me. I shall never deserve to lose it, and if I can at
any time be in a position to help you, make use of me to the
full. . . . These will be my only moments of happiness in the
future. . . ."

Wiping the tears that escaped her eyes, she withdrew to her
dressing-room; I had no strength left either to stop her or to
follow her.

Many difficulties still remained to surmount in order to establish my liaison with Sophie and keep it secret; there were even
greater difficulties in safeguarding it from an untimely end. My
relatives wanted me to travel, first in France, and then to spend
three months in England before joining my regiment, the
Noailles's dragoons, where I was commissioned as sub-lieuten-
ant. They were guided by the ideas that travelling is good for
youth and that it was wise to remove me from the perils of
Paris.

But the Queen's disposition towards me provided a weapon
to resist all attempts at sending me away, for, on the memorable
day of my presentation to her as an officer, the Queen had, more
or less, ordered me to stay at Versailles. She had indeed had the
kindness to say:

"We are not taking leave of each other, as you will, at least
for some time, continue to live here under my care. Take my
advice, and make but few trips to Paris; it will not be my fault
if you do not find life here as agreeable as you may wish. Behave
as you ought to, and you will have in me all the support you require. Dress more simply. This is your second embroidered suit
in a few days. Although fairly good, your income will not suffice
if your tastes exceed your means. What sense is there in this
headgear and these side-curls? Are you going to act in a play?
Simplicity of dress goes unobserved but wins esteem."

As may easily be believed, none of this has escaped my
memory. Such motherly good-heartedness from the greatest
of queens, and wisdom worthy of the noblest minds, were too
much the hall-mark of her speech to be forgotten. Had the
enthusiasm aroused by her words led me to repeat them to my
credit and to hers, I should not have cut so ridiculous a figure

as Mme de Sévigné exclaiming to the Comte de Bussy Rabutin,
"It must be agreed, cousin, that our King is the greatest in the
world," merely because Louis XIV had danced a minuet
with her.

It does not become me to estimate the extent of the Queen's
intelligence, or to what degree she displayed it in her actions,
but whenever I had the honour of approaching her and of hearing her, I observed in her words a wisdom and a poise worthy
of the best of minds.

I did not show myself again at Mme de ———'s on the day
of our talk, but (what was hardly better) I took special care
to bribe one of her maids and I succeeded. I had thus frequent
opportunities of seeing Sophie, and during three months no
suspicion entered her benefactress's mind. It was no easy task
at dinner to be often the third person between these two; only
in the presence of guests did talk ever cease to be embarrassing
and become general.

An event I had not foreseen nearly disclosed the whole
intrigue and hastened Mme de ———'s return to Paris, as her
duties no longer kept her at Versailles. She had once, in those
happy days of our intimacy, given me a bracelet of her hair.
I wore it for a long time. Sophie had sweetly claimed it as an
offering and (wickedly enough) I had given it her. I seize this
occasion to offer young men a useful lesson: they should never
buy present tokens of love at the cost of past favours, nor
sacrifice to the vanity, the hatred, or the whims of a new mistress, the letters, hair, or portrait of a former. This piece of
advice seems futile, but it is not so: it is closely consistent with
honour. For the young man who in such cowardly fashion surrenders what love entrusted to him at the time of the greatest
intimacy, will scarcely be more careful in his friendships or in
other circumstances of life requiring honourable dealings. Yet
this situation is of daily occurrence and may often make one
face this act of honesty, for women's eternal clamour for these
surrenders, to which they attach value in the degree they know
we ourselves have attached it, constitutes a trap they are themselves caught in and into which they like to see us fall. And
what if hatred of a former rival blends with this? Women hate
as they love, all so easily. They need so much agitation of both
heart and mind; this mind being always swayed by fickle emotions. They are fond of cruel tricks once their nerves are exas-
perated. These weapons, so harmful and so easy to handle,

suit their nature well. . . . Women are, with but few exceptions, light-headed, inconsequent, and at times barbarous beings.
. . . Yet are men so much superior? I much doubt it. Ah, mankind is worthless!

To come back to my bracelet, a fine pearl adorned its clasp,
which was engraved with the English motto "For ever," for, as
Diderot once remarked, love pictures everlasting constancy, but
human nature fixes an end to everything. There was no mistaking this bracelet. Sophie had put it away as something
precious at the back of her writing-table, but one day, having
taken it out in some haste while searching for something else,
she left it on her dressing-table. Mme de ——, who often came
into this room, happened to enter it that very day. The sight
of the bracelet, its recognition, the sense of being struck by
lightning became one and the same thing for her. I had not
told Sophie of whose hair the bracelet was made; I had never
uttered a word that might make her guess the nature of my
attachment to the giver. Honesty played a great part in this,
but I must not grant it the full credit. I had also feared that
such a confession might strengthen Sophie's opposition or even
prevent me from overcoming it; and since her surrender I had
not wished to grieve or embarrass her further. She had luckily
gone out when this fatal evidence of my unfaithfulness was discovered. The offended lady, with whom I was dining, never
said a word about it; but in the evening, finding herself alone
with me, she begged me to hand her back all she had once given
me as having no longer any value for me; she particularly insisted on this wretched bracelet. My answer of course was easy:
I could never part from what recalled a happiness of which the
memory was a delight; I had not deserved being asked such a
sacrifice. I thought the incident but a fit of ill temper and that
I had disposed of it.

But the next day Sophie wrote that she was lost: she could
not understand how the bracelet was known to Mme de ——,
how it was now in her hands, above all what importance this
lady could attach to it, but she added that the letter "E" on it
had seemed to throw a light on the matter which she would
like to repel, that for the rest she had denied possessing the
bracelet, and when told it had been found on her dressing-table,
she had declared it was there unknown to her; she could not
now foresee the issue of this frightful incident, but she was in
bed, prostrate; and, believing herself the bearer of the unfortu

nate fruit of our love, her state was such that she hoped never to recover.

What a position! We were far remote from those hours of bliss during which, after leaving the church, we had bestowed on one another all the proofs of the most ardent passion. Sin, or what society calls love's transgression, does not always run an easy course, and often carries its own punishment. I was in despair, but I felt it was for me to save Mlle de Lorville, and this idea gave me back some courage. I longed to confess everything; the fear of thus marking out Sophie as an impudent liar alone stopped me; for, I must own, I was deeply surprised that she should have had the presence of mind—I will speak plainly —the skillful duplicity to deny the evident truth, and to thrust aside such clear evidence by so flagrant an imposture.

But this course of action is the sole refuge for the weaker and more delicate sex when there is need of safeguarding the one secret that women can and ought to keep.

My resolve was soon taken; I did not go to Mme de ——, but I hurried to the kind M. Morand, who, though the reader has not heard of him for a long time, was still of the same disposition towards me.

I had previously written to Mme de —— to inform her of my loss, which I looked upon as a real misfortune, especially at the time when she had demanded the return of this very token of her favours. I had the audacity to ask her if she had not herself stolen it so as to enjoy my grief. Was this a serious theft or a practical joke? This claim of hers and this loss, both at the same moment, did not seem to me, so I told her, just casual coincidence. In any case I was deeply grieved and I called on her, for the sake of my peace and honour, to get me out of this dreadful perplexity. M. Morand, according to my instructions, followed close upon this letter to bear a note for the maid I had previously bribed and win from her the promise that she would tell her mistress she had found the bracelet in one of the rooms and that, having placed it on Mlle de Lorville's dressing-table, she had forgotten to mention the matter.

All this tissue of petty lies was clumsy enough, yet it met with as much success as I could have hoped. Mme de —— was probably not convinced, but she pretended to be. Life started again with its usual routine, and if one handsome face had not kept unduly serious, and Sophie's enchanting features had not shown dejection mixed with fear, no traces would have remained

of an adventure that made me behave with more caution until
Mme de ———'s departure for Paris, where she settled down a
few days later.

It was at this period that I became acquainted with a man
of letters who in no small degree helped on my taste in such
matters, though he was judged by his own age with a severity
for which another age will make amends. It is of M. Dorat[1]
I am here speaking, a man who with less wit and facility would
have been thought worthy to rank amongst the most distinguished literary men. He had an unquenchable thirst for fame,
an ever-renewed need of public favour, and so, constantly mistaking the true road to celebrity, he wrote incessantly and never
corrected anything. I put apart the poem "Déclamation," a work
that, jointly with twenty slighter poems and a few fragments of
his "Célibataire," gives him a name and saves him from falling
into the oblivion to which some obscure critics, who outraged
him in his lifetime, would like to debase him after his death.

A selection of his works put into two or three volumes would
contain but few blemishes and would prove worthy of admittance to any classical library. The main reason why he went
astray and could not reach fame, and why his life was strewn
with such misfortunes, disillusions, and bitterness as to send him
to a premature grave, was a mixture within him of two natures.
He was not really either a man of the world or a man of letters.
As a man about town he appeared, at first sight, a fairly odd
compound on account of the bad manners he had contracted
amongst low-class people and which he believed excellent, though
he had on occasion lived in polite society. On the other hand,
an unbearable light flutter which marked all his ways, finally
infected most of his works, so that his books became dangerous
models for the provincial youth or for the young man of the
capital who aspired to a literary career, for he would mistake
insincerity for favour, set to verse common love-encounters, and
use false jargon for painting still falser pictures of a society he
could not portray, but to which his one mania, above everything
in his writings, was to pretend that he belonged.

But when the first misgivings were conquered, when one became used to him, one was soon captivated by a real geniality
that no superficial veneer could hold back, by a mind both solid
and gracious and in no way dulled through this false glitter, by
learning far more extensive than was generally supposed, by the
wealth of his varied knowledge and of his pointed narratives,

but above all by the easy grace of his temper comparable only to that of his wit. In short, anyone taking the trouble to seek and find the man through his conversation and his writings was sure of meeting with reward. He perhaps hated but one man, a man who, though his superior in intellect, could not rival his wit, a man who is one of the glories of France since he has erected a monument which will live as long as the French tongue,[2] but nevertheless a contemporary who put himself odiously in the wrong by persecuting M. Dorat with as much animosity as stubbornness; this clearly points to M. de La Harpe.[3]

Dorat had been a mousquetaire, he was of noble birth and would have everyone know it; he had been fairly wealthy at the time he entered society, but he died in real poverty.

I have allowed myself to speak at length about this ill-fated man—and I purposely so call him, for ill fate was very much his lot in life and his memory has not yet been granted the repute it deserves—I speak of him with impartiality, for though I saw much of him at one time, I scarcely ever heard him spoken of afterwards.

I must still add, before concluding this long digression, that he had been spoiled by another man whose career, though much more singular and brilliant, did not end more happily: I mean the well-known M. de Pezay, author of "Zélie au Bain" and "La Rosière de Salency," who, assisted by his sister Mme de Cassini, rose to be a marquis, helped to appoint a cabinet minister, and, what is more, came very near to being one himself; he nevertheless died rather young and wretchedly from a courtier's broken heart, due to some hidden ambition or frustrated expectations. His story is fairly well known, so I have no wish to give it here; I shall only relate in this connection an incident that gives a true picture of M. de Maurepas [4] who could so well turn everything into a joke: his position, the King, the kingdom, and himself included.

The Duke of Manchester, later to be English Ambassador at the court of Versailles, went in his youth on what is called the grand tour through Europe. Dining one day with M. de Maurepas, and being seated next to him as the guest of honour, he enquired: "Monsieur le Comte, who is the gentleman at the farther end of the table [it was M. de Pezay] wearing an apple-green suit, a rose waistcoat, facings to match, and silver embroidery?"

"It is the King, my Lord."

"How is that?"

"The King, I tell you, sir."

The conversation ended thus, M. de Maurepas chatting with a neighbour, and the Duke's English pride not formulating anew the question that had met with so queer an answer.

But once dinner was over: "Monsieur le Comte," said the Duke of Manchester, "how came I to deserve the bitter sarcasm with which you met my question concerning this nobleman, in countenance so thoughtful and self-satisfied, to whom many people pay their court even in your drawing-room?"

"My Lord, I never use sarcasm; first of all he is not a nobleman, and I tell you again he is the King. I see that you need proofs, so I will give you some. He goes to bed with a cousin of mine, Mme de Montbarrey,[5] who rules Mme de Maurepas, the latter does with me as she pleases, I lead the King, so, you see clearly, that gentleman reigns." [6]

I must now come back to the time when I first became acquainted with M. Dorat. Sophie being gone, Versailles had become odious to me, yet I dared not settle at once in Paris for fear it should be evident I was running after her. My temporary residence was Le Désert, a charming spot, belonging to a man who, since my entrance into society, had bestowed upon me a friendship that never flagged, nor ever found me ungrateful. M. de Monville was totally unlike a financier except for wealth, his own being still considerable though much reduced. He joined the greatest elegance of manners to the best of behaviour; his mind, without being cultivated, was sound; he was one of those commonplace men who yet possess the qualities required to live exclusively amongst the most distinguished persons of their time in all conditions, and to meet with their approval. He was truly honest at heart, and never allowed either the pomp or the munificence he came in contact with to corrupt his ways. Had he withstood the boredom which consumed him in the midst of a fully comfortable life, he would have lived happily. His disposition was marked by some depression because he found most things in life wearisome. My heedlessness was very pleasing to his nonchalance, and his good nature much to the taste of my light-heartedness. He would sometimes get cross; I would then sing to him, in my poor way, a charming air whose words and music he had himself composed for a woman he once worshipped in youth and which begins thus:

In my sorrowful heart
Bring back some light of hope . . .

I do not know if I am mistaken, I do not know if the magic of the words lies in the memory of these happy fleeting days when they seduced my ears and spoke to my heart at the happiest time of life, but though neither the lines nor the music may be excellent I find them possessed of an inexpressible charm by which they hold me as powerfully as if they were the combined work of a Racine and a Paesiello.

Monville has since put himself in the wrong by remaining the friend of the Duc de Orléans [7] when to be seen in such company was shameful. But he never was in the secret of the Duke's crimes. He continued paying his court to a prince of the royal blood, whose attentions had flattered him and who, if without skill in his public misdeeds, yet had some wit or rather affability in private life. Some sort of weakness made Monville keep up the friendship; perhaps he also believed he might find it useful to ward off various dangers, for people who were no better acquainted than he with revolutions and popular risings must have thought that a prince who aspired to the throne would have enough influence to live on and grant life to his friends.[8] But the course of the floods which engulfed both tormentors and victims did not run that way. Nevertheless, pulling through the Revolution, Monville discovered the secret of dying in his own bed and of being shown mercy by the French Sylla and Marius [9] though they were merciless with every one else.

So it was at his home, Le Désert, a place made beautiful by both nature and art and everywhere bearing evidence to the exquisite taste of its owner, that I buried my grief, finding my only consolation in some occasional letters from Mlle de Lorville and in the charms of poetry which M. Dorat, whom I met at Le Désert, taught me to cultivate and cherish.

Having spent three weeks away from her I loved most, it was time to meet again at all cost, the more so since Sophie's letters caused me great alarm. She informed me that Mme de —— had not altered towards her, but appeared overcome with melancholy and sadness; that she spent the greater part of the day alone in her room, hardly seeing her most special friends. "As for me," Sophie added, "unhappy as to the present, more anxious still regarding the future, I scarcely dare survey my position. I can no longer doubt my condition, which it will soon be impossible to hide, but as all my devotion is yours alone,

and this means my very life, I shall follow no one's advice but
yours; indifferent both to happiness and to the criticism of society, henceforth I shall only rejoice in what gives you joy and
suffer in what gives you pain."

I hurried to Paris.

Mme de ——— received me with a kindness that deeply
moved me; her voice, though now less tender, was affectionate;
her looks, though less caressing, conveyed motherly interest.
Sophie badly concealed what went on inside her heart; she held
herself with constraint, breathed heavily, spoke in an ill-assured
voice, and, if I may express it thus, the clumsiness of modesty
showed in all her behaviour. Blushing had become her habitual
state, and the lilies on her lovely face gave way to the roses.

Thanks to the people with whom I was already in league,
I soon devised means of seeing her in secret; it was even more
easy than at Versailles, save for one difficulty causing me a
moment's pause: the bribing of the porter. The one maid who
was devoted to me had not enough moral sense to draw back
when she had gone so far; she made believe that my nightly
visits were on her behalf, and she generously sacrificed to me
her good name.

I was thus progressing on a path adorned with flowers, and
not yet considering what course of action one should adopt in
such a dilemma, when an important event came to put an end
to my hesitations. Women, even the most straightforward, are
always up to some wiles, and they take more time to hatch their
deceptions than we men. To this day I do not know whether we
were betrayed. After supper I had gone up to Sophie's room,
of which she had given me the key, and was waiting for her
by the fireside, engaged in reading La Bruyère; the time at
which she should have come had gone by, so I was impatient,
yet without anxiety. Someone softly knocked at the door, I
opened it, but imagine my surprise on seeing Mme de ——!

Her presence, however, put me more out of temper than
it embarrassed me. I was tired of pretence and of perpetually
acting so humiliating a part in front of a woman who had been
privy to my first transgressions. Our parts seemed to be changed;
as she was advancing towards me in almost queenly fashion, I
forestalled her.

"Well, madame," I said, on my side also acting a tragic
part, "like Athalie your wish was to see and you have seen,
but I warn you I want no reproaches."

"And you will hear none from me, for I alone should incur reproach."

These few words restored her full ascendency.

"But," she added, "I have no doubt the right to save Mlle de Lorville and to protect you from the dishonour of her disgrace. Thank me for having surprised her secret yet kept it sacred for both your sakes. You may not at present approve of the means I have used, but the day will come when you will be thankful, and this is enough for me." I wished to seize one of her hands, but she withdrew it sharply and left me without visible emotion or anger.

I remained, like a statue, rooted to the spot where I stood, until Sophie herself entered, in a state impossible to describe. Her features had aged by ten years, and no tears were left in her eyes. A long time went by before she could answer my questions, which poured out madly.

At last I heard that Mme de —— had asked Sophie to her sitting-room after supper, and had said to her pointblank: "The Comte de Tilly is now in your room, he is your lover and you are pregnant." The trembling Sophie tried to stammer a few words, only to kneel speechless in front of her judge, who, pushing her away, caused her to fall to the floor. But this first impulse was short-lived; generosity and kindness regained the upper hand: Mme de —— helped Sophie to rise and clasping the girl to her bosom brought her back to life and lavished on her the most tender care. It was after this scene, which lasted a long time, that Mme de —— came up to confront me. Then she went down again, spoke tenderly to Mlle de Lorville, and without further explanation advised her to retire.

This narrative transported me with rage. The night was given to tears and to the most fantastic schemes. I told Sophie that Mme de —— had been her rival, preceding her in my heart; at this her despair increased as I had foreseen. I wrote Mme de —— several notes which I tore up, all of them (I blush at the thought) breathing threats and vengeance. I at last resolved to ask her for an interview so as to learn what were her plans and how she intended to dispose of our love.

Having left her mansion at dawn, I sent one of my men about eleven to enquire at what time it would suit her to receive me.

I must confess I went to this meeting with the intention of loading her with reproaches and inhumanly abusing the rights

I had once possessed over her. This inconsiderate plan, I hurry
to say for my good repute, was not carried out. Her appearance
disarmed me, I was grieved at her pallor; her eyes, once more,
spoke to my heart through the tears bathing them.

I remember that having at last questioned her as to what
she intended to do, she replied: "All I can and all you wish."
That was wrong of her, because she never fulfilled her promise.
The conversation ended there. Sophie entered the drawing-
room; she was deadly pale. Mme de —— with her own hands
rouged the girl's cheeks, and covered her with kisses; at that
moment I loved the one almost as much as the other. At dinner
time, Mme de —— kept the conversation going with great ease
and kindness. As it was her day for a box at the opera, she
insisted on taking us there in spite of my entreaties, so we had
to comply. "Roland" was the opera given; all went fairly well
until this lively air which, even in ordinary circumstances, one
cannot hear without being moved:

> You know what fond regard and sweet devotion
> Were mine for her! How faithful and true my affection!
> But see indeed, to-day, these gifts so ill repaid!

At this moment Mme de ——'s face indicated deep sorrow;
Sophie uttered such a cry of pain as nearly drew the attention of
the whole audience to us. "Ah, madame," she exclaimed, with-
drawing to the back of the box, "God is my witness that I never
knew. . . ."

"Cruel child," replied the other, "I am convinced of it, and
I do not complain—"

"You see," I interrupted, "was I not right? . . ." and I took
them home.

Once back we sat in gloomy silence. Mme de —— was the
first to speak. "We are all of us guilty," she said, "myself more
than either of you. Let us put an end to reproaches and think
only of the present. Do not expect that, through cowardly complacency, I shall allow in my house a liaison of which the secret
is now mine, and is also, unfortunately, shared by other people.
Mlle de Lorville was for me a trust which I have badly kept,
but, to the best of my abilities, I must now repair both the
scandal I have occasioned and the evils meted out as punishment. She must go away. You are yourself on the eve of joining
your regiment, so the sacrifice will be less painful. She must, as
I say, go into the country; a trustworthy woman will take her

to one of my estates; there she will give birth to the unfortunate being she bears, and come back only when the sad secret has been buried forever; my rights over her are very limited. You will each work out your fate, and you will give thought: yourself as to what you wish to exact, and she as to what she will like to grant you."

I did not find courage to appeal against this decree so conformable to both honour and reason. As for Sophie, she had no will left.

Three o'clock in the morning found us still engaged in this painful discussion. I took my leave, in a state of fever, and with despair deep in my heart. The letter which I received when getting out of bed did not bring me peace; I give a faithful copy of it.

Soon after taking leave of you, we both started by coach. I shall go with Mlle de Lorville as far as twenty leagues from Paris and will stop from eight to ten days at D—— with Mme de M——. Please accept my pledge that neither temper nor jealousy has anything to do with my determination. I will prove it to you. Your happiness and hers will always be as precious to me as to yourself. If you will allow me to express an opinion, you will go back to Versailles and pay your court to the Queen before you take your leave. I am not the one to advise you as to the future, for you might have reasons for doubting my skill in the course of action I should trace; I feel on safer ground in wishing you happiness: which I do for all times and all circumstances of your life. Goodbye.

As a postscript: "I fulfill a promise in forwarding you the enclosed letter of which I do not know the contents." The letter was from Sophie.

Pages of tears and love entreating me not to forget her but to cherish her memory should she lose her life. My first impulse was to send for post-horses and run after her, the second to fall into an abject depression; and I should have given way to it without the Marquis de Senecterre's comforting friendship, for he behaved as an affectionate brother. The reader will see later how grateful I remained to him; had I been at Grenoble at the time of his last illness, possibly he might not have died.

It was Paris this time which had become odious to me, so I went back to Versailles. What turmoil of vexation and rage devoured me! And what deep anger my heart once more entertained towards Mme de ——!

"Ah," I exclaimed as I approached the palace, "what labour, wealth, and sweat have gone to the building of Versailles! How difficult it should be to tame the lion which roars in the menagerie! What a task it must be in our days to be Prime Minister of a country such as France: fulfilling the duties of such a position, having the skill required! But one thing is even less easy than these, that is to leave a woman who will not be left and teach friendship to outlive love."

I am not even now sure I was not then grossly unfair.

Real grief was gripping me for the first time in my life. The world seemed but a vast wilderness without Sophie to give it life. I could have said with Antiochus: "In the desert East who could my boredom tell!" [10]

But, such is the queerness of the human heart, ten days later I was unfaithful, though this infidelity was of the senses, which men are agreed to count as nothing. The incident would be worthy its place in a rather risky novel, but, nevertheless, its occurrence is an authentic fact.

Early one evening I had had supper at the inn "Au Juste" with M. de Rabodances, who was going back to Paris next morning. I was leaving the inn on foot, when, after a few steps, I was stopped by two women who at once parted company. I found myself alone with one of them, who in a faltering voice asked me to follow her. I replied to her coldly, but hearing her laughter from amongst the wrappings covering her head, and finding nothing vulgar in her walk or bearing, I thought better of it and tried to pull off one of her gloves. My curiosity was well founded, the hand was charming and beautifully tended. Yet nothing else could I see, though I heard a voice which was not that of a woman accustomed to prostitute her charms.

"What will be the end of this?" I asked her. "What do you wish from me?"

"To follow you," she replied, "and charm you if I can."

"I am not worth the trouble. Besides the task is difficult, no one is any longer attractive to me."

"You are blasé early in life."

"It is because I am not blasé that I do not wish to go with you."

"The excuse is specious."

"What language is this?"

"French, no doubt."

"Yes, but not the French of the street."

"Who told you I was of the street? Does one live in the gutter because one gets muddy?"

"Upon my word, I will see your face."

"Upon my word, this no longer pleases me. You shall not see it."

I tried to raise her veil, but she repulsed me saying: "You would grievously distress me if you tried to look at me here."

"Where then can I look at you!"

"Anywhere else but in this street where you seem to think I spend my life."

"Well, would you like to come home with me?"

"Where do you live?"

"At the Duc de Noailles's."

"I prefer not to go there."

"No one is there but the porter, a few servants attached to the house, and myself. I am staying there at the present."

"All the same I do not dare."

"I should have thought you bold."

"I may be just a little, yet not enough."

"Where else can we go?"

"In the Rue de l'Orangerie, if you are willing to follow me."

"I would follow you to hell."

"I am in no hurry to go there, but we may one day perhaps meet at that spot."

We started to walk; she had taken my arm. Thinking the matter out, I found myself rather ashamed; I withdrew my arm.

"You are not very civil," she told me. "It is too dark to be seen, there is but little risk of being noticed."

"It was not . . . for . . . that reason. I thought you could do without it, and it was more convenient for me."

"I am not worth a lie; at least so you ought to think."

"There is my arm."

"I no longer need it."

"You will grieve me if you refuse."

So she took it again.

"Do you belong to Versailles?" I asked her.

"No, I came here only a short while ago."

"From Paris?"

"No."

"From where then?"

"From Franche-Comté."

"Have you still any relatives?"

"My mother and my husband."

"Where are they?"

"My mother lives in Paris, my husband is far from here."

"Have you any profession?"

"These last few months I have been training for one which bores me much."

"Not much of a profession!"

"My mother once belonged to it."

"A most respectable little family!"

"So everybody says."

"Does it bring in a lot?"

"Very little . . . save honour."

"Oh, indeed!"

"I assure you."

"Do you meet in this way every evening men as docile as myself?"

"I suppose I could; but was it of this you were thinking?"

"Of what else?"

"You said a profession; this is only a pastime."

I literally did not know where I stood. We had reached the door of the house to which she was leading me. She stopped.

"Well, now [here she called me by my name], you must give me your word of honour never to speak of this adventure if you happen to know my features."

"And so you know my name!"

"As you see." (I was dumbfounded.) "Your word of honour," she repeated.

"Whether angel or devil," I replied, "I give my pledge."

She knocked; the door was opened, and we went in.

The room we entered was simplicity itself, yet not without a certain elegance; one might guess its use. My companion, no longer making difficulties, removed her hat and veil, to reveal an extremely charming face, though I had never seen it before. I told her so; she seemed delighted. I could not conceive how, with features so refined and moving, a gait so graceful, anyone could fall into this state of degradation; she had the face of an Héloïse worthy of keeping faith to a new Abélard. I behaved as he would have done before his misadventure. I was vaguely reluctant, for I was thinking of Sophie; but I was also thinking that in such a place one should not have her in mind; I succeeded in forgetting her.

It is impossible to bring more wit, I would almost say more refinement and bewitching loveliness, to a real love-encounter than this woman—for whom I find no fitting appellation—displayed in this passing orgy.

I was bewildered by this unexpected scene. Too young to imagine such things really possible, I drifted in uncertainty. I did not know whether a virtuous woman could play the whore to such a point, or if a whore could so much resemble a virtuous woman. I came to the conclusion that she was a well-to-do lady whom poverty had dragged into an abyss. But: "As well as virtue, crime has its stages." [11] Why had she not stopped? Why had she fallen so low? I might have forgiven her had she sold her favours to only one lover—but to solicit in the street! My heart was indignant with her, and I hated myself for succumbing to such gross seduction.

These thoughts, passing swiftly through my brain, made me decide to go. I took some gold from my pocket and offered it to her, not wishing to fix the price myself. But the whole adventure was to prove singular; she refused.

"Keep your money," she said, "but satisfy the woman of this house. The only thing I need do now is to give you a piece of advice, which it is no doubt in my interest to give, but which, nevertheless, will be in future of daily use to you. Always beware of your first impulse, whether it be of surprise or joy or shame; the man who has no control over himself, above all over his features, constantly gives himself away when his own interest demands secrecy. If you have only learnt that this evening, you will not have lost your time."

This was a riddle for me and I asked the key.

"But," she said, "my words have no hidden meaning, they are perfectly clear and positive."

I was like a schoolboy listening to his teacher; I believe I must even have looked very near to a fool. In queenly fashion she gave me her hand to kiss; she called, and made the woman who had opened to us light my way out: I put some money on the candlestick, and found myself in the street.

The next day I related this story to two or three men who were knowing in such matters, but they laughed at me; I decided it would be best never to mention it again.

I endeavoured to shake off the memory of this incident which made me so ill at ease with myself, but there was, I must be bold to own, some obscure charm pertaining to that evening and perpetually bringing back my thoughts towards the woman who had been the life of it. Above all her last words were always present in my mind, as I could not grasp their meaning.

Her advice (the reason for which will soon appear) to master any display of our feelings, brings me to one remark which may be stated here: namely, the fallacy of judging from appearances. This is the wrong way people generally have, for instance, of believing because a man blushes, that he is guilty or convicted of what he is accused.

I may take my own case. I have never been looked upon as being shy or easily put out. Yet, all through life, I have never been able to control my blushes, not only when I am openly charged with some deed or fault, but even when such imputation, however absurd, comes indirectly to my knowledge. Should I be accused of having murdered the King of Sweden, I do not know if I should be able, however ridiculous it would be, to refrain from blushing and embarrassment every time the matter was discussed.

This is due to liveliness and heat of the blood and to organs of delicate constitution easy to stir; it does not proceed from moral susceptibility, but is purely a physical and mechanical manifestation. But, whatever it may be, it proves a misfortune in polite society, for one is often judged by these doubtful symptoms, and I have even found myself unfavourably prejudiced by such signs, whereas, upon reflection, I more than anyone else should have known better.

I was at last approaching the day when I must join the regiment where I was to serve. I had gone to the house of the Prince de Montbarrey, then minister of war, to receive my orders, and the Prince invited me to dinner. Five women were in the drawing-room when I entered. I knew only three of them; M. de Moreton de Chabrillant, a man who has since played a most shady part in the Revolution, undertook to introduce me to the others. I should try in vain to express my agitation when I suddenly looked upon features so well known and so distinct. To believe that two people could be so much alike seemed to mark me for a lunatic asylum. I hid as best I could the excess of my surprise and tried for the first time to put into practice the advice so recently received. I could not, however, resist the temptation of turning my eyes often to this face, this waist, these arms and hands, which I found loaded with bracelets and rings I had not formerly seen there. The sound of the voice finished me. I was as agitated as she ought to have been. Yet, calm as the priest at the altar, she contrived to relate her whole story from her birth to people who knew it as well as she did, this clearly for me whom she wished to instruct. It was all done with unperceived art, in but a few swift words, and without a shadow of affectation.

It amounted to the fact that, married at eighteen to a man with whom she scarcely lived, she had spent three years in the country and then come to Paris to join her mother, who had rooms at the Luxembourg, and a post at Versailles that later fell to the daughter. She had now, for some time, performed its duties. I could not find strength to say a word. I was pronounced to be a handsome lad, very unassuming and with the most pleasing deportment; it might have been added that this same little gentleman was very abstemious, for he ate no dinner.

On leaving the table I tried to speak to her, she replied absent-mindedly in a few curt words. I thought her most impertinent and no longer knew if I had not been mistaken. At one moment, when my eyes were on her, she nodded as if to say, "Yes," but I could scarcely take this as an answer to a request I had not formulated. She was quite aware of this, and, as several people were admiring a handsome clock which appeared newly placed in the room, she stood up and, appearing very eager to join in the praise of its workmanship, she approached the clock as if to examine it more at her ease, then her finger on the dial found itself at the figure ten while she threw me a swift glance that had meaning only for me. A few minutes later, while speaking to the Comtesse de Blot, her voice, rising to a higher pitch, pronounced very distinctly, "I believe it is in the Rue de l'Orangerie," but soon, having resumed the conversation in low tones of voice, the last word she brought out loud again was: "To-morrow."

How could I any longer believe that I was mistaken? There was no possibility of now fancying it was only a dream.

It may be guessed that the next day I was punctual at the assignation which I felt convinced she had made. I arrived first, but did not have to wait long. For one moment I pressed her close to my heart, then felt I wanted to push her off. Catching hold of my hand, she led me away. I said a few words to her,

but received no reply. . . . At last we were in the same room.
"By what luck," she hastened to ask me, "have I found you
again?"

"What speech is this?" I replied. "I understand nothing
of it. Did I not dine with you yesterday?"

"With me? Where please?"

"At the Prince de Montbarrey's. Are you not the Comtesse
de——?"

"What story out of the 'Arabian Nights' are you telling me?
Are you ill!"

"But, come this way! Ah, you will no longer deceive me,
it is you right enough. . . . But, is it possible? For—yes—of
course you. . . . It is true, very true. . . . It *is* you."

"How ridiculous! Are you giving way to mad fancies? As
you please, good luck to you!"

"How is that?"

"Come, you are mad."

But, as I was at least very certain of her presence, I engaged
in more positive occupations; she appeared to be herself very
much occupied.

I beg forgiveness if I myself fall into the same fault I have
condemned in writers who have deluged us during the last fifty
years with licentious and, above all, ill-mannered novels, which
they believed in the best of taste—thus leading the lower classes
to believe likewise, and moreover foreigners, as I have already
explained. But, as regards myself, I have no choice. I write the
truth and, not being able to conceal it, I adorn it with the least
transparent veil. But I shall not be caught like these gentlemen
in the benighted and absurd position of wishing to convince the
reader that the hidden vices of polite society are its general
behaviour, nor the few mad conversations met with in some
boudoirs those of the drawing-rooms. Such society, if we are to
believe these authors, is composed of fops and wantons who converse only in the queerest, most inconceivable of jargons; as if
our school of politeness and good form—that of the best-bred
people of France—were after all, to judge from such portraits,
but a stage for light vulgarity or elegant absurdity. We ought
to disapprove of these pictures and their execrable taste more
than of a few isolated narratives of hidden deeds in immorality
or libertinage, which are neither a marvel nor a novelty in a
century that does not let modesty stand in the way of hearing
everything, and sees neither merit nor fault in saying everything.

But before shutting myself up again in the room from which I made this digression, let me be permitted a second one concerning two authors of my time, M. Dorat and M. Marmontel. I knew both intimately, especially the first. Both founded schools in portraiture and led astray a crowd of disciples. They followed Crébillon the younger, who had less talent than either, especially Marmontel. He was their prototype, the discoverer of a false kind of fiction, the inventor of a wretched jargon. And see now the army of their followers! What is to be said of these? Is it not doing Europe a service to deprive both these authors of a fame they owe to such tasteless methods? We cannot too soon open the eyes of the reading world to the disservice which these otherwise worthy men have done, and counter the mischief they have effected amongst the young people who imitate them.

With all their faults these two authors were masters of their tongue and really wrote French. When that excellent man of letters, Marmontel, is somewhere led astray and makes one of his heroes at a great dinner say, "Nothing is talked of in society but the very reasonable arrangement you have made with your wife; it is understood that she has taken back the Chevalier and you the little Marquise; it is known that you are agreed not to quarrel with each other about anything," such phrases can only mislead young and inexperienced newcomers, who, when they have once had the honour to be invited to a smart dinner, will soon realise their error. When the author says further, "And that she hands you the rhubarb, so that you may pass her the senna," a provincial apothecary would at most laugh at such a trite vulgarity and wonder how his drugs could have reached such good society. Yet, as I have said, these forms of speech, however tasteless and ridiculous, are good pure French and generally intelligible.

But, O mighty godhead of the French Parnassus, what has the beautiful tongue of Bossuet, Fénelon, Pascal, Montesquieu, Buffon, Voltaire, Corneille, Racine done to thee, to be so disgracefully distorted?

I open the writings of the new authors and read: "Des yeux vaporeux et veloutés; des robes vaporeuses; des goûts vaporeux; des cœurs calcinés d'amour; des lèvres ambroisiées; des roses d'amour tamisées; des larmes délirantes." Another speaks "de doigts parfilés par l'amour; de perfidies délicieusement traitées; d'un crâne sentimental; d'un roué pâli sous les rideaux de nos élégantes, du privilège que nous autres grands avons d'être de charmants tapageurs, d'une vibration des cordes retentissantes du cœur, d'une tendresse filtrée dans le sang."

Another allows the Marquis to write to the Chevalier: "Tu es dans tes domaines où tu te rouilles; ta végétation, loin de nos brillantes coteries, est un attentat monstrueux et dérogatoire à nos lois," etc., etc.

My pen will not allow me to transcribe further the sillinesses of this French-Iroquois language.

> Ce moderne jargon dont on fait vanité,
> Sort du bon naturel et de la vérité;
> Des mots vides de sens, affectation pure,
> Et ce n'est point ainsi que parle la nature.[12]

Our language, after reaching the climax of perfection, will become unintelligible, falling from that height, attained with so much exertion, where its masterpieces of clarity and elegance have placed it for all Europe. Perhaps a day will come when professors and interpreters will be needed to explain and comment the speech of the new school.

But to return to my assignation.

Nothing on earth lasts forever; I had to take leave of the siren who had seduced me.

"I was not pleased with your first gesture at M. de Montbarrey's," she told me suddenly, and with a distant air. "I might have forgiven you if you had been sensible enough to regain your composure, but I might easily have lost countenance through your embarrassment; for a man of wit, no one could be more clumsy."

"At last, madame, so it was you!"

"As you see."

"Allow me to ask you one question. On the first occasion of our meeting you could not have guessed I was going to be there. . . . Were you looking for me?"

"I was looking for pleasure." [13]

"Whom were you after?"

"The first man I should take a fancy to." [14]

"Great Gods!" I exclaimed, not being able to conceal some sort of fright.

"It is too amusing," she replied without embarrassment, "that you men wish to be allowed to do anything after having forbidden us nearly everything. We have but one means of re-

asserting our right, that is to do in secret what you pride yourselves upon doing in public."

"But you will lose your good name."

"Oh, not at all! Half-hearted sinning leads one to ruin,
but not if one goes to extremes, for nobody believes it. Besides,
do you think I am like you, totally lacking in skill? Come, don't
look so sorry for yourself, and so much like a schoolgirl. You
would be a very desirable lover if it were not for your grand
principles. But now that you know me, I am no longer worthy
of you; if ever we meet in society, I shall admire you as a shy
pretty young girl dressed up as a man, and you will show me
the consideration you ought to a woman of will who has made
herself just a little bit like your sex, but who in public will
never give up that decorum which is the chief adornment of
her own."

I was dumbfounded, I was speechless. She went on kissing
me; her logic could not convince me, but my senses were carried
away in spite of my reason and through some attraction superior
to my resistance.

"Alas," I told her at last, "I am very guilty, for I worship
another!"

"Tell me the story," she said.

"What would you think of me if I did? Would you not fear
I should be no more discreet as regards you with another woman?"

"That is true, but it is not the same thing. The attachment
which you mention is of a respectable nature, while my adventure with you is shameful and outside ordinary conventions."

"Have you then a conscience and remorse?"

"No doubt; I hide myself, as I would do were I to get drunk
on champagne in my room. There is no great wickedness in
either one deed or the other, but scandal is always a great evil.
Absurdity and madness are, at bottom, the order of the day
upon this earth; it is merely appearances that deserve to be
treated seriously."

"Great heaven, where did you learn all this?"

"Through some thinking and in my heart."

"I can scarcely compliment you."

"Good-bye," she said, placing one hand over my eyes. "Forget a good half of all this but remember me a little."

"I shan't be able to forget you."

"Ought I to thank you?"

"Just as you like."

"Good-bye. I warn you I wish to keep towards you a feeling that will altogether resemble friendship."

"And I, some gratitude. After all I owe you some. Good-bye."

"Good-bye."

If this narrative appears fantastic or exaggerated, I shall not complain, though I might tell the incredulous reader that I felt great hesitation before putting it down in these memoirs where I vouch that not a word, not a line, is contrary to Truth, unless it be by some involuntary failure of my memory. I might add that France is not the only stage to display such scandalous scenes, and that I am intimately acquainted with a foreign officer of high degree, whose veracity cannot be questioned, and to whom the same sort of adventure happened, with a woman of very high rank in one of the chief capitals of Europe. What does this prove? That woman can be depraved in all ranks of life as there have been virtuous ones in all ages and in all countries; but that everywhere those who move in the highest spheres of society behave and speak, at least publicly, with the decorum and decency of their station. No matter what inclinations or moral habits may be theirs, they expect and deserve as much consideration as well-bred men or the most virtuous daughters of their sex; for since they maintain the pretence of the same virtues, they demand the display of the same regard; and certainly society soon disposes of those men or women who openly transgress the codes consecrated in their circle, or their social conventions either in speech or behaviour.

I will add, to palliate the errors of the woman of whom I have spoken, if it is now possible to say anything in her praise, that I saw her many years later attached to a man very well known, but far from pleasant, whom she had the bad taste to love, while his passion for her knew no bounds. She remained as faithful to him as if he were her first love. No doubt he was the first to have found the way to her heart. Once, in Brussels, I remember spending in their company the most boring evening of my life. Although she was full of wit of many varieties, I gathered but the rebound of all the insipidity of a sentimental pastoral: they had forgotten I was there. . . . She had forgotten Versailles.

The moral constitution is like that of the body: liable to illnesses of which it can be cured.

CHAPTER VI

ON the eve of leaving Paris and Versailles for the obscure garrison town of Falaise I was not without many regrets at the memory of all that already filled my life. The Queen, of whom I went to take leave, assured me of a protection she did not aways grant, and of a good will she did not always exert, but she was sincere at the moment she condescended to give such pledges.

She had, a few days before, been greatly distressed, and was still much troubled, over a matter that may give an idea of her heart and prove how easily she would have won the love of her people, as she longed to do, had she been surrounded by advisers and friends worthy of her; to desire this love so ardently was already to deserve it. She did me the honour of asking if I had been to the Opéra on the last occasion she was there (two or three days previously).

"Yes, madame."

"Why was I so coldly received? What have I done to them?"

"Coldly? . . ."

"You cannot have failed to notice . . . but, in truth, so much the worse for the people of Paris; it is not my fault." She had tears in her eyes.

"Your Majesty places too much value on what may be just mere chance; besides, if the Queen will allow me to say so, in as high a station as hers, one should grieve only about good deeds left undone or bad deeds one cannot prevent."

"Very wise words for a scatterbrain, but when one has nothing to reproach oneself with . . . it hurts a great deal!"

Little did I think, as I left her, that such incidents were already the faint flashes preceding the thunder that was to reduce to ashes this throne her ascension to which she had considered as the highest favour of Fortune.

It may be fitting here to give some details concerning the Queen and the intimate circle she had gathered around herself through her own inclinations and likings. I shall thus mention that, before leaving the pages, I saw for the first time the Comtesse de Polignac, née Polastron,[1] a lady very famous since

because she stood high in the Queen's favour, and later on account of the hatred displayed against her by the French people
and the harshness of fate which held for her a premature and
wretched end. Count Jules, later on Duc de Polignac, shared the
brilliant fortune of his wife without having sought it or given
it a thought. It must not be inferred from this, however, that
he was unworthy of his good fortune; this would wrongly convey my meaning. He was an upright man and a man of honour,
who through his name and his family connections might have
attained any high position, but whose tastes and habits seemed
to mark him for a retired and peaceful life. His personal wealth
was only moderate and his aspirations not far-reaching. More a
friend than a lover to his wife, he remained satisfied with the
former title and showed no ill humour at having no other.

Fortune, on account of the features and the charm of his
wife, specially favoured him; he had paid no court to the goddess, but, in all common sense, he did not repulse her; he let her
gifts be showered over him without abusing them, though the
contrary has often been asserted. But, his sister Diane de
Polignac and her followers—the abbé de Balivière [2] and others
—caused envy, dissatisfaction, and bitterness to be meted out to
him and Countess Jules, who, if the truth be told, was not
so easily contented. This public dissatisfaction was already
secretly felt before the Revolution, but, by that time, it burst its
dikes and threatened to sweep them both away as its first victims. Neither M. nor Mme de Polignac deserved the hatred
that pursued them. I admit that they sometimes yielded to the
flattery and the pestering of their dependents, or paid attention
to pernicious advice, and that, being dazzled by the strokes of
fortune, they fell into errors and went often on the wrong
track; but has ever any court existed, or courtiers, real or sham
ones, who in similar circumstances have displayed less greed,
less pride, or committed fewer mistakes? Can it ever be an easy
task for any man to set himself up as a judge of human frailties
and measure their bulk, length, or goal? Must he condemn all
that is contrary to his own ideas? Must he not take account of
the position in which the accused persons were placed, and,
weighing the whole with impartiality, measure the breadth and
depth of the torrent that has swept them along?

The reproaches, the exaggerated accusations leveled at the
late government for abuse of power, despotism, and secret
arrests came either from men who had not suffered from such

measures, or from others who should rather have been thankful to those in authority for having mitigated their punishment by methods indulgent and fatherly.

Acts of injustice like those which dishonoured the cabinet of the Duc de Vrillière [3] and covered with shame those men and women who were his instigators, no doubt deserve the hatred and reprobation of the country. But nothing of the kind could be brought against the Polignacs during the whole course of their favour and power, which lasted for nearly fifteen years. What were the abuses of power imputed to them? Benefits conferred upon their friends; a title of duke and high offices at court for M. de Polignac; perhaps even wealth. But men seek wealth wherever it can be found, though it is more dignified to despise it.

The court's favours which were withdrawn from their opponents constituted, in fact, the Polignacs' abuse of power and their ascendency; it was this that gave them unlimited authority in the branches of administration; and, for many years, caused them to appear as the masters of royalty.

When Countess Jules was first presented at court, she attracted everyone's attention, not only by the charm of her face, but more still by those graces which make a greater impression than beauty itself. Her seductive features pleased all the more for being a gift of nature; not one small detail appeared to be due to art; nothing was unnatural. The advent of Countess Jules could not have happened at a more favourable time. The tender attachment which the Queen had so far felt for the Princesse de Lamballe,[4] and which this Princess returned with interest until her lamentable death, was beginning to lose some of its warmth and intensity. The Queen's heart, so it seemed, sought in a friend another heart in no way linked to the splendour of the throne. This explains why, from the first, she felt towards Mme de Polignac that sympathy which in matters of love or friendship is harbinger of a durable attachment.

The Queen, desiring Countess Jules's constant company, offered her the office of lady-in-waiting, and later that of mistress of the robes. But the Countess refused these favours, perhaps through indolence or some heedlessness, or maybe in accordance with the advice of friends and a little diplomacy. From that moment she could be attached to the Queen only in the quality of friend. Such a position was then a novelty; a friend who claims nothing from the crowned head could not fail to retain friendship for a long time. M. de Polignac, on the contrary, could, without obstacle or without being offended, take an office at court; he was thus selected as the ultimate successor to M. de Tessé, first equerry to the Queen.

This arrangement, of which the Comte de Tessé was not even informed beforehand, proved to him a dagger thrust, though he had no son who could have succeeded him. The wound smarted the more as everything was devised to surround with favours the man called upon to occupy his post, and to make de Tessé feel discredit and humiliation, the idea being that he would tender his resignation. But the Comte de Tessé had either enough fortitude or enough weakness to brave the storm and to keep to his post. This deed was in truth a bitter reward for one of the most honourable men of France, a grandee of Spain, a lieutenant-general, knight of the Saint-Esprit, grandson of a marshal of France, and the last offshoot of a family in which the post had been hereditary from father to son. But young queens care little for old courtiers and take little heed of such things.

The Comtesse de Tessé was the Maréchal de Noailles's daughter, but she could hardly make use of her family's influence to parry the blow, which undoubtedly wounded her all the more as it was rumoured she had entertained the idea of claiming the succession to her husband's post for her cousin, the Vicomte de Noailles. The Viscount, however, has solemnly assured me to the contrary. The Comtesse de Tessé avenged herself of this disgrace by speaking her mind freely, and henceforth she seldom appeared at court. Whenever she showed herself there she displayed a haughtiness closely resembling dignified vengeance. But she should have stopped at this and gone no farther. With a mind such as hers, which foresaw the trend of the revolution then brewing, she should have made it a law for herself to punish those who wished to make use of her to seek their own revenge upon her enemies; she should have borne in mind that, whenever one lowers oneself to philanthropic sentimentality, one is always punished.

This occasion of the appointment of M. de Polignac as successor to the first equerry obliged each of us pages to pay him a visit of congratulation. His fortune was at that time very modest, and he was living with Mme de Polignac at the hôtel Fortisson, Rue des Bons Enfants, at Versailles.

The distance was great indeed from this station to the splendour awaiting them when they came to dwell at the palace and daily received the Queen, the Comte d'Artois and even the King.

I should try in vain to render the impression the first sight of Countess Jules left on me. I was still young; she had just risen from bed in a négligée as white as snow. . . .

> Beautiful, unadorn'd, snatch'd from her sleep,
> In the last veil our drowsy beauties keep. . . .[5]

She had a rose in her hair and was in front of a mirror, which in giving reflection to her features seemed to double their charm.

I still remember it all vividly. What struck me most was the fancy that my eyes were thus beholding a princess about to act the part of shepherdess in some amateur play, a part fitting her to perfection. At the same time I was saying to myself: "Should she limp a little, she would much resemble the Duchesse de la Vallière, though, with more beauty, she does not possess the same languid and tender look." [6]

It is strange that this first and vivid impression made on me by the Comtesse de Polignac proved in no way lasting. I saw her several times later without being moved by her beauty, but I always remained under the spell of her enchanting carriage. Her walk was imprinted with a seductive, free grace that distinguished her in a peculiar manner from other ladies at court whose gait was only that of pride and vanity.

To the share of her husband had fallen an equanimity of temper that was revealed in his very appearance; a rare quality in any high station and one most commendable in all positions. Their friends did not possess the same composure, nor were they so serene; even the Comte de Vaudreuil,[7] who ruled the Queen, could not always rule his own temper. He had much wit and grace as well as a noble bearing; he was happy in the choice of his expressions and the turn of his sentences; he had all the ways of a great lord with something attractive about him. But he could be carried to extremes by his impetuous temper, and he also deserved the reproach, meted out to him, of taking too great a pleasure in speaking of himself. Yet one the more easily overlooked this weakness since few men ever had more right to take a leading part in an interesting conversation. From what I know of him and what I heard from others, I should like to question to what extent he influenced the Comtesse de Polignac; this would be the more easy for me since I could say of him that,

in truth, no man at court was ever more chivalrous, more munifi-
cent, or gifted with as many qualities denoting a beautiful soul,
even though one should admit that it was easier for him than
for most other men to display these precious qualities and possess
such noble inclinations.

He also proved himself an enlightened friend and protector
of the arts and letters. Always showing deference to men of
science and artists, he was gracious in his attentions to them and
served them with a zeal that enhanced the value of the services
rendered by both the Mæcenas and the client.

Yet this Comte de Vaudreuil, with so many brilliant qualities
and their counterbalancing human weaknesses, never succeeded
in obtaining the favour of the Queen.

What attitude should one assume here? Must one shudder or
smile at the rumours that in a certain degree have acquired
credence both in the provinces and in foreign parts? Must one
repeat that certain serious-minded people have always believed
in the existence of some private intrigue? But I have no wish to
harm the memory of an august person by defending her against
such calumnies.

The Queen did not do even justice to M. de Vaudreuil; she
felt towards him, as I could vouch, a sort of estrangement; not
to make use of the stronger word loathing; she was ready to do
more than not like him, and this because she had reasons for as-
cribing to him a strong influence over the Comtesse de Polignac.

The Abbé de Vermond [8] also hated M. de Vaudreuil with all
his might, and endeavoured to convince the Queen that the Count
was taking away from her Countess Jules's affection. Vermond's
hatred was well founded, as on several occasions M. de Vaudreuil had treated the Abbé in a manner to which the latter was
not accustomed.

The Queen's favourite had a brother who, like Mme de
Maintenon's brother, never gave promise of great worth; he
never achieved any other career than the one appointed to him
by chance: he played the violin and was more or less the humble
servant of his wife. This lady, née d'Espagnac, was, through her
great beauty, made to please and to hold captive, as indeed is
proved in one long passion she inspired and the tears shed for
her. She really had what is figuratively referred to as a slant-
wise coquettish air, for her head, being aslant on her shoulders,
gave her a languishing careless attitude not without charm.

The Queen's affection for the Comtesse de Polignac was not

always maintained at the same pitch; it could be compared to a beautiful day, not devoid of clouds and changes, but always ending on a fine evening.

Both the Duchesse de Fitz-James and the Princesse de Tarente were, for some time, the Queen's favourites. There was even a period when they received better treatment than the Comtesse de Polignac. This might make one infer that the Queen was no longer so ardent in her friendship. But, in this case, the attachment had become too strong a habit, had too closely entwined two hearts, for any trifling interruptions to loosen it and bring about the triumph of the Polignacs' enemies. This constancy does credit to both of them, the Queen as much as her friend.

The King himself, who liked to share the Queen's inclinations, always behaved towards the favourite with extreme consideration and kindliness, an attitude the more striking in a king like Louis the XVI who deserves the title of an honest man. He raised the Countess to honours, made her husband duke and a knight of the Saint-Esprit.

As soon as the favourite had rooms at the palace (they were at the top of the main staircase), the King frequently shared with the Queen and the Comte d'Artois the charm of her private society, and often enough spent thus part of the evening. But the King's company always placed a certain constraint over a party of young people who longed to free themselves from the trammels that the royal presence everywhere entails. This sometimes gave rise to a deceit, then looked upon as innocent. The King, who was very punctual, had the habit of retiring at ten; to hasten this the hands of the clock would be put forward and, success thus obtained, the circle of friends would, in the King's absence, revert to their unrestrained gaiety. I must admit that this little trick would be unworthy to-day of any court having a true sense of its dignity. But those who then allowed themselves such behaviour were too light-hearted to estimate its consequences. Let this be their justification; they certainly never viewed it as an evident indication of a gradual weakening of the support that must surround and maintain the majesty of the throne.[9]

The Queen, as was often remarked, wanted to enjoy and to relish the charm of friendship and the sweetness of private life more than any queen who ever ascended the throne of France; but, let it be said in passing, such enjoyments never befit either

kings or queens. There is perhaps on this count but one reproach
to level at the Queen and one which does little credit to her great
soul: I mean her cruel coolness towards the Princesse de
Guémené, governess to the royal children, from the time of the
unfortunate bankruptcy of the Prince de Guémené. No one can
deny that this Prince had behaved in a way difficult to excuse.
Nevertheless, there were excuses for his guilt. Had not the Queen
contributed to the downfall of this family? Was she without
blame? Had not her presence beguiled an unfortunate couple
who, launching into excessive expenses, had thus met with ruin?
Had she not accepted invitations to festivities and thus given
occasion for more entertainments? Perhaps she feared to show
too much interest towards two bankrupts against whom the public clamoured, in case the uproar rising from so many desperate
families might echo in the antechambers of the palace or even in
the throneroom. All this, however, cannot justify an entire lack
of interest. Although she never greatly liked her, so people said,
the Queen should have shown consideration to a woman who was
placed near her person in so important a position that the lady
could not have held it so long unless deserving the trust of their
Majesties.

When once the favourite was governess to the royal children
in place of the Princesse de Guémené, she became, in all respects,
the first lady at the court of Marie Antoinette and Louis
XVI. I will even admit that, through her intimate circle, she
exerted some considerable influence over matters of state by
causing the rise or fall of ministers; and this most often without
either rhyme or reason as to the public good.

When later the name of Polignac tolled as a death warrant,
the Duchess left France and through flight alone escaped the
danger hemming her in, yet only to serve the decrees of Providence. It was indeed written in the Book of Destiny that the
Duchess was to be punished for the errors she had committed
(and who does not commit some?) and for those attributed to
her, such punishment being the long agony, the imprisonment,
and the cruel death of her revered mistress. The news of that
frightful event broke her heart and shut it against any consolation. She found the end of her misery in a grave, and this grave
in Vienna, where she is regretted and mourned.

Her daughter, the unfortunate Duchesse de Guiche, followed her to the grave. She was as charming as her mother;
many people thought her even more beautiful, but this did not

appear so to me. She was more affected in her manners and had less natural charm. Hardship had deprived this beautiful flower of its gloss and sap; the wings of death came to break its stem. A stone now covers its roots; and what else remains?

I could have lengthened this chapter by seasoning it with anecdotes, but it might have been boring through superfluities. Our praises do not disturb the dust of the grave, but it would be both unworthy and deserving of hatred to break an urn and tread underfoot the ashes it contains. Neither flattery nor bitterness are to be found in my heart or under my pen. I believe I have said enough in thus showing certain facts in their true light and claiming their rights for people who were slandered and for a family mercilessly persecuted by hatred and fate.

I had started for Falaise with an oppressed heart, bearing in mind the Queen's words, while my own eyes were brimming with tears; and I may record here that I have never left Paris, or come back to it after an absence, without feeling acute grief or a deep emotion. Might it be that I had then the gloomy foreboding that, against my will, I should one day have to forsake both Paris and my native land at the most beautiful period of my life?

During the journey from Paris to Falaise I could scarcely account for such feelings: an oppressed heart, an inexplicable sensitiveness. But when one is scarcely more than seventeen vague forebodings and grave reflections do not leave on the mind a very lasting imprint.

I arrived at Falaise full of my marvellous adventure; very pleased with myself and perfectly convinced that I should go far. I felt almost like exclaiming: *"Sic itur ad astra!"*

The life one led there was very different from what I had so far seen, above all during those nine months when I had been absolutely my own master. To my lot fell: dragoons to worry now and again; officers to meet, who were often none too civil to newcomers; former legionaries whom one might scare by a mere word, or shock by too elegant an apparel, for they had grown old in inferior posts; a lieutenant-colonel (the Marquis d'Isle,[10] a distant relative of mine and one of the best officers in the army) to whom I was specially recommended; military routine to learn in all its minuteness; a rather ugly little town; a few pretty women, fairly decently watched over; others who needed no watching; men whom people from Paris were pleased to look upon as beings from another world—such is a brief sketch of what struck me without provoking delight.

Four months went by in all sorts of apprenticeships—the rest of my time I gave to reading good books. Social intercourse could not distract me, for I had the bad taste to care little for provincial society, which, since the Revolution, must be much less like that of Paris than formerly. I except two towns where I have sometimes lived, as will appear in due place, and where amongst both sexes one came across people who would have been excellent company anywhere; and certainly there could be found in France, in many big towns, a company worthy of the most refined and most fastidious people, with the one difference, it must be owned, of a certain tone, which was rarely quite the same.

Not that I wish to pamper the senseless vanity of some hundred men and women who in pre-revolutionary France claimed to be polite society *par excellence,* and looked upon themselves as the born dispensers of good taste, the leaders of public opinion, and anyone outside their circle as an inferior or a reprobate—this notwithstanding the fact that some hundred other salons were putting forth the same pretentions and merely by tolerating *ourselves and friends* easily boasted the same supremacy. Yet, in a final survey, there was almost as marked a difference between the style and language of the court and those of the town as between Paris compared with the provinces; and since some invisible link united the whole—although the composite was not always homogeneous—the result was a general politeness which was born from emulation, and which I should call a national school of behaviour. It is much to be desired that the recent upheavals have not impaired it, and that an all-powerful government will take care it flourishes anew.

However this may be, my exaggerated predilection for Paris, carried almost to a ridiculous excess, helped me to acquire what little learning I may have; for it is mostly during these interludes that I have given myself to general studies and to work, though work—on account of my memory and facility, perhaps also of a natural aptitude—was always less of a necessity for me than for many others, even in the midst of life's pleasures and dissipations.

CHAPTER VII

Et in Arcadiâ, Ego!

I ALSO have been a shepherd! I once led a pastoral life in the peacefulness of the country. I once danced with innocent peasant girls to the tune of a rustic pipe and in the very meadow where, a few years before, their mothers, now at rest in the adjoining cemetery, had kept time to the dance. Yet I said good-bye to such simple happiness to become infected by the corruption of pompous cities and of courts, to grow weary at heart through frivolous and guilty lapses, to prove myself a bore in fashionable circles which bored me even more and where I damaged the first of all treasures—my health, the only real inheritance of man, wretched dweller upon this earth.

A letter from Sophie had caused me to leave the garrison town where the reader last found me, and proceed to some of my relations who had an estate in the province of Maine. Sophie told me that she had been more fortunate than she deserved; that the whole episode was hidden in inscrutable secrecy, while she was now completely recovered and on the eve of joining Mme de —— at her country house previous to their going back to Paris four months later. This news made me resolve to bury myself in the country until the moment when I could join the object of a love now increased through absence.

So I arrived without notification at the house of my most civil of uncles, a man of honour in every sense, judicious though not brilliant, but of the noblest disposition. He had a decent income to which he added every year.[1] He showed more surprise than displeasure at seeing me. He assured me that his house was quite at my disposal. Yet he greatly feared lest life at his country-seat and the monotony of its surroundings should prove the death through boredom of a beau like me, though, in truth, not far away, were two towns[2] with fair populations. But at each the women were virtuous, the husbands boring and jealous, while everybody went to bed early; as for himself, busy as he was during the day with the management of his land, buildings, and domestic affairs, he was but poor company by the evening, being very sleepy long before ten; while his wife, a very pious lady, read only sacred books and spent a great deal of her time in prayers. Nevertheless the library, poor as it was, would be left open for me, nothing would be hidden from me, each day I could give orders for dinner so as not to grow thin through ennui, and the gardener would always be ready to take me on fishing expeditions, and the keeper out hunting. He added that there were often country dances where the prettiest peasant girls gathered under the supervision of mothers or aunts and their sweethearts.

To all this I replied that such a fabulous picture made an enchanting landscape; that I had come to seek the charms of virtuous society and the pure pleasures of nature; so I begged him to grant me his trust, upon my assurance that I was worthy of it.

My uncle's wife was not so much of an aunt that one could not easily pay court to her; but though still well preserved, she threatened me with her confessor at the first compliment I uttered. I had to yield to so much virtue. I vowed that what I had said was but a matter of form, so as to have everything in order lest she should in her heart accuse me of being unmoved by one who had still so much charm. She thanked me with un-usual modesty, and we never again spoke about it; but we had long talks about Saint Augustine and Saint Jerome, the first an admirer of the fair sex in his prime, the second almost as famous for his victories over a hot-blooded temperament and a passion-ate soul, as for his beautiful mind. She could not recover from her astonishment, and I became dangerous for her once she knew I had read the Fathers. She would exclaim: "You could have been a most virtuous man. Oh, nephew, what a pity!"

Dear soul! I know that she is still alive; [3] but these memoirs are too profane. . . . She will never read them. . . .

Thus, for every woman, one form of seduction lies in wait, one snare where the strictest virtue can be caught.

I started looking over the books in the library, which well deserved its bad repute. A few books on mysticism, some of La Calprenède's novels, Father Daniel's History, two or three vol-umes of Corneille, "Le Parfait Maréchal," "Le Grand Jar-dinier," "La Cuisinière Française," were its foundations. Fortu-nately it also contained "Les Provinciales" and a passable edition of Buffon. I began a serious study of the latter, whose theories and systems always appeared to me hardly worthy of confidence, and whose style it is more easy to extol incessantly than to find always faultless. I had often heard praises of M. de Buffon's harmony of style and rhythm, of his pompous way of reciting to himself and others the well-rounded sentences he had composed with so much art and labour; and indeed I acknowledge in them superior excellence, but I remain nevertheless convinced that he did not unvaryingly bestow such care during the course of his long and immortal work. For there are whole passages, I will dare to say, which are not only written with extreme negligence, but are burdened with blemishes one is greatly surprised to find, though it would be presumptuous and bold on my part to point them out.

I allotted myself tasks to fill my time: reading, hunting, a walk, some talk with my relations, whom I scarcely saw except at meals, divided the day. During the evenings, in the peace of the country, I made verses, and it is there I composed the first poem which was printed under my name, and of which the following extract was quoted with praise by journalists.[4]

> Sous Darius, un courtisan,
> Poli, galant, homme à bonne fortune,
> Autant que peut l'être un Persan,
> (Mais Chardin dit qu'il en trompa plus d'une) ;
> Ce satrape, en un mot, avec beaucoup d'esprit,
> Fut exilé, malgré tout son crédit,
> Dans le fond de la Bactriane.
> Le vizir Artabane
> Lui porta les ordres du Roi,
> Fit semblant de pleurer, et dit: Comptez sur moi;
> Vous savez combien je vous aime!
> Et quinze jours après fut renvoyé lui-même.
> Le premier fut cacher dans un triste manoir
> Sa douleur et son espérance;
> Car en Perse c'est comme en France,
> Un courtisan n'est jamais sans espoir.
> Il s'ennuya beaucoup la première quinzaine,
> Il envoya deux conviés à la cour;
> Il errait tristement tant que durait le jour,
> Et la nuit, le sommeil, pour adoucir sa peine,
> Ne venait point fermer ses yeux.
> Enfin, se résignant, il reprit son courage,
> De sa raison il essaya l'usage;
> Espérant un peu moins, il dormit un peu mieux.
> Il écrivit, il aima la lecture,
> Il aima ses vassaux, les arts et la nature.
> Il chassa loin de lui les regrets superflus,

Et dormit tout-à-fait quand il n'espéra plus.
Il aima son exil, il eut une maîtresse;
           Le mieux serait de s'en passer.
Le Roi le rappela, mais il eut la sagesse
           Et le bon sens de refuser.
Il mourut dans les bras d'une beauté fidèle,
A qui dans ses malheurs il s'était engagé;
Et quelque temps après, dans les plaines d'Arbelle,
           Par Alexandre il fut vengé.

I quote these verses because, as they are the outcome of my youth, they may give an idea of what I might have done as a poet, but for the various interruptions which have always befallen me in life. Rivarol, whom I quote with all the more pleasure and the more often since people have believed that I liked neither to praise nor to quote him, has often said to me: "These verses are in the fashion of those of your Dorat, who most likely has nothing as good in all his bulky collection." But he liked neither Dorat nor his talent, and I am far from accepting literally a judgement which is due to temper and on that account proves nothing.

This long epistle (for the extract is only one episode) was addressed to that worthy Dampierre, then officer in the guards, to whom, on my leaving Paris, I had promised to send verses. We had had literary breakfasts as guests of a man who since came to no good, and Dampierre, to incite me to work, had beforehand ordered me to work at this piece.

It would at that time have been difficult to foresee the fate he was preparing for himself and the death he encountered. He, kindly, simple, honest in private life, a man of honour and refinement, became, I do not know how, an associate of Monseigneur le Duc d'Orléans and sided with the Revolution. Brave as Cæsar, though lacking the talent, he deliberately sought death while in command of one of the victorious armies which preserved for France both her name and her territory.[5]

But to proceed, for I must return to my fields and my muttons, I became, as I have said, shepherd on Sundays. I danced with the whole village, but very soon noticed a pretty blonde who did not repulse my pastoral advances. She has since become a dancer on one of the leading stages of Paris, and has always been kindly disposed towards me for having taken her out of her village; had Fate finally placed her upon the throne of Golconda, I am sure she would have been as grateful as Aline.[6]

Country life has its charms; four months went by like a peaceful dream. Now that my passions are quieter, I often wonder why towns are not forsaken for the country and the life one could lead there? It is, though, only recently I feel such surprise, for I was for years unable to tear myself from Paris, or even to conceive how one could live elsewhere, save perhaps in the other great capitals of Europe where I have since dwelt.

Yet, if we were but to give it thought, how many worries, disappointments, trials, pettiness, and constraint would be spared us by not wasting days of small talk in drawing-rooms—those battlefields for ostentation, disparagement, unfairness, erroneous judgements, and absurdities—but looking to nature, and the free enjoyment of our real self, to offer us pure and unrestrained joys. How quickly we should learn to exchange noise and vain agitation for a solitude adorned by nature and the arts, brightened by friendship or cheered by a little love.

But cannot these things be found in fashionable circles? No.

There, you will be betrayed by the wife who might have loved you faithfully in solitude. You have conquered her heart and her senses, but out of personal vanity she must escape you: such and such a man is more in the fashion than yourself, such a woman is a famous rival; she wants to secure the first and to humiliate the second. You are fortunate if she does not become your enemy, for she will no more easily forgive you the wrong she has done you than the one you might have done her.

This friend of your youth, who in a quiet country life would have kept for you an affection worthy of the days of Orestes and Pylades, will amidst city turmoil forsake you at the first misfortune, or the first encounter of his pride with yours; he will carry off your mistress, and may wish to snatch away your very life to make his possession secure.

Art and literature, which could have been your consolation and which you might have cultivated like a master, will prove rebellious to all your attempts. You might have produced manly work or perhaps given birth to masterpieces had your mind matured in meditation; the splendours of nature and of an art most resembling them might have been accessible to you; but you will find yourself unable to grasp them in the midst of a society cankerous with falsehood, cant, and degradation.

Even you, divine beings, charming women, go dulling your beauty by the light of a hundred torches. Its flower will fade in a few years amidst night festivities fatal to your attractions, its bloom will wither through intrigues, while at ruinous gambling your heart will become the loser as much as your purse and face. You debase without caution all these stable charms and cause them to vanish before the time appointed by Nature; while, should you keep her laws and live in closer contact with her and her bounties, you would find within yourself and in quiet retirement an unchanging felicity. Take for this the word of a man who was once passionately fond of excitement but never found therein even the shadow of happiness and only approached this state at the moment he led a retired and peaceful life. It is in such sweet retirement that you will learn to seek and find your soul, to acquire knowledge and love of your own self and of the few beloved persons around you. Believe me, the tenderest emotions, the most enchanting sensibility, will become yours in this seclusion, and, having lived surrounded by kindliness, affection, and esteem, you will see your death honoured by tears, and regrets will follow you beyond the grave.

But my preaching will cure nobody. . . . I was myself for long incurable; I have idolised a life of agitation. As long as there are men, passions will prevail; and in a community organised such as ours, there will be coteries with the cup of bitterness passing from hand to hand. There will be ever fresh trials causing people to curse society life, yet not preventing the majority of men from living therein or from throwing themselves into it with a sort of fury.

When I went back to Paris I stopped at Alençon where lived a kindly governor, hated by his neighbours almost as much as governors ever are, though he deserved it less. He, too, died on the scaffold! The axe had a job with him; he was past sixty and of monstrous corpulence. His secret for this had been, during forty years, never to dine, but to eat raw, every evening, a whole ten-pound leg-of-mutton. He was an excellent administrator, a hard worker, and at heart a very obliging man, although, being spoiled like most of his type, he assumed the bearing of a proconsul and did good ungraciously. A wicked man with good manners would have found more favour. It must be admitted that such posts formed one of the abuses of the old-time monarchy, and it is much to be desired that their counterpart will never appear in a new order. But what human institutions are free from inconveniences? In what administrations devised by man will there not be ambitions ready to supplant others?

I recall that M. de Meilhan, formerly governor of Valenciennes, once told me at Aix-la-Chapelle a thing which much impressed me: "If governors of provinces had been drawn from the high aristocracy, they would have been too powerful." The check to their authority was to be found in their starting point and in public opinion, which always reminded them of their origins, and constantly threw them back, so to say, into their former personal way of life.

The confession contained in the sentence just quoted was modest enough for a man who made no profession of being modest and believed himself equal to the greatest writers on account of a few insignificant pages he had written with more ingenuity than learning. He generally betrayed an almost obtuse vanity.[7]

This M. de Meilhan also believed himself the greatest administrator in France. He once gravely related to me that upon the appointment of M. de Calonne as Chancellor of the exchequer, the King had sent for him. "In a conversation lasting two hours," he told me, "I proved to him that I had infallible means of saving the state. His Majesty appeared entirely satisfied, and I am sure I had convinced his mind. I thought that on the morrow I should be made Chancellor, France thus escaping the political wreck which is now awaiting her; but I was cheated by a mere courtier: I lost the position for which I was born, and a man of wits carried the day over a man of genius."

I come back to my governor of Alençon, of whom I speak rather at length because his wife, who invited company for games of reversi, was a queer mixture of vulgarity and decisiveness, and told me such an extraordinary story that it seems but yesterday I heard her voice whispering to me at supper: "You see that tall woman of a rather ruddy complexion, with whom the governor pretends to be in love, though really he cares for no one but himself, do you see her?"

"Yes, madame."

"Well, she is a roué's daughter."

"A very common thing."

"Not at all, a *roué* . . . a man broken on the wheel, I tell you."[8]

"What horror!"

"I will explain after supper, for I believe she is listening. We must have a few more rounds at reversi. Try not to win too many knaves of heart from me or you will not hear my tale."

In fact, once the company had retired, she told me that the

mother of this lady had been a fairly handsome woman in her time and for a provincial town, and that she passed for a model of virtue. The husband, whose business I do not recall, was often absent, and on one occasion, during a very hot summer, she was asleep in a first-floor room, her windows, overlooking the garden, wide open. This garden was bordered by a lake, and a highroad was the shore of the lake. A burglar, having cleared all these obstacles, arrived at the foot of her wall and throwing a rope ladder found himself by her bed. She was resting in attire fitting alone for a husband's gaze, granted that the husband is loved enough to be so well treated.

This burglar was a real one according to rules, but showed a tenderer disposition than thieves usually do. Having softly forced open an escritoire, a chest-of-drawers—goodness knows what else—and taken what he wanted, he had a mind to kill the lady who, having awakened, was already more than half dead. But, looking at her more closely, pity and a burglar's love came over him. He undressed on account of the heat, spent the night with her, left her only just before dawn, giving her back all he had taken, but adding besides a pretty little daughter to whom she gave birth nine months later; that was the lady supping with us.

The wife said nothing to her tender spouse when he came back; there are wrongs, even though involuntary, of which a well-brought-up woman never speaks. But she did all her best to make of him a tender and gallant lover. He, who had lost the habit, left her to her trouble and did not show enough conjugal wit to come to her help. Consequently, and above all since she came to hear that for other misdeeds her thief had been broken upon the wheel in the town of Domfort, she saw no other course left her but to retire to a convent, and there decently to give birth to the burglar's daughter; she previously wrote a very touching letter to her husband and consecrated herself to God under the protection of iron gates, which no thieves force open except those by whom one wishes to be robbed. She died about fifteen years later, and, as her daughter inherited her fortune, a Monsieur de P——, who had a government appointment, married her.

What terrible evidence that Fate rules everything upon this earth! What a horrible way for virtue to be foiled! What a strange and abominable burglar! Yet girls and women who hear the story might wish to fare as well if, during the heat, they still sleep with windows open.

This dreadful story brought me to these thoughts and many others. I started off the next day without the least offence to the governor or the lady his wife, towards whom it was quite impossible to be wanting in respect, but who did not fear thieves in the least and was supposed to have met several during her life. Amongst others was a M. de D——, who once had some right of access to the court of France, while he is now very comfortably married in another country, and who, early one morning, walked off with the lady's bracelet and sprigs of diamonds, on the pretence that beauty such as hers required no adornments. But I do not wish to make this chapter libellous. I have pledged myself not to compromise anyone still alive; initials are not names. This precaution reassures my scruples and, as it reconciles me with myself, I am sure to be thus on better terms with my readers, who for the most part, I certainly expect, are exceedingly moral.

CHAPTER VIII

It is easier to give one's life for a woman than to
find a woman worthy the sacrifice.

FRANCE is the country of duels. They are a national fruit. I have visited most parts of Europe, I have travelled in the New World, I have lived with army men and courtiers, but nowhere else have I met this disastrous touchiness, this sad tendency to believe oneself insulted and to long to repulse an offence nearly always imaginary. I know that this disposition is adorned by a pompous name, that it used to be termed showing more delicacy and sense of honour than other people, knowing at their best the exquisite shades of the art of life and the respect one owes to others and to oneself. But I also know that all this was founded on principles that are criminal when it comes to deeds, and blameworthy in essence.

Whence then comes this trait so peculiar to the Frenchman, who by disposition is too noble to be vindictive, but yet fights duels over matters for the most part so trivial that the phlegm of no other inhabitant of Europe would be altered thereby?

It is the result of education and of that alone.

In no other country is there a saying that "honour stands first and nothing else matters." Life counts for nothing if a gentleman of your own class has humbled your pride or looked condescendingly upon you. Life counts for nothing if your courage is under suspicion on the day of battle. Does your general seem to doubt it? Show no insubordination upon the spot, but on the morrow get yourself killed to convince him! Your best friend and yourself have had a discussion; you have shown some heat but in no way exceeded the limits of good manners, but some ladies maintain that your animation betrayed a touch of offence, and that you will be dishonoured if you do not strangle your friend or be strangled by him. Get yourself killed; for good repute is preferable to life, and it is better to die than for ladies to suspect you of any lack of courage, a matter on which they have expert knowledge. You have met with doubtful dealing at cards, but it becomes evident that it is a misunderstanding, and

both your opponent and yourself have cleared the remotest
clouds of suspicion; yet a certain gentleman has smiled cynically
and spoken in whispers to his sister, who passed on the words
to her cousin. Get yourself killed; for perhaps you will become
known for a cheat at cards, and nothing clears up such matters
better than a pistol or a sword. Yet do not entertain the belief
that your seconds will reconcile you. . . . They will be chary
of that lest they should themselves be accused of weakness and
become entangled in your disgrace; and so, bound by prejudices,
far from composing your quarrel when this could be done, five
times out of six they will make matters worse. Your wife is an
arrant coquette: get yourself killed by her lover, this will redeem her honour. A certain dancing girl who has already cost
you the selling of six meadows, four fields, and a wood of full-
grown trees, deceives you with a handsome youth who gives her
nothing: get yourself killed by this favoured rival, for valour
blots out all wrongs and vices, above all foolishness. Your
colonel, prompted by military zeal, spoke to you with too much
heat while on the field; say nothing when on duty, but find him
in Paris: kill him. It is possible that, having due respect for military rank, he will refuse to measure swords with you; and if
he reports the case, you will be sent to prison for twenty years
and a day, but nevertheless dishonour will be his and glory
yours, even in the dungeon where you will die of a most commendable death. You have seduced the wife of a worthy man
who, in the mood due to such a position, showed you less consideration than was his wont; he answered you back with harsh
words: kill him, for after having deprived him of peace and happiness, you scarcely need spare his life. And so on.

Are these pictures caricatures? . . . Hardly at all; they
are more true than believable, and I have not even mentioned
the odious set of people nowhere else to be found, whose special
pleasure was to foster a fight. A supercilious look from one of
these bravoes used to prove an insult dishonouring you almost
as much whether you sought vengeance or refrained. I do not
mean to say that these shady people, so easy to suppress, were
numerous, but they existed, and the fact was one more proof of
the national mania for duels and the presumption, almost openly
stated, that nothing was higher and greater than this kind of
valour, that its brilliancy covered all sins and, indeed, a scoundrel
who fought well was hardly a scoundrel at all.

Are people in other countries wrong to despise this beautiful invention, or are they guilty because their blood is more lazy in its course? No, though any form of excess should be avoided.[1] In these matters one must not be either too awake or too sleepy: *in medio stat virtus*.

As I have previously mentioned, I was going back to Paris; on reaching Chartres, I had just stepped out of my carriage while horses were being changed, when two officers of the King's guards, whom I had never seen before, honoured me by choosing me as their second in a quarrel they wished to settle at once. My uniform had most likely induced them to approach me, and they politely proposed I should instantly accompany them some little distance away from the town to witness their sword play. This proposal seeming to me entirely out of place, I frankly pointed out that it was my misfortune to be a perfect stranger to them, while the office they required was one I could grant only a close friend; that, besides, I knew no position more boring than being a second, save perhaps being a combatant, and I was not even sure I did not prefer the latter.

They insisted, claiming that officers never refuse such help to one another; they added that being anxious not to compromise a lady's good name, however unworthy she was of consideration, they were giving me the preference over people of mark in their town . . . and so on and so on.

I had great trouble to refrain from laughing at the dramatic tone in which this was uttered. However, since one of the men had a most attractive face and a noble bearing, and because their story might be amusing, I offered to remain three hours in their town, if they would accept the dinner which my valet ordered at once. I promised to listen to their misadventure and to try to reconcile them, pledging my word to be at their orders if no other arrangement proved possible. They accepted my invitation, adding—both speaking at the same time—that they would most undoubtedly have the pleasure of cutting each other's throat in my presence, for their affair was as clear as the day and certainly could not be arranged. The innkeeper, to whom I found time to say a few words, informed me that these gentlemen were from the town or some adjoining district, and that both enjoyed high repute and were the best of friends.

A strange friendship! I thought.

"Gentlemen," I said to them, "you cannot put much trust in my advice as I have not the honour of being known to you. Besides, my years are too few for me to boast of extreme prudence.

Yet I am older than my years, and I believe I know enough of women to give you advice and to suggest so simple an idea that I am surprised it did not occur to you. Either the lady on whose account you wish to come to blows is infinitely praiseworthy, or she deserves contempt. In the first case, in spite of all your precautions, the scandal you are making will dishonour her; in the second, she is not worth the blood you will shed for her."

"You speak with great truth," said the elder, a man about twenty-five. (His opponent was two or three years younger.) This speaker, tall, well built, and very manly looking, must nevertheless always have been in the wrong towards his rival, who, I repeat, had a bewitching face. "Nothing is more sensible than such general propositions," he went on. "They are, I should say, universal wisdom; but there are cases which in no way conform to ordinary rules, and so allow no choice to men of honour, and no considerations of prudence. If you wish to speak," he said, turning to the younger, "I am willing you should."

"No," replied the other, "you are speaking, and so long as you are accurate in your facts, as I am sure you will be, you can go on."

"Good. So I shall explain the subject of a dissension which brings us to take arms against each other in spite of a lifelong friendship." Then, turning to me and pointing to his opponent, "Monsieur was on the best of terms with a cousin of mine, daughter of a gentleman of this town. Their intrigue had lasted a long while, and, as is right, no one knew of it, myself less than anybody, for I had been away a year. He had promised to marry her, but family interests, which I am the first to acknowledge as very important, prevented him from keeping his word. His mistress—"

"Better say yours," interrupted the young fellow.

"If you wish to speak," replied the other, "I shall listen in silence; behave in the same manner or else let us stop. The time will come for a better fight than wrangling over words; besides, we owe civility to this gentleman, who is willing to listen to us though we have not the shadow of a right to bore him with our quarrel. . . . I was, then, saying that his mistress at the time ["Just so," remarked the young man with a nod] complained, lamented, and bitterly reproached him for having seduced her and not kept to his word.

"Matters had reached this point when I arrived. I very soon

noticed that my friend, as he then was, hid some sorrow in his heart and was obstinately silent about it. His reticence grieved me, but I respected it. Meanwhile I discovered that Mlle D——, whom I shall call Julie, had charms that moved me deeply; her disposition and her mind made her all the more attractive, especially when, after giving it thought, it appeared that her fortune, added to the little I had, would very much help my affairs. I was beginning to be bored by a military life; and, reflecting it could only take me as far as the Saint Louis Cross—which, according to someone's remark, it is as shameful to have as not to have—I felt the best I could do was to marry and leave the army. I told this gentleman of my plans, and far from deterring me, as was the duty of a faithful friend, he encouraged me in these thoughts. I dare say it is very convenient to make our friends shoulder our shame and to claim them as correctors of our errors, but, upon your honour I ask you, was this becoming conduct? and could I expect it from the man I have most loved?"

The speaker at this point stopped his tale, and fixed questioning eyes on me; but I replied by neither look nor voice. He continued:

"So I became Julie's admirer; and decided to marry her. . . . Peace reappeared in her soul, and the face of her seducer resumed its former serenity. My deluded friendship increased thereby, for I was stupid enough to think that my friend's troubles had vanished in view of my happiness.

"However, a distant relative of mine from whom I have expectations opposed my marriage for reasons he did not explain, but this was no surprise to me since the man is the most taciturn of all provincial freaks. I hoped to make him relent, and my fair one, whose interest it was to ensnare me beyond recall, offered me just as much resistance as was needed to increase my desires. At last she granted me the same favours she had shown monsieur, and either because she loved me less— which is quite natural—or because experience had taught her more cunning, she made me sign a formal promise that, come what might, I would marry her within a year. The appointed time ended the day before yesterday, and I should have scrupulously kept my promise, had I not been suddenly enlightened when on the very edge of the pit into which I was about to fall. It will be a favour to explain this to you.

"The treacherous Julie was acquainted with a lady of this

town who was suspected of having habits once much in vogue in Lesbos and which, to the shame of our time, have made alarming progress even in the provinces. They were close friends; people had joked, then no more was heard of it. Vague rumours had reached me, but I confess that this sort of rivalry gives me no ill humour, on the contrary it amuses me, and I am so lacking in morals as to laugh at it.

"A few days ago these two ladies went to a dance, and there had a violent quarrel for reasons not yet very clear. All we know is that fierce words were exchanged, and mutual threats of causing each other's ruin.

"The next morning I received a note from my fiancée's new enemy asking me to call on her. I thought it was in view of making up the quarrel and I hurried to her home; but you are going to see that it was something quite different. She handed me several letters, all in monsieur's handwriting; they had been entrusted to her by Julie, who had feared to compromise herself by keeping them. I felt indignant at the meanness to which vengeance had led this woman, but I nevertheless read the letters to my great profit, for I had occasion to convince myself that there exists in this world but a mere show of friendship, cut to the pattern of personal taste and interest. I learnt that, previous to myself, monsieur had enjoyed what was granted me only as a means of forcing me into marriage. In justice to monsieur I must say that all the letters show the most perfect honesty—I could almost say concern—when mention is made of me, but all are set on my marrying. There is even one where, after having feebly pitied me, monsieur enlivens his theme by two lines of poetry from I know not where, as I frankly own that my life has been too full for much reading; yet these lines struck me and I have retained them:

> The sin, when known, is very small,
> And when unknown, nothing at all." [2]

The speaker stopped, and I thought he had finished.

"These two lines are from La Fontaine," I told him, "and they contain the full justification of your friend, who did not commit the offence of urging you towards marriage so as to free himself of his difficulties, but contented himself with not deterring you. I find you very agitated while he is quite calm, which—if you do not mind my saying so—is a point in his favour. But allow me to ask what is the definite cause of your quarrel as matters now stand, for you are, so far, each within your right in not marrying the lady."

"I will with pleasure explain this to you," he went on. "My opponent pretends that I owe this discovery only to his ill luck and clumsiness in having written, and above all to the treachery of the lady who has now plunged Julie into the wretched position of which he believes himself the cause. He wishes to force me to keep my word, all the more as he sees for it a thousand reasons of propriety, etc., etc. He adds that I shall wed or the world is too small to contain us both, and one of us will have to leave it. But I insist that not only shall I not marry —a scheme which no longer deserves serious discussion—but it is he must accept the sacred bond, for he alone can redeem my cousin's reputation and mend the ills of which he is the sole agent since he was her seducer. Besides, this is the only way I can decently clear myself as regards public opinion, for people will look upon the breaking of my word as a sacrifice to friendship, while otherwise such behaviour would appear a downright fraud, since it is impossible I should myself reveal my cousin's baseness."

Quite against my wish, I burst into such violent laughter —in which the other officer joined me—that I thought it would give offence to the narrator.

"Could you," I said to the younger, "answer one question? Do you really, on your side, demand that your friend—for so he must remain—should marry?"

"Most certainly," he replied.

"Ah," I exclaimed, "it is a mania, a disease! It is madness, for you must excuse the word. Allow the whole truth to be put to you: your one thought should be to regain self-control. . . . The only grudge you should bear each other is that you have mutually deprived each other of common sense, for you must truly have lost all sense when you each think of forcing the other into a marriage that is no longer possible for either on account of the kind and degree of information you have both acquired. Seek a third man—this is your only course—who, in the innocence of his heart, will consent to a union neither of you can now contract with honour; and if the woman who separated you is worth the trouble, if she is pretty enough, remain calmly with her what you were before. I believe she would thank me for the advice I give you, could she hear me; and, take my word; this woman, and those of her disposition, do not deserve more consideration."

My views made converts of them. Before dinner was over they improved upon my scheme and swore eternal friendship. I saw them kiss before I took the coach whither they escorted me, overwhelming me with praises and thanks. They assured me that Solomon's knowledge was no greater than mine, and that my judgement was marked by his wisdom.

CHAPTER IX

There is no need to take much pride in the love of a mistress. Nature has laid such firm founda-tions for the traffic of love as to leave little room to merit. There is not one heart which she has not marked for another. She has not always taken care to bring together those people worthy of esteem: it is all a mixture, and experience teaches us that the choice of a lovable woman proves nothing in favour of the man to whom it befalls. It seems to me that such truths should make lovers modest and discreet. —La Bruyère.

*I*N Scripture the deceived man exclaims: "I said of laughter, It is mad, and of mirth, What doeth it?" This could be said of love even by the men whom it has treated best. What falsehood hides in love's illusions! What emptiness in its prom-ises! What disappointment even in its realisations! What noth-ingness in what one believes the best of amorous adventures!

I remember a time when, being accessible to every lie and every spell, I was childish enough to believe that a man must have great merit who could please women; that to find favour in their eyes presupposed a handsome face, elegance, skill, wit, and a thousand other fine qualities; a man being indeed justi-fied in showing impertinence and conceit if he could produce a long list of ladies he had betrayed and who had paid him back with interest.

A little later I was satisfied to think that if all these quali-ties were not required, at least a few of them were needed. . . . I came to know I had once more been under a delusion, and I ended by geometrically convincing myself that the man who on all counts is the most insignificant of his sex can make the most attractive of women lose her head. . . . But here is the blasphemy! I am not far from holding the belief that medi-ocrity all round is a recommendation to her. This assertion may appear harsh and ill-sounding; I should have no difficulty in supporting it by observations to my mind entirely decisive; yet my respect for the sex to which we owe the only real possession to be found in life (the positive part of love) forbids my bringing forth these scarcely polite arguments. The reader will besides see through these memoirs that three-fourths of my life having been devoted to the sex, and success having now and again been my reward in this pursuit, selfishness and conceit may, unknown to me, have something to do with my wish to permit at least some doubts upon this subject.

It is, however, remarkable that firmness binds women more than a fine mind and looks.

> Love gains one woman by the heart
> And a thousand by the eyes,

a poet has said; but one could add that there exists, so to speak, a well-known trick to catch them, and a policy of firmness—if I can put it thus—to keep them. They often resist the most handsome behaviour, and nearly always succumb (horrible to say) to the fascination of the roughest ill usage. Their beauty is a short-lived tyranny with which they unmercifully abuse those who are willing enough to be enslaved. They nearly always seek men who despise them, and are submissive only to those who do not flatter them. One recalls the words of a lady of high rank in Europe when her lover had one evening so far forgotten himself as to strike her; she confided next day to a friend: "I am now sure he loves me!" [1] The men who deserve it least generally attract them most, and a better proof than any argument of how false is their judgement, excitable their imagination, and vain both their minds and their hearts, is that the worst men are those to whom their constancy and memory pay the most lasting tribute. It often happens that a woman has never found consolation for being forsaken by a lover whom a mere whim would have caused her to send away a fortnight later.

Do not raise the objection that this is wounded pride; certainly pride plays a leading part in such wretched reckoning, but it is not everything. The way women exaggerate the value of what they have lost is similar to the giddiness which may seize one at some height above the ground.

But yet few triumphs are greater in their eyes than cruelly to leave the man who has given everything up for them, has placed in them his hopes of happiness and to whom despair at this betrayal of love is all that remains. In what bewitching way

they enjoy his grief, with what callousness—I almost said boredom—they witness his tears and trample upon his weakness.

This picture is not typical of the whole sex, although it
has been said that they are all alike: certainly there are exceptions. One can find among women models of high-mindedness,
exquisite sensitiveness, generosity, inexhaustible goodness, sweetness, courage, and virtue. I have known two who were far superior to the crowd so unworthy of them; one above all. . . .
Alas, my worship saw her soon lost! Eternal laws had decreed
that I should mourn her without ceasing and never replace her.
I had not deserved happiness so pure.

Oh, you who now live in my heart alone, you who will be,
I believe, the last thought of this heart worn by the grief of
your tragic and lamentable death, if you see my tears, if you
know my despair, beloved spirit! in some better world you
must have regretted your temerity and sighed over my deep
misfortune.[2]

So, then, I am not unreservedly your detractor, charming
beings, big and adorable children who would never be allowed to
rule over us could we preserve any particle of common sense
(granted common sense exists upon this earth). But I maintain that you are the lowest order in nature when you do not
prove its adornment; and those of you who lack one special
"virtue" generally possess no other. At the same time, as an
experienced moralist has remarked, the coldest and most rigid of
prudes can seldom look a very handsome man in the eyes without thinking of something which cannot be spoken. Appeal
against this sentence as much as you like; accuse me of gross
openness if this soothes your nerves, but show due respect for
my experience, for I have very badly employed my time, very
fruitlessly wasted my life, as wise people have told me. . . .
I have spent the greatest part of it at your feet. In my springtime, and even some while later, I was one of your most faithful dupes; under an appearance of light-heartedness I even
acquired a store of melancholy such as falls to the share of refined and tender souls. Misfortunes of more than one kind have
later darkened my soul, but this melancholia springs mostly
from the anxieties of possessing you, from my hopes deceived,
my relationships with you, the exaggerations of a mind en-
tranced then disillusioned, the wild fantasies of the lies connected with love, and all the inevitable sorrows attached to a
man who pursued you and lived mostly in the shadow of your
altars.

Ah, how long it takes for the poor pupil to become as learned as his master! When one begins to be your equal, the prime of life has vanished just as one would have found strength to teach you in return! Even those who know you best, and speak ill of you with the greatest insight, yet regret you as much as would the beginners and the least experienced.

> Car Vénus vous donna sa divine ceinture,
> Ce chef-d'œuvre sorti des mains de la nature,
> Ce tissu, le symbole et la cause à la fois
> Du pouvoir de l'amour, du charme de ses lois.
> Elle enflamme les yeux de cette ardeur qui touche,
> D'un souris enchanteur elle anime la bouche,
> Passionne la voix, en adoucit les sons,
> Prête des tons heureux plus forts que les raisons,
> Inspire, pour toucher, ces tendres stratagèmes,
> Ces refus attirants, l'écueil des sages mêmes;
> Et la nature enfin y voulut renfermer
> Tout ce qui persuade et ce qui fait aimer.[3]

I had not received any letter from Sophie since the one quoted previously, so the reader may guess with what impatience I looked forward to calling at Mme de ———'s mansion. This lady, to whom I seldom wrote, had postponed sending me news of Sophie until my arrival, yet I had no doubt that they were together in Paris. So I dressed in great haste as soon as I had left the coach and hastened to the fortunate house where I hoped to find the being who had taught me the use of my heart. Mme de ——— received me with the simplicity of an old friend. I hurried through all the questions concerning herself so as to come to the one nearest my heart: enquiring for Mlle de Lorville. "She is married," replied Mme de ——— as coolly as if her lips had said: "She will presently be here."

"Married!" I exclaimed in a terrible voice.

"Yes."

"And without letting me know!"

"She wrote to you, but I thought it best, for all our sakes, not to let you have the letter."

"For all our sakes! And who advised you, madame, to enter into our interests, our sorrows, or our happiness? From where comes your daring in disposing of my life? Is it because you corrupted it at the beginning? Know that I detest you and feel no more regard for you; above all, take my word for it, you will never see me again. . . . I am dead to you." She tried to answer, but I was already in the courtyard.

Alas, in fact, my eyes never saw her again. She was already struck by the fatal illness of which her face bore the imprint, and she died, as will be seen later, before my departure for Switzerland. My readers will likewise learn what had brought about an event so disastrous to my fondness; the whereabouts of this Sophie my heart will come to forget, though I loved her then with excess; and how I shall meet her again as a perfect wife and mother.

How had she agreed to this wretched marriage? How, after so much love and so many promises, had she forsaken me? . . . The answer is easy. It is the fate of seduction to awaken violent passion, but it is also its penalty rarely to give birth to such passion as will withstand regrets and reflexion. The woman who once confronted morals, braved prejudices, and defied the world for the man she worshipped, soon loses her illusions; in the seclusion of her soul she rediscovers herself, she sees the man who caused her ruin surrounded by poor esteem; contagion spreads to her, half of her love vanishes by degrees, the bitterness of reproaches soon corrupts what remains. . . . The unfortunate woman views only an abyss in her defeat, and an enemy in the author of her ruin. This sort of passion meets sometimes with another fate, but I urge young men to trust me: a few exceptions cannot destroy the general rule, such is the usual way with this kind of attachment. Besides, was not this Sophie—whose unfaithfulness surprises you —beset by the authority and advice of a person to whom she usually paid deference? Few people of either sex, in matters of love-attachments or friendship, have the strength to think for themselves and to resist outside influence. It seems that to love anyone we need the opinion and the ascendency of others. Few have the generous temperament that can steel them against obstacles, and above all against suggestions, so that they are the only judges of their own tastes and affections. There is scarcely a woman so carried away by an imperious inclination as not to sacrifice it to a friend's advice . . . or the disapproval, often through self-interest, of a clever rival. There scarcely exists a man who will remain faithful to a friend pursued by the slanders of public opinion. . . . It is generally difficult to make people believe good of their fellows. Yet the least effort, a single word, is sufficient to convince them of all the evil one wishes them to think. . . . The man who has falsely prejudiced you is sometimes reconciled to his enemy whom you do not know, while you are still influenced by the hatred that was forced upon you.

This brings back to my mind a story I heard from the lips of a witty woman, once maid-in-waiting to a famous princess.

One of her special man friends had begged her to hate a person of whom he gave the most horrible description; thereupon she started detesting in earnest a man she did not know, who had never wronged her, and she spoke slightingly of him whenever she could. A few months later this gentleman was introduced to the Princess just mentioned; the maid-in-waiting scarcely looked at him, turned her back upon him, answered him curtly, barely performed her duties, and, what was more, gave an unfavourable account of him to the Princess: all trusting to the word of her intimate friend, who at that very moment entered the room, retired into a window-recess to embrace affectionately the gentleman whom he had no recollection of having hated but a few months before, and seemed to pour his soul into the fellow's ear. Mme de B—— was lost in astonishment.

"But," she exclaimed, "you told me horrible things about him. I have treated him with contempt, doing him many ill turns. I thought you had fallen out with each other."

"That is true, so we had; but now he is the most decent of men, we are friends for life."

For such are your decrees, gentlemen of fashion.[4]

I now come back to what concerns me.

So I found myself without a mistress and in despair. All the evil I have thus far mentioned concerning myself, the reader has easily believed . . . perhaps complacently; I claim the same indulgence for the following story, which may not be so entertaining to the spiteful, for I feel it may do me credit.

A man who is still alive and who treated the Revolution as he did the court, that is to say bowed low to it on every occasion, offered to console me by making me share his exploits in a house where he had obtained admittance through the most objectionable means. He had seduced a young lady who was to be a great match. She had a sister, perhaps more charming than herself, for whom she wanted to find a lover so that the younger should have nothing to reproach her with. My go-between asked me solemnly to promise never to reveal my good fortune; when I had given him my word, he led me, one fine night, to the meeting place where the two fair ones awaited us. The elder was under seventeen. I took fright at their youth, their beauty, at the thought of a family of standing being thus deceived and dishonoured, at the monstrosity of such a seduction and the means devised to achieve it. But when I was alone with this youthful victim and saw her embarrassment, her tears, her displeasure at complying with her sister's advice, I promised myself not only to respect her, but likewise to protect her from the threatening danger. . . . Perhaps my virtue was in part due to my own condition, as I was then the prey to deep melancholy.

"Do not explain matters to your sister," I said to her. "Tell her that we suit each other splendidly, and are looking forward to other meetings. I shall come again soon."

Two hours went by in talk as decent as this interview was supposed to be the reverse; everything she told me, everything I guessed, made me more satisfied with myself, and encouraged me in the behaviour I had adopted—a generous behaviour, as I dare to term it, for this angel possessed all that was required to make me forget my best resolutions. I then showed great merit in keeping to these, above all as she would easily have become privy to my deeds, once the first hour was gone and her tears dried.

When affection begins to be felt, indifference wins a woman of experience, but sensitiveness and above all gentleness conquer innocence without much ado.

My partner, who had employed his time better or worse, came to fetch me away and assured me that I ought to be infinitely grateful to him, since he would lose his best friends were they to know he had given me the preference over them. I thanked him profusely, and we parted in the Rue du Cherche-Midi, where our carriages were awaiting us. If he reads these pages he will see that I recollect faithfully the least details, but he will likewise learn that which follows, of which he is ignorant.

I then lived in the Faubourg Saint-Germain, at the house of a bath-keeper, where the Bishop of Limoges [5] also had rooms. He was the most civil man, very simple and righteous, leading a rather retired life. During his rare journeys to Paris where he saw few people, he had lent me money and maintained he would convert me. I do not know to what extent his holy wishes were fulfilled on this last count, but what I am certain of is that I never gave him back two hundred sovereigns, and that I have never known to whom they should go. I do not lay

much scruple by this for it was the Church's money; and one
day, when I am rich, I shall give it over to its children *par
excellence:* the poor. I arrived at his rooms the next morning
as he was muttering over his breviary and drinking his chocolate. He was by disposition serious and playful in turn, and
knew neither pedantry nor worldliness. I started by taking great
care not to compromise the gentleman, who after all had sought
only to procure me pleasure; then I related the story from end
to end. Never have I witnessed such terror and disgust; and
only on this occasion did I see him devoid of all common sense.
The good fellow spoke of nothing less than going immediately
to the governor of Paris.

"But, my Lord," I exclaimed, "you are losing your head.
Do you wish to compromise me in this dreadful way when I
have placed my trust in you and you were so kind as to praise
me for doing so?"

"Not at all, everyone will think well of you."

"But what about M. de ——, whose secret I have betrayed?
And his family, whom you will plunge into mourning? . . . and
my broken pledge? the horrible scandal all this will make? Mlle
de —— for ever lost! For be certain that everything becomes
known in time, and that malevolence gets hold of our most secret
concerns. . . ."

He began to understand me and to grow calmer. So, after
a few more explanations on my part and some amendments on
his, it was agreed he would call upon the girls' father and that,
without entering upon any details, he would use the authority
of his calling and reputation to make this gentleman promise,
without further explanations, to start for his country estate
and there behave towards his daughters as was his habit, save
that, without delay and under some plausible excuse, he should
discharge one of their maids, who would be pointed out to him.
One of these young women is now dead, the other married; she
held her rank in society, but was swept away by the torrent of
the Revolution into some remote province where I suppose she
still lives.

My partner, a few days later, came to see me with a long
doleful tale, obligingly waking me up to inform me of the sudden departure of our sweethearts. I appeared very upset, and
he declared that we were much to be pitied.

He must, however, recollect that we had breakfast together,
and what a gay meal it proved to be.

I flatter myself he will laugh at the wholesome trick I played on him; I hope that he has altered enough to thank me for it; but he would be wrong to show anger, for I warn him—and others like him—that as I am dead to society at the moment of writing this book I shall submit to no responsibility nor challenge concerning the truth I put on record.

Everything at this time distressed me, saddened my heart and left me the prey to sufferings born of the recollections I tried in vain to dismiss. Though so young I was disillusioned. I decided to leave for Switzerland, to seek there the healthy air purified by the Alpine winds, to find peace for my blighted soul while paying homage to the spirit of liberty in the happy republics that gave it birth.

CHAPTER X

I *WAS* preparing to leave Paris when a man who was devoted to me suggested I should go to see some play or other which was attracting great crowds on the boulevards. He offered me a seat in his box with a woman he loved to distraction, and who was worthy of this love as regards beauty, though her heart and mind were not in keeping. However that may be, I agreed, and we were soon in our seats. A moment later the next box opened to admit two men and two women whom I did not know; one of these gentlemen began to laugh immoderately and to utter in a loud voice harsh condemnation of women of ill repute and loose principles, who were, so he said, a plague to mankind, and who, though deserving to be exiled from society, sought refuge in Parisian convents to bring disgrace upon these institutions, as they had upon the polite world.

As I was seated very close to this moralist, I ventured to ask him to speak in a lower voice. He complied with a fairly good grace, and I thought the matter was ended, but, having left the box between the acts, I was surprised, on my return, to hear the Comte du Touceville tell me he would need me after the play in order to chastise this gentleman for grievously insulting him. He thereupon left me for a short while, placing the tearful lady under my protection, while he ordered his footman to fetch a sword.

When the play was ended we saw the lady to her carriage; in all fairness I must say that she was dismayed at being the Helen of the fight. She briefly explained to me that this Hector was a country squire in her own province, who had been much in love with her, but, as such women do, she denied any acquaintance with him save one strictly honourable. . . .

There was, at the back of the Boulevard du Temple, a large open space full of deep cavities where, the adversary informed us, one could be at ease to *rip one another open* (for such was his fine taste in expressions). He asked ten minutes leave to call on a friend near by so as to borrow a sword. M. du Touceville came up to him to inquire with whom he would have the honour of crossing swords.

"My name," replied the stranger, "matters little; it is hardly known here. The truth is, I have offended you, and, far from regretting it, I am ready to do it again; since I am both ruined and betrayed, nothing better could happen to me than to perish at your hands or take your life."

I could scarcely contain myself at hearing such detestable reasoning and witnessing the insolence, or rather the madness, with which he uttered this speech. But M. du Touceville was as calm as innocence and truly could hardly be held responsible for the blood which was about to be shed. This engaging stranger had brought no second; I pointed this out to him, to which he replied with a swagger that he never took seconds, that he had fought twenty duels in his lifetime without dragging in a third person, and that, were I disposed, he would soon show me we could fight without seconds. Thereupon he made off at full speed, kindly informing us he would soon be back. Then Touceville declared, in tones almost as solemn as in a drama: "This man is dead, and here is his grave." He was pointing to a pit eighty to a hundred feet deep and a few steps from us.

The insolent fellow did not make us wait long. He came back bearing under his arm a sword of a length most certainly forbidden by honour and regulations. The Comte du Touceville did not allow me further remonstrances, but took off his coat and, quick as lightning, bared his breast for his opponent, who did likewise. One could see fairly well, but, under the pretence of seeking a better light, my friend gradually drove the stranger towards the pit I have mentioned. There, a few feet away from its edge, began a fight as desperate and as skillful as can be imagined; but suddenly Touceville, with one marvellous swift volt, brought his opponent to the brink and, as if he had awaited the moment, ran him through the breast, up to the hilt; then, catching hold of him with both hands and raging as a lion after his prey, he literally lifted the man from the ground and hurled him into the pit! . . . I must confess that my blood ran cold, and I was unable to suppress a cry on seeing the fellow fall into this abyss with a sword through his body. "Let us go," said the victor, "he no longer needs help," and, picking up the sword which the stranger had dropped: "A wretched evening and a bad exchange for him: we had better go."

This was certainly my opinion, but for a kingdom I could not have left without sending help, though I was sure it was unnecessary. Touceville walked on, lost in gloom. A state of dejection and almost regret had followed on the fierceness of the fight. I helped him along; he could scarcely walk as far as the cab to which I led him. I left him there, to run to the watch where, taking aside a sergeant and placing money in his hand, I told him that I had heard doleful cries at a place I mentioned.

I learnt later how useless this step had been, and that the wretch, as well he deserved, was quite dead.

As this work is specially devoted to recollections, I will give here an historical account of the hero of this adventure. I must throw a few flowers upon the grave of a man scarcely known by some, and known only to others through a bad reputation. I shall not hide his faults while I vindicate his memory from false accusations. I shall write about him what I positively know, above all I shall make clear that he was not altogether an ordinary man. The tale may prove instructive and beneficial to young men entering upon life with advantages which they abuse or unruly passions to which they give way.

M. du Touceville came from a very old family of Normandy which, though not eminent, was related to the noblest houses in this province. His ancestors, down to his great-grandfather, had been Protestants, and this religion was not the means of reaching favour and fame. His father, while very young, had been in command of a company of dragoons in Condé's regiment, but had left the army after having impaired his fortune. He made a mistake in later accepting some second-rate post of the magistracy in a town of Normandy; he turned it into a sort of business and managed it so badly that he proved himself below a position to which in all respects he was born superior; to complete the disgrace, he had to give it up. I speak of the father's post because, later, it served as a reproach against the son when people wished his ruin. He had been made a page to the Prince de Condé, and was pleased to have people think he had been in a more direct way attached to the Duchesse de Bourbon, at whose court he lived at the time of his entry into society. But as he has never said to me anything positive about the matter and as I have, besides, strong reasons to believe the contrary, I shall be the more careful not to stain this princess's reputation, now that days of misfortune have come, and since happiness is even more sacred than the proprieties of rank— though these indeed should be held so.

He had a pleasant face, above all imposing; he would boast

of two things, which did him harm, for they denoted a dangerous disposition, both ferocious and futile, though he was neither:
he took pride in being known for his duels and his luck with
women. He had fought several duels—a few of which caused
some commotion—one of the first being with the Comte de Durfort, who later became officer in the King's body-guard and
joined the Revolution at the outset. This quarrel had started at
Mme d'Espagnac's, close to the Invalides, where half Paris
was that day at a ball. The dispute arose concerning some office,
but peace had been restored; yet, the next day the ladies declared that it had been a most "scandalous scene," that the two
men had used "outrageous language," that it was "unheard of"
that they had not already fought, that both "were lost to honour," and were men to whom "one could no longer curtsy."

These gentlemen had indeed to give way to such strong
arguments; the ladies obtained full satisfaction, for the two
victims of their gossip met, each declaring deep esteem for and
friendliness towards his rival, though they were about to kill
each other for the love of a sex which whenever it wishes, creates
reputations, and whose decrees are law. So they set to in front
of M. de Foufai, who died since so tragically; they pierced
each other through by what is known amongst professionals
as an interchanged thrust, which kept them in bed for several
weeks, and for nine days at death's door; the one who was bled
the least had blood drawn seven or eight times.

I have just said that Touceville fought several duels, and
thus this insane boast was well founded. As to his luck with
women, the matter is not so clear, though he spared no effort
to make himself believe in it and to convince others. He had
mistresses, it is true, he even changed them often; but as quality in this sort of thing is better than quantity, and as all his
mistresses were generally litigious provincial beauties,[1] forsaken wives, ladies lodging at the Précieux Sang or La Conception,[2] dancing girls, second-rate actresses, I came to the conclusion—and I told him so—that what he had done in this field
(with one exception) was worth nothing.

His bearing offered a medley of manners copied from
novels, the stage, the court (for he had been there), and the
second-rate company with which he was thrown, so that he was
hardly equipped to be successful with women who were very
stylish or very natural; he could not deal with them in a fitting
way, he would speak of them in quite a provincial manner. The
same thing applied to a few arts, poetry and music, which he

loved without understanding. I have noticed that he even possessed some discrimination and taste; he showed bad form only
when he was in love.

Mme de Vierville of the Palais Royal was his relative.
She introduced him into the circle of M. le duc d'Orléans and
Mme. de Montesson at whose house he acted in plays;[8] his
acting was bad, yet, as he believed it very good, it was all the
same to him, though quite a different matter for others. This
led him to know endless verses by heart, which he would apply
to most occasions in life, very often, as many professional actors
do, spoiling them by giving them the wrong metre, either adding expletives or changing a word:[4] no one ever had so poor
an ear.

His unbecoming self-conceit, his absurd presumption, or some
accusation, either false or true, which gained credence through
his behaviour, caused him to be refused admittance at the Palais
Bourbon; a duel barred him from the Palais Royal more than
did his debts, which were given as a pretext, though M. le duc
d'Orléans would have settled these had M. du Touceville agreed
to go to India with a colonel's commission. He had, I believe,
at Le Raincy, lost money to M. de la Marck and M. de Gouvernet. He did not pay, angry words and bad temper ensued,
and he gave a thrust with his sword to M. de Gouvernet, in
whom the Prince was so interested that he did not consider it
beneath his station to intervene in this jumble. Asking M. du
Touceville to his closet he wished, as he himself put it, to re-
monstrate with him as would a father; the self-conceit and the
tone M. du Touceville displayed on this occasion brought him
to disgrace, especially after the wound to M. de Gouvernet,
which the Prince had done his best to avert. M. du Touceville
was requested to stay at home in the future, which he did after
he had written a letter more than unbecoming. He then looked
towards Versailles, where he had been presented, though he
never obtained a formal right of entry on account of the prejudice the King, from hearsay, was feeling against him. I know
that it has even been disputed (for what does not envy dispute?) whether he could claim his full coach rights; but I, who
saw M. Chérin's certificate and a letter from the Duc de Coigny,
cannot have the shadow of a doubt on this point. It seems to
me, however, that it hardly matters to-day, and I refer to it
historically as I would to the ruins of Palmyra, Athens, or
Rhodes.

He then turned to Versailles, as I have said, and for a few

weeks the Queen did not treat him too badly; but once so well on the way, hatred does not stop, since no doubt it took for its motto: *Nil actum reputans, si quid superesset agendum.*

It must be agreed that he played into the hands of his enemies. The past was recalled, a future invented the better to ruin him; people went so far as to unearth his father's conduct in that vile post the man had held—as if the son were responsible. It was even disputed whether he was of aristocratic birth.

He was the man least fitted to withstand patiently this reproach, however absurdly it was put. So he developed the mania of talking genealogy and of claiming loudly and often a relationship to the greatest houses of the realm. For a long time he even went about armed with certificates and heraldic credentials; the late Prince de Salm and myself, having put him to shame for this, he took our advice. This brings back to my mind a supper with one of the worthiest men of France, the old Prince de Bauffremont,[5] always so extremely kind to me and a man who, though he never filled any high offices, deserved them as much as any man by his virtues, and better than most by his birth. Touceville, who knew of the invitation, told me that he had often met the Prince in the past, and induced me to ask leave for him to come with me; this I did, and the permission was granted.

A few days later we arrived at the Prince's. After many greetings, "Prince," said Touceville, "the honour of being one of your family renders more precious that of meeting you once more. The numerous alliances—"

"Sir!" said M. de Bauffremont.

"Yes, we are connected, amongst others through the royal family; Hyacinthe-Maximilien du Touceville and Yolande de Bourgogne—"

"Sir!!"

"Yes, Prince. My house and the house of Bourbon having many a time—"

"Sir!!!"

The Prince de Monaco[6] was present, a great friend of M. de Bauffremont. He never in his life missed an occasion of making fun of someone; he would banter his footman if no one else came his way; so M. de Monaco, putting in his word, interrupted:

"Sir, you will so frighten M. de Bauffremont that his family will never dare to belong to your house."

Some newcomer was announced; the matter stopped at this point, and Touceville was the only one who failed to realise that he had been completely ridiculous.

After his misfortunes at court, he sold his wardrobe, which was truly very handsome; he would jokingly say that a black suit was good enough for town. I was once laughing about it; he answered me tragically: "I am like those kings who, after having grown weary of luxurious clothes in the soft indolence of courts, become warriors and wear for ever a simple army uniform." Yet he did not stand it long, and towards the end of his life I have sometimes seen him much decked up, above all when he was in love, or when he was penniless.

It would be unfair to believe he always spoke in that way. He sometimes could be most pleasant, and often displayed fine wit, which, however, in my opinion, was always spoiled by a something one is more easily aware of than able to describe. He had a great store of chivalrous spirit, which he exaggerated; a great respect for women in theory,[7] though in practice he lacked it; he was extremely strict as to behaviour on this point, above all for others. Having no sense of humour, he was either full of compliments or very abrupt, though he showed a marked leaning to mockery; but where he was eminently gifted during serious encounters was in his ability to hold his tongue, or, if I may put it thus, in his command of the situation when he chose to speak little or not to speak at all.

But adverse fortune pursued him; the kingdoms of this earth and their splendour being closed to him, he retired to provincial life; after some insignificant conquests amongst obscure ladies, he came back to Paris in possession of sixty thousand francs lent him by a German prince, who looked upon him as a second Vardes exiled by another Louis the XIV;[8] at four hundred leagues distance, one knows no better. He took a house and set up an establishment which implied an income of one hundred thousand pounds a year, and he went in for heavy gambling. Towards the end of his life, which had been like a stormy day brightened by a few rays of sunshine, he went for a journey to Brittany where he married a well-born girl, descendant, so he told me, of one of the first Knights of the Saint-Esprit as instituted by Henri III.[9] The fact interested me so little that I never verified it. The girl brought him some for-

tune which he came back to Paris to endanger. At last so many
ups and downs and changes were bound to make him old before
his time, and little was there left for him to do but die; it is
the decision Nature took on his behalf as she received him into
her bosom after a rather long and painful inflammation of the
lungs, the danger of which he soon realised and faced with
great equanimity, just as he did death, telling me twelve hours
before the end: "I am like these great actors who leave the
stage while they are still able to captivate the public. We live
in deplorable days [10] which will give way to others even more
frightful: I shall not see them. I shall not become the prey to
the infirmities of old age; I shall not waste away in the gradual
agony of a decaying body: I have not been virtuous, nor have
I been wicked. If He who allows us to be born deigns to concern
Himself about me, He will forgive me. I die as an honest man,
without weakness and without fear. 'As of old they would die
in Greece and in Rome.' "

It must be owned that he died very opportunely, even in
what concerned his creditors, whose only expectation from him
could have been a demand for further credit.

I believe that he was not yet thirty-seven. I am almost sure
he left from three to four thousand francs of debts: this was
dying at the right time and in good order.

I was coming back from a fairly long journey when I found
him at death's door; he was much moved at seeing me. He spoke
with perfect calmness of the few people who would regret him
and of the great number who had misunderstood him, he quoted
these lines from the Abbé Delille:

> When life is ending, who could help to cast
> A sorrowful and longing look at last,
> In hope of kindly eyes all dim'd with tears,
> And sight of one true friend to charm one's fears?

I promised him I should be that friend; I have kept my
word.

The portrait I have so far made of him has not been very
flattering, nor much to his credit, yet the fact remains that
he had very fine qualities which bound one to him. He was
a faithful friend, sparing nothing to serve those he truly loved;
and, what is most strange, he who seldom took good advice
for himself nearly always gave good counsel to others. His heart
was sound, and although his behaviour had not been above blame

I have known few men ready to make greater sacrifices or to brave more dangers if one uttered the word "honour." He lacked tact in many things, but his will-power nearly always made up for this and redeemed him; his jealousy in love could reach frenzy, yet was capable (I speak from experience) of giving way to friendship. His passions were all the more fierce since they sprang much more from his imagination and vanity than from his heart, honest from birth, or his mind, perfectly sound when neither touchiness nor pride led it astray. The only qualities that prevented him from attaining repute and position in ancient France were those difficult to find in a young man who without guidance and training begins life on so splendid a stage. I mean: enough force of character to appear as having less, enough wit to display only what is needed, enough good taste to remain simple and alarm no one, finally enough stable sense to avoid undue brilliance.

I had known him in his days of prosperity; I remained faithful to him through all his misfortunes; and during the twelve years of our friendship he has rendered me many a good office and given me proof of his untiring helpfulness and great devotion. I have always had much cause to be well pleased with him and none to complain. It is thus but justice I should have remained attached to him during his life; while the courage I saw him display at his death now mingling with these recollections makes, I must own, his memory precious. I shall even add for greater fairness that he was in almost every respect superior to many people who, after knowing him and meeting him, feigned to ignore him or despise him, which was most convenient, but ungenerous.

I have traced this portrait rather at length, my heart's disposition wanted it so. Touceville is one of those men who have left on me an unfading impression, though I am quite unable to find in myself the reason for this. I have often been reproached for the friendship I bore him, but it has always been justified within my heart. A man of great merit once mentioned him to me in England and showed surprise at my partiality. Another man, more distinguished in all respects, asked me in Berlin what could make this friendship so binding. "I have known him," he said, "and I have never discovered the secret of his worth."

This remark did not surprise me. Touceville could never be liked or disliked in moderation. But you must remember, dear

Prince,[11] that I have promised you two things: the first to prove you had never known him, the second to draw such a faithful picture as to convince you that your eyes alone beheld him: I have fulfilled my promise. If what I have said of him seems long and tedious to some people, they are careless readers who discriminate against others; his name is most likely distasteful to their ears, his memory holds no charm for them. Yet is there not something striking, I do not say in the colours I have used, but in the whole figure and the details of the man I have portrayed? Is there nothing worth study in the whims of his fate? Nothing to be learnt from the contradictions and varied aspects to be found in a temperament in turn so strong and so weak?

If this be not so, I am strangely mistaken and I beg the reader's indulgence, for I need it; but should it be otherwise, what does it matter whom my brush has portrayed? I am absolved. I will say more: I wish anyone, in days of trouble, a friend as devoted, with a heart as firm and a soul as tender. But, as the name of the Comte du Touceville will recur in these memoirs, the reader will judge him better from the facts than from long speeches.

I should like to write with method and coordination; but the flood of reminiscences often causes me to leap over long intervals to which I am obliged later to return.

The incident of this death has made me skip ten years. I must now go back to where I interrupted the course of my narrative.[12]

It has been seen how I left Mme de ——'s home on the last occasion I saw her alive. Some time afterwards I received from her a note well calculated to move the least sensitive heart. She reproached herself for the sufferings she had brought upon me; she did not try to justify her motives, since jealousy had defiled them, so she put the blame on a love that had overmastered her, but, being consumed with regrets and dying of an illness that the doctors had for long declared incurable, she asked to see me before the approaching end. I should have been a savage to pain her, yet I did not feel generous enough to console her while I was myself inconsolable. I started on my journey that very day, and replied to her only from Lyons, a few days before she died.

Thus, following a life agitated and restricted through boundless desires and ambitions, after a few moments of painful struggle individuals and generations sink into oblivion.

Just as in Nature an unchanging law gathers, around the summit of high mountains, clouds which forever trail one after another and disperse, some inexorable will pushes forth the great and wretched human family in its blind course towards an abyss across which no hand can stretch, and from which no foot can retrace its way.

What! has this wonderful being, this conqueror of Nature, this ruler over the elements, been cast upon this earth of affliction of which he believes himself the master, only to trample its dust a short while and mix his own with it? "Where is the dust, which has not been alive!"

Ah! what nothingness behind our vain agitations! what void in our deceitful pleasures, since Man, this wholly perfect being! —But let us stop awhile to consider. . . . Are this perfection so much lauded, this feeling of superiority so well established in our own eyes, anything more than the fantasies of our desire? Can we vouch that any one thing exists on this globe, still so mysterious to us and surrounded by other worlds at which we are left to conjecture since we have no geometrical data about them? Who can assure us that we are not lacking some sense the possession of which would reveal to us the inadequacy of both our organization and our destiny? Who has induced us to believe that the elephant and the beaver are not as perfect as ourselves, or more wonderful in the eyes of Nature and the Creator? Who can be sure that in their own language they do not daily boast their superiority and intelligence? Besides, even supposing we were the most perfect amongst the animals, would that prove we are so magnificent a production? so exquisite an achievement? or that our goal is immortality? Yet, indeed, we are born to immortality, for we are an emanation of the eternal substance, the offshoots of the divine Creator, who, having had no beginning, will have no end! . . . Had we been marked for extinction when our mortal shell perishes, would it be possible to imagine a Being having the power to bestow life upon us, yet mad and wicked enough to condemn us to it? a Being so great and cruel as to grant us breath, but with all the plagues that are its attributes and punishment; to give us an unquenchable thirst for happiness coupled with the need of mutually preventing each other from attaining it, and for peace and harmony in His universe, while man is always at war against man? a Being so inscrutable and so strange as to allow without motive or compensation that men such as Lavoisier, Malesherbes, and the Maréchal de Mouchy [13] should fall under the blows of a

Robespierre? Certainly, O most righteous and wonderful of beings, I am not deceiving myself; we are immortal! . . . This journey is but a step, this world but a trial.

When free from it we shall perceive that we were but the necessary parts of a whole too well conceived to come within our divination; that here below everything is despair and deception except virtue, and that, just as virtue helps to make us less wretched even upon this earth, it alone will secure the place of honour in a better order of things.

CHAPTER XI

Delenda est Carthago!

*A*LL those who have known great sorrows will agree with
me that travels are a palliative if not a remedy. Their
agitation neutralises grief, as it were, by keeping it on the
move. The open air refreshes the soul and brings it, unknown
to us, what I should call the dew of consolation. New objects
in their succession soothe the wound, closing it partially, if not
completely. Suffering is lulled in the peace of the countryside;
the grief-stricken man, who could not weep in town, sheds tears
and feels less oppressed; under a sky he admires and in a solitude bringing him meditation, he seeks a refuge against fate
or mankind; his thoughts ascend towards Him without whose
permission nothing can happen. He attains thus to the inward
conviction that a peaceful awakening will follow upon the agitation of our dreamlike and flitting life; he looks upon these
scenes, these trees, which one by one he leaves behind, as mere
shadows, and compares them to the insignificant succession of
events upon this earth, so that the goal of his travels becomes
the symbol of his course across life, of which the end is immortal felicity.

There are griefs, as I know, that are proof against all contrivances of consolation, and that one can control only by always
thinking of them and becoming reconciled to them through
tears. There are griefs dwelling within one's heart until death.
One knows that nothing will prevail against them; they are
domestic enemies whom we cannot—or perhaps have no wish
to—send away. They serve us a good turn: they sharpen our
sensitiveness on other sides; they make us heedless even of
calumny, and immune to the cruel deeds of civilisation. They
are a poison which also acts as an antidote. But I know, too,
that such griefs befall few men, that not everyone has received
from nature what is needed to be so deeply affected, that this
sort of suffering spreads over the whole life of a man, disposing
of it, absorbing it, vanishing only with his last breath, and perhaps even following him farther, if one carries memories of this
earth beyond the grave.

Travel may also bring amusement to the frivolous. When I started off I was not, it is true, in this frame of mind, but I was still too young to draw from my observations all the benefit one derives when older.

Other men have given pictures of this fortunate Helvetia, since then shaken and again made stable on its foundations. Even had I seen it better, I should not describe it, for this has been done too often before; but I have lived in it neither well enough nor long enough to speak of what I know so little. I had been a few weeks at Lausanne when duty and honour called me back to join my regiment, then in Brittany, and on the eve of being incorporated in the army which, so people said, was going to attempt a descent on England.[1]

This scheme—often conceived, then forgone, and taken up again—is, I believe, far from impracticable or fantastic, but proved to be an impossibility for a weak and clumsy government and ministers so worthless as to have allowed France within sixty years to lose her advantages, preeminence, and indisputable superiority.

If France were to endeavour to punish the affronts meted out to her and her inhabitants, she would have far too much to do. She might accordingly have waged an everlasting war against Europe, where perhaps not one nation is to be found that—however poor its claim—does not declare itself the rival or the born enemy of anything French. Our arts, our books, our civility, our court and luxury, the military genius of our nation, our theatres, our language, all these things, including our vices, have been exploited by other nations and have been an education to them. One might thus have believed them under obligation to us, but the debt has been repaid only by hatred and envy.

This work, as it progresses, will lead me to enlarge on this idea, its foundation and consequences. I shall do so as a free man and a philosopher who is neither a flatterer nor a despiser of those in power; I am not yet reduced to that.

I would add that, in spite of the obligations of Europe to France during three centuries, we have done much to draw Europe's hatred down upon us. The moment to discuss this question has not yet arrived for me. I will here indicate only the source of that hatred.

I might confine myself to showing that if we may be regarded as the tutors of Europe we may also be regarded as the chastiser, the scourge, and the peace-disturber of Europe. We have never used our advantages with moderation; we have nearly always been seduced to put vanity and renown in the place of simple good sense and modesty. Our lively character, our self-conceit, have made us hated, especially in the North, where people have more sympathy with reasonableness than with wit, where orderliness, rather than wealth, of ideas is valued, vigour rather than grace, where common sense is put before imagination, and solid phlegm before a cheerful good humour.[2]

But there is a nation which more than any detests us, which does not limit this hatred to contacts through the court, the salons, or travels, which does not feel towards us a mere sterile antipathy spending itself in words and idle scheming. The people of this nation have sucked at their mother's breasts the horror of all that is French, their execration is based on instinct, calculation, logic, conviction, and even good style, for they consider it good taste to exaggerate, when there is a chance, the hatred they feel towards us. This makes them dispute our possession of every possible thing, even in matters in which they have nothing to oppose us. They would like to see us wiped off from the earth, and though deep at heart they have full knowledge of our superiority at countless points and of our equality with them in all others, they pretend to feel more esteem towards nations who cannot compete with them. Finally they are a people whose hatred spreads its uneasiness to the rest of the world, and, having produced some very great men who have shown admiration for France in their speeches or their writings, they never yet have produced one loving her. After such a picture, need I name England?

Reader, do not blame me for digressing; if I had to do without it, I would forgo writing.

So it was either to get drowned or to invade the three kingdoms (which was plain justice), that I left Lausanne to hurry to Brittany. Neither of these fates befell me, but, may your delicacy forgive me! I caught a fever and the *itch.* . . . But I must not anticipate.

In two years' time I had contracted debts to the extent of some forty thousand francs, and was without a penny on the eve of this great expedition. I hastened to Paris to knock at the door of some money-lenders who, knowing that the risks were next to none, were delighted to oblige me at a hundred-

per-cent interest. There was no time to lose, but on the second
day after my arrival, as I was in my rooms awaiting one of
these honest fellows, a M. L——³ was introduced, a provincial
barrister unknown to me, whose father I had seen at some relatives', for whom he acted as business agent.

M. L——, who took such an active part in the Revolution,
and who, from what I read in the newspapers, would have much
terrified me in the days of his power, was a young man of in-
tense impetuosity but shy in appearance. That day, when he
entered my room, his face impressed me as interesting, his disposition seemed kindly when he was not irritated, his mind
cultured, his ways those of unassuming politeness.

If he acquired his hatred of the court on account of that
journey to Versailles where he went with me, and of which I
shall presently speak, I am almost obliged to forgive him. He
came to my rooms, and having stated his only claim to my good
will, which he kindly called my protection, he told me that,
being sure of my credit, he desired to ask my help in making
his fortune. I could not conceive what means were his or mine
for the purpose, but I listened.

The post of director to the library (I believe it was so
called) of the town of Alençon was vacant; it was worth two
thousand crowns a year and would give one the opportunity of
being of service to some people and of bringing trouble on
others: a pretty position in the provinces, and one few people
would reject anywhere. He had hurried off by stage-coach before
any of his rivals, and could think of no one but me, so he said,
who, on account of my connections with Versailles, could help
him in obtaining the post. This is funny enough, but what proved
even more so is that I did secure him the post. But let us proceed with due order.

Having told me all this he stopped, looking embarrassed,
as if the most difficult thing was still to be said. He then made
two or three attempts that led nowhere; at last he stammered:
"Monsieur le Comte, will you allow me to point out that I would
have great pleasure in putting down three—three hundred lou—
louis towards the expenses and the formalities that in all probability will be necessary?"

I hastened to reply, as if I had not caught his meaning—to
save myself the trouble of being cross—that the expenses he
was ready to face were entirely useless; that the one way in
which I could oblige him was such that no bribery was needed

to smoothe things along; but that, since I had to leave Paris in a hurry and had spent foolishly, thus placing myself in a difficult position until I was of age, I would accept his money if I met with success, provided he would accept my bond signed in front of a notary to repay him within eighteen months and with interest. He made me a deep bow and lent me the money, which was given back to him within a year through Master Bérus, then my business agent, during a transaction over a fairly important plot of land that I sold to one of my uncles, who, on account of its convenient situation and its size, chanced the risks of buying from a minor.

These details are minute—this is one of the drawbacks of the sort of books called memoirs.

M. L—— left me quite satisfied, after I had arranged to meet him on the morrow in the palace gallery at Versailles, where I was to spend the night.[4]

I found him at the spot next morning, and told him to stay where he was. He assured me he was extremely bored, and that all he saw seemed to him most extraordinary, he would love to have his post and be gone. I promised he would soon be gone, but I could not answer for the post, as I was doubtful if he would get it.

As for me, I took my stand in the gallery close to the door of the Queen's apartments, at the time she usually came out to go to mass. Having noticed me, she greeted me and honoured me with a few words, while she walked and I followed her. She asked various questions, then, after telling me that M. de Poix had left for his regiment, she ceased speaking for a moment, so that I made bold to tell her I wished to place myself at her feet and beg her Majesty to grant me one minute's talk. "Come to see me before five," she replied.

I gave back his freedom to M. L——, and fixed an appointment with him for half past four in the Queen's guard room; he went his way, and I mine.

I found him punctual at the meeting, but he looked dusty; for he had explored all the thickets, had dined poorly at one of the porters', and could not easily conceal some ill humour. I asked him to wait for me while I went to the dining-room. An usher informed me that the Queen was not within, but would presently be back; in fact, five minutes afterwards she came in.

"Good day. . . . Where did you have dinner?"

"At Mme. de Beauvillier's,[5] madame."

"Do you mean mine?"

"No, madame, at Mme. Adélaïde's."

"Does she invite people to dinner?"

"Yes, madame, at any rate myself, whom she has known as a child and with whom she does not stand on ceremony."

"If Monsieur de Champcenetz were at Versailles, you would have dined with him—that would be suitable company for you!"

"Madame, he has wit and much gaiety!"

"Oh, how charming! . . . It will take him far!⁶ But, monsieur, what do you desire? Come in."

"I beg the Queen to listen to me with some indulgence, for I may take a little longer than I ought to."

"Certainly I will listen."

"Madame, there has just arrived a gentleman—a sort of magistrate to whom my relatives as also myself wish well. He would like to obtain a post at Alençon; this post is vacant, the details are here on this piece of paper. The matter rests with Monsieur de Miromesnil. My gentleman is a decent man, and I should be delighted if he could secure this post. A word from the Queen to the Keeper of the Seals and it is evident—"

"Well, it is evident—"

"Yes, madame—that he could not refuse."

"Is that all?"

"Yes, madame."

"I will write. Give me this paper."

"Madame, it is very much crumpled."

"Give me this paper. Come back to-morrow at half past three, the letter will be ready. Good-bye."

"Your Majesty, I do not know how to express my gratitude. . . ."

"By behaving well."

I then returned to my protégé and said: "Sir, in this land, one should only reckon on things when they are accomplished. Yet your affair is going on well; you thought better of my influence than I did myself, and I shall be delighted if it turns out you were right."

"What, sir, you have spoken to the Queen all this time?"

"Yes, sir."

"But, sir, we were told in the provinces that the King and Queen speak so little that it were almost as good if they never spoke at all."

"Were you also told they were mute?"

"Not exactly that, but that there was scarcely anyone with whom they could talk, since etiquette required they should be surrounded by all the high dignitaries of their court whenever they granted an audience to anyone."

"Even if it were a private audience? I wager this is so! . . . M. L——, you may have been told many other things about them which are as true as that."

"Sir, I have read—"

"Yes, in books, facts of the same nature and the same truth. Monsieur L——, I only ask you as a reward for my little help not to believe blindly all the absurdities you will hear or find in print about this land. Those who could write to the point never write; those who scribble on paper over these matters are wretches who, from their attics, mislead public opinion, and have no notion of things as they are, nor of men. They hold forth in a dogmatic, peremptory way, and discuss matters of which they have not even the remotest conception; their ignorance and disorderly imagination open to them the doors of the palaces of kings and the cabinets of ministers. They try to picture a world they have not seen and which cannot be guessed, and find people as backward as themselves ready to believe them. What is deplorable is that amongst their dupes are men of fine wits who are seduced by the natural liking human beings have for distorted facts,[7] lies, and above all by the propensity for deriding what stands high in social rank. These lampoonists, I repeat, find dupes who in good faith, and in their right senses, give credit to imposture and errors because, from their standpoint, they cannot distinguish the real from the ridiculous, truth from falsehood. I must leave you, M. L——, and I advise you to refresh yourself by going this evening to the theatre. We shall meet again to-morrow at the same place at three o'clock; if you wish to see me in the morning, I am putting up at Le Juste,[8] and shall not go out before half past eleven. Good day."

Next day he was furious. He had been to the play, according to my advice, and shown himself there without a wig and wearing a black suit and cloak. Two scatterbrains had made fun of him; on coming out he was offensively pushed by a man who was escorting a very pretty woman; he complained loudly, and the fellow asked him who he was and what he wanted. M. L—— was simple enough to give a detailed account of himself. "Well," replied the man who had pushed him, "it is very good of you to

be all this, I am the Comte de Chabanon and I am in a hurry."
Laughing inordinately, he then entered his carriage.

"So this," M. L—— told me, "is the dreadful distance
which pride and foolish prejudices place between one man and
his fellows! To see myself being pushed, questioned, laughed at,
and yet unable to seek revenge!"

"What prevented you from pushing too, monsieur? Who
told you to answer his questions? and what prevented your
laughing? Why be so sure he would refuse you what you call
the opportunity to seek revenge?"

"Ah, sir, I am sure of it. . . . This Comte de Chabanon—"

"There is no Comte de Chabanon. There is a writer of this
name, an extremely pleasant fellow who plays the violin like an
angel and is in the run for the Académie Française, but he
knocks no one down, as he is not in so great a hurry. M. de
Chabannes who pushed you, quite unconsciously I am sure, is
a very handsome young man of most illustrious birth, the descendant of ancestors highly commended for services rendered
to their country. It is natural and fair that some of this glory
should shine upon him. It is like a torch preceding him; if his
life has blemishes they will be the more easily seen."

"But he should not knock me down."

"Certainly not!"

This was the beginning of the revolution, in the case of
M. L——. M. de Miromesnil completed it next day.

I went to the Queen's apartments at the time she had appointed; I was told to call on the Comtesse de Tavannes, a lady
in attendance at the palace, the same whose husband, then gen-
tleman-in-waiting to the Queen and since a Duke, had forsaken
her with these few words: "You ought at least, madame, to close
your door." She had been busy at goodness knows what with
M. de Montmorency. This is coolness, this is what is known as
correct style! He was a small white-haired man, rather sprightly,
though speaking little. I never could see him without thinking
of the Maréchal de Tavannes, one of the ferocious instigators
of the Saint Bartholomew massacre, the crime in our history
which makes me shudder more than any other. This Maréchal
de Tavannes, first a page to the King, had become one of the
dearest minions of Charles IX, and one can remember that during the massacre he rushed about the streets of Paris calling
out: "Bleed them, bleed them; blood-letting is just as wholesome
in August as in May." But these men, at any rate, never turned

murder into a speculation; they had no personal interest to serve in immolating their victims. Theirs was an atrocious zeal, the fanaticism of cannibals; but most of them honestly believed that so holy a religion could enjoin these heinous deeds and sanctify them.

But do not pride, ambition, vanity, revenge, self-interest likewise lead us to fanaticism? Wretched humanity!

Mme de Tavannes had retained some beauty and freshness, though she was rather plump. When I presented myself to her, she gave me a letter of the Queen to the Keeper of the Seals, then, after a few trivial remarks, she asked me: "Could I know what is the object of this letter?"

"The Queen will most likely tell you, madame; the great trust she places in you, the favour you enjoy with her, answer for this."

As she was little loved by the Queen (and I knew it well), my reply sounded like sarcasm, so the conversation languished, and I took my leave.

I once more joined M. L——. "Come to M. de Miromesnil," I told him. "I have your post in my pocket."

We arrived at this magistrate's home. He was drinking coffee with a crowd of gownsmen from the town and country.

His great gift for taking the parts of valets in comedy made me fancy that one of these, stepping out of a Molière play, was there, disguised as judge or commissioner, to play some trick on a guardian.

However this may be, M. de Miromesnil, whom I had often met at M. le duc d'Havré's and who was not a fool, received me with extreme civility, as he did M. L—— when I introduced him. But when I had explained the matter which brought my companion to Versailles, M. de Miromesnil's features as well as his whole attitude changed entirely.

"Zounds," he exclaimed, turning towards M. L——, "you have lost your senses, rash young fellow! You are asking for a post that is the reward of years of faithful service, that requires a degree of ability of which you have given no proof. You have misled Monsieur de Tilly's good faith"—this with a cunning look and a bitter laugh—"in persuading him to such an indiscreet step—"

"But, your lordship," said poor L——.

"Silence, sir!" Then, speaking to me as if to make amends for his sudden sally, "Will you have some coffee?"

"I do not want any, sir," I replied, "but I should like to give you a letter from the Queen."

"From the Queen!"

"From the Queen."

He beamed; he hastened to break the seal; but how gloomy became his face as he read!

"Sir," he said at last, "I am convinced that her Majesty could not know the difficulties—how it is, I should say, almost impossible. . . . Yet, my whole pleasure is to obey the Queen. . . . But I must confess it is bitter to fail in one's engagements. . . . I should like to know, Monsieur le Comte, why you are so interested in this man. . . . You will have your post, do you hear? but I shall take care it does not become for you a mere title, and that you do your duty."

"Your lordship," said M. L——, "I have too much honour not to fulfill all my duties."

"It may be so."

"It certainly is."

"Yes, yes!"

"Allow me," I said quickly, "to offer your Lordship my thanks and my respects. Believe in my gratitude; the good grace you have shown in obliging me will make it last for ever." He would have escorted me, but I was already gone.

"Ah, sir, how near I was to causing my own ruin!" exclaimed the provincial lawyer with a sigh. "How I longed to retort to this old monkey. Forgive me. I feel that I ought not to speak thus of the representatives of our rulers, but it is dreadful to be humbled in the dust without daring to rise. . . ."

"Rest in peace, my dear M. L——. Come, calm yourself; it is a slight storm followed by a beautiful day. You have your post. Is not this what you wished?" In fact, he had it, but he came to tell me a few days later that it had cost him twenty-five louis, I do not know to what secretary, to speed the matter up. I congratulated him on being quit of the clerks at so little cost.[9] He left Paris a few days later and I believe came back only to do much harm to these men and institutions whom he fancied had given him offence.

What social order, what institutions wrought by the hands of man, are free from wrong-doing, inconveniences, and unpleasantness? Is there a country or a government where power is not intoxicating? where it does not tend to make refusals harsher and diminish the worth of favours? In what system do rulers always endeavour to soften the lot of their subordinates or to make the hand which holds the reins and deals out reproof or good offices, do so with a lighter touch? The best administration —it will always be so—is the one offering the least evil. The most paternal government is that which endeavours to see every-thing at close quarters, though it cannot encompass all objects; which reproves the worst and encourages the best; which allows no unfairness it has knowledge of, though there are wrongs that must go without redress in any vast constitution too com-plicated to be grasped in all its branches.. The best adminis-tration is the one that prevents as much evil as it can avert, that seeks to do as much good as it possibly can, and that pro-gresses with fixed purpose towards a great harmony, though it cannot possess the boundless power of God, who alone can com-prehend the whole details of His handiwork.

After having once more placed myself at the Queen's feet, I hastened towards Brittany to join the army which under the command of M. de Vaux and M. de Langeron was to attempt a descent on England. The town of Saint-Malo looked like a camp, and its inhabitants were proud of this animation. Officers of all ranks galloped in the streets at the risk of running over women and children, while a few second-rate courtesans from Paris drove about in coaches. They had come at the request of the Duc de Lauzun [10] and the Prince de Nassau, who had apparently enticed them with fairer promises than they found fulfilled. It was with great difficulty that they returned to Paris and paid for their post-horses.

As for me, I had the satisfaction of getting myself several times soaked in the sea during practices for a descent, at which the troops appeared little amused. I was quartered in a village named Châteauneuf, if I recall rightly, and in the property of M. de la Vieuville, once a captain of the guards. I had scarcely any other distractions than occasional visits to Saint-Malo, where I lost my money, as I shall later relate, so that the very young men who accept a game with the first comer may benefit by the tale. The sole pastimes in the village, where the fair sex provided none and the countryside was neither attractive nor picturesque, were riding in the morning and some fencing in the afternoon.

Demoustier would not have found at Châteauneuf the in-spiration for his charming and tender verses on the death of a country girl:

Oh, springlike Beauty, flower so dear,
Why could not death respect your grace?
Must one so pretty end apace,
While still she brings delight so near?

    *   *   *   *   *

Some for a time will speak of you
As one so fair, so young; and yet
They will forget; and spring's sweet hue
Must soon your grave with turf beset,
And there, to stop his course and quest,
Ending his day, some huntsman spry
Quite unaware will seek to lie
Where sleeps the shepherdess at rest.

There was a cemetery at Châteauneuf, and old peasant women, perhaps there may even have been young ones—but certainly no shepherdesses. I caught there the ugly disease I have already mentioned; it came of its own accord, I know not how. In Brittany nothing is thought of it; several officers from my regiment shared my good fortune, which did not prevent my wishing it to the devil. Happily I was rid of it in eight or ten days. During these two months, which I spent in hope of qualifying for the rank of Marshal of France and of being the first to land on England's shores, I had leisure to convince myself that the experiment was purely honorary, and that we should have only our labour for our pains. To crown it all, a slow fever, which I believe befalls all newcomers in that climate, made me look as haggard and yellow as a ghost; and unconquerable melancholy consumed me. God knows that I was not afraid of the English, but some unaccountable foreboding told me that my grave was in this solitude. My illness resisted the doctor's skill and all the quinine wine available. Each day found me more wasted through premature decrepitude.

I went one day to Saint-Malo to chase away these gloomy thoughts. I meant to invite myself to dinner at M. de Rulecourt's, a colonel in command of a legion, who since died heroically during an adventurous expedition resulting in heaps of dead in the streets of Jersey where, with a handful of soldiers, he had attempted a descent.[11] I was told at his door that he was away at Saint-Servan, which gave little promise of my dining with him at Saint-Malo. I was going away when a gentleman stopped me, giving his name as the Baron de —— and assuring me that M. de Rulecourt would be back for dinner. He appeared to me, judging from the servant's air, to be a friend of the house, and he seemed to take it upon himself to welcome

me. We reached the drawing-room, and after he had referred
rapidly to a few topics of war and politics, he proposed a game
—just to cheer me up. He called for cards before awaiting my
answer, and won from me in less than an hour, one hundred
and fifty louis at rouge et noir. I had enough presence of mind
to remember that I was not to lose to a stranger more than I
could pay, so I insisted on stopping the game in spite of his fine
speeches and a thousand assurances of his regrets and of his
longing to give me my revenge. He displayed extreme prudence
in asking for an I.O.U. for the *trifle* I had lost, a document
which I redeemed the very next day so as to have the right
never to speak to the man or greet him.

This little incident, which in my state of mind was far from
pleasant, completed my utter disgust with the emptiness of our
monotonous life in this town, where the fever undermining me
was every day becoming more serious, and where my most
exciting pleasures, I must repeat, were either a horse or a foil.
This last recreation nearly brought me to a duel with a gentleman for whom perhaps it might have been a blessing to be
killed; I mean the Comte de Latour-Maubourg, whom a most
decided siding with the revolution and great misfortunes ensu-
ing thereupon have rendered famous.

He was then only known for his distinguished name, great
wealth, the Queen's favour—which had caused him at an early
age to become colonel, second in command—and by the generosity of his nature, or, I should rather say, his magnanimity,
valour, probity, and honour, which caused him to be chosen as
arbitrator in any disputes in our regiment. Never was a man
who was so universally loved and who deserved it more; never
did one see such simplicity and obligingness with brothers-at-
arms, nor less condescension towards the humblest subordinates;
he could, on occasions, stand up to his chiefs, and often as advocate to lost causes; besides all this, he was endowed with an
imposing figure and lovable features. He had started his military career with the Vicomte de Noailles and M. de La Fayette;
their political views became his, which most likely accounts for
his being chosen as escort to the King on the way back from
Varennes. Misfortunes and prison were his lot. If metempsy-
chosis is a real thing, and if under a new shape I visit the earth
again, I pledge my word to you, Maubourg, never again to judge
anyone before a whole revolution has put my valuations to the
test.

One evening, when I was fencing with him, he became heated

over a doubtful lunge which he claimed I had not acknowledged. I said I had not been touched; I perhaps was too hasty because I was sure of the fact. After a few more passes, he caused his foil to bend over my breast, exclaiming that apparently it needed that much to convince me. . . . I threw away my foil.

"Come," I declared, "let us see if you will have such luck sword in hand!"

He jumped at this, dressed in haste, caught fast hold of me by the hand. . . .

"Let us go," he replied. "We will fetch our sabres. . . . Then you will see!"

"You will see yourself," I answered, "but I would not be mad enough to choose a sabre to fight with anyone much taller and stronger than myself; besides it is a weapon at which I have no practice; let us take our swords."

"Very well!"

We rushed out. Two officers, of the sort who rise from the ranks, joined us and in the name of the King compelled us to put down our weapons, and did all in their power to reconcile us. Latour-Maubourg agreed to it with good grace; it was not for me to be more exacting than he, who was older, had more years of service, and was versed in laws of honour as much as any man alive. He pressed me to his heart, shed a few tears while I did likewise, and showing me more friendliness than ever carried me off to supper.

This exploit was my last during the campaign. I received a letter from a relative who was trying to arrange a very favourable marriage for me; he advised me to come and see him at his country-seat before I returned to Paris. The match he was thinking of was so advantageous that only a fool could have refused it. If I had followed his advice, what griefs and misfortunes would I not have spared myself through life! But what man can escape his fate? The lady he proposed to me, and whom I should have won, has since married M. de M——, colonel in the horse regiment of L——, and brought him sixty thousand livres a year; this incident, and above all my health, made me decide to ask the Prince de Poix for leave, though I gave my word of honour to join my regiment at once if ever the French flag was hoisted on Albion's shores. No one had hope of this; so I came back to Paris where I sent for a doctor, who in a short while gave me back my health and the full strength of renewed life.

Our expedition having failed, and all schemes for a descent on England being abandoned, everyone made for home. If I knew how the whole business ended, or what were our reasons for seeking peace and the conditions that made it secure, I should tell them. But I confess that I have not the least notion of the government's operations; and since with the years which have elapsed, and the time and the place from which I write,[12] I have no reliable information regarding matters now so distant, the most convenient and shortest policy is thus for me to keep silent. What I know is that Paris was overrun a little while after with English people who, as usual, were loaded with favours, comforts, and privileges, both at court and in town, because we have always been a magnanimous nation, but one lacking in character and imbued with a fondness for foreigners, who never return the feeling. We seek all that is far from us, exalt everything we have not (in complete opposition to other nations) and belittle what we have.

The new order of things has given birth to more robust national feelings, and has replaced a petty vanity by great pride. Let us be just to ourselves. Above all, let us put aside Anglo-mania, for I have never found Gallo-mania in an Englishman, never yet found one of that nation who, after having intimately associated with a Frenchman on the Continent, has willingly seen him again in England.

CHAPTER XII

*M*Y health was restored. Carried towards all the errors of a vigorous youth, an age in which there is as it were a superabundance of life, I was seeking pleasure. . . . Paris, towards which was then flowing the élite of France and of Europe, became also for me, as for so many young and even mature men, a whirlpool of dissipation, pleasure, and indulgence, if one may so call frequenting the theatres, the actors' green-room and the high-class Phrynes; gambling and attending dinners and exquisite suppers, balls, and concerts. All of these things did not exclude seeing what was considered good company. One could not then go to theatres and salons without having to occupy oneself also with literature, epigrams, and songs. I had myself attempted verse, as I have already confessed; I sought the company of wits—those in the fashion—and I came to sharpen my own against that of Champcenetz.[1]

We have seen that the Queen had appeared indirectly to disapprove my relations with him; it was because of his malignity, or rather of his biting sarcasm, which did not spare the court. The style of the day brought us together rather more than any frank and solid friendship; I often had sharp discussions with him. He attributed my facility to that faculty of retention which is called memory. This was one day the cause of some ridicule, which I brought upon myself. I was foolish enough to grow seriously angry because he accused me of having much of this faculty, making the accusation in the presence of two very formidable judges, one, M. de Rivarol, as much distinguished for wit as perhaps any man ever has been; the other, M. Chamfort,[2] possessing a fine taste very superior to his talent. My accuser, this unfortunate Marquis de Champcenetz whose head later fell under the revolutionary axe, was a little less imposing. He is certainly the man who has best proved to me the emptiness of reputations, the lucky chances on which they rest, and the ease with which a man may be acclaimed as a wit, when at other times the name is denied to men who are fully entitled to it. Let me not be told that he was not supposed to have much wit. I have been vexed for ten years by hearing society people talk to me of the epigrams, the songs, the letters, the verses that Champcenetz had composed, of his charming sayings, of the cutting sarcasms he allowed himself, of the jokes he had made. Living intimately with him, I know that he did almost nothing, and this almost nothing always required to be corrected, for the very good reason that he knew not a word of Latin, while his French was only moderate and his spelling ridiculous. Men of letters in their turn have spoken of his wit; they have said that his talk was striking; they credited him with endless *bons mots* which other people had made. Never was there so much impudence in depriving other men of their property, in peddling the wit of others, and all that assisted by a stammer which wonderfully served him. The Chevalier de Boufflers, on account of his song "Les Jeunes Gens," became the cause of a sword cut which the Vicomte de Roncheroles gave Champcenetz. I discovered the wounded man in bed, finding it a simple matter to have a sword cut of his own for verses that were not his own. In the song "Des dettes," about the Marquis de Louvois, Champcenetz's only part was to change the name of Louvois to that of Gramont:

> To $\left\{ \begin{array}{l} \text{Gramont} \\ \text{Louvois} \end{array} \right.$ according to rule,
> I owe some songs and some debts.

The epigram against Mme de Saint-Armande was a similar case. It was by Rivarol, who at last gave it up to Champcenetz since the fellow had taken it from him and had come to believe seriously that he had really written it; just as he claimed to have written "Chloé, Belle et Poète," of which I knew the author, "Si l'on achetait du courage" . . . and twenty others.

He maintained one day to that excellent and worthy man of letters, Florian, that he, Champcenetz, had written I do not know which of the fabulist's romances; we were walking in the Palais Royal, one beautiful autumn evening. The author of "Estelle" took it very badly and defended his property vigorously. "Very well," said Champcenetz, "let us say no more about it. . . . I—I ought to—have written it, for it is—not worth much and I am fond of it." The fact is that with a face which lent itself to the part he had assumed, he had some occasionally happy flashes of wit. He chanced everything, remembered everything, and took everything; he was gifted with inexhaustible gaiety—I use this word gifted, which is here rather out of place, because it expresses my idea—this gaiety was his wit. It did not forsake him even before Fouquier-Tinville; it persisted in front of his tribunal and condemnation. His malice was indefatigable and general, though he was a man of honour incapable of any serious and deliberate infamy. He was never so full of jokes as when he was attacking his family or himself; for the sake of a *bon mot* he would have found delight in making himself ridiculous. It is no wonder that the man aroused much laughter during his life who, before leaving it, when on the cart in which Robespierre piled up his victims, called out to the executioner: "Drive us safely, and I will give you a good drink." [3]

For the rest, he had very little imagination, an uncultivated and not very extensive mind, a shameful ignorance of history and of the classical writers even of his own country, an earnest claim to understand all the arts, about which he argued with an expert boldness well calculated to impose on those who knew less than himself.

I had the misfortune, and I confess it, to work with him during some weeks at a journal, now I hope almost forgotten, the title of which was not new: "La Chronique scandaleuse." I wrote the prospectus, which then made some sensation, soon stifled by louder clamours of a more terrible kind: the cries of the victims, the bellowing of the executioners, and the clanging of chains in those abysses which were beginning to open. It was impossible for me to send to the printer a single one of Champcenetz's articles without revising and correcting it, and I remember that one day I exhausted myself in vain without being able to make him understand that it was not a matter of indifference to write *quant à moi* like *quand, quando.*

For the rest this work in common, undertaken against my tastes and my principles for reasons needless to explain here, cost me dear, for it was the sole cause of my departure from France in 1792 to avoid the dagger of the sieur Fabre d'Églantine and the vengeance of M. de Condorcet, discontented at having been pilloried in that journal. [4]

The reader will perceive I often indulge in long digressions, but what does it matter if I come back to him?

I was saying, then, that one evening I arrived at Rivarol's (it was I think about the middle of the year 1791, Rue Notre-Dame-des-Victoires). He was in a rather badly lighted room with MM. de Champcenetz and Chamfort. I reached the neighbouring room without being noticed; he was talking with his

usual facility, rapidity, and magic; they were listening with attentive admiration. The conversation, which had certainly begun
with some dissertation on the sovereignty of the people (then
his endless and everlasting subject of thought and discussion,
as grammar and style became during the last years of his life),
had changed to the debt that the moderns owe the ancients.
I remember that Rivarol, in one of the sayings so easy to recognise for those who lived with him, summed up in these words:
"And it is fortunate for most writers of to-day to have a good
memory, just as it is unfortunate for their readers."

I think I might do well to record as nearly as possible the
whole dialogue of these gentlemen, giving to it as much as I
can, after all this time, of the order and the form which they
themselves gave; for I do not deny that I have a good memory
—though I have lost at the age of nearly forty the better part
of it. I have as much as people ought to have who possess some
intelligence, and I shall explain presently my idea as to what
I believe memory to be.

CHAMPCENETZ. Ha ha ha! it would be a good thing if
M. de La Harpe had never read anything, and that the Vicomte
de Ségur and the Abbé Delille had never talked except to each
other.

CHAMFORT. You are too severe on La Harpe, my dear
marquis.

RIVAROL. And too indulgent to the other two.

CHAMPCENETZ. How is that?

RIVAROL. By making mention of them.

CHAMPCENETZ. A stunning memory is Tilly's, you have no
idea what a lot he has retained!

CHAMFORT. Better than that: he has wit and imagination
. . . fire and force.

CHAMPCENETZ. Observe please that most of this is in quotations; except for his jargon about women, what he gives one
are shreds of poetry, bits of prose, and then, to give himself
the air of a scholar with a Latin name, he quotes you Horace,
Virgil, and passages of Tacitus in which Martin [5] assured him
the other day that there was a barbarism of which poor Tacitus
was not guilty.

RIVAROL (*brushing his forehead with his hand*). At all
events that was not a feat of memory?

CHAMPCENETZ. It would be better to be Tacitus than to
quote Tacitus like that.

CHAMFORT. The Comte de Tilly would not have said that!

CHAMPCENETZ (*laughing*). You are taking his part.

CHAMFORT. That would not befit me, but I acknowledge his wit; and if he had been born in an inferior station and could have been given a serious taste for work and patient application, I am convinced that he would be a distinguished writer and himself a man to be quoted. Do you find his conversation so ordinary?

CHAMPCENETZ. I? Not at all; I often find it very extraordinary.

RIVAROL. Bravo! "Lay it on, nephew; you are doing wonders!" [6]

CHAMFORT. I thought you were amongst his friends.

RIVAROL. He would ask you what this means.

CHAMPCENETZ. Oh, but enough! Is one a man's enemy because one thinks he has more memory than wit? . . . though I don't say he lacks this.

CHAMFORT. Don't quarrel with him, for he will perhaps dispute that you have either.

CHAMPCENETZ. I shall speak ill of you in the Petit Gautier. [7]

CHAMFORT. And suppose if after reading it I do not consider you have spoken evil of me?

CHAMPCENETZ. Very fine! But what the devil, Rivarol, you say nothing! That is no fun; at first I made you lively.

RIVAROL. People who give themselves up to women never do any good. Softness and dissipation kill the most vigorous talent. It is certain that Tilly was not born without gifts and facility; he specially has vigour. See how he can laugh at you when you don't want him to, and not laugh when you want him to. Besides he knows enough to make you seem ignorant. . . . Come, don't say too much ill of him, for I should not like the spirit of contradiction to lead me so far as to take his part.

CHAMFORT. Ha ha!

CHAMPCENETZ. Well, I am done for! A fine thing to ask your opinion.

TILLY (*entering*). You were saying then that I have nothing but memory, you whose only merit is to make thefts with yours!

RIVAROL. Ah, good evening!

TILLY. Who told you so? You do not know how to read. You speak of quotations; do you know anything about them?

CHAMPCENETZ (*laughing*). I warn you that you are angry, and that a mere joke—

TILLY. Your laughter is as thick as you are, and your jokes

are as thick as your wit. For the rest I may tell you that I take little account of that wit. . . . I even scorn wit since people grant you some.

RIVAROL. Gentlemen!

CHAMPCENETZ. Never mind, it is amusing.

TILLY. I defy you to make it so to me, for a fool always bores me.

CHAMPCENETZ. This is in good taste!

TILLY. It is what is needed to reach its aim.

CHAMPCENETZ. Monsieur de Tilly, you must answer for this. . . .

TILLY. Monsieur de Champcenetz, I will answer for it, and what is more I will see justice done.

CHAMFORT. But, gentlemen, this is a quarrel! . . .

RIVAROL. Upon my word it is the height of absurdity. How could you be angry over a thing which at bottom means nothing? And then . . . why give an ear to it?

TILLY. One cannot help doing so with you who are always talking. It is a kind of monopoly which at all events what you say justifies.

RIVAROL. The praise is a charming corrective.

CHAMPCENETZ. Yes, yes, but he puts you down as a mo— mo—monopolist.

RIVAROL (*laughing*). And you a stammerer. But that is better than to take offence.

CHAMFORT. No one here dreams of doing so.

CHAMPCENETZ. We are acting a proverb.

RIVAROL (*turning to me*). Then laugh.

TILLY. At what?

RIVAROL. At yourself, for having lost your temper so ill-advisedly.

CHAMPCENETZ. Who prevents your laughing at me?

CHAMFORT. One cannot sacrifice oneself with better grace.

TILLY. These are his ordinary tactics, to offer up himself so as to be able not to spare others.

CHAMPCENETZ. Very well, I must be taken literally as to what I say of myself.

RIVAROL. And all the rest should be looked upon as fiction.

CHAMPCENETZ. But here is an afflicting reality! It is pouring with rain.

RIVAROL. The Comte de Tilly has a cab, I am sure he will see you home.

TILLY. And Monsieur Chamfort also.

RIVAROL. That is needless, he does not mind rain.

TILLY. Besides, how could we be three in a cab with M. de Champcenetz?

CHAMPCENETZ. An epigram! a mere nothing . . . but it does one good.

TILLY (*laughing*). I shall see you home this evening, but I shall kill you to-morrow.

CHAMPCENETZ. I should prefer you to kill me this evening and see me home to-morrow.

We had to laugh, and make friends; that was the end of this ridiculous evening, ridiculous because I took offence in a fit of foolish vanity over what ought to have amused me and been of benefit by prompting me to cultivate my memory better if he was right, or by showing on future occasions more wit if he was wrong. But, as Montaigne says: "Vanity has been allotted to man, and everything deceives him in the end; he runs, exerts himself, flees, hunts, follows a shadow, adores the wind, the profit of his day is chaff—and that chaff is praise and fame."

I thoroughly proved in the end to M. de Champcenetz that I had kept no resentment, and I did my best to rescue him from the executioners who have since sacrificed him. But he could not be shaken and assured me that though he knew the fate which awaited him he would never forsake his books and his engravings to go and play the wandering Jew over Europe; that he loved life, but indolence still more. I know that after I left he had an interview with Brissot [8]—I do not know by what means —who promised him his life on condition that he kept silent. This was to ask the impossible of Champcenetz. I am sure that he even saw Condorcet, and that conditions of peace were signed between them. He justified himself apparently at my expense, but my spirit forgives his ghost. Through a friend of his and of mine he let me know that he was peaceful and that he believed he would *pull through*. He was arrested under Robespierre, who had promised him nothing, and would only grant him death for some pun reflecting on the Republic, which perhaps was not even his. In truth he was condemned for having conspired through jokes. He had my regrets. He was mischievous only in speech. The judgement which I pronounce on him cannot be put down to any personal motive. He was not in my way in any respect. He placed his happiness in provoking laughter, and I should detest to pass for the finest wit of France at that price. He attracted me, and would even have inspired friendship if I could have believed him capable of returning it. I wish he were alive, even should I be condemned to praise him. But now he is dead, I owe him only the truth.

But I believe I promised myself and the reader a definition of memory. It is an aptitude to retain what strikes us, what we clearly conceive, what pleases us, and especially what has an analogy with our ideas and knowledge. It is, in some sort, a superfœtation of ideas which we beget upon our own. A fool may recollect just as well as an intelligent man that on such a day, at such an hour, he saw someone fall off a horse, etc.; but I never met in my life, I do not say a fool, but a man indifferently average, who has read with profit, and has recollections which are correct, useful, mature, and ordered. A man has already intelligence who understands that of others, and a very good intelligence if he discerns what deserves to be retained; his æsthetic penetration is very great if he can preserve the deep emotion aroused by beauty, such treasuring being memory; finally, he who can make others share and enjoy, through a conversation in turn gay and solid, the treasures which he has acquired and made his own, shows insight, accuracy, and judgement.[9] In a word, a memory which is not the simple repertoire of a parrot is one of the prime gifts of Nature; she bestows it only on her favourites and on those to whom she has otherwise given much.

Rivarol, for instance, had a prodigious memory. Lively feelings, an extreme love of the beautiful, had engraved on it nearly everything worth being retained in the great authors, ancient and modern. But these powerful aids, while fortifying his conversation, had not disturbed its originality, nor mixed any alloys with this gold; it was a statue of which the draperies and ornaments equalled the beauty and added still more charm to it.

It was in Berlin that I witnessed the extinction of this brilliant star, which in northern regions had lost its fire, this star of which the often varying light had yet shed abroad so much brilliance. I have to some extent in another work [10] described how during the last months of his life people succeeded in making us quarrel. I shall repeat it with more details in this when the time comes, but that circumstance will not make me unjust to one of the finest spirits Nature ever formed.

Thus of these three men not one remains! Death reaped them all before their time.

Two of these were very remarkable men, and one of these

two still more distinguished and extraordinary than the other. Not one has raised a real monument to commend himself across the ages to succeeding centuries. Chamfort had not perhaps the talent, though he had infinite wit and a still more exquisite taste. Rivarol had an excessive indolence together with a stimulating pride, an incurable idleness over which his prodigious vanity could not triumph, to which the momentary successes of conversation provided a pleasanter food than an uncertain and remote fame; I dare to say that he gave out his genius in speech and exhausted it. His wit was extremely delicate, and one could not get angry at his sharp witticisms, blended as they were with a smile full of grace. They were often meant ambiguously, hiding a kindly interpretation. Like his saying to M. de Florian, who was carrying his poem "Numa Pompilius" protruding out of his pocket: "If one did not know you, with what ease one could steal from you!" He was fond of rings, cameos, stones, or anything which might recall those classic times to which his mind and thoughts so truly belonged. The Vicomte de Ségur once lent him an antique ring bearing the head of Cæsar. Having noticed it on his finger, I praised it. "It is really fine," he said. "I am sorry the Baron de Bezenval did not bequeath it to me, but upon my honour I shall keep it. Cæsar never once surrendered."

He is, as I have said, dead, and nothing remains of that vivid flame which animated him. Thus all passes in rapid succession on this singular stage where we figure like shadows in mirrors that are soon broken.

Ludimus, interea celeri et nos ludimus horâ.

All enigma! Who will solve it for me?

CHAPTER XIII

*The most practiced man cannot easily hold on
to the thread which will guide him out of the labyrinth of certain treacherous sirens. Skill, cheating,
false promises, cunning, assumed despair, lying pro-
testations of everlasting love, are twisted ways out
of which one can find no issue.*

*I*N the midst of this life of excitement, even more than of
pleasure, which I was leading since my return to Paris, I
was in no want of anything and not one thing went in want of
me save this need to love in order to be loved. . . . I wished
to dispose of my heart. Fortune and luck served me better than
skill or foresight could have done. One day, driving from Passy,
my cab drew near to the Esplanade at a pace such as Louis XV
had declared he would forbid were he M. de Sartines, lieutenant
of police. I had lined up close to a carriage that suddenly collapsed as if by magic. A frightened woman screamed, her valets
went to her help, and she was taken out of her coach none the
worse but for the fright. . . . She was beautiful in all possible
ways, as could clearly be seen. . . . I had offered her my arm
before she knew if she still possessed both her own; and forgetting to ask me who I was she quickly answered all my
questions.

If she reads this chapter, such a beginning must not alarm
her. Let her be reassured; I shall not even put down the first
letter of her name. What I shall say of her could be applied to
a thousand others. For instance that she has since married a
man of fashion who believes he has never been duped by a
woman, even in the smallest affair, while she, by way of keeping
the balance even (for balance governs the world), made him
pay in the same money he had bestowed on others—she played
on him all the tricks at which he had been a master. No one
will learn from me the name of the town where she had lived
previous to coming to Paris; nor the truly dreadful event which
caused her to leave the country, and how she lost her husband
before she had had time to loathe him. Nor will I—but I must

stop. . . . Be reassured, O you almost pagan beauty, I shall
not write down a libel nor one dishonourable imputation even
when I name or indicate people so clearly as to cause them to
be recognised. As to your name, nothing pointing to it shall
escape me. Nature has moulded all faces on the same model,
yet one characteristic and positive feature distinguishes them;
this feature which suits you well, which would give you away,
I shall not portray. My pen will never defame people save those
who are already infamous in the estimation of their contemporaries or of posterity.

I shall call you Cécile (it is as pretty a name as any) and
I shall say: Cécile had been to the rue Saint-Dominique to pay
a call and was going home to dine at Passy where she had taken
a house. This she related to me in a much troubled voice; I knew
the rest. Thereupon, very modestly, I stated my name. I might
as well have called myself Pompey or Cæsar; she had not heard
of me. I tell it to those who set value on themselves, it is a
lucky thing to be little known, especially by those women whose
imagination loves to run wild and to nurse fancies.

"Madame, you see this cab. Will you trust yourself to me?
I drive moderately well. It will be an honour to take you home,
and instead of a reward one grief will be mine, that of losing
you so soon."

She murmured a few words, beautifully expressed, but which
I cannot recall . . . and there she was beside me.

"Monsieur, I beg of you, drive more gently."

"At a walking pace, madame, if so you wish. My happiness
will last the longer."

"Servants are dreadful, not looking where they go; truly
I think I shall dismiss my coachman. It is entirely his fault."

"Madame, I shall engage him."

"For what reason, monsieur?"

"Because I owe him my happiness."

"What happiness?"

"That of hearing you ask this question."

"Would you please put your horse to a trot?"

"No, madame."

"Why not?"

"Too great a responsibility is now mine. But if you want
the reins, madame, it will be a joy to be driven by you, and I
give myself up to it."

"I have sometimes driven, monsieur, but in this dress people would think me mad . . . and with somebody I have not the privilege of knowing. . . . Give them to me, monsieur."

She took the reins, lowered her head, and with charming composure drove me at a fairly quick pace into a courtyard to the foot of a flight of steps flanked by stone balustrades. Two gentlemen walking on the terrace made an outcry.

"Monsieur, will you do me the favour of dining with us?"

"Must I, madame?"

"There is no must, monsieur, but I should be delighted."

"And so should I, madame."

I offered her my hand, she related her story. We were in a drawing-room. Monsieur l'Abbé was pleased to see me; a fat gentleman in green would have kissed me had I allowed him. . . . I should love to draw his portrait, but I shall not give in to the temptation, which might prove dangerous.

Dinner was served; we talked little, the fat gentleman less than the others; he hastened to remark that he took but one meal a day, and ate greedily. The Abbé, seeing what an antagonist was his, hurried to a laughable extent, and ate enormously.

"Monsieur," said the hostess to me, "do you know M. de la Tour-du-Pin, the colonel?"

"Yes, madame."

"Do you know his wife?"

"Not very well, but I have met her and I know she is a daughter of the late K——g. Is he so privileged as to know you, madame?"

It was the Abbé who after an interval replied: "In the old days we saw no one but him."

"Ah," said the other, "do you remember? . . . You even wanted to fight with him; it would have been a joke, an abbé fighting a colonel!"

"It would have been most ridiculous," said Cécile, "it would have been worse than the colonel in 'Le Cercle' [1] who did embroidery work."

The Abbé pulled a face, sought refuge in his plate and spoke no more. The fat man would have laughed could he have spared the time.

As for me, I could easily see that there was some mystery I alone was unable to unravel, but Nature has endowed me with a perfect indifference for secrets which are not entrusted to me, and I could not foresee that a most important part was awaiting me in this adventure. When each of these gentlemen had satisfied his stomach, a hidden tyrant to whom they appeared to immolate inordinately, the conversation chanced to fall on acting and the well-known preeminence of our stage. I possessed enough general notions on the matter to enable me to give an opinion; but since I had not then sufficiently investigated the subject nor travelled much, and as I only like to speak of things I have studied with care or learnt from experience, I did not take so active a part in this discussion as I should to-day, now that I am convinced that the ancients never had a Molière, and that the great tragic authors of France have surpassed the classics and improved on what they borrowed from Sophocles and Euripides. As for the stage in other countries— But why treat of a question so closely related to national pride in every country? Why provoke so cheaply the animosity of foreigners? Why try to convince them that they are wrong in their ways of feeling pleasure and emotion, of giving in to laughter and to tears? Who can judge of the likes and dislikes, or the peculiar conventions of a whole nation? Who can display such excessive pride as to say: "All you approve of is second rate, I condemn it. Only amongst us are to be found models of what is great, beautiful, pathetic, and natural; your tragedies are inflated monstrosities; your plots lack art, truthfulness, method, and restraint; your comedies are anæmic, insignificant, their intrigue being either weak or deficient"?

Foreigners would reply:

"Such vanity is odious, even if it were well founded. It is nearly always the hall-mark of ignorance and a proof of prejudice. But is it fitting you should teach us how to enjoy ourselves or to display emotion? Are you the controller of our very life and of our feelings? Is your estimate of our manners, intelligence, customs, and tastes correct enough to enable you to know, without risk of being mistaken, what is most suited to us in this climate of ours? Was your judgement of us moulded and modified through the principles of an education similar to ours, or the influence of the same prejudices? Are you the Supreme Artist? Do you live in our bones or think in accordance with our code of morals? Are you in the secret of our habits, our primary concepts, our positive ideas: in a word are you in the secret of our organism?"

"But nature is the same. . . ."

"You think so but we do not believe it. Keep your nature to yourselves and the pleasure you find therein; leave us ours, or what we conceive as such, as well as the joys it brings us."

"But you have translated most of our plays, often the least good, and constantly put them on your stage."

"This proves we are not exclusive, nor as contemptuous as you are; that one taste does not forbid another, so that we widen the circle of our entertainments while you would like to restrict it. This finally is proof we are fair to you while you are not so to us."

"But our superiority cannot be contested."

"Nurse that idea, but do not tell it to us, for we should not do so about ourselves even if we thought likewise."

"But most of the best foreign writers have owned it in their books. Lord Chesterfield, one of the finest minds England has produced, has said: 'There is not, nor ever was, any theatre comparable to the French theatre.' " [2]

"Lord Chesterfield may be right or he may be wrong, but drawing up a general theory in the seclusion of the study is quite a different thing from winning the casual approbation of the crowd in every-day talk and the ordinary course of life. Besides, such an assertion is susceptible of being carried further by reasoning, and of being mitigated by counter and minor facts. . . . In a final survey the French stage may be preferable—in reality superior—but we have legends, fictions, customs, fancies, and ideas concerning beauty that move, suit, and satisfy us more. In a word, we alone are competent to judge these, and we do not admit that you are. Keep your rules, your pride, your comparisons, dislikes, elegance, delicacy, and prejudices—reason itself, if you wish to; and we shall retain our ways of seeing and feeling, the sort of emotions that stir us most, and the entire stage-craft which is our very own."

This is what I could have said to Cécile; I would have silenced these gentlemen. . . . But I did even better, I went to the Opéra as there was still time. I did not ask leave to come again, since if one has dined with people, one owes them a call. This I paid a few days later, and, to spare all idyllic details, I shall relate only that in the course of a fairly reasonable time I became the most intimate friend of the house, where I met no one but provincial folks, save two people whom I believe deserve a special mention.

One was the Marquise de C——, a witty woman, immoral to excess, and at one time worse than a courtesan, yet the same who, when "Les Liaisons dangereuses" was first published, had her door closed to M. de Laclos, whom she had often received, saying to her porter: "You know that tall, thin, and rather bilious-looking gentleman dressed in black who comes here often? I am no longer at home to him; if I were alone with him I should be afraid."

She apparently believed that he had moulded Mme. de Merteuil on herself. She was scarcely worth more than that lady and she became as ugly.

We have from her one excellent repartee which has been wrongly ascribed to Mme de Créqui: "Indeed, the Baron is a sot, but he is not a fool."

It is also about her, I believe, that the Maréchal de Luxembourg's wife used to say: "Her eyes always have that expression it gives us much pleasure sometimes to see in our own."

The other person was the Prince de Broglie,[3] son, grandson and great-grandson of Piedmontese noblemen in the service of France, where they had built up a fortune surpassing their expectations, and nephew of a man who died too soon, since in true merit he was superior to all the members of his family. One might have thought that M. de Broglie would have been in duty bound to prove one of the most ardent supporters of a monarchy that had done so much for his family and likewise promised everything to himself. One might have believed this the more readily since he ought to have felt the need of preserving this inheritance of fame which his ancestors had handed him and to which his way was so clear.

But it turned out quite otherwise: he, the son of a marshal of France, of an hereditary duke who possessed the only diploma which in France throws lustre upon the title of imperial prince, found a revolution and threw himself into it as would a philosopher whose fortune is to be made; he became one of its victims[4] because he was blind enough to believe in his personal merit when he had ceased to be a part of the governing class.

What is most remarkable is that, in this very house, we one day had a sharp argument concerning abuse of power, which he termed the foresight and wisdom of those in authority. So he was then the champion of despotism, and I the friend of freedom. This is, in fact, what I have always been, though it depends what meaning is given to words. But it appears that his political creed has since undergone great transformation, while I have remained faithful to the one I have solely and constantly professed; my line of advance has been firm and straight. I had disinterested principles; his, probably, were merely the outcome of circumstance and egotism. I have always

thought that the greatest misfortune for a whole nation is to
overthrow its rulers through violence; I have always been convinced that the worst government that governs, is better than
any visionary improvement purchased through anarchy and all
the ills to which it gives birth. But I have always dreaded
despotism, and have had a horror of oppression; I have always
preferred equality before the law to disparity resulting from
prerogatives, and though I uphold social hierarchy, I detest an
excessive use of distinctions which goes beyond limits set up by
reason and true justice.

My argument with the Prince de Broglie concerned a M. de
La Serne, captain of foot, who believed himself offended by a
staff officer whose credit at court and power over public opinion
were far from imposing. One evening, meeting his rival in the
street, the captain fell upon him sword in hand, thinking he
could brush aside rank distinctions, since he considered his
honour at stake. His adversary, though armed, refused to defend himself, and, from love of order and rank, lodged a complaint. The subaltern was arrested, imprisoned at the Abbaye
Saint-Germain, and there blew out his brains.

This problem presents two aspects, so it is not surprising
opinions should vary about it.

The way to discuss the matter seems to me as follows:

In former days an officer who had nothing to look up to but
his profession would rarely venture to risk this, and sometimes
things dearer than life, in order to challenge one of his chiefs,
unless he had received such an offence as would leave a lasting
stain upon his honour. If the chief had so far forgotten himself
that the despair of the outraged party seemed justified, opinion,
both of the public and in the army, would judge the case and see
justice done, admitting that he was cowardly enough to refuse
to fight and to have known beforehand he would do so.

Only on the assumption of a very serious insult, a case exceedingly rare, would a subaltern, first resigning his commission
and becoming a civilian, reclaim his honour from the man who
had taken it from him. That is what happened to the great
Condé. He had insulted a mousquetaire at the battle of Steinker-
que, and nobly offered him satisfaction. They met, both drew
their swords, but the mousquetaire placed his at the Prince's
feet.

In such exceptional cases, which hardly ever occurred, the
colonel or staff officer who appealed to superior authorities the

better to crush his victim twice, was judged and condemned by the most formidable of all tribunals—public opinion.

But then, particularly in France, what abuses did not spring from this! What an overthrow of all notions pertaining to rank and to passive obedience, the chief support of an army! In the last resort, it is to general good will, which renders verdicts final, conscience, which never deceives, to public opinion, which may go wrong but can be guided, and finally to the absolute necessity of restoring honour when it is truly endangered—that alone should be referred a decision in cases so infinitely rare that it would be best had never one instance occurred in the French army.

That is why I once disapproved the exaggerated chivalry displayed by the Vicomte de Noailles [5] when in command of a regiment of the King's dragoons. One day at table he stated in front of several officers that he would despise a colonel who refused to fight with an officer he had offended (this expression left too much latitude; he should have said *insulted,* and even then these were fine words of little worth). "But," he added, "I should mercilessly cause the ruin of any man who challenged me while on service; though in Paris, in mufti, I shall always be at the disposal of any man who may ask me for a stroll in the Bois de Bologne." (His literal words, but most out of place from a commander.) This statement was heard and remembered by M. de Bray, a captain, who some time later believed himself offended. He claimed satisfaction, was granted it, and gave his chief a thrust with his sword. Noailles sought no other vengeance than having his victor promoted to the grade of second major on the occasion of his own transfer to the command of a regiment of the light horse, which it was then fashionable to seek. M. de Brienne, the War Minister, at first refused; Noailles insisted, claiming that M. de Bray, one of the best officers in the regiment he was leaving, was indispensable to him in his schemes regarding the new corps to which he was called, and that he would only accept on this condition.

Here is vengeance to which few people can rise!

Since I am on this subject of the Vicomte de Noailles, I shall enter into other details about him.

His gifts and his ability are not sufficiently known. I give my word that he was not one of those vulgar and ordinary personalities one so commonly met. He lost his peace of mind, repute, and life through an unrestrained craving for celebrity, and a longing to surpass his brother-in-law,[6] as a rival of whom he had willingly and to his own undoing set himself up. This brother-in-law possessed more steadiness, perhaps even more moral worth, than Noailles, but he was certainly far from having a mind as strongly organised or an energy as powerful. The Viscount played a tame part in the Revolution, since no party placed much trust in him, as he told me himself; he was never given charge of vital interests, and on the other hand he lacked eloquence on the platform, though he did well in a draw-ing-room.

However, his political views were only second-hand and borrowed; they were not only in direct opposition to the prin-ciples of his education and the advice of his relations—worthy representatives of another century—but they were just as little in keeping with the leanings of his own heart, with his intel-lectual tastes and spiritual aspirations. I know this from the conversations I held with him when he no longer had any interest in hiding things from me, for was it not acknowledging this to say: "Once I thought the Revolution unavoidable, but that we could guide it; later, being carried away beyond what I had fore-seen, I thought that it would be better to follow the Revolution than to allow myself to be crushed by it." In fact, all one needed to do was to make a *noise,* and the means of attracting attention, if anything could still cause a surprise, was *to go in for democ-racy* when one was born to be a pillar of the throne.

This false attitude is the reason why he left no precious memory of himself, nor acquired any striking fame amidst our civil dissensions; and he felt this so keenly that he only resigned from the army, where he then served, and escaped to the United States because this newly born army made of disparate elements was unruly and clumsy and *would not permit a man to seek death as he pleased,* a glorious death being then what he most sought. If he had had a little patience, occasions to display his gifts would have been forthcoming, and I do not doubt he would have been worthy of following in the footsteps and of emulating most of those great generals who reorganised the army and brought victory to the colours of France while defending her territory.

He never left France or any other country after the Revolu-tion without inserting in the newspapers the day and the time of his departure. He used to call this an offer to square up accounts in all directions.

I have known few men more able to cling to strong views and to carry them out with more tenacity, vigour, and wit; few men whose gifts of friendship inspired me with greater confidence, and whose determination when he was not your friend proved to be more dangerous. I shall later speak of his private life.

Besides, he died as he was fated to do, sword in hand: such was his star, such was his destiny! There had once been a time when he cared little for life; he had withdrawn from it for a while; death took him at his word on this second occasion when he once again showed himself indifferent. He was a man of fine courage, I repeat—one of those manly spirits seldom met with even in France.

I recall a rather curious trait that will give an idea of the exaltation of his soul and of his freedom from prejudice, even before the Revolution. During the American war, he had been lieutenant-colonel in a Soissons regiment; a captain in this regiment had been wounded through the chest by a bullet which killed a grenadier standing behind him; he could not get well, and, a long time later, he came to Paris to claim the Saint Louis Cross. He was covered with wounds and had a most imposing face. For a few months he dragged in and out of public offices without receiving anything but promises. One day the Vicomte de Noailles had come to the Vauxhall, where I was chatting with him, when he chanced upon his former captain (for he now had the King's regiment). He ran to him, put his arms around him, and asked him what he was doing in Paris.

"Monsieur le Vicomte," replied the officer, "having several times called at your house to have the honour of paying my court, I have never been lucky enough to meet you. My wounds cause me horrible pain, and I am asking for the cross."

"Monsieur," said the viscount, "I am grieved at not having seen you sooner. I go very little to Versailles, and very seldom meet the ministers, but I still have enough credit to see that justice is done you. I myself do so now"—he put his own decoration in his pocket—"for I do not want to wear this cross in front of you as long as you do not have it." The captain received the cross a few days later.

Once more let me show how anything singular tempted him. He knew that I had good reasons for complaining of the Maréchal de Ségur and the Maréchal de Stainville in connection with an action which had been referred to the Marshals of

France sitting as a court. He asked me, in the early days of the Constituent Assembly, to draw up a memorandum against their administration of justice, which he called inquisition. I consulted a few books and handed over to him some pages on the encroachments and abuses of power of these high officers of the realm. But is it not delightful that this son, grandson, great-grandson, and nephew of four Marshals of France should show his affection towards their kind in those cruel days by formulating such a request in front of the first prince of the blood?

I speak of him without temper or partiality, for the recollections I keep of him are too mingled with friendship to allow me to be oversensitive regarding events which became disastrous for me. My mind is now free of them, but he had played too direct a part for me to retain any illusions concerning a friendship he had promised me and which he betrayed.

We had not yet reached that point at the time of my argument with the Prince Victor de Broglie, an argument not mainly concerned with the isolated case of M. de La Serne, which I never knew in all exact details, but with the more general proposition of a despotism that Broglie favoured and I rejected. He has not since maintained his principles at such a height, for, not content with fighting in the ranks of Freedom, where he would have had me by his side, he went over to the flag of Rebellion and proclaimed himself a rebel.

CHAPTER XIV

THREE months passed by the side of Cécile in the security of a happiness to which I could not foresee or wish an end. Her charming face would sometimes betray a vague anxiety I could not understand, her heart seemed oppressed by a weight I could not lessen, but when I expressed a longing to share her secret, she assured me she had none. She appeased my uneasiness with so much skill and goodness that it vanished. Twice her door was shut to me; yet my love was not then subject to those fits of tyranny, rage, and jealousy which I was later to display, I am ashamed to say, more perhaps than most men. . . . I now blush for them when there is no longer need to blush. Cécile had succeeded in convincing me that family difficulties concerning her alone were the cause of all that surprised and alarmed me in her, that she was happy and owed her happiness to me. . . . We easily believe such things. Self-conceit is an accomplice we treat with much regard. And to quote one of our most lovable and most classic of poets: "My sole belief was sweet caresses!"

Yet indeed I had noticed with uneasiness that one of her maids, the girl most in her confidence, could not be won over either by kindness or gifts. The truth is that she hated me because she wished to help another from whom she had received much money and hoped for more.

I was thus unsuspectingly nearing the end of an idyll that was to have a tragic conclusion. To paint this picture I shall go back to colours I have used before in another work (when I never thought of starting on this one), where I mingled truth with fiction, blending together the descriptions of several periods and adventures that concerned me as well as a friend who was dear to me.

It was night, and after the first ecstasy of love, I was sweetly drinking in the memory of a joy too soon ended, when I heard a loud noise and a curtain was raised which covered a door opening on an adjoining room. It was L. T——.[1]

"You will not survive your triumph," he said. "Get up and defend yourself. I know that you have a sword."

Cécile, at the same moment as myself, had jumped out of bed; he pushed her aside with so much temper and violence that I was enraged. I rushed for my sword, and we fell upon each other with the fury of two tigers. I do not need to say that the fight was unequal since one of the men was in an attire which a chaste pen cannot portray; and so I was wounded before I had time to recover my wits. Cécile filled the room with her screams and endeavoured to place herself between us, when, less blinded with anger and my hand more steady, I hit my adversary square in the chest. . . . He staggered and fell.

It was then I discovered that the object of our worship and the cause of our fury was herself wounded below the breast and bathed in her own blood. What hand had spilt this blood? . . . I still do not know.

M. de L. T., a former rival who had long since lost the rights of a favoured lover, had bribed the maid to sell him her mistress's secret and to compromise me. This girl had taken flight at the first screams and warned another maid.

Picture my position: a beloved woman drenching with her blood the bed which had known my bliss; at my side the lifeless body of a man I knew well and had always esteemed; floods of blood on the floor; myself covered with my own; our swords lying there; chairs and lights knocked over. . . . More than twenty years have not dimmed the memory of this night of desolation and slaughter, the horror of it continues still. Soon I no longer saw anything. I was seized with frightful convulsions and a moment later lost consciousness. This deathlike state lasted twelve hours, and when I recovered my senses I found myself in my rooms surrounded by doctors who spared no efforts to bring me back to a life I at that moment hated. The surgeon told me he had been awakened by a man who had guided him to a carriage where he had found me. There he had tried to examine my wound, but his guide had prevented him, and soon after reaching my rooms the fellow had disappeared, promising my valet that he would come again in the evening.

In fact, he came again; he was one of Cécile's servants and informed me that her state was not serious, but that the baneful perpetrator of so much evil would most likely pay for it with his life. So far he had been looked after in Cécile's house, but they intended to move him to his rooms in the darkness of night.

It was not, however, until some years later that M. de L. T—— died far from Paris; I do not know from what dis-

ease. He had deserved to perish in this duel, or rather this
attack for he was entirely in the wrong. I know of nothing
more ungenerous and absurd than to force a woman to be bound
when she no longer wishes to be, and to abuse her past favours
to exact new ones.

Cécile asked to see me as soon as we were both better; she
wept a great deal, assured me she had adored me (for it is
thus people love), and gave me such bad explanations for everything which had happened that I have never been entirely enlightened. She then fixed a time to see me the next day, but she
did not keep her word . . . for when I arrived she was gone.
We have met on several occasions since, and as if by mutual
agreement have never entertained the thought of reviving a love
which had died under such tragic auspices and left me so disillusioned.

I needed to divert my mind from this gloomy event. I was
fairly well acquainted with an Englishman, to-day a member of
Parliament, who was going to Brussels, so we set out together.
I journeyed through these rich districts favoured of Heaven
and priests, and finally settled in the capital after having visited
Austrian Flanders and Brabant with as great an interest, though
I know not why, as I should have found in the classic soil of
Italy. I have nothing extraordinary to record concerning my
stay in Brussels (1784), where the arts were then only moder-
ately cultivated, society rather out-of-date, and where women
loved without refinement and men without pride.

I saw many officers and very handsome troops, reputed to
be more skilled than ours, which had degenerated, people would
say, since the famous days of men such as Condé, Turenne,
Luxembourg, Villars, and the crowd of heroes to whom the reign
of Louis XIV had given birth. It was said that they (our troops,
of course) had lost some of their former military brilliance.
I was not personally convinced of this point for two very good
reasons: first, because I could recall the battles won under
Louis XV and was not scared by the perpetual contention of
Rossbach, Rossbach, and always Rossbach, where I knew quite
well that a brave but none too skillful general had fallen under
Frederick the Great, who in himself was worth more than an
army; and secondly, because I knew that the French army—
where reigns a courage which perhaps can be equalled but never
surpassed, where amazing intelligence is found by the side of
genuine national impetuosity, where two corps as undeniably dis-

tinguished as the artillery and the engineers have reached the highest degree of perfection—because I knew, I repeat, that such an army contains all the elements for leading men to the greatest feats of war, which bring them victory.

Those learned tactics which the French troops were supposed to have lost, they have now found again . . . or is this another brand? It must be agreed it is well worth the old.

I walked through many gardens, visited many castles and parks, among them Laken and Belœil. The first was adorned by exquisite gardens. Belœil [2] was the delightful estate of a man remarkable in all the ways which bring celebrity, and lovable through those qualities and charms which cause one to forgive superiority: I mean the Prince de Ligne.

On my way back, I spent a month in Paris before joining my regiment at Metz, where I journeyed in so queer a fashion that I believe no one ever thought of it before: namely, in a hackney coach, this being as good a story as that of the Prince de Nassau, who used to give bills of exchange at every relay.

But what proved less cheerful was that on my arrival I was sent for ten days to prison by order of the Maréchal de Broglie, as many days as I had extended my leave while in Paris. I well deserved it, because my delay was due to a ridiculous wish to witness the first appearance of an actress who seemed very gifted, and was to act at the Comédie Française. She has not proved so good as she promised, but it is useless to give her name and wound her pride to no purpose. I know that she believes herself excellent, and I am sure she would do better if she could.

The Maréchal de Broglie is known to everyone, as are the battle of Bergen, his obstinacy, and his love of duty.

Another officer for whom great achievements were predicted was also in command in the Three Bishoprics. [3] This was the Comte de Caraman, then lieutenant-general, and often looked upon as future War Minister, a man who seemed marked for the highest military distinctions. Though he never had many great opportunities of bringing forth his gifts, which were reinforced by a constant and thoughtful study of military matters, both public opinion and that of the army were in the main favourable to him. He is one of these men whose careers were checked by the Revolution when he had but to stretch his hand to reach the highest distinction. He had had more difficulties to put up with than most, for he was not favoured by the Queen, and out of envy for his happiness and success, people reproached him for what he could not help, the fact of his not being of illustrious birth. He was a man of high and strict moral principles, and had married one of the most honourable women of France, who I hope would pass muster as to birth, since she was a Chimay, sister to the Prince of that name and to the Prince d'Hénin. She formed with her charming daughters a family of angels. M. de Caraman was enabled by his immense wealth to keep a large establishment. His house was a godsend in Metz for anyone who appreciated the charm of good company.

The Comte de Darmas, the one who became a knight of the Saint Esprit, also held a commission in this province. He was a staff officer who dealt fairly, honourably, and courteously with those who served under him. I met him again in Berlin in less fortunate times, always the same simple, upright, and resolute man even in days of adversity, proving thus that he could dispense with Fortune's favour.

The least ridiculous and the most amiable of the commissaires' wives (in fact she was not really ridiculous at all) was a Mme de Pons, who gave excellent receptions which she herself sufficed to adorn. She belonged to the best circles of Paris and had all their ways, and though she had not perfect beauty she had charm and parts, which for a long while attracted a man, the comte de Gand—to-day lost to France—who combined a good education with elegant accomplishments, gentle gaiety, and genuine courtesy. I hope that the grandees of Spain, his colleagues to-day, value him as much in Madrid and the kingdoms of Granada and Valencia as if he had been born among them, and show the respect due him. If these lines should come to his notice he will recognise in them an expression of my friendship, a poor memento of my feelings towards him which I have wholly preserved.

In this gallery of recollections I must not forget a man with whom I was little in contact and did not like, though this will make me the fairer to him: I mean the Vicomte de Ségur.[4] He was the son of a minister who was not popular in the army because he did not display as much good nature in these functions as he had shown striking valour on the battlefield. The Viscount himself was not much thought of in the Noailles regiment, where he was colonel second in command, but he knows as well as I that this proves nothing against him. He could make pretty songs, and others not so good, which he sang with less talent than he thought he possessed; but he had exquisite manners, when he was not sarcastic, and perfect elegance when he did not give in to what I should frankly call foppery had I loved him more.

On the whole, he was a very pleasant man and really worth more than one might expect, considering how he had been spoiled. He has written many books wherein he displays more elegance than art, more ease than talent, but which nevertheless assure him a place amongst those writers who are men of fashion and follow two careers at one time. There has come to my hands a volume of his poems written while in Paris, which I read in my journeys north; in it are to be found a few pieces of the good old days in excellent taste. I have also read his work "Sur les Femmes"; he is worthy to speak of them, he whom they have so well treated. It is fair that after having attracted them so much he should endeavour to make them loved and appreciated. This was erecting a monument of gratitude, and was work fitted to his bent, but the talent is uneven. . . . I look upon it as a book that needs to be done over again.

A few days before I left France he read me, at his house, fragments of an opera that seemed to me extremely pleasant; I hope he gave it to the public. . . . I remember also a conversation I had with him in the King's apartment in the Tuileries during which he displayed very sensible views and great loyalty, though he gave his reasons for his mistrust and disapproval of the decrees regarding emigration. I may here assure him, on my honour and as the result of experience, that I now side with him. And if it can give him pleasure I swear in all good faith—and without disparagement to the worth I set upon his writings—that this viewpoint was the mark of even better judgement than is displayed in the composition of his best works.

I shall not here mention a man whom I knew very well and who was then at Metz in command of a foreign regiment. I have never had a very favourable opinion of him, although he had gifts, but I was far from believing him capable of the heinous deeds which have left a stain upon his life and honour in all the records of the French Revolution. This man was even more the disgrace of one party than he was the wonder and abhorrence of another. As his house has given a king to one great nation and is allied to almost all the crowned heads of Europe, it is useless to renew his shame, which brings a blush even to his followers and to his relatives, who have disowned him.[5]

The time for returning to Paris was drawing near. I found in this thought an excitement similar to what one feels on seeing one's mistress after an absence. The nephew of the Swan of Cambrai,[6] a little less pure and virtuous than his uncle Fénelon, offered me a seat in his coach, and we came back together. My joy lasted only a short time, for on my arrival I learnt an event which caused me great consternation and which, instead of creating the scandal it should have occasioned, has never been made public.

A friend of my youth had a sister who should have been a great match; she was a few years older than we were, but I had often met her in former days. She was very beautiful, and still more attractive because of the accomplishments she had acquired. She had been sent to school at a convent at Arras to be near a rich aunt who had a country estate and proposed to leave her a huge fortune. A nobleman of the county of Artois, a very good-looking man who owes to this advantage the great wealth he has gained for himself in a northern court, had the sad privilege of climbing over the walls of this holy retreat, or perhaps simply of having the doors of the House of Our Lord opened to him. Whatever may have been the means he used, the result was that two girls of good families, and perhaps also a nun who never said anything about it, found themselves left with embarrassing and costly tokens of his love and daring.

The young lady we are here concerned with wrote to her aunt that, her health being out of order, she needed good country air. She was taken out of her convent; and hardly had she arrived at her aunt's estate, when she secured some powerful poison, I do not know how, and was found dead in a romantic way at the foot of a tree in the park. Her brother, a prey to dark despair, thirsted for vengeance, but his family, conforming to principles of honour and delicacy, forced him to silence his resentment; and threw a veil over what they called their disgrace.

His friendship raised this veil for me. I feared anything might result from his grief, and kept watch over him for six weeks as over a child in delirium. I have never seen deeper wretchedness; one man alone in this world ought to have felt even more wretched than he.

It was about this time that a book appeared which caused a prodigious commotion in the public, and more disturbance in many heads than would the most licentious pictures or the most

obscene works. This book has set its author at the crossroads
between blame and praise, contempt and esteem; between distinguished men of letters and those who make a fatal use of
their gift as writers; between the great delineators of vice and
the corruptors of every virtue. It is a book for which its author
has not feared to claim a moral purpose, though it is an outrage
to the morals of the whole nation; it is a book that every
woman admits having read, though it should have been condemned by all men as deserving to be burnt by the hand of the
public executioner; and yet, in its kind, it is worthy to rank with
classic works in the best libraries. I believe this clearly indicates "Les Liaisons Dangereuses."

I speak to-day of this work contrarily to what I then
thought, for I reproach myself with having passionately admired it, and above all with having lent it, when first published,
to two or three women who more readily concealed such reading
than they did the practices they learnt therein.

I longed to know M. de Laclos,[7] but this longing, like all
those which have no serious foundation, quickly vanished. It
was not until many years later that I met him, and even later
still before occasion arose to lead me to discuss with him his too
celebrated novel (which strictly speaking is not a novel at all),
and to learn from his lips what was fable or truth in this elegant and cynical production. To say everything at once, I shall
transport myself for a moment to a much later period than that
which I ought to follow in the natural course of this work.

In 1789, M. the Duc d'Orléans (from whom I had asked a
favour which only meant the reading of some document) had
fixed an early appointment with me at his little flat in the Palais
Royal. I arrived at half past nine in the morning, and already
found at his rooms Messieurs Heymann and Travanet, with a
third gentleman whom I did not know. Travanet told me that it
was M. de Laclos.

Who could have dreamed, knowing these three men and
their origins, of ever seeing them together? They were so
totally ill-assorted, and they were even more at odds with the
first Prince of the blood. However that may be, I hastened to
seek an opportunity for addressing a few words to M. de Laclos,
although I had by this time quite forgotten his "Liaisons Dangereuses," since I had my own. Our conversation was not long,
the Prince sent for me, and I only reappeared with him in the
midst of the company to find a great gathering of people and a

lively discussion concerning a new pamphlet by M. de Calonne. I thought no more of M. de Laclos, and I did not see him again for nearly two years, when I met him in England whither he accompanied M. the Duc d'Orléans on a strange mission. From the drawing-room of Mme de Coigny, M. de La Fayette had dispatched the Prince to London to explain that he was no longer wanted in Paris.

This is not the place to describe in detail the revolutionary activities of Laclos, or to be occupied with the degree of influence he exerted over a prince whom friends and enemies led to the scaffold by the same road—that is, by drawing him hither through the bait of a throne on which he would have been alarmed and astonished to be seated. Here, I wish only to speak of the author of "Les Liaisons Dangereuses." I attempted once or twice when in London to learn from him the whole mystery of his book, because I was convinced that such a book cannot come into a man's head without preliminary data. But he politely evaded my questions and gave me no satisfaction. At last boredom delivered him up to me, serving me better than his own pride or my curiosity could have done.

We were at the levee of the Prince of Wales who, conforming to his princely custom as one of the handsomest men of Europe, spent a long time at his toilet and was late in arriving. M. de Laclos had no very courtly manners but all the gloomy impatience of a philosopher or a conspirator, in spite of his apparent phlegm, and preferred to talk rather than pull out his watch and feel fidgety. Here is very nearly what he said to me:

"I was in barracks in the Island of Ré, bored by the training for a profession which was never to bring me great promotion or great consideration; after having written some elegies of dead people, who will never hear them, and some epistles in verse, most of which will never be published (luckily for the public and for me), I resolved to write a book which would be quite outside the ordinary trend, which would make a sensation *and echo over the world after I left it.*[8] One of my friends, who bears a name celebrated in the sciences,[9] had had several very notorious adventures which only lacked another stage. He was a man specially born for women, and for the wiles at which they are past mistresses. If he had been a man at court, he would have had the reputation of Lovelace, and would have been even more successful. He had taken me into his confidence; I laughed at his *pranks, and sometimes helped him with my advice.* I knew him to have a mistress who was quite equal to Mme de Merteuil, but it was at Grenoble that I saw the original of whom mine is only a feeble copy, a marquise de L. T. D. P. M.,[10] of whom the whole town used to tell stories worthy of the days of the most insatiable Roman empresses. I took notes, and firmly resolved to make use of them when time and place allowed. The story of Prévan had happened a long time before to M. de Rochech—a high officer in the mousquetaires; it brought him discredit, though to-day it would be laughed at. I had also put on record several little affairs of my youth which were rather spicy. I blended all these varied fragments together; I invented the rest, especially the character of Mme de Tourvel, which is not ordinary. I bestowed as much care on my style as I am capable of, and after some months devoted to finishing touches, I threw my book among the public. *I hardly know what has happened to it since, but they tell me it still lives."*

I forget what I replied to him, but what he said to me, I remember, and I have here repeated.

Since I have made this digression, why, before throwing myself eight or nine years back, should I not at once express in a few words my feelings about this production, considered simply with respect to its literary merits and the nature and danger of its pictures? My opinion on this subject, which I never heard discussed, will not rest on that of anyone else.

In the first place, there was very great art in presenting Mme de Merteuil as so corrupt, for in this way she contrasts better with the angelic candour of Mme de Tourvel, and even Valmont appears less wicked than she; the author is correct in this, since though women are better than we are, they proceed along the path of vice much quicker and much farther when once they have entered it.

On the other hand, it is a great defect to have given to each character a style of his own, which is not the same thing as to have impressed upon each a distinctive physiognomy. The result is that, by the side of a page written in the finest manner, we find a misplaced childishness, or inexcusable carelessness, which are not so much contrasts as blots. The portrait of Mme de Tourvel is adorable, and has caused the youth of both sexes to shed many tears. How many young girls would rather die like her than live like her odious rival! There indeed is a homage to virtue. How many young men have dreamed of such a mistress, have knelt before her image, have prostrated their imag-

ination before her shadow! There again is a tribute to real love.
But this, however, is the only part virtue has in this book. The
remainder is a shameful conception, offering pictures more rep-
rehensible than those of Aretino (which are hardly ever in bad
taste and often truthful), while in the main M. de Laclos's
pictures are exaggerations and caricatures, which those persons
who know no better have taken for a startling description of a
certain class. Under this aspect, the book is a wave of the revolutionary floods which have submerged the court; it is one of
the thousand flashes of that storm, though nobody has suspected it, and most readers will think the idea exaggerated and
perhaps ridiculous. This, the author has never owned to me,
but a sworn friend of the Revolution such as he, knew it only too
well, for in the midst of this conspiracy each man had beforehand fitted himself with a part at court, in town, in the provinces
or in the army. Even the death of Valmont has no moral significance, since in its kind it is worthy of severe condemnation;
the intervention of Father Anselme is a sneer at his calling; even
the servants will gather therein a training in vileness and an
incitement to corruption; and above all, the part played by this
innocent girl who behaves exactly as do the most scoundrelly
women, who makes her mother appear ridiculous, and sets such
bad example to all young girls, is the last stroke of the brush in
this picture drawn with a skill on all counts blamable.

The style, by dint of being so natural, is at times weak, but
nearly always elegant, graceful, and concise. All the different
parts of the plot fit into one another with an ease that conceals
labour. These vices, so monstrous if we give them thought, seem
quite simple as we read. The author carries us on, and we free
ourselves from this blending and participation with his mind
only when we have run the full course and discovered the goal.
In a word this work springs from a brain of the first rank, but
a corrupt heart and a spirit of evil. Under a new social order
the book has lost some of its interest; nevertheless it will live as
long as the language.

If any reader is surprised at this long diatribe and this new
analysis of an old production, it is because he does not feel
as I do; this work has not reacted upon him as on me. He has
not seen its effects in the same light, because either he is too
insensitive or myself too impressionable. He looks at "Les
Liaisons Dangereuses" as a novel which one closes in youth when
once it is read, while I contemplate it as one of those disastrous

meteors which appeared in a blazing sky at the end of the eighteenth century.

Let us go back to Paris, to the side of my grief-stricken friend, then spend a few weeks with him on his estate, afterwards leave him partly reconciled. For what does not time achieve in these matters? . . . From there, a short stay in the province of Maine on an estate which, as a minor, I cannot sell but where I arrange for some trees to be felled and find a buyer, for I sell them at a ridiculous price. Then once more coming back to this huge abyss, the capital, which swallows up everything, I soon squander this money, the symbol of a youth spent with even less discrimination . . . of this youth whose beautiful days vanish like a restless dream.

My family was dissatisfied with my forestry transaction. My father, whose hands were full enough with his own affairs, thought fit to meddle with mine on this occasion, but this made no difference, since I retained the net product of my pre-majority deed. He even wrote to the Prince de Poix, a very sensible letter, to ask him to upbraid me vigorously and force me to rejoin my regiment. This step met with no success; he sought consolation by buying from the Prince de Guémené the office of high bailiff in the dependency of Monsieur, the King's brother, and claimed the reversion for me without asking my consent. If I had had a say in the matter, I should have had him well reprimanded for this foolish deed, which cost him a fair amount of money, and concerning which the Comtesse de Tessé told him she could scarcely congratulate him on his acquisition, since one no longer heard of seneschals, except in Molière.[11] My father nevertheless gave costly entertainments in his province, and thus adding to what he had spent at the christening of my stepbrother, to whom Monsieur and Madame Elizabeth were god-parents, he burnt his last boats as regards his money affairs—already so muddled that they could not stand more confusion.

I had lost all taste for the great adventures of love, I sought lighter pleasures. I had become regularly acquainted with the Muses, so I wrote a good many poems which I buried in some periodical depositories, and, to do everything in due form, I went in for gaming, which before I had never liked. The Comte de Genlis gave me a start. He had a house on the Place Vendôme where men of good company, and others who were not so, resorted for play. Fortune, who always makes sport of newcomers, just as women respond to their first wooers by coquetry, trapped me by letting me win at the outset, but I soon paid for the deception hidden behind such favours. I must, in fairness to M. de Genlis, say that he was anxious on account of my youth, and made me some fine speeches on the baneful practices taking place in his house. He begged me to enjoy myself, to have supper, but to keep my money. The opportunity confronting me was, however, more powerful than his eloquence, even had it been like that he has since displayed in the Convention, where he proved to be no more convincing nor of better faith.

My visits at his house, and at that of a President de Champ —who received a similar set of men, and women of all stations, ages, and colours, was looked upon askance by my relatives and by other people of influence who wished me well. I almost entirely neglected these good people, and they made free to call me a good-for-nothing, an appellation no one should use at random, even in jest, when speaking of young men, for they at first resent the name, then end by making light of it and by giving it sanction through their indifference. But if in youth one comes near to deserving contempt when one shows contempt for public opinion, later on it may be permitted to take opinion for what it is worth, and to throw ridicule on these censors who are often more disreputable than the victims of their onslaught.

The winter was given to such activities in these houses, to some love-adventures, inglorious and short-lived, and, on a few occasions, to seeing good company wherein, in spite of myself, I would impolitely yawn, finding no pleasure with people who no longer found any in me.

The Comte de Genlis, who became afterwards the Marquis de Sillery, was not an agreeable man. He was looked upon by men of fashion as being cultured, though he was no more this than he was a statesman during the Revolution, so that, as is often the case, the reputation he had acquired was the reverse of the truth. He was, for instance, accused of lacking courage, which was distinctly an unfounded absurdity, since he had numerous wounds, had fought brilliantly in India, and had (in spite of silly talk about him) made a fine stand at Ushant as did his Prince, M. the Duc d'Orléans, of whose guards he was captain. He was brother to the Marquis de Genlis, a man looked upon as more ignorant than the Count, though I found him not only a thousand times more agreeable, but also much more cultured, for he possessed the foremost of all sciences—a knowledge of the world and men—as well as the most useful and practical of attainments—the secret of always pleasing. Among other surprising feats he had preserved exquisite manners, worthy of the most refined court, and could still use the language of distinguished women, though he had long since talked only that of courtesans, and he remained a model of good taste amidst the excesses of a disordered life that would have corrupted any man not essentially born for true Attic graciousness and polished elegance. His talk was unpretentious, but to listen to him was nearly always profitable, yet he could sometimes display an ignorance he would himself have laughed at, had it been pointed out to him. I cannot render the impression I have kept of him better than by saying that he seemed to know a great deal, but evidently not by mere book-learning.

The two brothers thought highly of each other, though few people tendered them the same regard; yet it was difficult for anyone to escape being charmed by the Marquis and it was impossible not to love him. If one had set him up in a pulpit of vice in opposition to the greatest preachers, he would have made virtue hateful. There exist numerous witticisms of his, some which I could quote, and others which I would not, though they are worthy of some ears. He had a pedestrian philosophy, which I know served him well during the Revolution. At fifty years of age he still made real conquests amongst ladies, and never took it ill that his own wife should become a conquest. His family has produced men of wit, dating from the Chancelier de Sillery, who was no fool in his day.

The member of the family who, in that way, gave it a distinction which will survive the name, is Mme de Genlis,[12] known for her royal pupils, her books and their success, though like her husband (Genlis-Sillery) she ceased writing during the Revolution. I often dined at their home while the first Assembly sat at Versailles; he would sometimes urge me to outlive everyone in fame, and then would read me memoirs (he had an unfortunate facility in making notes on everything) of which I do not remember a word. This was his gentle way to send me off to sleep, the last word in politeness . . . a most touching attention towards a guest. I could to-day no doubt pay him back with interest, but he sleeps an unbroken sleep which no idle talk of this world can interrupt.

He was one of the advisers of that unfortunate Prince who was more a vile man than an atrocious monster; but posterity will have the right to muddle the two things. Besides, M. de

Sillery did little harm to his master, who placed slight trust in him, and made use of him at the end only as one plays on an old and wretched instrument through sheer habit. M. de Sillery died on the scaffold, bowing low to the rabble, a simple task for a courtier, and going the full game with his confessor, which is far more out of the way for an ungodly man.

I have said that I was losing my money; I lost it so well that by the end of the winter I had done as bad business as M. Necker, newly appointed chancellor of the exchequer, was preparing for the monarchy.

One evening I went on to the home of this President de Champ—already mentioned, carrying there my boredom and thirty louis. Five of them still remained in my possession when the Marquise de Soudeille, my host's niece, asked me to take her in to supper. I offered her my arm with the noble indifference of a gambler who, though weary of the present, is still polite by habit to beauty of the past, a fitting instance with this lady since she had hurried to lose her youth. A certain M. de Poincot, who had been installed at Versailles as croupier at the Queen's gaming-table, noticed my prolonged bad luck and my young face. "Go in to supper," he said to me, "and give me your five louis."

I did not hesitate; I was not even sure, so much was I used to ill luck, that I had not lost them before I handed them to him. I returned to the drawing-room about an hour later and saw in front of him a pile of gold to which I never thought I had the least right. I believed he had soon disposed of my offering and begun to win on his own. He went on staking with prodigious coolness, never saying a word to me or looking in my direction.

Some time later, "Don't you think," he said, turning towards me, "that it would be madness for you to claim the remainder of this bank? *I advise you to withdraw.*"

"Sir!"

"You are winning much."

"Is this money—"

"Yours. *I* have not played all the evening."

"You are joking."

"Well, at any rate it is not a bad joke. . . . Don't have any qualms, for I give you my word this money is yours."

I threw it into my hat; there were more than twelve hundred louis. Was he not a most estimable man? And what a charming way to make much out of little!

The name of M. Necker, newly appointed minister, has come at the tip of my pen; I bring it there again no longer to escape me.

He had at first only been working under M. Taboureau, whom he soon reduced to a dislike of the post and to a longing to leave. Ambitious men know how to reach good positions; they know more: they have the knack of getting others out of them. Everyone remembers M. Necker's beginnings, his fortune and the course he made us run. It is not beside the point to remark here that it is perhaps the first time that a gift for writing, combined with a good head for figures, has led a man to the post of minister and to honours. He united the skill of a specious financier to that of a solemn and eloquent writer; the special quality of his writings is a glow of virtue that seems to spring from the heart, and would be more striking still if pride was not nearly always close at hand to tarnish it.

The nation was already becoming restless when he brought into the ministry the germs of discord, the elements of faction, the ferments of strife, which were to seethe under his hands and to crowd between his virtue and his ambition, between his semi-talent as administrator and his vices, between the inclinations of his heart and the designs of his pride.

The French people were weary of a happiness that bored them because it was peaceful, and that had no value in their eyes because it lacked brilliance. Discontented men turned towards the future, for they mistook tranquillity for bondage; being idle, they discussed everything; they were not unhappy, but they felt that life held no glamour, and the nation longed to come to its own again. Unbelievable as it may sound, under a government so peaceful and kindly everyone was agitated in advance, as if there really existed a struggle between serfdom and tyranny.

This is what I witnessed.

The hand that was chosen to hold one of the reins of the state was not calculated to steady the course of this runaway chariot. It was not difficult to guess that a man who had risen from the ranks of subordinates, who was used to the minute details of a narrow philosophy, a calculator, a wit, would do either a great deal of good or a great deal of harm—or rather could do only the latter. It was easy to realise that a republican would have but a clumsy and tepid liking for the monarchy; that a Protestant would feel poor zeal towards a Catholic state;

that a bourgeois from Geneva would not side with the French nobility; that being odious in the eyes of the Queen and the court (except his own party), he would try to become a sort of King, and that if any attempts were made to exclude him from the council-board he would become a council in himself.

We know the last pages of his story; we have seen the state melt away through his experiments, and a whole kingdom vanish under his innovating hands. Such was his baneful work, such is his destiny, such is the muddle he created. As a crowning achievement he made Mme de Staël.[13]

I know that he felt remorse. . . . I know that his death was not hastened thereby, but I have been told that his repentance was deep and sincere, and that it followed him into the mausoleum he had erected for himself and his helpmate in a life of unconquerable pride. It seems to me almost evident from this that if he becomes minister in another world he will be wiser, and there is reason to hope he will not there marry; but this does not absolve his memory from blame in this world.

This same year stands out in my recollections on account of a queer adventure with the Prince de Poix,[14] then my colonel, who throughout his relations with me has displayed a constant wavering between a brotherly attachment and a coolness which, like the sea, were well ordered in their rhythm; yet it is comforting to me to have definite proofs that for a long while now friendship has remained ashore.

But this friend has often made things as difficult for me as would a dangerous enemy; we must, however, remember the precept in the Bible which enjoins us to forgive offences, and even more must we forget the inconsistencies due to frivolity and a hot temper, which, however, left no traces in an excellent heart. One must joyfully sacrifice to twenty long years of friendship the memory of a few indiscretions, even though they might have had consequences. To have shown repentance for these, to have made amends, this is as good as not having committed them.

After this short exordium, I come back to the point where I left my narrative.

I was at the Bal de l'Opéra, offering my arm to a pretty masked girl whom I had taken to supper. . . . I was not to leave her until long after the ball, at least such was the promise she had given, though it was not fulfilled, for nothing frightens Love and the Graces more than Mars in anger. M. de Poix

caught sight of me and pounced on me in loud anger to scold
me at the top of his voice for not having joined my regiment,
to reproach me with some debts (for which also the King knew
how to blame me), to declare that it was more fitting to train
horses at the regiment than to boast embroidered clothes, etc.
All this happened in a moment, and it seemed to me that the
roof of the Opéra had fallen upon my head. Even the most
kindly and placid of readers will feel that I was bound to think
this blowing-up out of place; so I replied with insubordination,
as if I had been a Marshal of France who had won victories.
M. de Poix, who was then accustomed to see things giving way
to him—he has since met with more resistance—lost his temper;
he called in a police sergeant from the Gardes Françaises,
Mazoger by name, an old knight of Saint Louis, an honest
fellow whom we all loved. "You know me," he said. "I am the
Prince de Poix, governor of Versailles and captain of the
Guards; here is the Comte de Tilly, officer in my regiment, whom
I am within my right to send away from Paris—as a matter of
fact his parents want me to. Arrest him." I was beside myself;
had any man then attempted to carry out this order he would
have been badly received; but I was spared this trouble. "My
lord," said Mazoger, "I have indeed the honour of knowing
you, but I cannot possibly obey you on this occasion. With due
respect to you, I receive orders here only from my proper chief,
my lord marshal Duc de Biron."

At this I laughed up my sleeve and lost myself in the crowd
so as not to prolong this unheard-of scene; but my pretty partner
had taken fright, the screech of the hawk had caused the dove
to fly, and I was not able to catch her in my net again. Full of
rage, I asked Monville to allow me to spend the night at his
rooms; he came home two hours later and tried in vain to pacify
me. At five in the morning, I hired a hackney-coach and hurried
to the Rue de Varennes to ask a friend to accompany me to the
Hôtel de Noailles and act as my second; but his wife, about to
give birth to a child, was far gone in labour. He advised me
to call on another officer of our regiment who was in Paris, a
Baron de Froman, a great gambler and sorry jester, who at once
consented. I have learnt since that the Duchess de Duras, hearing
a carriage stop at the front door and a loud knock at such an
early hour, had looked out of her window, and seeing, at such
an hour, two gentlemen crossing the courtyard, one of them
wearing an embroidered coat, a feather in his hat, and a sword

under his arm, had believed that paladins had come to claim
some fair lady her brother had carried off.

We arrived at M. de Poix's, who had only then gone to
bed, and found his servants quite opposed to waking him after
the fatigues of the ball. We assured them he could not yet be
asleep; we were shown into his bedroom.

I tendered him my resignation and told him, without more
ado, that I reckoned upon his giving me the satisfaction to which
I was entitled.

No one has ever doubted his courage; he has proved, during
the sittings of the Constituent Assembly,[15] that he was as brave
as both his father and brother, whose valour was so striking;
but it was not at this moment a matter of courage, but of pacify-
ing a hot-headed young man and the agitation of a scatterbrain.
He burst out laughing, and very kindly invited me to sit down,
while he sharply reprimanded M. de Froman and advised him
to withdraw. When we were alone, he remonstrated with me as
would a father, and brought me partly to agree, quite civilly,
that he was not in the wrong; he spoke of the interest he felt in
me, kissed me, and begged me to let him go to sleep. I left his
house convinced he was perfectly right; but friends, women, and
my afterthoughts, made me change my mind. I then resolved
never to join his regiment. I told him of this, and having some
days later gone to Versailles, I had the honour of paying my
court to the Queen and made bold to entreat her to help me in
obtaining a captain's commission in the dragoons.

I was about to explain my difficulties with the Prince de Poix,
when she stopped me, saying that she was willing once more to
do as I asked, but that she was better informed than I thought,
that my behaviour was bad, that M. de Poix had spoken of me
in a very unfavourable way, and that she advised me to alter
if I did not wish to lose her favour. She was kind enough to
allow me to state my own defence, and before I took my leave
she seemed almost convinced by my justification. However,
M. de Poix has sometimes regretted, so I hope, this too hasty
and unjust action; such regret he several times afterwards expressed to me, and to-day, since the importance of these matters
has vanished and power has been rent asunder, to-day, as I
write this story as if ten centuries had made the facts antiquated,
I recall the injustice only to forget it, his friendship to thank
him for it, and his regrets as being to the credit of both of us.

I will end this chapter with an atrocious story which, though it is rather foreign to my subject, belongs to the period and to the history of mankind in all ages and countries as well. It is one of those deeds which point to the shamelessness of man and the frightful dominance of passions, which make one feel contempt for our scanty virtues, and horror for the vices, the crimes, and the dispositions of the human heart, often more abject, more ferocious, than the blind instinct of lions and tigers in the desert.

There was then in Paris an Irish peer, a warm admirer of Shakespeare, Lord Mountnorris,[16] who has since committed suicide most dramatically for having been called a *fortune-hunter* by some English newspaper. This was seeking death after the manner of his favourite author, by cheaply mixing tragedy and comedy, and because of a mere appellation concluding his own drama in a terrible and ridiculous fashion. It was quite natural that, not being rich, he should try to make a marriage through his title and on account of the deserts he imagined he had. He believed himself a great orator and had for a long time abused the patience of the Irish Parliament, where they had at first yawned at his speeches and long since stopped listening to them.

One day, as he was delivering a long speech on the home policy of this kingdom, a matter which the other honourable members thought they knew better than he, everybody left the House. He always spoke with his eyes shut while his restless eloquence carried him beyond himself, so he noticed nothing. He thus held forth at his ease, and after two hours of unchallenged argument he summed up his speech by offering thanks to the House for their flattering attention in listening to him, attention which he was quite aware they had not always granted him (to the great detriment of the state) in those debates concerning matters of the highest importance which his patriotic ardour had led him to approach.

Having thus spoken, he closed his mouth, opened his eyes, and sat down. He then observed that there was only one listener in the hall—the man sweeping the floor. He was fond of relating stories, yet never told this one.

But to come back to mine, from which this anecdote about Lord Mountnorris has carried me so many miles away.

I was preparing for my first journey to England and seeing as many English people as I could. I then fancied that they liked us well when they were not fighting against us, and I bore a grudge to my parents and teachers who had advised me to hate them. So I one day found myself in the company of this pleasant Irish peer who, as soon as I entered his rooms, tackled me on Corneille and Shakespeare. After this dramatic exchange of thrusts, he invited me to dine at a new restaurant, just opened in the Rue du Mail, where there would be many foreigners, especially a chosen number of inhabitants of the Three Kingdoms. I accepted, and we went. Soon after our arrival, a general protest arose against a M. de C——, a high officer in the Irish brigade, on account of a guest he had brought whom everyone viewed with horror. This guest made such an impression on me, as soon as I heard his story, that I uttered an involuntary exclamation which drew the attention of the whole company.

This monster, with the face of a very handsome man, had remarried at the age of forty a charming woman who was not yet eighteen. He had a most promising son who unfortunately conceived for his stepmother a fatal passion which she shared. It was not the first time that a son has been preferred to his father by a sex with whom youth is the first of charms, whatever may be said by some sentimental women. Certainly it would be better to love only what one ought to love. But who amongst us limits himself to duty? For whom has duty more attraction than its opposite—than that which is forbidden to us? *"Pauci quos ejus amavit Jupiter."*

But let us leave morals and continue. This young man and his stepmother endeavoured to subdue that dangerous attraction which mastered them; the son even went so far as to beg his father to allow him to travel. The permission was refused. The result which might be expected followed: they succumbed, were happy—and guilty. The father, learning the truth (for what is not seen by jealousy, which is able to see even what does not exist?), concealed his resentment in order to revenge himself elaborately. The unfortunate young man foresaw his fate; he set out for a town near his parent's estate. The outraged husband intercepted a letter, forced the unfaithful wife to confess, compelled her by the promise of a generous pardon to call his son back, and himself pretended an absence which he failed to carry out. The lover fell into the trap, where his heart led his judgement; he flew to death on the wings of love. The barbarous father entered the room which ought to have witnessed transports of tenderness, reproached them with their crime and their treachery, and in spite of the weak efforts of the distracted woman blew out his son's brains. Then, dragging by the hair his griefstricken wife, who was a few months pregnant, he trampled her beneath his feet until he believed he had completed a cannibal's vengeance on her and on the seed she bore in her womb; nothing survived his barbarity. The monster wandered through Europe in order to escape the laws of his country and of outraged humanity, but he could not escape from himself. His branded forehead bore that sign of reprobation which the first-born of the first man carried, imprinted on a face which no longer dared to gaze at heaven after Abel's murder. His heart was a prey to those torments which Cain has bequeathed to the most abandoned of his posterity.

I have no word to express the terror inspired by this tiger, who was walking and dressing and eating like any other man.

What then is this disordered passion, love, which softens the heart for a moment and often hardens it for the rest of life, concentrating the mind on a single object, and isolating it from all others? What is this solitary passion which kills other attachments and severs itself at its height from all other affections? This passion which gives birth to a daughter more relentless than itself—jealousy! Jealousy, this Fury eager to tear her own breast, impatient of peace and of happiness, seeking only excuses for her own torture, living on suspicion, fed only by fears, wearing herself out to learn what she burns not to know, and wishing to know that which she has so much interest to ignore. Frightful Fury! Eldest daughter of Hell! giving to a father the hideous courage to staunch the thirst of thy cruelties, to assuage the frenzy of his egoism, in the blood and on the corpse of his child! What man has ever been spared by thee even from tormenting the woman he idolises?

My eyes never rested again on this cowardly murderer, but I saw him for a long time. . . . He is there! . . . I see him still.

A few days afterwards, I set out for England, carrying my nineteen years and five hundred louis.[17]

CHAPTER XV

Tros Tyriusque mihi nullo discrimine agetur.—VIRGIL.

I REACHED Calais congratulating myself on the speed with which I had made the journey, after having worried the postillions as if I had been a plenipotentiary on a high mission, who has to account for every minute.

I put up with the Sieur Dessain,[1] who kept a better house than any of that kind in Europe. I asked for his best rooms: he told me that he had no others; for the best supper: he assured me that a bad one had never been served at his house. I informed him in a haughty voice that money was nothing, and that it is ignoble to take it into consideration; a few days afterwards he made me see that he was quite able to appreciate that point. I stayed there eight days and behaved as foolishly as if I had seen a stream of Pactolus flow in front of the windows, and the Sieur Dessain dealt with me as one accustomed to deal with scatterbrains and to profit by them.

An English lady, since known in Paris for her beauty, was also staying in the house. I did not fail to put myself on the right footing with her, and to pay her attentions; I was even not too seriously repelled. But as she had the whim, through a fit of insular eccentricity, to make me go up to her room by a ladder (literally), though she was lodged only a hundred feet away, I did not care to break my neck for the sake of a maid with whom she pretended she had to be cautious. Since then, many men have very peacefully reached her by the staircase.

My companions on the crossing were a man of much wit and culture of whom I preserve such a pleasant memory that I reproach myself for not having seen him more often since; a pretty young lady suffering from seasickness, whom I looked at very little, because I was suffering even more than she was; and I do not know what freak in the style of M. Desmazures,[2] who wearied me even more than did the crossing.

I was struck by the ugliness of the town of Dover, though it is compensated for by the beauty of the women of the people, especially (though it is low taste to say so) of the servant girls,

226

who in the county of Kent constitute a class all the more worthy
of esteem since it is generally from it that recruits reach London
for the cloisters of Venus, whence women often pass to the
temple of Fortune, the English being the people who most
readily marry their mistresses, asking the smallest account of
their past, and very little of their present. The philosophical
mind is an unprejudiced mind.

The beautiful art of cookery is highly honoured amongst
the English. They talk much on the subject, yet know little about
it; but as their food is wholesome and plain, one quickly becomes
used to it and feels all the better for it. They are sure that they
alone know how to dine, and that they are more difficult to
please in this matter than any other people, though I do not
know in what other country one fares as badly. With the exception of a few individuals of good standing who have travelled,
the English are convinced that French food is poor and scanty,
while really their dinner, in all corresponding social classes,
would in France appear detestable and insufficient.

There is not, on the whole, in spite of a great many qualities, another nation that is so superstitious in its customs, or
preserves more carefully a crowd of prejudices, of which some
are essential to a people drawing its strength from its national
spirit, but most are absurd and even ridiculous. It is a stable of
Augeas that ought to be cleaned; such prejudices should be
shaken off with more eagerness than is employed in perpetuating
them.

I do not wish either to satirise or to flatter the English; I
will say about them what I have observed, and what I have
learnt through living at different times more than five years
amongst them, from my first youth to my mature age. If I am
not severe enough for some tastes, or sufficiently laudatory for
others, that is because I have undertaken to write nothing but
the truth, and I have promised no man to nurse his whims, his
prejudices, his partialities, or his hatreds.

I reached London without having been bored for a moment,
for nowhere does one travel with more ease. One never has to
wait, or to exhaust oneself in abusing the postillions; and the
beauty of the countryside and its peaceful fertility make you
fancy that you are travelling in a garden in which a novel tint
of green deserves a new name, and beneath a sky refreshed by
sea mists enriching a land where the sun is mourned for three-
quarters of the year.

London is one of the finest towns of Europe if one considers the extent of its streets, its public squares, and the immense ground it covers. Its footpaths bring comforting thoughts to philosophical minds; they are evidence that consideration is taken of the public and that common mortals count there for something. But it is only a second-rate town if one looks for the palaces, the notable buildings, and the monuments which ought to adorn the capital of a proud people that likes to be thought, and is believed to be, so rich. I beg our neighbours' forgiveness, but London, which in fact is only a monstrous and ungainly protuberance at the summit of their empire, is not an agreeable town where the art of life is understood—I do not say as in Paris, for there is no comparison—even as well as in many large towns of Europe. London is no place in which to live.

Not that it is to be believed that the English are as unsociable as most foreigners reproach them with being. It is as easy there as elsewhere to live in good company if one is such oneself; and if there are people in England who bear out the accusation that the English are considerate on the Continent but disdainful in their island, this is because there exist everywhere persons who are unpretentious away from their own fireside, but who resume their native insolence on returning to it. This is by no means, however, a general reproach to be made against the English nation. Intimate relations are not formed readily simply because an undemonstrative and sensible people, who keep their distance even with fellow countrymen, as befits their temperament, cannot bridge that distance in two days with someone whom they have never seen before.

It is in Paris that it is difficult for foreigners to enter really distinguished houses. I except the mansions of princes expected to receive all comers who are entitled to bore them because of an important name, and certain houses like those of Mme de La Vallière, the Maréchal de Biron, and perhaps M. de Soubise, which were in a way opened to all travellers arriving unexpectedly, without knowing where to go in spite of their station.

The King's ambassador in London was at that time M. d'Adhémar, one of those men whose good fortune is a reproach to chance and an encouragement for intriguing mediocrity. He had originally retired, on account of a wound, to a small fortress town where, being a subordinate officer, he seemed to have little prospects and lived on his small pay. But M. de Montfalcon (for that is the name he then bore) suddenly became a man at court and what is popularly called a lord—this after the age of thirty and without having been prepared for it either by his situation or his expectations. While at a health resort, he had become intimate with a court lady who advised him to come to Paris, so as to entertain her with his love and to bore the War Minister with his claims—for he had sketched out I do not know what wonderful scheme of military tactics. He could sing rather well the ditties of Collé and other song writers, and he circulated some poor songs he had himself composed. Deficient as a lover as he was in business, he used flattery with women to replace the chief means of seduction, which he lacked.

It was his military good fortune to obtain from the Duc d'Orléans, to whom he had been recommended by his patroness, the Chartres regiment of infantry, where proper discipline needed to be restored. Truth obliges me to say that he made of it a very smart and well-drilled regiment. He was thoroughly hated there, because he not only displayed the tyranny of a man who reaches command late and from afar, but also the vanity of an unkind disposition and the pettiness of an evil mind.

As he claimed that he was of the house of Grignan, and no one troubled to dispute the claim since the family was extinct, he took the name of Comte d'Adhémar, and found himself fitted for all possibilities, even for marrying Mme de Valbelle, the widow of a man[3] who had had an amiable celebrity. She held an office at court and was badly rewarded for this whim of the altar.

It is by no means proved that M. d'Adhémar was not all that he claimed to be. The man who most contributed to his good fortune, and one entirely incapable of supporting a good action by a lie, the Comte de Vaudreuil, has positively assured me that public opinion was unjust regarding Adhémar's birth. It was worth much more than his person, and the genealogist Chérin had no doubts about it.

However that may be, everything opened to him at once. Then a brigadier-general, he embarked on a diplomatic career, and was appointed the King's minister in Brussels. A little later, the household of that unfortunate saint, Mme. Elizabeth, being established, we find him there in a high post. The last stage was ambassador in England. He would have refused it, if he had dared, simply from his dread of the sea. The climate, the sooty atmosphere, ruined his frail health during his embassy; and rage at not having been made a knight of the Saint-Esprit as quickly as he expected made of him a sort of revolutionary. Towards the end of his life he joined the National Guard and died at his country estate a few leagues from Paris, discontented with the court, which ought to have been much more discontented with itself for having made of him what it had.

Such was the man by whom the virtuous Louis XVI was represented in England when I arrived there. He maintained a fairly good house, but more in the style of a rich private citizen than in keeping with the high state held by his predecessors. The English made fun of him, and the French, accustomed by old tradition to the splendour and noble expenditure of their ambassadors in foreign courts, were astonished and grieved to see this position so badly filled. Their estimation of the public man was not much improved by their way of viewing the private man, who was constantly the victim of their sarcasms, and the injustice of these outbursts came near to absolving him in the impartial eye of reason.

At that time, one was almost as fortunate to be French in a foreign country as it has since become embarrassing to have only that recommendation, especially if one combines with this the ill luck of having been a man of standing in one's own country, and of having belonged to the old order of things, which, even in its ruins and ashes, arouses envy and jealousy.

At that time, however, there was not the danger which later arose of being deceived by adventurers. Only those who were introduced by their ambassador could find entrance at court and reach high honour. At a later date, foreign countries swarmed with French people of a class capable of utilising the misfortunes of their own land to spread abroad lies and calumnies: people who, for their own benefit, gave out that they were victims of a revolution which in reality could not have touched them since they had nothing to lose; people who constantly talked of things they had never seen, and of high positions they had never occupied but knew only by hearsay, and which often indeed had never existed; people who called themselves the heads of the nation, though they were really its other extremities, and made our credulous neighbours believe that they had been driven out of their great estates for their fidelity to the house of Bourbon.

I could name many examples, but out of pity shall spare them. I shall content myself with a few general indications. Thus I have met a colonel of the regiment of Berry Dragoons (which never existed), and a superintendent of the house of Mme Elizabeth (who never had one). They had no shame in letting themselves be called "monsieur le colonel" and "madame la surintendante." An emigrant who condescended to supply me with shoes that pinched gave me his word of honour this was impossible as he had been a brigadier-general (he was not yet thirty). I know a woman who gave out that she was lady-companion to the Comtesse d'Artois, and had really been a milliner all her life in a Flemish town. A great German princess invited to her table, for over a year, a self-styled former colonel de la gendarmerie!

The Comte de la For—— recognised a former valet of his playing the fine gentleman at a small German court. He took him aside to bring him to reason, but without wishing to betray him. The former valet had acquired some little credit at the court; he denied his valetship, threatened to use his influence to have the Count expelled, and very nearly carried out his threat. In northern countries I have seldom met a French teacher or village vicar, a pedagogue or priest of any sort, who had not in France been near to becoming a bishop, or been the nephew of a bishop, or at all events belonged to a highly distin-guished family. I have never spoken to a French governess who had not been a girl from one of the best families.

Foreigners were mostly delighted to enter into relationship with such noble ladies and gentlemen, to receive them into their houses, invite them to their table, and entrust to them their children. They were enraptured with their manners and ways of speech; it flattered them to think they had the nobility of France in their servants-halls and kitchens. These bourgeois gentils-hommes never failed to have their mouths full of it and easily out-talked the real émigrés; a Montmorency with weak lungs would have cut but a pitiful figure beside them.

This is what I call a coalition of foreign lands with the French Revolution at home. It helped to pour contempt over the old régime, to degrade the unhappy émigrés by piling up favours on rascals and cheats, to tread further underfoot a nobility already driven out—in a word, to introduce twenty revolutions in place of one.

To return to M. d'Adhémar, I found at his house the only Frenchmen of note who were then in London; the Chevalier and the Comte Alphonse de Durfort, the old Baron de Wurmser, and M. de Bouillé,[4] whom I had then never seen. He took us to court where the King, with the noble simplicity and the extreme goodness that marked him, treated us all equally well. He showed particular attention to M. de Bouillé, precisely because he had displayed against England his brilliant gifts and valour, for superior merit arouses admiration even amongst those enemies who are the least inclined to recognize it. And M. de Bouillé was then received in all English homes with an enthusiasm and esteem all the more flattering since they were spontaneous.

In fact his conduct at Dominica, Saint-Eustace, and Saint Christopher, had not only been perfect in the military sense, for he had crowned his victories by a generosity of which there are few examples and few imitators. He might have tried to build himself a fortune, but he sought only fame, and found it. The city of London gave him a banquet; they offered him a sword—a gift more worthy of him than the wealth he had disdained. He had been fortunate all his life, and his star has only paled under the unique and solemn circumstances in which the destiny of France triumphed over him.

The English court was simple and dignified, larger than at Versailles because it was easier to be admitted to it. The King and the Queen displayed remarkable kindness and even courtesy; the women in general were fairly beautiful, though some uglier than anywhere else. Two things must be owned: one is that there are perhaps more beautiful women in England than elsewhere (Nature having been at great expense to make them, though she has often refused them charm, which is here imperfectly replaced by outward ingenuousness); and the other that when an Englishwoman sets out to be ugly she goes beyond anything—as if to cheer other women. The men dress in a fairly expensive way, although generally an embroidered coat and a sword seem more to embarrass than to adorn them. The Englishmen look best in morning dress. It is in this attire that we view them as masters of fashion in Europe.

Saint James's Palace is assuredly the most wretched hut ever inhabited by a great king, though it is true that the rooms inside are harmonious with the style of building. I would say almost the same of Windsor, if it were not for its picturesque site, its forest, and the great memories it recalls. What can one say of that fool of a Smollett, who, after having travelled through France, was not struck by that crowd of palaces and royal mansions, gardens and parks, their splendour and their pomp, and who on returning to England stated that the palaces of the French kings, beginning with Versailles, were pigeon-houses compared to those of the kings of Great Britain? It is true that this poor hypochondriac saw nothing in Rome itself worthy to fix his splenetic and jaundiced eye, and that the queen of basilicas, the church of Saint Peter, found no grace before him. He even persuaded himself that Michelangelo must yield to Wren.

There is an English peer who has no doubt that the French people live only on frogs; and often in the streets of London, at the sight of a foreigner, one hears the expression, "This heathen French dog." The English ought to decide that it is time to throw aside these ignorant notions, which make them in certain respects a backward people. But this animosity, hatred, and prejudice, it may be argued, are more necessary in that island than on the Continent. That is as much as to say one must throw oneself in the fire in order to get warm. Excess is in all things ridiculous. In my opinion, nothing shows so cate-gorically the unquestionable superiority of the French nation as this striking injustice of our neighbours, whom in our own noble and impolitic pride we commend on all occasions, even in those matters in which they are least deserving.

Our books bear witness to the justice we render them; they show our indulgence even more than our equity; our theatres have echoed with their praises; we have left nothing undone to spread abroad English history and literature, the progress of this nation in science and art. It might be said that we have under-taken to interpret their fame to Europe, while they only seek to deny us everything, to question what even the grossest bad faith could not question without betraying itself. They never present a French character on their stage except to degrade it and expose it to the laughter and the contempt of a coarse and ignorant populace. When there is any occasion of rendering justice to the bravery (I do not say to the tactics) of the English troops, we have done it with an honesty which belongs to that noble and generous frankness of the French nation, which is never jealous. As for them, they are jealous of everything, refuse everything and deny everything. I can never forget how, on the stage at Sadlers Wells, an Englishman brought a dozen Frenchmen to their knees, and six Englishmen broke through whole columns of Frenchmen and took them prisoners. They were the giants, these were the pygmies. My neighbours, well knowing that I belonged to the pygmies, listened and laughed with joy and content. I, for my part, liked saying to them in a cold-blooded way: "Yes, gentlemen, and such has been the case in Flanders."

But to return to my first stay in England: I certainly cannot be silent concerning a woman so distinguished that she was at that time the queen of London. Beauty, fortune, birth, rank, and the esteem of everyone, disposition of mind and of character, bearing—everything worked together to assure to her in society a kind of supremacy that no one disputed. She was the Duchess of Devonshire. I had been only two days in London when I dined with her at M. d'Adhémar's; I own that nothing has struck me more than her presence, the dignity of her bearing, which was full of grace, her way of entering a room, and that surplus of beauty which seemed in some way to encompass her. She kept us waiting till nearly seven; if she had arrived earlier, she would still have produced a sufficient stir. But I knew her little feminine artifice, and forgave it on seeing her. From the first moment my heart was her accomplice and imposed silence on my stomach.

I have said that it is not in London that one ought to live, and that fine buildings and beautiful houses are scarce there; but one cannot overpraise the country, the kind of life which the people of standing live there, and the genially hospitable luxury which they display. The traveller is never tired of visiting and admiring one beautiful country-seat after another, especially the parks and gardens, which are unique in a manner unknown or badly copied in the rest of Europe.

One can compare France and England only by opposing them, alike in private manners and external forms, in ideas and in words. I will attempt to set out these antitheses.

In France, before the Revolution, dwellings were sumptuous with a certain lordly luxury, and offered more commodities for daily life than were found in England, more idle servants in the halls, more mirrors, bronzes, furniture, gilt. In England reigned an opulent simplicity, a country life nearer to nature, houses with more rooms on the ground-floors than ours, and these meant to be shown, but upstairs a few incomplete, wretched bedrooms, which must be hidden (though all the time one heard the word *comfort*); they boasted more men in the stables, more daintiness in the furniture, which is simpler and scarcer, and sometimes more pictures.

In some English country-seats, there is drinking, racing, and hunting; one goes to the country in order to forget the town. In France one found exquisite fare, music, walks, solitude, reading, theatricals, rehearsals, and wit in the drawing-room; all this filled up the time and made it fly. . . . One made love when one could; in a word one lived as in Paris.

English manners are simple, natural, and sometimes a little lacking in refinement; French manners were more polite, more elaborate, more elegant, sometimes perhaps approaching affectation, yet the morals of both societies were much the same.

The English eat like people who make a business of it, and at such leisure that one might think they have no other. Their table, simple and substantial, becomes animated only after those who ought to be its ornament have retired, and when wine has produced that noisy effusiveness which is regarded as an aspect of frankness and as the fine side of the national character.

Meal time was for the French a necessary relaxation, but over which always presided urbanity, elegance, and a decent conversation, in turn solid and gracious. We lived like people for whom drunkenness, far from being respectable, was unforgivably ridiculous, for whom women embellished every assembly and every moment, and for whom that ugly word *eat* (though we understand it better than other nations) was only a word which indicated a need. Up to the age of fifty the table was but the adorned path leading to tenderer and more essential pursuits.

In England, women, being neglected, make love only when their men can spare time for it. In France women were chiefly occupied with repelling advances or anticipating them. Englishwomen yield to the voice of Nature, French women engaged in a combat where they feigned to be conquered by skill. Relationships of this kind in England are either of very long duration, or else merely passing affairs, because there are so many obstacles and so few occasions. In France women surrendered with some difficulty in order that they might not be abandoned on the following day; even coquetry was foreseeing enough never to be in a hurry. But the occasions were so many, owing both to the spirit of gallantry and the manner of life, that one seldom had the inclination to continue the same union for ever. The English seek, in love, but a distraction; for the French it gives an aim to life.

In England the mental outlook is just, not very extensive, and offers an element of geometrical dryness; the language is concise, devoid of ornament and that aptitude for superfluity so necessary to conversation. Reason is thus less easily ensnared. In France, while judgement is just as sound in serious matters, the need is felt of showing more wit in what is spontaneous, more profusion and fluency in conversation, more adornment and amiability in speech; language is enriched by this luxury which it welcomes. More polished through wit and graciousness society repels everything that is not thus stamped, and from these swift and far-reaching explorations the mind is sometimes obliged reluctantly to recoil on itself. In the pulpit the English make God descend to the simplicity of human speech; the French try to raise themselves to him by the sublimity of their language.

Our stage is for Europe and for us a school of politeness, good behaviour, and reason, a display of all natural happenings, gay or pathetic, which, helped by a pure and chastened style, can, and straightway do reach the heart and mind of an audience no matter the nationality. But the stage of our neighbours finds grace only in their own eyes, furnishes pictures only agreeable to themselves, and makes an impression only on their own senses.

The eloquence of their orators is purely logical; it is all rational and comes from the head in an appeal to the reason of the hearers. It disdains, or it does not know, the devices of rhetoric; it is a stranger to the impassioned abandonment of those great emotions that reach the heart as well as the mind. What seems to prove that the methods of their eloquence are more due to poverty than to intention is the instance of Mr. Burke, whose eloquence is entirely French and who is placed by them in the first rank of orators; it is true that they have rather reproached him with his declamation.[5]

The eloquence of our orators always shines by its lofty character, the choice of expressions, the knowledge of the human heart inspiring it, by digressions sometimes foreign to the subject but leading back to it and determining its success; in a word by a burning enthusiasm and an adorned discourse which echo long afterwards in words carrying conviction and victorious sentences that become familiar quotations.

The English understand business better, and we the arts. Their courage is as solid as ours, but ours is more brilliant. They are a nation shut in one corner of Europe, we are at the centre; thus their influence is by the way, ours is direct. Similarly our towns are more opulent and their countryside is richer.

English literature, estimable in many respects by its great efforts of patience and philosophy, is in general dry, barren, and

above all without variety. The *toto divisos orbe Britannos*
always makes itself felt. By seeking originality their authors
have often fallen into eccentricity. The desire to be profound
makes them dig down into an idea in every direction and the final
development is often obscurity, sophism, or paradox. Constantly
aiming at the sublime, they often only reach the gigantic, and
their art is nearly always opposed to Nature, which yet they
specially wish to copy.

History, being a positive matter, is better suited to their
rational methods, although they do not put into it all the dramatic spirit it admits; it is the field they best cultivate, when
not poisoned by national or political prejudices. Their novels,
which are so much talked about, are only a description of the
manners of their own island; the passions displayed there are
indeed those of mankind, but the livery is that of England.

The epic form, eminently suited to writers who do not mind
what risks they take, and to whom it is the same whether they
rise to heaven or sink into hell, has naturally found amongst
them a poet who stands out. Milton (as I have observed in
another work) when he is in a happy mood of inspiration and
carried away by his subject is the most sublime of poets, without
excepting Homer and Tasso, though I much prefer to read the
last named. "Paradise Lost," while it is full of passages that
give the highest idea of its author's genius, and presents the
loftiest aspects of the human spirit, yet has dreary passages,
vague and diffuse, which offer neither elegance nor vigour. If this
Englishman had lived nearer to us, if his genius had not been
absorbed by party spirit in the calamitous days when he lived,
if he had had in more fortunate surroundings the time to polish
his verses, if he had not sometimes abused his inspiration and
overdriven his Muse, he would have reached the last degree of
perfection and received the laurels of the epic. He died without
fame! But the English soon claimed it for him. . . . They are
not the people to disregard any means of bringing credit to
their nation. They are more fortunate with Milton than with
Shakespeare, for their British Homer almost justifies what they
assert about him.

But how far it is from the good books the English have
to those treasures of literature of every kind which France possesses, and which have made her language supreme in Europe,
other nations becoming her pupils, from their poets to their
philosophers and moralists, from their orators down to their

most frivolous writers. When I hear it said in other countries
that the fine days of French literature are over, I agree that it
is so relatively to ourselves, but deny it by comparison with
others. Voltaire and Buffon lived yesterday, the ashes of Saint-
Lambert, of Thomas, of d'Alembert, of Marmontel are still
warm; Colin d'Harville, Picard,[6] and others have written comedies such as are not produced elsewhere, and which are everywhere translated; without counting a crowd of young writers
whose talent is still stifled on account of factions hardly yet appeased, but who will perhaps achieve as brilliant a fame as our
great masters. Indeed is it quite sure that, when fifty years have
passed over the ashes of La Harpe and the Abbé Delille, they
may not be counted in that gallery of superior writers of whom
my country is proud? Men taken in the mass must, like individuals, seek rest, especially after a storm, and I cannot see how the
French could go further in the cultivation of letters, since they
have long ago reached the summit; our great masters can hardly
be surpassed. Were we to depart from the path which they have
opened, we might rashly be led astray; to imitate them is for us
a sufficiently fine inheritance.

But there are arts in which the last degree of perfection still
awaits us; that this full harvest of laurels will not escape us is
clearly indicated by the general enthusiasm which has taken hold
of our expanding nation and by the immense store of treasures
which we have made our own.

The ideas of the French and the English on the point of
honour constitute another characteristic difference. In France,
as I have already remarked, duels were a frequent mania; in
England a duel is a rare necessity. The English are brave, but
they have a sentimental morality that leads them to avoid shedding blood, and the man who does not fear to settle his own
fate and take his own life hesitates to expose himself for a slight
offence to death at the hands of his fellows. The prejudices of
education also favour this wholesome horror; and the custom of
boxing, common among the lower class and not always unknown
to the others, quenches that ardent zeal for the point of honour
which is carried so unreasonably far amongst us. I have seen a
peer of the realm boxing with a baker, who certainly did not
spare him, in the lobby at Covent Garden; *populi stante coronâ.*

These instances are rare, but they exist. There is yet another
reason why men avoid single combats, that is the extremely common use, I might say abuse, of wine, which often gives rise in
the evening to quarrels that are settled next morning by the

simple statement: *"I was in liquor."*[7] This confession settles everything and is not meant to convey an unfavourable opinion of him who makes it, while in France it would have doubly dishonoured any man who had had the simplicity to put forward such an excuse.

In France to try to compose a quarrel is to make it worse and to discredit oneself to no purpose; in England the great point is not to shed blood uselessly, not to put oneself in the wrong with others or with oneself. An Englishman who dies wants to know why; a Frenchman consoles himself beforehand by thinking of the grief of his friends and the tears of his mistress. English laws are very severe against duels. . . . Ours also were severe, but they carry out theirs, with the result that duels are rare but serious. Amongst us one often went to the Opéra the day after having killed a man in the Bois de Boulogne. Amongst them, unless a duellist has triple right on his side, a duel is followed by exile, to avoid being dealt with as a murderer. These differences naturally fit the character of the two nations, and prove that the government and policy which suit one cannot be adopted by the other, except by short-sighted beginners in legislation. Thus, among the evils the English have done us and for which they take credit, I put at the fore this ridiculous mania of aping them which they have inoculated us with, though once they used slavishly to copy our fashions and, as Mr. Burke has said in his picturesque way, dress themselves in our frippery.

Thence in our young men, and gradually in the whole nation, have been born contempt for our ancient proprieties and our consecrated etiquettes, a confusion of ranks which has led to their subversion, and an abolition of distinction in dress once so useful to influence unsteady imaginations. All these things are now replaced by new customs and ways of dressing that place all men on the same level and do away with subordination: that is to say with habits of respect matured by tradition.

To complete this list of oppositions, it is not out of place to bring forward the contrast offered by education in the two countries, to point out the awkward and stiff pride of their young men, so unskilled in the art either of addressing or of greeting, and to contrast this meaningless and passive attitude with French vivacity, sometimes too expansive and too noisy, and often, under the cloak of graciousness, not sufficiently ripened by wisdom.

There is need to explain this rough stiffness of the English, their cold reserve, their inability for elegant manners, the almost total absence of wit in their conversation, and a bashfulness inherent to their nature; there is need to bear in mind that it is connected with their climate, their ways of life, food, language, and government, but especially their geographical position. One might show conclusively that, in spite of the fascination which they have long exerted, they form one of the nations of the world whom in many respects Providence has least favoured. One might observe that everything there develops later and is finished earlier than elsewhere, so that the best men of the nation, those who have to think for the rest, begin to be essential and useful only after thirty, in the midst of a generation whose members divide their time between newspapers and hunting, by way of distractions, and wine which sends them to sleep and uses them up before their time; so one might almost conclude that here we have a mathematical nation for whom life is nothing but a short process of reasoning.

Nature never gives everything; the gold of her favours is always a little alloyed. Why cannot a Frenchman's wit, which commonly flows with so much impetuosity in his prime, always keep within the limits marked by prudence and reflexion? Other nations would not then have grounds to comfort themselves by sometimes denying us solidity when we seem too fond of brilliance, or protesting that our countrymen cannot display sound judgement until they reach maturity, because they exercise too much light and pleasant wit. Thus it seems on the whole that but for a few exceptions, an Englishman in his youth is boring and bored, and often lives and dies in that state; and that the Frenchman, while in youth frequently unbearable, usually becomes a real and distinguished man as he reaches his prime. The first sometimes achieves distinction, which is too rarely embellished by amiability, the second needs to throw off the fire of youth before he finds wisdom, that beneficent wisdom which in the English is the result of a phlegmatic temperament, and in the French a victory over nature.

The glory of the English, which in them has often taken the place of every other, both at home and abroad, is their national spirit, that patriotic and virile energy which collectively makes of them a great people. Taken in the mass, it is an imposing attitude, which added to the barrier of sea that surrounds them imparts to them a wild and rugged vigour. Each individual merits a small share of that consideration which their whole organisation deserves, for is not one tempted to grant most to those who give and demand the least? Certainly the French possess a public spirit that yields to none, but as their national strength is more real they speak of it less. Every Frenchman is conscious of what he is worth, and rather boasts about himself; this is displeasing. An Englishman affects to forget himself and boast of his country. The English are all united in a conspiracy with the sole aim of palliating their defeats and their weakness, exaggerating their successes and their strength, in short of exalting their country as a lover praises his mistress; that is wearisome, but it is not so displeasing. If I were to seek a way to explain the Anglomania that has made the circle of Europe but is now declining, I should find it in that calm and quiet pride with which the English have made the world a battlefield and come forward especially as the rivals of France. One might believe, to hear them talk, that their claims were just, and their pride was a virtue which all must admit!

But the chief trait of the English character is their rooted hatred of the French, their contempt for all other nations, the cold egoism which would immolate the whole human race on the altar of their country in order to satisfy their insatiable ambition and maintain themselves on that height.

English ships are on every sea, volcanoes which bring ruin to every nation, devouring vultures on the crags of their island looking for booty and prey. Speaking as a cosmopolitan and a friend of humanity I assert that if the English will not confine themselves within the limits set to them by nature, reason, and sound politics, we must turn against them for the general welfare that famous axiom of Cato: *Delenda est Carthago!*

If England can rest satisfied to be ranked high amongst nations by virtue of her constitution and her weight in the political balance, by the spectacle she could present the world of a people prosperous in its trade and ingenious within the boundaries of justice; if she could be content with the honour of having given birth to philosophers, several great men, and to Newton, an adornment to the whole of mankind; if she could through the prestige of ancient esteem and the chances of prosperity still within her scope, limit herself to rebuilding her tottering credit, restoring her threatened existence and winning back the confidence she is everywhere losing; should she resolve, in short, to enter the path of justice, good faith, and moderation, then let her live and continue to present to us a people unique and

sturdy in their persevering energy. But should she fail to exchange a spirit of flighty ambition and conquest for wisdom and
broad-minded common sense, she has scarcely time so to mend
her destiny as to preserve its guiding principles and replace the
shaken foundations of an edifice which is more specious than
solid, and which will suddenly collapse.

In this sketch, my pen has not been guided by hatred and bitterness. I am relying on truth, though a Frenchman cannot forget that it is English politics which have given rise to the French
Revolution in order to reduce the French nation until two last
survivors slay each other at the same moment.

I have visited the towns and the countryside of England; I
have seen her magistrates, her officers, her courtiers, and the
general population; I have moved by turn amongst all classes,
high and low, and I have convinced myself that there is no
method of extirpation, when used against us, which the English
do not regard as justified and sanctified. Their motto is *Dolus
an virtus, quis in hoste requirat?* [8] It is clear to me that they will
employ any means that lead to domination, that for the English
their island is the world, and that freedom and humanity have no
claim on the rest of the earth. [9]

Now I will offer, at my own expense, an example of the
severity and inconvenience of English laws, an inconvenience the
English admit, but which in a predominantly commercial country they believe to be compensated by advantages.

As disorderly at nineteen as I have been nearly all my life,
I had given a bill for two thousand crowns to a certain Mr.
Smith, steward at Monceau, [10] this transaction being carried off
in my easygoing way, which I should call magnanimous, could
there be magnanimity in displaying the sorry wit of doing such
sorry business as to lose for oneself both freedom and peace.
These two thousand crowns were the price of a phaeton and two
horses Smith had sold me, and the bill, payable at eight months,
had been signed about two months before I left Paris.

Some time afterwards, M. the Duc d'Orléans, then in close
touch with the Prince of Wales, reached London. As I called on
him one day, I found Smith in the hall; he said many charming
things to me and seemed delighted to see me. I never mentioned
the rag I had given him since, according to a universal principle
—"Who has credit owes nothing." A few days later, when I
was supping at M. d'Adhémar's with the Duc d'Orléans, some
race was spoken about. I was grieved at having no horses. The

Prince told me to ask Smith, "who would do anything to oblige you."

I thanked him profusely, and next morning Smith came to me. Two hours later I was on horseback, followed by a groom. Towards four o'clock in the afternoon I returned to dress; on putting foot to the ground I was accosted by a gentleman whom I did not know, and who had two evil-looking men with him. He came close to my ear and assured me that, being his prisoner, I must accompany him. Cold sweat froze me; pulling myself together at last, I asked for whom he was looking. I felt bewildered when he informed me that I was arrested on the complaint of Mr. Smith, and that I must, he insisted, follow him at once. I was much inclined to resist, but my landlord made me realise the danger of doing so. As I drove away with this portly gentleman, he did me the honour to assure me that, since I had become quiet and sensible, he intended to proceed in a friendly manner, and as I was so well disposed he would send away his two acolytes. He condescended to tell me that this was quite a natural and simple occurrence, very ordinary in London; he recited a list of most distinguished people, English and others, to whom the same thing had happened, and he explained that the main point is always for both sides to behave civilly. I interrupted him to ask where he was taking me.

"To very comfortable lodgings," he replied seriously, "*a sponging house.*" (A very correct name, for there they squeeze your purse as one squeezes a sponge; it is a sort of anteroom to prison.) "One stays there," he continued, "for a few days, before being put in prison. But as you owe nothing, and since you say you do not wish to pay, I advise you to send for an honest lawyer, a friend of mine, who in two hours will get you free."

"But, sir! think of the horrible reports which will be spread about."

"Not at all; it will not be known, and even if it is known it will not be spoken about."

"I was invited to a grand dinner."

"You will soon have a dinner, and then you will have supper."

"But what explanation can I give my host?"

"You forgot."

"That would be polite!"

"Say you were ill."

"That would be dishonourable."

"There is no pleasing you, sir: you always say the same thing. I have already told you that this happens every day to the best people in the kingdom. *I tell you what,* Lord—— wished to sleep with the wife of Sir W——, an absurdly jealous man who never left her side, and his lordship, determined to have a quiet night, had the baronet arrested for a considerable sum which he did not owe, quite certain that the baronet *would bring an action* against him and make him pay heavy damages: that is the hole he got into."

Here I could not help laughing.

"You see," my guide said, "now things are going better. *You behave like a man.*"

Reaching an ugly door in an ugly street (Wild Street), we got down. The door was triply locked behind us, and hardly had we gone upstairs when I was asked what I should like for dinner, what wine I drank, and if I preferred *small beer* to *porter.*

"I want a lawyer and Mr. Reed. Let me have a pen and paper. I will give you five guineas if I do not sleep here."

In less than an hour the two gentlemen arrived. The advice of the lawyer was that I was quite wrongly arrested, but that it was necessary to begin by paying, or else find bail.

"I will go bail," said the good Mr. Reed.

He was accepted. After I had signed many papers, complied with other formalities, and paid ten or twelve pounds costs, I went home at eleven o'clock in the evening, mad with rage.

Next morning I hastened to M. d'Adhémar to tell him of my adventure and to ask his advice.

"The Duc d'Orléans," he replied, "set out this morning for the country; he is coming to my house on Thursday. I shall warn him; I want justice to be done to you; it is horrible! You will tell him the facts. . . . Do it with moderation, respectfully insist on the dismissal of this Smith, and I am sure you will be pleased with the result; he is too much a gentleman to refuse."

The day came. I approached the Duc d'Orléans, I asked for a brief interview. "M. de Tilly," he said to me, "I know what you wish to speak to me about. The Comte d'Adhémar has told me about it. . . . Smith also mentioned it to-day. . . ."

"Is Smith still with you, your Highness?" . . .

"Yes, certainly. . . ."

"Then, your Highness, he has not told you the truth, and I cannot believe that you know. . . ."

"Monsieur de Tilly, if one owes money one is in the wrong, even with Smith."

"I do not owe him."

"I beg your pardon, you left Paris owing money to him and without warning him; his bill, which I have seen, will fall due in two months; he has been told that you were going to Italy. . . . Paris is, besides, a bad place for him to obtain payment from you. . . . England offers him every facility in this matter. . . . I disapprove, but he has profited by the occasion."

"What logic, your Highness! . . . If it were not for my deep respect for you, I would not hear another word. . . . I take the liberty of asking you if this reasoning comes from Smith."

"It is *mine* and *his*."

"I will refrain, your Highness, from giving it a name."

"Sir!"

"Your Highness, let us simplify matters. . . . Does your Highness intend to dismiss Mr. Smith, a wretch who has clearly insulted me, and who without asking me first for the money, which he had not the right to demand, has suppressed a bill not yet due in law, only to bring forward the debt, and has caused the arrest of a French gentleman who met with this misfortune simply because he had the honour to come and pay his court to you?"

"I cannot dismiss him; there is no disgrace in this in England; he knows my affairs in his own department better than I do myself; he is very necessary to me . . . and, to tell you the truth . . . I cannot see that he has failed towards you."

"I have fulfilled my duty, your Highness. From now on if I have the misfortune to do something which may displease you, if the honour to be in your employ proves no safeguard for Smith, please recall this step I have taken."

I did not wait for a reply, but with a deep bow left him where he stood in the window recess. He remained there two good minutes, pretending to be looking out.

M. d'Adhémar forsook the people he was talking to and took me into the next room, where hung a fine portrait of Mme de Polignac by Mme Lebrun. "Well?" he said to me. I repeated all that I have just written. I owe him the justice to say that he was indignant. "I shall speak to him again," he said.

"Sir, I am full of gratitude, but I warn you that before twenty-four hours are over, at all risks, I shall kill Mr. Smith, even at the Prince's door. I shall have post-horses ready, and you can, sir, take my most sacred word on it."

"That," he replied, "would have no common sense, and in a country such as this is scarcely possible. Be reasonable, if you wish me to concern myself with your affairs. . . . Keep calm."

After dinner he had a long conversation with the Duc d'Orléans; the Chevalier de Durfort, though not liking me, took my part. . . . A few moments later, the Prince, coming up to me, did me the honour to say: "Sir, I shall dismiss Mr. Smith." I bowed. When later I saw him make for his carriage, I followed him. "I beg your Highness to be assured of my gratitude. I am fully satisfied. I implore him to keep in his service a man who has the good fortune to please him."

"You wish it so, sir?"

"I beg it of your Highness."

"It is to you he will owe it."

Next morning Mr. Smith was announced; I would not see him. During the rest of my stay the matter was never mentioned again. The Duc d'Orléans, whom I met every day, was cold but polite. Long afterwards, in the presence of that unfortunate and regretted Lauzun, he spoke to me laughingly of this incident: "Between ourselves, you were wrong." I denied it. I told the story over again; he persisted. The Duc de Lauzun went so far as to say to him, asking his pardon, that it was impossible "to view more falsely so simple a matter." We could never convert him; in all this he could only see "the debt itself"; and the love of money, of that gold which he has since spent with a prodigality so abominable, so fatal to his whole house, finally corrupted his naturally sound judgement.

A stay of five months in London seemed to me a long exile. What should I have said if I could have unveiled the Book of Destiny and read there that the twelve best years of my life would be wasted in banishment far from Paris, to which all my restless thoughts carried me back? At that moment, when I was prepared to leave the English capital, a love-adventure (for what other business could I have at that age?) induced me to hasten my departure.

I had been to spend the day at a country house, a few miles from London where I had to return after supper. Finding by my side at table a lady much spoken of at the time, whose lover, whom I knew fairly well, was then travelling in France, I persuaded the friend in whose carriage I had come to go back to

London alone. When I saw the lady leave the room, I was careful to go before her, and, having reached the foot of the main staircase, appeared to be genuinely at a loss how to get back to London. What I had foreseen happened: she offered me with some hesitation a seat which I hastened to accept. The journey was fairly long, but on these fine sandy roads, six horses travel quickly; there was no time to lose. I hurried to bring the conversation to its real object, and to say that I was reduced to be either impertinent or foolish. Finding myself no further advanced by these remarks, I risked a more audacious action, which was repelled by a vigorous defence, until I found a point of approach so responsive that I never let go before it only remained for me to obtain a second victory. The first had been stolen under such unfavourable circumstances that it was merely justice to claim a more comfortable conquest; but she maintained that I was a monster, a thief (delightful moment!), and that nothing should be granted me, that I had obtained one useless victory, which would only deliver me up to memories, evil conscience, and regrets. She dealt out in short those numerous commonplaces which, always the same on such occasions, resemble the shoes of Theramenes that fitted all feet. Meanwhile I had reached my door, not having succeeded in being driven to that of the offended fair one, who did not fail to use the specious pretext that she could not allow me to enter her house in front of her servants at three o'clock in the morning.

It may easily be believed that on the following day I appeared at her house; they told me she had gone out. Two days later the reply was that she was in the country. I wrote; no answer. My imagination being spurred by resistance, to see her again became a need, I have almost said a happiness. I sought all occasions for it; I found one at a ball of the Duchess of Ancaster. We had by then changed parts: I was bashful, she looked confident. I wished to speak and to reproach her; her silence was a graver reproach. I sought an explanation; she avoided it. I displayed feeling, passion . . . real emotion had seized me. She seemed conscious only of the danger of such a situation in the presence of witnesses.

"If I were not already bound by a relationship which I believe is unfortunately too well known," she said at last, "I should listen to you here, and it would not matter if anyone noticed; but I do not belong to myself, and I implore you to spare me and to respect yourself."

I gently insisted; I tried to remind her of my rights, but she said: "You have no rights: it is I who have the right to complain of you; but this is not the moment or the place for reproaches. I promise to receive you to-morrow afternoon if you will come to my house before two o'clock."

She then moved towards some ladies and joined the company, leaving me half dumbfounded and half delighted by the assignation I had thus stolen.

The night seemed to me a long vigil, the following day a year. I was given to a thousand contradictory thoughts. At one moment I longed for the pleasure of seeing her again; the next minute wounded vanity prompted me to disdain the occasion she had offered. Desire won the day. . . . I was at her door, I was announced, she was alone.

"You are free," she told me, "to abuse my position, to condemn me to the necessity of avoiding you, or to acquire an everlasting title to my gratitude, my friendship, and above all my esteem."

"Free!" I exclaimed. "If you leave me the choice, I feel myself incapable of any generosity."

"There should be no choice," she replied, "when on one side there is all my esteem."

"And on the other—all my love," I hastened to interrupt. . . . And carried away by imperious emotion, by uncontrollable desire, I was in her arms. She loved me . . . I could almost believe it . . . I could at all events think that she had ceased to love another.

"You have willed it—you have basely brought me to it," she murmured in a low voice, putting her hands over her eyes. "You have led me to despise myself for life. . . . The attraction of a moment, one first misfortune and offence, overbore my best resolutions; but be assured that you will have degraded me in vain, that you will never see me again—never. . . . No more than if we were separated by death."

I tried, it may well be believed, to oppose this idea; I threw myself at her knees, when herself falling at mine, she begged me with an accent and gestures that I am unable to describe, to forget her, to flee from her . . . to reassure her by the most sacred oaths that I would never again disturb her peace, or abuse her weakness. She maintained it was barbarous to afflict a heart possessed by another, when there were so many women ready to give their whole hearts to such desires and such daring.

The sound of her voice, the expression of her features, her attitude, some tears—everything urged me to this solemn oath. I swore it. . . . I was faithful to it. I made only one condition, the gift of a tress of her hair, which she refused—then called me back to give it me. This I soon sent back to her, and she returned to me once more when she knew I was setting out for Paris, asking me to keep it for the love of her.—I have it still; and when in 1792, pursued by men who were pretending to regenerate France by way of carnage, I sought to save a victim to their fury and risked the danger of returning to my house, after an absence of three days, to rescue some letters, a few portraits, packets of hair—memorials of the loves of my youth —her souvenir was one of those which chiefly decided me to brave death when life was so little worth disputing. Since then I have seen one of her near relatives; I have been in a position to be of some help to her, and I found happiness in doing so; but I have often reproached myself with having been so lacking in generosity, or so little attractive, at the time of my contact with her.

This adventure, on reflexion, has often struck me as being very unlike our own manners and customs. It is seldom that a Frenchwoman values herself so little as to give herself thus quickly; seldom does she yield to a surprise of the senses with such abandonment and softness; still rarer is it to find a woman who, having granted her favours cheaply, possesses the virtue necessary to repent of it so soon. I speak of those who are worthy the name of women. The second assignation and the second weakness are still more extraordinary. That gallantry and wantonness should after that send you away may not be surprising; but who would expect to receive this dismissal from a heart faithful to its inconstancy? It was like a homage to virtue, yet wantonness and corruption would not have taken any other course. I remember that the Marquis de Genlis said to me one day: "I have had Mme de —— only twice; the first time it was for my sake, the second for hers. I never went back to her afterwards; there was no one left to oblige."

In France it needs much care, much skill, much planning, sincerity, and art to conquer a woman worthy to be attacked. One might believe that there were certain formalities to fulfill, all equally necessary, the last as much as the first. But success also was frequent, unless one was a beginner, or the fair adversary one of those dragons of virtue who have sworn never to fall. There were many of this kind, but with them an experienced man never compromised his reputation; he soon discovered what he might reasonably expect, and retired before the world learnt of his accident. Only a few novices came to burn their incense on an altar where the inexorable divinity fed on victims.

In other countries, many women resist a plan of attack, or a whole system of seduction, yet succumb on a single occasion born of a chance that will never occur again. The Frenchwoman possesses a methodical virtue that is no protection against an accomplished enemy; other women by the help of one or two prejudices often resist passion and skillful scheming, yet fall suddenly under the influence of the moment.

I have noticed that you invite a Frenchwoman to love you with the words, "I love you," while the same words may almost invite a foreigner to defend herself. One might say that one has to call out her weakness.

All this, I repeat, is applicable only to the women who are worthy of mention; amongst all nations there is a refuse of their sex and of ours not worth studying. Together with highway robbers, they are the dregs of a nation; they are like the wall raised between analysis and contempt. But I have also noticed amongst the women who merit regard—and I honour them without distinction of country, whether in England, Germany, or France—that they are always nearer perfection than the best of men. I view them as an adornment to their own sex, an object of veneration for ours; and it seems to me that they suffice to balance the extremes of vice by the realities of virtue.

For the rest, let those who will read me accept this from me (if they are happy enough not to know it)—that there is neither happiness nor glory in these seductions, whether easy or difficult. Let them learn once for all that the former displease the heart and inspire disgust, the latter dissatisfy the conscience and lead to remorse. Misfortunes, slanders, dangers, frightful calamities are nearly always the legitimate punishment of both; loss of life and of honour often their reward. The brilliance and the pleasure of these guilty relationships are false and lying; shame and grief are their indispensable outcome; so let it be known that this scandalous commerce so flagrant an outrage to morality, which is not dealt with severely enough and is too often laughed at, gives birth to sufferings, evils, and adversities of a special kind which other vices and crimes are powerless to produce.

No villain is as disillusioned as the seducer; the heart of no other being in creation is so faded, so withered by remorse, and gnawed by so many vultures as that of the man improperly named *homme à bonnes fortunes,* when he descends the last steps leading to the grave. I shall say more. He was already crowned with misfortunes when youth left him. No profession involves in a short span so much *deconsideration;* if this word is not French, I shall still use it, in place of the juster but harsher word *contempt.*

CHAPTER XVI

Chiama gli abitator dell'ombre eterne
Il rauco suon della tartarea tromba;
Treman le spaziose atre caverne,
E l'aer cieco a quel romor rimbomba.
          —TASSO, CANT. IV. ST. 3.

*T*HIS trumpet of Tartarus everlastingly summons those flitting shadows we name the human race; to obey its gloomy
sound the children of men are hurled in floods along the road
leading to the kingdom of darkness. This is where swift dreams
of happiness are carried off; where enemies and the sharpest
darts of adversity sink into oblivion, along with our hopes of
fame and ambition, whether deceived or gratified; along with
the meaningless false things that delude us from the cradle to
the grave, whether we sit on a throne or in the peasant's hut.

Such, then, are the primary conditions of life; such is the goal
awaiting all our schemes, thoughts, meditations, all our riotous
designs, which battle amongst themselves as do the waves of an
angry sea. This is the reef against which, amidst everlasting
silence, founders this frail pride we have in our frail greatness,
and where are wrecked the last endeavours of these active and
potential faculties which subject the past, present, and future,
and the whole of nature, to the memory, the power, and the investigation of man: himself an admirable piece of workmanship,
yet so limited that he can neither value himself nor explain himself away, any more than the clock is aware of itself which yet
obeys, points out the time and strikes the hour unknowingly.
Was it worth while for anyone to swell this procession of ghosts?

On my return to Paris, I laudably decided to pay off my
debts and to accumulate no others. The Queen, to whom I had
the honour to pay my court on coming home from England,
spoke to me with some of her former leniency concerning my
affairs. She added laughingly: "The last straw would be if you
developed a mania for travelling. M. de Lauraguais used to say
he went to England to garnish his mind; you might say that you
went to disgarnish your purse."

It must be admitted that a sum of over twenty thousand crowns in debts was no favourable evidence of my caution and economy. I came seriously to consider a rather desperate plan I had for long thought of adopting. I set out for Maine and entreated one of my relatives to purchase of me a piece of land which it suited him as much to buy as it did me to sell. He raised many objections, owing to the difficulty of my being a minor; I made some concessions, and he consented; I found myself relieved of my debts and enriched by some cash which my quieted imagination pictured as a treasure upon which wisdom alone was henceforth to draw.

This premature sale turned out, after all, a most wretched piece of business, since it brought about an incident in which I placed myself completely in the wrong, punishment following swiftly. The consent of an uncle on my mother's side was needed to render actually legal the agreement for the sale of a plot of land relinquished by a minor, though in the end I managed without it. I had almost, but not quite, reached the legal age. One day, on leaving parade, I met M. de Chassilé [1] taking a walk, and I confronted him in the presence of several officers, asking him imperiously for the third time whether he consented that I should conclude the transaction I had submitted to his approval. As I was speaking with marked energy not unlike impertinence, he replied:

"No, sir; no, once for all; and please control yourself and try not to forget who I am." He looked fierce with anger and was furiously handling the pummel of his sword.

"Better yourself recall who I am," I replied, "and how greatly my father honoured you by marrying your sister."

He makes for me. . . . Our swords are almost drawn. . . . People step in between us. This ridiculous brag, for which I beg forgiveness from both reason and common sense, cost me over a hundred thousand crowns. A month later my uncle was married; it served me right.

I stayed awhile at Le Mans. This town was then the scene of a tragic event that left on me an impression all the more lasting since I was later to love to distraction its unfortunate heroine. She is one of those people who cause a judicious mind to feel disheartened as to the possibility of a trustworthy reading of history, since even events which have happened under our very eyes elude our most reasoned deductions. This adventure is of a nature to support the contention that scarcely anything matters at all, not even affection, since there are circumstances which leave the heart in a perpetual doubt as to the reality of the dearest attachments, as to the price we should set on them, and the amount of affection we should give in return for what looks most like love; since there exist chances we cannot ward off or foresee which lead us of necessity to be either grossly unfair or grossly deceived.

A man of much wit and above all of an unusual turn of mind, a man who, in conversation, could display on all subjects a confidence and originality born of some fair knowledge of science had, at thirty years of age and though he was far from handsome, attracted a charming woman who was only twenty and in whom youth was one of the least advantages. This was the Chevalier de Dolomieu, then quartered at Le Mans in the dragoons, and the less known brother of the famous Dolomieu.[2]

He had to go for a few months to Dauphiné, and felt much reluctance at leaving for a while the fair object of a love he had confided to me, less—

> Through self-conceit in bold excess
> Than overflow of tenderness,

two similarly common causes, both almost equally unjustifiable, which lead to indiscretion. One of his friends, a very handsome young man, self-assured with men and ridiculously bold with women, thought this a favourable opportunity for capturing a forsaken stronghold. His manners were of that audacious bad style which meets with success when not thoroughly disliked, and there was about him an elegant ease that rendered him equally attractive to the wanton woman as dangerous to the strictly virtuous one. Did the Marquise de Br—— succumb or did she come out victorious from this conflict? This was never known; a year of intimate conversation with her has in nowise enlightened me on this point, even when, moved by such jealousy as I can feel as much towards the past as for the present, I spared nothing to win knowledge of a secret that most men would have looked upon as of little consequence. But I have never thought it a matter of small importance to know well and to rate highly the woman one loves, to weigh her heart by its former attachments and to learn therefrom the amount of love and regard one owes her; to discover in these previous affections what trust one can place in her present feelings, and by means of such com-

parisons and observations to reach an estimate of one's chances
of happiness or misfortune at her side.

Should this remark appear sheer nonsense to some men, I
smile at the thought; should it appear so to women, I am sorry
for them. Yet I know that love is a matter of such importance
to but few people; not many would take all that trouble. Happy
are those who only seek easy pleasure in love-encounters, the
roses without the thorns, those who manage life too skillfully
to blight their happiness with analysis, or again handle love too
expertly to allow it to evaporate in subtleties, and its bloom to
fade under reflexion.

On my part, I was less fortunate; I have followed a path
in life which leads to no recognition: that of a man specially
devoted to women. But if an overdose of recognition—laurels
which are usually bestowed much at random—is not to be
granted to every man in full measure, he could hope to find consolation in his own self-respect provided he might at least seize
happiness or (since such does not exist upon this earth) the
semblance of it. As for me, I never reached it; I wasted my
youth in the torments of a too fastidious imagination. . . . I
was too hard to please. I exhausted myself in unreasonableness,
anxiety of mind, mistrust of my heart, and all the storms of restless and discontented emotions to which a mere nothing would
bring consternation, and which many favours could not yet sufficiently reassure. I was constantly complaining of love, yet had
no other pursuits. I have never found love to hold what I had
promised myself it would, yet I have always feared it would
take away from me the little it had granted me. I have never
derived rest from the strongest attachments of my life. I have
often, in spite of myself, brought sadness into my heart and
grief into another's. . . .

Strange contrast! One should deserve less love on this account, yet one is loved the more; and greatest is the happiness
when tears have been most abundant.

Love—is the serious plaything of big children.

Indifference—the deathlike sleep of wicked hearts.

The longest life—a short-lived lie.

This young officer, whom I have deserted because it would
be odious to me to write without holding converse with my heart,
was called M. de Ma——. He had acquired a sort of provincial
fame on account of his too excitable bravery, of his fair success
in his profession, and the vigorous advantages of a handsome

figure which would have given him a name anywhere had his education been more finished.

One evening, after he had supped at the house of the Marquise de Br—— in the company of some of his chiefs and the best society of the town, he hid behind a screen in the hall, and when he thought Mme de Br—— and the servants had retired for the night, he made for her bedroom and tried to open the door. He had the key, but was not successful in his attempt as the door was bolted on the inside. He first begged Mme de Br—— to admit him, in the name of their love, which she seemed to treat with contemptuous indignation; then he changed his tone. He reminded her of her promises, spoke of his sacred rights, overwhelmed her with insults and abuse; he added that she was locked in with a favoured rival, but that vengeance would be his on both of them in a way which henceforth would throw fear in the hearts of all unfaithful and presumptuous lovers. Upon which Mme de Br—— appeared at her window and called her servants. Scandal and confusion reached their height. Her butler and her coachman tried to seize M. de Ma——; he drew his sword and defended himself like a lion. Finally, about two o'clock in the morning, he was thrown into the street, defeated by numbers, his sword broken, himself injured, though his cruel lady had begged he should be spared. The screams, swearing, and confusion had attracted some undesirable idlers, in front of whom he uttered unheard-of and disgraceful accusations. To these he put a finish by throwing into the court-yard a key which he claimed as that of the bedroom, and which he declared had been given him in more propitious days during the absence of a rival who had returned two days before.

The Marquise de Br——, at her wits' end and desperate, dressed in haste, took her coach and hurried to the commanding officer, a sorry jester in this sort of adventures in which he often figured as the hero. But, being a relative of the fair accuser, he listened gravely to her tale, was moved by her tears, and promised her swift justice fitted to the boldness of the offence.

He immediately sent an under-officer and a few dragoons to seize the mad young man who sought to rape women he had never possessed, or those who no longer wanted him as a lover —which are one and the same thing if a man is fair to the sex.

The chief had him locked up in the prison of a monastery, previous to reporting the case to the minister and deciding his fate. But our energetic scatterbrain, foreseeing that he would at least be degraded, and obeying despair as much as weakness, sent for two of his friends, proclaimed his right to seek revenge for betrayed love, and shot himself twice through the heart. He lived for another six hours in frightful agony, which he begged should be cut short, but to no effect.

Mme de Br—— had sent post-haste for her husband, who was then absent, and he had immediately started at full gallop and mad with rage to avenge his wife's honour, whether she was guilty or innocent. He certainly owed at least that much to himself; but he was quit with the coach expenses, for he arrived to be present at the funeral of the man whose life he might have taken or who might have shortened his.

This ending ought to have satisfied him as much as the other. As for the Chevalier de Dolomieu, calm and silent, displaying no fuss, he had the incident explained to him, though it was rumoured he was the cause of it and had witnessed it all. The Marquis de Br—— took his wife's part with the fearless intrepidity of a man confronting public opinion and believing in virtue. He defended her against the judgement of a whole province let loose—which, having two victims offered for immolation, would not choose a corpse; he defended her when she was wasting away with grief; he gave her the courage of her innocence, or the greater courage to affect innocence.

For was she innocent or was she not?

If we assume her guilty, did she deserve the torrent of abuse that I saw poured over her when, carried away by youth, I raised a bold voice in her favour, thus evoking her gratitude later transformed into love? If she was innocent was M. de Ma—— worthy of the widespread pity meted out to him in a large province inhabited by several people of consequence and many others of good family and wealth?

It seems to me hardly probable that a woman who has betrayed an absent lover (it is a great mistake to go far away from the beloved!) should not, on his return, use all means in her power to rid herself of a dangerous substitute, should not claim back a key she had handed over, should cause a public scandal, call her servants to defend her outraged honour, rather than trust herself to the generosity of the two men whom she has favoured. For at the worst she in all likelihood would rather surrender at discretion to her lovers (though there are ways of avoiding this) than to her servants and the whole town. Then again it does not seem probable that a young woman who has never before appeared depraved should break forth with such energy, have her seducer thrown out of doors and herself lodge a complaint, when even her acknowledged innocence and the proved justice of her claim could not suffice to save her from blame.

It seems to me incredible that, since she mourned the loss of her good name, she should have remained stubborn in her indifference to the death of a man who, she thought, had but passed sentence upon himself; that she should never have given herself away by a word, a gesture, or during the most confidential talk, so that I was not able in the course of over a year, and under the sway of tender emotions which such an avowal would have heightened, to obtain from her anything but an unwavering and positive denial.

Is it likely that, if their liaison had existed for a few months, no one would have suspected it within such a restricted sphere of action, where this woman attracted attention and the man was notorious for his boisterous ways and his indiscretion? How could neither the friends of the latter, nor the servants of the former (I inquired into all this) have had no indications, no revelations to offer?

Is it probable that at her death, to which it was my misfortune to be witness and unwittingly contribute, a woman so gentle and so easily alarmed should have gone to her last sleep with the look of innocence, and without uttering a word which might have unburdened her of this baneful secret or be some small atonement for this sad mystery?

This is one side of the problem.

On the other hand is it credible that a man should throw himself into a whirlpool of misfortunes, which he must have foreseen, without believing he was within his right in daring to face them, without the pretence of past favours and the excuse of reborn desires? that, since he was always employed in these pursuits, he should select a woman the better placed to ruin him because of her position and surroundings, and the most likely to expose his presumption by the clamour of her opposition? that he should persist in an attempt to enter a bedroom where he had no title to admittance, where he suspected a rival, and that he should wish wantonly to confront a man against whom he had nothing to object?

Is it credible that he should fly into so real and sudden a rage on account of purely imaginary rights and a presumed insult which caused him so to forget his manners as to put up a

lion's defence against a group of valets over whom victory
could mean only shame? that he should so degrade himself as
publicly to bring dishonour on a woman of whom he knew
nought but her virtue, and that he could commit the infamy of
throwing her back a key he must have stolen, without even the
shameful justification of regretting its use? that he should
threaten with his vengeance a woman who owed him nothing,
and a man whose happiness it was his place to respect if it did
not deserve his reproaches?

Is it credible that he should call two of his friends and with
tears of despair declare his anger legitimate; that he should burn
letters he does not show but swears to be mementoes of love
from the woman who causes his death, and finally that he should
kill himsef, still persisting to the very last in his fury of de-
nunciation and accusation?

This is the other side.

It is the mystery.

Did a woman deserve contempt who, having had but one
lover, remained faithful to him? What is more: should she
arouse hatred if, having fallen twice, she refused to give herself
again, since she had returned to her first choice?

Must one pity excessively a man who on our first supposition
was a monster let loose, and on the other an enraged man lacking delicacy? But society does not look at things so closely; it
absolves the dead and condemns those who remain behind; it
gives praise with due compunction; it approves, but with reser-
vations; it judges without pity, and blames by a flash of instinct.

The Marquise de Br—— recovered; she and her family
withstood the storm; she kept a good house, so people came
back to her; if she had been a nobody without the advantages of
fortune, she would have been hopelessly forsaken.[3] I advised
her to go to Paris, that abyss where stories which in the province
are the subject for long-drawn gossip are quickly effaced and forgotten and give food only to the fugitive talk of the moment.
She believed me.

She had awakened in me an ardent love, which I had the
modesty not to mention to her, seeing her present state of mind;
she was grateful to me; later I was rewarded.

To visit Italy had been, from early youth, one of my live-
liest desires. I yielded to it, and with no unusual incidents I found
myself on the first of February, 17—, quite naturally at Lyons,

that populous commercial city which it is one of the good works
of the new government to have restored from its ruins.

There is nothing remarkable in Chambéry, a small town with
a population of at most ten thousand inhabitants. The only observation to be made about it is that it was the retreat of King
Victor-Amedeus in 1730, after his abdication and his marriage
with Mme de Saint-Sèbastien. Before reaching Turin one feels
dejected at the sight of the great number of people with goitre
for which Savoy seems the cradle. But with what delight the
eyes rest on that superb town of Turin, so regularly and uni
formly laid out on the banks of the Po, from which one of the
most beautiful streets in the world borrows its name! The
savage Attila razed it to the ground in 405. It claims to-day
eighty thousand souls. It had belonged to the house of Savoy
since 1278. It was three times conquered by the French; first
under King François I, known for his valour; a second time in
1640; and at last during the revolutionary wars, this time becoming for ever an integral part of the French Empire.[4]

Although the King's palace is one of the finest of the residences of crowned heads in Italy—on account of its splendour
as much as its good taste—yet it is in no way very extraordinary;
the town theatre, however, is one of the finest anywhere, and
the citadel is a miracle of its kind.

My stay in Turin does not permit me to supply clear information about the manners and customs of its polite society,
but, from what I saw, decorum and nobility prevailed in its
social life. The court set an example to a wily and frivolous nation, which was thus led back to more dignity and seriousness
through the character of its crowned heads.

The fair sex at Turin, generally speaking, owes a debt of
gratitude to Nature.

From Turin to Milan the road is adorned by numerous
country houses, and the beautiful plain of Lombardy offers a
widespread and magnificent scene, enlivened by a crowd of interesting towns where the only improvement one might desire
is better inns.

Milan, the third in rank amongst Italian cities, counts I believe more than a hundred and fifty thousand inhabitants. But
the annals of mankind are mostly records of the misfortunes, the
follies, and the cruelties of the inhabitants of our planet. This
glorious city was pillaged about the middle of the twelfth century; its site was turned to plough-land and salt given to the

ground in place of seeds. Hideous barbarity of conquerors! Prodigious industry of the conquered! Man possesses a frightful and marvellous faculty for annihilating and recreating everything except himself.

So I was in this Milanese province, once conquered by François I and for ever a sore in French history, since the battle of Pavia where the pick of France's nobility perished and her king was made prisoner, only regaining his freedom by breaking an oath he had given under circumstances which almost absolve him from perjury: a baneful battle which gave Austria the possession of this land covered with the laurels we had watered with our blood!

Milan contains several buildings that deserve attention. The canal, which joins the town to the Adda, is the chief means of irrigation for its territory. Public and private art galleries offer many fine pictures. Its aristocracy is noteworthy for its courtesy and in hospitality displays much magnificence. Its women (one must always return to the sex) display attraction and charm.

To whom would not this sky bring back the memory of the famous Gaston de Foix, that dazzling hero, nephew of Louis XII, and governor of this duchy? He was but twenty-four when he perished in the arms of Victory and carried to the grave a fame which usually is the reward only of captains whose hair has become white with the years.

I received at Milan a letter which put a stop to this journey in classic lands, and I was obliged hurriedly to come back to France.[5] It contained the news of the death of my grandmother on the maternal side, for whom I grieved, though I was to get from her a fairly considerable inheritance. I came back to the province of Maine more quickly than I had left it, so as to set my affairs in order, and I found myself fairly rich, could I henceforth have been wiser. I once again saw the Marquise de Br——, whose charm and misfortunes had so moved me; she was still sorrowful but accessible to consolation. I found her as fresh as a flower, and her face, expressing sensitiveness and melancholy, lent her irresistible attraction. She knew to what extent I had taken her part; I loved her too well to remember this, she loved me because she had not forgotten it.

From this attachment were born the results that were bound to follow: endless misfortunes, quarrels amidst a united family, insulting talk from the outside world, which we learnt to disregard and which ceased because we were proof against it. Calumny chiefly feeds on the resentment of it, which even enhances slander. Some time passed before the husband—whose friendship I had been careful to cultivate—had sufficient proofs to create a scandal, always superfluous when it comes too late. He was a man of honour dissatisfied with the court, against which he thought he had grounds for complaint for the simple reason that an uncle of his had had grounds for satisfaction. For one stupid singularity of ancient France was the belief that court favour is family property. The husband to whom I refer here had some sort of rights which he grossly exaggerated and of which no notice was taken because he was not overgifted and did not push himself forward; he consoled himself by a sharp turn about at the Revolution; it was like seeking distraction with the birch. He had been madly in love with his wife, whose feelings towards him were those of friendship and esteem. The bonds uniting her to him had already slackened; the certainty of my happiness severed them. The way he secured proofs of what it would have suited him best to ignore is unique.

There was to be held at the theatre what in the provinces is called a *rout;* if you like, a *bal de l'Opéra*. At supper we had all agreed to go, except M. de Br——, who declared himself very tired and ready for bed; he hoped we should enjoy ourselves. But he did not keep his word, for putting on a fancy costume and a domino he went to the ball, and recognised us easily, though we were as effectively disguised as himself. We two had at first wandered about the ballroom, but soon sought a seat during a talk enlivened by such sensuous feelings as build up the life of love—its quarrels, its reconciliations—and form, I am ashamed to say, its greatest, perhaps its unique charm.

A masked figure followed us, and settled down on the same bench. . . . Was he dead? No, without ceremony he was asleep on my shoulder. The most amusing things become boring in time, so after a while I pushed him away, begging him no longer to take me as his pillow. He stammered some words of excuse in an effeminate voice, then fell asleep again with the same rudeness and in the same position. I had, it so chanced, decided that during the evening Mme de Br—— should be reproached with too much coolness towards me and warmth for another. I complained, although in whispers, yet in the voice of passion and with the gestures suited to youth consumed by burning love. The tiresome domino, immovable, encumbered me . . . all his weight pressed upon me, while now and again a stray sigh escaped his oppressed chest. I pushed him back with annoyance, having long paid no heed to what attention he gave the conversation because of that I brought to it myself. He moved at last and pressed me close. Mme de Br—— stared at the domino, looked him over from head to foot . . .

"Good heavens," she whispered to me in fright, "I am lost! It is my husband!"

"Impossible!"

"It is he."

"Let us go."

We got up; he followed us, tried to grasp my arm; I freed myself roughly; a party of people came between us, and we lost ourselves in the crowd; he never found us again. . . . But imagine my despair and embarrassment. Our talk had been clear, it would have been so even to an indifferent listener.

We put our heads together, and she hesitated to go home. She wanted to take refuge with her mother, or her sister in Paris, and to ask for an amicable separation. I was against this plan, advising her to assume a calm and assured attitude, to await what would happen, and to deny everything.

She was not forced to this, for her husband on the next day started for Paris, to watch over a lawsuit that did not require his presence, and only when half-way through his journey did he write a cold and dignified letter. He told her that his absence would be long, that he wished to be informed of the time she would choose to join him, so that he might come back to Le Mans to look after his house and his money affairs. It was evident he dreaded a scandal, that he wished to spare his son's mother, but that he had decided no longer to live with her, or at any rate not while he had to dispute her with her lover.

Love, which makes up for everything when it is strong enough, afforded her consolation in a situation the disgrace of which she could not easily hide from herself. I was everything to her, and I felt more than ever her slave since she had taken such risks. A new letter from M. de Br—— informed her that he was in wretched health, feeling his strength giving way, and that he feared he could not live long. Other people of the family confirmed this news. She had too much heart to rejoice, but she dared to look forward to a future we had not foreseen. We both dreamed, without telling each other, of one day being indissolubly bound together. Her private income was quite important. I tried to reason with myself, for there nevertheless remained that incident of M. de Ma——, who died for her after so tragic an adventure that a bloody shroud covered his uncertain spirit. But I thought it difficult to marry her only because she was rich. She, for her part, dreaded lest I should refuse her. Half her days were spent in weeping, while I sat at her feet and questioned her on the cause of her tears, partly guessing, however, what it might be. At last our hearts, feeling less oppressed, understood each other; we talked openly about it in one of those happy moments when love is the more faithful for being the more indiscreet.

But He who mocks at our schemes and rends asunder our hopes had ordered otherwise. This preparation for Hymen was to be transformed into a ceremony of mourning. A grave was awaiting the woman who looked towards the altar. That was to be her bridal bed, the harsh bed where mankind is put to sleep. She was to rest there long before the husband whose place at her side her deluded imagination had reserved for me.

Sad recollections! lamentable pictures of which the colours are still vivid after twenty years! Punishments proportioned to the aberrations so frequent in my life, and casting upon it so much bitterness, have brought me misfortunes and enmity, and dismally caused my life to wane.

I had spent fifteen hours by her side without leaving her, and had then, against my wish, gone to be bored at a dinner party. There I received a note from her, written in an enfeebled hand: "Come, do not lose a minute, I am dying." Neither seemliness nor consideration stopped me; I uttered a cry, and rushed out without taking leave of my host. I reached her. Alas, life was almost gone from her brow! Her sweet and tender eyes were dull and wandering; all over her adorable face were the imprint and colour of death. Surrounded by medical men, she was placed on a bed set in the middle of her room, amidst confusion and disorder. Fainting fits, at the rate of ten in the hour, were in turn taking her from us and giving her back. Savonnières,[6] who has since lost his life through a generous and faithful death following the events of the fifth of October, tried to pull me out of this room which I filled with my lamentations. One of my relatives, Mme de Fondville [7]—whose beauty, famous in her province as in Paris, has kindled so many passions, and who, as a new Ninon, saw the triumphal car of her charms surrounded by worshippers to the very end—was also by the death-bed and advised me to retire or at least control my awful despair; but, on my knees by the bed, I held a cold hand in my burning one and grieved on till night. They then demanded that out of decency I should retire to my home; I dragged myself to the rooms of one of Mme de Br——'s maids, where I was kept informed of her state at every moment of the night, though in spite of all skill it remained unchanged. She at last gathered up what strength was left her when morning came, and sent for me. Slowly, and with great effort, she entreated me to forgive her such a death. She clasped my head to her bosom and, bathing it with tears, she explained of what rash imprudence she had been guilty; she had been weak enough to fear the world, and heaven was punishing her; she had wished to avoid giving birth to a being not yet formed, and three weeks previously she had taken a drug which a surgeon had assured her offered no danger, but she firmly believed this was the cause of her death. She requested that, without seeking information and bringing trouble upon this man, I should keep the secret unbroken.

She assured me she had faithfully and solely loved me, and had fallen into only one other error that had not been prompted by a guilty passion. She grieved over the unhappiness to which her death would deliver me, making as it were tender excuses, and bade me take without delay all my letters, which were in a drawer she pointed out. She entreated me to see that she died, and if possible was buried, with my portrait, which she wore on her heart inside a locket. . . . She kissed it again and again, and ended this speech—punctuated by her tears and my sobs— by begging me to be heedful of her husband, to show regard for his grief, and to avoid scrupulously all occasions for quarrels which would leave an indelible blot upon her name.

How easily death seems to come to those who wish not to go! How hard it is to die when one ought to do so, or when one wishes it! I was carried unconscious from the house. An hour later she was in a better world, and I remained alone in this one, having no courage to leave it nor emotion left to enjoy it, but filled with horror at her death and my own life.[8]

When she had breathed her last, Mme de Fondville and M. de Savonnières, who had then been with her, busied themselves with me; they brought me back to consciousness. Mme de Fondville, that excellent friend, kept me in her home; she coupled her grief to my despair and distracted me from my sufferings by sharing without trying to weaken them; two days later a postboy arrived; he was preceding M. de Br—— by a few hours.

. . . Mme de Fondville entreated me to retire into the country; I emphatically refused.

Savonnières added his entreaties to hers; I opposed them.

"Are you sure," he told me at last, "that nothing exists at her home which might discredit her memory? Have you recovered everything which could, in the hands of a husband, speak against her, all that might heedlessly break his heart, both as husband and father?"

"Everything except my portrait, which she desired to take away to her last resting place."

They both protested; he immediately left us and hurried to the house of mourning where he approached the bed in the midst of the women keeping watch, and, pretending to seek assurance that all was indeed ended, detached the locket which he brought back to me. This was a renewed affliction, I could almost say a new object of terror.

Through a false sense of honour, I remained for some time in the town, but then tore myself away from a place where M. de Br—— affected such indifference as to win back every heart to the unhappy woman who no longer heeded this world. I bade farewell to a city which was about to consume all that remained of what I had so much loved, of her whom it seemed I should always worship since now death had taken her from me. I went to seek seclusion at the country house of a wise man who, in a a beautiful solitude, chose to forget his contemporaries and all their schemes. He comforted me, both with his mind and heart, yet could not instil into mine the blessings of his wisdom and the quietude of his old age. He offered to follow me to Paris; but to make him forsake the peace of the country and the freshness of his woodlands for noise and mud, to make him exchange so much quietness for all the agitation of which he had taken leave, would have been badly to repay him for his care and kindness; it would have been a refinement of ingratitude. I went alone. Only my grief held me to life; it cast an inexpressible spell over one who had no happiness save that of having none. I should have had less regard for myself if I had found more consolation.

The sweet vision of her I mourned long saved me from any new love. More than six months later, as I was at the Palais Royal one fine evening, I heard her sister burst into peals of laughter while talking to a man I knew; I felt (it was no doubt exaggerated) a sort of indignation and anger. It seemed to me that this mirth was an insult to her memory; I should have liked nobody to laugh in her family. I went home in a mental and physical state impossible to describe; I was bled several times and this simple incident, I do not know how, reopened my wound so deeply as to bring me to the brink of the grave. It was some time later that I saw the Marquis de Br—— at the Prince de Condé's house. He scarcely looked at me, but I could not take my eyes off him; he brought her back to me so powerfully that I was near loving him; he seemed undisturbed and behaved with propriety, though he appeared to eat too much. Alas, I wanted to give away my heart, with all its regrets and emotions, to everything that had belonged to her, to all that surrounded me. . . . But the dead seldom leave long memories behind; and tears are soon dried that fall on the marble slab of the tomb.

At about this time Mme de Fondville died. Her end followed a painful and slow illness. I was attached to her by many ties, and wanted to return her friendship with the same attentions she had bestowed upon me, but I arrived only in time to witness the death of a woman well worthy to leave a name on account of her remarkable mind and a face which was even more so. She never entered the winter of life; hers remained a prolonged spring right on to sixty.

It is a fact that shortly before her death she might have inspired a most violent love in a certain young man whose education in all ways she could have undertaken as well as any woman in France. She had exquisite taste, and was able to adapt herself to every circle of life, though she was born in the best. She had spent half her life in the provinces, but whenever she was in Paris one would have believed she had never left town. She had very distinguished friends, especially the last Maréchal de Duras, MM. de Thiard and Le Voyer, who were not men to be infatuated with ugliness or to encourage stupidity.

The town of Le Mans became unbearable to me after her death; though I still had in the neighbourhood some property interests, I resolved never to return to it, and I kept my word. Mme de Fondville's tomb was situated not far from that of the unfortunate Marquise de Br——; in the end their dust may mingle. Sadly, yet almost sweetly, I forced myself, before I took my leave, to visit these two monuments which love and friendship led me to regard as sacred. It was towards midnight and during a night as gloomy as my heart.

As I entered the cemetery where sleep in their everlasting

rest these two women, one above all so dearly loved, my hair stood on end, but the eternal luminary of night, which so far had been veiled, began to throw light on this precinct of death. I fell to my knees to thank our Supreme Master for this light, and I dared appeal to Him for her repose and mine. I know not whether my voice, stifled by sighs and tears, ascended up to His throne or descended to the graves, but some sort of peace and tender devotion suffused my heart, pouring into it the solace of religion, and of that compassion which is a credit to mankind. I rose with less guilty impulses and more inclination to virtue.

Have I been wrong in lending this chapter the dismal aspect of Tartarus? . . . I alone survive of all those I have named. The portraits I have drawn in this chapter are all covered with mourning crape . . . a funeral veil which even the hand of Time cannot raise! To praise you, above all, loving Émilie, and you, my dear Dolomieu,[9] both early attachments of vanished happy days, and to bring tears amidst the cypresses growing by your graves, a more skillful and accomplished hand than mine was required. It might have lent more splendour to my recollections, but could not either add to or efface the bitterness. My first homage to your shades is to believe that it is but yesterday I have lost you, and that I shall never find consolation for this loss.

> Car si facilement les morts sont oubliés!
>   Si promptement les larmes sont séchées!
> Avec tant de dédain l'homme foule à ses pieds
>   De ses amis les cendres dispersées!
>   Qu'on a tort de croire aux regrets,
> Lorsqu'on sera parmi les ombres éternelles!
>   Qu'il est peu d'amis très fidèles,
> Et que peu de tombeaux sont ornés de cyprès!
> Moi je veux élever un monument durable
>   Aux souvenirs de mon printemps;
> L'amour et l'amitié donneront à mes chants
>   Un intérêt ineffaçable.
>   Je saurais défier le temps
>   D'anéantir l'histoire mémorable
> Des ces penchants si doux de mes premiers beaux ans,
>   Et d'une larme intarissable
> J'écrirai ma douleur sur les marbres parlants
>   De ce sépulcre impénétrable
>   Où mes amis dorment avant le temps.[10]

If these verses are not good, I see only one reason for it— perhaps one excuse: what one tries to do with the heart does not come up to what one should only do through talent.

CHAPTER XVII

Even of oneself one grows tired in the end,
No love for self left, if no loving friend;
The tedious days insipidly flow by,
And leave behind no memory when they die.[1]

*H*OW difficult it is to respond once more to life, and the delusions which cause us to love it, after an event so disastrous as to abide within consciousness to our dying day! Pleasures become mere seductions of which we must beware; it seems that Fortune can only set snares; hope, and even thought, no longer have wings; we seem rooted to the spot where unhappiness met us. Imagination tries again to rise towards new dreams, but falls back disheartened, since joy is no more and impotence causes despair. Just as a wounded bird might once more try its wings only to come to the ground bathed in its own blood. Yet the hand of Time, which mitigates all sorrows, at last metes out increasing consolation, for some hearts a cure, and for others a palliative. For my part I bear with patience the griefs which time could not cure.

A woman, who was never more than a relative, but who could read my heart and was pained at my sadness, tried to dispel it by finding me a wife. She proposed two matches offering no grounds for a refusal, for they provided me with ample freedom of choice; the less advantageous one was yet excellent. I decided in favour of the one promising the most comfort and happiness. I paid my court, without eagerness, though it appeared sufficient, but when there remained only to ask for and claim my reward, I gave it all up through some caprice of my head or of my grief.

It was about that time that my father, having carried out his scheme of settling on a pretty estate in the valley of Montmorency, came to live there close to his friend, the Commandeur de Champignolles, of whom I have already spoken. I made my home with him; he displayed good-hearted fatherly regard towards a grief the depth and continuance of which he could not understand. His kindness on this occasion is what has most en-

deared his memory to me. For I have never been influenced by
the voice of blood, and I confess that to have been begotten by a
certain person is but a scanty obligation to love him, if he has no
other title freer from chance and more essentially the outcome
of his own will.

My stepmother, like most women, was much moved by the
sight of a despondency due to love. Such a condition conceals
great dangers to the sex, for it swiftly leads to love for the man
who was at first only pitied. I did not myself remain unaffected
by the interest she took in me; but, at the first intimation of too
warm a feeling towards her who had so endeavoured to dry
my tears, I resolved to go away. I did it without making any
disturbance, and after a few months in this sweet seclusion,
I left to seek diversion from my thoughts by tiring myself with
hunting in Normandy. While making my way there, I felt a
sudden impulse to become a Trappist and bury my life in this
Thebaid.[2] I entered the solitude of the monastery where my
imagination had hoped for wild scenery and melancholy gloom;
but I found there neither the silent peace nor the drab desert I
had dreamt of through books. My fervour cooled, my grief was
disillusioned, a voice within me exclaimed: "Spirit by turns
profane and sacred, you tender and merciless Rancé, in your
gardens where these wretches are bent in labour, your Order
holds nothing of the solemn and religious charm my youth had
lent to it. On these insignificant pale faces I see no vestiges of
love or repentant ambition, no ravages of ardent passions. This
is silence in life without the peace of death. . . . You also, you
have cheated me!"

Great kindness was shown to strangers inside the monastery;
they gave me the room once occupied by the Duc de Penthière.
The recollection of his virtues did not reconcile me to the bad
fare which had been his and now was mine. I might have grown
used to living on bread and water, but never on the uneatable
food which was served. That of the mind was scarcely better;
the library contained many books, but of a bad selection. My
vocation was irrevocably dead by the third day. The story of one
monk, alone aroused my interest, for he was almost the only man
whose face was romantic and bore the marks of those great sufferings which instil in the heart a love of solitude and a hatred
of the world. I had more than once questioned him, while he
waited upon me as was his duty, before he condescended to
comply with my inquisitiveness.

I now leave him to speak:

"My name is Barbazan; I was born in Toulouse. My story

could be the subject of a *cause célèbre*. Before I came to join this flock of wretches who make amends here for the daring of their reformer, I had served my country. My father was a magistrate known for his stern probity. This austerity, becoming in a judge, had found its way into his inner life, and made me dislike the calling for which he intended me. Through one of my relatives I obtained a commission as lieutenant, and left the town where I had been born. I returned however after a few years, and became attracted to the charming daughter of a friend of my family, a judge in the supreme court, whose wealth was by far superior to ours. My father was the first to declare it would grieve him to see me paying my addresses in such a house, and that the more advantageous the match with his friend's daughter, the more need was there not to expose myself to a refusal or to the suspicion of greed. The young lady was instructed to the same effect; it all ended by an interdiction of any further meeting on our part, and, to make this more effective, our parents themselves ceased to see each other. But love, which thrives on difficulties, prompted us to overcome them all, and brought us together under cover of night. Heaven at first appeared privy to our deed, and did not betray my mistress through the disgrace of pregnancy; yet at last it wearied of protecting us. The crime it led me to commit was involuntary, but it leaves me an object of horror to myself: I killed my father. I was going up a back stairway; in the pitch darkness a strong hand gripped me, and the word 'scoundrel' is the last I heard from lips whose voice I ought not to have mistaken. I had a pistol about me; I killed on the spot the daring aggressor who had tried to fell me. As I told you, it was my father. Hearing the report, people appeared with lights; I made my escape, jumped on horseback and left the kingdom.

"It appears that my father, having gained information, had, without warning his misused friend, secured means of taking me by surprise, in order to confront me and put me to shame. His integrity could admit of no compromise with my passion. He had obtained a *lettre-de-cachet* for my arrest, and was going to offer me the choice between starting off to the West Indies, or languishing in prison until the death or the marriage of the young lady, whose disgrace, he hoped, would remain a secret. He thus deliberately wished to snatch from me both happiness and freedom, when in my ignorance I took his life. These details came later to my knowledge.

"For a few years I wandered about Spain. I heard that the

woman I had misled had buried her life in a convent; I thought I could emulate her. I preferred to die in my own country and under a hair-shirt, rather than to linger ignominiously begging a pittance amongst strangers. I have, for the last twenty years, endeavoured to make friends with myself, but I never find relief from my crime. I cannot grow accustomed to my grave; the road which leads away from life is not here a gentle slope; the penalty of expiation exceeds too much the crime of having been born, the path towards death is too steep, one has to trudge through too much suffering."

His tale, delivered with a southern accent which, I know not why, commands attention, was simple and curt. He seemed pleased once more to be silent; if his eyes could have known tears he would have wept. This I did in his stead; and that very evening left a retreat where prevailed a gloom sufficient to cause despair, but not to move the soul to such pensive sadness as raises it towards God.

A gentleman of this district proved to be fairly well equipped for hunting; his neighbours shared his sport and the expenses. They welcomed me, as if they had known me all their lives, and treated me as if they liked me. I remained with them for the greater part of the season, galloping by day in the forests, and in the evening (what is neither in very good taste nor very edifying) getting drunk with them. Night would then come to offer deep and needed sleep. Thus I learnt to forget a little and to acquire really good health. Such is to be found in the woods, in robust sport, far from the sybaritism of great cities, far from the fascinations and the musings which make one soft.

But what a poor gift life must be since our greatest comfort is nearly always to shake it off our mind!

Amongst these rather wildly and riotously joyful children, I became acquainted with an elderly man who had retained the vigour of younger years and could with impunity join the young people in their sports and pleasures. I say pleasures because they also went in for love-making, or at least what resembled it. This gentleman was M. de Nocé, great-nephew of the Regent's favourite. Fifty years previously he had joined the mousquetaires, and had known there many people of the best society; he had not lost the manners which are not found in the forests by hunting boars and stags. Can I ever forget that he then foresaw the Revolution?

"Sir," he would say to me, "open your annals; we are a

nation born for tragedy, yet for a long time none has taken place but on the stage. La Fronde, the religious wars, even the Saint Bartholomew's, these are tame compared to what awaits you. What stories you will have to tell if we meet again on the other side of the grave! The Queen is disliked, the King is weak; the ministers are incompetent and corrupt; our finances—the excuse for most revolts—are exhausted; the army retains the fame of former glory, but the great generals are dead and leave no pupils. For you there is still the stage, the finest in Europe, also some minor poets, some talented dancing-girls, and your courtesans, who would be the most seductive sirens upon earth if your wives could not give them points. All these fine things, however, and hair-dressers and cooks, are rather degenerate offshoots of the greatest nation in the world, as we were once in the greatest of ages, the days of Louis le Grand. These are not elements of life for an empire. France will perish, sir, *and during your lifetime*. She is like a worn-out blade which needs tempering in fire, and, in its degradation, to be steeped in blood before it is remade."

"I quite believe you," I told him, "but I shall not see it. It is an inheritance for our nephews."

The mistake was mine. He was wise.

I ought before this to have mentioned the journey of Joseph II to France.[3] But since it was not till my return to Paris that I noticed the first strong suspicions which marked the Queen out for the hatred of the people, because she was presumed to have given to her brother important sums of money, I only now speak of this monarch.[4]

It would be easy to bind myself to precise dates, but I confess I have no memory for such; I should find it unbearable to seek, at every minute, the help of outside sources, always so boring even when they are reliable.

I shall have the opportunity, and I will not disregard it, to refute the absurd slanders heaped upon the Queen; but to *deny everything* would serve badly both her memory and truth. I shall allow for her weaknesses, but when once I have sorted out lies from real facts she will retain no more frailty than befits her sex or any human being—yet enough to be pitied by the most insensitive souls for having been more ill-fated than the most guilty heroines in history, or any fictitious characters in novels. But, in the main, if I reject these popular and slanderous rumours, impartiality obliges me to say that I have grounds (the authority for which I cannot divulge without compromising an illustrious family) to believe that, either as loans or gifts, the Queen handed over to her brother sums which he was as guilty to accept as she was to offer. These sums are far from amounting to the figures party spirit and malice made them out to be; but when could voracious lips, feeding on gall and imposture so as to discredit both private and public individuals, ever voice the decrees of justice and moderation? Besides, if this accusation is founded, as I think it is, the Queen was betrayed by a blind attachment to her house.

I now come to what I believe to be the real character of this strange monarch.

He was too good for a throne to which he proved no credit. He had gifts superior even to his station, which he was yet unable to fill; all his care went to the army, whose glory waned under his hand; he wore himself out sitting up late over reforms and schemes for the splendour of an empire that declined during his reign. This prince, so superior to the majority of men, was yet a more indifferent ruler than most kings. He was in theory a great philosopher, but in practice a powerless administrator; wishing to remedy abuses, he added to them, and through contempt for love in the manner of honest men, he relished vulgar debauch as the lowest of his subjects might have done.

He went to war against the Turks, when his one thought should have been to win the respect of the rest of Europe for his military power. This war only weakened his army instead of rendering it more martial. He was more a soldier than a general; without perhaps having all the courage of the one, he lacked the great qualities of the other, such gifts as he possessed not being in a prince sufficient justification for a love of war, though in the eyes of nations they are a brilliant excuse for it.

His experiments were disastrous both as supreme magistrate and as law-maker, and he lost credit through trying new ways of winning it. Eager to be popular, he succeeded only in being singular and even feared. In a word, he reigned as a man would who—having studied divinity, the law, rhetoric, and philosophy —had reached the throne by means of a rebellion without knowing beforehand that it was his inheritance.

He arrived at the court under the name of Count von Falkenstein, glad to see his sister, the Queen, whom he loved; he went away discontented because he loved her less after having seen her on the throne of France. One might have believed he

was unaware she was there, and had been ignorant of the importance of such a kingdom; he was unable to hide his ill humour at
having so powerful a brother-in-law.

What no doubt did him most credit was the immediate estimate his shrewd envy enabled him to reach of what such a
country could be and could achieve. He was alarmed by the
wealth and resources of the state, by the flourishing condition
of the provinces, the numerous towns, fortifications, arsenals,
dock-yards, ports, etc. He was above all offended by the splendour of the capital.

He affected popularity as was his habit in Vienna, thus surprising the learned men; and he displeased the philosophers
because he showed them it was not difficult to be one. He displayed extreme simplicity and moderation before a nation accustomed to know its princes by their magnificence, which is a
protection for rulers against fickleness and disloyalty.

He went to Luciennes to see Mme du Barry, the famous
royal mistress, who will stand out in the Revolution as the only
woman who did not know how to die when that was the fashion.
She had been the enemy of his sister, and had indecorously
sought occasions to wound the Queen. He thought fit not to
remember this, and the Queen was most displeased. He even paid
an insipid compliment to this ancient beauty. Mme du Barry's
garter had become undone, he picked it up, and, as she was lost
in apologies, he exclaimed that "emperors were not too great
to be servants to the Graces." Emperor Charles V of Spain had
picked up Titian's brush; this was for love of art. Edward, not
satisfied with having handed back her garter to the Countess of
Salisbury, made it the emblem of an order of knighthood; this
for love of his mistress. Joseph II was content with saying a
stupid thing, for a dull compliment out of place is nothing else.

He was less gallant at Lyons where vexation and ill humour
took such hold of him that he harshly remarked to some distinguished ladies of the town assembled to see him: "Well,
ladies, you see me! I warn you, I am neither Adonis nor Hercu-
les." Words one would call coarse from lips to which one dared
to apply the name they deserved. Ruder still was his remark
to a gentleman who, wishing to be useful, cleared people out of
the Prince's way: "Did I choose you, sir, as my master of ceremonies?" This again at Lyons where, I repeat, all he saw appeared to throw him into an absurd rage he was not skillful
enough to hide.

He longed to take his departure, and that was to repent
having come. His attitude towards the King remained throughout the visit that of the most obedient courtier, and he behaved
to the courtiers as a most polite equal.

He went away with a heart full of envy, hatred, and the
positive design to do us as much harm as he could; he had sufficient will to keep his word, but he lacked the necessary genius.
Had he been alive at the outbreak of the Revolution, he would
at first have been its ardent advocate, and notwithstanding his
ambitious schemes and the political welfare of his country, he
would have opposed it only when too late. It is true our history
might not have been stained by the Queen's death; he would have
had enough influence through his acquaintance in philosophical
circles to redeem this august victim. Had he, however, failed
in this, and the Queen been submitted to the frightful fate meted
out to her by cannibals, he would, I am convinced, have sacrificed his whole army to the last man, perhaps even through pride
exposed his very life as emperor, the better to satisfy the vengeance of a brother.

Everything was to be bizarre in the fate of this prince; he
never had a friend (except perhaps Marshal Lascy), though
he pretended to lay aside royalty and every day to live more as
a man than an emperor. He felt a tender affection for his
nephew's first wife, a marriage he had arranged almost in spite
of his brother, afterwards Emperor Leopold, who held other
views for his son, or at least did not share Joseph's. But it had
become necessary to obey a brother who could bestow thrones to
his heir and who himself threatened to marry.

This charming princess died prematurely in the midst of
the unhoped-for splendour which seemed to have come to her
hand only to break like a fragile toy. She was universally
regretted.[5]

The Emperor, out of the affection he bore her, and perhaps
also in order to do nothing like other people, died on the very
day of her death, and left to his brother a dazzling but much
entangled inheritance. This has since been made more secure
and solid by means of an art which is not ordinary: that of
defeat. For defeats have been of much value to the Austrian
monarchy, or even proved more profitable than victories which
would have aroused envy, and (though this sounds almost incredible) they have in no way tarnished the brilliant exploits of
its brave troops, headed in later days by one of those heroes [6]
so numerous in our country.

The death of Joseph II left people free to think that he had lived either too long or too little; he had had time to conceive disastrous schemes, but not to carry them out; yet a few of the weakest parts of these plans might have acquired strength if once they had been combined in a whole.

This prince will puzzle history; I have seen men of sound judgement who had had the honour of being much with him, but whose penetration and impartiality were nevertheless at a loss: they would have been hard put to tell all the good that was in him, or enough of the evil.

I retain, from all I was able to gather, that he was a man more surprising than admirable, more singular than rare, more amiable than attractive, more brilliant than solid, and more extraordinary than great. He was a genius with more enterprise than vision, and vision greater than wisdom; in a word he possessed a thousand fine qualities which are of no use to kings, being for them superfluous, and lacked those which in a prince are absolutely necessary. He resembled those comets which light up the sky, but lay waste the earth in passing over it.

I come back to his unhappy sister, whose mistakes and faults it is wise to acknowledge in order to vindicate her from the monstrous accusations with which her life has been blackened, and to clear her memory for posterity of the mire which so absurdly soils it, through back-stairs gossips, or libels which most likely originated in the same quarters and should have died there.

My respect for her sex, her misfortune, her reputation, and the triumph of truth will lead me with no hesitation to approach the most delicate aspect of her life: the long series of lovers for whom her wanton hand exhausted itself in throwing a shameless handkerchief—this if we are to credit the voice of many scoundrels whose information was manufactured in garrets where, in the pay of the Furies, they wrote down the echoes of ravenous slander.

It is difficult, even in a circle of intimate friends, to decide with certainty whether a woman has yielded to the lover she is credited with. If she be skillful, if he proves neither clumsy nor indiscreet, if above all—which rarely happens—they have an equal interest to seek secrecy, even the most experienced onlooker may well be deceived. A man, even one most lacking in principles, rarely takes the initiative in indiscretion; it is nearly always the woman who betrays a secret she asks us to keep. We give her this promise, whether we are honest or not, but she a

moment later confides in a friend who all the more readily
spreads the story abroad since she has also pledged her word not
to do so. The happy lover, having thus an excuse, may then abuse
it; his pride, and sometimes also his feelings, may cause him
to reveal the mystery of an attachment that will offer sport to
malice long after those who entered into it are bored with each
other. Nevertheless, I have witnessed in society a thousand instances of mistakes, of misunderstandings, and erroneous judgement. A man is given a mistress who is not his, another is denied
the favours of a lady whom he had enjoyed longer than was
his wish. I have seen a woman conceal one or two lovers from
an outside world that six months later made up for its ignorance
by unfairness. I have often seen two people, equally concerned
in keeping secrecy, enjoy for a long time, and perhaps for ever,
a happiness where love is strengthened by the delights of mystery. Concealing veils can be devised for this sort of union as
for most things upon earth; and few men could be found who
do not carry to the grave the knowledge of some deed that will
never be disclosed. I know that a contrary assumption is generally the one to prevail; yet, by the side of this, there is room
also for mine.

It is clear that ordinary lovers have numerous chances of
escaping indiscreet curiosity. What chances then will curiosity
have of viewing people so remote that even the best eyes can
scarcely reach them? what chances of forming an opinion when
its only guides are distant and uncertain lights, so that everything concurs to lead it astray? Curiosity will have few chances
if honour and life be at stake, perhaps for both lovers—for the
man who must seek safety in circumspection, for the woman
placed in so high a station that she can make love only on the
brink of an abyss. Will they commit a blunder? neglect a single
precaution? betray themselves by avowal, or by seeking a confidant? Where is the person who took them by surprise? Let
him who saw them together come forth. If any accomplice was
admitted to this fearful secret, the weight of such responsibility is so enormous that indisputably it would guarantee discretion. Argus himself would fail to catch red-handed such a
daring woman who has all to fear, yet finds security only so long
as prudence feeds such fear and caution guides her pleasures;
he would fail to discover her lover, who even in the midst of
happiness must dread discovery at least for his beloved, admitting he be strong enough not to dread it for himself.

Where is even part evidence of these numerous imputations, of all these presumptions and outrageous indictments? Where are the foundations for these suppositions, and the guiding threads in this labyrinth? What hand discovered them? what other took them on? The men who might have had the right to speak, accustomed to silent deference, have shown no inclination to talk. Discreet and reserved as to facts they might well know, they guarded themselves against mere conjectures. Who then elaborated this concert of calumnies and blasphemies? Who else but subalterns, intriguers, scribblers, low wantons, idlers in cafés, who were all in a better position to know what was happening in Peking than what was done at Versailles or Trianon. Unfortunate Queen! You have been unjust to me, who should not show surprise at this as I have been so to others, to me, who in your brilliant circle was only a small insignificant speck. At some proper time I will show how and why you were unjust, but now my sensitiveness to justice will not lead me to use the colours of prejudice. I shall avenge your shade with the weapons of truth, and if some people may pretend that this truth itself accuses you, Europe, hitherto so misinformed, will see that I vindicate you.[7]

The young Queen, then the Dauphine, on her arrival at Versailles found herself constrained by a ceremonial and a strict etiquette for which she was not prepared. No court in Europe, not even that of Maria Theresa her august mother, provided so many spare moments for idleness, imposed so many necessary limitations to the rank of queen, or displayed such unchangeable uniformity in the deportment of its crowned heads, a deportment almost enjoined by the routine-like deference of the courtiers. I should say in passing that in no country (and this may be one of the causes of the Revolution, which no revolution will, however, alter) has there been so great a distance between man and man, or has the supreme rank soared to so lofty a height.

Beauty, talent, and charm find no advantage in concealing themselves behind pride; it is sweet intercourse will give them their full value. It is difficult to convince a young princess that it is a better policy to make oneself respected than loved, that to be bored is more useful in the long run than to please. The Dauphine, finding herself at the first the idol of a great nation, could hardly have thought so much love would change to so much hatred, that it would prove an unforgivable crime to laugh when one is queen, or to welcome to one's side, by the throne, friend-

ship, pleasures, and the unconstraint of private life. This was
the first grievance, the first word uttered by the voice that later
accused her.

Her presence on the terrace at Versailles, where beautiful
night festivities and sometimes music enticed her amidst a crowd
who delighted in seeing her, was a new pretext for evil minds
to seize. She would often appear there without the escort which
a queen of France drags in her train, but never so much alone,
never so devoid of respectful attendance, that any except fools
could find fault with her behaviour. Yet the first weapons to
wound her were sought in these festivities. The balls of the
Opéra, those at the Town Theatre, the intimacy with which she
honoured Mme de Lamballe, her lasting friendship for Mme
de Polignac opened a new field for fresh accusations. Her dislike of the restraint and strict observance of formalities pertaining to her station was mistaken for contempt and forgetfulness
of her duties. Although no woman knew better than she did
how to perform her part of queen when she so wished, the independence of her ways was interpreted as moral looseness, her
dislikes were looked upon as fits of wanton temper, and her
kindness as a sign of guilty lapses.

The King, who possessed a thousand estimable virtues, had
few of those which compel love, and still less those attractions
most compatible with the tastes of the feminine mind. The
Queen, absolutely devoted to the King (as she so well proved
when misfortune came), felt at first more bound by duty than
drawn by an affection that adversity was to render more fervent
and tender. This attitude was a homage to virtue such as a heart
essentially devoid of virtuous leanings could not have paid.
Boredom, which has such hold over certain souls; the springtime
of stormy youth, which has so many fights to sustain with the
senses and passions; the forced idleness of the great, who being
wearied by ceremonial feel much in need of rest in quiet friendship; the atmosphere of adulation surrounding a woman twice a
queen by virtue of her rank and her charm; the swarm of courtiers young and old, hiding their feelings out of respect; these
things will always besiege a beautiful queen and prove enervating unknown to herself.

Women are excellent judges of the effect produced by their
charms: this princess knew positively, especially on two occasions,[8] that she had inspired love the expression of which had
only been repressed through the exercise of will, a sense of pro-

priety, and the possible danger. Most women would have behaved with consideration towards the men whom their charms
had wounded. She showed no contempt for feelings which are
a homage to a queen as to a shepherdess; but at court, where
these two men were of high standing, she displayed only the
mildest interest in them. Had she had a pronounced leaning to
gallantry, could she have been hard put for choice, since the
court offered some remarkable young people? Her aloofness and
coldness towards young men were on the contrary distinctive
traits of her character. The only man one has to acknowledge,
since she singled him out, was at least forty-five: the Duc de
Coigny.[9] He was neither handsome nor a man of much wit. He
had what was better: a kindly countenance, exquisite manners, a
fine bearing, a mind simple and judicious, a calm serene politeness, a sincere heart neither corrupted by high position nor
spoilt by favour. Loved by everybody he himself hated no one.

This attachment lasted long; the Queen remained faithful
to it without, so I believe, any motive of passion. She afterwards
had to dispute the man she so esteemed with a woman whom he
later married, but she did it with kindness and moderation, and
this woman was never ill used by her. Envy and malice had
little to seize upon. The Queen was reserved, the Duc de Coigny
simple and quiet. He never abused her favour either to boast of
it or to advance his fortune, which remained practically what
it had been except for the peerage granted him after their
friendship was severed. He was the first to withdraw from an
intimacy which alarmed him, and to which so many would with
pleasure have sacrificed their lives. She was affected by this,
remaining for a time offended, but had the generosity to forgive.
She honoured with her unwavering friendship this man who no
doubt had not sufficiently appreciated the supreme happiness,
for such I view it, he had sought in the autumn of life. He pretended that the suspicions prevalent at court would before long
find their way to the heart of the one man whose ignorance it
was his concern to prolong; on one occasion he thought himself
lost. . . . How could a man remain amiable when thus plunged
in terror? He conceived that it would be the height of skill and
caution to show himself engrossed for a while by a dancer at the
Opéra. The King heard of this, as it was meant he should, and
publicly teased the Duke about it; this was presumed sufficient
to avert suspicion. M. de Coigny congratulated himself on so
clever a scheme, but the Queen expressed her opinion severely.

She disdained a safety resulting from such fine precautions, bitterly taunted him on his bravery, looked askance upon him, and ended it all with a friendship that never abated.

Wounded in her pride, she never dreamt of replacing him by another; she sought and found happiness in her task as mother.

Am I condemned to run through the absurd list of presumed lovers who never approached her nearer than the Great Mogul? Must I begin gravely by disposing of these frightful slanders? Must I seriously assert that they are all as absurd and devoid of reality as her love encounters with the Duke of Dorset,[10] whom she had nicknamed "the old woman"; with Dillon, whom she for one moment treated with kindness, but who straightway disgusted her with his fatuity; with the Duc de Liancourt, who was a sort of favourite but of no consequence; with Prince George of Hesse-Darmstadt, in whom she interested herself on account of his sister and because he was a German; with Roure, whose death particularly affected her; with Lambertye, officer in the royal guards, whom she noticed a short while (as if queens were not allowed as well as common mortals to find a person more or less attractive without exposing themselves to odious imputations); with a M. de Saint-Paër, to whom she showed marked consideration because he loved a woman pleasing to the Queen; with a Comte de Romanzof; with an Englishman, one of the Conways, since Lord Hugh Seymour; with the Duc de Guines; and to complete at last this ridiculous list, with the Comte de Vaudreuil, and the Duc de Polignac, of whom she could and would not have thought? Wickedness and stupidity have added to the aforesaid lovers—as fantastic as those who might have been found for her in the moon—others whose existence I should find it both unbearable and superfluous to challenge.[11]

Poor people! To be so convinced that if a queen of France had an uncontrollable leaning towards gallantry she could have satisfied it despite her rank and the unconscious but ever-present supervision of the court, or of her own private household! Not even a Ninon placed on a throne could have succeeded amidst such organisation; she would have been forced, by degrees, to learn virtue.

Yet this place of high favour, which calumny has filled so easily, had been occupied once, and was now vacant. The man destined to win the Queen's confidence, to be the last one admitted to her intimacy and the most deeply, the Comte de Fersen, was about to appear.[12]

His father, who in Sweden belonged to what was called the French party, had been in command of a French regiment and later became a lieutenant-general. The son, when starting life, found himself in the best position to acquire some knowledge of public affairs; he had been entrusted to the Baron de Breteuil as attaché to the French embassy at Naples. Later he obtained the command of the Swedish Guard attached to the King and received a fairly high pay, secured for him by the Queen. He was one of the handsomest men I ever saw, though with an icy countenance, which women do not dislike if they can hope to give it animation. I do not believe he had a very distinguished mind, but what he had helped him to behave with calm and moderation in the difficult position attained by him. He was fond of music, arts, and a peaceful life; he lived without intrigue and without seeking renown; if anything at any time caused one to suspect the high degree of his favour, it was his attitude of greater propriety, greater respect, which perhaps slightly partook of the courtier's affectation.

Yet it was not affectation; his whole art lay in his ingenuousness. The Queen never varied in her feelings towards him; this long and tender constancy in itself best refutes the infamous conduct of which she has been accused. The King placed his trust in M. de Fersen when he planned his flight to Montmédy.[18] After that disastrous journey the Comte de Fersen narrowly escaped proscription, and he later retired to his native land where he was employed on important and secret missions. The Queen was wise in such a choice; she selected a man who never compromised her, never lent fuel to the flames of hatred that devoured the reputation and the very life of this ill-fated princess.

Her two tender affections, I have described . . . but I maintain outright, and I am ready to answer for it with my life, that for these alone will she have to account to the Supreme Judge—if such trifles are deserving of blame and punishment, and if the last years and the death of so illustrious a victim have not been sufficient to absolve her in the eyes of Heaven and posterity.

It is with grief I draw this picture of the truth; but only those who misjudged her should blush at it, those who forced me to drag her out of the grave to enlighten slander and crush lies. It is painful both for my heart and my code of honour to deal with such strict justice towards the affronted dead. Such an apology was bound to wound, in spite of myself, the soul I wish absolved. I have fulfilled a painful duty to which my work led me. I have considered it laudable that those unfeeling ashes should be disturbed to provide me with this page which, if it may be used to reproach the Queen on two counts, will do her justice in a thousand.

Men will be found (is it not always so?) to ask me what business this is of mine, what was my mission. I disdain to answer if they fail to understand both my indignation and my motives.

Someone [14] whose friendship I value, and in whom I cannot suspect ill humour when my reputation in matters of heart and mind is in question, once remarked to me that "if one grants two men as favourites to a woman seated on a throne, one holds nearly the same view as those who attribute to her a dozen lovers." But this way of reasoning is more specious than solid; it would prove of no value in regard to ordinary women; why should it be applied more mercilessly to a queen? Truth weighs us all in the same scales; I have had no hesitation in opposing truth to imposture, which I hope thus to have crushed. If the amount of credence which I think my opinion deserves is denied me by some people, if the integrity of my motive is doubted by others, I shall refer the case to what alone consoles me when no reproaches are due: my conscience. I have been just out of necessity, and I do not trouble to inquire if people will cease to be as just towards me out of envy or design.

It is time to return to what concerns me more personally. I tried to recover that peace of the soul the absence of which is the prime misfortune. I endeavoured to seek distraction in study and *belles-lettres*. I wrote a comedy in five acts and in verse, which I was afterwards judicious enough to reduce to one act, and which later was accepted by the Comédie Française, merely owing to Mlle Raucourt's reading. I was no longer at hand to preside over the fate of my play, and I do not know what became of it; my mind was given to very different matters. While I was working at this comedy, M. de Bièvre, I believe it was, took me to see Mme d'Angivillers,[15] whose reputation for wit had made me desire her acquaintance. I found her far superior to her reputation, not only for wit but for a thousand other qualities of much greater value. She received a company all the more interesting for being greatly varied, since it brought together courtiers, men about town, and numerous writers. It was at her house that I read my play to some few people who seemed pleased with it, and I owe my bent for literature to this lady's encouragement. She fortified a vocation that had been shaken by the mortifications with which a writer's life is filled, and weakened by other considerations liable to affect a man of the world.

My heart still unhealed, I went one night to the Bal de l'Opéra. I was there pursued by a masked lady who, besides abundant chatter, revealed details of such imposing beauty as to give one a favourable impression regarding her face and the other charms left to conjecture. Her conversation was enjoyable and in the best of taste, so I had no hesitation in promising to wait for her at the next ball on the amphitheatre steps, where we agreed she would give a sign and meet me about one in the morning. She kept her word. So we wandered about the ball-room, and emulated each other in wit and tender words. My curiosity and infatuation increased. The most melancholy disposition of the soul can be transformed by contact with certain attractions, and the most powerful remedy, if one can bear it, is a new love. It appeared too that I was gaining ground with her, and I began to find some charm in the adventure; on her side the stranger assured me I had discovered the way to her heart until then very fastidious in bestowing tenderness. . . . It was most touching! She added words urging extreme prudence, for the situation was delicate and required the greatest caution since a single mistake might mean the loss of her reputation, her happiness, her very life.

All this was very nearly true. I was nevertheless vastly annoyed (above all at the time of the third ball) by the thousand precautions she took in order not to be recognised, and the difficulties she placed in the way of my burning desires. The night of Ash Wednesday was selected for bringing me happiness. It came at last, this appointed night. We hired a carriage and, choosing byways, we arrived in front of the small door of a rather wretched house. I found myself in an apartment lit by the faint glimmer of a night-light. Complete enjoyment was placed within my reach; it would not be gallant on my part to-day to declare I was not made very happy.

The day which followed on my felicity brought to my lodgings someone I scarcely knew. He informed me that he was sent to me by a man to whom but few people in the kingdom would not feel bound to show great respect, and that I was requested, the next day at nine in the evening, to find myself in the main courtyard of the Luxembourg. I had no hesitation in promising to keep the appointment, and no longer doubted the truth of the story when I saw a man coming towards me whose features and voice I could not mistake.

"M. de Tilly," he said to me, "I sufficiently trust your honesty and discretion in asking you to meet me here. You can no longer remain in ignorance of my position as regards Mme de Bal——; I am fully informed concerning you, I even know that you do not really love her, I also think that if you had guessed who the lady was whom you approached, or rather who approached you, the probabilities are you would scarcely have sought such an attachment. Give it up for my sake, I beg of you; it cannot be a great sacrifice on your part, and my gratitude will be yours. If you wish to make the favour more complete, keep this meeting of ours a secret."

I first denied everything, as I was bound to do, and protested I should immensely value a happiness which was not mine; but I finally assured him I would not stand in the way of his enjoyment, and that he should no longer have occasion for even suspecting me. We parted good friends.

A marked regard for other people's wishes, a great docility in my disposition, a complete control over my passions, were not then virtues of which I could boast. I was scarcely the man to surrender to calculation or to consequences I had foreseen. But I was not sufficiently under a spell to cause unnecessary grief to a man whose appeal moved me; I owed him much, and he placed great value on what I apparently appreciated badly. . . . My surrender was not very meritorious.

Women do not forgive us for renouncing their favours, though they themselves so pitilessly withdraw them. I eluded a few rendezvous by means of bad excuses; I flattered myself that pride, helping common sense, would bring this lady to neglect me as I was neglecting her. But I was asked to supper. This sort of invitation did not appear to me to have consequences. I thought it would be extremely absurd to be on bad terms with a person who seemed bent on being my friend at all costs. The day came, I made my appearance and was led through two badly lit rooms where I saw no one, then into a secluded closet where three women were seated. One of these gravely got up and closed the door. Someone lifted a cushion from the sofa; three napkins tied in big knots were taken from underneath it; before I had time to know where I was, these Eumenides fell upon me literally to murder me. I put my hand to my sword in the hope of keeping such Furies in awe, nothing affrighted them; I ran, I tried to escape, I jumped on chairs; they followed me, reached me. Had I possessed Orpheus's voice, I could have fancied these bacchantes were reserving for me his fate. At last I caught hold of two candlesticks and in my exasperation set alight one woman's dress, the skirt of another. . . . I applied the flame to the curtains. Inhuman shrieks followed this attempt to kill me. . ... They opened the doors, they ran away, they called out, I made my escape and, sore with the blows and bewildered, I reached the street. Such are women! Wicked, weak, and queer!

All this did not fill the void in my heart. My passionate and bereft soul needed to find new energy in one fixed purpose.

A vague ambition seized hold of me; I thought it would be fine to train my mind to some knowledge of diplomacy since the state, asleep through a long peace, did not claim my arm. The Queen once more was kind enough to help me with this plan, and obtained for me the authorization to seek for government employment. This dull work, so lacking charm, disgusted me after a few weeks. My instability, the unreliability of my will, caused people interested in my welfare to withdraw from me; this indifference in others, finding its way into my own heart, made me lose courage. I was perhaps meant (people have told me so) for a swift and distinguished career, had I known how to moderate the passions that led me astray, and how to curb a spirit of flame that consumed me.

But I felt that ambition is, of all passions, the most barren as regards happiness; the enjoyments it brings are as dull and gloomy as is ambition itself, which one can indulge to the full without ever reaching gratification. Ambition is, like hope, always restless but with even less stability; it ignores the charm of repose. Everything seems an obstacle in its way, and not one thing appears to be a goal worthy of its efforts.

CHAPTER XVIII

*The wise man alone disposes of his fate; others
do not lead, they are swayed.*

*T*HE man who, on a bold skiff, has a hundred times braved
the ocean and only miraculously escaped its abyss, yet
trusts to it again. The huntsman who is carried through the
wood by a runaway horse, and dragged along a track which, like
another Hippolytus, he drenches with his blood, may be healed
of his wounds. Coming back from the grave, and still weak and
ailing, let him hear horses neighing, dogs barking, the sound of
the horn and the cries of the whippers-in, and out he goes, eager
for new pleasures, which are new dangers. This old man, whose
shrivelled hands are emaciated with counting gold, once reaches
the brink of the grave; he surprises a covetous heir numbering
his sighs and looking forward to his last breath; he sees him
squander, in anticipation and desire and craving, these treasures
so painfully amassed. . . . The old man gets up, becomes half
alive, and once more puts on clothes. . . . Is he going to enjoy
what he still possesses of life? Will he use this gold which another covets and longs to waste? No, he begins to hoard once
more; he grows faint and haggard over the strong-box where
the Fates will snap the last silken thread of his life, while his
imagination perhaps takes fright at the cost of his funeral.
And the young man who has from youth prostituted his heart
with wantons or victims of his lust, who has spent his life running after women and made a trade of seduction, will he ever
know any other course? The same errors keep him spellbound;
he will die as he has lived, dreaming of women when his hair
is grey, entertaining fancies on that point alone, and bitterly
disillusioned by reality on all others.

Since my loss and its effect upon my soul, I had imagined
my heart closed to love and the numerous perils it engenders.
I daily resisted its attacks; or rather, scarcely moved, I had not
even the merit of resistance. My grief, though altered in form,
so wholly absorbed me and proved such a gloomy enchantment
that I thought it guaranteed unshakable indifference. Fantastic

device! Deceitful hope of peace! It failed me by the side of a woman from whom I feared no danger.

It was the fashion amongst young men of a certain class to frequent the actors' greenroom at the interval between two plays, for there would be found the prettiest women on the stage. Mlle Adeline,[1] whom I had met when Senecterre was devoted to her, had then reached the height of her fame in her art; she was not the greatest of actresses, though she possessed marked talent, but was unquestionably the most seductive of courtesans. She would have been queen in a country of bayaderes. Her face was not such as either sculptor or painter would look for, but of a sort to wake to life the most blunted senses, and to stir a sleeping satyr from exhausted intoxication.

A figure, a carriage, of which the secret was hers alone, were in harmony with her conversation, often rather free, but not going beyond a decency that, in view of her eyes and her whole person, seemed foreign to her. This is so true that, in spite of her dislike for all licentious expressions even at moments of complete surrender, popular opinion, somewhat against her, credited Mlle Adeline with shameless ways of speech, and a dissolute private life in complete contrast with her nature and disposition. Hers was a reputation like thousands of others—the very opposite of the real truth.

At the time of which I speak she was living with a man who was loading her with presents and who had but to wish to make her wealthy for it to be done; and he wished it. This was M. de Veimeranges,[2] who had on several occasions been thought of as a possible minister of state. But he had finally attained power only through his rather despotic influence over the Maréchal de Ségur and above all M. de Calonne, and in this way had found open to his cupidity two almost inexhaustible sources, from which he drew insatiably. It cannot be said he had wit, but he had a good head, great aptitude for work, much patience over financial schemes, this before his love for this siren proved an intoxication rendering him practically inapt to business and capable of any stupidity, for it came at an age when one becomes a child again, and when the passions are stronger and men weaker. He was in repute for his skill at wording clear memoranda, with which the Academy might have found fault, but which, in matters of administration, were as they ought to be: reaching the mark, throwing light over debated issues, and presenting them in all their varied aspects. I have myself seen only a few

of his letters, addressed to the object of his worship, who made
rather free to laugh at them; they betrayed the most obtuse
idolatry and were scarcely written in French; I give my word
that spelling was not even there.

Such is the truth.

Fame! repute! public favour! you are but often the loud
echoes of deceit. Fortune, oh, blind goddess, your judgements are
unreliable, your favours without significance.

In the midst of all this, several people of my acquaintance
were besieging his mistress, not seeking to take her from her
lover, but nevertheless finding some pleasure in making fun of
him. For mortals are thus made: people who have no share in
our esteem are yet of some use to us if we can humiliate them.
Adeline, regarding herself as the widow of her dead lover,
Senecterre, and being thus separated from someone she had
truly loved, was in no hurry to find him a successor. She was
faithful to his memory, as well as to Veimeranges since her heart
was empty, but was hesitating about a new choice when one of
her suitors, a man full of a good opinion of himself and deeming
his person irresistible, imprudently enticed me almost in spite
of myself into the greenroom between the two plays. My melancholy moved Adeline, my reserve provoked her, the charm embodied in her whole person fascinated me; before I was myself
clearly aware I was conquered. She straightway desired to offer
me the vacant place for which rivals were contending; I allowed
myself to crave its possession. I made her promise to receive me;
and after having danced attendance upon her with a skill and a
purity of behaviour that would be creditable in a passion conceived for a virgin or another Présidente de Tourvel,[3] through
relating to her my last adventure, I began a new one. "So weak
are mortals, and no better can be."

This liaison, which at first was but a means to pleasure, soon
became a real attachment, and the more surely held me captive
because circumstances helped to strengthen it through opposition. A few people seemed to take upon themselves the duty of
keeping me within its bounds by prematurely and clumsily forbidding it. Opposition lends us strength where sheer indifference would cause us to surrender. *"Nitimur in vetitum semper."*

People who took some interest in me, or pretended to,
leagued themselves together to snatch me from a great danger
—so they said—and to save my morals from being wrecked.
The most exalted lady of France, I might have said of Europe,

did not think it beneath her to send me some bitter comments. Noxious and uncalled-for slanders took hold of this part of my life and embroidered it with the most absurd and false colours. Like those poor mortals who were thrown to the beasts, I found myself offered as pasture to that part of the public whose life is spent in soiling the lives of others. Mlle Adeline, it was said, deceived M. de Veimeranges, and I deceived them both. It was added that I was ruining Veimeranges by using Mlle Adeline's ascendancy over him. This was the only explanation people could find for my obstinacy in attaching myself to a person who could in nowise justify a passion that was blamable and ridiculous because it was serious.

The truth is that all those who had known her had fallen hopelessly in love, and that besides being extremely attractive she was less vicious (although she had faults) than many women who are well spoken of.

It is also true that M. H—— de St. Foy, so well known in Paris on account of his speculations at the Bourse, at the gambling table, and in stock-jobbing, had come to offer me, so he asserted, a clean profit of two hundred thousand francs in a transaction between himself and the Abbé d'Espagnac. These gentlemen would advance me ten thousand francs as the first installment of my share. H—— de St. Foy gave me a card on which five numbers were indicated, so far as I can recall, for it would be difficult for me to describe faithfully a transaction that was foreign to my habits, and that I did not quite grasp. The idea was to get Veimeranges to write on the card five corresponding figures. Mlle Adeline at my request undertook to approach Veimeranges, feeling convinced as I did that she was doing me a very great service. She handed me back my card on the following day *duly honoured.* I took it to a M. P. de C——, a money changer, who scribbled I know not what upon it. I finally give it back to M. H—— de St. Foy, who some few days later placed in my hands twenty-two notes to cash, each worth a thousand francs, and added long explanations, which I scarcely followed, to make clear to me an error of five hundred and thirty thousand francs, the result of which meant a net profit of only sixty-six thousand francs, the third of which was twenty-two. The late Barrème could not have bettered such reckoning!

It is even more true that I never asked Mlle Adeline, even by way of loan, for the smallest sum of money, a base action from which reason would have saved me had my heart been inclined to succumb, for I am deeply convinced that pride would have caused her to refuse, and contempt led her to leave me. And so, in the letter I found myself compelled to write to the Queen, though I begged her to forgive me for calling her attention to such abject details, foreign to one in her station, I wrote, amongst other things: "My honour, which I respect even more than I do the Queen, if this were possible, obliges me, madame, to seek justification; prodigality that squanders money may have been one of my failings, but never baseness that receives. . . ." It will presently be seen how I was driven to write this strange letter.[4]

Nevertheless I grew more and more attached to the woman to part me from whom all means seemed fair. This persecution won her my whole heart, and changed into passionate love what might have been only a mere fancy. A lady of much wit, a friend of mine or rather of my family, sent me word to call upon her and embarked on some pointed arguments to convince me I ought never to see Mlle Adeline again. For lack of good reason she fell to insults, which made me laugh because she was ugly. She summed up by asking what difference I saw between the smartest courtesan in Paris and the miss of the Rue Saint-Honoré.

"The latter," I replied, "having no education or refinement is a danger only to your footman, with whom she lives; the former, adorned by a thousand attractions will, ladies, charm your friend, your brother, and often carry off your lover or your husband."

This reply pleased her but little, indeed not at all, for it so happened that her husband, of whom she was childish enough with a face such as hers to be jealous, was ruining himself for a dancing-girl who made fun of him, though he gave her twice what she was worth; or, rather, this was the very reason she laughed at him.

The Queen in the meanwhile (for she must be mentioned again in this adventure where her name ought never to have been found) was so unjust as to wish to dishonour a young man by one of those sayings which, falling from the throne, killed on the spot those who were crushed by their weight:

"I no longer take any interest in M. de Tilly, who lives openly with an actress at the expense of M. de Veimeranges, who, it is said, robs the state."

One half of this statement was nearer the truth than the

other. Veimeranges drew money from public funds, and I from a patrimony which I was alienating every year. He, lost amidst the gaieties of Paris and on rather bad terms with a conscience far from clear, pretended not to have heard these big words which echoed afar; but I heard, and wished to hear. I appeared at Versailles, *pallidus morte futura.* A prey to a despair I did not conceal, and with rage in my heart, I hastened to the Queen's first lady-of-the-bedchamber in order to obtain an audience; in the afternoon she informed me that it was refused. I addressed myself to the Duchesse de F——, lady-in-waiting, who may recall the incident; the Queen sent the same refusal. I wrote the following letter:

MADAME,
It is with a surprise equal to my despair that I learn of the remarks your Majesty has made concerning me. Since respect does not debar truth nor the care of preserving one's honour, a treasure more precious than life, I will make free to tell the Queen, even if it causes my ruin, that no doubt unintentionally, she has behaved towards me with the most deadly injustice, and one without remedy.

You once thought fit, Madame, to learn from me, as well as from several people who have the honour of approaching your Majesty, that I was born with some wealth; I was even born with an abhorrence for all that is degrading and vile. Prodigality that squanders money may have been one of my failings, but never baseness that receives.

I beg the Queen's forgiveness for coming down to details so unworthy of her, but my honour, mortally wounded, forces me to this . . . my honour which I respect even more, were this possible, than I respect your Majesty.

I will confess, Madame, that an attachment you thought fit to reprove may truly have called for rebuke, but I shall never believe that it deserved so public a censure, and one coming from so lofty a place as your Majesty's lips; above all it did not deserve the slanderous accusations of which I am the inconsolable victim.

Calumny, Madame, spares no one in France: it aims at everything, even the throne; your Majesty knows this; I have seen her in my youth grieving over it; yet she so lightly believes it to-day when it concerns me. The Queen credits it as if, having reared me, she suddenly found me deserving her hatred after all the kindness by which she honoured me. . . . The Queen credits it as if she were

ignorant of the ways of the world in the high station where
Providence has placed her.

I shall henceforth, Madame, refrain from showing myself in the presence of your Majesty, as I have been doing
for some time already, although she has been kind enough
to let me know that her displeasure did not extend to this,
and that she had simply refused me an audience because
she had nothing to say to me. Heaven, Madame, would
have fully gratified me had your Majesty always thought I
was only worthy her silence; my life would not have been
poisoned and my reputation tarnished.

If this letter, a weak echo of an inconsolable grief, is
to bring persecution upon me, I respectfully protest to the
Queen that, after what has happened, nothing else can
affect me: the Queen has robbed me of everything, even of
the power of winning back her favour, which could not
compensate me for her esteem.

I ardently desire, Madame, that no deep grief will ever
afflict your Majesty. People in high stations have their sufferings. My wishes are for the happiness of the Queen who
has so cruelly brought discredit upon my youth, and I fall
on my knees before her throne to beg forgiveness for the
details to which I have been forced to bring her down.

I remain, etc. . . .

My friends foresaw the Bastille for me. I awaited it, but
showed no surprise at escaping it, for I had felt no fear. I said
good-bye to Versailles, and never returned to it except in days
of calamity, when only danger was to be found there. The Queen
was then astonished at seeing me back amidst what she perhaps
believed to be exclusively her party, while I looked upon it as
that of the entire French nobility. Her tardy favours left me
unmoved; I was surprised only at her astonishment; yet, in fact,
it fitted her disposition, of which the chief blemish was that she
could not forgive nor overcome prejudices.

Can those who are rulers ever display too much caution in
censure or rebuke that may cause a whole life to wane? Can
they ever fear showing themselves too sparing in condemnations
that so greatly influence other people's opinions? too much
afraid of any injustice that might distort an innocent man's fate,
delivering him defenceless to his enemies' passions, and to all
the contrivances of hatred and envy, never so virulent and active
as when the man who provokes them exposes himself by displaying pride, or does not win them over by his mediocrity?

Those whose power is law should almost dread to express an opinion as regards guilty persons, for one word from their lips has often proved too severe a punishment. They should reserve this outstanding penalty of social death for people whom public opinion has placed beyond the pale of society on account of crimes for which the law has no decree, but which the commonwealth denounces in the name of mankind and of an imprescriptible and eternal justice.

Unfortunately, at the moment I write, this power has practically fallen to pieces in the hands of kings; authority, even when as despotic as in Asia, has lost too much spiritual value to represent justice. In old times its sentence was punishment, and its bit of ribbon a reward. In those days an ideal was a force; but these great driving-powers are now shattered, buried under vast ruins. New beliefs have emerged from the wreckage, and old ones have changed like the universe itself.

For my part, I appealed from this royal decree of proscription by patience; with calm and disdain I appealed to truth, which does not always triumph but which consoles. Those who knew me, and the healthy-minded portion of the public, did me justice; others, always ready to believe in evil, are not worthy of the trouble to convince them of good. In the depth of my heart I became the Queen's mortal enemy, but I respected myself enough never to mention her, or else to do it with deference when it was already ordinary and culpable to utter her name with lack of regard. The Revolution and the misfortunes befalling the Queen converted me as swiftly as I had been estranged; I had no need to guard myself against desires of vengeance, and of this I am to-day proud. I congratulate myself on having for long past remembered only her greatness of soul during that dreadful storm and the shipwreck in which it ended.

There was I, then, still so young, lost in this huge Paris, lacking a profession, an aim, a guide. The queenly hand which had deigned to place my youth under its protection was now withdrawn. I drifted about, discouraged, having no plans, no projects, feeling as uncertain as the traveller who hesitates between two roads and ends by setting out along the worse. There was I, imperturbable but inwardly soured, lending sanction to a few wretched words of supremely unjust allegation by my indifference and by the levity and the mistakes that ensued.

I have dwelt at some length on this part of my narrative; those days and that period were to prove decisive on the course of my life. I no longer listened to dreams of ambition and advancement, for I was thrown amongst the half-truths of a life of pleasure. Even the longing for other men's esteem deserted me, since it could be bought only by renouncing enjoyments rendered necessary to me through habit and, sadder still, through abuse. When the social order was overthrown I might have had to mourn the loss of fortune in every respect if I had as diligently applied myself to making it as I had to losing it.

What would my imagination have preserved of it? Perhaps bitter regrets. What has it retained of the contrary? Memories of much pleasure—now vanished as do all things human, but the charm of which still dwells in me—and the sense, more consoling than disheartening, of having lived a full and complete life, where pleasures, too frivolously no doubt, filled my time and unquestionably bestrewed my path with many mistakes, but a life that in a final survey was never tarnished by any truly guilty deed.

Does this mean that one should choose such a life? Let young men take my advice and abhor it. May they rely on my word: this life will bring them only emptiness, disappointment, and confusion, misfortune, bitterness, and a discredit that is never formulated but clings to all those who stupefy themselves in vain pleasures and remain strangers to useful duties—those, in a word, for whom time has only wings but no honorable track.

To come back to my love for Mlle Adeline. It was passion in full sway, and she responded to it. If it is permissible for a man to trust a woman's feelings, especially one who was so made by our sex, I have no doubt that she loved me, though she was reproached with loving nothing. Veimeranges wore himself out in outbreaks of useless jealousy; he tried all means of getting me out of the way; nothing succeeded; he was too subjugated for her to fear losing him. At last he appealed to me directly, and attacked me by two methods which were very different in form, but which might have had the same result. The first was to cause half a house to fall upon me. Do not look upon this as a joke, it is literally true: I shall prove it.

I used to leave my cabriolet a hundred yards away from the house of his faithless mistress, and if his coach was still in her courtyard after midnight I sought refuge in the Prince d'Hénin's house, which adjoined. Whether the Prince was at home or away, there I could always find a fire, a light, and some books. Veimeranges had discovered this retreat by means of spies, always easy to find for those who have money, and one evening, as I was making my way there, a huge lion, a helmet, a cornice, and I cannot remember what other ruins or trophies, were hurled down on me by a man posted on a side wall of premises owned by the sailor Paul Jones,[5] who was then away. All this came to a dead stop at my feet and covered me with glorious dust. Had I been hit, it would have meant at least three months in bed, and nothing comforts a rival more than a withdrawal of such a nature. There was nothing to do but to laugh, and walk in the middle of the street.

Two months later I had an appointment with Veimeranges, though I cannot recall how this came about. He behaved towards me in fatherly fashion, and told me that it was dreadful for a man like me to busy himself with nothing but love-making, and that chance having granted him some credit he would be only too pleased to use it on my behalf. If I wished to obtain a colonel's commission and go to India, he would make sure of my getting it, with a hundred thousand francs to pay off my debts. I escaped his offers and flattery as I had escaped his lion and cornices. As all this, however, was really annoying, and I was as much in love as I have often had the bad habit to be, I frankly told Adeline that she was rich enough, that I was disgusted with this sharing, and that I begged her to choose between Veimeranges and myself, since I was resolved to take my leave if she did not send him away.

She complied, I cannot say with the best grace imaginable— but still she complied, and that meant much.

Veimeranges felt a grief that would do credit to a youngster, but appeared ridiculous in an old fool. It literally brought him ill luck. Some public scandal, the nature of which I do not remember, caused him to lose much of the consideration he had acquired and landed him at the gambling tables at Versailles, where he went to the bad. He merely vegetated, rather than lived, in obscurity and almost disreputably; I believe even that he no longer remained as wealthy as he was supposed to be and himself thought he was. Men launched in big business, and those gambling on a large scale, scarcely know what wealth is theirs, and for how long they possess it. Then again Fate likes to second men whenever they fall upon a victim, and skillfully joins the conspiracy which a man's good luck must finally form against him, just as the tallest oaks attract the lightning because their high tops are so near the storms.

I again met Veimeranges on a few occasions long after I had
freed myself from my bondage to the woman who had divided
us. He lacked the wit to forget, and he had not forgiven me.
Whenever I appeared, his eyebrows bristled up, and he looked
like a sick wild boar. My smiles were wasted upon him, he
longed to bite.

But to proceed.

My Circe and I still loved each other, so that it was a joy
and edification to behold; but we had lost the talisman of our
love, the delight in deception, and that still greater of facing
obstacles. We quickly realised this, though not a word was said.
Mars and Venus, beyond compare, loved each other so long
and so well only because of the fury and distraction of the crip-
ple Vulcan, previous to the famous adventure of the iron net.
The net we fell into was that of boredom, one of the most
frightfully entangling.

This attachment had lasted a little over a year when my
false mistress gave me as partner that diminutive Sartine,[6] who
has since fallen like others under a Robespierrean blade. Paris
courtesans made game of him as a miniature machine for pro-
curing money, and I have to reproach myself with having on
several occasions caused him grief, almost still pestering him
right in the sanctum of matrimony.

Since this partnership was unpleasant to me, and I found it
most difficult to countenance this new speculation of my perfidious mistress, she simply dismissed me, though no lightning
had foretold this thunderbolt.

After a night given to tenderness, I had left her, sure that
she was mine, as much as La Châtre had felt about Ninon after
her *billet*.[7] But to my surprise a letter came from Adeline as well
as a sweetmeat-box adorned with her portrait, which I had forgotten at her rooms. The letter contained a quite formal dismissal, a very solemn farewell. It was written as letters in such
junctures have always been written since the beginning of the
world and will continue to be until it ends. She reckoned on my
friendship, she promised me hers . . . all quite charming! She
regretted taking this necessary step and, like Zémire's father,
would set out on a journey . . . a very long one perhaps. All
my imperiousness then asserted itself; vexed at being dismissed
so flatly, I grew mad in my vengeance and love. I wanted post-
horses at once; then no longer wanted them; my whole day was
spent hunting for Adeline in this huge abyss which my eyes will

perhaps never behold again—in this Paris where, strictly speaking, she no longer was, since she had hidden herself away in a small house at the Champs-Elysées. Pride soon took the place of weakness; the heart like the pulse is intermittent. I longed to forget her, a thing not easy to do when one has been forsaken. . . . If women but knew the truth they would be our tyrants even more than they are. A fortnight went by during which I exhausted myself in impotent rage; then, for a change, I fell ill.

At last came the news that she was back, that she had been seen. I obtained an interview and a promise was made that *if I would be calm,* she would devote herself exclusively to me. This cool assurance, too little concealed, killed my love on the spot and left in my heart no other longing but for revenge. I at once set about it, and to make sure of my success, paid court to her most deadly enemy. This was Mlle du Fayel, almost as lovable a person as I have ever found in any social rank, possessed of enough charm to make one forget her gallantry, and of a face pretty enough to fit her wit. She had belonged to the same theatre as Adeline, but had been dismissed for some atrocious crime she had not committed. They hated each other and lived practically in the same street; so it was a perfect vengeance and on the spot. I planned my attack so skillfully that on the very same day I was to love them both and receive their favours. I wrote to one that I had suddenly to go into the country, and to the other (Adeline) that I should be at her disposal for the evening. All went well, and there was I once more a new lover to my former mistress. Tender promises, ecstatic passion, renewed assurances of an undying love, delicate excuses for the past, nothing was lacking. The morning came bringing despair. . . . She had been so happy; it was odious to part so soon.

"So you love me?" I asked her.

"More than ever."

"You no longer wish to leave me?"

"Rather die."

"Well then die, for you will never see me again. . . . Forget me," I added in dramatic tones. "I love another."

She wanted to scream, to protest, but I was gone.

How inexhaustible are the resources of self-conceit! I was cured because I had been able to gratify my vanity and to let my imagination dwell on the usual theme, which eases one's mind at love-parting:

"You can no longer see her, but it is the dictum of your will;

you yourself erected this barrier; it was you, and not she, who said, *'We shall no longer meet!'* "

Lovers, weak lovers, who never found consolation at having been dismissed (I have known some, and such still exist), if on the very day of your misfortune you had forestalled your traitorous fair one, you would have remained as serene as an innocent virgin, you would have slept the sleep of the just, no crystal fountain would have been as pure as your soul. To win the start —that is the whole secret. *Hoc opus, hic labor est.*

That very evening I dispatched a message to Mlle du Fayel. I informed her I had returned and enquired whether I could invite myself for supper that day and breakfast on the morrow. She replied I would be expected. I duly arrived; midnight went by, the hour for love had come. . . . We were almost dropping off to sleep when knocks were heard which shook the house. A chambermaid, scantily clad, wished to know if she must open the door. Her mistress replied in the negative; it was too late. A coachman, clumsy or won over, had introduced the ravaging wolves inside the fold, that is to say, Adeline with M. d'Hénin, who, having had supper at her rooms, wished, he said like a booby, to make her see reason and bring me back to her feet.

"Open," called out a furious voice from the hall; "open, worthless rival who took my lover from me! And as for you, monster [that was I], *you shall see!*"

There followed a speech from M. d'Hénin; silence on my side. Astonishment, dignity, and an answer from Mlle du Fayel —threats of a complaint to the police for violation of domicile at an undue hour, and occasioning scandal in a respectable neighbourhood where her irreproachable virtue had won her consideration; more speeches on both sides of the door. . . . The apple of discord between the two fair ones!

I slipped on scanty clothes, and found a little stairway to an upper room: the Graces' laboratory, abode of cosmetics and all the secrets of the toilet, the arsenal of my divinity's most triumphant weapons. I was scolded for having thus entered the vestry of her temple, but I had no wish to appear more conspicuous in a story which could become too public.

After long parleys, the forsaken Adeline, leaning upon the Prince's arm, flanked by a friend, followed by a trusted maid, and preceded by a valet bearing a light, retreated in battle array to a very pretty house she had just had built close to this spot. I had risked my life, for I was frozen; so, waving a good-bye to

M. d'Hénin from the window, I went back to bed, which was but fair! The rejected lady was childish enough to become ill from vexation, and when for a week on end she had seen my cabriolet ostentatiously at her rival's door, I thanked Mlle du Fayel for her courtesy and went elsewhere.

If Adeline had had the wit to affect complete indifference, my vengeance would have been accomplished and I would not have pushed it further. But I heard that she was making a great commotion about it all, and that she was deeply wounded. Here was a new motive for making love to a pretty lady belonging to Adeline's theatre, and one whom she heartily disliked. This was Mlle Rosalie, now married to one of those martial men who saved France from invasion. The Marquis de Genlis had received her first favours. "Dear friend," she had told him on leaving his arms, "if it never brings me more pleasure than this, I have chosen a wretched trade." Some time later, vexed at having been forsaken by the Prince de Saint-Mauris [8] in favour of Mlle Thévenot, who had rather bulgy eyes, she exclaimed on leaving the Opéra: "It is easy to see this man is an arrant courtier, he will touch no food but at the Œil-de-Bœuf." [9]

Mlles Adeline and Rosalie were not on good terms; there had been a greenroom quarrel; there was particular jealousy over admirers and rivalry in elegance. I displayed much perseverance in endeavouring to win this blonde, not given to pining, for she was so secured within the boundaries of a passion for the Prince de Monaco,[10] that she repulsed my advances with a propriety entirely out of place. But no woman in France was ever more warm-hearted and hot-headed. I quickly won her interest by giving her a faithful account of my whole adventure and making her share my resentment. After a few weeks of hesitation, the surrender of Adeline's portrait and two or three of her letters secured me as much happiness as may be found when one's wishes are fulfilled.

The proud Adeline lost her head at the terrible news, her despair knew no bounds. Several solemn messengers were dispatched. She had already (which is most amusing) put on widow's weeds to ask audience from the Governor of Paris in order to claim back her portrait fallen into the hands of a light person to whom a faithless scoundrel had basely sold it. At last, after the most laughable parleys, it was decided, stipulated and agreed that the ladies should meet; that Mlle Adeline should appeal to her rival's generosity, while Rosalie, with all the dig-

nity fitting the occasion, should hand over the sacred pledges;
that finally I alone should retain the reputation of a vile monster amongst the ladies and Nicæas of our time. A treaty was
signed between the two mighty contracting parties; constant
friendship was sworn, a close alliance contemplated. No clause
praising me was inserted in this document, and the pleasure
which the versatile sex finds in slandering us is so contagious
that my new mistress related horrid things about her dear lover,
proclaimed me inordinately guilty, and joined in a chorus with
my former love. When I saw her again she had so absurdly
relented that I had quite a hard task to regain the ground I had
lost. So it was my luck to be the means of bringing these two
together. . . . Trust to women when your back is turned—
even when you are present! . . . An amusing thing, too, placing one's trust in friends!

As Troy fell, as the Macedonian Empire came to an end, as
so many other memorable things perished that are counted important and yet are nothing, so came to an end this great passion
for the most famous of courtesans. Alcibiades, Socrates, even
Alexander, and many wise men and heroes who were worth
more than I and yet *were not worth much,* loved and celebrated
those charming girls, who could not equal ours, though they
were the queens of witty Greece. Glycera, the flower-seller of
Sycione, whose very name moves the heart, was she not praised
and idolised by the numerous lovers whose brows she garlanded
with laurels and roses, entwined and wreathed by her beautiful
hands? The memory of all these girls is sacred to hearts born
for love; the syllables forming their names have reached us
through the centuries and are found on all the pages concerning
love. The events of their wholly erotic lives have echoed through
posterity, since love is looked upon by the greater part of mankind as the real meaning of life, fame being but a delusion;
finally their portraits are found in every collection, in every
heart. . . . Why should I alone keep silent concerning their
sisters of to-day, women who perhaps have surpassed them? No,
let a dismal censor, an austere reader, disapprove my faithful
narratives and, thinking them unworthy of history, throw over
my pictures the specious veil of decency, my modern Phrynes will
lift the veil and I shall erect a frail column to their memory,
since I cannot build them a temple as was done in Athens where
the Greeks had as good a knowledge of true merit as our most
fastidious thinkers of to-day.

To speak quite seriously, this passion for Adeline, of which twenty years later I strive to write lightly, held me powerfully and with the most unbelievable sway. It was followed by a few years of enmity which she did not conceal, but which on one occasion in my life gave way to a sincere reconciliation, offering me proofs of the excellence of her heart and of a sensitiveness keen enough to silence wounded vanity, which for women and even for most men is the root of everlasting hatred. Since love was no more, we no longer quarrelled, and, to be fair to her, I should like to say that she was far superior to the opinion people had of her and could not be surpassed in the great art of fascination, at which, beyond compare, she was skilled. Her seductions would have turned the heads of men who despise my weakness and believe themselves much wiser.

My new establishment with Rosalie worked marvellously, but the fine sky was darkened by many clouds. Prince Joseph de Monaco was not the only rival whose competition I had to neutralise. Another man, generous and lavish to excess, all with the most excellent heart, the Chevalier de la Curne, loved to distraction the woman I greatly loved. Since he forestalled fair Rosalie's every wish, he claimed a reward that the greatest gifts of Plutus cannot always obtain; I remember that he was the man for whom *friendship founded on esteem* reached its greatest heights, to use the words of the charming deceiver who could cheat the three of us; but of what use is friendship in opposition to love? It is coupling weakness to strength, the innocent lamb to the fierce tiger; it is answering the laments of a sick man by empty wishes for his health. In the course of time this much adored woman found herself with child; each of us dreamt of fatherhood and felt his heart ready for the illusion of the ties of blood. A daughter was born; it was said she resembled me; my knowledge extends no further and never will, unless a good many things concerning which we are condemned to ignorance upon this earth are revealed to us on the day of resurrection.

Rosalie was a charming person, pretty, witty, spirited, sensitive, roguish but essentially kind-hearted.

I must relate two incidents that picture her better than any long explanations. M. de Fronsac, who was gentleman of the King's bedchamber, and on this account inspector of theatres, had a mania for demanding most imperatively the appellation of "your Lordship" from anyone who belonged to the stage and

came directly under the control of the first gentleman of the
bedchamber. One day, in the greenroom, as he was severely
reprimanding Rosalie in front of several people, for I know not
what reason, she made a low curtsey and replied laconically:
"Your Lordship is a liar!"

So far, it was good, or bad, as you wish; but I had not
meddled with the matter. Next day I met M. le Duc de Fronsac
at the Comédie Française as he was mounting the stairs and I
going down.

"I entreat you," he said to my great astonishment, "to teach
Mlle Rosalie the respect she owes to me, or I promise you it
may be long before you sleep with her, for I shall have her
locked up for six weeks at La Force."

"I cannot conceive," I replied, "that you should consider it
my duty to teach actresses what respect they owe you, any more
than I consider it yours to keep a record of those I sleep with."

He paused, then went up, and I went down.

When I was at Rosalie's rooms, one morning, I received a
note from a woman who desired, she said, to love me; she
appointed a meeting at the Arcades Soubise on the stroke of
twelve; she would wait for me in a fiacre, not daring to trust
her servants. Rosalie, seeming quite indifferent, enquired whom
the note was from.

"A creditor," I told her. "Boring like all those idiots."

I hastened to get up, rushed to my room, and dressed most
elegantly. Wings took me to the rendezvous, I entered the ac-
cursed carriage, I knelt at the feet of the woman my imagination
pictured as nothing short of an angel—a thick veil covered her
face—I spoke of burning desire . . . I wished to give proofs.
. . . A hundred blows fell upon me, a load of insults: it was
Rosalie!

"It pleased me," I explained coldly, "to lend myself to a joke
which seemed to amuse you. Do you think I did not know
you? . . ."

I took her home, not feeling much at ease. We were on bad
terms; but that was delightful since we had to make friends again.

Rosalie well deserved my undying friendship, and my heart
faithfully kept it for her. It has followed her in all the courses
of her fortune; I know that she is happy and has reached port;
I rejoice at this as if such happiness were my own. I shall have
occasion to speak of her again and to do homage to her generous
soul and her excellent qualities.

Does the reader remember that Sophie de Lorville whom I passionately loved in early youth when the heart is so easily pleased? Not that she needed the allowance so often made in early life; she would have bewitched the most untamed. I had had no news of her for a long time. My heart lived without her but had not forgotten, for there she reposed. Having become the widow of a very kindly gentleman whom she had married rather against her will, she asked me to pay her a visit on her estate, a hundred leagues from Paris. I was greatly moved on once more seeing this face across which love and melancholy not only had passed but seemed irrevocably to dwell. I found her heart just as I had left it; her body alone had been given to another. We understood each other from the first moment, and after a few words concerning her husband we never mentioned him again.

"He was," she told me simply, "an honest man who loved me more than was right; any other woman would have been happy."

We were overcome by emotion at the thought of Mme de ———, whom we more regretted together than we had apart. In solitude one can but weep, while the tears which now came to me at the memory of my first love were such as I had not sufficiently shed over the ashes of this friend of my youth; my spirit and hers were now reconciled. Unhappy woman, your only crime had been to love too dearly a scatterbrain who did not deserve you.

Sophie was quite indifferent to the rumours my presence in her house might set up; her plan was to go and live in the south of France where she had been born. As she had money of her own she had decided never again to give up her freedom. Her husband had left her all his wealth, and their only son had died in the year of his birth. The outside world probably thought her happy, but the constraint under which a heart such as hers had languished marred her freshness for a long while. The bonds uniting her to a man she had not loved still pressed with all their weight upon a melancholy disposition; and the slow and wearing patience of resignation had drained from her the spring of happiness in which frivolous people believe so readily, but of which souls of a fine mettle justly despair.

She thus regarded the matter when a man to whom I have since united her, and who deserves her, came to settle on an estate near by. He brought with him Cazalès,[11] who served in the same regiment, being then a young officer in the dragoons, and of no consequence, not having yet revealed that rather lofty eloquence he came to display at the Constituent Assembly. He did not himself foresee the reputation, rather exaggerated in my opinion, which his daring and untiring voice not a little contributed to establish. He would then have asked nothing better than to sigh in that same voice with which he later thundered; but his whole being could only make Sophie wary of encouraging him. His ways, his style, were too much in opposition to hers. The man who became her husband loved her before he heard her voice, and guessed what she was as soon as he saw her. This divination was mostly of the heart, although he has much wit to which he adds an exquisite sensitiveness, the result of training in the arts. Few people display so many gifts, above all those useful in charming women's ears, which are so near feminine hearts, whereas in men they are quite distinct, making it difficult to impress them by an appeal to sensibilities alone. I did not know him at all, but I was won over at sight by one of those inward promptings which a tendency to mistrust perhaps leads me unduly to hold back. He showed a confidence in me that he might have thought it best to defer; I accepted this as if it were my due, and responded to this trust as if I had beforehand been under obligation to justify it. He never enquired whether I was the lover of the woman he proposed to make his wife, but he entreated me to second him in this task as if it were impossible I should be an impediment. I helped him with as much good faith as if she had been a stranger to me. He gave me detailed information about his income, for he seemed convinced that what I should accept for her she would accept through me. He offered to share with Sophie what counted in the province as a fairly considerable fortune; but he brought her a better dowry still: a good husband on whom she could lean in full trust during the journey through life, and a fine and noble disposition to be her consolation during our brief span, which yet is too long if people grow old side by side without the blessing of mutual esteem and the sweetness of friendship. I set myself to reason with her, I applied all my skill to convince her; it was not an easy task. Even a woman quite devoid of vanity, and over whom one has the greatest rights, only moderately likes to be told: "I love you well enough to wish to make you happy with another."

Her astonishment was such as in another woman would have

been almost spite, and she refused even to listen to me. I insisted, she grew sad. I tried to use the arguments so expedient for methodical and lukewarm natures, to bring her to feel that a thing which pleases for a while cannot be put in the balance with what will be useful for a life-time, etc. She replied that it was only fair I should have such views, and that, having spoilt her life, I should go to some trouble to embellish it. She was grateful to me, but could not offer any hope of success; some tears explained what was left unsaid. Those discussions made me the more firmly adhere to my plans of pure friendship and her prompt marriage, an idea which took full control of my mind; I lost no opportunity, using as much delicacy as I could, to bring these two together. I begged M. de V—— (it is the name she bears to-day) not to despair of a victory which perseverance aided by wounded feelings was sure to win.

What the reader is now to read helped M. de V—— better than all my endeavours.

An acquaintance of mine, a judge at the Paris supreme court, had a sister married to the president of a court of justice in the nearest town to Sophie's estate; and there Sophie had a lawsuit of no importance, but which she did not wish to lose. She told me about it, expressing regret at having neglected people of whom she would soon be in need. I undertook to see the president's wife, and explained what relation I had with her brother. On arriving at the town, I went straight to the judge's house, which was near the court. The lady received me with all the attentions one displays for a man from Paris. She was extremely pretty, and but for a rather solemn and affected gravity—a contagious disease in judges' households—she would have been a most captivating woman. I started to pour forth a load of platitudes on my delight, her face and charm, and as it was long since she had heard such impertinences she thought them in the best of taste and above all viewed them as the language of great passion and the undeniable token of love by surprise.

Her eyes thanked me, but with an air of discretion and serenity which ought to have inspired good behaviour; but since I am unfortunately bolder with women than one should be, I used such tender words, and tackled her with so much impetuosity and luck, that in spite of a few entreaties stifled by kisses the president's wife granted me in half an hour what, as has long been agreed, should not be given for at least a month. Most seriously disconsolate about it, she was shedding torrents of

tears and calling upon death to ease her despair, when that most
estimable of men, her worthy husband, entered the room. I had
entirely regained my self-control, and was in due form consoling
her, so it could not be guessed I had caused her grief; yet I own
that the sight of a ghost could not have flustered me more, and
that, while I hesitated over the course to adopt, I simply gave
to my countenance the expression of a sorrow sharing and composing that of someone else. But she, with that genius of women
which at solemn moments never forsakes even the least experienced, called out to her husband: "This is the Comte de Tilly,
sir; his visit moves me deeply; he has received letters from
Paris telling me that Mme de Bel——, my best friend as you
know, is so dangerously ill that at the time the mail left her
death was expected at any moment."

Confounded, full of admiration, but in the posture of astonishment which makes one look like a fool, I just managed to say,
with a sort of sigh: "Only too true!" Thereupon the president
delivered in a doleful voice such a long and fine speech on life
in Paris and the recklessness of young women which leads them
to a premature grave that I fully composed myself again and
displayed the blamable impudence of improving upon all he
had said. I made up a most detailed story of Mme de Bel——'s
illness, of its beginning, its progress, its nature, and the changes
in her condition. . . . I gave a bulletin for each day; I named
the doctors who had seen her, the mistakes they had made, for
which she most likely would pay with her life; I gave the names
of the people who had called twice a day at her door with a real
concern, so rare in this age of selfishness, that my misanthropy
had thereby been reconciled to mankind.

The credulous judge listened to me, his face melting with
emotion; I grew animated, and perhaps was on the point of
saying more excellent things, when I noticed with what appearance of perfect honesty the president's wife was following my
lies. Such embodiment of falsehood in this woman who listened
to me with tearful eyes, measuring me with the skill of the most
famous courtesans, brought home to me my favourite opinion
concerning the inexhaustible wealth of perfidy inborn in the sex,
and froze me with ghastly admiration.

The president, with a good grace, asked me to dinner, and
I was delighted; but the mistress of the house declared that she
would retire to her room for she positively could not eat anything and company was odious to her. She apologised to me in

well-chosen' words and with eyes rivetted to the floor, but this did not prevent mine from telling her how much her whim annoyed me. A lieutenant-colonel in the cavalry and the prior of a monastery made their appearance, so we were four at table. The monk had preached in Paris during his youth; he recited some fragments of his sermons which I recognised as being those of Father de Neuville; [12] great admiration was shown for the profusion of antithesis, precisely the defect of that orator. The officer spoke with knowledge concerning his profession, the president dwelt on some very famous *causes célèbres,* and I reserved for them at dessert various scandalous anecdotes the heroes of which I portrayed under the darkest dyes, denouncing them as plagues against whom society, rising in protest, should seek justice. The whole affair ended by coffee with eau de la Côte, and in a most provincial fashion I was once more in the street by four o'clock, laughing in all bad taste at what had caused the tears of the president's wife. I marvelled at the way a man of good society can find an excellent dinner with people he has never seen, and possess their wives without preliminary formalities, while in this best of all possible worlds some men lack provisions for a dinner in their own homes and cannot possess their own wives.

Admirable is the policy of human societies, proving to the most obtuse heads what progress civilisation has made and how far ahead we have moved towards that systematic perfection which is presumed to set us apart and distinguish us from the other animals whom the Creator of all things has given us as companions upon this earth!

The happy magistrate of whom I had been the guest had promised me to give his full attention to Sophie's case, which appeared to him completely just. So I returned to her quite radiant concerning my mediation, which I explained to her, and concerning my adventures of which I said nothing. M. de V——— made no progress, though he spent the whole day at Sophie's house and never wearied of playing the violin and the piano, or singing half the day, since he had noticed that his music (Sophie was herself an accomplished musician) lost him less ground than his person. He was advancing so slowly in this race for love that I grew even more impatient than himself; but he was not the man to take a woman by surprise, or to create an opportunity. He sought marriage with the innocence and the purity his grandfather had brought to the deed, and he

spun out his pastoral romance with a delicacy he had learnt
in some book or other. I would find him rolling melancholy eyes
at the piano, while his whole soul went into his voice, and song
and gestures implored the sweet tyrant to relent.

All I dared do was to give him advice, convinced that the
best way to strengthen a woman's resistance is to beg her to
be weak.

As regards myself, the Evil One tempted me to go back
to the town and visit my tearful lady. The president had Lunel
wine which he preferred to Romanée; he had praised it eloquently. Out of politeness I had drunk a few glasses without
mentioning that it was but schoolboys' wine, sickly, tasteless and
without body. I pretended to like it prodigiously, and there was
I, addicted to wine, and Lunel wine! I seized this excuse to
call upon him three days later and invite myself to dinner. I had
clearly foreseen that the afflicted lady would at last sit at table
and that a judge has business to attend to after dinner, so that
I would outlast his stay.

The president had talked of me to his wife, showing great
enthusiasm for a young man he represented as having escaped
the evil examples and corruption of our age. Her mind had thus
retained only what seemed good in my frightful behaviour; the
other half had been obliterated thanks to a readiness common
to all women for believing themselves so prodigiously irresistible
that there is no foolish deed on our part they should not forgive.
I had displayed impromptu wit, and for this she was pleased
with me, since reflection can correct a first impression. Women
love courage, and audacity resembles it. Any great commotion
fills these delicate beings with wonder, all singularity quickly
makes progress and havoc in their minds. The president's wife
looked at me with anger tempered by respect; I begged forgiveness by an air of haughtiness. She drew aside her foot which I
sought during the whole first course; but when the conversation
led me to speak of a great grief which had obsessed me for
some days, the rebellious foot naturally sought mine to ask the
cause of this; the hand followed under the table; the heart had
preceded it.

A certain means of never failing near a woman, would be to
die for the whole sex and come back to life. . . . One would
then possess them all!

Vain fancy of a diseased mind, this longing for all women
—many a man finds one too much.

Adorable sex, do not take too literally the jokes which the adventures of a guilty youth suggest to me. Without you, who could wish for life? You, and you alone, smooth the way for us in this vale of tears where we journey a short while without knowing where it leads. Your voice is our solace. Our desire to seduce you makes us wicked in dealing with you, but renders us better men in practically everything else. You lend brilliancy to our mournful and dull existence; and the monster you fail to move to tenderness is a wretched outcast on this earth. Men would devour one another if you were not the intervening angels to show them that they have hearts.

Such is the truth, the rest is mere trifling.

This long-drawn-out dinner came to an end, and we were left alone as I had foreseen. I embarked upon a well-reasoned justification and accounted for my behaviour by an irresistible attraction, a sudden feeling which had carried me beyond myself. I had to hear reproaches to which I gave no heed, since I knew them well: what she told me I could have said to myself. She assured me that my victory would create no precedent. I demonstrated that such behaviour would be unheard of, disadvantageous, and indelicate; I proved that for a virtuous and sensitive woman to whom such a misfortune had happened, the only way of making amend was through an attachment justified by its intensity and duration. She declared she had not shared my feelings, had not been party to my crime. I agreed up to a point, but gently brought her to own that during the whole length of dinner she had been my accomplice; I reminded her of the charming treachery by which she had saved me in relating the story of her dying friend; how I could have caused much embarrassment if I had been cruel enough not to keep up the happy imposture. . . . She blushed deeply—she knew not what to say. I had no wish to press her further, so this contest between modesty and desire ended in a silence of which every minute was well employed by me; I broke its spell, amidst half-protests on her part, only to vow that I wished for no happiness that was not shared; and I was made happy—happy for two months without disturbance or clouds. . . . Two months, have I, said? This on account of an absent sister who was daily expected and whom public opinion declared charming: I was waiting for her.

"Time may cast a veil, but also rend away." A wretched lackey saw us, and to feather his nest, warned the president, who nearly died of grief and would have given his life to preserve the ignorance this brute had taken away from him. The president would trust only his eyes, so hid himself and also witnessed. He did not kill me. Like Joconde he took the wisest course and spared the life of his unfaithful spouse; but, being by profession more talkative than Joconde, he made us a speech worthy of a Roman orator, summing it up by forbidding me the house and by threatening his fainting wife with the convent.

From that moment I thought but poorly of him.

On the evening of that stormy day, the lady wept . . . she wept so much that he came near to offering her apologies, near to believing his eyes had deceived him. He took her into the country, for there are occasions when solitude is indicated. This, as far as I know, is the only vengeance with which he pursued her; I have heard that he was even wise enough never to refer to the incident.

That brought him back some of my esteem.

Lucky are the husbands so favoured by Nature as to submit with so much wisdom and caution to the common fate! The president proved himself beyond compare in this respect. He was the type of those incorruptible magistrates of the Golden Age. Sophie won her case although I had interested myself in it.

Yes, the husbands are not rare (and one must admire and envy them) who are so fortunate as to rise philosophically above vulgar prejudices; who can with stoical unconcern defy an accident (in itself a mere nothing, even if a man becomes aware of it), and who do not for this frighten away the doves of love which soar over the nuptial bed. Blessed life partners of wives even more blessed, since woman's sweetest pleasure is not poisoned through fear, these precious husbands are not the born scourge of the lover, not the torturers of their delicate spouses, not the artisans of their own misfortune or, which is worse, of the indelible ridicule that pursues the man who loses his temper. They are, in a word, privileged mortals whose prime virtue is indulgence towards an idle sex whom we have excluded from the field of worldly ambitions, from all the serious business of life (though it will often meddle in this), and to whom we grant only one occupation, that of love—which it would run the risk of never knowing were love met only in marriage.

These compliant and respectable husbands consider it a fairly useful aim in a rather tyrannical institution to seek a friend for days of trouble, a sound adviser when the mind is disturbed, and healthy children to cheer one's old age. Such a husband has learned the most useful art in a household: that of not probing too minutely into intimate matters, of abstaining from any strict reckoning in regard to the heart of the woman who perhaps did not know him before her sacrifice, of refraining from searching with suspicious hands the abyss of woman's frailty, in a word the art of a noble disinterestedness when facing lapses natural in a state so remote from nature.

Such did the president prove to be. La Bruyère has written that if a man but knew what his most intimate friend says about him, he would end the friendship. And I say: "What husband could be happy with his wife who sought to know what she hates, what she regrets, what she longs for?" The president never inquired.

I was waiting, as I have said, for his sister-in-law, but my clumsiness (there is always clumsiness in being caught) caused a commotion and came to Sophie's ears, for anything evil is always spread abroad. She announced to me her intention to marry; I was expecting this, for I had no longer been urging her to it.

I wished to carry the news of his luck to M. de V——; he knew it already. I was displeased that he should have left me thus in the dark, but he easily justified himself at Sophie's expense, since she had asked him to keep silent. "And so," I sadly said to myself, "I no longer have her full trust; even the best of women is deceitful!" But she had so much to reproach me with that I lacked the courage to complain of her. I was glad to have her marry this honest man, yielding thus to my entreaties and his perseverance, yet I would have wished longer opposition on her part. The revelation of this secret longing of my heart came all too late. But I quickly conquered this guilty and painful feeling and made one final effort to hasten the happiness of the man I neither wished nor was able to view as a rival.

I myself led them to the altar. Sophie, deadly pale, could hardly stand. She no doubt thought of the church at Versailles and of all those fragile edifices we had fancied were erected to an everlasting love. When in an altered voice she uttered the "I do" which gave her wholly to another, her eyes sought mine to ask if her lips were to form the words. I turned my head away; tears filled my eyes, and I hurriedly left the church before the end of the ceremony, not to have to reproach her with perjury. My first efforts to overcome the grief I had brought upon myself proved fruitless, and I was not able to quell an impulse of unfairness which caused me to say to her: "May the barrier now erected between us not lose me your friendship as lightly as my other rights have been taken from me!" This reproach was supremely out of place; a fainting fit which for long withstood all attempts to relieve it was her only reply and my punishment. Such were the last symptoms of an absurd jealousy, the last sparks of a dying fire, the last words of a love gone awry from its foundations, which never ruled over my happiness as it might have done, thus to save me from the perilous encounters that dashed my youth to pieces. Farewell, dear and loving Sophie, you who first moved my heart with unknown emotions, you who first caused me tears of thwarted love, farewell. The closest friendship will unite us till death, this is my consolation; once more farewell. May you enjoy the great happiness you so well deserve. That wish embodies all others and is a guarantee for complete felicity.

CHAPTER XIX

I LEARNED at last that this much-desired woman, Mme
L. C——, beautiful sister of the president's wife, had returned. As I dislike farewells, I left behind a letter for Sophie
and her husband, and quitted the house at daybreak.

> You will both find here the expression of an affection
> that will never change and of my wishes that your life may
> be as peaceful as mine is troubled. I have arranged for
> you a happiness that I myself renounce, the greatest of all
> —that of living united to a being one esteems and loves,
> with the certainty, which brightens the future, that separa-
> tion will come only with death. May you live again in chil-
> dren worthy of you! Children are a gift of heaven, when
> they do not come as a punishment. Yours will certainly be
> your solace. Born of you, can they fail to be well born?
> I envy you this felicity which I do not feel myself fitted to
> deserve; for to enjoy it one needs a constancy that the
> passions and turmoil of the world have deprived me of, a
> faithfulness of heart that my volatile nature took from
> me, and that bad habits leave me unable to acquire again.
> I need your friendship to console me for my sacrifice, and
> I ask it of you until I prove unworthy of it; that is as much
> as to say that it will be mine until my last moments. I am
> leaving you; but all that is best in me, all that is most
> sensitive in my soul, will still be at your side.

I went away from this retreat as if I was to regret it, as if
everything which had there grieved me had not been of my
own doing.

This facility of man to be swayed by events, attaching himself with so much impetuosity, and later forgetting with so much
resignation, is one of the most singular attributes of his nature.
This aptitude to change, so predominant in our kind, though
varying with the individual, this disposition to love with idolatry
what we will one day neglect with cruelty, this belief that the
possession of an adored being whose name we will later hear
with indifference is one of the necessary conditions of our life,

this power of becoming a stranger to anyone we once looked upon as another self, of losing interest in what has been the sole object of all our thoughts, of finding the heart empty of feeling for a privileged person who once stirred its most secret depths, this inexplicable versatility is one of the most insoluble problems of man's disposition, one of the most obscure enigmas of his entity, and perhaps the capital accusation to bring against his whole nature, since it constantly leads us to reflect that our affections are but rubbish, and man's ego but a wreck.

I should like to know a man who had loved but two women in his life; it is permissible to attempt happiness a second time. I should like to feel that adverse circumstances alone parted him from them, the course of events always more powerful than man and carrying him along. I should like to know that he never saw either of the two again without excessive tenderness, without being moved at hearing their names, that he spoke of them only with devotion, or better still that he avoided speaking of them; and that finally, keeping their memory sacred, he became invulnerable to the sex, inaccessible to love or anything which takes its shape and usurps its name. If I were blessed with good fortune on earth and he were in misfortune, I should make him my friend. My trust in him would be instinctive and boundless. Were he poor, I should trust him with my wealth; were he to benefit by my death, I should without hesitation place my life in his hands. Even without God, without faith in heaven, without peace on earth, that man would still be an honest man. Who would mistrust him?

It was beginning to grow dark when I entered the town. I learned there that Mme L. C—— could not contain her indignation against me, that she made indeed more fuss about it than was fitting for the interests of her sister, whose misfortunes she reproached me with. I learned that she was rigorous as regards moral principles, and that she entertained horrible prejudices. What grounds for attack! for seduction! What good reasons for a hot-headed person such as I was at that time to neglect nothing that might secure me sweet vengeance on her, to omit nothing that could make me beloved by her! It needed thought, calm—and a scheme. I spent a whole night pondering over it.

I sent to ask her for an interview about a matter of the highest importance, and in the name of a stranger who had not the honour of being known to her, but who was spending a few hours in her town and had revelations of the greatest interest to make to her. My messenger informed me that she was hesitating and asked to be first told the name of this mysterious stranger. This led me to call upon her straightway, assuming the name of the Comte de Chantenay, from one of my estates.

I found a woman who not only possessed all the charms I expected, judging by popular opinion, but others I had not anticipated: that is to say, a voice, a style, a bearing that enchanted me, combined with a general appearance and an expressive face that impressed one in spite of oneself. But when it came to telling who I was, I found myself compelled—with all the symptoms of modesty and regret and my eyes fixed to the floor—to resign myself to an outpouring of commonplaces on my great boldness in coming to confront her in her very house after having brought grief and mourning into her family. She begged me to leave with an insistance that suggested hatred, not imagining, she said, that I could have any communication to make to her of sufficient interest to compensate for the aversion she was obliged to own she felt for me. "If I had deserved it," I replied, "I could not console myself."

"What," she said sharply, "were you not?—but we will not recriminate or enter into any explanations; we need only agree, monsieur, that we have not and cannot have anything to say to each other."

Then, with a curtsey full of dignity, she walked towards her boudoir; but that is what I would not allow. Falling on my knees between her and the door, I dared to take that hand which would so calmly have signed the decree for my death, as was apparent from the anger in her beautiful eyes and the change in her voice. She drew it back with a sort of terror; but taking advantage of my strength, I retained it, adjuring her to listen to me. She agreed in order to avoid the greater evil of being in such close contact with me. Those were the words which she had the extreme severity to use. I felt at last that it was time to exalt my pride and to rise above such trivial second-rate abasement.

"Madame," I said to her with some show of arrogance, "what I hear from you is new for my ears. I do not know of what wrong you talk to me, I never had any with you. What I have to impart to you concerns you as well as your sister's reputation and mine, and I have the honour to inform you that you will listen to me. I have the right to claim this after the adventure which has caused such ridiculous and misplaced reports

. . . and I shall not renounce this right. For the rest, I do not wish to do this to-day; you are not in a condition to listen to me, and I no longer feel able to speak of a subject that requires on my part calm and care, as well as on yours."

Seeing that she was astonished, I thought to soften her, and, knowing that the quickest way to secure love is to speak to women of an old attachment and of one's sensibility in a former relationship, I hastened to add: "I had hoped that an affection to which I had given up my whole heart would be the last of my life, which was to be spent entirely beside her to whom I wished to consecrate it. I had thought that near her would end my quest in the peace of mutual affection, where I dreamed to find at last, after having been so often deceived, the kind of happiness for which I was born and which can be met only when love is shared—the one goal for the wishes of a soul such as mine." I here wiped away a few tears which I had not shed. "A fatal event," I continued, as she did not interrupt me, "has countered all my prudence and overturned the edifice raised in my heart. I yield to a fatality that has robbed me of everything, but at least, to my last hour, I will make full amends to her who for my sake has lost her peace of mind. Her honour will be a sacred trust that no human power can make me sacrifice."

After this pompous bombast, supported by animated pantomime, I thought it time to withdraw, leaving behind two impressions: one of deep emotion, which is always infectious, and the other of a pride that disdained what it had seemed to desire.

I had acquired a sort of friendship for the prior of the convent of ——, who on his side had conceived a devoted attachment to me. He had a cook who would have done credit to anyone, and a magnificent library that he had finally come to regard as his own. I affected to find him as learned as his books; in a word I established a serious friendship with him in as short a time as is usually required to lose the friends one has. He ruled his house, which was not wealthy, in a very despotic manner. I requested lodgings from him and secrecy; he gave me the one and promised the other. Finally, after a few days, I informed my fair inhuman lady of my intention of calling on her, very sure this time that I should not be refused. I sent word, however, that this would be my last visit before my departure for Paris, and one which would clear up everything. She agreed to receive me.

"I had thought, madame, that the business relating to an

event too sad to be recalled, which had prolonged my stay in
the country, would be brought to a conclusion to-day, and that
the *papers* which I had to put in order could be handed to you
at once [here her face expressed amazed surprise]; but my
health now hopelessly ruined, my heart, which knows no peace,
and a new storm that *during the last few days* has come to
agitate it—everything is prolonging a work which, however
simple and light, yet seems to me beyond my strength. . . . I
need a kind of effort to set me on my path and to raise me from
my gloom."

She was unaware, she stammered, how it could be necessary
she should be concerned with my arrangements; but anyhow
. . . since I had demanded it . . . with such peculiar authority,
she would go into the details . . . which seemed to me so indispensable. . . . She was not prepared for the idea of *having
a page in my novel* (that is literary, I said to myself), and could
not imagine what should lead her to enter into relations with
someone (she begged my pardon) with whom she had so little
wished to have any. . . . However, she was *impelled* to take
a step to which she had many objections! . . . Nevertheless, I
might be assured of every civility which was consistent with her
duties (her duties! she had none, she was a widow), and in
spite of her first resolve I might trust her in all things that
would be in accordance with her principles (fine words! I
thought).

I had kept my eyes on her nearly all the time, except in the
intervals when I thought it was useful to let her own have a
chance. Mine were dim, laden with grief and oppression. As I
had not much more to say which would fit my scheme, and
wishing besides to induce a strong emotion I risked a fainting
fit, which had a prodigious success. For not daring to ring she
hastened to proffer such help as the most zealous anxiety could
suggest; she had started to unfasten my clothes when I considered all had gone far enough; whatever is overdone fails in
its effect. The lucky appearance of a few tears, which came to me
I know not whence, completed the illusion of this truly pathetic
scene. Their source was, I believe, the sudden thought of all the
trouble I was giving myself; perhaps also they resulted from
the prolonged fancies into which I had suggested myself, almost
as an actor, when he plays from his heart, sheds the tears which
the poet has put into his lines. What I observed with delight,
was that she showed as much emotion as myself. Having cov-

ered her hands with kisses, I fastened up my clothes, made a few apologies for my deep and legitimate emotion, and left her —with the look of a man who is going to meet his death. She remained motionless, buried in thought.

Two days later, I requested the prior to go to see her. He was told to say that I could not have this honour myself, for I was kept to my room by a violent fever. Since he believed this to be my state, he delivered his message in a way that aroused all the sympathy of Mme L. C——. She seemed touched by my indisposition, and shortened a visit which, it so appeared to him, put her ill at ease.

I took the step of writing to her that I had brought ruin upon myself in seeking to fulfill an indispensable duty, for such she would feel it to be if she knew of what nature it was; that in wishing to meet an obligation imposed upon me by regard for her sister, one moment had decided my fate and left me nothing to look for in the future but misfortune and despair; that there were passions born of chance which left but weak traces behind them, but that there were also sudden and indestructible impressions, punishment from Heaven itself, for which there were no remedies on earth; that, having so ardently demanded an interview with her, to renounce it without telling her why I must seem unbecoming and unreasonable; that I nevertheless entreated her to excuse me, since I had good reason for no longer braving a danger which I had not foreseen; that I begged her not to attribute to romantic and eccentric ideas my resolve to flee from her, since I had learned by sad experience that I must either see her always or never approach her.

Her answer, which I had not expected, said in effect that I was better able than she to judge the reasons which had made me wish to approach her, and those which had altered my decision; that she approved, *though with regret,* a course which seemed wise to her; that she ventured, nevertheless, to ask me not to leave without handing over to her the papers to which I had seemed to attach so much importance, and which I had assured her closely concerned her sister; that in my last letter there were many things unintelligible to her, which she gave up trying to understand; that, for the rest, she thought me more worthy of happiness than she was at first inclined to believe, owing to an involuntary but natural prejudice; that she begged me not to doubt she had largely overcome this, while the idea of the injustice she might have done me led her to form the most sincere wishes for my happiness.

After this, I found myself justified in presenting myself to her, as if I had changed my mind with some effort and had yielded to her roundabout way of inviting me.

How happy she was to see me again! I discovered that immediately in spite of her struggle to conceal it. But when she looked well at me, that light of pure joy was swiftly transformed into a cloud of sadness.

It was nine o'clock in the evening of a gloomy and rainy day. With my soul and my eyes appearing still more gloomy, I entered her presence dressed in black, without powder (which was then unknown), seeming to have cut my hair which was hidden within my collar, pale in consequence of all the water I had drunk during the day (an infallible method with me of becoming as pale as I wish to be), bearing on my cheeks the traces of a few drops of gum arabic diluted and slightly dried, which most naturally resemble tears recently shed, and with a humble and lowered brow.

I placed in her hands a packet with black seals, which I begged her not to open in my presence. I asked of her only the favour of listening to me attentively. She was in no state to interrupt me; she was Silence and Fear changed into a statue.

"The errors of my youth, madame—and I congratulate myself on this—have had no incurable influence on my heart, which was born sensitive and good [fortunately I was telling the truth]. If death had not separated me from a woman who had deigned to love me as one loved in the Golden Age of the world and of virtue, I should still be at her feet [it was true]. If those who since then have condescended to listen to me had been faithful, or had not been torn from me by circumstances independent of my will, I should myself have been a model to imitate in the sort of attachments which time justifies, and which are sanctified by their duration. But early environment, the depravity of our time, some advantages which I abused, a general relaxation of principles, which weakened my own, the puerile vanity of feeling proud of aberrations that ought only to produce restlessness and remorse, the society I have frequented, everything I have seen or heard, perverted my youth and corrupted my heart before I had entered on the wholesome road of experience and had discovered for myself the way of doing good and avoiding evil. Your sister was the last victim of this insatiable desire to possess the whole of your sex, which was implanted in me by nature and encouraged by fashion and by the ease with which one success leads to another if one devotes

oneself exclusively to following this miserable career. Such is
human weakness—that one pursues what one blames, and that
this sad propensity to guilty seduction becomes an irresistible
need even when one disapproves of it. I am punished for it.
. . . I have never found happiness. No, never have I secured
that happiness to which my disposition had visibly called me.
. . . The world believes one is enjoying oneself, but the heart
belies this; a worm is gnawing beneath the rose leaves. . . .
I am about to complete my punishment by leaving a life—"

"What, monsieur!" (This with a piercing cry, and she paler
than I was.)

"A life for which I feel horror since I have seen you,
madame."

"How is that, monsieur?"

"I will put an end to all this and bring solitude between the
world and myself. I have known that deceitful world far too
well; the gift of your heart would alone to-day reconcile me to
life. . . . I am not worthy to possess you. . . . The sudden
and extraordinary effect which you have produced on me is not
sufficient excuse for the alliance of crime with virtue. . . . But
there is no longer any question of that. For a long time I hesitated over this course to which I was irrevocably bound by the
misfortunes of the springtime of my prematurely faded life—
especially the misfortune of a new passion by which I am imperiously overwhelmed. . . . I shall bind myself by vows and
make my way towards peace, or else towards death, in the shade
of a cloister. The worthy prior is directing me in this path,
along which I endeavour to walk with fervour. I leave behind
only one memory which poisons my life, but it will smooth the
path of penitence. It is itself my vocation."

I was silent; it was high time.

"But I am truly upset to see you in such a state [a singular
expression, I thought]. What has led you to so desperate a
resolve? Would it not be wiser to wait until your health is
restored? For the physical state influences the mind more than
people think. You are not well; you are entirely altered, even
since we last met. Of what insurmountable passion are you telling? Is it possible that with control such as you have exercised
over yourself, and unfortunately over others, you should yield
with so much weakness to an impression that you ought to struggle against before considering it unconquerable—before adopting a life so eccentric, so little in harmony with all your tastes?

Beware of a false vocation. Beware of the gate of the desert, for on its threshold one must abandon hope."

"How well you put it, madame! But your mind must fail where your heart alone could best advise me. You might—"

"What might I?"

"Bind me to life again by restoring to it a value it no longer possesses."

"Alas, what can I do?"

"Bring me back to virtue."

"Begin by recovering your common sense."

"Where can I find it when I have lost it through you and while I am still seeing you?"

"Is it not enough to have made my sister unhappy?"

"Your sister! By what comparison are you profaning yourself?"

"My sister is a very lovable and distinguished person."

"I agree, but she is a woman. Your nature is of another order; if it were not so, would not her eyes have cast into me that devouring poison, that inextinguishable flame, with which yours consume me? My bruised soul," I exclaimed, falling at her knees, "has no refuge saving you or death, unless I raise an eternal wall between us! Do not altogether forget an unfortunate being who, unable to live beside you, conceals himself in solitude in order to live without distraction with your image."

Her head had fallen on my shoulder, she bathed me with burning tears. That was the moment, a moment which perhaps would never come again . . . I seized it.

My triumph was consummated, she was still in a swoon; my packet with its mournful seals had fallen to the floor. I hastened to put it back into my pocket; and Eau de Cologne, which she perhaps mistook for tears, reopened her beautiful eyes. She fixed them on me with more embarrassment than anger.

Her candour was such, and I remember it with tenderness, that she disdained those customary scenes of reproaches and remorse, and all those affectations after the defeat which are as old as love and its victory. She only said: "You will at least renounce that fantastic plan, and I alone will be unfortunate! . . . But how could I be unfortunate if you do not forsake me?"

Most men think that women all give themselves in the same way; ordinary women believe that there is but one way of giving oneself. It is a gross and ignoble notion. Even beauty needs a

magic charm to ennoble its fall and to rise from it again. It is
this afterthought when triumph is over which makes the difference for a man between being in love and not being in love.
A woman with an ordinary face who gracefully gives her final
gift has the advantage over her who has only her attractions
to abandon without that innate delicacy or that imperceptible
skill which creates an enchantment prolonged beyond pleasure
and strengthened by reflection; Venus has need of art to unfasten her girdle.

This art, or beautiful disposition, was possessed by Mme
L. C——.

Our days followed on in that sweet security which happy
nights spread over the only happy days of life, when that cruel
disease—now prevented by inoculation—came to mar a face
that I was beginning to adore. I did not leave her. I did not go
out of her room during the whole illness, which was long and
acute. By exposing myself for her sake and lavishing attentions on
her, I became the more attached. I gave no thought to a danger
that shared with her ceased to be one. What man would fear
to die with the woman he loves? She was delirious during the
whole time of the eruption. She would call me, I was at her side,
she did not recognise me. My despair was at its height, but it
was a despair that did not find me insensible to being present to
her thoughts in the midst of such cruel suffering. But the most
frightful of all awaited her: the surprise and the terror at seeing
herself disfigured, the consternation in which her mirror plunged
her, in spite of all that I could oppose to that severe looking-
glass which reflected so sad a truth. I swore to her from my
heart that she had not changed for me. She replied that she
knew I would prove true, but she also must be true.

I did not understand at first the full sense of these words;
a few weeks later I had the explanation. More sincere than I,
she retired into a convent, whence all my entreaties could not
snatch her. She begged me to return to Paris, protesting that
if my feelings for her were maintained, she would come back to
me and would abandon her plan. I offered to marry her: I was
sincere. She was more inflexible than steel. I departed, thwarted
and unhappy, and was to feel still more so on learning that she
was taking the vows—vows which robbed me of her for ever.

What magic lies in obstacles! What power in impossibilities!
What impatience both arouse, what inconsolable regrets, when
desires are in vain!

The Revolution found her in this retreat; at the moment I now write she is in a convent in Germany. May she feel herself as happy there as in the days when I knew her adorned with all the charms of youth and beauty. And if she has any tears for those fugitive moments of our youth and that beautiful country which we have lost, may they flow without bitterness in a dreamy melancholy more delicious than gaiety.

It so came about that Divine Grace employed my profane hand to touch her, much as the humble artisan may work at the precious porcelain vases which are used on the tables of kings.

The Comte de Maillebois [1] was then on one of his estates, meditating on the injustice that had prevented him from becoming a marshal of France; at all events that was the favourite subject of his thoughts and his conversation, which for the rest was occupied with a thousand other things more interesting for his friends. He had often invited me to come for a rest in his retreat, which for him was adorned by the presence of a woman of wit whom he had adored and believed that he still loved. [2] She had with her a very pretty friend for whom the line of La Fontaine, "And her grace was lovelier still than her beauty," seemed to have been made. I only saw her as one sees the last ray of the sun, which the clouds soon cover. She left twenty-four hours after my arrival, leaving with me a beautiful drawing, the work of an angel or her own, for which I nearly got myself killed long afterwards. Stopped by robbers in the neighbourhood of London, I abandoned with the best grace possible my watch and a few guineas, but was so obstinate in retaining a little rosewood casket containing trifles and especially this pretty drawing, which gave it value, that one of these gentlemen became ill-humoured enough to discharge his pistol through my carriage window before taking his leave.

I have not forgotten her talent and the pretty hand which cultivated it, and still less forgotten that, in love with the models of antiquity and its costumes, she used to dress as they have attempted to dress since, and as was formerly done in Athens beneath the beautiful sky of Greece. She was the first woman whom I heard argue in France that all Europe was badly dressed, alike as regards grace, comfort, and health. She wore a white tunic as her only garment, with a pink scarf crosswise under the breasts; her only head-dress was a flower. There could not be a more beautiful figure, better outlines, more naked without indecency; it is impossible to give any idea of a way of dressing so attractive and so scanty. . . . There was but little distance between her and happiness. She had the extreme goodness to draw up a little memorandum explaining the whole scheme of her wardrobe. I showed it in Paris to a few ladies among my friends, who were not brave enough to adopt antique grace and reasonableness; but it must be admitted that to make such an attempt one needs a better climate than that of Paris, where so many beautiful women have been mowed down since, like early flowers not sufficiently protected against an inclement sky.[3]

It was also at the Comte de Maillebois's that I saw the first lines that I have read written by the hand of Louis XIV, eight pages about the famous adventure of Mme du Rumain, who, having become pregnant in her husband's absence, came to throw herself at the King's knees to beg him to save her honour. She told him that she believed she was addressing the worthiest man in his kingdom, a compliment which much pleased that great monarch. He delivered her a little lecture on morality, fitted to the occasion, and obliged her in the way she desired by sending her husband to the frontier, where he was retained all the winter. This king of immortal memory wrote down the anecdote using initials, with remarks on gallantry full of good sense and truth. "How easier far it is to preach than act."

This manuscript was intended for M. du Maine, though I cannot see what use it could be to him, any more than I can see how it came into the hands of Desmarets.[4] For the rest this document, as I verified, was perfectly authentic and was recognisable by a sort of loftiness and authority in the style. The King was as capable of writing well as of thinking well on matters which were, so to speak, within the immediate range of his power, as witnessed by the famous instructions to Philip V, many letters to his generals and ministers, and also—what is a strong proof of his talent in writing—the happy aptitude for the right word which has caused so many sayings of his to be quoted and remembered. *"Invenit verba quibus reges deberent loqui."*

I have therefore not been surprised as so many people by seeing the announcement in the public papers of the "Œuvres de Louis XIV." I am convinced that he wrote with his own hand a volume worthy to be handed down to posterity and very superior to that which has been spun out as being his, though not worthy of him, under the title of his "Œuvres."

"I dare say," the Prince de Ligne wrote to me, "that we are of the same opinion about the 'Mémoires de Louis XIV,' which contain something of the cook, something of the monk, and something of the instructions of a mother to her daughter. I imagine that they found a few notes in his handwriting and then diluted them in this bad style."

On leaving the Comte de Maillebois, with whom I had spent days I found very instructive, I set out for Paris, where I tried my best to throw off all the provincial reminiscences which weighed me down. One of my first distractions, offered to me by chance on coming out of the Opéra, was a pretty Mme de L——, whom I had known in Maine, and afterwards at the house of Mlle de Coulanges, whose beauty was admired by all Paris, and who was mowed down like a flower before her day was half over. (At the time of her death she was adored by the Prince de Bauffremont, who came here to warm the ice of winter near the fire of dawn. It was he himself who led me to her house without suspecting that I should play on him the trick of a page, although I was no longer one. That is what happened, and if I have not spoken of this adventure in its proper place, it is because it proved to be nothing but a very brief liaison, brought to an end by dissipation and indifference, and because it is too petty and above all too tedious to relate everything.) I saw Mme de L—— again, having had but a glimpse of her at Mlle de Coulanges's before her marriage. She was just as attractive, but more mature, having developed all the graces and charm she was then promising. I found her now displaying a piquant assurance and bearing acquired through marriage, and more becoming, in my opinion, than the bashful or real affectation of a young girl who approaches love and repells it. I had previously attempted to come near her, but had not taken any risks in face of the obstacles placed by her mama, a woman of limited ideas who was frightened of everything where her daughter was concerned. I ought to add that the mother—who on that day was accompanying her daughter whose husband was away—still possessed all the perfections of beauty, but a beauty that was every day losing something and rapidly approaching its decline. There is a fortunate period in the lives of women when their charms are, so to say, stationary, when their eyes, bright with the fire of youth, command Time to pass by, and Time obeys them. There swiftly follows another period when every minute withers the flower, steals an attraction, destroys a seduction, when every moment effects ravage. They are still desirable, to-morrow they will be less so, the day after they will not be so at all. Every moment is precious then. Every occasion to return to youth and its pleasures, before leaving them for ever, is treasured. To deliberate is not for such a woman . . . she hears but one call: "Enjoy yourself."

Such was the position of Mme de L——'s mother, and her ideas on this important point were in conformity with my own! Severe for her daughter, who still had time ahead, she was indulgent for herself, who had none to lose. All this was very fine but too antique, and I quickly decided to yield to her pretentions but not to permit her to be in the way of mine. I began by telling the young lady that I had adored her for a long time, but that her mama would not allow it because she desired to claim my attentions for her own benefit. I told the mother that she had inspired me with a steady passion from the first, but that her daughter had her eyes on me; that having been born unusually sensitive, and possessing only one heart to be touched, it was impossible for me to open it to two loves; that I implored her to believe in mine, and to take it as natural that I should affect a gallant air towards her daughter to reassure her pride, so she would leave us in peace.

The young woman was mistrustful, but her rival yielded, for people will often display fierce and noisy virtue just because it is not theirs which is being besieged. I therefore applied myself directly to the elder of these virtuous ladies; and when she had listened to my coaxing I warned the other, who acquired proof of this through a prearranged discovery. It was then that in order to purchase silence and peace it became necessary to give up a clumsy adorer who seemed unable to protect himself against simple curiosity. Our plot was never suspected, so behold my homage brought back to its first and natural destination. But, as traitors must be punished even by means of their treachery, I made the frightful mistake of consoling the forsaken lady, unknown to the younger and prettier one; I came very near to no longer loving the latter through loving the former. So, to make an end of it once for all, I, a few weeks after, wrote a letter that was sent to both of them. The same leavetaking astonished them simultaneously, the same farewell reduced them to tears, and this fine idea which had come to me so easily, restored freedom to all three of us.

Mme de L—— was shocked at what she called a rascally

trick, but she had the good taste to laugh at it afterwards (what will not youth laugh at?). But her lady mother was angry (I have just told you that at her age one will not allow joking on this subject); she manifested a despair much too dramatic for the occasion and for the time which I had devoted to her. I know that she has not forgiven me.

These ladies were living at the Choiseul Mansion; the father held a position in the office of the duke of that name.[5] The agreeable Mme de L—— might very well have been the daughter of that minister, an intelligent man but a rake, and a spendthrift who, in the pay of foreigners, prostituted France during a term of office which was evil for the state and a humiliation for the kingdom; yet his name cannot be tarnished with the crime imputed to him of having cut short the days of the unfortunate father of Louis XVI. The Maréchal de Stainville, his brother, was a harsh man, full of hatred and of less worth than the duke. I shall describe him when I come to an event which, it goes without saying, turned to my disadvantage, since I was wrestling against his stupidity and injustice.

I had resumed my Paris life when, crossing the Palais Royal one evening, with the Marquis de Genlis, I was stopped by a woman who requested us to follow her. I refused to do so; Genlis professed to find in her charm and a grace and bearing worthy of a better fate. This made me laugh the more, and I prepared to walk away without foreseeing that a most pathetic recognition awaited me. It was my Aline (everyone has his own),[6] she who in one of the most charming villages of France had received my first homage to love beneath the heavenly vault. How could I avoid going up to her room and listening to the narrative of her adventures? They were simple, but the natural result of her misbehaviour and mine. What she had done with me she continued with others, and her parents had driven her out. Dissipation starts by being a timid child, but becomes a giant who grows unceasingly until coming to grief. She had finally settled in Paris, that abyss in which all vices conceal themselves under the same garment, and after varying luck had fallen into poverty from which she would not easily emerge.

She wept as she told her story and moved us, especially me, for I could not hide from myself the part which I had had in the life of disorder she had led. Genlis, with that generosity which was natural to him, gave her all the money he had on him, delighted, he said, to make amends for the misdeeds of a friend, hoping that someone would another time take charge of his own. As for me, I did better, as was my duty; I sent her to the Faubourg Saint-Jacques, to S——, famous for his skill in curing that disorder which makes pleasure a danger; then, having provided for her journey, I married her to a gamekeeper who asked her forgiveness for his infidelities, made in advance of her due, in the shadow of the bushes and forests. I do not know if she confessed to him the formal receipts she had accepted in anticipation.

Why could I not always repair through good deeds, so easy to perform, the evil which it has sometimes cost me so much to commit, and which it is often impossible to wipe out? To make amends is the virtue of those who no longer have any other.

This time of my life was remarkable for two habitual dispositions of my mind, which it was a hard task to struggle against, and over which I have with difficulty triumphed: the constant thought of death, without precisely fearing it, and, as an involuntary relief, dreams of an unbridled imagination, thriving on chimeras and delusions, and creating nothing but castles in the air. It was often impossible for me for long hours and even days to detach myself from a situation in which my imagination had placed me. One day I would fancy myself the general of a victorious army, the town was taken by assault after prodigies of valour: I tempered the fierceness of the soldiers, and my clemency was admired by the defeated enemy. Another day I was king, my court was the most brilliant in Europe. I appointed the high officers of my kingdom, I made mentally a list of the names; the men I thus distinguished accompanied me in my fancy. I often met the greatest difficulties in the innovations I planned; this was an object of serious meditation. I encouraged the arts and only moderately protected men of letters, because I knew their ignorance of the world, their presumption, their ingratitude, their impatience of authority and subordination. I gave fêtes; that is almost an obligation for a king, after he has fulfilled his other duties. I was mindful of the splendour of the throne, because this concerns its preservation; those who deny this are fools or partisans who delight in degrading what they hate.

Sometimes, transformed into a Christian orator, another Bossuet, I thundered from the holy pulpit, I terrified kings and nations by my august eloquence, and my eulogy of greatness fallen to dust served as a revelation of its emptiness. Another day, as the preferred lover of a great queen on whom my imagination bestowed a power without limit and a beauty without blemish, I had driven away my rivals; the universe was at her feet, and she was at mine.

Another time I carried my madness (as it would have become if I had not taken care) so far as to transfer my life several centuries ahead. Able to clothe myself in whatever form pleased me, I wandered across Europe under various names and filled it with the fame of adventures by turn glorious and enchanting, and all more or less prodigious. The most deplorable part of this mania was that I could not be rid of any such idea when once it took a strong hold on me. It would follow me into society, was proof against all distractions; it rooted itself in my imagination, which it isolated; it lived there during my sleep, often preventing me from being restored thereby, and when I awoke it was still my leading thought, if indeed it was not the only one. Thus to abandon oneself to a fixed idea is the highroad to insanity.

After having believed oneself to be Tancred, Alcibiades, Bajazet, Louis XIV, Demosthenes, one would end like that miserable wretch who was shut up for calling himself God Almighty. That poor man was sensible in all other respects, and I do not see why they treated him so severely. He had a mad idea, I admit, but have we not each of us our own? Many people have had more pernicious and fatal ideas—especially some who held among us a share of the authority which this innocent visionary believed was his to exercise both on earth and in heaven.

I resolved to forbid my imagination these deceitful excursions, and to guard myself against the peril of creations so fantastic by never allowing my mind to dwell on these dangerous transfigurations; on the contrary I forced it to seek the reality of life instead of the emptiness of the waking dreams of a madman. I had much trouble in overcoming this familiarity with immensity and space, and in acquiring a distaste for this mania of a boundless horizon. So full is life of bitterness from which man's nature delights to seek escape!

I emerged from these constant abstractions only to think of death, though without being terrified by it. Nevertheless, with its melancholy fingers, it withered my life. Such thoughts spoiled anything fortunate that happened to me. What does this existence of a day matter to me, I would say to myself, or anything which may brighten or degrade it? What have I to do with what men call happiness or misfortune, glory or shame? What interest can I take in the illusion of an hour which death will to-morrow terminate? Can I have a smile on my lips and joy in my heart when everything bears witness that I have been condemned to the greatest of misfortunes, that of being born? when everything shows our incapacity to exist? when everything attests that we are nothing but living dust which the wind of death will soon disperse? This most beautiful work of Nature, this woman whose beauty is so finished, has allowed me to taste all the favours of her love. What little happiness there is on this earth, if any there be, I could have found in her arms. . . . I came near to knowing it, but for the poison of thought. These delightful walks, these smart gatherings, these pompous ceremonies, this ball, this supper, this play, were about to interest me, to move and to flatter me, but at a bend in the avenue, behind a pillar, in the shadow of a mysteriously lighted boudoir, even seated at the festive table, I have seen death. . . . I have even seen it on the lips of that beautiful woman, who is to-night so full of laughter, but who to-morrow will be its prey. . . . It is everywhere, and we are all dying! So why should I be deeply impressed by something which can leave no trace? Why should I attach a price to fancies without value, since they are without substance, to fancies more perishable than the leaves of the trees, which are born anew, and more fugitive than the sand, which the wind bears away but brings back again? I read a book which touches me, which would move me if I allowed it to do so. . . . Death is at the end. . . . Is it worth while to finish it? May not death interrupt the reading?

Can one be flattered by praise, or can one deserve it? What belongs to us in all that? Is there anything here below that does not lack the essential attributes of perfection—strength, and duration? Can anything good be discovered in so brief a span? And, if finally something approaches what we imagine to be perfection, is not that a thousand times more lamentable since nothing is possessed with the power to endure? Come, I exclaimed to myself, there is no substance in life, nothing but mere appearance without body and without foundation, and mankind is only a family of ghosts! I am not really sure that what I call *I* belongs to me more than what in another I call *he*. There is nothing true but death, if that word itself is not a vain sound, since it is impossible for anything which does not exist to cease to exist.

Such were the two enemies which I had for a long time to struggle against and which in the end I almost rid myself of, but not sufficiently to prevent a great contempt for life remaining, a deep foundation of melancholy formerly hidden beneath appearances of heedlessness and frivolity, but to-day showing itself naked. Great joy or great surprise in others always astonishes me, and I protest genuinely that it is only with pity I hear people forming plans for the future, or treating seriously the affairs of this life, which is but an uncertain, mysterious, and wretched void. This is only too sound a concept for anyone who bears in mind what constitutes man's nature! It is the legitimate induction to be drawn from our littleness, our knowledge, our ignorance!

There are men who have never given thought to this; there are others over whom these reflections glide as over a sterile soil which yields no fruit. They know by morning this mortal envelope may perish, and yet this evening they are as arrogant as might be a God in the full knowledge and pride of his immortality. They have the certitude that not one thing they pursue or obtain in this world is worth the exertion, the sleepless nights, or the mean deeds resulting from ambition and cupidity; yet they are moved by the remorse of indecision, the anguish of denial, the agitation of hope, the impetuosity of triumph, the vanity of success, the excitement of joy! They know that nothing is lasting, yet they behave as if they possessed the privilege of eternity! They have discovered that honours are of no account, that no gold or treasure can buy one hour of life, that it is only a senseless hoarding of mere metal which survives us; they have in a word discovered that all upon earth is smoke. Yet I see them forgetful of this eternal truth; I see them lavish of scorn, sparing of good deeds, bustling in order to cut a figure in this world, as if they supposed this life to be everlasting.

There are two men in each of them (perhaps also in myself); every object has two sides, we all are like so many Pentheuses.

> . . . *vidit Pentheus*
> *Et solem geminum et duplices se ostendere Thebas.*[7]

We see double; often, alas, we do not see at all.

So farewell, illusions of a fame which I now and again have dreamed of! Farewell, regrettable deceptions of love to which I so long devoted my life. Farewell, you brilliant fancies of the imagination which often created glamour for me upon this earth where some few phantoms creep along and generations of deceitful shadows! I know how void are your promises; the veil covering your emptiness has been fully lifted for me. This farewell which my pen traces here, this renouncing of all your deceits, comes from my heart; it is the last farewell. Stage without foundations, drama offering us no sensible plot, no known ending, you no longer can provide a part for me. Barren meadows yielding only colourless flowers and tasteless fruits, I shall no longer wander about your precincts, so wide and yet so closed-in. I am henceforth without illusions, I have lost interest in all things. . . . I no longer believe that there is any distance between the Pantheon and the gemonies.[8] I have surveyed this world; its senselessness has followed me everywhere; I have known kings and their subjects, I have visited nations, I have felt at their keenest all human affections: in a last analysis, there is *nothing*.

After so many feverish agitations I found a woman who had borrowed her features from an angel, goodness from some god;[9] I was imagining that such sweet affection was about to lend charm to what was left to me of life— I must stop, once again confronted by the worthlessness of my last deceived hopes, by a disastrous event which gave birth to such grief as will follow me to the grave. This grief has so broken my heart that when slander seized hold of the facts it found me as insensitive to its riotous fancies as I am to all the pretences at consolation. I have more than ever felt the immeasurable void that presses on us from all sides, the mere thought of which should pacify our hunger for honours during life, and quench our thirst for fame after death.

CHAPTER XX

I saw one of those women who, as if by miracle,
combine all the perfections of which the ancients
shaped their ideal of Beauty. I saw her and felt
suddenly as if struck by lightning; my heart was
taken from me. This woman spoke; I heard as it
were a man's voice, and my heart at once came
back to me.

*O*H, triumphant magic of a melodious and moving voice,
what charm is more bewitching and compelling? Beauty
of voice, how powerful is your grip upon us, how penetrating
your attraction! You claim the heart, you enslave it, not to leave
it free again. You are, in relation to words, what grace is to a
shapely body, what wit is to flesh. A beautiful voice enhances a
mere trifle on the lips of an ordinary woman. And its absence
would strip of beauty the speech of an angel. . . . Endowed
with the soft and flexible stresses of a sensitive voice, ugliness
is no longer utterly ugliness. Without a charming voice the most
handsome woman ceases to be handsome for me. She does not
even regain her beauty if she once more returns to silence. For
where is the barbarian who can make love without speech? . . .
Harmonious tones of the voice, echoes of a heart seeming always
moved, I would rather be deceived through you, in the darkness,
than hold in my arms by the light of the sun a fair one whose
manly voice scares love and puts pleasure to flight!

It was at the Champs-Elysées that I saw the type of woman
who makes one fastidious when looking at any other, and whom
the heart still follows when the eyes have lost sight of her. This
stranger completely filled my thoughts; I forgot all the rest.
I was in despair of ever seeing her again, when one day at Issy
at the house of Lady D——, who was then in France with her
charming daughters, I saw but one person at a big gathering of
people. She was the goddess of my heart, the charmer of my
wits. What unhoped-for delight thus to meet her again! . . .
to feel sure that I was about to learn her name, sure that
I should soon place my homage at her feet. She hardly spoke,
she was English, and I waited a long time before the spell was
broken. Heavens, how shattered it was! From what height did

not my fancy fall? Her voice was that of a man, a man who would deserve to be reproached for it, and for whom such a voice would prove an obstacle with any woman whose soul had a delicate ear. She was no doubt aware of my forwardness at the Champs-Elysées, and of the effect the second meeting had upon me. It must have appeared strange to her that I did not make use of this opportunity; but I could not approach her, nor wish to know better the woman whose voice I had heard far too much. She became for me like one of those ruddy fruits, so inviting with its fresh colours, which you open to find that the worm has eaten the core; or like some flowers, still gay as in their first bloom, but whose scentless calyx is already faded. My heart said to her: "O handsome statue! What a fatal gift is a voice to you! If the gods had made you dumb, what yearnings would not go towards you! But you speak, and one forgets you!"

I could not, however, take my eyes away from her. I went on listening to her for a while to make sure of my misfortune. When a man is about to fall in love with a woman, if he discovers an imperfection in her, how eagerly he tries to convince himself of it; he wants to know if he can love her. My decision was soon taken; I withdrew, but sadly, as one does on losing a friend who has betrayed our trust and deceived our hopes.

Before loving another woman, a few adventures kept me busy; I will sketch them rapidly, because I do not myself find them of great interest. For instance, a few weeks given to Mme de S——, who perhaps attaches even less importance to their recollection than I do. I was one day dining with the Colonel S——, who lived in furnished rooms at a hotel of the Faubourg Saint-Germain, when we heard an uproar and commotion. I learnt, on making enquiries, that distrainers wanted to arrest Mme de S—— who also lodged at the hotel. I came downstairs, and as there was not a minute to lose I proffered my watch, my horse, my cabriolet, and, I believe, even my groom in payment, or at least as a security. The rascally people with whom I had to deal chose to look upon all these as worth only fifty louis. Colonel S—— lent me twenty, which, added to what I had on me, secured the freedom of this dark-eyed beauty. So she believed herself bound in gratitude to me, while I avoided her out of propriety.

But a few days later, when she cleared her debt, the situation became very different. I made an excuse of having to thank her for accepting my help, and I went to see her. I had been receiving my reward for about a month when one day I saw Polastron arriving at her rooms with his violin, for, although he was a colonel like others, he always had it in his pocket, or under his arm or—on his tongue. A sort of languor was all he had in common with his sister and his wife, two remarkable women; he was wasting away through secret grief. When I noticed that we were two, I politely questioned him, displaying interest, and he answered me from an oppressed chest and with tears in his eyes. I addressed some reproaches to our mistress and left them together.

Very soon after this surrender, Simolin, Minister of Russia, solemnly boasted to me of the happiness he enjoyed with a Mme d'Al——, who had come all the way to Paris to ruin him; she was arriving from the town made more than famous by the plague, and the glory which accrued to Bishop Belzunce on account of his pastoral self-sacrifice and abnegation.

Simolin, with his wig daintily curled, believed himself loved (everyone believes this); he wanted witnesses of his bliss; he welcomed me at his fireside where I did him all the harm which a young and handsome man can bring upon a fool who is neither. Not that he lacked ability and intelligence in his profession, but the art of business is different from the art of love: any state matter, any official document can be more easily dealt with, without making one run the risk of being laughed at. I was his mistress's lover without his noticing anything. I practically told him so myself; he made an absurd disturbance, yet ended by growing calm. But I, at supper one day with his mistress, began to weary of this peace and her charms; and since she picked a quarrel with me on account of an enamelled Héloïse upon my watch—which she insisted was a rival I ought to surrender to her—I shammed a bleeding of the nose, retired into the next room, took up my hat, jumped out of the window to the ground below, then to the boulevard, leaving her at table, where she might truly have awaited me to this day had she not died since as the wife of the Comte de Custine, a general who was guillotined while in the service of the French Republic.

Ladies! . . . Now comes a very different story! . . . Indulgent and warm-hearted sex, grant me forgiveness for the great sin of my life! I was rather forced into it, as you will see; however, I pass judgement. . . . I look upon myself as extremely guilty, and I beg from you a forgiveness which truly I do not grant to myself.

There was once upon a time a very pretty woman who was looked upon as very virtuous. She had been born far away . . . in a country where women are more desirable than beautiful, and have stronger senses than sensibility. This one had charms, perhaps even a heart. Her husband used to spend his nights at gambling, so much so that he lost huge sums and impaired his fortune in this pretty Paris where, as elsewhere, one should gamble only with people one knows very well, unless, which is still better, one does not gamble at all. I had met the lady his wife and even started a sort of romance with her at some balls at the Opéra, a vast and appropriate field for affairs of this kind. She defended herself sufficiently to stir love for a while; then she had given in. Not wishing to confide in a maid (a course I greatly approve and commend to all women who might do otherwise), she herself would open the little door which led, as well as a larger one, into her room. The darkness was great, the way was roundabout, but all this secret and difficult affair amused me as it did her. It would have lasted long and ended in all decency had it not been for a misplaced saying of hers which put into my head ideas I would not otherwise have conceived. One evening as I stumbled on account of the darkness, I complained about it with a slight show of humour. "You would prefer," she said in an almost severe voice, "to enter my rooms full lights on, in view of my servants and perhaps of all Paris; but I am fully decided not to be compromised, and to act in such a way that no indiscreet talk, even on your part, can be believed."

A thunderbolt falling at my feet could not have astonished me more than these words. I leaned against the wall struck by stupefaction, dumb with surprise and anger. She sought my hand, which repulsed her, and I reached her room without having uttered a word, and with but one idea in mind—that of taking my leave with dignity and never returning. But this lofty vengeance would have required a control over myself I did not then possess by the side of a woman as desirable as she was, and of whom I was master. Besides, kissing and cajoling intervened; she declared it was an innocent joke, though to me it was a very bad one. Yielding to my senses, my heart grew calmer. But when I returned home, I put my thoughts together and all were against her. I no longer felt generous enough to forgive. It is then D—— came into my mind, an officer in the royal guards having all possible reasons not to love the Revolution, though

he went over to it swiftly and deeply from the first. This D——
had once acted towards me in a most handsome manner; he
was loved by a young lady, daughter of a painter. I found her,
what she truly was, very pretty; no sooner had I mentioned this,
than he gave her up to me, though he had some trouble to make
her agree. Perhaps he was tired of her, but one must not analyse
motives too intimately, or search too deeply into a kind action;
nothing would otherwise be left of most human deeds. I did
not long benefit by his kindness, this little person soon taking to
the stage somewhere in the provinces. We both have this to reproach ourselves with, and, what is worse, the fact that she
turned out a wretched actress, which makes us all three the
more guilty.

As regards D—— I had often expressed my gratitude to
him and had promised to repay him if occasion occurred. So
while I was pondering over the recent insult I had received and
the necessity of vengeance, my thoughts turned to him. He was
passionate; I knew that his temperament was sufficiently sus-
tained to enable him to take my place without giving me a bad
name and, what is more, would fit him for the part of impro-
vising his good fortune and the lady's punishment. He had
almost my build, and I sometimes carried during these nocturnal
encounters a huge muff in which to hide my face as a protection
from the cold. There was no need of much ceremony in the
dark, so I resolved to lend him this muff and to give him full
instructions. When it came to the act itself, I planned it all with
so much care that I even supplied him with the scents to which
my fair one was accustomed.

To proceed with my tale in due order, I must say that I
had some trouble in making him agree, though he at last gave
in when I had told him her name, and after he had reflected that
if he should be discovered all that could happen would be to find
himself shown to the street. He set out, therefore, after midnight to this dangerous encounter. It was February, and with
head well buried in the kindly muff he uttered no other sound
when the door was opened to him than the shivers of a man
who was cold. He caught hold of an arm, and resolutely followed his guide. I had instructed him in all the ins and outs of
the place. At the top of a flight of steps was a dressing-room
the door of which remained open so as to throw light on the
corridor; there would be found a marble bath, a small cupboard
on which burned a candle, a few chairs, a sofa, a table bearing

flowers. I had warned D—— that at this spot only was danger,
but that it was great.

He was to hurry ahead, quickly make a survey of all these
things, and knock over the light as if through clumsy eagerness.
Then he would take hold of her before she could collect her
thoughts and reach her bedroom (this I had often carried off
with success during the beautiful early days of our liaison).
He should, above all, lead her to the most comfortable seat
available, and there reap a victory that could be explained by a
rush of warm passion and love, which is never displeasing.

He managed it.

He has assured me since that she was given no time for any
suspicion, nor to express the thought of it. A little confused,
but still more proud, she found her feet again and went to her
bedroom. D—— boldly followed her and hastened to conceal
himself (at least this is what he said) in the bedcurtains. She
saw him go by, as light as a shadow, and shuddered, beginning to guess the horrible truth. She threw herself in distraction
upon him, in spite of his efforts, scanned his features in the semi-
darkness of her alcove, and tried to make him speak. At last,
discovering her misfortune, she screamed and fell fainting at
his feet.

He picked her up and placed her on the bed. There he tried
to use a comforting remedy he pretended he had; but she came
back to life, defended herself like a tigress, poured insults upon
him, bruised her face and breasts in her despair, spoke of nothing but death and poison, in short said all the mad things that
come to a woman when her mind is deranged. He threw himself
upon his knees: his repentance was abhorrent. He wished to
speak: all justification was an outrage. He tried to make love
to her: he became a thousand times more odious. At last, having
exhausted himself in fruitless explanations and useless endeavours up to three in the morning, he took the key, and by himself reached the street with a great deal of trouble, for she had
lost all sense of prudence and fear, and disdained to facilitate
the escape of a monster issued from a monster even more
hateful.

Such was the end of this idyll. It must have taught the fair
lady a sad truth—that one should never by words out of place,
and above all insulting, provoke anyone to perfidy. It must also
have convinced her that payment for an evil tongue is nearly
always an evil deed. I confess, however, in all the humility of

my heart, that my deed was nevertheless inexcusable, and I have always regretted it as a blot upon my life.

The Prince de Salm [1] had at that time the whim to give a ball to which he invited half Paris; so many people came whom he himself did not know that he said to me jokingly: "A number of people here may look at me as a guest."

I, who knew him well, was less surprised at his joke than at all the platitudes I heard him utter at the dawn of the Revolution; they brought him to the guillotine and justified all the evil that was said of him, though it was not entirely deserved. A more unlucky reputation was never known. His courage was questioned, though he was covered with duelling wounds. When he had squandered a huge fortune and faced ruin, his probity was challenged. He was looked upon as *not to be trusted* at the gaming table, though he had there lost vast sums of money. No one dared deny him wit, but he was found devoid of common sense; and though he possessed more sound culture than many people, his conversation interested none. Does this mean that we refuse to place confidence in a man's mind if we mistrust his character? This prince, whose haughtiness soared sky-high, was yet always expected to behave in some mean way, as if the public tried to seek compensation for his pride and to chastise it. For haughtiness is so unnatural a feeling, and in essence so forced, that when it subsides it does so unguardedly and gives way without discrimination.

After spending his whole life in upholding the aristocracy, scarcely ever speaking of anything else and finding no society good enough for him, he opened his arms to the vilest demagogues and died a victim of his mob worship. Having once played the part of prince in the style of the Comte de Truffière, [2] he embraced principles for which a good bourgeois would have blushed. The scaffold put an end to this struggle between vanity and meanness.

However that may be, during the whole night of the ball I interested myself in Mme de R——, whom Parisian society insisted on calling beautiful, but in whom I have never seen anything more than charm. I believed myself at the threshold of love when she told me she would be the last to leave the ball, but would then take to her coach and drive forty leagues without a stop, for her brother-in-law was dangerously ill at one of his estates. I did not know him well enough just to drop in at his place, besides the moment seemed inopportune; but I had in

early youth often been to Rouen, which is near by. This town
boasts a regiment, a good theatre, and the prettiest women in
a province where many are found. At all events I could be sure
of spending there three agreeable weeks. So next day I took my
departure. After my arrival I enquired (all this by means of
the servants) at what date Mme de R—— would dine with
L.C.D.L.R., and I arranged to call the day before, reckoning
upon an invitation to dinner for the next day. My expectations
were not disappointed. What astonishment upon seeing me! I
was asked why I had come there. I said that my journey was
due to a most important business, an affair of great moment—
and I added on leaving the table: "It is but for you I came."
She wanted to scold me . . . but how could it be done in front
of other people?

On the following day I resolved to go shooting—though the
weather was frightful, and I am not much good at this sport.
I walked three leagues, and now and then fired at occasional
game, but my hands were pure of innocent blood when I arrived
at the farm to which I had been directed. From there I dispatched to Mme de R——, just as in a comedy, a valet, who
fortunately was then mine, with a note that revealed a perturbation truly touching. Having dressed as a peasant, he was to
choose what excuse he liked, but he would risk his head if he
came back without having delivered his message. She absolutely
refused to see me in secret, but should I care to pay her a call
I would be welcomed. I felt that this would lead nowhere, and
that only a risky device, which she would feel would compromise her reputation, could further my plan. So I wrote once
more and frightened her with the consequences of my despair
if she did not consent to come and speak to me at the farm
where I had established my quarters. I promised that I would
then immediately take my leave. The unfeeling woman at last
agreed to come, which made matters very different. What I said
to her any man would have said in my place; what she replied
was also as it should be. She entreated me to go away; I begged
her to come again. My wish was granted without helping me a
step further, except for a few caresses which desire managed to
steal, modesty to repulse. Nothing could have been more proper.

My trusted servant (I must say it to his credit) was not
wasting his time. More resolute than his master, he was on the
best of terms with Mlle Leblanc, one of Mme de R——'s
maids. He succeeded, thanks to the warmth of his entreaties,

in getting me introduced inside the manor house, and, what is even better, inside her mistress's room at supper time. The obliging maid asked for only one condition, that I should promise on my honour never to admit she had helped me in my bold scheme. Picture me then behind the curtains, looking like a thief, and trembling as if I were one. At last she comes to bed, for such is the conclusion of every day. She is in bed; a candle gives a faint light; she is reading "Clarissa," so atrociously translated by the Abbé Prévost. I show myself, she screams to frighten the dead; I crave a forgiveness that she does not seem disposed to grant; I protest my innocence and declare that my respect and my heart leave my senses powerless to attempt the outrage she fears. But she with dignity orders me to withdraw. I demonstrate the impossibility of this, and ask as my only favour that she bear with me until daybreak at which time I shall leave, pure as the dawn itself from the crime she supposes I intend. Long parleys ensue; I settle on a chair, then gradually on the edge of the bed; and towards three in the morning, after all the oaths of an impotent man, I take possession of it as if I had been the late M. de R—— himself.

I had acquired all his rights by the time I jumped out of the window to return to the farm. I slept there in a sort of loft, where the miller's wife had made me a bed which I could not offer to share with her, since the testimony of her virtue was stamped upon her face in characters of galling ugliness. I believe she was much annoyed by it; ugliness is a great disadvantage, a sort of misfortune—only less so than extreme beauty. Several nights were thus spent in wakeful hours, followed by several days which had to be given to sleep, so as to restore the balance. But these nightly visits becoming dangerous for her and tiring for me, I went back to Paris ahead of her, less than a fortnight after leaving it.

One might infer from what has just been said that Mme de R—— was a light woman. This would be a mistake; she never gave proofs of this before or after. But circumstances are stronger than women, even those women least given to weakness. Chance brings the best resolve to naught; and it is especially in love-encounters that events are the results of surprise and opportunity.

On her return I found her constrained and ill at ease, and I tenderly pressed her to open her heart to me. She owned with some confusion that she had betrayed sacred ties, that she no longer belonged to herself, but was bound to Victor de Broglie, the first man to whom she had pledged herself. She could not forgive herself for having broken her word, though she reckoned on my honour, not only to refrain from abusing her trust, but to allow her to return to an attachment which she confessed she still held dear, and which she could no longer debase by further unfaithfulness. I eagerly claimed a portrait, which was granted with good grace; and, choosing the only means of being regretted (if that is possible when one is dismissed), I withdrew like an honest man, leaving her to this insignificant rebel whom I have described elsewhere, and who like many others paid with his head for the mistake of worthlessness.

This momentary intrigue was in no way flattering; it vanished like lightning, and like it left no traces. I could put down my success only to post-horses, to a prompt and daring plot that placed in my power a stronghold provided with all the means of resistance. Capitulation was not followed by any result. My triumph was that of cunning not of merit; it was a surprise, not a conquest. I was sacrificed to a poor coxcomb, and I could but think myself little attractive, since he was not sent away on my account. But he was the sort of lover of whom one cannot take leave, for they always hold one end of the chain they make you bear. Everlasting tyrants, they fall upon a heart and seek to devour it, as the insatiable vulture preyed for ever on Prometheus. You might suppose that there was but one woman in the world to whom they had confessed their inability to find another; and that they had compelled her to enter into a life-contract with their lack of generosity. This sort of man cannot be dismissed; a woman may be vexed at having chosen him, but will never be able to congratulate herself on being quit of him. I abandoned her to that slavery.

There are some periods of life when we could easily believe Fate keeps an eye on us and enjoys at our expense all the evil tricks that malice can contrive. No doubt the reader must have noticed that for some time I had had no luck; the remaining part of this chapter will show that this was a settled matter, and that my star had waned. But it must be admitted that we too often blame Fate for our own mistakes, when heedlessness and misconduct are the real enemies to accuse.

I sacrifice myself with a good grace for the instruction of youth, even if the teaching which I provide them with may sometimes make me feel somewhat ashamed.

I had become a slave to a Mlle B——, a pretty and enticing lady best known by the short-lived felicity during which she had ruined the Comte des ——, though she was none the richer for that. Money wrongly acquired brings no prosperity; and it is the fate of money earned through easy vice to be spent on other vices that do not reckon with the future. Mlle B—— was living in the Rue Bergère, and I had ordered my cabriolet to call for me at nine in the morning in the Rue Montmartre. Having waited in vain for it until ten, I decided to go home on foot, resolved to give a sound scolding. But I had to relent when I discovered what was the matter. A M. M——, to whom I owed a thousand crowns, had appeared a very honest man on the day he lent them to me. But as he had since asked them back from me with great tenacity, I looked upon him as completely ridiculous and replied to him as Don Juan to M. Dimanche.[3] He then came to an unheard-of decision, and during my absence on this love adventure had the criminal impudence (I was then convinced he was in the wrong) to have seals affixed to all my belongings, in spite of my servants, who offered a praiseworthy resistance; lodgings, stables, everything were sealed. One could not have carried away a horseshoe or a slipper. As in those days I had few scruples, I hurried to this honest man's house and talked about killing him (though one could kill nobody in France, where there were good laws for all—whatever has been said to the contrary). He hid himself; and his daughter-in-law, who was six or seven months gone in pregnancy, had a fright for which I ought to have been punished. After this commotion, I threw myself into a hackney-coach and hastened to M. Le Noir, then Lieutenant of Police. I related to him my whole misfortune as being a most absurd incident, thoroughly deserving punishment, and highly insulting to a man of my condition. He listened to all my feeble platitudes with extreme politeness and sent a man from his office to fetch M. M——. When the fellow appeared, he was invited to accept a bill of credit to be paid with interest within a year; and the magistrate added that he would answer personally for my debt. As may be well believed, I sincerely thanked M. Le Noir, after M. M—— had left, and satisfied the latter before the bill became due. A few affronts such as this would disgust one with the bad habit of making debts.

One familiar demon who did not spare me set himself to following me. This demon was not one of those propitious spirits who sometimes guide us towards good, sometimes tease

us to relieve monotony and give time swifter wings; my demon
was the Devil incarnate, who had perched himself at the back of
my cabriolet. I was one evening driving out by the side of the
virtuous Mlle Guiraud, of the Opéra, and speeding I know not
where, at such a pace as I would fetch Dr. Bouvart or Dr. Portal
if my best friend were dying. I encountered a travelling house
pulled by two heavy horses, which a coachman in a black livery
was driving. I naturally wished to get ahead of this grotesque
machine, but the coachman, in an impertinent way and treating
cabriolets as equals, refused to let me pass. I struck a blow of
my whip at this bold fellow who was not keeping the straight
road, thereupon the rascal, quite unperturbed, swerved to the
right, and in the movement I made to avoid being crushed I
fell from the top of the rampart in the Rue Basse Saint-Denis,
where—building operations being in progress—the parapet had
been removed. This was a drop of at least thirty feet. My
cabriolet was in the moat; the horse was all wounds; the groom
had been thrown fifty feet, his head broken, several joints dis-
located. His screams were enough to frighten all the district,
and half the inhabitants rushed to the spot.

The stage princess had fainted, after two shrieks to rend the
hardest heart, and more moving than in her best parts. She
bled copiously. It was impossible to know whence came these
torrents of blood . . . luckily it was from the nose. As for
me, bruised and sore all over, entangled in the reins like another
Hippolytus, my hat crushed down to my chin, my whip in a
thousand pieces in my torn hand, mud covering me from head
to foot, my clothes in rags, I lay prone on the overturned cabriolet. Out of pride, I wished to stand, I fell: I struggled and
found my feet. I started to run after the scoundrel, who must
perish at my hands. He had put his elephants at a gallop, and
I lost sight of him. I did not even know to whom this lordly
henhouse belonged. I ended all this by fainting, with all the
honours of a swoon. I was carried to Charland, apothecary to
the Duc d'Orléans. It was midnight before I reached home; we
were all bled. My rage and confusion were at their height.

I got well at last; one must, after spending many mortal days
on a sofa. Enquiries reveal that it is M. R——, Governor of
C——, or rather his horrible coachman (the coachman of a
lawyer . . . a governor!), who had proposed to reduce me to
atoms! This shameful catastrophe can only be washed off in the
wretched fellow's blood. I rush to his home, I enter the court-

yard, I have a pistol in my pocket, I fall upon the impudent coachman with a hundred blows of my stick before they drag him from me. Then his master appears, and in my blind rage I wish to throw myself upon him. He speaks, recognises me, stammers on. I show such bad taste as to pour insults upon him, to offer him a sword, pistols—goodness knows what! He excuses himself, says something about his calling—which presumably, like the church, has a horror of bloodshed. His wife also shows herself. Insensibly I find myself in the drawing-room; everyone is weeping; again I am on the verge of a swoon. I believe some-one throws water in my face, which helps me to regain consciousness. I wind the matter up by a show of feeling. We apologise all round, and I dine with them three days later. The most touching friendliness is established. However, the Governor remains somewhat pedantic. His wife, far from pretty, talks incessantly of the court where she has never set foot, and is full of that part of the province where she holds her own court and which produces wine much superior to that drunk at her house. These considerations, put together, drive me away from their society in less than six months.

Now comes another drama, less tragic, but almost of the same kind! It is again connected with that treacherous carriage known as a cabriolet, which ought to be forbidden anywhere but on the highroad.

I was coming back from Saint-Mandé with the Comte A. du Luc, when in the Rue Saint-Antoine a gentleman wearing a braided red coat threw himself under the horse's forelegs as if for the pleasure of it. He was carried off like a wisp of straw. I drew in the reins, in spite of du Luc's objection; we stopped (a mistake I have never made since), we proffered help, apologies, and money. We soon found ourselves surrounded by the mob which at that time would grow fierce at the sight of a carriage, as it has since at the sight of palaces and mansions, and always will in connection with anything it covets but cannot have. This mob clamoured angrily, threatened to smash the frail carriage to pieces and to hamstring the horse. We were much embarrassed when a horse-dealer, who was in the crowd as a mere spectator, proposed to lead us to the police magistrate, who would decide what indemnity was to be offered to the injured party.

The words police magistrate sounded offensive to us, but a swift expressive glance from the fellow made us agree to place

ourselves at his mercy. With the skill of his trade, he took hold
of the horse, jumped into the cabriolet, followed us at walking
pace, and, vanishing with the animal before we had reached
the magistrate's house, made straight for du Luc's mansion.
When we arrived at the police magistrate, that official was very
busy with affairs of his own and excused himself from seeing us.
He sent his substitute, a vulgar and stupid rascal who without
enquiring into the business was contemptuously preparing to
institute proceedings, meanwhile letting loose rather unmeasured
language. The situation changed, however, when we swiftly
threw open the doors, pushed the brute who opposed us upon
a chair—which he broke with his weight—and called for the
magistrate in a loud voice, until he appeared with the majesty
of a judge in his most exalted functions. We gave our names,
and he condescended to become an entirely different man. He
immediately took all necessary steps to put an end to this odious
adventure; nevertheless he wished to summon the wounded man,
who was no longer to be found. He was a well-to-do man, who
had been dragged along by the crowd but had proved to be in
as great a hurry to leave us as we were delighted to be rid
of him.

There remained the unruly crowd which had to be given
satisfaction, just as if it had anything to claim. It was with some
difficulty that this mob was made to believe we had left the
building by the rear, and more than an hour went by before it
all dispersed; but at last it withdrew, falling back with much
rumbling as do waves breaking on the shore. The magistrate
was a man of pleasure and of good company; he had a marvellous dwelling and perfect manners. His wife appeared, and she
also was pleasant to look upon; beauty had not yet deserted a
face where it had dwelt for long; and during the few hours we
spent with these people we felt that no other lady could be
more lovable. But what was most remarkable in the family of
this local Minos, was a niece who had just been rendered more
beautiful through weeping. He was drying her tears when we
entered his room. Du Luc, always peculiar, took it upon himself
to say that since luck had granted him the pleasure of paying
his court to these ladies, he would enjoy it a while longer. It was
in vain I pulled him by the coat, almost tearing it, he settled
down to stay. The magistrate was not displeased at this, and
thought he could do no less than propose we should do him the
honour of sharing the family supper. My companion in mis-

fortune, who seemed to arrange the evening entirely on his own account, replied by a torrent of compliments which all meant yes.

While we awaited a supper truly unheard-of as to munificence and quality (the wedding feast of Camacho [4]) our host thought it fitting to share with us his family's secrets; he wished to inform us of his domestic troubles. His worthy spouse (every woman is a painter) made of them an even more touching picture. They had married the young lady to an officer in the engineers, who not only had done nothing to make her happy, but amongst a thousand other bad qualities had the abominable one of beating his wife. "That would not matter," she exclaimed, "if only he loved me!"

The ingenuousness of this dear little woman, in the presence of strangers, appeared to me as sublime as Racine's manner, which is, towards the sex, what that of Corneille is when dealing with man. Thereupon followed a long discussion on men who beat their wives. I seized this occasion to express my unspeakable horror of such reprobates, and was rewarded by the full admiration of the mistress of the house. But an amendment came near ravishing it from me, for I declared that though it was frightful and in very bad taste to beat one's wife it was permissible in the case of a mistress, this being very different. The magistrate's wife protested, but added that these *creatures* who so lacked the sense of duty as to welcome *gallants* did not deserve *much consideration*.

"And notice, ladies," I exclaimed with some eagerness, "that the wisest of mortals, the divine Socrates, one day without any qualms gave a beating to a courtesan, though he disdained to use this discipline with the scourge of his life, his Xantippe— the domestic harpy who brought desolation upon him, put his wisdom through the hardest trials, and would have scored a triumph had she been granted the honour of a slap in the face, the favour of a fillip, and the pleasure of being pinched. This great man, too knowing to place himself thus far in the wrong, left her to be so situated. 'I married her,' he said to Xenophon, 'because she is good practice for my patience, and by enduring her I learn to put up with whatever may befall me from other people.' Socrates alone," I went on, "could say such things, ladies, for if one may consent now and again while at home, to swallow a bitter medicine for the sake of health, it does not follow that one must submit to drinking wormwood when dining with company."

The ladies laughed much at my comparison of marriage to a bitter medicine; and I made them easily own that it was such and nothing better when it failed to be the sweetest thing on earth.

"Nevertheless, sir," said the elder lady, "I have on this matter ideas that you may consider antiquated if it pleases you, but I think and will always believe that a man, husband or lover, who beats his wife or sweetheart, and a woman, married or not, who lets herself be beaten are monstrosities. As for me, if I had had anything to do with lovers in my youth, and an impudent fellow had dared lift his hand to me, even had I adored him, I should not have struck back, because this would be base, but I should have summoned to my help the law and my fellow creatures. I would rather have brought ruin upon myself by revealing the fact to your host here present; I would have severed chains so unworthy, and delivered the monster to the execration of both sexes."

Her simple-minded rage hugely amused us.

"You must remember, madame," I went on, to complete her indignation, "that it is above all queens, empresses, and famous princesses whom one ought to beat—of course when they deserve it. From them, more than from others, the least injustice is a crime."

"How, sir, queens! If I were a queen and if, placed on a throne, I were foolish enough to take a lover and he committed the audacious sacrilege of striking me (the very word makes me shudder) I should have him hanged!"

"Not at all, madame. It would appear exciting to you, and you would love him the more; just as one of the greatest empresses who in modern days have held a sceptre said one day with much warmth to her trusted confidante: 'Congratulate me, dear friend; since yesterday I know that I am loved; he struck me.' It would be just the same with you, madame; this forgetfulness of propriety would appear to you what it really is; the full measure of tenderness grown frenzied, the last proof of exalted passion. You would be thankful to the man whom you had raised to your station, for loving you enough not to fear you; and you would find him possessed, as would your whole sex, of the greatest of attraction—that of rough handling. Besides, there are various ways of beating; a man of good society does it in a fashion not that of Billingsgate. Also it must be extremely rare. What is abused loses its value."

As I witnessed her astonishment and that of these good people (except du Luc, who swore I was a monster and capable of acting according to my words), I gravely went on: "I am going, ladies, to explain to you my views on this delicate matter. To strike one's wife is a stupid atrocity. She is your children's mother, she bears your name, you should respect her as yourself. Bound to you for life by vows, at the least very rash, and the outcome of an essentially vicious institution, she is to be pitied.

"But the woman who in possession of her full faculties and freedom is not bound, except by her inclination, has no other ties but those of love, no obligations but of her own free will, no need to cheat but her own bent, and no excuse for tormenting you but the wickedness of her disposition; the woman whom you love after a prolonged and deliberate choice, whom you are the less inclined to leave because you are quite free to do so; this woman who, lavish in all the refinements of passion, has enticed you through all the lures of love, who has made herself indispensable to your pleasure, necessary to your very existence, who by means of voluntary oaths she does not keep has extorted from you promises to which you are faithful; in a word with such a woman in whose company it is a torment to live, but from whom it would be still a greater misfortune to be separated, why should it not be allowed, when one has exhausted every ingenious means of persuasion—those of the most delicate tenderness—to try, moderately and gradually, some of those attempts at violence which look like what is called . . . a beating? This with the purpose of producing one of those great commotions which restore order, impressing her by what at the worst will leave deep traces but might truly bring a harvest of blooms and healthy fruits in those fields of love where brambles, thorns, and thistles were about to take root.

"She weeps straightway; this means a great deal; she will be kinder on that account. Her lover is on his knees to her (a few hours later, so as to give time for the lesson to bear fruit). He ends by weeping for having been obliged to profane the altar where he burns incense. What a happy transition! What a useful contrast! This mingling of tenderness with severity, of strength with weakness in a man much beloved who is not in the wrong, is most efficacious. Sweet reconciliation follows, sunshine after a storm. She will display tender pride in forgiving her victor, who humbles himself! There will be enchantment in all the words now to be uttered in confused exchange. Happy man! How much he will be loved if he is lovable!

"Though if you speak in cold blood, ladies, to an honest man, asking him to beat one of you—you who are under our protection, whose weakness is your defence—every man of us will protest with the horror inspired by a wicked deed. We shall all flare up in a body and fume against the scoundrel who dishonours our sex and does outrage to yours, for such is the first impulse, the general theory. But how far it is from a cool-headed discussion to find oneself suddenly at grips with jealousy, and all the madness of love! Besides, as I have had the honour of explaining to you, this is a device one must use sparingly, a severity one must display only at the most critical junctures, when one is more than right with a woman who has for long been in the wrong. One must do it in good style and ask forgiveness in even better style. One must know how to weep and be past master of a thousand subsequent achievements in the great and beautiful art—of winning forgiveness."

The niece swore by all the gods that she had never heard anything more sensible than my speech. The magistrate kept swallowing champagne in great gulps, as a man to whom all this talk had for long been foreign. Du Luc, emptying half of his wine under the table, pledged him with perfidious zeal; and his virtuous wife, who had never known the storms of youth, stuck to her opinion, as insensitive as cold ashes that no longer retain or kindle fire.

We did not take leave of these kindly people until one o'clock in the morning. The magistrate longed to see us home, but, being solidly drunk, he made one body with his chair. The ladies, who had been thoughtful since the outline of my principles—though I assured them it was but a joke—and whom du Luc's fooling had amused, for he had natural wit, appeared full of wonder at so unexpected an evening. They said good-bye to us as to old friends one regrets to part from, and would have shown us to our carriage had we not threatened to carry them off. It would have been inhuman to act so and to abandon the magistrate to his valets in the respectable state to which his hospitality had reduced him. We all promised each other to meet again. Perhaps this will happen in the next world!

The demon who for some time had set ablaze all my affairs was not yet gone to sleep. Read on!

I had ceased to frequent the greenrooms of theatres, when

one day I walked into that of the Théâtre des Italiens in order to speak to that charming Rosalie I have previously mentioned. I was sitting close to her when Mlle Colombe, Adeline's sister, appeared. She had taken Adeline's side in her quarrel with me, though I forget why, and she thought we were enjoying ourselves by joking about it. Eventually she insulted us, she dared to use threats and raised her fan to strike. On this I got up, took hold of her by the arm, pushed her out on the steps which led from the greenroom to the stage, adding at the same time: "I know that I am wrong to pay any attention to you, and to compromise myself, but perhaps someone will be mad enough to take your part, for which I do not care any more than I do for you."

It happened that the man for whom these words might very well have been intended was M. de Lubersac, nephew of the Bishop of Chartres. We had been brought up together and were great friends, but for some time I had noticed a change in him and felt sure he had let himself gradually be influenced by the impression she gave him of me. She hastens, she bestirs herself, she seeks her lover, enjoins him to avenge her, and has no trouble in overheating this impetuous young man, too much in love with her, and perhaps also with the idea of a duel. Lubersac meets me at the theatre doors; he has with him Dampierre, so well known since, and another officer of the king's guards, a friend who since has also acquired celebrity in another and quite opposite direction. Lubersac displays an excess of temper, declares that I owe respect to a person who has the honour of receiving his favours, asserts that he will make me repent. He is all the more vexed because, as his friend from childhood, I ought to have shown him more consideration, etc. . . .

There was in his protest something true and reasonable, but as it was expressed without moderation or courtesy, I answered laconically that since he took this tone I regretted not having done even more. In conclusion a meeting was arranged for seven o'clock the next morning, in the Place Louis XV. When we were all there the Comte de Lubersac, my friend's elder brother, whom he had brought with him, came towards me. He served in the French guards, and both his reputation and his manners were excellent. I was fond of him and had always preferred him to his brother, though I had known the latter much longer. He said to me that he was in despair about what had happened, that it grieved him to see us armed against each other, but, since this misfortune had gone so far that it was irreparable, he flattered himself I would not take it ill if, out of consideration for his brother, he had decided to act as his second. The Marquis d'Aigle, my second, replying to this, insisted on his withdrawal, declaring that it was unbecoming to be second to one's brother. But I put an end to this talk, kissed him and begged him to stay.

So we came to blows in front of M. Beaujon's house where, after having fallen upon each other with great fury, I gave Lubersac a thrust high in the chest which, although it did not go in deep, knocked him over. Mad with rage, he got up at once and soon wounded me seriously under the right armpit. . . . We had to stop at this. The blood I was losing would not have prevented my going on, but I could scarcely stand. Reconciliation thereupon followed, but I could never make him agree that the motive for our fight was hardly worth such commotion. We had, however, made a cheap show of ourselves, which did us little credit. In my wish to hide this accident as much as was in my power, and to prevent publicity, I harmed myself by going to the Comédie Française that very evening. But next day I had to resign myself, and on many subsequent days, to being bored on a sofa. The born devotees of duels, the ladies whose sympathy belongs by right to the man who has just fought one, came to keep me company. They bestowed care upon me during my convalescence, and favours once I was cured. The indulgence of the boudoirs consoles one for the disapproval of the drawing-rooms.

One morning, to my great surprise, there arrived at my rooms M. Restif de la Bretonne,[5] whom I was not aware that I knew, and with whom I had no connection. He reminded me that he had seen me at the house of a Comtesse de Beauharnais,[6] who held what was wrongly called an academy of wits, but where one met good society, both men of the world and men of letters, though the worth of the latter was very uneven. I had myself been there two or three times. But I hate affectation as much as I like wit, and I had never gone again. The author of the "Paysan Perverti" told me that he had frequently heard of me, and that he had come to ask me for some *erotic anecdotes from my life,* in short *some striking adventures* susceptible of being displayed in a work of great length which had been in his mind a long while, and which he wanted to write for posterity and not for his contemporaries, of whom he was *wearied.*

I had to laugh at the object of such a visit; it would have been absurd to be angry; but I told him that my life was frightfully barren, though I thanked him for his kind attention. I assured him I had enough taste to be aware that I missed a precious opportunity of rising to fame in the next generation, and entreated him to reserve his good will and his pen for me in better days, and to believe that, since he had looked upon me as a promising subject, I might one day help his scheme by furnishing him, in a future I looked forward to, anecdotes worthy his fresh colours and his original touch.

My compliments charmed him, he was himself even more delighted with his works. He did not hesitate to confess that the "Paysan Perverti" was a book of outstanding merit which would live as long as a language he had emboldened *to speak of everything,* and as long as Nature herself, whom he had caught *on the run.* He congratulated himself on having been ignored by a *dull* and *puny* century. The calumnies of journalists and academicians who were not his equals were his first title to immortality. I replied to it all: "That is true." I bowed, and he took his leave.

Nevertheless he is a man whom it is difficult to judge; one would implicate oneself too far in greatly praising him, yet it is easy to be unfair to him. Some of his productions seem to come from a man in delirium, unintelligible to his readers and to himself; yet, in other places, you find him original and stimulating, while displaying a wit which lacks taste but on this very account comes all the nearer to being genius. If you happen to open one of his works at random, you may find it difficult to decide to read him; but there is scarcely one of his books you will not finish if once you have started it. One comes upon pages often so extraordinary (in the best sense of the word) that he keeps expectancy alive to the very end, though it is often disappointed.

He nearly always chooses ignoble subjects, and if he treated them in superior fashion that would be a specialty and his justification; but the chief reproach from which he cannot be absolved is that he is nearly always coarse and indecent, that he delights in pictures that often wound modesty and delicacy as much as taste and reason. Although his powers of invention are varied and prolific, I shall not praise his imagination, for it is easy to make a show of this if one let it run at random. But even if some delicate and fastidious people smile at me, I own to having

read all he has written, making my way through the bustle and
sometimes the filth that render him no company for the squeam-
ish reader, and I confess that, if I have frequently shrugged
my shoulders in scorn, I have often laughed, shuddered, and
wept.

Indeed, the "Paysan Perverti" is the work of a man of
power. The vigour of manly genius, however unruly, prevails
throughout; the abundance of an excessive but rich imagination
gives life to these pictures, which few hands would have chosen
to draw. It unfolds itself in scenes of which taste and delicacy
may disapprove, but which are suffused with a forcible art one
must admire. Restif de la Bretonne is the Teniers of the novel,
his book is "Les Liaisons Dangereuses" of the common people.

I must not forget three days spent most agreeably in the
valley of Montmorency in the company of M. de la Harpe.
I specially sought during some of our walks to gather his opinion
of several men of letters then living. I remember that I induced
him to alter his views on Restif de la Bretonne, this not by arguments but through quotations. He at first hardly condescended
to mention him; I chose numerous passages from the "Paysan
Perverti" and made him own that it was most extraordinary to
find so much gold in that dunghill. I knew his aversion to
Roucher's talent; it was in vain I sorted out sixty to eighty of
the best lines from the poem "Des Mois"; he practically knew
them by heart, and with that pure taste [7] which he was one of
the last to preserve, he rejected most of my protégés. With his
eaglelike gift in literary criticism, he tore them to pieces. Then
came the turn of Rivarol, who at that time had produced next
to nothing. He was perhaps better known for his "Chou et le
Navet" than for the canto of Dante's Inferno which he had
translated or his "Épitre au Roi de Prusse" and his "Discours
sur l'Universalité de la Langue Française" which won a prize
in Berlin. Although there was in this last production a great
wealth of style, and boundless wit, the whole was marred by a
heaping up of comparisons, metaphors, and images, often more
brilliant than just. Altogether this work is, nevertheless, well
planned and carried out with elegance and precision. At the time
of which I speak Rivarol was in my opinion a promising writer,
giving all possible tokens of a fine talent. M. de la Harpe did
not share my views, and certainly he was sincere in his severity.
"He may have," he told me, "the mind of a distinguished man
of letters, but he has not enough will to become one; he is a

French improviser." Rivarol has unfortunately done almost everything that was required to justify this forecast uttered by our Quintilian.

La Harpe was, on the other hand, a decided admirer of Beaumarchais. The latter having insulted me in verses which are as poor as they are little known, and inserted invectives in a gazette printed by a certain A——, I replied to the author of "Figaro" (as was not in very good taste) by a dozen lines in which there was more virulence than talent. A woman of his acquaintance and my own led him to think I had written two very poor couplets which Champcenetz claimed as his, but the true author of which was really Bouville, his comrade in the guards. I showed my verses to M. de la Harpe.

"Trust me," he said, after hearing them. "Burn this; make friends again with Beaumarchais. He is a man with a fine mind; one should quarrel only with fools."

"Do not set this up for me as a commandment," I replied. "You would put me on bad terms with half the world."

What gall has not the author of "Warwick" been given to swallow! He who weighed each man's reputation for admission to the temple was refused any merit for himself. Practically all his literary verdicts will prove final for posterity, yet people have doubted whether posterity would acknowledge him. He has written a book that will remain for ever a classic, a book that does credit to French literature, which absolves an epoch verging on civil discords, or foreshadowing them, from the accusation of being powerless to produce any new work worthy the good old days; yet, in spite of such indisputable claims, his repute was long open to question. This is what befalls a man who dispenses fame and passes judgement upon the living. While he decrees what is smoke or wind, his peace flies away with these. La Harpe has preciously preserved our traditions of beauty. From out a sea of blood that threatened to engulf it, he brought back to shore our inheritance of that exquisite taste which is revealed in great works and forms the code from which we learn to imitate the masters without copying them. In a word la Harpe ought to rank as an excellent writer and a most useful rhetorician.

Yet he scarcely enjoyed repute at all, and was much grieved at leaving part of his work unfinished. He lived exposed to bitter quarrels, a prey to the uneasiness of thwarted ambition, exhausting himself to obtain a seat which was disputed to him; and he died at the moment when his gifts were beginning to arouse envy, and when his contemporaries no longer dared to deny him some part of the justice that future generations will see done to him. Such were the fruits of so many nights given to work! The reward of so much labour! The faded laurels for the diligence of a whole lifetime! . . . And I who write these lines, who had thoughts of fair dealing towards me? Who has granted me a rank and who will decree what it should be? I have written pages which I have seen translated into foreign tongues, but which few people ever mentioned to me, while many more never knew them at all. It is true that I have composed a few songs, which, to my consolation, have been sung all over Europe.

Oh, vanity of vanities, who will grant me the fame which a rather sparkling imagination, a style both wiry and easy have perhaps deserved? Where is the man who will duly appreciate attainments for which I care no more than I do for renown? To him I surrender my entire "self"; a whole man who claims no credit as exclusively his own if he happens to be worth anything; who despises both modesty, which people accept at its word, and self-conceit of which they make fun. So I beware of dreams concerning posterity,[8] which bothers me even less than do my rivals. I free my tomb beforehand from any ostentatious stone which would set forth my claims when, in absence and darkness, I shall be no longer anything but silence and dust.

CHAPTER XXI

Such presumptions of youth as self-assurance and trust in oneself, as the belief that anyone must have merit who attains favour and success, are things you will laugh at yourself, when you become enough of a philosopher (in the worthy sense of the word) and once mature thoughts take for you the place of a multitude of illusions—illusions that vanish with the springtime of life in men who are not fated to remain big children to their dying day. For then you will be more intelligent than you are now, you will even set no great store by what intelligence you have had so far, and scarcely by any intelligence whatsoever.

*H*OW short-sighted is the young man who, in the prime of passions, in the fever of virginal delusions, welcomes with complacence all sensuous gratifications, all the compliments of false friends and the praises of his treacherous mistress! How aware he is of what powers he possesses and even of those he does not possess! How easy it seems to him to please! How seriously he looks upon the business of displaying wit! How hard he works to appear agreeable! But he succeeds so little only because he wants to succeed so much. Others shine more than he does, because he wishes to throw everyone in the shade. He is always falling because he is constantly desiring to rise. He sets value on matters that when older he will disdain. A word wounds him, a word delights him. He ventures all on chance and yet grants nothing to chance.

Reckless during this time of life meant for happiness, he feels any reverse an insult from Fate, while success is the reward of his merit, the result of the wisdom of his plans. He takes fright at nothing but his wounded pride; nothing stops his vanity, nothing consoles him but his self-conceit. What trust in men and in things! There are no delusions for him. He attaches importance to everything, at the same time esteeming everything less than himself. How he believes in life! How he loves it in order to worship himself! It is true that now and again he disdains the whole world, but it is only when he is

dwelling upon himself; the next moment he again sees the world
through an enchanted prism. A day will come when it will be but
too easy for him to lose interest in most things, despising them,
and himself more than any; a day will come when he will be no
longer astonished, seduced, ravished, or flattered, not even at
having acquired enough true philosophy to acknowledge the
truth before reaching the grave.

That time has arrived for me, I call heaven and earth to
witness; and yet I have lived through the intoxication of a
multitude of illusions, to the point of causing my friends to
quarrel with me and my enemies to triumph. Now I will continue the narrative of those often shameful conquests which
ought sometimes to have inspired me with modesty rather than
pride, and oftener brought me to salutary reflections.

> When I myself applaud,
> Me people hiss abroad.

The nephew of the Swan of Cambrai,[1] who had no voice
like his nor his frank simplicity, did what for a man of forty
must have been as difficult to do as to write "Télémaque." He
kept a miss who maintained she was not one, because her father
had I do not know what employment in finance; she was a
Mme Bauvilliers, who completed his ruin. She was extremely
beautiful. It is not usually about ugly women one is foolish to
that extent, though this has sometimes happened; for nothing
has such bad vision as the heart—it even misleads the mind.

This siren, whom the Abbé Delille had not disdained to cele-
brate in verse (which was even more than to have loved her),
had fascinated this poor Fénelon, a man who had been guilty of
all the mistakes one could think of, but who with natural wit
and a fine figure had so far known how to defend himself with
women. She made fun of him, as the custom is, and had given
him as partner the best dancer in Europe, Auguste Vestris;[2]
or rather the latter played the chief part with her, and Fénelon
was his understudy when it pleased Vestris. The first, like the
rich man, was seated at a splendid table, the other picked up
the crumbs that fell from it; the dancer was able to enjoy everything to satiety; the Marquis de Fénelon lived on scraps, and was
able to make love only in the room he would furnish for her
and on the day of offering it. His rival, in fact, was the king
of the palace, while he spent his life in the vestibule.

He wearied of this trickery and changed his attitude with

strange suddenness. He begged me, very mysteriously, to accompany him to the Comédie Française, and not to leave him, so I firmly believed he had on some affair of prime importance, and I prepared myself to respond to his trust, when I saw him pounce upon young Vestris like an eagle upon his prey, with all the imprecations men have borrowed from hell. I made him feel ashamed of his anger,[3] and led him away. He told me at length of his love, which had gained such tragic power over this hardened soul that he shed tears. I listened in admiration. He begged me to see his inhuman lady and to teach her fidelity. She, knowing all that had passed and trembling for the danger run by the young god of the dance, came to ask for me at my door, and solicited my mediation; my path was clear. I advised her to practice concealment with more skill, and I joined example to precept. She soon forced me, however, to renounce her favours, for she was guilty of the clumsiness of calling me by the Christian name of the only being who ruled her heart, in one of those fleeting and happy moments when she ought certainly to have known, at least, that I was there. I left her to dance a pas-de-deux with him whom she was constantly betraying, and for whom she betrayed others.

All her family had a mania for amateurs and artists. Her sister, prettier but not so beautiful, had taken for Travancourt the place of his wife, but she made fun of him the year round with the most amiable of European singers, Viganoni, though at least she never ruined Travancourt, who was proof against ruin. However, he later became game for the Revolution, and its whole weight was needed to bring him to die like a pauper. Fortune acted according to rule with Travancourt; it had taken him from the mousquetaires, devoid of wit and money, and deposited him destitute at the edge of the grave with the genius of a good reckoner. His wealth which reached him so quickly only to insult him on the way, evaporated in the crucible of philosophers and cannibals, and lasted a few months less than his own life.

Ancient chronicles tell us that the Sire de Pons was renowned for his gallantry and famous for his courage and misfortunes. A new Ulysses, after having been the plaything of gods and men, he reached his home unrecognized. Wounded at the battle of Mapoure,[4] he returned to find his wife rather less faithful than Penelope, and was greeted only by his dog. One of his descendants, the Vicomte de Pons, for long happier than himself, met with a worse end, since his days were cut short in the revolutionary butchery of that epoch so rightly called the Terror. Like his illustrious ancestors and like all heroes, Frederick II excepted, he adored ladies. A heart burning with all the fire of love animated this gracious but rather frail body, which, however, lived on too long, lived till those organized massacres in which grieving France saw the purest blood of all classes flowing on the scaffold. That of the Vicomte de Pons mingled with the floods just shed.

To go back in time: before the Revolution, the Vicomte de Pons loved a certain Mme de C——, little known in Paris but the most celestial of houris in the paradise invented by Mohammed. When I asked him with a careless air and voice some details about this person, whose side he seldom left, he replied with the same apparent unconcern that she was a provincial and was going away in a few days. This reply, which was not a reply, could not satisfy me. I followed the traces of this almost unknown beauty and convinced myself that she was an angel, although living in a convent. I even discovered that she had numerous pleasant talents which enhanced her beauty. The Viscount was no longer of the age which is specially suitable for love-making; he had even begun to reveal a little of that fragile lack of substance indicated by the nickname given to him of *pompon*, alluding to his dress, his manner, his whole person, which had in it something of a gaudy plaything, although he was on the whole an excellent man. I had feared more difficulties than there were in approaching his mistress, to whom before long I confessed the secret of my passion without writing to her. I hold it a principle that one must never compromise oneself by a letter, a living and silent witness, unless she to whom one addresses it is condemned to discretion by a sense of danger. For this reason I have all my life felt esteem and respect for a very skillful man who, I am assured, began all his love letters with these words, or their equivalent: "The charming confession that you have made to me of your feelings. . . ." "The manifold proofs that you have given me of your love. . . ." "The emotion which I was so fortunate as to inspire in you. . . ."

How could I not approve of a method which frightens that most daring being in the world, a woman: and which compels loquacity to silence, and indiscretion to secrecy? It is truly sublime!

I was torturing myself to reach some decisive result when chance, which sometimes works better than wisdom, came to my help. Everyone knows that M. de Montesquiou[5] was one of the most exalted men in France, that he was immensely clever without having, however, sufficient title for admission to the Académie Française, where he nevertheless was received. Everyone knows how ungrateful he was, and that he only concerned himself at last with the public finances when his own were in a state of hopeless disorder; everyone has seen also that he proved to be as poor a republican general as he had been a cunning courtier during the monarchy; everyone knows that he was related to an abbé of his name, a thorough intriguer, whom many people have taken for an honest man, while every party believed him on its side. He stole a good reputation, he usurped that of a man of wit (I am still speaking of the abbé), because intrigue and cunning, sweetly adorned by a few commonplaces, took its place for him. Everyone has seen him finally (I now mean the general) die forgotten by a nation which remembers only what is essentially great. But what apparently fewer people have seen is that this descendant of Clovis was when in love an abominable tyrant. He displayed at once both the hypocrisy of cold indifference and the exacting insistence of the most jealous lover; the reasoning of a bore and the whims of an old fool; scarcely acknowledging to others the rights he had over a woman, but concealing to himself those she had over him, and trying to forget his fondness of one moment by ill treatment at another. The heart and the senses in him were opposed; he tortured his beloved as if she were his exclusive property. His visit was always to be expected, yet was always put off; like a weary sultan he would hold the handkerchief in his hand but never let it fall.

He had for a time attached himself to the widow of a man whose unquestionable gifts had not saved him from dying in poverty, from which his name alone ought to have saved him. But does wealth imply deserts? Is it ever a reward? Is it not more often merely an indication that one has trampled everything in the dust to obtain it? And if a man of surpassing merit so often lives in poverty, is this not most often a reason for his dying in it? So there was this widow, hardly in possession of the necessaries of life, and longing for its luxuries, sacrificing her heart to her head, bartering discomfort for unhappiness, misfortune for crime, estranging one half of herself in order to

degrade the other for the sake of a few hours of luxurious
life, which consoles the sex for everything. Happily this union
was not of long duration, and she had the tardy courage to go
and vegetate in the provinces after having thus prostituted in
Paris a name which she would have respected if she had believed me.

But if ever she were to read what I write . . . I stop my
pen, for I do not wish it to become a dagger in a heart whose
native virtue was debased only by misfortune and succumbed
only to circumstances. Let it be enough for me never to have
led astray her whom I blame, but to have given her counsels
of virtue just as if I had cultivated it myself. I did wrong in
claiming from her favours of a kind foreign to love, which she
was worthy to inspire; but greater harm had already been done,
and I was not too particular. M. de Montesquiou had often
advised her to retire to a convent; I persuaded her, through
the kind of power I had over her, to agree to do so.

So, to go back to my story. She came to live in Paris and
settled only a hundred steps from Mme de C—— whom I
loved to distraction, a familiar phrase which is true when one
is young. They soon became acquainted, and friendship served
love. It was agreed beforehand that the Vicomte de Pons was
not to be received at the newcomer's house, even if he wished it.
The pair were soon one in heart; and this affair of mine, which
I could have made a success alone, progressed much more swiftly
under the protection of a woman who was the born enemy of
another's virtue and the most persuasive of pleaders. Ah, truly,
if it was the tongue of a woman which brought about the fall
of the first man, how much more readily would she not have
used her tongue to lead astray one of her sisters!

I had won my case and the Viscount had lost his without
appeal; but I wished him to know this, and Mme de C——
did not wish it. Her idea was to drive us two abreast, mine was
that he should be vexed and clear out. I set myself, therefore,
to commit all sorts of indiscretions, which was not difficult. He,
to my great astonishment, would take no notice; that was less
easy. Entertaining thoughts of vengeance against her, and
against me, and against himself, he pretended to be at peace
while hell was in his heart. So, in the sufferings of others there
is consolation for one's own! Ah, human nature, some of your
secrets are hideous!

Mme de C—— was not a woman of much intelligence,

but one felt more pleasure in what she possessed than regret for what she lacked. Exceedingly cunning, this wit of hers showed only in her eyes. She never told lies so skillfully as when she told the truth. Her looks led you astray and prevented you from believing her. Her skin, of a dazzling whiteness, almost passed into her smile, and that smile seemed to lend candour to her soul. Her delicate blond hair cast over her enchanting head a sort of perfidy . . . but the perfidy of a child. A suppleness of walk, which the Italians call *disinvoltura,* gave her an irresistible charm; one could not have believed that so much voluptuous nonchalance could have left her time and strength for deceit. She was as inconstant as the waves of the sea, and resolute to obstinacy. All her enjoyments, I say all, came from her head.

The husband whom fate had given her rendered all these fine qualities more than superfluous. He was an ignorant and stupid man; he ill-treated his wife before she had deserved it. She decided on drastic measures, and gave him opium of which he nearly died; while he was in this unnatural sleep, she ran away with ten louis in her pocket, went twenty leagues on foot, and at last reached Paris from the depths of Béarn in a sort of country cart. When she used to relate this fantastic story, with a grace which I should like to put into the writing of it, one was surprised that she survived. She landed at the house of M. Amelot, who was then cabinet minister; she was somehow related to him, though he would perhaps have maintained the contrary if she had been ugly. . . . But she was pretty enough to tell the king that she was his cousin.

Having looked at her, the worthy secretary of state promised her safety and protection; but three months afterwards he quarrelled with her, tired as he was of cherishing hopes that she had never given him. It was a good chance for the husband to punish the runaway, and to accuse her, if necessary, of poisoning him. At this crisis she found the Vicomte de Pons, who was looking for her . . . at all events he was looking for a woman who would make him forget another of whom he retained the most painful memory, a Mme F——, who had shut her door to all her admirers in order to keep herself exclusively for the Sieur Nivelon, a dancer at the Opéra. Five years spent in a temple where so unworthy a successor was now officiating was a subject of melancholy reflections for the Viscount, who was born excessively sentimental. So he had met, at the right moment to distract him from his griefs, a bewitcher who was in need of a support against a former tyrant; he had reassured her with his fortune and his credit. It was time; the legal owner had hastened to Paris to claim his victim, but he found someone to stand up to him; he went off as quickly as he had come.

The Vicomte de Pons, with his soft manners and his light-hearted ways, was steady in this sort of relationship. He was a man very substantial in trifles and very serious in futilities; dress was for him no light matter—he would stand no joke when in love, and he never wore a badly cut coat. On a small scale, he was *elegantiarum arbiter*. If we had had ministers with as thorough a knowledge of their business as he had of his, and as skilled in administration as he was in the matter of waistcoats, footwear, sticks, buckles, elegance of dress, the management of a stable (even of his own finances), the upkeep of court carriages, etc., France would still be as she was before 1789.

When the Viscount was really in love, he was all attention and tenderness as in a pastoral; when forsaken, the gloomiest despair undermined his soul; when betrayed, he thought of nothing but vengeance. This time it came promptly. He caused a letter to be written to the husband to the effect that his wife was alone, without support and that he could come and fetch her. For the husband to set out and to arrive were one and the same thing. The vulture was already at the gate when the dove heard of it. She threw herself into the arms of her natural protector, but the Viscount, with refined cruelty, told her that he loved elsewhere and that he *had no more horses in his stable to ride to death*.

I was her only hope and to her stood for everything. M. de Montbarrey, imperial prince as he was, grandee of Spain, ex-minister of war, did not on that account enjoy much consideration nor any great credit since the death of M. de Maurepas. He had, however, enough influence to get her out of this situation. I knew him well, and knew that he was kind in accidents of this sort. I brought her to him and left her to his care; he took prompt measures which justified my expectations, and saved her. He made no claims for a reward, so she had not the embarrassment of a refusal. She played the harp and sang for him, while loving another. I was not that one for long. Was this her fault or mine? That is a question no longer worth considering. . . . People have assured me that she now is in Switzerland, not far from the beautiful lake [6] immortalised by J. J. Rousseau and his trout. She is somewhere about thirty-nine years old;

I wager that she is still charming; she helps her face by her mind and still more her mind by her face. May she find enjoyment where her star has led her! More than anyone she needs pleasure. She has for so long a time invoked it and hoped for it.

I am not without some remorse over this incident, which may have had a bearing on the tragic end of the Vicomte de Pons by throwing him back into the society of 'Mme de Saint-Amaranthe, whom for a long time he had seen less of. He was included in her proscription. But could Pons have escaped? He was burdened by his name and guilty of possessing an income of forty thousand crowns. With the poor intelligence Nature had granted him and which fear had still further shrivelled, he jested mildly at the beginning of the Revolution which devoured him, and produced various arguments for not leaving France. His indolence made him an arguer, and love of wealth and life a poor politician. Killers and killed were both alike unskilled in the science of government.

I had not been to Versailles for several years when—having formed the plan of a second journey to England which I later carried out—I went to ask for a passport and a ministerial letter to the Comte de Montmorin in the Rue Plumet. He obligingly told me I should find them ready on the following Sunday if I would call for them myself. Since he in his department entertained petty ambitions, cultivating the minor virtues and the kindness of the King, which he ill recompensed, he believed that I was likewise an assiduous courtier for whom a dinner four leagues away would not be out of place. Yet I certainly went up for a moment to the Œil-de-Bœuf,[7] and found myself there talking to several people, especially that blind caterpillar Moreton de Chabrillant, when suddenly the conversation degenerated into a quarrel. It had at once to be put an end to, if only because of the sacredness of the spot; so a challenge was given and accepted with equal gravity.

Béon and his cousin, the Marquis de Chabot (who was called Big Cat) made me feel the absurdity of crossing swords with a man whose sight was so poor that he had kissed at midday at Fontainebleau a colossal Swiss guard whom he took for a fair dancer from the Opéra. At Metz he rode full tilt into some troops which he took for a bright green meadow refreshed by a few showers. As a result of a serious quarrel he had been made to attack a red cloak placed on a pike. His adversary, who stood ten paces away, declared that he was wounded; the seconds, who connived at this comedy, persuaded him that honour was satisfied. There was not much glory to be won in such a fight, and the quarrel ended with a breakfast: the worst is better than the best duel.

This quite insignificant anecdote may amuse the reader by showing in a ridiculous light an individual whose numerous vices have not been sufficiently pronounced to be worth remembering.

Now for something less serious!

I was one day at the theatre of the Rue Feydeau, in the box of that unfortunate Baron de Grimm,[5] who was often hoaxed at his own table, who was made ridiculous by a nickname because he wished to shine in the drawing-room while he only belonged to the anteroom, and at whom people would laugh though he was not so much ridiculous as good-natured. He had little modesty, I agree; but in this respect also people expected the impossible from him. To satisfy those who called themselves his friends, but were really his cook's, it would have been necessary that he should post himself as lackey at the back of his own coach, like that millionaire at the time of the Mississippi system. They were not easy to please!

So I was in his box, the next to one occupied by an English lady more noted in London for her grace and beauty than for her virtue. I had met her several times at Commander Boniface's, a born boarding-house keeper, and recognized host to all foreigners in Paris. I already knew her well enough to be able to pursue the acquaintance. I had even seen her on another visit to Paris, when she had refused to me what she had granted to others; but I had not had the luck to please her, that was all. However that may be, this new occasion was favourable; to the melting melodies of Paesiello or of Cimarosa I thought I might with better advantage blend words of a tenderness this time openly declared. I had reason to believe, in fact, that my cause was prospering. After a few preliminaries in a low voice, she appointed midnight as the happy hour of fulfillment. The temple was to be furnished lodgings in the Faubourg Saint-Germain.

I arrived to the minute. A sort of chambermaid received me and encouraged me, in barbarous French, *to go to bed;* she added that "mistress," delayed by important business, would be back directly. I supposed that on returning from the theatre she had given orders to this trusty woman. I waited more than an hour, however, before availing myself of the liberty I had been so cordially invited to take. I went to bed, I read as if I were at home, I slept till morning without extinguishing a single candle. How queer if I had set fire to the house! Eleven o'clock was everywhere striking next day when I began to realise the situation.

The same woman peeped through the door with the carefulness of someone who fears to awake a sleeper and left a very short note which said that a series of unheard-of accidents had upset a charming plan, as would soon be explained to my entire satisfaction, and that I was to go to Chantilly [9] in the evening and settle at the coaching house, or at all events to leave word there to say where I was to be found.

I made my arrangements with some ill humour, but nevertheless I went to that beautiful spot of which only the name remains, but which ought to be restored by a hero, since it was once inhabited by heroes. With the docility of a fool who could hardly be worth deceiving, I did everything the ungracious woman had prescribed. Twelve hours afterwards I began to realise that I had been duped. I came back feeling very wild and by no means proud of myself. She had taught me discretion, and if I had been in the mood to follow her I should have danced attendance and lain down in all the beds of France. I took the liberty six years afterwards to acquit by a bad joke, on the banks of the Thames, the bill of exchange which this beauty had drawn on me by the Seine.

Was there so much wit and Attic salt in this insular mystification? I do not think so; but I am too much concerned in the matter to be entitled to an opinion. It is a lesson for youth for whom the grossest baits are good enough traps, since presumption goes hand in hand with stupidity, and self-conceit is the most deceitful of microscopes.

Let us go back to Frenchwomen. I will first speak of Mlle Arnould,[10] so well known for her repartees. She had seemingly been very witty before I knew her; many *bons mots* from her lips were repeated to me by others, but I never heard them directly from hers. I saw her rather frequently during two or three years; yet I did not once catch her in the act of a piquant or witty saying, although she was said to have much felicity in this direction. But wit has its grand climacteric; it declines like the body, and gradually passes away, though less rapidly than beauty. I was always expecting what I had been told, and only finding what she actually said: gleams, never brilliancy; a fluttering, no great stroke; a very ordinary conversation, never a saying one could retain. She had deceived her admirers, who in their turn deceived the public because they did not dare to confess they had themselves been taken in.

Her suppers were worse even than her conversation and her alleged *bons mots*. One went to them just as one expected the others, out of habit. Her circle was generally composed of people who aspired to be witty, who made verses as a pastime, or sometimes seriously, which was comical; of some distinguished men of letters who came there for a little distraction, believing themselves in good company because there were people in the room with high-sounding names; of a few pretentious people of quality who liked to rub shoulders with men of letters, though they could hardly read those they received by the post (what a detestable pun!); of a few travelling sightseers who wish to see everything and whose country is everywhere; of a few courtesans who had shown a bit of wit or found a few fools; of some actresses who had had talent or, what is better, showed promise in that direction; of men of importance who were no longer considered important; and finally of a few others whose importance could not be injured by a supper more or less. The Comte de Lauraguais,[11] author of "Jocaste," no longer went there, insufficient admiration having been shown for his tragedy, an enigma more obscure than that of the Sphinx overcome by the son of his heroine.

I met there Molé, that inimitable actor, who was charming even with all his defects. The lines of all his parts were almost equally good as he delivered them, though he committed the great mistake of mutilating nearly all the verses by meaningless exclamations and had accustomed the public to a kind of stammer which was not without charm, though it infected several other actors who had not his talent for making imperfections attractive. But other days bring other customs, and I fear that he has carried to the grave the secret of his art [12] and the colours in which he painted a special society of which even the tradition is perhaps destined to be effaced. His tomb also conceals an uncommon immorality, some ridiculous vices and others that were hideous. But an actor is not obliged to win the esteem of the public in order to obtain its love.

The day when I saw him at Mlle Arnould's was destined also to make me acquainted with a Mme R——, his stepdaughter and his mistress, and perhaps in a way his victim. She had the face of a Roxalane, the falsity of a novel. . . . She

was perfidious with all her might, and in every one of her mo-
tions and each of her limbs. She was the daughter of Mlle
Dépinay, since known at the Théâtre Français under the name
of Mme Molé, and of the Marquis, afterwards Duc de Villeroy,
who despite his crawling ways and littleness was murdered
on account of his immense fortune, when Fouquier-Tinville was
minister of finance and the executioner his head clerk. Her
parents had married her to R——, a third-rate comedian, who
was clever enough to realise that his father-in-law was a roué
and his wife a consummate coquette. He soon separated from
her, and had abandoned her to some men of good society, who
all, without knowing it, including myself, shared her with Molé.

She was neither beautiful nor pretty, but she had unspeakable charm; it was for her the word "desirable" was invented.
She was not intelligent, but so cunning that she imbued me with
a supreme contempt for all artifice. Without being a distinguished actress, she embellished several parts and spoiled none;
she enjoyed a reputation for good behaviour and a quiet life,
which almost made her a comedian even in society. The public
had become used to seeing little of her, for she had arranged
to draw a half salary at the Comédie Italienne, yet scarcely
ever to appear, having bought the favour of old Camerani,
the director of this theatre, by granting the greatest of her own,
a kind of favour that she liked to have supposed she accorded
only with much difficulty; her hypocrisy had made many dupes.
But the sad truth is that, no matter who one was, it was always
necessary to dispute her with the husband of her late mother,
that Italian satyr who would have disgusted one with Venus if
one had had to love her in company with him. This is the woman
whose hidden depravity and whose skill in vice had built for her
a reputation far more favourable than that enjoyed by most of
her fellow actresses who were infinitely less corrupted.

Whether on the stage, in palaces, at court, or in society,
whether of queens or shepherdesses, princes or magistrates, the
brilliant courtier or the simple citizen, Reputation no longer
imposes on me. I have heard the false blast of her trumpet; I
have gathered the lies of her hundred voices. I no longer prostitute my ears to her; my brow has blushed at my credulity.

And yet this was the woman I was going to love, and who
at first sight turned my head. She brought to Mlle Arnould
and her house all they lacked. Mme R—— shone there with
her colours and her charm. For a long time she kept me hovering

from hope to rebuke and from severity to hope, feigning love
for me one day and repentance the next, as Penelope would
always undo her work. My desire was so extreme, my impatience
so keen, that when she displayed one day some interest and fear
on my behalf, because by an involuntary movement she had
almost wounded one of my eyes with her scissors, I very genuinely begged her to put that eye out. . . . Thus thwarted passion can reduce one to a state more stupid than madness. For
indeed we know what madness is, and all our pity is granted
to this extreme wretchedness of fellow creatures who die before
they have ceased to live. But the other state is one of absolute
degradation, absence of dignity and will power, for which there
are neither tears nor pity. This siren had at that time taken as
her lover a very vain and very commonplace schoolboy, who
would not admit she could deceive him in the smallest thing.
Would he not have discovered it? Was she not faithful since he
was adorable?

The presumption of youth is only equalled by the blindness
of love. How explain to a young man, and even sometimes to
an old one, that his mistress has betrayed him? A kiss destroys
all reasoning, obliterates all reflections, dissipates all fears. Self-
conceit can even give the lie to one's own eyes. Nearly all my
life I have gone to the opposite extreme: I have been mistrustful; I have met perfidy half-way; I have dreamt of it beforehand; and my mistresses have nearly always taken on themselves
to give me proofs that my dreams were those of a man wide
awake. I was one day talking about this with Mistress B——,[13]
one of the most distinguished women of America. "Believe me,"
she said, "you have made bad choices!" "One cannot do anything else, madame," I said, "among the women who allow
themselves to be chosen."

I had reached that point in my languishing love for this
Merteuil [14] of the stage when an unforeseen and most remarkable event occurred to awaken her sensibility and to delay an
ending that I found a sort of pleasure in spinning out because
I was so sure of it.

Here a rather long digression is indispensable.

Two causes to which no sufficient attention has been given
have had a powerful influence in bringing about the revolution
and our misfortune. To take the first:

The proofs of nobility by four descents required of any man
who wished to serve as officer in the army could not but cause

discontent amongst the upper bourgeoisie and the newly created
nobility. Men of a rich, educated, and well-brought-up class were
thus refused access to a career which it was only fair to let
them enter after the nobility had been placed; for though under
the monarchy this profession was primarily that of the aristocracy, no such condition should ever have been made into a law
of the state. Its application should have been left to the discretion of the generals, the minister of war, and finally to the sanction of the highest authority. It would have been easy to make it
a matter of exceptions, and such a tacit convention should not
have become a rigid rule. That was a mistake of the Maréchal de
Ségur,[15] one of the unskillful acts of his ministry; it was a short-
sighted view.

Now for the second cause:

This was the lack of foresight and the blunder of another
Marshal of France, neither braver nor more honourable than
M. de Ségur, who of course was both, but who had more ideas
of chivalry in his head, and the courtesy and the bearing of a
great lord. . . . But let us forgo portraits and the partiality of
gratitude to come to our goal.

He (I mean M. le Maréchal de Duras) made the King agree
to the decree so called of the "coach-rights," that is to say that
it was required of those who wished to have the honour of entering the King's carriages (to make a début as it was called) and
following upon this, to be presented to him, to give proofs of
their nobility back to the year fourteen hundred without traces
of new ennoblement. All very good, very simple, but why publish it, so to speak, with the beating of drums and the blast of
trumpets? Why make a rule tending to prove to one third of the
nobility of the kingdom that they cannot and ought not to be
admitted to pay their court to their king—to that king who—
the sixty-third of his house, and head of the most ancient monarchy in Christendom—suddenly insists, before anyone can approach him, on preliminary conditions the other sovereigns of
Europe would not have dreamt of even in delirium, since the
first obligation of royalty is before everything to be accessible,
I would almost say to be popular.[16] But let us admit the principle; I quite agree to it. The King should have been free, as a
private person is in his home, to allow in his carriages, or to
supper in his private rooms, only the people whose presumed
ancestors had trodden the dust of the Holy Land, washed themselves in holy water in Palestine (where a man of my name, the

old Chevalier de Tilly, killed twenty-six infidels with his own
hand, which was apparently twenty-five times bigger than mine),
only men whose forefathers had died of hunger, thirst, and ex-
haustion in Syria, only the remainder of that purest French
blood shed in torrents at Massoure in those days of delirium
and grief which have caused incurable wounds to the monarchy
—to this I subscribe without appeal, without ill will, whether I
am called Montmorency or Gorsas. But still, were not the names
entitled to this honour (names more or less historical and harmonious) perfectly well known and in no need of fulfilling such
a condition, which it was impolitic and superfluous openly to
impose? Could not the King have been at liberty to select,
amongst the people deemed unworthy of appearing at court,
those he could welcome and those he should not admit? Was it
necessary to promulgate a law humiliating to the greater part of
the provincial nobility and rigorously carried out only against
them? A law which did not affect a peer of the realm or the son
of a marshal of France, or even a chevalier of the Saint-Esprit;
a law which brought out of their mansions great landowners
whose presence was the life of their countryside, but who, out of
pride, would come to seek ruin in Paris in order to be able to
tell their discontented neighbours that they had just returned
from Versailles, though their quaint appearance had there provoked laughter, and their backs, apparelled at the cost of a
meadow, a wood, a vineyard or a mill, had borne witness to
their bad taste.[17]

This law often caused quarrels between the best of friends,[18]
especially among women, because one lady would describe to
another, with superb complacency, what had happened at the
queen's ball on the previous day, how much she had enjoyed
herself, what a success her dress had been; how ridiculous it
was that Mme de R—— should love the Prince de B——,
who had been staring at her all the time with such stupid eyes;
how inconceivable it was that Mme de L—— could have chosen
anyone like M. de C. G——, who certainly was an excellent
man but one with whom it was absurd to fall in love; how ravishing the Queen had been; with what kindly grace she had asked
her news of her mother-in-law, etc. . . . All of this as much as
to say to her greatest friend, by now her enemy: "You were not
there, my dear, and never will be; and if it were not for the
chatter with which I overwhelm you in tender superiority, my
angel, you would have no more news of that country than of
what is happening in China!"

This law has made more enemies for the court than the deficit in our finances, which never found friends ready to obliterate it or make it up; this law, in short, has armed the nobility of the province against that of the court, incorrectly called the highest nobility if antiquity is constituent of such nobility. For there were at court, amidst the most illustrious names, many very modern lords—granted that one can be a lord, as it was spoken of in those days, when one is scarcely a man of quality; and this I take the liberty to doubt absolutely.

Many families for which the proofs demanded by the court were child's play might yet have found some difficulties in supplying them, owing to the loss of patents of nobility, which had not been preserved since they were of no use for ordinary emergencies. Other families have been ruined through sending agents abroad at great expense to explore archives, registers, and charters. They have sometimes secured in that way not only evidence of their past nobility but of their present poverty. All this fostered rebellion in some heads, and in others discontent; vexation and confusion on the one hand, pride and irritability on the other; a concealed jealousy of those families who had reached favour, while others had the same rights if the conditions had been but fulfilled, etc., etc.[19] Such mistakes, blunders, wrong enactments were to prove the germ of dissension and evil!

These two regulations have given birth to revolutions already armed like Pallas; to rebels, who sprang from two discontented classes, the most active in the kingdom—the top of the high bourgeoisie and the medium nobility. The new nobility did not then consider themselves authorized to complain; they were, so to say, isolated, and joined in only when the Revolution had sounded the tocsin of violence and fury and afforded them a choice. Add to this that the highest offices of the state, especially in the army, were given almost exclusively to favourites of the court, and you will have the best explanation of a revolution more extraordinary in its consequences than singular in its principles.

But this subject will recur in due course; I am now wandering too far from my own.

My grandfather, as has been said at the beginning of this work, was of a sufficiently ancient house to supply all possible proofs, but had only had need to produce those required from pages.[20] He had been one to Louis XV, and had followed him to his coronation. For twenty-five years he was captain in a cavalry regiment at a time when a man of quality did not con-

sider that it was indispensable for his rank to command a
regiment, or that all members of his family should.[21] It was not
then possible for any fool to threaten to abandon the King and
the state to their unhappy fate if he was not made a colonel.

During the ministry of M. de Monteynard, a Comte de
G—— demanded a regiment, declaring he would resign if he
was refused. The minister coolly sent for three men who were
in his department. Their names were none other than Lévis,
Rochechouart, and Beauvilliers. They had all three been serving
for twenty years, not one of them had a regiment.

"Gentlemen," said the minister, "the King is about to suffer
a great loss; this gentleman is going to leave the service, but
as people like you still remain with his Majesty he will find
consolation."

This incident does all the more credit to M. de Monteynard
since M. de G—— belonged to Dauphiné and was his relative,
and what is more, was a brother of a Commandeur de G——,
rather a comical creature, but an estimable man, who never left
the minister's house, especially at dinner time, and always said
we when referring to his chief.

The old Prince de Beauffremont, always teeming with anecdotes, once told me an amusing story of the Comte de Saint-
Mauris, belonging like himself to Franche-Comté, and of this
good commandeur.

M. de Saint-Mauris, being displeased with the court, as
often happens when one has lived there a long time, had retired
to his estate; but having a grown-up son marked for a high
fortune because of a great name, he thought it was sheer infanti-
cide to sulk any longer. He set out for Versailles and on arriving
went direct to Mme de Pompadour, with whom he had formerly
had a considerable degree of familiarity. He was well received;
that very day she arranged for him to have a conversation with
the King, and he had the honour of supping with him in her
rooms. A most lucky position for a resurrected man! The Commandeur de G——, who knew nothing of this, met Saint-Mauris
in the corridor, boasted of his credit, protested that no one was
more anxious to serve him, spoke of their ancient friendship and
the good old days, and added at last:

"My dear Count, chance has given us much credit, and a position in which we can oblige many people, let us know what you
wish for your son, and be very sure that we will do everything
to put you back in the running and be useful to you in some

way. . . . Speak, my dear friend. . . . What can we do for you?"

"Give me a pinch of snuff."

To return to my grandfather—this worthy old man was covered with wounds, honourable scars, which he liked showing me in my childhood; he had married a girl of quality, related to a man of her name much esteemed at court and in the army, who might perhaps have become a marshal of France if he had lived ten years longer. She was a woman of ordinary ability and intelligence, but of a courage, frankness, and virtue that recalled the days of old. I am all the more to blame for not resembling them since I remember them perfectly and my early childhood was spent beneath their wing. My grandfather never showed such pride as to arouse hatred, though he possessed the noble and simple dignity of a man who knows he is of illustrious birth and finds himself acknowledged as such everywhere, especially in two great provinces [22] where he was universally respected. He set great store by this favourable circumstance, but with such moderation that it was forgiven him; whereas my father, who talked of nothing but the maternal stock of Percy and Harcourt (and even maintained that the duke of the latter name did not belong to the real family), whose head was always full of the ancient kings of Denmark, of which pure blood we descended, as well as of that of the Bourbons which runs in our veins, would have made Wittekind's [23] genealogy hateful, and poured ridicule on the blood of Saint Louis; at all events, if he had enjoyed sufficient favour and credit as to render his vanity more striking and more dangerous.

However that may be, my grandfather never personally concerned himself with genealogy, nor put his own much in order. When he retired from the army he took his numerous family to his estate in Normandy, and there lived on an income of ten or twelve thousand livres, acquiring the reputation of being one of the wisest and most honourable noblemen of the neighbourhood. The Marquis de Tilly-Blaru, lieutenant-general and grand commander of the order of Saint Louis, knowing that a branch of his family was settled a few leagues from Alençon, came with the Marquis de Scépeaux, who had been a friend of my grandfather, to spend a few days with him and ask leave to take away two of his children, hardly yet out of boyhood, although the elder was already in the Noailles regiment. He intended to guide their first steps in the army and to make them

begin in the life-guards of his own brigade. This choice, honourable as it was, was not to my grandfather's taste. He gave in
to the request of his relative, and head of his house, only after
a formal promise that one of the boys would shortly obtain a
cavalry company and the other a sublieutenantcy as "exon"
(exempt) in the life guards; and this the Marquis would take
upon himself to secure when the time came. The old Marquis
de Tilly-Blaru was not the man to boast about imaginary credit,
but was well able to keep the promise he had made, being in
high esteem with the King and having much ascendancy over the
last but one of the Dukes of Villeroy, captain of the guards. So
he took the boys straight to Versailles, the elder being then seventeen. But both were far from having reached the usual height
required from the guards who have no longer any intention or
prospect of growing taller; so when the King saw them he began
to laugh, exclaiming: "How small they are!"

"Sire, I beg your Majesty to remember that they are my
relatives."

"You are right; people of your name are not measured by
height."

It is perfectly clear that a man who comes of his own free
will to seek another on his estate, and who almost by force takes
charge of his children, and tells the King of France that they
are of his house, is quite convinced of this fact.

My father at the end of eighteen months left the life-guards
to enter the Light-Horse School, which was then very fashionable. Though he had a handsome appearance and courage, all
that was needed to succeed in the army, he left it to marry at
the age of twenty, as if Mars and Venus had not always been
on the best of terms! Or rather, to speak seriously, he left it out
of that spirit of insubordination, restlessness, and inconstancy
by which his whole life was disturbed. He was one of those men
who find no rest but in the grave. His brother, quieter in disposition, methodical and steady, a man of the strictest honour but
of limited intelligence, made no way and awaited idly the cross
of Saint Louis in subaltern posts in the army. He later died as
a captain in the Noailles regiment, just before his promotion to
be either a major or lieutenant-colonel. One of his sisters, sunk
in deep devotion, which offered much hope for the next world,
did nothing but pray in this. . . .

See how insensibly families decline! Their vigour and health
fail like those of empires or of individuals; everything on earth

decays. Here then was a branch of an ancient and distinguished tree which was not throwing out very vigorous shoots and whose leaves were not very luxurious. Who will give it new sap? Who will restore to this fine tree its ancient distinction? Who will cause it to blossom again? Who will bring beneath its shade another generation to perpetuate its interrupted fame and to renew its ancient lustre?

I, perhaps (so people used to predict), I, without doubt, if I had had the courage to display ambition, the skill to achieve a method, the patience that leads to success, an aptitude for a steady life, the misfortune of having no passions, or the tedious firmness for controlling them. The revolution, as I have many times said, might thus have found me a model of goodness. I might have choked with vexation beneath its ruins, and the hand of pleasure could not have rescued me. Oh, Candide, Candide, you were right! All is for the best in this best of worlds.[24]

My parents and the Comte de Tessé, first equerry to the Queen, perhaps entertained this idea when he offered and they accepted for me an appointment as page to the Queen. As I have already described everything that concerns that period, I now return to it only for the sake of the incident to which I wish to bring the reader.

I belonged to a family in which I had heard so much talk concerning heraldic science and genealogies that I had no doubt my own was in order. One of my uncles, to whom I wrote asking him to send our patents of nobility to Chérin, was himself so convinced that they were strictly in order that he replied I should make my début at the time of his next journey to Paris, which was to be soon. He arrived in fact with bundles of papers which, added to those already in the hands of M. d'Hosier,[25] categorically convinced Chérin "that we were as noble as the King but which, nevertheless, could not authorise him—since in all conscience he must do his duty—to grant me the required certificate on account of gaps and interstices which, with a little expense and research, it would be easy to fill." He indicated more or less where the missing documents could be found; he suspected that it would be in the Tower of London, in Denmark, and at Vareville in Normandy. A certain Abbé Guérin was sent at great expense to recover these papers.

The day for my début was approaching, and M. de Tessé had arranged beforehand with the Maréchal de Duras that I should have the honour of being presented to the King on the following Sunday. That done, there remained the royal family, and finally, in the course of the same week, the princes. I carried out this heavy duty[26] (it was a heavy one at my age, but two persons of my family had urged me on) with the least bad grace that I could, with fine clothes for which I long owed my tailor, and with awkward or bashful bows which were not those taught to me by the representatives of Terpsichore. I made no mystery of the irregularity in my papers; it was an indifferent and remediable matter. Happy youth, so prompt to blush, is yet a stranger to the concealments of vanity; it is later that one blushes from pride when pretentions of every sort, pressing one every day, have taken the place of the heedlessness of youth, which knows no foresight. I had made bold to mention the matter myself to the Queen, whose reply, as kind as it was simple, was that "persons of my family and of my name having entered the court carriages, and myself having been presented, was all that was necessary for the present, and that I had ample time before me to put myself in order as regards the rest."

In spite of this I at once set to work. I spoke to the Marquis de Tilly, who was so sure I was related to him that he had paid calls with me. He assured me that he would gladly do all he could for me, but that since our families had been separated for several centuries he did not believe his patents of nobility would be useful to me. Thereupon the Abbé Guérin brought some others back from London where he had been sent; he asked for more money to make another journey, but this requisite was refused. I now felt indifferent to his success, since it was no longer of any use to me, and I proposed to wait until my finances were in a more respectable condition, and I could myself go to England. I have always, from earliest youth, enjoyed travelling, as if in anticipation; for I confess I had no foreboding of the interminable journeys to which Providence later condemned me. The fact remains that in this occurrence, by openly proclaiming my difficulties over a matter then deemed so important, by further neglecting to procure the documents which, with some little trouble, I could have secured, I was to find myself faced by a serious duel which Fate chose to postpone for twelve years!

The Abbé de Tilly-Blaru had had to complain of either my father or one of my uncles. He was, or thought he was, a great genealogist, and much concerned with his name, his family, its distinction, and its antiquity. He had been at some seminary or

other with Louis Prince d'Aremberg, who was not claimed by
the church, which handed him over very completely to the profane world. Prince Louis, having met me at the house of the
Comte de B——, Minister in France to the Queen's brother, the
Elector of Cologne, said to me very distinctly, but attaching no
importance to it:

"I know the Abbé de Tilly very well; he makes out you are
not a relative of his."

"If he means by the word relative," I replied, paying little
attention to what he said, "a cousin-german, or something as
close as that, he is entirely right, but we bear the same name,
and the same arms,[27] and though separated from time imme-
morial, we have the same origin." The conversation dropped.

Intrigued by this assertion, impelled by a restless curiosity,
I went a few days later to the Notre-Dame monastery, where
the Abbé de Tilly lived. After the first greetings I straightway
stated the object of my visit. He told me he had not positively
uttered the words I reproached him with, but that some in-
vestigations he had made led him to believe we were not related.
He did not mean that my family was worth less than his, but
that he was almost convinced we were two distinct families, and
that relationship was due to chance and not an act of will, etc.
I expressed my surprise, assuring him without ill temper that I
proposed to establish a truth of which I had no doubt, or else
admit I was powerless to prove it.[28] We separated with the
rigorous politeness of mutual pride.[29]

I will not enquire how the Vicomte de Tilly-Blaru's passions
came into play, what hand fed the fire of discord already lighted
by circumstances of which I was ignorant. However this may
be, he was impetuous, ardent, perhaps discontented with his
luck, for he had not attained the position he deserved, nor been
granted advancement; but since he was brave to rashness he
felt impelled to stand for his branch of the family by bringing
legal action against me, the whole affair preluding with a peti-
tion to the marshals of France. No course of action could have
been more useless, for after my interview with the Abbé de Tilly
we had decided, my family and I, to obtain an authentic pro-
nouncement on the question from two genealogists who would
handle all the documents. I had notified the Marquis de Tilly,
who had assured me he was no active party to this quarrel. Such
a step would have been much quicker than a lawsuit, the dilatory
procedure of which delights the public and often decides nothing.

But it was written in the Book of Fate that the question was to
be decided by the sword and ended by a duel notorious throughout France.

The deep friendship which to-day unites me to my opponent
of that time, the relations which have sprung up between us and
which the recollection of bloodshed has further cemented, forbid me to go into subsequent details or any odious recriminations
at which friendship takes offence and which are despised by men
who have crossed swords in an affair of honour.[30]

I shall limit myself to a rapid summary of all that apper-
tains to this great episode of my youth: a scuffle in a public
place of which I myself informed the King and the royal family
by means of a letter; our appearance before a court of marshals
of France; the promise we gave not to fight in France evaded
by a journey to the frontier; a serious duel; a pretty, loving
woman, greatly perturbed, hurrying post-haste after me; another who wished to mend our quarrel before I departed; my
return to Paris; M. le Maréchal de Stainville's attempt to have
me arrested at the Opéra; the romantic and perfidious Mme
Ray——, to whom I sacrificed much for love while she surrendered her virtue; the pursuits of the Provost Marshal; the
Comte de L—— carrying me off to his estate in Normandy to
enable me to avoid these; a police officer coming to fetch me
thence on behalf of the most amiable tribunal in the world; the
devotion of my friends,[31] which my heart delights in remembering; my cross-examination by the marshals of France, to which
my replies were simple and dignified; the interest shown me by
some members of this tribunal; the railing of some others; my
three months' imprisonment at the Abbaye Saint-Germain; a
few love-adventures in this gloomy abode, to which I brought
such merriment that their lordships [32] were vexed; Desprémesnil
coming to offer to take my case before the supreme court, which
was impatient to play a trick on the most distinguished institution in the state; my freedom restored, thanks in a way to the
kindness of the Queen, who did not wish me to know of it, but
who had thus spoken on my behalf: "If M. de Tilly is to be
prosecuted I will not allow it; but a few months in prison will
do him no harm."

Later Sillery came to report to me a repartee from the Duc
d'Orléans to the Maréchal de Stainville: "The marshals are free
to forgo honour in this affair, but they will not succeed in bringing dishonour upon M. de Tilly."

Finally followed the exhilarating feeling which comes over a prisoner who once more breathes freely. There is the whole story in a condensed picture, the shades and details of which would prove too minute and tedious.

I shall go into details only concerning an episode that will naturally lead me back to the thread of my narrative. I have said, referring to Adeline, that she wished to make up our quarrel before I left for the frontier in order to fight. It was on the very night of my departure that I saw her again and spoke to her for the first time after many years, in one of the prettiest boudoirs of Paris, where she displayed towards me both friendship and sadness; I tried to cheer her up and to make her love me, but she felt almost horrified at my proposal, as if her rapture could bring me ill luck, and mine prove to be that of a dying man. I recall that on coming home I unsealed my will to bequeath to her a handsome sweetmeat box which had been handed back to me with my portrait a few days previously.

As for Mme de Ray——, whose surrender was delayed by all this, finding herself sad and perturbed through my absence (at least she condescended to assure me it was so), she carried superstition to great lengths; love can be more superstitious than devoutness. The forecast of fortune-tellers was sought concerning the issue of the fight; cards were drawn and drawn again in confirmation. Upon these mysteries of a magic born of the devil followed more sacred ones; masses were sung; the holy sacrament of the Saviour of mankind celebrated; a well-paid priest entreated this divine victim of our sins not to let me become one in battle.

At the first fortunate moment which placed me in the arms of this society comedian, she displayed all her arts of tenderness: eyes dimmed with tears marked sensibility, difficult breathing came from an oppressed heart; a few stammered words were lost in a sigh, and a swoon in an armchair came with good grace and most suitably. It was all done in due form!

When I went away under friendship's protection, the post, during this my short and last stay in Normandy, brought her twice a week news of my regrets, my love, and my hopes. She never replied, and I was vexed at this. She assured me later, when I saw her again, that it was due to her inability to describe her emotions adequately. But, in reality, this angel of darkness had feared to supply me with weapons for a future and inevitable break; she was imbued with the prudence of wicked hearts; in a transitory love affair she was far too knowing to send letters.

When I came back to Paris with my police officer, who clung to me with the assiduity of personal interest, I yet obtained from this fellow the permission to betake my heart to my new love. Since he had no need of the said heart, but only of my body, he was satisfied with my word of honour that I would deliver this back to him within two hours. So I flew to seek new favours from the charmer, and I seemed to lose in her arms that freedom which I was soon to lose in truth through my captivity. But this she promised to come and cheer, and so make me forget it; she kept her word all the more easily since her adorable lover, whom no woman ever dared betray, was then away at the regiment where his merit had brought him to be second major.

But man's happiness is a fragile thing, especially when one wishes to drive two women abreast along the path of pleasure, a course I have heard indeed condemned by numerous people still stuck in the rut of ancient prejudices. The fair Rosalie, towards whom gratitude should have kept me from giving her a rival, noticed one day, in what would be called a hall except in a prison, a token of a faithfulness which never was mine, that is to say she recognised a little dog belonging to Mme de Ray——. She turned back, reached her carriage, and went away . . . but like a Parthian, leaving an arrow in my flesh. She spread the news of my liaison with this comical prude, and swore by the Styx she would never come again; her rival swore to the same effect and kept her promise. If some other kindly souls had deprived me of consoling attentions, I should have remained alone, just because, in a corridor, a dog had yelped and caused dismay.

The roses and lilies of a Mme M—— and a Mlle Saint-Y—— came to adorn and perfume my solitude. But you above all, worthy spouse of a follower of Neptune, charming Bourg——, accept the expression of my everlasting gratitude. You looked like Cupid, who was not as graceful; you charmed away upon his wings the long hours of captivity; boredom vanished before one of your smiles, your kind attentions, like a magic talisman, brightened my brief bondage, and the memory still enlivens my exile.

CHAPTER XXII

SO I came out of the den where I had been hurled by a sort of inquisition to which members of the French nobility had to submit without being aware of it, and without complaining, since they took pride in being tried by their peers. I had now to give thought to no less a matter than calling on these gentlemen, the marshals of France, in order to thank them for having been so glaringly unjust. For it had been an injustice, even if one admits their supremacy as judges, which was but a gradual usurpation of state functions totally foreign to the original dignity of their duties, as I am convinced I have satisfactorily established after a perusal of dusty authorities, which I quoted in a memorandum I blame myself for having handed over to the Constituent Assembly. Such a supremacy, at the best, was under the monarchy a defiance of the laws—which we had not broken, since we had fought outside the kingdom—and laws should always be of an even, dull uniformity and of a strict equality, both in their principles and their application. Besides, who were these men who thus reaped advantages from the fact that an office of the crown, purely military at the outset, had degenerated into a judicial and civil authority whose abuses were notorious and whose verdicts caused it to be hated without being respected? Were they the marshals of France, burdened with the laurels they had really gathered, or bedecked with those they were at least presumed to have reaped? No, nearly all were lords of high birth, and they had obtained this lofty distinction at the end of their careers, when their weak hands, enfeebled by age and infirmity, were soon to let it fall. Never having studied law and procedure, their innate honour and knightly loyalty were not beacons bright enough to enlighten them. This office was for them more in the nature of a costly burden than an honourable duty or an attractive occupation. Difficult points were solved by a pedantic master of requests, nearly always a born enemy of aristocrats, who, if not corrupt, was, to say the least, unequal to the task he was called upon to undertake— that of dispensing justice and of imparting knowledge in matters often either beyond his sphere or not in conformity with his principles, his tastes, or his education. If he happened to be mercenary, or hot-headed, or open to bribery, it was even worse confusion for both the judges and the contending parties.

Below this was found an army of subalterns barring all access to the court, and never easily throwing open its doors except with keys of gold. They would sell their support and information, the petitions that secured an acquittal, and the false reports that guaranteed a condemnation. Such was this crew of scoundrels, issued from the mire to plague those who should have come under their notice only for respect! This shameless gang quenched their thirst with tears and fattened on iniquity. Robbers all, they used but one weight and throve on gall, extortions, pilfering, and rapine.

These hideous facts were acknowledged as true even by several of the marshals of France. The courageous Maréchal de Duras more or less admitted this during the call I paid him to tender my thanks. He went into some details which convinced me he knew full well the law-court where he sat and its obnoxious ways, and would have seen its abolition without displeasure as that of an office entirely distinct from the fame and supreme reward due to soldiers. He treated me in fatherly fashion and kept me to dinner, not a matter of indifference since he was perhaps the man in France who most liked good living. I told him that he had too much resembled Cæsar in his youth to punish me for having done my duty, and that I knew his opinion had been favourable to us. He listened with a smile to all my bold assertions about the Maréchal de Stainville, and the fact that he did not stop me was a sufficient answer.

I found him delightful to show such little liking for his colleague, and to be still young enough to allow me so to forget myself. He clearly recalled how he had been on duty the year [1] of my presentation to the King, and had himself presented me. Young men drove the old ones out at a rate terrifying to both; he was sorry to hear I had left the army, which was in France the only profession for a gentleman; I must make haste to go back to it and push ahead smartly so as to become myself a marshal of France and then have the pleasure of proposing and perhaps bringing about some fine reforms in a tribunal with which I did not appear infatuated,[2] etc. . . . All this was said with extreme graciousness, yet with perfect dignity.

I had not yet paid my call on that Hungarian corporal, the Maréchal de Stainville, the chief instigator of this little prosecution. I come to it.

"You do not owe me, sir," he told me roughly, "any thanks. [To whom did he say this?] If my opinion had prevailed, you would have lost your head on the scaffold."

"I hope, Monsieur le Maréchal," I replied, "that this would have been a task beyond the power of your court, had I even been deprived of friends, family, and acquaintances. There are still laws in France other than the law of the sword of the provost-marshal."

"Sir! . . ."

I repeated my words, but deference prevents me from entering into the details of this affair: "I have fulfilled a duty, as I was enjoined to do, in coming to call not on M. le Comte de Stainville, but on the marshal of France." [8]

During this speech he eyed a certain gray woollen jacket he was wearing as a dressing-gown; he was gazing at it either with humility or fondness. I am inclined to think that it was the former feeling, for he condescended to stammer some excuses for having received me in that state; a deep bow on my part left him free to go and attend to his toilet. It certainly required attention, though he could scarcely be embellished thereby.

This sullen fellow had been drawn into the service of France through his brother, who was already a minister. The Queen had helped to raise him to the rank of marshal of France on account of her gratitude toward the Duc de Choiseul (on whom it was impossible to bestow a marshal's staff) for her marriage, which she still looked upon as a gift from heaven while it really was one from hell. This worthy man, who would have had my head cut off, had scarcely displayed enough ability for ordinary garrison duties. In Austria, after fifteen years of active service in the regiments of Kollowrath and Loewenstein, he had become an inefficient lieutenant-general. He had not deserved the rank of field-marshal in the emperor's army, so he was not granted it; and the marshals of France had little deserved to find him in their midst, though there he was. Yet one must have the courage to mention the fact that this high command has been sold for bare gain in these later days, and other military grades as well, too numerous for an army that in proportion to our territory and power was far too small. Many favours were squandered, including the collar of the Commandeur of the Saint-Esprit, which was granted to people surprised at wearing it, to others who themselves admitted they deserved only the title of simple chevalier, and to some few others whom public opinion regarded as deserving no reward at all. The peerage was the only high distinction of which the last reign was sparing, be it said to its praise. Nothing is a more unfailing indication of the approaching downfall of an empire than the bartering away of the highest rewards in the state.

M. de Castres, M. de Guines, even the Duc de Châtelet, called to distinctions attained by right of birth, were but dukes through inheritance or by writ. The Duc de Coigny was made a peer . . . and one was free to believe it was but a compensation for the office of first equerry, which some reforms of economy had caused him to lose, giving to M. de Lambesc the two offices combined in his own of gentleman of the horse. This de Lambesc has shown since what gratitude was his. While in Brussels, where he would pose as a foreign prince because he began to despair of France, he showed his good taste by speaking of "your king."

"Whom do you call your king?" exclaimed Mme de Matignon, who excelled in this sort of eloquence. "He was almost more *yours* than the king of anyone else! You held too good an office and were too well paid to fail to be sure of that." She might have added: "It turned your head." If this branch of the house of Lorraine, which settled in France as far back as 1500 and came to the peerage as early as 1527, was not French and subject to the King, nearly all of us could then find something to say for claiming a country elsewhere. Pitiable! But ingratitude and pride are not generally very logical. This brings back to my mind an anecdote which is not generally known, but of which I am sure. M. de Poix, then Governor of Versailles, and captain in the guards, was not always an altogether discreet courtier. He incurred a most severe rebuff from M. le Comte d'Artois, but he nobly extricated himself, and without impertinence:

"If the house of Lorraine had met with success at the time of the League it might have happened, your Highness, that he would now be king [he meant M. de Lambesc] and you gentleman of the horse."

"What would you then be?" retorted the Comte d'Artois, "a groom?"

"No, your Highness," replied the Prince de Poix, "I should still remain what I am, a nobleman."

This was the smarter as an answer since these Noailles are a very ancient family, even though their favour at court and the vanity with which they made use of it have often caused envious malignity to say they dated but from yesterday.

It was about this time I made a discovery that grieved me and explained several riddles the clue to which had often bothered me. President de Nicolai informed me that someone bearing my name had been arrested and taken to the La Force prison by his creditor. Although the president's duties had hardly any connection with such affairs, he added that he knew from his secretary, whose brother worked under the Lieutenant-Governor of La Force, that this man was an abominable fellow, and in particular accused of forgery. I hastened to see a magistrate, and having been received with much consideration, I obtained from him complete facilities, and went to the prison. There, furnished with his pass, and escorted by a lawyer whom he had sent with me, I saw a man of the vilest appearance with a most ignoble face. I made free to tackle him straightway, at all risks, in the most deliberate manner; I had a full report written of his stay in Paris during the two previous years and of all the detailed circumstances leading to his arrest. He literally threw himself on his knees, confessed all his crimes and his real name.

He was called Le Blanc and was a creole. His mother had for long been intimate with the Comte de Tilly, a general who had for several years lived in the West Indies. Thus this wretch had had the whim to adopt his name. I had all his statements and confessions legally recorded, and felt at peace only when he had been sent away from Paris and forbidden to return. I know, however, that he has been there since, and actively employed under Robespierre.[4] I suppose that, if he had ever found me again on his path, the kind of interest he would have shown towards me would have increased my chances of the scaffold.

Society tattle, resembling renown, and a duel which had made a sensation could but promote my affairs in my dealings with the sensitive sex, whose delicate perceptions render them easy to move in such various ways. I was kept very busy, I could have been even more so. But a keen anxiety tormented me; I felt about the future I do not know what vague apprehension, which has been only too fully explained since. It was a formless cloud I could not see through; I suspected it to hide a storm, just as during days of excessive heat some physical reaction or discomfort foretells lightning and thunder.

I had one day been to thank the Duc d'Orléans for the interest he had shown towards me, and I heard at his house a conversation that disturbed me against my will. I found him surrounded by people, several of whom were men of honour, but thirsting for repute and burning with an eagerness only restrained by prudence and personal interest. Others were there for whom all means were equally good that opened the way to fortune, and their theories clearly indicated that, defying consequences, they would stop at no obstacles. Finally there were some, for whom the ambition of seeing their names associated with useful and memorable changes mitigated or concealed the dangers therein, who dreamed of nothing but reforms, liberal ideas, an English constitution doing away with abuses,[5] the checking of despotism, and a restriction of the power of the court and its agents.

The mantelpiece in the Duc d'Orléans' study was encumbered with pamphlets, *cahiers,*[6] and schemes drawn up by his scribblers, where each dreamer had set down his Utopia. The first words he said to me at this visit were: "Be reassured, such oppression will become impossible; there will soon be honest and simple laws which cannot be interpreted according to arbitrary whims. The *lettres de cachet,* the bastilles of all sorts, will not exist for long." As I mentioned to him that I was going to spend a few months in England, he interrupted me with emotion: "Truly! one will soon be able to go there and anywhere else without asking leave and without fear of being refused."[7]

I was amazed at the words full of vengeance which came from the lips of the first prince of the blood, but I had no time to recover from my astonishment, for I had no sooner entered the drawing-room than I had many other fine things to listen to. Thus the Vicomte de Noailles said, with the feverish zeal characteristic of him: "It must soon be made easier for any soldier to end his days as a marshal of France than it is today for an officer to become one." This because I had led the conversation to the marshals of France, an everlasting theme with me at that time, and the only tribute I ever paid to the disease.

Yet it was only as I was leaving the Palais Royal that I became fully aware of the uneasy feeling such talk, so strange in those days, had left with me. The ghost of a revolution—the character of which I could not have described—and that of a grief-stricken monarchy appeared before me. To speak without metaphors, I protest that, from this date, I believed in an approaching civil war; this was the one vague premonition which the present gave me of the future. On the next day I hurried to the Vicomte de Noailles, who had just helped me to make friends again with his brother, the Prince de Poix, and told him of my feelings.

"I do not believe anything of the sort," he replied. "We shall be guided by our *cahiers* and we shall push a little further ahead. The King wishes to do good; he will help us; and if it must end in a fight, that is good for the health: we shall fight."

Noailles had a strong revolutionary vocation; he was M. de La Fayette's brother-in-law and was jealous of him as being preferred to himself; he wanted to put him in the shade, as if his rival had called forth such tactics from envy. This "noble" passion had sprung up in him in society, at court, in the regiment where they served together in their youth. It had grown stronger in the United States whence they both brought back chimerical notions, the seeds of which had always been within them: I mean, a scheme for equality and freedom, badly defined and wrongly conceived.

But to come back to my journey to England (1789-90). I felt the need to travel, especially to England; I have had since too much time and opportunity to gratify this whim; but I felt then I do not know what uneasiness within me. It seemed as if I did not wish to witness the prelude to our public calamities, nor to see these last beautiful days which were to shine over my country and over Europe, so soon to be shaken to the foundation —beautiful days to which a long darkness succeeded. What I have preserved of this experience is that there is within us a voice which does not tell us the future, but falters out prophecies about it, so that we are conscious of aversions and antipathies we can ill define, but which the future justifies all too well. Such was, for instance, the feeling of deep and unreasoned hatred I always had towards M. Necker, dating from his admission to a career to which nothing called him except presumption on the one side and blindness on the other. Such again was the scorn I felt from the very first for M. de Calonne's diplomatic and financial gifts, to such an extent that, though I then busied myself little with such matters, I said to one of his most zealous supporters [8]: "I hate him as much as I do M. Necker; he is merely a clever man and he will prove the finishing stroke."

Yet, even with such men at the head of the state, putting forth their delusions and their experiments for its rejuvenation, it would have been difficult at that early date to detect the Revolution in all its details and fatal consequences. But it was only too easy to see that, with no guiding thread to help us, we were entering an inextricable maze over which the Minotaur and Death were keeping watch.

A king full of vices and immorality might perhaps have saved us; we were about to perish under one whose weakness rendered his virtues ineffective. In France, to argue about authority meant undermining it; to investigate thoroughly in view of reforms meant certain destruction. It is especially in these matters that good should be done without being advertised, unless one wishes evil systematically to be born out of every improvement. M. de Calonne, whom I have known well since, and whose easy grace and agreeable culture have pleased me, laughed much in London, when I told him one day, at M. de Luxembourg's house and in the presence of Mr. Burke: "The King should have given you the office of conversationalist in his private apartments rather than that of cabinet minister in his Council. He should have asked you to make a *note* never to speak to him of your *notables.*"

It may be guessed that these words were not said as curtly and nakedly as I write them here; but, however wrapped up they may have been in qualifications and flattery, I fear that if he laughed loudly it was only on the wrong side of his mouth. . . . He laughed! He should have shed tears of blood. . . . But no one would acknowledge having done wrong; he accused M. Necker, who in his turn consoled himself by thinking ill of M. de Calonne. The latter accused also the Archbishop of Sens. I listened to one after another; of course not one of them was guilty, but each passed that sentence on the other which posterity will pass on them all. The future will have due cause to be strictly equitable, since in politics as in administration a man is as responsible for the evil he does not prevent as for that he actually commits, for the evil he purposely perpetrates as for that he allows through his incapacity. Inexorable history no more readily forgives those who brought dishonour upon their office by means of crimes than it does those who wrought such dishonour because of their stupidity and their inaptitude in fulfilling their duties.

It chanced once when I was still very young, heedless, inconstant, and little prepared to discuss the ability of a minister of finance and his duties, that I was staying in the country as the guest of the Marquis de V——, who was an enthusiastic admirer of the Genevese statesman. I left almost on bad terms with my host and his circle because I went to sleep during the reading of Necker's "Eloge de Colbert," which I had read long before, and because, on waking up, I had declared it was written in the style of a refugee and with the ideas of a charlatan.

The reader may judge, then, whether my love increased at the reading of his report on the finances of France, where he sets himself up in opposition to the King and has the insolence to ask that judges should pronounce between himself and his Majesty. I had read his character in his books, and knew him as if I had lived with him. When I saw a foreigner, a bourgeois from Geneva, a Calvinist, managing the finances of the kingdom, and that a Catholic kingdom, where his advice was required even on matters foreign to his presumed accomplishments, I had no doubts as to his pernicious influence on our destiny. A few virtues, embarrassed by emphatic phraseology, did not reassure me; his frankness, if ever he had any, could not have made up for the absence of those great components of a statesman's ability which are not to be acquired on the dusty benches of a counting-house. But when there came his convocation of those baneful States General which, all through youth, I had heard condemned by one of the greatest statesmen France ever had,[9] when he delivered that pompous and emphatic speech in which he expounded a completely subversive scheme, a whole system of government in which he hoped to concentrate power in his own hands, then one could only shudder and feel pity, unless one was a dissident or a fool.

Thus it is a fact that I did not at that time measure the extent or the depth of the abyss which was then opening, though I had forebodings. History, which I had read carefully, seemed to predict a revolution which it was to be my fate to study and to know. If in this work I do not write concerning it any of the particulars I am so well acquainted with, it is that I view this as too odious a task, the horror of which I could never overcome even if I had been blessed with the genius of Tacitus. The stage and the actors in this drama are still too near to us.

I shall, then, quickly pass over the early months of a crisis unparalleled in the annals of the world's history, and limit myself to mentioning a few anecdotes or some incidents which, while concerning me personally, are more or less connected with the events that marked the Revolution.

It is very strange, for instance, that after I broke with Veimeranges on account of Adeline, we never spoke to each other again until the beginning of the Revolution, and it was well

for him that he did then. I more or less had the privilege of
saving his life, in a church where he was cutting a rather poor
figure, through finding himself caught in a crowd and mixed up
in a very unequal argument with a citizen in office, who had
formerly been a coachman to Mme de Polignac. This gentleman
would accept no bargain, he aimed at the head; his eloquence
was far from polished, but of a kind well suited to the greater
part of his audience. I remember in particular that he had transformed Veimeranges into a member of the Austrian Committee,
the most terrible of accusations coming from the mob, even
more dangerous than that of being an aristocrat. He demanded
nothing less than a domiciliary visit to the house of this *blood-
sucker* feeding on the people, as he expressed it, where tons of
gold would be found; he called him another Foulon![10] Veimeranges, who had never been a good speaker, was in a state of
agitation that might have led him straight to a lamp-post. His
heavy face had assumed an expression of stupidity, his gaping
mouth stammered clumsy justifications more compromising than
silence, while a deadly pallor settled on his ruddy brow—all
indications of crime seeming to justify his condemnation; it was
the involuntary confession of a man guilty of malversation who
forgives his executioner.

The time of which I speak is that of the three or four days
previous to the King's arrival at the Hôtel-de-Ville, when he
came to have the tricolour cockade pinned to his hat. In all
probability the plan had not been that he was to go through that
day so easily; but turbulent factions were once more checked;
the cup of bitterness which, like our Saviour and with the same
resignation, he was to drink to the dregs, had not yet been filled
to the brim; not one single drop was to be spared him. Now he
was once more allowed to return to Versailles, the better to be
steeped in the floods of the Revolution. He brought back to his
palace both life and insults, but the sceptre was no longer to be
found there. The gates of the capital were closed; men, more
frightful on account of their looks than their weapons, paraded
the streets and called at every door, bidding the inhabitants to
assemble at the district headquarters or at the People's-House.
God's sanctuaries were chosen for these early meetings, as if it
was natural to man in the midst of public calamities and the
crimes that follow in their trail, to seek divine protection and
make signals of distress from the foot of pillars which are the
means of transit from earth to Heaven.

After vainly trying to get away from Paris, I thus arrived

at the church, on the following morning, in the company of the Duc d'Aumont, Sartines junior, and Morinval; we were, as if by popular consent, straightway appointed to important posts, a military secretaryship falling to my share. This small test has yet convinced me that if all the people who held or had held important positions had then remained in France, the Revolution would have taken another course and produced other results. However that may be, I made use of my growing credit to help my old rival when he seemed unable to help himself. I jumped upon the table and, thanks to my lungs and a few words harmoniously arranged, I had the former coachman thrown into the street with some injuries, and poor Veimeranges temporarily secured in a side chapel from which I rescued him on the sly before he had had time to say the prayers fear might have suggested to his piety.

To do him justice it must be added that he hit upon a happy financial stroke, for after my speech he exclaimed: "M. le Président [M. le H—— and M. Suard of the Académie Française were both president] I am a good citizen, I place a thousand crowns on my country's altar."

This was eloquence à la Veimeranges, à la Beaujon, people more profuse of speech than Cicero and all the rhetoricians. It might have been better for this unlucky man if he had died then; at all events he would not have found a kind of death more horrible than the one he sought of his own accord, by throwing himself into the street from a fifth-floor window some time later, in order to escape the henchmen of the Reign of Terror.[11] In that ghastly fall came to an end this dense lump, and he breathed his last in a hospital.

Some time later, as I was one day dining in Versailles at the house of the Duc de Biron, I talked with an animation and felicity that caused Mirabeau to exclaim as he left the table, although his views were quite opposed to mine: "My good friend, come over to our side, and I promise you fame and wealth."

"Would that save me," I asked him, "from remorse and the gallows?"

But indeed the fame of the orators was putting all else in the shade. The only subjects of conversation were the speeches of Mirabeau and Barnave, this Barnave whom Mme de Tessé should have refrained from calling Néronet [12] on account of his famous repartee.

M. de Robespierre (as Mirabeau gravely called him all

through the first Assembly, in contrast, it is true, to the offhand way in which I have often heard him refer even in the same speech to Louis Joseph Bourbon, called Condé)—M. de Robespierre, I say, was talking to me one day of the need of hanging every year some hundred or so of those people who wore court dress. That tiger! Was he wrong? Another day, while I was chatting with the Vicomte de Noailles in the Avenue de Paris (during the three first months), Robespierre accosted us, and after heated arguments about politics did me the honour to say that an aristocrat such as I was in great need of being hanged. That time he was not right, and I did well in going away that he might not keep his word.

It was from all this, and from talk I had heard, that I wanted to take flight, when Sir John Lambert, whom everyone has known as a wealthy banker in Paris, entrusted me with a commission to London. He was an extraordinary man in all respects. For instance, he loved only women of a dangerous thinness, in whom a complete flatness of breasts might lead one to question their sex. As I arrived at his house at supper time to fetch his letters, I found arranged in rows of armchairs a collection of mummies with whom I would never have adorned my drawing-room; they were the most skinny specimens from the Opéra ballets, and the nearest to skeletons among minor courtesans. I was astonished to find a man so wealthy and so voluptuous surrounded by what should have put desire and pleasure to flight. He had about him a few friends who also pretended to like it, but who at heart knew that a reasonable plumpness is quite a different incentive from wasting and phthisis.

One man alone, the Vicomte de C——, sincerely shared this taste for osteology in the living body. This man has often maintained to me that for a woman to be desirable her waist should find room in her two black velvet bracelets, that those charms which are an indication of so many others should be absent, and that what remained ought to be devoid of fullness. A very marked taste, one may say, for angular bodies and an assertion which rested upon nothing!

At that supper there was a certain Abbé d'Arcès, a shameless parasite, profanely fawning on the master of the house, and after enumerating the prettiest women in Paris who were so ill-advised as to display fine breasts he named Mlle Lebeau and praised her as if she were without this charm, although she had enough of it to have escaped his eulogies. He extolled her as an actress most pleasantly gifted, and as a courtesan who gave promise of reaching great heights. He related about her a scandalous story I cannot now recall, full of roguishness and wit, of piquant and original taste. I slightly knew this Aspasia, and had never viewed her in that way. I felt ashamed of my unfairness and wished to ascertain whether I had really been guilty and, if so, to make amends. That is to say, I resolved to make love to so lovable a person in order to see if she would really yield all that her panegyrist had promised, and not to let her go before she herself took leave of me, a matter swiftly arranged when one sets to it in earnest. I did not rest until an occasion had offered itself for me to speak to her and obtain permission to go to her rooms in order to intimate my wish to stay. She lived (as it is commonly termed) with F——, son of the Chevalier de M——, an honest and handsome young man whom she would have loved if to deserve it were a sufficient reason to please women of her kind. But women such as she are faithful to no one. Alas, not in any class are they so, frightful as it is to say! If tackled with the necessary degree of skill, patience, and seduction, even the woman who most trusts in the inexorableness of her virtue and the misfortune of her temperament will yet yield, if occasion and a suborner of her mettle happen to come her way.

Since I was seeking an opportunity of meeting Mlle Lebeau, it soon came; it was at the Salon [13] where she moved about like a connoisseur and where Champcenetz and I approached her as amateurs. There are always natural things to say to talent and beauty. As she was at the time fully engaged—if not with ruining F—— at least with unsettling his fortune for a long while—a sort of faithfulness springing from fear made her at first resist me. But it proved a matter of but a few weeks, and we had no sooner come to a friendly arrangement than she blushed at her fright and laughed at her scruples; she was a worthless creature from whom not much was to be expected. People have assured me that she behaved horribly during the Revolution. Can I be surprised at that? Her heart was such as to carry her far. So she piled up a fortune and could be to-day what was formerly called a *dame de paroisse*. She was as pretty as her name, and most diverting; but what proved to be less so was the tragic adventure that caused us to part. We had been most affectionate during supper, and love was awaiting us in an

alcove which had already witnessed my happiness and that of
my predecessors, when I do not know what incident or what
words happened to disturb so touching a peace. She nonchal-
antly took the gold scissors out of her work-bag, and then and
there, quite genuinely and with a good grace, stabbed herself
in the breast, "which Love had carved to ravish every eye!"

Blood flowed; she was deadly pale; she was at the point of
death, she said; I feared it; I called out for help. My agitation
was greater than hers. I covered with kisses and tears this bosom
which would have caused Sir John Lambert to flee. A sleepy
chambermaid appeared. She took me for the murderer of her
mistress, who was kind enough to put her right. I rushed into
the street, brought back a physician, who considered it rather late
in the day to stab oneself with scissors. He hoped the wound
would not prove fatal; this hope was torment since he would
swear to nothing. He prescribed a balsam of a pestilent odour,
promised to come again, and left me a prey to despair, uttering
words as tender as any of Céladon's best, and weeping more
than he could, while she, as staunch as Cato, reflected upon
death. Dawn came to put an end to this wretched farce. I ran
to warn one of the heroine's friends,[14] and this lady, casting
aside the apparel and gait of the queens whose rôles she sometimes acted, came to play that of nurse at friendship's bedside.
My idea was to call twice a day as long as danger lasted, and to
ask for my dismissal on the first morning of convalescence. But
a M. de L——, as much in love as a novice, and Mlle Raucourt,[15] infuriated by the lust by which she was always overcome
near the poor wretches she had soiled, consulted together (at
least so I presume) to have me sent away during the illness itself,
the circumstances and the danger of which these kind souls
exaggerated.

One little clique in Paris, rather poor society at that, soon
received their cue; it was agreed that I was monstrously in the
wrong. It was odious to have rendered an angel of sweetness so
disconsolate; it was unforgivable to have reduced kindness per-
sonified to suicidal despair. . . . I had to think myself lucky
that they did not decide to say I had murdered her. Little
account would have been taken of her own confession to the
doctor, and his personal examination, showing that she had
stabbed herself. . . . Let slander have its way, some mud will
stick, someone has said.[16] This is a dreadful truth that daily
experience endorses. I got off at less cost (except for one small

intimate circle); it was rumoured that I had not obtained the least favour from her, that she was in bed with a violent fever following upon a frightful scene, the result of my vexation at her virtue.

To be flatly dismissed by a woman, of whatever class or standing she might be, has always been highly unpleasant to me. This is a weakness which my reason reproaches me for, but has not been able to conquer. I have painfully endeavoured all through life to laugh at so trifling an accident; but I have never achieved complete triumph over myself. All went well during the day, when the effervescence and bustle are a stimulant that helps one along, but I would collapse in the evening. Night has, if I may put it thus, an enervating quality inducing in the soul all the soft feelings, such as remorse and sadness. These give birth to vexation, which prompts wounded pride to all sorts of follies, such as believing one loves what one has never loved at all.

On this occasion I allowed a few days to elapse; but I wrote a sentimental and apologetic little note when I heard she was cured. It was left unanswered. I asked her to send back my letters and my portrait; silence again. I threatened to come and fetch them myself; renewed display of silence. I then rushed to her rooms, I went up in a rage, I pushed everything out of my way. I asked for Mlle Lebeau, she had gone out, all doors were opened for me. I behaved very wrongly and with so much bad taste as to break or knock over furniture in her bedroom, and the only excuse I can find for that to-day is that I intended to wrong her in such a way as to make it impossible for me ever to see her again. Such was the farewell I took on leaving this pretty face which hid, I fear, a wicked heart, an arid soul, and a sordid avidity. Like all Paris I have since seen her again on the stage, where she displayed gifts that her charming face set off still further to advantage, but I have never again exchanged a word with her.

Some time afterwards I at last started on that journey so often planned and then put off. I went a second time to England where later I have lived more than I could then have foreseen. This country is famous for its philosophers [17] and its public-spirited citizens, just as we are for our arts and our warm patriotism. The English are rivals we could never esteem too much if we could love them enough. They form a great nation which for its own fame and advantage ought to be bound to ours through everlasting peace—this in the interest of Europe and out of love for humanity.

On the eve of my departure I spent a few moments at the house of La Vaupalière, where heavy gambling was in progress. I found there M. de Montesquiou, who was at the time meddling in the public finances only because his own were in irretrievable disorder. I saw him lose enormous sums of money that in the course of the night reached the figure of a hundred thousand crowns. He left the house only to go to the Assembly and read there a report on the finances of the realm. Just as if Aretino should speak on chastity!

I set off with you, my dear Morinval, friend so affectionate and so faithful, whose natural wit could have charmed away boredom during a much longer journey. It was soon after the fifth of October, so hideous a date in our annals, and when the cowardice of the Duc d'Orléans had already landed him on the shores of the Thames, so as to escape the censure of the French nation.[18]

CHAPTER XXIII

Nescio quâ natale solum dulcedine cunctos
Ducit, et immemores non sinit esse sui.
—Ovid.

WHAT a deep impression the attraction of one's birth-place leaves in the soul! How far more delightful is the balmy air of one's own country than all the perfumes of Arabia! The unlucky man who renounces it must be driven away by misfortune before he exchanges a foreign land for the place where his cradle was rocked, where he played in childhood, where he lisped the first words of a beloved tongue, and whose dust is mingled with the ashes of his forefathers. To leave one's country for long is slowly prolonged torture; to leave it for good would prove immediate death could one foresee with certainty that misfortune.

The journey from Paris to Calais, although swiftly accomplished by the side of a dear friend, yet caused me great sadness. I could decipher a sort of savage mistrust already depicted on most faces. An austere or unruly patriotism animated everybody, some people displaying it too openly, others appearing too constrained in disguising it. This journey, which no imperative necessity was as yet forcing me to take, disquieted me at heart, but I should have felt even more disquiet had I not undertaken it. I needed to divert my thoughts under another sky. I argued within myself that I could see France again whenever I wished, that the unforeseen events which later were to close its gates to me were improbable. But although I have always disapproved the emigration movement, as I might show by all my writings at that time, I nevertheless had a misgiving of inevitable exile. It was almost impossible not to become involved in the general rule, or to find oneself at grips with dangers, and above all with the disgust at one's own position, the discomforts of which were to increase as time went on.

With such bitter thoughts preying on me, I found myself more unhappy than I had ever believed possible in those former bright days of my youth and its frivolities. I marvelled at the way my judgement had ripened in the school of early misfortunes over which my sensibility, previously awakened only by the pleasures of love, now brooded with a dismal fascination. Since we were making history, and since our period was to blot out all others, I viewed my century with melancholy terror, not only on account of the advanced times in which we lived, but because one always exaggerates matters that concern oneself. The things I had read made me fear what would be read about ourselves.

Here I wipe away my first tears, the first that ought to be given to one act in this vast tragedy in which more or less all Frenchmen have been actors as well as victims. Such calamities will never again overcome mankind; in no country will one ever see again opportunities for a similar revolution.

On my arrival in London, I found the Duc d'Orléans. He was less despised there than he ought to have been. The French Revolution still found at that time in England many earnest supporters, many others who feigned to admire it, and finally others whose personal interest it was to uphold it. The opposition of a prince of the blood to what was termed the court's despotism appeared sublime; his participation in sweeping away abuses was viewed as magnanimous self-sacrifice. People questioned the evidence regarding his crimes, and a lingering consideration for his rank, supported by his wealth, threw an even thicker veil over the iniquity of his politics and of designs which were not yet proved. His house was a meeting-place for many distinguished men belonging to all parties, not only that of the opposition, but even of the ministers.

These people, divided on all other points, were united in what concerned a good dinner, where Mme de Buffon [1] sat as hostess and was the main attraction among the prince's brilliant company. The Duke was on the lookout for newcomers to England and, failing their approval, would endeavour to secure at least politeness from those who of old owed him respect. He had even come to fear that people in the street might no longer courteously acknowledge his greetings, which were given with much hesitation. What he had gathered about me through the Marquis de Sillery (Genlis), what he had heard from my own lips, the principles which I openly professed, all this ought to have convinced him he was not to count on me in any way. For though he was still a prince to me, since he was of the same blood as my masters, he had nevertheless behaved too vilely for me not to prove equally vile were I to pay him my court. Some personal reasons, which have always exercised much power over a soul made as mine is, had caused me to leave my card at his door at a time when I was sure he was out. The first time he saw me at the King's palace he greeted me in such a flattering way as to make me feel ill at ease; one might have thought I had deserved this, and that I was a budding conspirator. My cool and constrained countenance must have convinced him he had distressed more than welcomed me.

He probed me again on another occasion and finding himself fenced off by my respect, or at least what resembled it, he became my enemy, according to his fashion. M. de Laclos, with whom I readily enjoyed a chat because he was, although more dangerous, at least less conspicuous, told me that "his Highness" had let fall a few words betraying dissatisfaction with me. I pointed out, choosing my words with circumspection (for it was a difficult confidence to impart to one of the Duke's spokesmen), that in view of my position, of my contact with so many French people among whom I lived, let alone my own way of thinking, it was impossible for me to follow another course; and I made him more or less agree (he who was so well placed to know) that his prince was for everybody a *liaison dangereuse*.

A most exalted personage [2] with whom the Duc d'Orléans was still on very friendly terms had welcomed me most kindly during my first visit to England, and again at the beginning of this second visit; now he visibly changed towards me all at once. Pitt, who then saw a great deal of him, told me it was the result of unfavourable hints dropped by the French prince. I thereupon came to a resolve, and going up to the Duke at a rout at Lord Luc——'s, I said to him: "This country never brings me luck, your Highness, in my relations with you; once before you vexed me through a stable quarrel; to-day you wish to make a prince dislike me. . . . I solace myself as to this, but I beg you to look upon me as a dead man, or else I shall trouble you to kill me."

M. de Luxembourg, who had done all he could to ward off this rising-in-arms, and who as my friend showed me real interest, soothed me and took me away. A few months went by; the Duke's eyes, which I did not seek, everywhere avoided mine. But one day, just about the time when Boinville brought him orders from La Fayette with which he did not comply,[3] the Duke appeared in the pit at the Opera House, where I was already settled. He was too near my seat for me not to bow. He suddenly threw this remark at me, with a sardonic smile: "Yet M. d'Aiguillon *gives good thrusts with his sword.*" [4]

I thereupon replied sharply: "And is your Highness as skillful?"

He lost countenance and grew pale, for shame would turn him pale as modesty makes another blush. He started talking to someone else. . . . As for me, he never spoke to me again; it is true that upon my return to Paris he tried to have me murdered, a fact which did not prevent me from rendering him to the end whatever justice was his due. It has been said, and it will go on being said, that the Duc d'Orléans was a monster. Certainly that may be maintained as a general proposition, but if he is judged by isolated facts or details of his life it might require modification. His pliable character disposed him to all possible crimes, as well as rendered him fit for a few virtues.

Let me give some typical sallies of his and some anecdotes which will make him better known.

A man of my acquaintance, from whom he had accepted an invitation to dinner, reminded him of his promise:

"Will his Highness pay me the honour of dining with me to-morrow?"

"No, sir, I should be pleased if you would do it with more ceremony, and I give you three days' respite."

Another time, as he was losing money at Dresnay's house, all in good grace, for he was a bad-tempered player only when he won, someone proposed to have a bet with him for a hundred crowns.

"When I desire to bet, I shall tell you."

"It is possible, your Highness, that then I may no longer want to."

At the conclusion of a long dinner, the Duc de Fronsac, practically drunk, used "thou" when speaking to him, which was impossible and absurd had Fronsac been his ordinary self. The prince, rendered sober as if by magic, said to him: "M. de Fronsac, we are spoken of as being friends: do not let us be spoken of as being ridiculous." There was a gracious elegance in thus taking upon himself part of the ridicule which could reflect only upon the man whom he reproached.

As he was one day M. Le Voyer's guest, either in Paris or at his host's country house les-Ormes, the conversation fell upon a quarrel between the great Condé and the Comte de Rieux. The latter having been struck by Condé, had used his plate as a weapon against the hero of Freiburg, Nordlingen, and Lens. Condé was for that exiled to Chantilly, and Rieux sent to the Bastille for a few days. M. de Voyer was of the opinion that they ought to have fought a duel, in spite of the King's opposition, and he finally asked the Duc d'Orléans if he thought likewise. "I do not pride myself," replied the prince, "on having an opinion about what could never happen to me," and turned his back on Le Voyer. I heard this story from the Comte de Lauraguais, who witnessed the incident.

A stupid Chevalier de Saint Louis met him as he was alone and going up the steps of the Palais Royal. Accosting him, the Chevalier exclaimed: "I believe I have the honour of speaking to his Highness the Duc d'Orléans."—"I do not believe you believe it."

I know many more repartees and sayings of his which make me feel sure he must at heart have been very much astonished at the company he kept towards the end of his life.

It was easy to sway him and to convince him, because he had little intelligence and was, besides, very credulous. He made up for this lack by excellent taste and a sharp and light humour which never betrayed his moral depravity. His excessive self-conceit, coupled with an even more extreme carelessness, led him to commit a thousand mean deeds, from which this very self-conceit, which is a distant relative of pride, ought to have protected him; and as he was timid as well as shamelessly impudent he did not know how to draw back when once he had gone astray. Eminently impressionable and revengeful, it was by these two passions he was driven to the crimes to which he was urged. He committed them without remorse, but with ill grace, for, as I have said before, if they did not frighten him, they nevertheless seemed to worry him. This is all the more easily explained, since the demagogues with whom he lived in the later part of his life, and from whom he sought distraction in torrents of champagne, were repugnant to his vanity as prince; and of this he possessed a fairly good allowance, though he had far too little pride as a man. Indeed, he was endowed with as much vanity as a man could have who attached importance to no single thing, for he believed in nothing. . . . Since he had an unsound mind and a heart seldom moved, it became easy, after his early revolutionary errors, to bring him to think he could no longer hope for pardon. And as his vindictive feelings knew no rest he

imagined that the court would know no pity. Mirabeau, who at
one time intended to make him at least a lieutenant-general of
the realm, so as to reign under him, chiefly impressed that belief
upon him. One could have led him to almost any crime by assuring him it was the last, and one which would absolve him of all
others.

This prince, although timid, was a free-thinker, in the broad-
est and most dangerous sense of the word: he cared for none of
the things of this world, not even for life itself, which he has
been accused of loving too dearly, not even for money, which
he collected without delicacy in order to spend without discernment. Crime and virtue were one and the same to him, discredit
or consideration were but creations of the mind, all human
actions a matter of indifference. The material pleasures of life
had value in his eyes; they were the only metaphysical certitude
he had acquired concerning what we encounter in this world and
hope for in the next; he was so constituted as to find his fill of
pleasures before he had become weary of them. Gall would have
said that he had the voice of a tippler rather than that suited
to conspiracies. This is true, since Nature granted him the one,
and those who managed him grafted the other upon it. As he
was heard one day to declare aloud, and in bad taste, that public
opinion was not worth a farthing, some people thought he had
thus set his own measure and proclaimed his own worth. But
those who have known him and have been aware that he was a
good father, a good husband (with the exception of a few
infidelities such as never cause unhappiness to the woman who
is kept ignorant of them), an indulgent master who never could
refuse anyone face to face, a man fond of private life, those
people might say correctly that he was an immoral man lacking
character, but might be inclined to add that less severity on the
part of the court and public opinion, a better education, and
good counsellors would have endowed him with the appearance
of an honest man and the repute of an amiable and easy-going
prince. His imprisonment, the Revolutionary Tribunal, his trial,
his journey to death through the streets of Paris, the scaffold,
even his own execution must have been for him, *badaud* that he
was at the core, a real stage display. He had seen many heads
fall, notably the most sacred of all; he had inspected the work-
ings of the guillotine as those of a rare device; he must have
viewed the preparations for his own destruction in the same
spirit and, so to say, stood as spectator at his own death.

I have perhaps spoken of this prince at too great length; but without him the Revolution, which was not of his own making, could never have become an accomplished fact; after M. Necker he stands out as most guilty.

The Duc de Luxembourg, who, once the first presidtnt of the nobility, had left France after the meeting of the three orders— an event he had tried his hardest to prevent—was also then in London. He was far more intelligent than has been generally acknowledged, and displayed a lovable and attractive disposition. Many people had imagined he would side with the innovations; his stormy youth when Marquis de Royan, and even the mistakes of his father, had unfavourably prejudiced many minds as regards his likely conduct in such solemn circumstances. The uncertainty was brief, it took him little time to choose. Nevertheless, I have often heard it said that he hurried far too much and had, in his departure, displayed pusillanimous haste. Such is the opinion of men for whom any opportunity to find fault is always precious; it is not mine.

Through compliance with the King's wishes he had been forced into a course of action he had always opposed with all his might. He had once, during a long conversation with his Majesty, victoriously expounded all the dangers of calling together the three orders; he had proved that by this very act the monarch's authority would find itself deprived of protection and support, while the people's will would rule, knowing no moderation nor obstacles. Louis XVI, whose judgement was too sound not to feel the strength of these arguments, yet did not allow himself to be convinced. Accustomed as he already was to giving in, on all points, to a revolution to which he was later to offer himself for sacrifice, he silenced his reason out of a love for what he believed to be the public good. He gave orders; as a faithful subject one could but obey.

M. le Comte d'Artois, uneasy about the future of his exalted brother, sent a pathetic letter to the order of the nobility, which helped to end M. de Luxembourg's irresolution. He had fulfilled his duty as a subject, he had sacrificed his own opinions to those of his master, he had actively lent help to a course of action that both his judgement and his conscience disapproved; who could exact of him that he should further sanction by his presence and, what is more, by his deeds, decisions he had censured and a scheme which both his heart and his mind altogether condemned? He chose to live in peaceful obscurity rather than

remain any longer on a grand stage where he would have liked
to hold the boards as much as anyone else, but where he soon
realised that in view of opinions then prevalent one could act
only a vile part. He remained consistent with himself and
showed greatness of character. This is how I heard him expound
the matter himself, in its principles, and without bragging or ill
temper. Those who put his departure from France down to
fear should have credited it to his sagacity.

I do not forget that it was at his house that I for the first
time saw and heard the famous Burke, who had become his
friend through M. de Calonne. I have elsewhere printed a
testimony of my gratitude for the touching way in which Burke
welcomed me to England after the tenth of August, and all the
heart-felt and sensible things he said concerning my country's
calamities. His heart was as lofty as his gifts were remarkable.
English to the backbone, as he was right to be, he paid signal
tribute to the French nation, which he esteemed because he
knew it well; to its literature, its arts and fame in various ways.
When, some time later, he became convinced that I knew English, he asked me, in front of M. de Calonne, to make a translation of his book, which all the more needed translating since
it had been done once before. I excused myself for reasons I
did not give him, for the real one was that a good translation
reflects little credit on the translator, though a bad one does
him much harm.

Burke, the orator of the opposition benches, had changed
his attitude as soon as he realised that opposition was in itself
a danger to the state. This defection astonished some people,
calmed down some others, and rallied a good many to the
throne, his own example proving better than any parliamentary
speeches could do the necessity of standing close to it. It is well
known that he foresaw all the consequences of the French Revolution from the outset, and that, if there are in his eloquent
book some exaggerations, which too much rhetoric still further
makes evident, this work remains nevertheless the prophecy of
a real statesman, a proof of his fine enthusiasm and a monument
to his great gifts. He was perhaps even more ardent in conversation and more abundant. He loved to relate his political
career, and to fire his conversation with the warmth of his old
speeches. He used the past as a touchstone to judge the future;
he earnestly admired the English constitution, though he could
detect in it a few errors inevitable in things human, but he worshipped it as the palladium of a great people's liberties.

Amidst numerous passages of the highest eloquence which I remember of his, I always think of the speech he delivered at Bath or Bristol in disapproval of the American war, and when he had against him the mass of the people. He appeared at a meeting of the electors to deliver this speech, often reputed his masterpiece, in which he explained his attitude. He began with these words: "Gentlemen, I decline the election." In an eloquent peroration, referring to the death of one of the electors, Mr. Combe, struck dead suddenly during the electoral campaign, he spoke these words: "What shadows we are and what shadows we pursue!"

I declare that as early as 1790 I heard him sum up the French Revolution in two hypotheses, and explain it by reasoning which revealed it entirely as it later unrolled itself, on to the advent of the Consulate. He had seen everything except the gigantic stature of the man who would fill up the abyss.[5] Young as I was, my ears were open, and, helped by my own reflections, I thus received a training from him which has at least saved me from being astonished at anything.

The Duc de Luxembourg, without any affectation, avoided the Duc d'Orléans, whom he despised, and came only in slight contact with the French ambassador, for whom he had no esteem and who hated him. The latter was the Comte de Luzerne, brother of the navy minister of that name, but with very different principles. One had just cause for surprise that the court should have appointed him to this embassy, which had now long fallen from its magnificence. He was, morally and physically, a person of much clumsiness, but of so poor an intelligence that he had never met any obstacle between his ambition and his promotion. He respectfully kept up with the proceedings of the Constituent Assembly, always answering its stupidity by his own baseness, and he would call himself *monar-chien* to be ever ready to destroy the monarchy. He had formerly been minister of the King in the United States (which, to tell the truth, was scarcely the way to the embassy in London) and had badly digested all he heard there. All his ways were contemptible and ambiguous, and the one man he compromised more than himself was the King of France. He was in good faith only over his mad infatuation for a Mme Saint A——, an astute courtesan and mistress to Lord Ch——, who acted according to rule, for she made fun of him and of a love that made him look still more ugly.

As he was more attached to his post than lucky in the means

he employed to keep it, he was soon forced to resign, after giving one of those thousand oaths which were then demanded without any expectation that they would be observed. This he had not foreseen, still less his death, which happened soon after. I can never forget how M. de Luxembourg would take pleasure in tormenting him by expounding theories of despotism, and how Luzerne defended himself *with two Chambers and a balance of Power;* all this put forward laconically because no man can long talk irrationally, yet keep an appearance of reason. Good folk! To argue out at sea about the building of a ship when the one which carried them had sprung a leak and was on the rocks.[6]

In that drawing-room of the Comte de Luzerne, where those light encounters took place, a few women chatted with a frivolity to match this fencing. There was the Duchesse de Laval, red as a fighting cock and sour as an unripe crabapple, angry at getting old, bitter at never having been pretty, although she would have you treat her as if she had been so. There was Mme d'Ossun, sister to one of the Duchess's former lovers, a man who had played that part with all the women who could promote his fortune. Mme d'Ossun was an interesting, sentimental blonde, almost beautiful, who had to uphold a reputation of virtue. She had married a highly estimable man of probity, of whom Louis XVI was rightly fond, as he always was of all honest people; Ossun had been appointed delegate to Russia in the place of the Comte de Ségur. There was, again, a little Mme de La Luzerne, née Mon——, who looked rather like a ruffled squirrel whose nuts have been taken from it. But before the ladies, I ought to have mentioned M. de B——, who never disclosed himself, or very little, and who, cold and reserved as a prime minister, seemed to have some secret knowledge of his ultimate future that nearly cost him so dearly. He was the watchful spirit in this household.

As far as such life went, it provided me with a vast field for study and observation in various ways; yet the ardent passions of youth needed some other food. I then most pertinently made the acquaintance of Mistress Pove,[7] a woman of eccentric and piquant character such as is often met with in England, and of a beauty as out of the ordinary as was her disposition. The adventures these qualities brought to her would not be unworthy of appearing in a novel.

Of a respectable family, she had, when a girl, once gone on

a journey to Canterbury with her mother and one of her sisters. A man of quality belonging to the county of Kent conceived a wild passion for her. Three women in a post-chaise going along the highroad can keep no one in awe, above all if their driver has been bribed. So, towards the evening, they were stopped by some men whom they took for highwaymen, a common nuisance in England, where, however, the natural kind-heartedness of the nation nearly always prevents murder. This does not alter the fact that these constant holdups and robberies cause many unfavourable reflections concerning a government otherwise so excellently conducted. But without entering into details more fit for the police, let it be sufficient to say that the frightened women were made to leave their coach in great haste, and that amidst the uproar and panic the young Cecilia was thrown into a post-chaise which drove off swift as lightning and took her (so at least she believed) to Devonshire. There she was kept in seclusion for a few months, having to submit to the caresses of a man who frightened her with his love-making and his threats. Then her ravisher took her to Ireland, and, after loading her with presents, gave her back her freedom, and went off to Italy.

Whatever she told me to the contrary, it seemed to me that she had grown accustomed to her bondage, and that her tyrant often knew how to win forgiveness, for it would be valuing too highly the power of fear to explain thus the silence of the offended party, as well as that of the law to which she could have appealed. An Irish peer was her second lover; she thought this a matter of course after what had happened to her. . . . One can never too deeply imbue young girls with the idea that the start of life is its most interesting part; it is the prelude which influences the making of one's future for good or bad. Lord D—— worshipped Shakespeare, and his taste for reciting verse amounted to a mania. He burdened Cecilia's memory with all the most famous passages from the poet and imparted to her voice a declamatory tone, and to her body a habitually dramatic movement by which all her gestures were affected. That was the only blemish to spoil a beautiful and magnificent figure.

The gallant man had a nephew with a pleasing face, who had read few verses and never wrote any, but who was twenty, a lucky age when one can show little wit in most things and yet appear to have much. He served his dear uncle with a rascally trick, for suddenly one fine morning he carried off his unfaithful mistress; and, to play the game to the full, he gave her a child. He travelled a little with her and brought her back to London, where he studied law and she gave birth to his child. A son— who, as he has proved to me since, meant little to him—came to strengthen ties already so mixed with numerous others.

Mr. Pove (this was the nephew and seducer's name), caring less for fatherly duties than for their attractive preliminaries, endeavoured anew to seek mothers in wives of a temporary choice. Cecilia heard of this and did better than to quarrel; she took her revenge. (Nothing is so bad a training for virtue as to begin life by being raped.) She left him for a wealthy man who could give everything happiness might wish for, and who would have done so, had she not gone suddenly back to her lawyer, from whom apparently she needed to be parted in order to feel that she loved him. She was cooling in her love when they came together to dine with C——, in former days colonel of an Irish brigade in the service of France. I was present at the feast; and after having much looked at her I told her I should come to love her; she assured me she would be pleased to pay me back. A week or so later she told me the same thing by a kiss on the lips, and soon after by her whole body. The result was a very lively pastoral. The shepherds in "Astrée," [8] on the banks of the Lignon, could not have done it. She would spend with me six hours a day, without detriment to many a night.

Mr. Pove, lost as he was in the busy life near Temple Bar, in the drunken atmosphere of taverns and gambling dens, took long to realise the dreadful truth. As soon as he had knowledge of it, he cheered his grief with a joke of peculiar taste, which I found detestable. He did me the honour of sending me his offspring; I received his child together with a letter. The former screamed, the latter said nothing except that it was only right not to part a mother from the fruit of her womb, and that he would be much obliged to me if I took care of them both. I believed him mad, and I advised the woman whom I had heard him call his wife to make sure of this by flying to Hector and bearing her little Astyanax with her. This she did, and I en- treated her to remain for good by the side of this unnatural father whose views seemed to me too queer.

She followed my advice for a while, but her inconstancy soon placed her in the arms of a strolling player who acted as lead in tragic plays. She had fallen in love with him in the part of

Romeo, in which he had made his début either at Drury Lane or Covent Garden. Having become his Juliet, she followed him to Scotland. She took there the parts of Mistress Siddons, whom she did not throw into the shade, though she was more appreciated than this great actress by a baronet who, enthralled by her charms, offered her his heart, which she rejected, his wealth, which she despised, and finally his name and his hand, which she had the kindness to accept. She has deported herself all the more virtuously since, in the respectable part of spouse, as her husband, acting a tragedy with her, has kept her locked up nine months in a year in a tower which is not enchanted. "What baneful peace for gifts so great."

Why are such marriages, so uncommon in France, so frequent in England? Are there not two plausible reasons to be found? The first being that our neighbours set less store by birth than we do; the second, that, more fastidious than we are as to what is expected after marriage, they are less so as regards what has preceded it. These are opinions which can both be defended, though they are more a matter of feeling than of judgement. . . . On my part, I confess that, though I might find pleasure in leading my neighbour's wife astray, I should very much prefer my own to be chaste on reaching my bed, and that she should thenceforth live free from blame in my house. I further confess that of the two evils, I should prefer the least: which would be to have chosen a wife who misbehaved herself after I had married her, for in this alternative her improper conduct would in fact be independent of my will, and I could not have foreseen it. In the other alternative I should knowingly become a party to her shame and defy the disgrace of both past and future. Who will dare decry celibacy, which escapes this last danger and preserves one from all others bearing on this question? Alas! there are unfortunately too many weapons against it, independent of the reproaches incurred by it from social institutions; it makes life a burden and turns death to gall. Children of Eve, while you are young, let yourselves be deceived by women so that when old you may be consoled by their tender attentions! Their voice is no longer deceitful when their hair has turned white, and their weak hand is yet a support. At the approach of death, man, burdened by the weight of years, staggers; woman is less enfeebled because she has expended less energy; when the end of the journey comes she relieves her companion, saying: "I shall marry again."

But a point on which Englishmen are without question wiser than the French, is in the matter of courtesans. Not a single one in London makes a show of costly luxury such as often scandalises all Paris. Not a single one boasts a house built from the ruins of those of twenty idiots who, while these ladies disport themselves on golden beds, would sleep in the street if their creditors did not see to it. Not a single one, driven in a triumphal chariot, appears in the front row at the theatre, glittering with the diamonds of prostitution, to give offense to public morals, alarm respectable matrons, and proclaim to the daughters, by an eloquent silence, that there exists one vice better rewarded than all the virtues. One can in London, as in any other town in the world, buy *ready-made love,*[9] but none of those who sell this commodity have risen to such heights of opulence as I have seen certain *misses* amongst us. Most Englishmen confine their affairs to the usual type of such accommodating beauties, form an acquaintance with them for the hours of pleasure, and seldom bind themselves by a lease of faithfulness; they enquire more about their health than their constancy.

I have known many a man of mark whose mistress lived at a procuress's, and who would rather visit her there than take her away. If now and again a man removes his mistress from such a place and furnishes rooms for her or takes her to live with him, it is because there exist upon earth secret sympathies and ties. It is then that seduction reaches its full height; such cases often end in marriage. It must be granted that their streets and their theatres are swarming with these inferior followers of Laïs, openly displaying the cynicism of gross debauchery. But this seduction is bereft of peril; it is impotent vice whose symbol is a barren tree. In this sort of thing, this most fastidious of nations might, and indeed must, be reputed the most corrupt.

Mistress Pove was the only idol at whose feet I burned incense during that journey. It would be making bad use of my memory to recall any other objects of more fleeting attraction.

I renewed in England my acquaintance with a lady renowned for her learning and her love of *belles-lettres,* Mistress Montagu.[10] She had erudition and was what the English call a blue-stocking. Exclusively English, like most people of that nation, she had a passionate love for her country amounting to fanaticism, and she valued nothing but Shakespeare and works springing from British soil. She would honour us with some esteem, but so second-rate that I disregarded it. Yet she displayed exquisite politeness towards foreigners, whom she welcomed at a big and handsome house, especially putting herself to some trouble with the French, who alone, so far, had found favour in her eyes. She had more than once taken up the cudgels against Voltaire—who condescended to lend himself to such playfulness—in favour of her hero Shakespeare. In these lively discussions she had risen to all the exaggeration of credulous enthusiasm which partiality may reach even in the arts. And he had replied with a moderation which he cannot always be praised for having displayed, but which he knew how to blend with extreme politeness when he spoke to women—or to men whom he wished to treat as he did the sex. And thus this old gladiator, playing with his opponent, neither of them very young, he, the wolf, and she, if not the lamb, the sheep to be shorn, would instruct and refute her, but never once convinced her. She condescended to have a tender heart for Corneille; but her disease was desperate: the unfortunate woman did not like Racine! And to prove herself even more guilty she pretended to understand him. This excellent woman could view the Achille of "Iphigénie" only as a French beau, and looked upon "Athalie" as a tale for children. . . . She lived and died entertaining such thoughts.

You who, born in her country or in other lands than France, may have the misfortune to share that barbarous opinion, take my word for it, you have no ear for the music of this great poet; you have not unravelled the mysteries of his genius. I fear one must have been born French wholly to understand this great man; yet he will rise in triumph above all those unfair decrees which most people of all nations put forth. Being equal to Virgil and greater than Euripides, he will forever remain the delight of all intelligent men who have felt his genius, and he will prove the despair of his weak imitators. But for this, dear lady, one must possess the French tongue better than you knew it. One must not exclusively relish tombs, stakes, scaffolds, cemeteries, imps, and witches; one must have been early initiated to all the refinements of his style, the delicacy of his expressions, as well as to his faithful pictures of the storms of the heart; one must love the Greeks and delight in their theatre to be able to enjoy his pure fancy, to be ravished by so natural an art as his, the truly Athenian mechanism of perfected tragedy. Ah! let us leave this Shakespearean literature to those for whom it suffices. Let us be satisfied to have brought back to life a Greece envious of our stage, to have introduced more philosophy and pathos into our drama than there is in that of the ancients, and to have surpassed them in their own science.

I agree with you, madame, that Shakespeare is a great man and a fine painter, but he has not achieved a single picture, nor erected a single monument that, while displaying his genius does not also bear witness to the bad taste of his century and especially his own. The roughness of his age has so far found its way into all his works that one may be allowed to doubt whether he would have shown more taste in another age. You know it well—one pays for a fine scene with two acts of boredom and for one true picture with twenty that are unnatural. Your own nation, madame, is divided as to his merits; a great many of your countrymen do not appreciate him as highly as you do, another class of them do not approve of him, and Mr. Hume, one of your most distinguished writers, said that he appeared all the more gigantic because he was so deformed. In France we give more reasoned thought to our pleasures; a few draperies thrown over a shapeless model do not reconcile us to a colossal statue lacking gracefulness and proportion. We have been rather rashly accused of being frivolous, we who can be charmed only by correctness and reason; it is true that we demand elegance.

I do not think I have yet mentioned the gambling houses of London, those dark haunts, the anterooms of Hell; they are so numerous that every street offers a snare for inexperience and cupidity. They alone would deserve a chapter if I could find time and the inclination to penetrate into these dens of desolation; it would need a pen of steel, dipped in blood. One trait will suffice: they are more noxious and more dangerous than ever were those of Paris. Drunkenness, the predominant vice of the English, gives birth to more daring swindlers and more docile victims. Besides, in France (except in the lowest type of gambling den) there were nearly always women at these gatherings, and although they were not the best company, the habits of their sex restrained the desperation of the most ferocious gamblers. For the rest, I have seen in London such a passion for gaming seize the foremost ranks of the nation that the heaviest losses have been incurred in the highest society and amongst the most distinguished women. More than one lady has in a few nights wrecked her whole life and that of her family. But it is not of this class of house I wished to speak, though it is sad to be exposed by sheer chance and fashion to courting ruin in order to live in good company. I had in mind to mention only those low dens where anyone can enter forthwith and be robbed without ado.

If I were king, two scourges would disappear from my kingdom: gambling and begging. . . . One might maintain in good faith and with sound logic that gambling is more odious than theft; the thief is known as such and punished, the gambler is honoured; he thrives on the tears of the fallen, yet society grants him full honours.

My recollection, if so I wished, might lead me to draw a picture of a very conspicuous personage.[11] I might perhaps succeed in portraying him in his real likeness, in spite of the mobility of his moral disposition, and the inconstancy of his manners. But there are proprieties which nothing can make us forget; they allow me to say only that some men Nature has treated with such liberal munificence that her favours counteract fickleness and its mistakes, and that her gifts survive systematic misconduct. This was more or less explained to me by an old courtier [12] whom I knew too little, his acquaintance coming too late. He still displayed the good taste and style of the lords of the good old days and complained that in England people of his rank had forgone this ancient demeanour for a style both petty and spare which the frivolity of fashion had introduced.

"Sir," he would say, "we used to dress in former days from your wardrobe; but the fashions you sent across to us from Calais to Dover were not only graceful, they were dignified. I spent my youth in following them more or less closely, for I have always felt an aversion to rushing rapidly to extremes. I have retained of that, in my riper years, a certain *French touch* which marks my gestures, my bearing, and even my speech to an extent that has sensibly softened *our insular stiffness*.[13] There exists *a happy blending of what is best in the two nations, and this should be* cast into shape and adopted by all the decent people on each side. . . . *It is to this study I owe the little worth I possess.* . . . I see to-day most of our young men transformed into stable-boys; politeness, a virtue in which we have never greatly shone, is disappearing. Our nation retains only *eccentricity of character,* but this is so varied that here more than anywhere else one man stands out from another. That, however, is not enough.

"A young man in our days thinks himself sufficiently English if he speaks with enthusiasm of his country, without really knowing what great things his country has achieved. He believes himself a Roman because the common people have boxing bouts at the crossroads; and he delights in cock-fights because they are a symbol of war. Our unconquerable navy is brought into all his talk. He keeps on his riding boots three-quarters of the day, and gets drunk in order to do something. He would willingly, as they did in Rome, make himself vomit before sitting down to dinner; but to take off his hat would not seem to him civil; and the best of styles appears to him, on those rare occasions when he enters a drawing-room, to treat women in the worst style, *by using oaths in front of duchesses, and stretching out on the sofa instead of seating himself.*

"*You have, on your side, made even a poorer bargain:* you have tried to imitate us, which was doing what is most opposed to your nature. What might present no dangers here, will be full of peril in your country. *I have travelled in France; your nation requires decorum, and that each class should keep strictly to itself.* An inexplicable mania has caused you to forgo *this polite dignity so characteristic of the French nobility;* you have bridged the gaps which should remain wide open. I look for *your great names;* I enquire if *they still figure on a grand stage,* I am informed that many bearing these names *hide behind the curtain or in the wings and are unable to act any part;* I ask if there still exist *a Montausier, a du Guesclin,*[14] *a Sully, a Turenne,*[15] *a Couci, a Fénelon, etc.* The reply is, yes. What are they doing? Nothing, sir. These people ought to have continued the tradition of their ancestors. I go further, the King, your master, should have *compelled them,* in some way, to emulate their ancestors. I should have given them high posts, even had they been burdened by them, and I should have obliged them to keep up their ancestral station, at least in society, and to remember their fathers without causing their children to blush."

"Very good, my lord," I exclaimed. "It is all very fine. . . . The Great Chatham himself could not have spoken better. You are as spirited as the knights of old, but it is the last spark of a fire you will try in vain to rekindle. The days of analytical philosophy have arrived. More than ever, great families need to-day to win back credit through great deeds; fine gold must sometimes be spread anew over the letters of illustrious names if one wishes to make them readable again; and I very much fear that in order to win respect no name is now high-sounding enough if no fine qualities go with it. No order from the King can give back great men to a house that no longer has any; just as there is no gardener who can cause a plant to grow if the seed is not in the ground. Ancient names are like old castles; when the foundations are undermined, it is difficult to renew the façade. Europe needs a new education to guide it in its new ways and to replace its ancient prejudices, which, while bestowing consideration on some people, acted as a brake on others, and so protected us alike from license and slavery.

"But truth is to be found only in a middle path; for if we tread underfoot ancient institutions, we shall learn to our cost that what are termed prejudices are the indispensable conditions on which rest society and the vital parts of the body politic. Yet, on the other hand, a sleepy aristocracy that feels no obligation but to display its titles in arrogant repose [16] must learn that it is stricken at heart and doomed to perish; just as a nation where public opinion [17] no longer has any force must become the prey of arbitrary power and fall into the hands of a despot. So we must reinforce our reasoning on the foundation of a compromise, and not claim that great families should always produce great men, but insist that when they do they should be treated with more veneration; that is to say, to demand of the people respect towards the nobility, but of the nobility respect towards itself for the sake of the people. In a word, my lord, long wars [18] or new customs, otherwise the eighteenth century is the hegira of our destruction."

As I was coming away from this conversation, partly feudal and partly philosophical, I met the Marquis d'——, officer in the gendarmerie, murdered so ferociously since on one of the estates of M. de Cl——. His clothes looked frightfully unkempt, an indication of the deepest poverty; his eyes were hollow, his face haggard as if already livid from the death he was to undergo. Since I was lucky enough to provide him with the help which in his hunger he gave me no time to offer, he assured me that out of gratitude he would make my fortune. Urging him to explain himself, I found he had lost his mind; I could scarcely laugh when he whispered in my ear that he had found the philosopher's stone and the art of never dying.

"Do not offend me by expressing doubts," he went on in a tragic voice, "or you are not worthy of making the acquaintance of the most eminent prophet, the Chevalier de Saint-Yldro, who is no other than the successor of the great Cosma, who handed over to him at Memphis, more than a thousand years ago, his secrets and his art, previous to joining Jesus Christ. The Chevalier demands blind faith, and with the best will in the world I cannot put you into touch with the master, and make you share his invaluable bounties, unless you bring him a docile heart."

I pinched myself to make sure I was awake. I asked him to come with me to a café (the Cocoa Tree) to prevent his preaching on the pavement, *populi stante corona*, and to let him expound further both his theory and his madness. He continued: "The man who transmutes metals into gold, and gold into diamonds, the conqueror of death, will prove to you beyond doubt that he was present at the siege of Constantinople by Mohammed. You will see his wife, Princess Irene, whom idiots will tell you was beheaded by that same sultan who had raped her. For this is how history is written and, what is worse, how it is read. But hear something still more astounding: my master, who will become yours, was at Palermo, at the Sicilian Vespers, and not having been able to pronounce the word *Ciceri*, he received there ten dagger thrusts, five in the heart. He pretended to be dead, and then went off by boat. You will see his genealogy; he is a descendant of Ægialeus, brother to Osiris, and through the female line he comes in direct descent from Isis. The brilliance of the greatest reigning families is very faint, as you see, compared to this; but what will touch you more, a man of feeling such as you are, is that he, and he alone, was the *Man in the Iron Mask*.

"You may well imagine, dear friend, that I only impart to you such special details in my strong belief that you will become one of us. . . . What am I saying? I see by the attention you pay to my words that you are already with us and listening to me with your heart. Well, learn then, my fortunate friend, that benevolent philanthropy is a natural virtue in the immortal chevalier. Towards the year 1640 he journeyed to France in order to bring thither such important revelations that, if they had been made use of, we should have escaped the Revolution, this Revolution which has left me without a shirt to my back. He was treated as you have just learnt because he told the truth to that rascal Mazarin, and finally, after that, to the proud Louvois, whose victim he became. He still preserves a liking for dainty linen and a mania for using the point of a knife for tracing hieroglyphs upon a silver plate. But in the end

he acted again the part which had met with such success in
Sicily: that of a corpse. They buried him in that Bastille, which
has since been knocked down by boobies. He saw to it that
Cagliostro, who was then his valet, but who has since . . . but
then he was . . . faithful, and his master was disinterred
through his care, and went to rest in Pekin for a few years,
where the Princess Irene was waiting for him. There he became
prime minister. These adventures are not," he told me, nodding
his head, "at all ordinary."

"No," I replied, "but a man who never dies is even less so."

"Excuse me," he replied, "it is more common than you think;
we are fifty-six in the universe; you will be the fifty-seventh, and
the figures will reach sixty: there the master's power of dispensation does stop. Jesus Christ, to whom he will introduce you,
and whom he sees at least once a week, alone has after that
the power of immortalising; but we have been warned that it
is only under most peculiar circumstances that he makes use of it.
You will be quite free to enter into communication with persons
of your family, dead these fifty years, or to see once more a
friend or mistress for whom you mourn. He will make you so rich
that after a few days you will feel no more pleasure in being so.
You see me rather shabby, and the loan you have kindly obliged
me with bears witness that my finances are for the moment in
disorder, but you must know that the Chevalier has locked himself up in the dark-room all this week. He is at work with the
philosopher's stone on behalf of two northern monarchs who
will bring Louis XVI back to sit once more on his rather worm-
eaten throne, as it was called by M. de Mirabeau at an evening
séance where people made free to laugh at him. To-morrow my
master will reappear, scattering forth gold dust, looking more
striking than the opal and more brilliant than the sapphire born
of his hand."

The Marquis d'—— stopped speaking. I was stupefied; he
was in earnest!

"I had always believed until now," I told him, "that God
or His Son did not show themselves in such friendly fashion to
the elect, and that if one had once seen them, one lived for ever
in their glory; I had always thought that the philosopher's stone
was to be found only in a well-ploughed field. I confess that I
was not quite prepared for the idea of immortality upon this
earth, and I have often given thought to the inconvenience it
might occasion in the long run, especially if one were so rich

as to have nothing left to desire but death. I nevertheless congratulate you upon your intimacy with a personage who will help you to find again what you seem to lack, health and money. I say health, for I do not suppose that your friend wishes to render you imperishable, and yet leave you in poor health, which would be more dreadful than not to live at all. I know quite well that life is like a mistress of whom one complains all day long, yet goes to bed with every night; but still, she must not be a burden if she is to prove a benefit."

"Look here," he exclaimed, interrupting me, "you talk jestingly and seem to laugh at me, which I do not like. Let us put a stop to it. I can smash your doubts to atoms. Where can I meet you the day after to-morrow, about six in the evening? Please tell me?"

My only risk was boredom; yet it might be curious; I accepted.

The disciple was punctual, but was no longer the same man. His lifeless eyes had a new light in them. His dress was almost dainty; he had apparently enjoyed some rich wine. Drunk, as he almost was, he appeared less mad, and his earnestness less gloomy. He came to fetch me in a coach.

"Where are you taking me?"

"To the holy of holies, to Chelsea, where the vicar of the Highest is to-night holding a séance almost in your honour and that of three believers. You are still lacking faith, but you will soon be converted."

How keep from laughing? How could I foresee the way this show would end? How could I control my astonishment at seeing a man who had always been well balanced, suddenly transformed into a credulous idiot? But poverty paves the way to all forms of helplessness and accounts for all its consequences; and even without poverty there is no damage a fixed idea may not do to the mind. Pascal, the great Pascal, always saw an abyss gaping on his left side. It is clear he must have seen it once and fear made him fancy it for the rest of his life. Why should not the Marquis d'—— have seen a river of gold flow at his feet? His master was a scoundrel. . . . But then so many honest men have been that! Has the hermetic philosophy done as much harm as another philosophy which I do not wish to decry too much, because it has been blamed for too many things, and since there are some formidable journalists and some distinguished men of letters who wish it let alone at present, and not made a scapegoat? It must be sufficient to repeat that amongst alchemists, magicians, and people who are nothing of the sort, there are many rogues in the world, indeed a very great many, and no complete virtue anywhere. Cato would get drunk; Brutus was a usurer; and Marcus Aurelius in his youth had found thieving a pleasure.

My absorption in these thoughts did not prevent the progress of our carriage; we alighted at the door of an out-of-the-way house, and were admitted to an entrance hall hung with black draperies and lighted by a silver lamp. The steps which led to the drawing-room were also of the same mournful hue; as was the livery worn by the servants. I saw thirty people from all countries who spoke to one another in whispers and in all tongues.

The great man, the owner of the place, had not yet appeared. D'—— informed me that he was in his private closet, at grips with inspiration, but that, while we waited, his own duty was to introduce me to the Princess born on the stroke of eleven on the evening of February 15, in the year 1436. All the diamonds of Golconda and Masulipatam shone on her head, arms, bosom, and dress. Since there exists a paste which so faithfully imitates diamonds that one must be a lapidary not to be mistaken, I shall not undertake to estimate what degree of confidence one could have as regards the Princess's adornments. But her dress was a delightful success; this crazy woman was pretty. I was likewise introduced to Lord B——, crazier than she was. He was an immortal and a sub-delegate. She spoke with charming grace, but since one judges a woman, even when looking upon her, more with the imagination than with the eyes, her beauty seemed no more genuine than anything else; her charm seemed to me another imposture.

At last the two leaves of a door opened noisily, and a man of tall stature appeared. His sunburnt face was pleasant, his eyes were piercing, his walk studied; he swiftly looked at all the people with more cunning than cajolery. There is no need to say that my sponsor introduced me with comical deference. I lent myself to this, and the master gave my hand an affectionate squeeze, which proved all the more cruel since I have a liking for rings. His first question confounded me. *"Will you love me?"* asked this sorcerer. As I made no reply, d'—— hastened to do so for me, declaring that my fervour had been edifying to him, and that my silence, my surprise, and my faith were equally great. So I was kissed, which is contrary to the custom in this land; I showed some reluctance, the interpretation of which was left *ad libitum*. Our man, having led me to a sofa, made me sit close to him and proceeded with methodical enquiries regarding my age, my country, the day of my birth, my aptitudes and ardours towards the fair sex, all of which became matter of minute investigation. I replied all wrong, and nearly all the information I gave was opposite of the truth.

Suddenly the twenty candles which had given light to the room, went out as if from a magic breath, and I saw appear a ghost of supernatural height, dressed in white, with a red-hooded cloak from which dripped blood staining the long robe. A phosphorescent light played like snakes about his head and sufficiently lighted the room to add to the horror and spare us nothing. This spectre muttered a few strange words that caused the master to shudder in a most natural way. In the middle of the room a furnace, three to four feet wide, was set upon the broken stump of a marble pillar. The metal which it contained was boiling noisily; smoke of a transparent greenish hue rose in spirals to the ceiling. Some of the gentlemen raised cries of rapture, though I might easily have interpreted them as of rage. The sub-delegate compelled them to silence, and pious meditation prevailed. My neighbour was lost in ecstatic contemplation, but was roused out of it by a terrific and prolonged clap of thunder, followed by pitch darkness. Then a faint light from a few stars in the ceiling pierced the gloom. Jesus Christ, bearing his cross, appeared to us. A melancholy expression, but truly divine, showed in his eyes. On his hair, of a golden hue, was a crown of thorns. The cross, of prodigious size, and seeming to me made of wood, he suddenly threw at his feet; it broke like glass with a sharp noise. After wandering about the room he touched me on the forehead. Then he turned towards the audience, and said to them in Hebrew, French, and English, "that he would leave behind peace and his spirit amongst them, and that he entreated us to live united as brothers and to believe ourselves always under his eyes."

A dust of gold, sparkling from his hand, flooded us with torrents of light and gave forth a fragrant smell. The Chevalier then stood up, and finally threw himself upon his knees; he gathered fragments of the cross, and respectfully raised them to his lips before locking them in a golden casket. Jesus Christ put forth his hand to him with great kindness, and they walked

off together to the most deserted part of the room. There they
held a long discussion in low voices. Soon another clap of
thunder was heard and we were once more in darkness.

When God had gone, such light was again granted us that
the room where we sat appeared to have burst into flames. The
conflagration of the palace of Armida could not have been more
dazzling. It gradually died out, but what remained was sufficient
to lend light to the descent from the middle of the ceiling of a
gentleman dead these last fifteen or twenty years, and father to
one of the members of the audience, who had asked to see him.
The scene was a caricature of that of the commander in "Le
Festin de Pierre." [19] He called his son in a loud voice and invited
him in Italian to draw near without fear. The son left his seat,
wished to kiss the author of his days, and fainted. The Chevalier
rang a bell; again darkness. Two valets entered at last, bearing
candles, and every possible attention was bestowed upon the
Marquis Massimi of Milan, who had fallen in a swoon. I do
not know to this day whether he was taken in or was himself
playing a hoax, but his fright appeared to me to be genuine.

The master, having once again kissed me unasked, placed
two fingers upon my forehead at the place where Jesus had
touched me, and I was congratulated upon the composure I had
preserved during this august ceremony. I was assured that at
the first assembly—for this was only an imperfect semblance
of it—secrets would be revealed to me which ordinary people
were far from suspecting, and that I should become affiliated to
the great occult lodge and proclaimed immortal. As I passed in
front of a looking-glass, I saw a golden mark upon my forehead;
my first impulse was to wipe it off, but instead of vainly trying
to rub the skin off, I patiently let it alone.

A handsome supper was served. The guests tackled it like
hungry men and discoursed of cooking and gastronomy like distinguished amateurs. I saw that immortals eat like other people;
could I be surprised at that? Have we not all of us heard of
the banquets of Olympus? And is it not proverbial to speak
of "a feast of the gods"? I was seated by the Princess, who kept
the conversation going with much wit. First we spoke of indifferent things. Not one word recalled what had just passed, not
one allusion. But at last, someone congratulating himself upon
having on the previous day reconciled two persons of his
acquaintance who had wanted to take each other's life, the
famous Chevalier told us that two of his friends had given him

a great deal of trouble in that way, and he even owned that he had never completely brought them together. "They were," he said casually, "Francis I and Charles V of Austria. I was the trusty friend of both. I undertook twenty journeys to make them listen to reason; it was quite against my advice that the battle of Pavia was fought." No one else laughed, but I was seized by laughter I could not quite suppress. "This is wrong of you," said Princess Irene, "even more wrong than not to let your forehead alone; the mark will go of itself."

After supper we went to a rather larger gallery which, with its display of flowers and shrubs adorned with weapons and trophies, was on a small scale like an enchanted forest. The shade of Francis I was summoned; this was punishment for my smile and the last fraud this charlatan produced against incredulity. The French monarch obeyed; he appeared in answer to the voice calling him. He was mounted on a dapple-grey horse richly caparisoned. Admiral Bonivet and some poor devil of a squire, as little known in death as in life, came with him. The dress and bearing of those military days, the weapons, all were in keeping, and, if I may say so, were true to that period. I must even confess that the personage looked like the best portraits I have seen of this royal knight. He wore his beard long after the fashion he had introduced; and, what is more, it badly hid the wound which had made the lower part of his face unshapely. He wept over the misfortunes of his house. Then he came down from his horse, and his squire handed him two swords saltirewise; he offered one to d'—— and the other to me. "May you," he said in a tremendous voice, "handle it nobly and usefully!"

I confess that this scene had a prodigious effect upon my imagination, which wine and the Princess's eyes had already heated. Once again I cannot praise too highly the art and the pathos bestowed upon this serious farce; I could believe it was but yesterday I witnessed it. Above all, were not the two swords a striking symbol of the future and of the cause we were then defending? They were of so fragile a composition that they broke in our hands.

Francis I went away amidst the flourish of martial music; and Princess Irene immediately gave us a warlike song which she sang to her own masterly accompaniment.

"It is thus that in leaving I wish you farewell," said the Marquis d'—— to me. And we left the house.

"Well, sir?" said he to me in the coach.

"Well, sir! it is all very strange, more extraordinary than anything I have ever seen; but your master, as you call him, is neither a sorcerer nor immortal."

"You will believe in his power when you share it; blessed with wealth and years, you will give me news of all this in a thousand years' time!"

We had arrived at my door; we agreed to meet again soon.

My sleep was disturbed; I was not mad enough to find anything supernatural in the events of the evening; it was however impossible not to be astounded after having been so much moved. The enormous expense which the machinery of all these fables involved, a stage erected on so huge a scale, gave one constant food for thought. The next morning I was happy to find that I no longer bore a mark upon my forehead, no more than many worthy married men who have good reasons for finding this part of their heads less smooth and more protruding. As I was engaged in these thoughts the secretary of a foreign prince was announced. This appellation appeared to me quaint; but the servant assured me the visitor refused to give another. He entered; I at once recognized one of the leavings of the supper of the previous day. He was bringing me a receipt for thirty guineas for my installation.

"You quite understand," he told me with a forced grin, "that a man who makes gold does not need other people's money, but this is a *talismanic matter;* it is what we call the *Crucible's maidenhead;* it is the quota belonging to the *secondary spirit* which promotes *germination;* it is the *primordial seed* of the *universal harvest.* Finally it is a *philosophical formality,* for, it is as well to tell you so, in a fortnight from to-day, your Excellency will be richer than you might wish."

My mind became enlightened; the clue to the enigma was given me. I sought an answer; I found it simplest to ask him politely to call again; my door was henceforth closed to him.

"You are perfectly right, M. de Saint-Yldro," I thought. "You do make gold, but you would be soon reduced to copper if your dupes protected their money as I do mine!"

I learned afterwards that an English peer and a very rich Neapolitan who had followed him from Rome vied with each other in courting ruin and in helping the master, though they were unaware of that, to ruin others. One must also mention the charms of the Princess, which, when secrecy and a favourable occasion made it desirable, likewise were proffered.

As for d'——, his faith and zeal were such that there was no longer any remedy for his madness; besides, what risks could a man run who had no possessions left him but a black coat and a stomach? I was made to listen to his argument about the most illustrious of men and to his grievances concerning the inconstancy of my behaviour. He could already use all the quibbles of his school, and I saw that his case was desperate. I simply assured him that such magnificent discoveries were repugnant to my reason, for they baffled my defective organs, and I made him agree this was a thing I could not apparently conquer, since I was willing to forego so brilliant a future. He no further understood me when I confided to him that such huge treasures frightened me even more than eternal life, though I wished it for him. The poor wretch would have done better to hunt for that, than to return to France to find a most frightful death.[20]

Lord L——, son of the Earl of D——, who had been in a position to know the alchemist Saint-Yldro, gave me some information about him that enabled me to retrace the first steps of this adventure.

He had been born on one of the islands of the Archipelago, from a Greek father who had made a fortune in the diamond trade. The son, having been up to mischief, had run away to Smyrna with a handful of pearls, and diamonds, white, red, green, and yellow. There he had become acquainted with a professor who had robbed him, and paid him back by giving him lessons. Then he had knocked about the world and found scope for his activities in Italy, at that time the natural stage for charlatans. While in Florence, he became acquainted with a courtesan born to help him; he made of her the Princess Irene. When he had reaped an abundant harvest in that country, and devoured some of the church's wealth by means of two cardinals who later reported him to the Inquisition, he came to London, but did not remain long among these sensible people. I know for a fact that his immortality *died* (momentarily no doubt) in Cartagena. His widow, during his absence, retired to Cadiz; she there hides her diamonds in a useful obscurity and, under another name, busies herself with music and love; her voice is her art, and her eyes are her allurement.

My interview with Francis I brought me bad luck. A few weeks after having had the honour to pay him my court, I caught the disorder of which he died; I mention this with a blush. If I had given my thirty sovereigns with a good grace to the secretary of the Great Maker and paid my attentions to Mme Irene, I might have left England without this shameful memento. But those who blame passions and passing attachments do not know what they condemn or what they enjoin. There is nothing more treacherous than idleness, and everything becomes a snare to the young man who seeks pleasures which have a false semblance to love. I was obliged to confide to a man of the medical art that I had made a mistake. He was scarcely more skilled in his art than his colleague who had attended Francis I, and he tried his best to send me to that King's court in the next world. Luckily I was obliged to leave for Brussels. The disciple of Æsculapius received my money, and gave me a little box which was to work miracles for my health before I reached Brabant. This expectation was more than disappointed, and I found myself all the worse for having carried out his instructions. He had not, however, put it down on his prescription that I should be robbed in the parish of Dartford, ten to twelve miles from London. Three mounted men, with veiled faces, imperiously requested me to give them my money or to let them blow out my brains. This could have been done all the more easily, even against their will, since on awakening as the carriage stopped I found the muzzle of a pistol against my face; it is true that the same attention was paid to me on the other side. These three travellers were in so great a hurry that they condescended to let me off after I had given them forty guineas, my watch, and that of my lackey. I rejoiced at such success, and after landing at Boulogne I immediately made for Brussels.

Here an English friend helped me to choose a skillful man who gave me a new lease of life. He cleared away traces of my error and granted me absolution for my sin, this after a retirement of two months; the penance he inflicted on me was severe, but well deserved. I had ample time to become convinced of the wisdom of the motto, *Latet anguis in herba,* which I could have translated by "The snake hides beneath the flowers." For sixty days I pictured death as being drawn from the very fountain of life, and had genuine cause to remember that Heaven has decreed that man shall not drink nectar except in a cup half full of bitter wormwood.

CHAPTER XXIV

That daring man of Genoa
Set forth with mad wild urge
Another world to discover,
And brought back another scourge.

*C*AN this really be true? A Chinese [1] scholar has assured me
that one of their emperors died of it nine centuries ago.
Semiramis was charged in her time with having given it to both
her husbands, and even to her son. Many other examples might
absolve Columbus of the burden of this execrable importation
which is marked out for the loathing of a great part of Europe
under the name of *mal français,* though we received it only at
third hand. It is true we infected the North of Europe with it.
It is still more true that we are not liked, and that some good
excuse is always found to abuse us. Besides, if governments
would take pride in a vigilant police supervision, this hideous
scourge would soon be exterminated. . . . But I will not ex-
patiate on a matter which in no way comes within the scheme of
this book. I certainly have no objection, now and again, to
portray Love triumphant, but the description of its evils is not
in my line.

By virtue of my youth I had regained the favours of Hygeia;
I went to Aix-la-Chapelle to make sure it was so. Its salutary
waters have a special advantage over others, that of never
doing much harm in any case, and always doing much good
so long as they are not contra-indicated, and that they seldom
are. I cannot too much recommend them. The place itself indeed
is not attractive, though so beneficial; it has the solid sort of
beauty of a comely but slovenly woman. There are many other
spas where one goes either to pass the time or because a mistaken physician has prescribed them, and from which one comes
back to pay during the rest of one's life for the mistake of a
moment.

In this city where so many emperors were crowned, though
it has now fallen from its ancient estate, I found excellent company, and I sought to repair, in my own eyes, the kind of shame

caused by the bad choice I had made, and especially the consequences that had followed it. I resolved, I do not say to attach
myself to Mme d'A——, the wife of a foreign general, but to
occupy myself with her, while having nothing else to occupy
myself with. She was not a perfect beauty, nor very young, but
such charms as still remained led me to believe that she had
once had more and might still please. And her mind, without
being cultivated or of wide range, had rather a piquant turn.
It was she who uttered a witticism I have sometimes heard
unjustly attributed to others. A man whose face and manners
were displeasing to her was wont to pursue her in the Assembly
Hall (the Redoubt), particularly at whist where he had taken
the habit of sitting behind her. "Sir," she said to him one day,
when she had been losing, "I am not rich enough to have you
always so near to me."

I found it too easy to share with her the dangers of my
convalescence, which, fortunately, was not infectious. She would
willingly have attached too much importance to this relationship of a season, had I valued it more than I made clear to her;
but she soon became as reasonable as I was. . . . She soon
indeed had the better of me, for she gave me as partner a
churchman who had formerly been an officer and a courtier.
I say she made him my partner because, coupled to other evidence, I can advance the ill humour he suddenly showed towards me when we had previously been on the best of terms.
A violent quarrel resulted, though after so long a time I cannot
now tell which of us was in the wrong. All I clearly remember
is that he was carried away by temper, and that I went beyond
him, in the presence of the Baron de Batz and the Comte D——.
If M. de la C—— had been a country curé, I would have taken
quite another line, but with a man of his name, and one who had
once almost reached the rank of colonel in the dragoons, it was
necessary to combine two codes of behaviour.

The Comte d'Egmond, a lieutenant-general and a knight of
the Golden Fleece, was then at Aix-la-Chapelle. He was a man
of noted loyalty, who, having all his life displayed the energy of
a thousand fine qualities, had ended by falling into a weakness
common alike to those who are and are not heroes: an inju-
dicious attachment, followed by a still more unfitting marriage.

> If thou rememberest not the slightest folly
> That love made thee fall into,
> Thou hast not loved.

What star has not paled at the rising of some woman? He had married an Irish girl who had at first been on the footing of lady companion to his late wife. She claimed to be as noble as the King, though public opinion persisted in thinking otherwise. I have even seen a song in very bad taste which attributed to her the lowest origin. When the floods of calumny are let loose over someone who arouses envy, no dam will stop them. What is certain is that she was not a suitable partner for a man of his position. But since she followed him into exile, softening its bitterness with the most tender care, and was his consolation and happiness to the day of her death; since indeed, with no great intelligence, but with an easy, equable, and thoughtful disposition, she had so accustomed him to the charms of this union that he could not long survive her, we must conclude that towards the end of his life he had really made a very good match, and was a better judge of what his heart needed than two of his lifelong friends (notably the Duc d'Harcourt), who would have nothing to do with him—very absurdly in my opinion—because he had married to please himself.

It is the duty of friendship, no doubt, to offer good advice to a friend who commits a folly; but it is the proof of friendship to pardon it, and above all to excuse it in society once it is done. Besides, what is pride of birth compared to an affection that is to colour the whole of life? "As ghost to ghost, I am your equal in the grave," said one dead man to another. Can we not say the same in life? Are men much more than ghosts? Why should not one freely choose the ghost with whom one wishes to journey until reaching that bourne where all vanish? The Comte d'Egmond, in spite of all this, was generally esteemed; I decided to go to him. After putting him in possession of all the facts regarding myself and the Abbé, I asked his opinion.

"Matters have gone so far," he replied, "that I advise you to fight with M. de la C——; but at the same time you must remember that to kill him would be very blameworthy, and to be killed by him really ridiculous. You have to reconcile all this." The advice was in fact rather complicated; but I set myself to simplify the question and I succeeded.

I persuaded the Baron de Batz [2] to act as *our* second. M. de la C——, whom he had warned, arrived at the appointed spot where I was awaiting him, and deported himself as in his most military days. De Batz first placed us at a distance of ten paces from each other and declared that we were both to fire at an agreed signal. I stood my adversary's shot, but he reproached me with not having fired on my side. "You are welcome to have another go," I told him, "but I do not fire *when I am in the wrong.*" He tried to insist, asking me with much firmness to take no account of his calling. "I have not said a word about it," I replied. The Baron then took charge of him, made him take my arm, and we turned back. I went to dinner with M. d'Egmond, and he approved of what I had done. "All very well, sir," I said to him, "but you give praise to me which should be given to Fate, for if Fate had let me be killed I should have been nothing but a fool."

Mme d'A——, after this unequal game she had made me play, began to love me to distraction. For my part, I realised that I should never have any serious feelings for her since I felt no greater attachment to her after the danger she had made me run. I had planned for a long time to go to Maestricht to visit M. de Maillebois. He had long led me to think he would receive a high post where I might count on a commission near him, both honourable and pleasant. This was a fine pretext for throwing off a very light chain which now held me only by a thread. The Marquis de D—— having suggested I should accompany him, we set out for Holland where we arrived safe and sound, except for some of those troubles common to all travellers on bad roads, with bad postillions, bad horses, and a bad carriage.

I had specially intended on this occasion to read to the Comte de Maillebois a history of the revolution I was then writing, with the idea of continuing it through the succeeding events as they occurred. Contemporary history is so difficult to write that in following this method, outwardly clear and attractive, I should have been reduced, even had I possessed the pen of a Tacitus, merely to a slender diary, insubstantial and without evidence for the coordination of facts, the sources of which are hidden from men who witness them at too near quarters. There is a special optical illusion needed for the great scenes of life, as for those on the stage, and the spectator's spyglass, even so, can be focussed only on one spot to discover these: viewed from too near, everything is confused; from too far, everything is dim. So I threw my manuscript in the fire. This paternal severity was quite in place, for that fierce party spirit, which spoils even the finest things, so prevailed throughout the work that everyone to whom I then read it gave me praise in all good faith and in excess, though at another time these same people would perhaps have picked a quarrel with me over a mere hemistich or a song.

I came back from Maestricht full of sadness at seeing a man of real merit fallen towards the end of his life into the nets of an old woman, a born intriguer,[4] the sight of whom was a sufficient condemnation of him.

Shall I ever forget how strange it was at that time to hear the *émigrés* indulging in dreams? Every week no less a scheme was put forth than that of returning to France on the following week, granting pardon to one party, punishing another, furnishing the King with a minister vigorous enough to save him from his own weakness *during the rest of the reign,* organising the army on a much stronger basis, mulcting Paris by transferring the seat of government to Lyons, or elsewhere, etc. Innocent castles in the air—so consoling to men who had lost everything and most of whom were destined to find nothing more than a grave on foreign soil. There prevailed such disorder in most minds that I was openly blamed for having dared to say that Mme de Maintenon (who had been mentioned I cannot recall in what connection) was the one blot on the reign of Louis XIV, a king whom no one is more ready than I to call great. Everyone listened to me with marked indignation, and M. de Rabodanges, leaving the room at the same moment, exclaimed as soon as we had reached the stairs: "You have made an unforgivable mistake. I cannot conceive how anyone as reasonable as we all know you to be can attack a memory so closely bound to that of one of our greatest kings. These subjects are sacred, young man, and in such times as these it is not permissible for a good Frenchman to dispute them."

"Mme de Maintenon sacred!" I exclaimed. "And what of Father Le Tellier?"

"Likewise," he replied.

"Well," I said, "have it your way; but be careful not to speak ill of Mme de Pompadour and the Duc de la Vrillière. . . . And I will especially inform against you if ever I hear you speak slightingly of the late Louis XI!"

"Ah," he exclaimed, hiding his face with his hands, "what indecorous jokes from one as staunch as you!"

The well-meaning simpleton!

That was the means, no doubt, which such people proposed for driving back the floods they had let loose! But, reader, I am about to speak on my own account—remain seated if you do not wish to follow me—for I shall give myself the pleasure of saying (especially nowadays when there is a league [5] formed to praise in the lump and without discrimination everything that wears the livery of religious hypocrisy) what a vile woman that Mme de Maintenon was. I can the less repress the desire to do so, since I have just been reading letters and memoirs in which everything that can do her honour is piled up with affectation. and everything that might make her really known is cut out with partiality or disguised without shame. They do not dare to say outright that she never had any lovers, but they infer that it is more than probable she was exempt from such weakness, and that it would be impossible to produce any names with certainty.

"Eat a whole calf, sir, and be honest," the Duc de Montausier used to say to the Dauphin, who was excusing himself for not eating meat on Friday.

"Take men, my dear woman, but do not persecute them, do not deceive them, do not sacrifice them to your ambition, or your idleness or your hypocrisy; do not employ base tricks to rise, in the name of Heaven, from the position where Heaven has placed you. Be *honest* with *them,* and with yourself." This is what I say to you, Maintenon, and what all decent people will repeat, in every country, down to the remotest posterity.

Come back to us, Ninon, and tell us what you know about it, come and confound the panegyrist—you who saw more clearly than he does in this matter—for *she* was your friend. You had her trust . . . you lent her your house, without fear of what might be said. . . . However much a dissembler, she was still a woman. She must have talked to you—on the first occasion at all events. The most reserved heart is never entirely on its guard in matters of love or what resembles it. Villarceaux, Miosans, Vardes, Richelieu, come back to life for us and reveal this truth which it is so *unimportant* to know. And you, King, whom she abused, and whose ministers she seduced in order to lead you astray, could you but defy the grave, would you not yourself proclaim that she alone cast gloom over the end of your immortal reign? Victims of her intolerance (though she was born in your faith), come back to life again to give the lie to the writers who adulate her. Generals and high dignitaries of the realm, you who were compelled to abase yourselves before this ancient Sibyl; [6] princes and princesses of the royal family who were degraded by enforced familiarity or by homage, both alike unworthy of you, come forth to protest against flattery and

imposture. Whether she had lovers or never had them is a matter of little interest; it was likewise quite simple that she should
offer herself as vestal to a monarch whom she debased through
the sole mean deed that can be brought against him throughout
his whole reign: all this can be explained. But can anyone approve the historian who deceives the living out of respect for
the dead, and, because of intrigue, speculation, or party spirit,
does honour to vice by adorning it with the attributes of virtue?
who talks to us of the goodness of heart, the sensitiveness and
the soulful qualities of this elderly sultana, who behaved shamelessly to Mme de Montespan, was a consummate hypocrite
with the King, a tyrant in her own household, and a persecutor
of the Protestants? For such was the vain upstart who by means
of false humility thrust her mediocrity into the greatest matters
of state; who protected Chamillard during the ten years of his
blundering ministry, which yet did not open her eyes [7]; who
basely sacrificed Racine after having brought him forward; who
poured forth her gall in all religious quarrels, displaying the
insensitiveness of a stone, in spite of a pretence at specious and
exaggerated almsgiving; and who was finally impudent enough
to find herself bored in the high station where impudence itself
had helped her to rise.

Will you have a sample of her sensitiveness? See how, sati-
ated with splendour in the midst of luxury and wealth, overwhelmed by those things which perhaps inspire more indifference to life than extreme poverty, she scarcely replies to the
most tender, touching, and noble letter of the Duchess of Mantua
(born a princess of Lorraine and French) whom she had known
from her earliest youth—that Duchess of Mantua who, unhappy
in the extreme without being blameworthy, had only placed herself in the wrong by begging the help of this old gnome whom
she was not born to supplicate. Listen to what this sensitive
Mme de Maintenon wrote to the Duc de Noailles: "Mme de
Mantoue is at Vincennes; I believe she will see the King in my
room once her exile is over. They say she is improved in looks
and very sensible; for the rest she is a Princess of Lorraine,
and useless; she is beginning to fall into disrepute."

So far it might pass. But let us read another letter sent to
the same Duc de Noailles, who was worth more than his aunt:
"The Duchess of Mantua is dangerously ill; she will do no harm
by dying; she is embarrassed and embarrassing. So what reason
is there for her to live?" You are speaking here—old vixen,

staining alike the private and the public life of Louis the Great
—of a virtuous and sensible princess (as you admit yourself),
beautiful as an angel, who was dying in her twenty-fifth year!
. . . You recommend the grave to her! . . . And you, vizir in
petticoats, raised from the dust to a throne which shook under
your weight, and where you have dishonoured your king for
all ages to come, what are *your* reasons for living? I see none
to account for your birth and your long life, save the inexplicable
fatality that rules over the world, and from time to time offers
us strange spectacles. I can explain away your existence only by
the assumption of one of those evil geniuses who, at marked
periods, are sent to disgrace the greatest of kings and to foment
the fall of the greatest empires in preparation for some inevitable future.

I have written these pages moved by indignation, and now
throw down the pen; but I will not strike them out even if they
lead me to quarrel with all the Rabodanges [8] in the world.
"There," would here retort, if he had read this passage, the
little Abbé S——, who was then at Aix-la-Chapelle, and passed
as the author of a good book they say he did not write—"there
is one of those diatribes which deprive a work of sponsors.
I have been present at some of your readings, sir. You have a
brilliant and sinewy style, you draw in fine lines,[9] but allow me
to say that you please few people, for you write for all parties."

"I write for truth, Abbé, or at all events, for what I take
for truth."

"A false notion, sir! In a world such as this, as in a deliber-
ative assembly, one must adopt a side, and give oneself altogether to it even if it is bad—never deviating from the course
once adopted."

"There is nothing straightforward and exalted in such a
plan."

"It succeeds all the better for that."

It was thus that everything went to prove that the Revolution came into being for people who did not deserve it and
against people who deserved it all too well.

I will quote another eccentric person, a M. Senac de Meilhan, formerly Governor of Valenciennes. "I have had long conversations with the King," he said to me. "I almost succeeded
in making him appreciate my views. The state was about to be
saved, as could be fully expected from a man of genius; but they
preferred to me a merely clever man, M. de Calonne, and the

monarchy collapsed. When we return to France they will have to come to me."

This worthy man took to his bed long before he died, and never left it; that was his best piece of work, though he had done much in his time. Such solemn pride and such calm self-conceit have never been surpassed; it would be difficult to find anything to compare with them.

Rivarol, who was a giant compared to this man, is the one instance of pride equal to his. Not that, in spite of the common notion, I recommend modesty to men of great talent—justice will be done to them after their death—but nine times out of ten they are caught in the trap while they are living. This much extolled modesty is like those ancient coins which are treasured like medals, but if used as cash it can be only at a loss.

There is a story about this M. de Meilhan I shall not pass in silence, now that he is dead and that his vanity will not be hurt. A moralist might find in it another instance of the ever-lasting truth that passions in a weak cipher are more dangerous than those of a man of power and strength, while hypocrisy is more troublesome than vice which knows no caution nor shame.

A printer in the town had a very pretty wife. We used to call her Mme de la C——, for she resembled her. She was likewise given to a free life, but I do not know whether she married again while her first husband was still alive. Such a course of action depends on what relish for independence and what degree of spirit one is imbued with, for to divorce in order to marry a lover is an edifying deed. Several of us had been happy with her (I am speaking of the printer's wife) and had no reason to complain. A decent woman has much trouble to find a discreet lover; one who abandons herself to several can hardly hope for a secrecy with which she seems to dispense, though a man of honour should always be bound by it. Yet, certainly, we had behaved wrongly in telling one another of our good fortune, which was ceasing to be one because of too much sharing. M. de Meilhan heard our indiscreet talk and wished to profit thereby. He looked rather ridiculous as a lover, but not everyone needs to please in order to find a mistress. And so he dressed himself more carefully, walked up and down beneath her windows, and applied himself to look at her so that she might look at him. He displayed his ring, he threw a tender kiss, and since he was an author he also wrote. His letter, like his love, was absurd; but the little bourgeois woman noticed that it smelt of powder *à la maréchale,* and that there were rose-coloured vignettes on the gilt-edged paper, with "Loving and Discreet" beneath, and that the seal was *L seule.*[10] She could not fail to puzzle over that. *"L seule?* I have it! *Elle seule. She alone!"* Very new and very touching, was it not? Well, what would have failed in the Faubourg Saint-Germain succeeded in the workshop, that is to say, in the little room at the back of it which the "fair lady" [11] called her drawing-room.

A few days later he very mysteriously drew me and the Vicomte de C—— aside. "Gentlemen," he said, "I know that you sometimes go to the so-called Mme de la C——. I wish to warn you that you run great danger there. I have been nearly murdered by her husband, whom she had concealed under the bed. I escaped only by leaving my purse and my watch behind. It is a den of thieves; be careful never to go there again." This story, told with all the semblance of fright and an appearance of concern and frankness, made us think, and the Viscount declared positively he would never set foot at the printer's again. I was at first of the same opinion; but after recalling to mind the proofs I had of the guilelessness of this woman, her sweet and facile disposition, her terror at the thought of being caught by her husband, her abandonment, and her good faith at those moments when the body reveals the mind, I concluded without a struggle that M. Governor was guilty of a shameless and clumsy calumny, and that this woman was neither a monster nor the accomplice of a murderer.

I went to her next day. I remember that I took with me a little pocket pistol, perhaps more out of habit than as a precaution against fear, for I do not think I even loaded it. Everything happened as usual, and I then repeated M. de Meilhan's horrible story. She laughed at first like a child, but when I reached the most important part of my narrative she became indignant at her accuser's wickedness. She confessed to receiving him twice, in a proper and decorous way; but he had pestered her to perform with him horrors that made her shudder. He had thrown himself at her feet, and offered her all he possessed as the reward for her compliance in chastising him; he had especially begged, as the *ne plus ultra* of happiness . . . a cut with a knife! Oh, man, pitiful man! She had assured him he filled her with terror, and that if ever he or his knife reappeared at her house she would risk the consequences and inform the police. Furious, and trembling at the thought of being discovered, he had hoped by his absurd story to frighten men probably as weak as himself, and to hide from them a secret that apparently would not have been betrayed had it not been for the precaution he took to conceal it. Many people more or less openly made fun of him about it. I own that it did not seem to me a matter for laughter, and I acquired an aversion for him.

What is not the heart of man capable of, when corrupted by social devices? You, who strut like a peacock, be humble, whoever you are. The beasts of the field, which man subjugates to his own ends, are in their instincts less detestable than himself. The Governor consoled himself by a definition of luxury, which he alone, he said, had discovered, and by a translation of Tacitus which he alone could translate. He had undertaken to render this author more concise. What I read of it was intolerable, save for some mistranslations which made one seek, and find, others. I had for a long time wasted my breath upon him, but after the horrid discovery I had made I left him in the hands of another comic personage, though of a different sort. This was a worthy counterpart to the Marquis de Tuffières, but a man of recognised loyalty and knightly honour; he was a boaster, and of a thoroughgoing sort, but this amusing pride had preserved his integrity from all blemishes, and had been a support to him throughout life, maintaining him at the height of his rather exalted concepts of what constitutes the dignity of a great lord. I refer to the Comte d'Escars.

His hair, dressed in a careful and frothy fashion, crowned a long thin face, proudly contemptuous in expression. His coat was tight-fitting and short, the waistcoat embroidered, while ancient trinkets adorned breeches of a pale colour. From early morning he wore shoes with little gold buckles over the instep; his hair was gathered in a net, called a toad, at the nape of the neck; other ornaments were a pretentious stick, the hat he carried under his arm, a pleated cambric collar in which a little diamond shone from afar like the Œil-de-Bœuf itself, and the *cordon bleu* [12] which swelled up beneath the hand placed in the waistcoat; the man walked with measured steps as one who shows off, and looked like a lean courtier who has failed in his last suit. He spoke in the tremulous tones of confidential hesitation, but with noble gestures, and paused a dozen times in fifty paces, so as to emphasise with thumb and forefinger the sense of every sentence. Apart from all this he was the most pleasant man in the world, speaking much to the point about everything,

knowing as much concerning good fare and the chemistry of a
dinner as he did about his family tree and his Horace, and being
as much of a gourmand as a man ought to be who had once
occupied a position such as his was in the household of the King
of France. Listen to him:

"Our alliance, four hundred years ago, with the Royal
House was no dishonour either to it or to us. . . . There has
been much injustice towards the Noailles family [18]; the rapidity
with which they have won favour in modern times has provoked
jealousy, as if they were merely people of yesterday, while they
are all the more old aristocracy since they belong to us. They
stand high in the Limousine region, and they easily rank first
after us. . . ." And here would follow a quotation from
Horace, and then another from Tacitus; for he knew Latin
much better than the pedantic Meilhan. His gallant brother
also knew it equally well.

This latter had from the outset of the Revolution become a
staff officer in the army of a power which has succumbed beneath
the victorious legions of the conqueror of the world. Never was
a man more obliging, more ready to help anyone; a man so
singularly well informed that he was an excellent judge alike of
a good dinner and a good book. As a brave officer, he was so
passionately in love with his profession that he could make it
hateful to those who served under him. He had the good sense
to return to his native country (which it would be best never
to leave) before the downfall of the one he had adopted from
force of circumstances, and where he had not always been
treated with the consideration he had never ceased to deserve.
But in what country of Europe has there ever been any flattering consideration shown to Frenchmen in exile?

I had spent three months at Aix-la-Chapelle; this was
enough; I came back to Brussels, a city which, without boasting
first-rate attractions, yet offers many resources. Besides, I knew
there a good many people and associated especially with the
English, as never fails to happen to a Frenchman when he meets
them on the Continent, in spite of the innate animosity of the
two nations, which esteem though they do not love each other.
Any relationship thus formed has all the appearance of lasting
friendship, though, as both sides know, it will not survive the
crossing of the Channel. If it sometimes turns out otherwise,
the bond of affection is all the more steadfast on account of the
prejudices which have had to be overcome to establish it. I have

besides noticed that the most distinguished men of each nation
are readier to render justice to each other than those passionate
foreign admirers who have so warmly adopted either of the
two countries as to praise enthusiastically everything in the one
and to belittle furiously everything in the other. Their prejudices
strike deeper, and their partiality is more exclusive than those
of any enlightened Frenchman or Englishman. That may easily
be understood, for the foreigner who thus becomes infatuated
with France or with England may be said to be a man who looks
upon himself as without a country, since he feels no esteem for
his own and has attached himself to one which his opinions made
him select. In a word, this man loves the one country because
he hates the other, and having perhaps little intelligence and
liberality of thought, and being accustomed to the manners and
customs of one nation, he cannot overcome prejudices perhaps
acquired in youth or developed under the influence of an early
friendship or a first love either in Paris or London. For when
a feeling is once received without examination, as a sort of
idée fixe, it becomes at length a lie that is mistaken for the truth.
Of course, it is simple enough for a Chinese mandarin or a Russian boyard to make a choice between England and France;
I have in mind here only those clumsy and intolerant fanatics
who would make one hate Elysium if they undertook to praise it.

In Brussels, at the house of the Chevalier de R——, Lord
of Lima, I met again a Comtesse de G——, beautiful in an insignificant way. The Chevalier was foolish enough to spend money
on her, yet with the moderation of a calculating man. He believed himself loved by her, and was in fact adored in that
fashion women have ordinarily with men of sixty. Her foremost
need was to deceive him, and I promptly made myself her accomplice; but, since she was not the woman to defy him, at his first
suspicion she left me, and with such Flemish coldness that it
was impossible to say which of us she treated with most
contempt.

This flirtation was but a prelude to a very real attachment,
of which the consequences were nearly tragic. To free me from a
very embarrassing position, it needed nothing less than the intervention of the man in whose hands the higher power temporarily
rested. This passion took so strong a hold on me that it drove
me across land and sea, was disastrous to me in various respects,
absorbed my thoughts so completely as to become for a time
my sole interest, and finally landed me back, more idle than ever,

exactly where it had found me. I alone am entirely to blame in this affair, and no one ever went to so much trouble to put himself in the wrong. It must be admitted, however, that the woman with whom I went astray justified by her grace and personal charm all the follies I led her into and those where she dragged me in her wake.

There was in Brussels a very passable French theatre: *"C'était d'assez beaux yeux pour des yeux de province."* [14]

All who entered the Duc d'Aremberg's box (and Prince Louis d'Aremberg admitted nearly everyone he knew) had been struck, as I had, by the really celestial beauty of a young woman who came to the theatre almost every evening accompanied by an Englishman. She seemed about seventeen or eighteen years old, and her figure was even more seductive than her beauty of face. Who was she? This was what we all wanted to find out. It seemed to me that the best way of knowing her was to carry her off, once for all, from her everlasting Argus. I endeavoured, therefore, to attract her attention so as to compel her to see how much I was interested in her. I wished her also to notice that, if I observed reserve, it was due to a fear of compromising her peace of mind in the presence of her father, her uncle, her guardian, or whatever the gentleman might be; and he might be anything.

When I felt sure that she understood me, I waited impatiently for a day when she would be accompanied only by an elderly woman who, of late, sometimes replaced her mentor. Unfortunately it was raining as if all the floods of the sky had been let loose. I nevertheless waited for her in the street, and fell on my knees in the mud at the moment when she was about to enter her carriage. "You might think me mad," I said to her, seizing the bottom of her cloak, "if you had not already read my heart and seen the torture to which I am condemned since following your steps. Will you have pity on a love I cannot conquer, and which will cause my death unless you share it?" All this pathos is laughable enough when the mind is collected, but one must never spare warmth and dramatic speeches with women, especially when they are young. Those who are old and corrupted will not allow themselves to be thus caught, and indeed they are not worth the exertion, so that one spares oneself the trouble.

"Sir—sir—I shall be lost. . . . Rise."

"It is I, madame, who will be lost if you do not speak to me.

. . . I ask only a word, a moment, and I shall leave your presence for ever if I do not succeed in convincing you."

"Sir, allow me to pass. . . . I beg of you."

"Where may I see you?"

"Nowhere."

"I shall follow your carriage."

This she had already entered, and it darted off. I followed at a run. The distance was short, and I saw her go into a house. With a tip to the lackey, who refused it at first but quickly grew tame, I learned the girl's name and numerous other details of interest. The main point was to have a talk with the lady's maid. My new confidant induced her to come and speak to me under a doorway, where I declared to her the extreme purity of my designs and emphasised how lavish would be my gratitude. She asked me to go away at once, above all not to confide in a lackey, but to come back to the same spot on the following evening at ten, when she would do all in her power to assist me, so far as honesty and her principles would allow. She added that I must certainly be the gentleman of whom her mistress had often spoken to her. This last remark won for her a kiss and a louis, and I left feeling as happy as if I had had a rendezvous with her mistress.

No more doubt as to success, I said to myself; the girl's maid is backing me; to-morrow I shall again see the servant who lives close to my own beloved, whose hands every day adorn her charms, and every night remove those adornments of which she has so little need. . . . She has spoken of me? . . . We love each other! It is evident. . . . A mutual sympathy was drawing us together. . . . This attachment must be permanent, must be the last. . . . Or at all events it must not be like those numerous wan flames of love that have often consumed me, only to bring into my heart a false warmth which degraded without appeasing it.

Let no one think I am exaggerating. Twenty times in my life I came to such resolves, but bad habits always got the upper hand. More like a schoolboy than anyone I know in matters of love, I was yet supposed to have a brazen heart that found pleasure only in deception, and could know desire but was too worthless to love. Was this surprising, since in public I affected to belittle those feelings which most held my interest? False shame and evil examples led me to adopt the language of a reprobate, though I could be kind-hearted almost to foolishness, would welcome the most tender emotions, and was worthy to enjoy the happiness of the fastidious man who has loved but one woman. And so a man may spend his life making himself appear wicked, while the really wicked people take him at his word. He thus acquires an unfavourable reputation; his fellow men notice everything that gives support to such discredit, and deliberately overlook what might destroy it. If he ever attempts to have such judgement reconsidered it is too late; he finds it engraved upon tables of brass where no room is left to record facts that are honourable. Repute has spoken, and it is untrue to say that she has more than one voice when what she first utters is evil.

If anything could make us merciless towards women, it is the thought that they deserve no indulgence because usually they show none. In polite society they are the public executioners of the drawing-room, just as the common women of the Revolution have been the high priestesses for the atrocious vengeance of the street mob. Their cruelty hides behind their weakness, and the man who is wounded seldom seeks them there. If he does break through that frail intrenchment, they tax with cowardice the man whom they have themselves in safety so attacked in such cowardly fashion, while some fools of men, whom they will sacrifice to-morrow, side with them to-day in their clamours. For men are wont to turn against their natural ally and join women in the persecution of a fellow man to whom, could the sex but think twice, it would spare its darts. These arrows, however, would lose their sting had not male hands drawn tight the bow of delusion. To grow old nursing delusion might be the best of good fortunes, but it is a consolation often denied us; so let us live with nature and the dead. . . . There are trees and books everywhere!

I was punctual at the rendezvous, as was also the officious waiting-maid.

I learnt that her mistress was a girl of good family (Mlle de Saint-F—— de V——), born in Corsica. Her mother was Scotch, and on her death-bed had entrusted her daughter to an Englishman among her relatives, Mr. B——n, who was now travelling with her. This precious charge had fallen into generous hands; he had treated her as a daughter up to the time when, having fallen wildly in love with her, he tried to abuse his rights and his position. He experienced more resistance than he had expected, but in her eyes there was a long way from

resisting her guardian to making a bold declaration in favour
of someone else. That was what the maid told me, and what
I had vaguely conjectured. Nevertheless an interview was the
aim of all my desires. My sponsor assured me that she had
aroused the fear that I might do something desperate, and that
the dread of being compromised seemed much to disturb her
mistress. I left her only after she had promised she would
obtain for me an interview on the following day, either by
cunning or persuasion.

She succeeded beyond my hopes, and introduced me into
the sanctuary. There I sought by every means to soften the
divinity to whom I had consecrated myself. I heard from her
lips that her heart was free; that she knew that to embark upon
an attachment of passion was to renounce happiness; that she
had yielded to the pleasure of begging me herself to give up for
ever my scheme for bringing her to share my feelings; that she
believed I was too honourable to make her pay with the peace
of a lifetime for a few moments of pleasure which her guardian
would soon know how to mix with endless bitterness, etc., etc.
. . . It was my turn to discourse—when the guardian arrived.
I had just time to disappear behind a worm-eaten screen into a
closet as cold as the weather outside (we were in January),
where it seemed I stayed twelve hours. I actually was there for
at least four hours, Mr. B——n having prolonged a laconic conversation far into the night. When I reappeared, Mlle de V——
was so frightened, and I was so frozen, that I needed little
persuasion to go quickly downstairs, looking round at the door
to make sure I was not followed. The maid, who held a light
to show me out, very decently offered to meet me in the street
the following day.

But on that day it was a miracle I was not killed; I was
never in greater danger. At such moments one escapes only by
a special dispensation of Divine Providence. . . . The incident
still seems to me as if yesterday. I had taken lodgings in the
house of a wild fellow who was only fit for doing foolish things
and advising them. He worried me to mount a horse he had
lately bought. It was a marvel, he declared, a paragon of all
perfection; beauty, gentleness, safety, his horse had all these
qualities. I do not think he had entertained any idea of seeing
me break my neck; it was simply that in his clumsy timidity he
wanted to find out what his acquisition was worth at the risk
of someone else. I was no sooner in the saddle than the wretched

beast started to jump, to rear, to struggle; and it all ended in a battle won only by vigorously giving him the spurs. The Vicomte de C——, who was with me, advised me to dismount, arguing quite wisely that to go riding on a restive horse was most tiresome. I rejected his counsel, and we set forth.

On reaching the ramparts we met the Comte de Gr——. He jumped a ditch; I followed him. Not only did my fine mount fail to clear it, but he fell in the middle, rose and galloped off, while I was thrown out of the saddle, my foot remaining in the stirrup, and thus was dragged, more unluckily than Hector, three times round the Brussels ramparts—without exaggeration for ten good minutes. Fortunately I at last fainted, and my foot freed itself of its own accord when once I ceased to struggle. There are so many things like that in this world, which one gets only after renouncing them. . . . I was put to bed and copiously bled; and I remained in a state of stupour for twenty-four hours. My bed seemed to be drawn by six horses; I was turning round and round in a narrow enclosure on the edge of a precipice; and—as I have always recalled with surprise—I remained constantly in this physical and mechanical position, though my mind was quite clear all the time. For nearly a week I could not overcome this sensation of hurried jolting which took me travelling post-haste on the parapet of an abyss, though no terror of my past accident was mixed with this uncontrollable phenomenon. I would sit up in bed and gaze at the floor, which nowise looked like a precipice; and, the moment after, my closed eyes would summon up the same delirium, though in every other respect my mind was unaffected.

Mlle de Saint-F—— de V——, whom I shall henceforth call Mme de V——, heard, as did the whole town, of my accident, and was moved at it. When I began to feel better, the faithful waiting-maid, well concealed in wraps, came to obtain news of my health so as to report to her mistress. I wrote to thank Mme de V——. My letter was well received, as also was I when shortly afterwards I was able to come myself, and I had the happiness of being convinced that a lover who has once begun to please a little pleases more still when he returns from the brink of the grave. Nothing could be more tender and affecting and fresh than all that was said and sighed for an hour on end. In view of such emotion I proposed we should never part again. This caused hesitation. What was to be done with a guardian invested with unlimited authority who was

everywhere entitled to reclaim his ward? I should be prosecuted for abduction; I should never escape the vengeance of
a man who would have law and reason on his side, as well as
the rage of frustrated love in his heart.

I begged her not to trouble over the last item, and after
much effort, with entreaties and refusals and tears [15] (without
which there is no love), she agreed to allow herself to be carried
off. I prepared everything; I had a carriage at her window at
midnight, and she threw into it a few indispensable clothes.
Then, with the lovable fugitive at my side, by turns trembling
and reassured, we flew towards the seaport where we proposed
to embark for Holland. All was well so far, but what woman
does not, through thoughtlessness or some rash deed, stir up
trouble, or, by some inconsequence, cause suffering to the man
who unites his life with hers? My fair one carried away with
her a girl of sixteen whom she had made her bosom friend—
the daughter of a merchant in Brussels. In the excitement of a
hurried escape by night, and the joy it caused me, I paid small
attention to the little one thus snatched from her family, and
to the very natural consequences her disappearance would have.

This was to prepare for myself two bad affairs in place of
one, and to complicate to no purpose a case that was bad enough.
To make the story short, I must say that we found a ship which
bore us without mishap as far as Flushing. It is there, and
there only, that the goddess which the poet Crudeli has per-
sonified in a charming sonnet, made for a young beauty of
Milan, took leave of her whom love had placed in my charge.
I was M. de la Tournerie, travelling for pleasure with his lady
wife, and a relative under her care. Our escort consisted of one
waiting-maid and a lackey, who were guilty of no indiscretions
during the whole journey. I would wish as much luck to anyone
who is obliged to be dependent on his servants and to entrust
to them his secret. We made our way to Middelburg in Zeeland,
and I soon had the happy prospects of an addition to my family.
But travelling has always been fatal to the propagation of the
race; the jolting destroyed my progeny, and my proud hopes
were not renewed. The flower lightly touched by the morning
dew never again opened its calyx.

Our days went by with the rapidity of happy nights. The
town of Middleburg offers but few resources; but in the dawn
of a passionate attachment one prefers (at least I do) silent
walks with the beloved person to more lively pleasures in the

midst of people to whom one is indifferent. Someone who had seen me in Maestricht, at the Comte de Maillebois's, spread about the town of Middelburg the news that I had arrived there. This rumour reached the Grand Pensionary of Zeeland who, donning an embroidered green coat and arming himself with a most remarkable hunting knife, came to visit me one afternoon accompanied by two evil-looking alguazils, who followed him right into my anteroom. He argued eloquently that it would be highly dangerous for a government to allow a foreigner, whatever his rank and condition might be, to come and settle under a false name, that the better known his name was the more he was bound to acknowledge it, at the risk if he failed to do so of being suspected of designs against the safety of the state. He begged me also, in view of his zeal for public propriety and morality, to show him my marriage certificate; and to declare besides, in a legal document, why I had changed my name and decided to settle in the good town of Middelburg; what in short were my views, designs, projects, and plans. . . . I interrupted this verbiage by begging the worthy man not to overheat himself; that it was not my habit to travel with my marriage certificate in my pocket; that surely he must be silly to think that I should show it to him even if I had it with me; that I had not in any way chosen to settle in his town, where I had found nothing but some excellent codfish; that during a stay as short as that I proposed to make at the Cloche d'Argent, where I was doing nothing but spend my money, it was a matter of indifference whether I was called Peter or Paul; that I had dreaded the respects he might have wished to pay to my wife (he saw I was making fun of him), and that to bring to an end a visit which was already too long (he wrinkled up his forehead and contracted his brow in a particularly hideous way) I would condescend to show him a few papers which would sufficiently explain everything.

Saying this, I placed under his nose a passport from the Comte de Mercy, Governor of the Netherlands, and a few letters from the Comte de Maillebois, whose name would be familiar to Dutch ears. While he was glancing at them through his spectacles, I asked him curtly to give himself no further trouble and to leave me to the peace of conjugal enjoyment, reproaching him with some acerbity for the dangerous commotion his sudden appearance had caused to a newly married wife, whom his stern countenance had upset. I informed him that dawn would see me leaving these walls where his authority prevailed.

He was vexed at this, and replied that it might please me to say so, but it was his duty to delay my departure until he had received a letter from M. de Maillebois, specially addressed to him, and containing a satisfactory account with full particulars of my journey and of my stay incognito in Zeeland. I assured him I was delighted to find him so reasonable, since I should now be able, as had at first been my intention, to stay a week or ten days longer with him. I begged him to sit down while I at once wrote, to hand over to him personally, the letter to M. de Maillebois that would restore me to liberty; "for," I added, "I regard myself as a prisoner of war in the citadel you command with such distinction in peace time."

He remarked with much sagacity that the French like to make fun and are very amusing. I protested that he was himself more amusing than anything I had known. After this compliment, which he looked upon as pointed and flattering, he took his leave with many apologies and bows, all as ungainly as possible. But, as he proceeded with more bows while he withdrew backward in a most polite way, he lost his balance at the top of the dark staircase and rolled a long way down before finding his feet again, with the help of his two acolytes. I professed not to notice his accident, and after repeating once or twice, "I wish you good evening, sir; be careful," I closed the door and turned the key. He certainly heard this and realised it was not with me he would find medical help if he broke his neck.

I ought to have guessed that all this was not natural, and that this magistrate was acting for some hidden investigator. That was really the case. The guardian had sent after us one of those honest folk who are always ready to undertake a dubious errand for money. However that may be, I chanced in the evening to meet the Comte de R——, colonel of a German regiment in the service of the United Provinces. I had known him at Spa, and he was now garrisoned near Middleburg. He accepted my invitation to supper with my wife, whom I very quickly acknowledged not to be my wife. I narrated to him the foolish visit of the pensionary, and we laughed over it. He undertook to procure passports for me on the morrow. This I refused; there was nothing left for me but to remain; besides I did not want to leave before victory.

M. de Maillebois's reply arrived without delay. The pensionary had the decency to bring it to me himself; he offered me the alternative of going away or staying. There was no doubt as to my choice; I took leave of him that very moment, and informed him my departure was arranged for the following morning. He had become so exquisitely polite that he pressed me to dine with him on the next day; but as his invitation did not include Mme de la Tournerie I felt obliged to decline.

To leave Middleburg was not everything; it was necessary to go somewhere else. The conscience of a ravisher holding to his prey is not much more at rest than that of a criminal. What am I saying? Is he not one? I thought that Ghent might offer a safe asylum; I proposed to deposit Mme de V—— there, while I went alone to Brussels to see how matters stood and to entrust my secret to M. de Mercy, from whom I could expect indulgence and good advice. So we took a carriage in the best of weather, to embark at Flushing. But it was a treacherous calm; during the short sea-crossing we were assailed by so frightful a storm that the ship was nearly lost. We landed at last at Sas van Ghent, in the midst of thunder and lightning, with the heavens in league against us, as remarked my two female companions, both terrified and half dead.

More adventures awaited us there.

The law now claimed "these ladies," kidnapped from their family by a seducer. I was careful not to offer the slightest opposition. "These ladies" were two travellers whom I had accompanied to Holland; their family seemingly had good reasons to make sure concerning them. The law would decide, from Mme de V——'s depositions, whether she was guilty or if others were. . . . It would establish whether Mr. B——n had the rights over her he took on himself. . . . Especially it would ascertain whether he had expressed feelings merely fitting with the duties he had assumed at the solemn moment of the death of his ward's mother. Such were the brief observations I conveyed to the two or three black owls who were instituting proceedings. I had time to talk as much as I wished with the two frightened beauties. I assured Mme de V—— that I should use all possible means to stifle the affair; that my whole being, my whole soul, remained with her; that my days were going to be filled with but one thought; and that either Mr. B——n would perish at my hand or put an end to me, if he refused to forsake his tyranny and his lawsuit.

See how passions reason! The man was a tyrant because he wished to carry off a woman I had myself carried off against all laws, human or divine, a woman whom it was his duty in honour to protect against a seducer who was leading her astray.

That indeed was what an inner voice one can never stifle whispered to me; but I silenced it by arguing with myself (and with some sort of right) that this protector had tried to be as guilty as myself—even more, since he was bound by sacred obligations which were no weight upon me—that I was even acting the knight on behalf of this persecuted beauty, was the avenger of betrayed confidence, serving the unfortunate mother who from heaven looked down with anger at the perfidious man who had disregarded her dying request; that the law case he was instituting against me was but an excuse for his hatred, and a trick of his love; that he was making use of justice and the law only to bring back to his feet a disarmed victim; that, in a word, since she had forsaken virtue, it was simpler and less scandalous for her to continue doing so with me whom she loved, than to face new persecutions and end by being more guilty with B———n, whom she did not love.

My affection for her added strength to these reflections; it felt still further stimulated by opposition, and the fear of losing her rendered her a thousandfold dearer. My honour, offended by this public procedure, inflamed my imagination, and I came to think that the accusation of seduction would be hushed up on account of the praise due to the rescuer.

Such was the reasoning by which I executed a deed as criminal as it was inconsiderate. I could not succeed in altogether deluding myself; but a guilty man has made a good bargain with his conscience if he is granted a few moments of doubt and a few hours of respite.

At all events I reached Brussels very determined to prove that I was right. Hardly had I left the carriage when a man I knew who was much esteemed by the Comte de Mercy entered my rooms. He advised me not to lose a minute in winning this minister to my side, and undertook to introduce me to him at once. He did not conceal that there was a strong feeling against me in the town, but what I was most reproached for was carrying away Mlle P——— (that little girl of whom I no longer even thought), and that this would cause me many difficulties. His opinion was that the lawsuit about Mme de V——— was a matter to settle with pistols; he added that he was convinced Mr. B———n would be agreeable to a settlement of this sort, but that it would be difficult to make the obstinate and thick-headed merchant listen to reason, since his daughter's honour was for him part of his business transactions and he wished to restore it intact to the shop.

I declared, in all sincerity, that he would find that honour exactly as it was when she went away, for I had not even enquired from the wearisome little creature of what sex she was. He seemed delighted by this statement. I believe, on my honour, that he feared I had raped two Sabine women at once. Reassured on this point, he was ready to advise me to plead that I had myself been carried off. The fact is that at the time of our going away my privacy had been broken in upon by this conceited little prude, who had entered my carriage without permission.

It was especially this detail which I went off to explain to the Comte de Mercy.[16] He received me with severe politeness, but gradually unbent, and at last, having listened to my justification, was more than ready to promise me his support. He made me understand that I must in the first place absent myself, or take refuge with some people I could depend on and not go out.

Before profiting by this wise advice, to which I finally conformed, I proceeded immediately to Mr. B———n's and found him about to go to bed. I told him I came to demand satisfaction for the infamous use of my name, in I knew not what legal proceedings; that it was true his ward, who no longer wished to be so, had left him, but in no way by my act; that I was aware she had sought by flight a refuge from the attempts he had made upon her, and his rough usage of which she complained; that I trusted reflection would restore him to a proper sense of justice and prudence; and that I expected him during the next few days to inform me of his decision by the medium of M. de S———, who was with me. The depositions of Mme de V———, I went on, "will make you understand, sir, how much it is to your interest to put a stop to a suit in which, instead of being the accuser, you may find yourself the accused. . . ." He was about to speak (he had already stammered something), when I went out, assuring him that this meeting would not be the last. S——— threw me a significant glance and remained behind.

The friend who had warned me on my arrival had no difficulty in persuading the little P———, whom he had found oppor-

tunity to meet, to write that it was against my wish, and in a
way unknown to me, that she had left home; that she had not
been able to forsake the protector and friend who was escaping
from the persecutions of Mr. B——n; that every respect due
to her sex had been shown her; and that she was coming back
home as innocent and as much pleased as if she had been for a
walk of an hour or two with her papa and mamma, etc. Care
was taken that this authentic testimonial should reach M. de
Mercy; he was waiting for it before bidding me to reappear.
On her side Mme de V—— deposed altogether in my favour,
and this wonderfully helped to cool Mr. B——n's hostile agitation. I feel sure that I owed to her sensible behaviour, more
than to threats, the fact that the worthy guardian desisted and
withdrew his complaint. I dined publicly with the Comte de
Mercy, in spite of a few good people who thought he ought
to have kept exulting vice in check; and the old Princesse de
St——, no doubt wishing to embarrass me, said to me in a loud
voice: "So you are back! What fairy tales! We heard that you
had carried off a young person."

"Do people say that? Now that we have both returned, you
from Paphos and I from Middelburg, they will say so no more."

This provoked scandalous laughter, for though she was I
do not know how much over sixty, she wore a youthful wig, and
jewels of the previous century; she rouged copiously with a red
as bright as a cartwheel, and her face was like a mummy's.

All was not yet over. I had to win back my sweetheart and
to complete the folly for which I had received absolution.
Negotiations were started with Mr. B——n, who at first stoutly
refused. He ended by leaving her a free choice. I took him at
his word, and he conducted me to her. In my presence he told
her she was the absolute mistress of her fate. I was full of
triumph. But I must confess that after he had put a paper in her
hands and said a few words to her in a window recess she not
only hesitated but burst into tears. I made for the door, when
she suddenly seized me by the coat, then gently let her hand
drop with some confusion. Was the paper a promise of marriage, some letter from her mother? I do not know; I never
shall know, for in later days, even at the most intimate moments,
I was never able to obtain any satisfactory information from
her, and it was useless to exert pressure since she could easily
substitute for the truth any invention she pleased.

That scene cooled my ardour; I was even moved by the

deep affliction of Mr. B——n, who showed not only much feeling, but also a degree of moderation that in a sense won my heart. Besides, I did not like the state of anxiety, the sort of uncertainty, in which I saw her, though a recollection of her sudden gesture in the presence of so disturbing a witness—this instinct which made her come to me as I was about to leave the room— came to soften me and to disturb my judgement.

I have many times been left by a woman, among others one whom I worshipped, but it was at a later date than I now speak of. It would seem that, in a rather long relationship, this woman had applied herself to proportioning her goodness, her tenderness, everything which is binding in a union of this kind, to maliciousness, hardness of heart, and proceedings quite revolting. The day on which we separated was the very day on which we had vowed never to leave each other. Seldom had she taken so much trouble to bewitch me. In losing her I sank into utter nothingness; she had depopulated my world. I wandered about all day long, day after day, thinking of nothing, wishing for nothing, able to remember only her good qualities, those which might cause me to weep for her until I breathed my last. I was inconsolable, I feared for my reason, imagining that such grief could have no end but in madness.

That was the fate awaiting me if Heaven had not prompted me with a simple idea, which may perhaps seem childish, but which I look upon as the finest device of my reason since it helped to save it. I drew up a concise and detailed memorandum, a methodical list of her barbarities, her black deeds, her cold treacheries, some of the atrocious words which had escaped her (she was the prettiest, the sweetest, the most sensitive, the most lovable, the most attractive person in the world when she wished to be so, I might even add, when she did not wish it). This list, a formal deed of accusation, I would read over to myself all day long. I carried it about with me constantly; I learnt it by heart. When other memories came into my imagination to defy those on the list, I unfolded my paper, I read it aloud, I grew animated, I succeeded in hating her . . . so at least I believed. But soon, regaining her ascendancy, she would pursue me victoriously from the other side of her power, and if I had not then wept I should have died.

But at last I believed myself secure; four months had gone by, I locked my memorandum in my desk and fancied I hated her. For three months longer I had no need to read my beneficent document. . . . She hardly ever came into my mind, or if I thought of her it was with indignation and something finer than hatred. Reader! seven months had gone by; three of these had witnessed my victory—you might believe me cured. . . . I thought the same. It was eight o'clock in the evening of an autumn day; the town in which I was living was big, but at that time rather deserted. At the corner of two broad streets I saw two women, one dressed in white with a scarlet Cashmire shawl. My eyes could not leave her; I seemed to detect in the air the scent she had the habit of using; she said to her companion "Ah, it is so and so [my name]!" I proudly walked by, but that voice, which I had not heard for so long, pierced my heart like a dagger. A few paces on I turned round. . . . Good God, what became of me! Not only had she also turned, but, rooted to the spot, she was gazing at me. She fled; as for me I leaned against a milestone, to avoid falling to the ground, as cold as it. . . . Then I dragged myself home with tremendous effort; all my old wounds were once again open! I had to write, to rewrite, to read and reread that fatal list before recovering what I had lost; and I never completely felt my mind restored until I had forsaken the spot where that enemy of my peace lived, and assured myself that there was no chance of meeting her again on this side of the grave.

Readers, especially those of you who are women, if I were to tell you all the good that woman did to me, to give you all the proofs of her love for me, you would not understand how I was ever able to find consolation. If I admitted you to the secret of some of her deliberate, treacherous deeds, of several of the vile tricks with which I have to reproach her, you would not conceive how I could ever have regretted her for a moment. But how have I come to write all this in anticipation? I now know why. It is the result of what I was relating concerning my longing to be reunited to Mme de V—— and how it weakened as soon as I noticed her uncertainty, but straightway revived at the recollection of a passionate gesture of hers which brought her back my heart. For thus we stood, she, Mr. de B——n, and I.

Yet, even in this position, I could propose a riddle that would puzzle those who do not know the human heart. I had developed a liking for another woman. I was about to have a new mistress; or at all events it only rested with me to believe this and to give her that name.

A lawyer in Brussels had a very pretty daughter who was

not unkindly disposed towards men. Wrapped up in a cloak, she had several times accompanied me, or any other Saint-Preux, to a garden outside the town, where, like Julie in her châlet, one ate strawberries and cream. Meeting her one morning near the castle, I invited her to come with me into one of the deserted courtyards. Without any warning I told her that I had sorrows, that I had done ill in giving up easy pleasure for days of bitterness and anxiety. I see now that this was not a gallant thing to say, I do not know if my remark wounded her; she smiled in a peculiar way, but nevertheless agreed to a rendez-vous for the same evening at eleven. I was to whistle the tune: *"Où peut-on être mieux?"* She promised to come down and let me in.

I was punctual. I whistled, and whistled again. But I might have set the whole opera of "Lucile" to whistling variations, no one would have come; so, led by instinct and impatience, I approached the door and found it ajar. To push it, to go up the stairs lightly, to enter the hall on tiptoe, was the work of a moment. As I prepared to open the door behind which *Rose was breathing,* I suddenly felt myself caught by athletic arms in an embrace which nowise resembled that of love. I struggled; I found myself the weaker; I was overcome. Pushed violently towards the stairs, I struck repeated blows at random. One arm felt broken. I kicked like a wild beast; I was ruthlessly thrown down, my arms tied behind my back; I bit and my hair was pulled at almost to make me bald. A knee was dug into the small of my back; my bound hands drawn together by a running knot, I was pushed down the stairs at the risk of my life, and after I had been thrust into the street in a more than uncivil way, the door was shut.

I was never in such a rage in my life, and hope I never shall be again. I knew not what step to take. To knock at the door was as impossible as it would have been ridiculous. But to return home with my hands bound behind my back! Still it seemed better to confide in my lackey than in anyone else. I arrived home without being seen, and was obliged to degrade myself with a lie to a servant, who was simple and honest enough to believe me. I told him an unlikely story of thieves who had attacked me, and he could not get over his astonishment that they had not more completely rifled me, and that I had come back with my watch. It was a remark a child might have made. Perhaps he thought, "My master is a liar." Oh! what a noble profession it is sometimes, that of *l'homme à bonnes fortunes!*

I finally decided on an explanation with Mme de V——;

the manner and the tone with which she assured me, and repeated to Mr. B——n, that she could be happy with no one
but me, removed all scruples, and would have sufficed to ap-
pease the most sensitive conscience. I owe it to Mr. B——n
to say that he gave proofs of a fortitude I should not have
thought him capable of. . . . He was manly in the best sense;
he even affected to display, in this last scene of his part as
guardian and sorrowful thwarted lover, the luxury of exalted
generosity. He called Heaven to witness to his desire that the
responsibility I was taking upon myself might bring me nothing
but happiness; that I might never have to repent my choice of
chains which reflection might have prevented me from accepting so whole-heartedly.

He went so far as to say, but in a sensible and disinterested
tone, that he doubted whether I would long find felicity in a
bond I could not break without guilt or preserve for any length
of time without realising that it was irksome; that the beauty
of Mme de V—— was as I viewed it, which is to say very great,
her mind lovable and gracious, but her character inconsequent
and frivolous; that her youthful effervescence and the instability
of her tastes offered no guarantee to inspire confidence, or,
rather, were unfavourable indications; and that if any uncertainty was to remain in his mind concerning the opinion he had
long formed of her the rashness of the step she was now taking
would confirm it. He had no wish to emphasise, he continued,
the numerous other reflections which came to him; he feared
to be thought too interested a party; but he anxiously hoped
in all the sincerity of his heart, that this conversation would
for ever remain in Mme de V——'s memory, so that she might
devote the future to disproving it. Then, more especially speaking to me, he called upon Time to be the arbiter and judge
between his fears and my hopes. Mme de V—— was weeping.
He looked at her with cold eyes, his face pale with the gloom
of repressed grief. I thought to myself: "There is still time
to pause; I ought to give her back to him; but they would now
be too unhappy . . . and so should I."

He invited us to spend the evening with him, gave me full
information concerning his ward's family, asking me always to
treat her with kindness, whether or not she deserved it, and to
allow her to write to him sometimes. He took a portrait from
a casket, and believing that I was rather touched, hastened to
say that it had been painted for her mother a few weeks before

her death, by Plymer,[17] . . . and that if I really desired to possess it he willingly offered it to me.

I would not have accepted, had my life depended on it. I thanked him by a low inclination of the head; to reply with a nod was thus possible, words would not have come. After two hours of such anguish, and of a torture that served him as a revenge, we took our leave. He promised to come and bid us farewell next day at dawn. He never came. I still thank him for that! I set out for Paris where this second Helen was to torment me; and I found out even during the journey that the woman whom we have disputed to others is far more attractive and interesting than the woman who is given away to us.

Those who are exclusively guided and ruled by that domestic madwoman, Imagination, do not preserve two hours on end the same reasons for feeling happy; yet their troubles are ever-lasting, for the madcap varies them endlessly, even in the face of Reason, unable to oppose unbridled Imagination, who leaps through space while her cold rival looks carefully where she walks.

So I was coming back to that Paris I had feared never to see again, having left it for nearly a year and a half. It had seemed to me a century of exile. Ah! if I could have foreseen how I was to become the plaything of land and sea, the victim of men and things, and the long future awaiting me where banishment would see its boundaries extended alternately through despair and hope, what then should I have said about fate?

France, when I re-entered it in 1791, was veiled in even deeper crape than before. I took rooms in the Chaussée-d'Antin, to live there with Mme de V——, to whom I brought but little company, for I tried to make her acquire a taste for seclusion, the chief warranty of feminine fidelity being the absence of opportunities for infidelity. Yet I none the less had cruel fits of jealousy, because men whom I considered my friends did not fail (even those who ought to have recognized what little right they had to do so) to attempt to seduce my mistress. One may expect, eight times out of ten, that it will be precisely one's best friend who will play us the worst trick of this kind, because he will have the greatest opportunities, and we suspect him least. Most women like to make a success out of what seems improbable; and to that taste is added an innate attraction for something which most resembles treachery. (Adorable half of the human race, do not protest! Those of you who are excep-

tions to this rule will well understand me; those who lend it
sanction will understand still better.)

I once again met some of the leaders of the Revolution whom
I had known previously; from the conversations I had with
those who played important parts on this sort of stage, as well
as from my own observations, I concluded that civil war was
about to be kindled, or that at all events there would be a long
struggle between a distracted monarchy and an impossible republic until there arose a man able to disband the madmen and
murderers and to bring back order.

The impotent King, coming to the Tuileries to give himself
up as a prisoner, had proved the full extent of his weakness, and
himself signed his abdication and his death warrant. Nothing
could any longer impede the success of legislators transformed
into gladiators on a bloody arena, for the only way to bring
them to yield was to oppose them. In vain had Louis XVI
accepted a constitution, a true mockery of royalty; in vain had
he uttered these touching words: "I will begin early to prepare
my son for the new order which circumstances have brought
about," etc. Outrage followed upon outrage, and the inexhaustible chalice was as bottomless as eternity. Left alone with the
Queen and Mme Elizabeth, victims reserved like himself for
capital punishment, the unhappy King saw himself forsaken in
turn by all his family. His aunts, whose advanced age might
have made them more generous in bestowing consolation and
less sparing of their own lives, had prudently retired to Italy.
Fury and affront watched at the gates of his palace, and his
heart would have known utter loneliness had his griefs been
less unrelenting.

Every humiliation had been heaped upon him; he had shown
himself able to rise above all outrages, yet tyranny pursued him
on all sides. He was not allowed to go and seek a few days of
rest at Saint-Cloud; while yet King of France he had to engage
in a scandalous struggle in the courtyards of his palace in a
hand-to-hand contest with Parisian mobs who cried shame upon
him. He had, with tears in his eyes, to give up the chance of
breathing the country air a couple of leagues from Paris. Yet,
forgetful of himself, he felt real alarm only for the safety of
a devoted servant [18] whom he rescued from the furious mob
by a gesture, some few words, and entreaties.

M. de La Fayette played fair on that day, and was not
able to obtain from the King that he should seem free in appear-

ance when he was not so in reality. Royalty, that tutelary divinity of the French people above all others, now resembled a mutilated statue still left standing the better to bear witness to its degradation. The King seemed to be living merely to be a target for cowardly insults aimed at every crowned head; he stood as representative of all the European sovereigns who were vilified in his name, and disgraced in the person of the *doyen* of the kings of the earth. Even that right which makes all others precious, the heavenly prerogative of granting pardon, had been snatched from him; the choice of his servants and representatives, the nomination of his ministers, in practice no longer belonged to him. They went so far as to dispute his right to salvation in another world; his conscience was violated.

Mirabeau, who had become the man of the court as soon as he was no longer allowed to stand for the people, had no time to keep the promises he had made and to enter on the task he had proposed to accomplish. It seemed that over this revolution the genius of evil, in full power, was always watching, and that all efforts at restoration and the will to do good were met by a barrier of steel reaching from earth to heaven!

Mirabeau (whatever they may say) died by poison. It is certain that the excesses he indulged in a few days before his illness rendered it more dangerous; but he had long been accustomed to such excesses, he thrived on them. His athletic constitution would long have withstood them if more efficacious methods had not been sought to do away with him. His body was opened, it may be objected, and no traces of poison found. It may be maintained that all poisons leave traces; I still persist in saying that he died poisoned. Less than ten days after he had proclaimed from the tribune that he would combat and unmask men fomenting sedition he felt himself suffering (as he told a woman of my acquaintance) from a lassitude he could not define. I have, besides, other indications about which I am silent—for I do not wish to be libelous, and it is best not to say too much when one cannot say enough. The King sent several times to enquire about him, and I myself found at his door a man who was greatly trusted by the Queen. The court took no trouble to conceal its grief at his death.

With the loss of this man of guilt, whose reputation in less than a year was to have been redeemed, collapsed the last hope of a monarch whom everything conspired to deliver over to the most terrible fate. Mirabeau died with the resignation and the fortitude of the just. Taxed as he had been with lack of courage, he yet displayed in his last hours a courage that was simple, noble, and without ostentation. He was accorded a magnificent funeral. Even the best citizen deserving reward from his country, or the worthiest man in a vast empire, could not have gone down to the grave honoured by more regret, surrounded by more public proofs of the gratitude and esteem of his countrymen.

As I witnessed this pompous funeral, I thought to myself that no man, simply by the mere deeds of his life, has the power to win esteem for himself during a lifetime and after death; that this giant of genius and immortality had no more wished for such honour to be shown to him in the unconsciousness of the coffin, than he had been free to avoid languishing in a dungeon at Vincennes and wandering for years about Europe, deprived of social standing and even of consideration. Likewise, upon witnessing the exhumation of his body, the scattering of his ashes, many must have thought with me that a nation gone crazy can no more confer true honour than it can inflict public discredit; and that the likes and dislikes of the mob are well portrayed in two sayings, one of Mirabeau himself, the other from the lips of Cromwell. The former had once exclaimed that there was "but a step from the Capitol to the Tarpeian rock." The latter said to his son-in-law Ireton: "Fool, to take notice of the applause of the rabble; they would applaud even more if we were on our way to be hanged."

Great and ever true lesson to be learnt from the two greatest leaders of factions in all modern times. Yet an unheeded lesson.

CHAPTER XXV

Destrictus ensis cui super impiâ
Cervice pendet, non siculae dapes
Dulcem elaborabunt saporem:
Non avium, Citharaeque cantus
Somnum reducent.
—HORACE OD. III, I, 17.

HAVE you ever watched a child playing on the brink of a precipice? He gathers some little flower hidden in the grass and runs in merriment along the edge, which may suddenly give way under his feet. He vaguely knows there is danger so far from his watchful mother, whose loving voice often calls him back; yet he persists in frolicking near the abyss, thus enjoying for the last time the pleasures of incautious childhood. For he will fall into the chasm, his instinct is not sufficient to save him, he will disappear for ever.

It is thus that most people were living for the day or the hour, in this Paris where so many of them were to meet with a frightful death; where soft and dissolute living, and various forms of intoxication blinded society to a future terrifying to people who were not children, or even to those whose simple instincts urged flight from a volcanic land holding no promise but of eruption, lava, and death. Yet an apathetic crowd persisted in living upon such a volcano, and gathered the pallid flowers still to be found on its summit.

Like so many others, I was in the procession of this ghastly folly. To heavy gambling, love-making, and jealousy, I added, to complete this list of fine qualities, a fervent zeal for Bacchus, and I discovered that the best thing about life was to forget it, since anxieties of many kinds must always sit at the banquet with us.

> Seest thou the wretch at that Sicilian feast,
> Given by the tyrant; when he fears it least
> He finds that friendship's mien is treacherous hate's,
> And tastes with terror the delicious cates,
> Raises the golden cup, and when his eyes
> Glimpse the suspended sword he almost dies.

These beautiful lines by the Abbé Delille, picturing the joys pertaining to man, his disquiet, his fears, and even his hopes, yielded a still more tangible meaning. So that everything might be in keeping with so peaceful an existence, my home life provided me with all the anxieties of an ardent love and all the anguish of jealousy. Every day I conjured up new ghostly fears which Mme de V—— had in no way, I am sure, helped to create. So it seems that the days went by amidst quarrels which it was as easy to begin as to end in reconciliation. The inconstancy of her disposition rendered the one as natural as the other. So long as love and feeling presided over this stormy alternation, such life was both horrible and charming; but when after much mutual pestering we began at last to feel weary, one hope alone loomed in our future: freedom.

But events of quite a different kind came to render me insensitive to my own troubles; I forgot them. The King resolved to leave his capital[1] at a moment when one least expected it, though such a decision should have been daily awaited. This unfortunate Prince sought a last chance of salvation in a step that would naturally come to the mind of a captive king deprived of all the attributes of authority, which essentially consists in recompensing the good by encouragement, and repressing evil by terror. But having long fallen under the blows of evil persons, the victim became conscious that the hour of sacrifice was drawing near, and tried to ward it off.

Louis XVI tendered to the Assembly a report that at the time was thought partial and exaggerated, as if there were any other fault to reproach him with in this declaration, which posterity will look upon as moderate, but the fact of having felt compelled to write it! The world at large knows the result of this attempt, which further riveted him to his chains. It is known that, stubborn in his opposition to the homicidal doctrines which caused torrents of blood to flow over Europe, he would not have a single drop shed on his behalf; he preferred to be brought back to his capital as a victim bound to the chariot of the popular victors,[2] and degraded for ever in the eyes of the mob, which can no longer respect what it has once been called upon to revile.

This event and its results had filled me with horror and uncontrollable sadness. I no longer took any interest in my own affairs. But just as I had resolved to free myself from an uncomfortable position, and when I was even rejecting the sweetness it could still offer me, a revolution took place in my household such as at every moment was unfolding itself all around me.

I had a valet in whom I had complete trust. One day I discovered him handing to Mme de V—— a note that she hurriedly hid with confusion. Someone's coming in at the moment gave her time either to conceal the paper or to destroy it. Later she had the impudence to maintain she had never received any such thing; this was like trying to make me believe I was blind. My trusted servant had the effrontery to support this lie by his corroboration. I dismissed him; that was simple enough. As to Mme de V——, I assured her I would forget the incident, would even abstain from searching deeper into it, if she condescended to own to it; but that we should have to part that very day if she persisted in a falsehood which degraded her by humiliating me.

"I consent to this," was her reply, which surprised me more than it brought me grief.

"Where do you wish to go?"

"To England, to rejoin Mr. B——n."

"Are you sure that he will happen to be there to take charge of you?"

"To take charge of me! . . . That is my business."

"Very well; I shall take you as far as Calais and not leave you until I have seen you on the ship."

She goes to join Mr. B——n again I thought; he still loves her. And what of myself? What if I were to discover, when it is too late, that I still love her, still need her? . . . Let me be a man, and see if she will come back. And I noticed, during the two days she spent in preparations for her journey, that she was the prey to a hesitancy as great as mine, appearing in turn completely at ease, or else more than melancholy. We left Paris; the journey found us full of tender politeness and kind attentions to each other. But we neared our destination, and an hour before the last farewell she said: "Here is that terrible letter; it is from Mr. B——n. Read it, he only writes about my family and gives me news of them. See if there was need of all that scandalous uproar you caused. But at least I do not want to leave you without taking your esteem with me."

"I have no wish to read it; nothing it contains will efface the wrong you have done by concealing it so long from me, receiving it in secret through corrupting one of my men who had always been faithful to me, above all by joining him in a vile lie. This tardy confession does not make your fault greater, but cannot repair it."

Her eyes filled with tears, and I found myself equally weak.

"What will become of this?" I asked. "Do we still love one another?"

"I fear it is so," she replied, "but, be that as it may, believe me, we must persist in our plans; after what has happened, we can no longer hope for happiness together. . . . If, however, you wish me to, I will now go back."

"Good-bye," I said with much effort. "You are a thousand times right; let us be firm enough to hurt each other for a while, for fear of doing so without end. Making it up could not bring us new sweetness or heightened delight. There are limits for lovers which they must not stray beyond in their quarrels lest love comes back to them transformed into a feeling that has all the drawbacks of hatred."

"Well, then, good-bye!"

"Good-bye! Let us at least remain friends."

"For ever!"

"As long as life lasts!"

We did wisely, as we both agreed when we met again. I have not now seen her for many years, and I regret it. The foolish things we both did, her striking beauty, her lovable yet peculiar disposition, all these powerfully bring back to me those stormy days which never knew any interlude of perfect calm.

I have learned with much satisfaction all that later came to give her happiness; I do not know whether I should describe thus her marriage with the Prince de Salm.

I returned to Paris, relieved of a burden, yet crushed by a grief I could ill define; I was widowed of a habit. One of my friends helped me to recover my wits, without the need of great eloquence. He granted me that she was charming, but that, with her disposition and mine, we should in any case have come to part, and that time, making the separation more than ever necessary, would also have made it more bitter. For it may happen that after having lived with a woman out of love, yet feeling one could leave her, one ends by remaining with her out of habit, which renders parting an impossibility. I felt sure of all this, but it was a consolation that another should have the same assurance. There are moments and periods when a trifling idea acts as a light, when the most natural remark from someone else turns to our benefit, just as the slightest support may prove sufficient to prevent a fall. It is as if a man needed to hear truths repeated to him which teach him nothing but what he already well knows; very much as in conversation phrases are used which mean nothing, but which we cannot do without.

Fortune, by lavishing on me temporary favours, caused me regrets. I won a good deal at *trente et un;* with this money, I felt, I could have made Mme de V—— very happy, so that she would have loved me all the more. The woman who feels entertained is more disposed to become attached than the slave who is bored. But new schemes in our endless tragedy offered themselves to my frightened eyes. The King's downfall was called for; the fierce Danton organised at the Champ de Mars gatherings of a rabble that rumbled like thunder and could be dislodged only by another sort of thunder. The blood which was then shed proved the death-warrant of the unfortunate Bailly,[3] who had not learned through the contemplation of the heavens the mode of the earth's revolutions, and who most likely had encountered in the dusty volumes of his study a fact he over-looked, namely that a mob, in dealing with former favourites, knows but one behaviour and one gift: ingratitude and then death. This blood helped to fertilise the germs of later devas-tating insurrections; it was the lightning foretelling the thunder of the tenth of August.

War was about to be declared with as much imprudence as futility in the grounds for it. But did it matter to such men what the consequences would be? Would not the defeats of our army offer the most specious excuse for killing the King and the monarchy?

I had long been marked out for vengeance by the most fero-cious leaders of the demagogic party. I had had a quarrel with that wretch, Fabre d'Eglantine; I had treated him with true feudal superiority, against which he had not appealed, but which had imbued a soul such as his with unconquerable hatred. A war of the pen against M. de Condorcet increased the dangers that awaited me. Many well-meaning people still persist in their esteem of Condorcet, whom I look upon, in the honesty of my heart, as one of the most dangerous writers brought forward by the Revolution. I shall finally dare to mention that I used then to write (even on to the end) with a boldness few men have cared to emulate, and which was perhaps then as indis-pensable a condition for success as talent. I seldom went to bed, and it was especially at this period that I lost the art of sleep. That art to-day seems to me more precious than any other, now that I would so much like to forget in sleep the uselessness of my life and its numerous sorrows. My day was given to gambling and part of the night, the rest went to write articles that have been carried away by the winds and have proved no help; probably only my enemies have not forgotten them. It was one more weapon for their hands.

While I was still the prey to a vague and gnawing anxiety that feared everything except death, I went everywhere, to clubs, theatres, promenades, yet belonged nowhere. Paris had never before been so dissolute a town, a den where all sensual passions sought gratification; one lived there in the midst of excess. It seemed to be foreseen that the duration of all these enjoyments was to be restricted by the grave, or by the misfortune of unbelievable happenings piled up over the heads of victims reserved for that fate. People threw themselves on the pleasures of the moment to get their fill.

Here must be given room to my last love attachment in France, witnessed by a sun that for me will no longer rise again over this privileged land; for it appears I am one of the few condemned never to see it again. But since an inconceivable destiny has excluded me from the clemency of a great man, whose advent to power I was amongst the first to acclaim, when fear might still be entertained as to its stability; since I am disowned by a country where I have hailed him as a redeemer, a country of which foreigners have often bitterly acknowledged me as an idolatrous worshipper, I have only resignation to oppose to the tyranny of Fate, who has decreed in her harsh book that after I had wandered in foreign lands, sometimes on inhospitable shores, my forgotten ashes would not sleep with those of my forefathers![4] May those who have caused the gates of France to be closed to me (and I have the consolation to know that *it is not* the conqueror of Europe) find there all they have deprived me of, and remain unacquainted with the burning fever of hunger for one's native land, and that wearing need of shedding tears on its threshold, of falling on one's knees to God upon its frontier!

As for you, young, moving, and beautiful woman who in that fair France received the last homage of a heart wholly yours, when disastrous days brought you to fall a victim to the axe, I tried everything (you would proclaim it if you could still speak) to save you. The tale of the tender feelings I entertained for you, of the last true pleasures granted to my departed youth, will close the too lengthy list of my errors, will complete

the cycle of what both morality and reason look upon as guilty
passions. . . . In less than a year from now I shall no longer
be French! . . . Yet I shall always be so at heart. The stamp
remains for life; death alone may efface it.

Who has not known Mlle de Saint-Amaranthe and her
mother, doubly famed on account of her family and her disorderly life? [5] This mother, born of aristocratic stock (Mlle de
Saint-Simon d'Arpajou) had been married to the Sieur de Saint-
Amaranthe, son of a chief collector of taxes. The husband himself was a captain in the cavalry, and a very wealthy man, though
this qualification would not have been sufficient to win Mlle de
Saint-Simon if she had not played at a very early age some mad
prank in imitation, it is said, of her mother's behaviour in the
town of Besançon where they lived. It seems that these ladies
kept to one pattern.

M. de Saint-Amaranthe was a madcap, possessing, as I have
mentioned, a considerable fortune which yet was too small for
his tastes. He took his wife to Paris, and was in a short time
ruined by his friends, whom he did not select from the best
society, and by his mistresses, whom he took from the Opéra.
These ladies skillfully drained him dry, and sent him to die as a
cab-driver in Madrid, where Fénelon told me he found him at
a stand in front of a church. He recognised him, gave him the
preference over others to drive him about (which was bold
enough), and also bestowed charity upon him. His wife, more
pretty than beautiful and more desirable than pretty, had some
distinguished lovers, amongst whom the late Prince de Conti
behaved most handsomely towards her; I know several others
whom it is as superfluous as it would be out of place to name
here. The result was that she lived in turn in the midst of wealth
and in the most straitened circumstances, the ups and downs of
a life of intrigue. The best society, side by side with very mixed
company, was constantly found in her house.

On the whole, I recognised in her a gift more difficult to
cultivate than is generally believed, that of compelling friendship to outlive love. This surprises me the more because, as she
was so unsteady in disposition and possessed next to no greatness of heart, she seemed to have few qualities to bestow in a
disinterested and chaste friendship. But to be able to judge
her correctly on that point, one should at some time have been
her lover, and this honour was never mine. Now and again I had
frequented her house, where from my early youth I had been

taken by the Vicomte de Pons. The Viscount, having spent the
greater part of his life with her (so far as his habits at court
and his duties allowed him), found death at the same hour that
she did under the blade invented by Doctor Guillotin, that
honest physician who, thinking his art had not killed enough
people, lent laconism to destruction, and even attached his name
to his murderous invention. For the rest, many people have
died who were more to be pitied than the Vicomte de Pons. It is
pleasant to make one's exit from life in the company of a
beloved person.

Mme de Saint-Amaranthe had a daughter, spoken of later
in Paris as an angel of beauty, who, renowned in life for her
charms, made her death famous by her courage at a time when
it was difficult thus to attract attention, for everybody sought to
die, as did the Roman gladiators, with style. . . . I almost said
with grace. I had admired her when she was a child, but had
not seen her again for some years. On my return from my last
journey I found that these ladies were running the most brilliant
and frequented gambling house in Paris. A skillful cook; a bank
for *trente et un* garnished with enormous funds; a gathering
of all that could be found in the way of men worth knowing,
in days when there were fewer houses of high order and less
support in the best society; a tone in the house as decent as if
no gambling took place; the charms of the two hostesses (for
the mother, although eclipsed by her daughter, had nevertheless
her value) ; other women whose class I could not ascertain any
more than their virtue, but who were most of them pretty;
everything contributed to make of this house a charming assem-
blage into which one would stray several times a day. For my
part I saw Mlle de Saint-Amaranthe, and really noticed no one
but her.

I had, however, to pay attention to what the Vicomte
de Pons was telling me, for after having avowed to me during
the childhood of the girl that she was his daughter, now that
she was eighteen he declared she was not. I hope, for his sake,
that having deceived himself with fancies of his fatherhood, he
came somehow later to know very precisely how empty these
were, for he had serious designs: he wished to make her his
mistress. I teased him about it; but finding him quite seriously
depaternalised I never mentioned the subject again; I rested
content with having a thorough talk with the little one. I first
enjoined her to keep my secret, then depicted with pathos the

heinousness of incest. I found her disposed to look upon it with the greatest horror, and I obtained from her the promise that she would try seriously to consider what share of her feelings was my due in view of my zeal and my advice. The Viscount kept his eyes on me, and looked bilious and mistrustful. He could hardly conceal his ill humour, which I pretended not to notice; but since he had a great influence over the mother's mind, which was better than his own, he represented me as the most dangerous man in her drawing-room.

Mme de Saint-Amaranthe would have raised no objection to her daughter's having a lover, but did not wish it to be me. Thereupon the girl was cross-examined, tormented, warned against my "devilish tricks"; and, as was natural, my prospects improved all the more. However, even if the gall of the Vicomte de Pons might have caused me to rejoice, the anger of the handsome mama frightened me; the time had not yet come to laugh at it. So I spoke to my angel only so far as politeness made it necessary; but we exchanged letters. I warned her that within limits I was going to court her mother. This idea hugely amused her. My aim was twofold, first to show the girl how easy it would be to succeed with a woman who was only strict for her daughter, and also to spur the latter to jealousy so as to bring matters to a head. No woman, even when fully warned that the affair is but a jest, can see without mistrust the man she loves engaged in a sort of rehearsal with her rival.

In fact, my plans, which succeeded almost to the point of frightening me, and brought against the Viscount the accusation of being very short-sighted, at first amused Mlle de Saint-Amaranthe but soon caused her ill humour. Every day I handed her a letter. Nothing more easily whets thwarted love than tactics of this kind. My letters were written with blood, a few drops from a slight prick; she replied in rouge mixed with water. I noticed the trick and sulked; then she wrote with ink, and I recovered my good temper. We should never encourage the cunning and crafty sex to ridicule us even in trifles; the victim of their poor jokes soon becomes that of their deliberate contempt. On her side, she clearly intimated that I was to leave her mother's heart at peace, and declared to me that this sham war wearied her. So I told the mother I suffered from my chest, and that I must diet on milk. But since I often dined with them and displayed an appetite to evoke remark she realised I was making fun of her and became cross. The moment came when the fair

one I worshipped in silence understood (as I had foreseen) that
she had to make up her mind to grant a little sooner what she
had resolved to give me some time later, for it was possible her
mother might place new obstacles in the way.

B——, then so famous on account of his absurd grief at
not being a man of quality—though his income of one hundred
thousand crowns ought to have afforded him consolation—had
a small flat in Mme de Saint-Amaranthe's house that he used
as a dressing-room, or even to spend an occasional night. He
lent me the key of it. One evening, when the two ladies came
home from what had appeared to me an endless opera, for I
was with them in their box which I had left before the fall of
the curtain, Amélie, true to a promise, came to join me in the
darkness; she arrived with beating heart just as I was beginning
to despair of her coming.

> *Odoratos nexa capillos,*
> *. . . vestis tenuissima, cultus amantis.*

I heard the signal agreed upon, three knocks on the door;
I opened and gathered Flora in my arms; for she was like the
goddess of the garden, in truth fresher than the posy adorning
her bosom. Moments far too swift having gone by, she went
downstairs again to the drawing-room; I followed some time
later, as would a modest victor who wishes to defeat suspicion
and to allow a girl's shyness to regain composure. Mme de
Saint-Amaranthe, prompted by some maternal sympathy, which
no doubt magnetised her unknown to herself, never showed me
more tender attention. She asked me, in a voice that was in
itself a caress, where I came from so late.

"From paying an indispensable call," I told her, "during
which my sole compensation has been constantly to think of
you."

"That is most polite," she said to me, "but nothing is indispensable in this world save to avoid being bored. As for calls,
no one pays them nowadays."

"Mine," I replied, "was of those few man has always paid
since the beginning of the world and will continue to pay until
it ends."

"I have no wish to know more," she said demurely, her
eyes avoiding mine.

"You are the person in the world whom it gives me the
greatest pleasure to obey."

During the whole of the evening she was full of charming good humour; just like a rather vexed hen transformed into a dove. Some of her atomic force still gravitated towards me; I was the son of her instincts, despite an antipathy born of her reason.

As for her lovable daughter, the angelic Amélie, she was like a rose come to life on its stalk, its crimson hue grown brighter now its petals have been gently opened by Zephyr.

Nothing remains concealed for long. Amélie had a young brother, since murdered at sixteen by Fouquier-Tinville. What does not youth notice? He suspected our meetings; he kept watch near the door, and saw her come out of B——'s rooms; he did not leave his observation post until he had likewise seen me go down; and that same evening he revealed the whole affair to his mother.

It may be guessed that the discussion I had with her was stormy; she did not spare me the names of monster and seducer. The latter produced little effect on me, for I was sure I did not deserve it, having been duly informed that another, protected by Mme de Saint-Amaranthe herself, had undertaken that task. I was requested never to set foot in her house again, and was told that the daughter would be sent to a convent to atone for her crime. I admired how eloquent Mme de Saint-Amaranthe could be in her fury, and how high-principled she was while in a temper. It was virtue, having nothing to win by faltering, which preached a lesson to vice caught red-handed. When she had vomited her rage, I replied quite gently that I doubted whether she had the right to place in a convent a daughter who had chosen a lover suited to her taste, since on a previous occasion she had acted wrongly in accepting one who was not; that on all other points I should take my orders from Mlle de Saint-Amaranthe and never from herself. Having said these few words, I withdrew, pursued by a din of insults, of doors angrily banged, and crockery smashed.

I warned Amélie of what she would easily have learned without me; I intimated that the moment had come for us to part if she did not summon will and spirit to her help; I reminded her that she had often promised to display these qualities if ever we were discovered. She did so beyond my expectation; her maid came to me that very afternoon to report that, after a lively encounter with her mother, Mlle de Saint-Amaranthe sent me word she would expect me at seven that evening.

I did not make her wait. She told me all about the outburst of
temper and even the entreaties she had had to contend with;
and how her answer had invariably been that her past had
secured her the right to dispose of the present, and that she was
resolved to take any step, even that of leaving her home, rather
than allow herself to be tyrannised over; that, helped by me,
whom she had informed of every particular concerning herself
since her entry into society, she would find ample means to
regain her freedom; that the luxuries and superfluities in which
she was steeped contributed little to her happiness, for all she
required were the conveniences of life with the man she loved,
and I would be in a position to supply her needs; that, besides,
ten thousand crowns entrusted to the notary, M. Tr——, were
her property, and would more than suffice for the kind of life
most to her taste.

Such wealth of arguments, supported by tears, greatly frightened Mme de Saint-Amaranthe, while the knowledge that I
knew her secret so deeply disturbed her that she agreed to
relinquish her authority from that day and to look upon her
daughter as a sister who could expect only advice. She merely
expressed the wish that the girl would never repent having so
soon shaken off the yoke of a mother's prudence. Meanwhile
her first advice was that I should be fetched at once, so that
Amélie's own lips should tell me of my good luck; and when I
left my sweetheart's side she bade me give my first call on the
morrow to her mother. To this I willingly agreed.

It was a lamb I found, a most docile lamb. I might have
believed I was her son; she begged me to entertain such feelings; she added she felt sure I would not compromise her daughter and that she would use all her influence to make the attachment a lasting one, for constancy and time would thus redeem it.
I was Amélie's first love, and she flattered herself that my affection for the girl would at last bind a heart which had always
been restless. She attempted some explanations on another delicate subject: she gave me the name of the seducer (I knew it
already) who had, by means of gold, bought the favours of
beauty and innocence sacrificed to him. Amélie had not really
been coerced and was to have married the man who had abused
her simplicity. The mother could assure me, in all sincerity,
that she had so little joined in this plot that she had even
scorned to ask what had happened to prevent the marriage,
as well as the reasons for her daughter's aversion for the man

she had at first chosen, etc., etc. I allowed her to speak as much as she liked, and I appeared to acquiesce now and again with a nod, but looking incredulous enough to leave her in my power and prevent me falling back into hers. Though at heart she hated me, she loaded me with promises of everlasting friendship. I swore she was what I most loved in the world after her daughter; this was deceiving her, yet I felt no hatred. I tried to convince her it was especially my esteem she had now conquered. As nothing was further from the truth, it was now my turn to lend weight to this assertion by all the oaths that might support a lie. I did not find her over-credulous.

Thus, when I left her room, we were precisely in the same position as when I entered it. But what a difference as to behaviour and all that pertains to appearances! Renewed friendliness, consideration, harmonious concord, delicate attentions— these everyone could notice. I dined at her house, I caught her eyes wishing my death, but she shook my hand on leaving the table to thank me for not having once looked at Amélie. It was impossible, she remarked, to conceal possession more naturally. On my part I thanked her; but my praise was flattery, it was that of her master. I might, however, state that for a woman of her experience she was much mistaken, since as La Bruyère, I believe, has pointed out with wisdom, to look always at each other, or never to do so, brings about one and the same suspicion in other people's minds.

We had loved each other for three months, feeling it was but a day, or sometimes as if we had done nothing else all our lives. But three months of happiness are a long spell in the longest career. How many men have died without three months of happiness! A swarm of would-be husbands suddenly appeared. One had a rather handsome name, but his face was hardly so; another was the son of one of the King's former ministers, but that was all; a third, Sartine, whose father had also been far too much a minister, was already a candidate, though it was much later he entered on this disastrous marriage which led him with her to the scaffold—a fate he might well have encountered alone, since it was then as common to be guillotined as to catch a cold.

As for me, since I did not want to marry but only to keep what most husbands have so much trouble to obtain, I became gloomy, unapproachable, and a prey to such suppressed jealousy that I turned mouse-colour in complexion. At last the storm

burst, quarrels followed upon quarrels. I had won, as I mentioned, huge sums of money; I squandered most of it in this
very house, the reef on which my peace and happiness were to
be wrecked. A man is not amiable who feels jealous before so
many people. And women have the unique knack of seizing upon
any ridiculous trait and expressing their disgust for it. They
have a special aversion for any suffering they have themselves
caused.

The idea of getting married, though she had done almost
all she could to render this impossible, became an obsession with
Mlle de Saint-Amaranthe; the mother gave her support, and
I cannot blame her for this. The hope of thus acquiring social
standing stole into Amélie's heart; she thought that she could
attain it with the addition of a husband, for she had some fortune of her own. This indicated a thorough knowledge of the
period of which the motto might have been: "We have done
with pedigrees. . . . We will discourse about your virtues some
other day; at present show us your gold."

However that may be, the sensitive Amélie, having duly
learned her lesson, begged me to listen to her with the attention
Augustus claimed of Cinna; she imparted to me her resolve
to marry; she was too sure of my heart to imagine I wished to
cause difficulties. She entreated me not to come to see her again
for some time, and to answer as would a man of honour any
question that malevolence might ask about her. She remained
at heart what she had always been towards me from the time
of our coming together; *I would find her again;* death alone
could destroy the feelings she experienced for me. She wound
up her speech, as many a woman has done before, by asking
me to give back a portrait which was too poor a likeness of
her, and some letters too devoid of brilliance for me to value
them.

I received this honeyed dismissal with fair stoicism; I was
ready for it and felt myself more than able to cope with the
situation. I thanked her for having thought so well of me as
to be sure no sacrifice was too great for me to face when her
fate in life was in question. I told her pointblank that I should
consider her house as *for ever* forbidden to me; that no indiscreet act of mine would blight her bridal wreath; but that
though indeed her portrait was as she so justly appraised it—
too little like her to be worth returning—it yet contained so
much of her that the idea of its passing into other hands was

bound to be painful to me. She volunteered to break it; I answered that I was superstitious enough to feel reluctant at such destruction of painted works, which often foreboded a more real destruction. As to her letters, I had given my oath to my first mistress, and to one of my grandfathers when death summoned him, never to give back any, and to this general rule was now added in her special case a more tender consideration, an indefinable feeling that made it impossible for me to part from testimonies both so flattering and so instructive. For, while they would bring back to me her former fidelity, they might blind me to her inconstancy. I kissed her hand with the respect of indifference; she showed me out as one would an ordinary visitor.

I will not, however, hide the fact that I was for long deeply grieved; I took good care she should not know it.

Since I now had only duty to think of, I became a more assiduous courtier in days when death threatened those in authority and nothing was to be gained by such assiduity. The Queen, though she had not entirely overcome her prejudice against me (which she could never bring herself to do at any time or for anyone), nevertheless showed me great kindness when I went to the Tuileries, either at the hour of play, or at other times to offer her my respect. She one day paid me the compliment of saying that she had read all I had written since her misfortunes began; she gave me to understand that it delighted her to see me so faithful in spite of her severity, but that she feared such daring might do me harm without helping them. I replied that daggers were indeed difficult to ward off with the pen, but that as long as I could make use of mine I would write at the prompting of my conscience.

The most remarkable thing about it is that she never spoke to me again but on one occasion (the twenty-first of June). My zeal and my steadfastness apparently disquieted more than they reassured her; it is true that she constantly held converse with those who had declared open war against the throne. *Make yourself feared*, such is the guarantee for all success. But it showed poor knowledge of the human heart to try to tame through condescension men who took note only of her hatred, her prejudices, and her fears; men who, true to their scheme of destruction, saw in their dealing with the court only the chance of striking more accurately. Pitiful victim thus to display more courage in losing herself than was needed to save

herself, never to have a fine impulse, a great idea . . . to
wander at random without plan, without aim, without fixity!
Unfortunate court, whose only supporters were useless or dangerous, while its enemies were so clever that one had to wonder
how ferocity could be coupled with such intelligence! Advice
was asked only from men who could offer none but the worst;
whenever a strong man appeared, he was sent away. Seldom
indeed did any come forth, since little confidence was placed in
the King. It is rare to see strength willing to help weakness
which deliberates when the hour has come to burn one's boats.

That day was about to dawn which would heap more insults
upon Louis XVI than either prison or scaffold: that twenty-first [6]
of June, another stain on our annals, which for a few hours
transformed the King into a hero when his august forehead,
profaned by the cap of license, more than ever proved itself
worthy of the diadem of Saint Louis. For to confront that
armed mob which broke into your palace because it knew there
was no longer any danger in insulting you, which claimed your
crown because you had already surrendered it, and your life
because you were not defending it, this, I say, needed courage
and magnanimity—as you came forth unarmed against these
furious gangs and faced a death that seemed inevitable. And
yet you saw, illustrious martyr, that such courage and magnanimity served your purpose and stood you in good stead. For
the murderers who would have slain you in some obscure corner,
had you hidden yourself behind the battered doors of your
palace, stopped when you opened them yourself, and almost
fell to their knees. That one moment must have fully reflected
its light upon the last deed of your reign; in the purity of your
heart you had preserved your presence of mind; you were aware
of what marks the people, and what marks a king. All advice,
all lessons, all reproaches were summed up in that dismal scene.
. . . Perhaps there *still* was time to give an ear.

Sublime courage was also displayed by the Queen. That of
Mme Elizabeth proved as lofty as her whole life in its smallest
details; but one utterance from her angelic lips makes of this
princess the central figure in the history of that day. The infuriated mob mistook her for the Queen, and as someone tried to
enlighten them, "Do not undeceive them," said this saint.

Are not such words the height of sublimity, an admirable
blending of loftiness in speech and nobleness in deed? [7]

Those four hours of violent affronts, unparalleled in the

history of nations and an offence to the good name of France as much as to royalty, should have taught those who still loved virtue and kindliness, those who still possessed human hearts, that it was time to leave a land where all one could attempt against flourishing crime was to snatch away its possible victims. Every day I came to this resolve, yet some secret power prevented me from carrying it out.

I who had so much opposed emigration, was it dignified that out of fear or impatience with all these horrors I should concede by my conduct what I had denied could be justified? Was it generous to forsake a king who was forsaking himself, and to leave by his side only the men who worked for his downfall and thirsted for his blood? Should not one who had so long been faithful to the monarchy during its decay be present at its obsequies? My weight could not make much difference in the scales; but had they not so much fallen to one side of late because too many people had had the same thought?

While I was thus pondering, the month of August one thousand seven hundred and ninety-two was about to emerge from the immensity of time, and to be swallowed up again into it together with an overturned throne.

Until that dreadful epoch I had kept faithful to my promise of never seeing Mlle de Saint-Amaranthe again; but some hideous foreboding of the fate Providence had in store for her came suddenly to disquiet my heart, which once again flew towards her.

Vergniaud, to whom an unforeseen circumstance had previously brought me near, had left nothing undone to induce me to leave France. He foresaw all that was to happen, even to his own death, yet for honour's sake, and out of laziness, he persisted in the course he had once chosen. He was not given to admitting this, but he frankly imparted it to me some twenty times.

On the eve of that terrible day I once again saw him. It was midnight; I planned to go home and burn some papers, but felt myself irresistibly drawn to Mme de Saint-Amaranthe and her daughter. To give them useful advice, to enlighten them concerning a situation they were not perhaps fully aware of, appeared an easy task. To brave dangers so as to spare them some, to share with them existing perils in rescuing them from greater still to come—this seemed to me another duty that it would have been a delight simply to fulfill. I summoned

one of their valets, made him show me into the room adjoining
the drawing-room, and there wrote them a few words in pencil,
asking them to leave their company and come to me for a
moment. I was received by them with emotion, almost with
tenderness. Their first words were: "Are you in need of us?
Has something bad happened to you? House, money, friends,
help, we offer you all; everything we have is yours." All this
proffered so swiftly and in such a tone as to leave no doubt
concerning their sincerity.

Telling them how touched I was, I made them sit down.
I remember that I placed myself at Amélie's knees. I told them
that what they wanted to do for me they must make haste to
do for themselves; that it was time they should take measures
to leave Paris, which was about to become a stage for events
beyond calculation, for inescapable calamities, particularly for
women; that the great fortune they had gathered, so useful in
other days, would now only be their ruin. I offered to secure
for them passports for England early next day, and to accompany them. I promised on my honour that, on our arrival in
London I would take rooms far from theirs, and that they
would find me the most unexacting friend, just as I had been the
most discreet ever since a tie, far too precarious, had been
severed.

Mme de Saint-Amaranthe said that her affairs were not
such as could be arranged so quickly. She could not leave her
money interests in the lurch, nor her house to be plundered; she
would find it more dangerous to leave France than to remain.
How many victims had been murdered while taking flight who
would have been overlooked in their quiet corner, etc.

Then she held out her hand, and her voice softened as she
uttered the word "Good-bye"; she walked out of the room,
leaving me alone with her daughter. Amélie assured me she
was not happy, that her heart was still mine. She gave way to
a marked display of feeling, but asked me to judge for myself
how impossible it was for her to sever her fate from that of
her mother. "I feel certain," she added, "that this act of resignation will cost me dear, and that I shall be the victim of her
obstinacy."

Then she came forward and kissed me; I felt my face wet
with her tears; I held her close to my heart and again begged
her to come with me. "I cannot," she replied, and drying her
beautiful eyes she slowly withdrew. . . . . I ought to have held
her back . . . to have dared more to convince her.

I can still see her white dress caught and torn by my foot as she drew away; I see it still as it fell in soft folds on the floor, and higher up moulded itself to the heavenly waist and the enchanting outlines of that beautiful body now separating from me for ever. I see again, and I shall always see, that angelic face looking back to comfort me with a smile made all the more moving by eyes brimmed with tears.

It was our last meeting, my last contact with the woman most universally famed in France for her unequalled beauty; a ravishing being whom Nature had taken pleasure to adorn with her most precious gifts, only to display them to the earth for a moment, so that those who constantly invoke her name find nothing left there to compare with her.[8] She could prove weak, but was essentially good and sweet, with a reserve of noble pride which under proper guidance would have enabled her to love only what was equally noble. She had more intelligence than was generally believed, for she was reserved and inclined to conceal her gifts of that kind; and, moreover, people find it difficult to grant such qualities to a person who is already eminently superior in other respects. She was imbued with such delicacy as women alone can possess, and which the most witty often have in less degree; though it must be admitted that delicacy is never found in women entirely devoid of wit. She died with such heroic courage as to inspire her family with it, for each member would have been ashamed not to emulate one who had so much cause for cherishing a life which yet she contemned, as much as she despised those who snatched it from her. She was unsparing in her judgements of others, which she would deliver in low tones; she could even be very hard on people whom she did not view with a woman's eyes. She would sometimes say to me that people who find everybody to their taste risk suiting nobody's taste. She belonged in a word to that type of women of whom no one has a right to speak but those who have been in intimate relationship with them, because by these alone are they really known.

The event I have just pictured, that last interview, has left me still more attached to her, and deep within my heart perpetuates her memory better even than the ties of another nature once uniting me to her. That attempt of mine, which some imperious feeling had prompted, I view as the proof that she had never ceased to be dear to me, and that, indeed, the foreknowledge of her misfortune was the voice of a love which had never died. It pleases me to remember that what I rediscovered in

her heart after a fairly long separation is ample justification
for all she had left in mine. She comes back to my imagination
as I saw her during that last evening, imbued with a more
subtle charm than in the most delightful moments when unveiled
love surrendered her to all my rapture.

Ill-fated, adorable being, how much, under a foreign sky,
have I not wept over her death, her ghastly and premature end;
I could not forgive myself for not having taken her in my arms
and carried her away nestled close to my heart while I smoth-
ered her protests in kisses. . . . I was indignant with myself
for not having saved her in spite of herself. The blow which
had struck her, likewise struck me for long after. . . . I lived
with her spirit. . . . I could not even bear to hear her name
mentioned. . . . Now, I love to speak of her. I could speak
of her for ever. Sometimes, I picture her on the stage, dazzling
with a beauty which has never been effaced—which none of her
rivals could equal; at other times comes a vision of her as the
bloody victim of the most atrocious savagery, and I could well
cry out inwardly from "Macbeth": "All the perfumes of Arabia,
all the waters of the sea, could not wash away this blood."

This murder, shameful even amongst so many others that
also reflect shame upon the mob which sanctioned them by its
apathy and its presence—this murder, so far from legal, was—
after that of Louis XVI—the most smarting blow dealt to my
soul during our political upheaval. A few years later I attempted
to put into verse, which I am the first to acknowledge as far too
poor, the story of her courage and of the death which made
her great, as well as the magnanimity of her last words, which
merely caused surprise to her executioners, since nothing can
move such men.

CHAPTER XXVI

The cloud-capped towers, the gorgeous palaces,
The solemn temples, the great globe itself,
Yea, all which it inherit, shall dissolve
And, like this insubstantial pageant faded,
Leave not a rack behind. We are such stuff
As dreams are made on; and our little life
Is rounded with a sleep.

—Shakespeare.

*P*OSTQUAM *res Asiæ, Priamique evertere gentem im-*
meritam visum Superis . . . , so we repeat pompously
in our trivial knowledge of the days when these empires flourished. We do not realise clearly enough that the inhabited part
of the globe is but one spot, and that we shall always ignore
what nations dwelt at other spots, which were once populated
though no traces of man's existence are now to be found there;
but we know of places where the remains of several ancient
civilisations are mingled with an earth no hand will any longer
plough; places where are buried the vanity of their glory and
the skeletons of their buildings. We possess dates, facts which
we call history (usually an agreed fable), and landmarks situated in the interstices of our uncertain traditions to which our
memory recurs.

All this is adorned with the pompous name of science, as
being an exact knowledge of antiquity and the ways in which
the forefathers of man used to live. Yet it would be best, once
for all, to agree that we know nothing, that our restricted history has perhaps no more authenticity than it has breadth; that
races, kingdoms, catastrophes of all kinds of which we know
nothing have followed one another upon an ever-changing earth;
that we boast of inventions which some thousand centuries previous to us had reached a perfection we no longer bring them to;
that great and useful things have happened under the heavens
which will never be disclosed to man. What we call the childhood of the world in relation to us was perhaps the first stage
of its decrepitude; it is possible that several of the most reputed
historians have been romancers, or have not lived at all; that

the man who is supposed to have written an epic composed only
a song, perhaps could not read, or did not even exist; that a
presumed kind-hearted emperor has really been a tyrant; that
another famous as a ferocious oppressor was adored by his
subjects; or again such and such a queen was a courtesan, and
Glycera an empress.

Thus we might come to acknowledge that, during centuries
we cannot fathom, events may have happened a thousand times
more interesting, more gigantic, than all we have read in our
deceiving books. We might thus no longer dare to decide
whether the earth has not once been a million times more populated than now; whether more people have not been wiped from
it than have remained; whether life was not once more peaceful
or more disturbed, more uniformly swayed by either crime or
virtue; whether its essence was not better known, and our destination after death more clearly understood; whether this very
death, which causes us constant anxieties and reflections, did
not then hold less terror and surprise.

We might even not dare to surmise whether the secret relations between heaven and earth have not once been more clearly
seen, as well as those between man and his Creator, a knowledge
of which could alone explain to us our destination and the designs of God. And we might have to draw from this the natural
conclusion that all we see has perhaps no existence; that it is a
mere optic reflection due to the disposition of our senses, and
not a revelation of the truth. Thus our pride and laughable
boasting would abate; we should at least not hesitate to confess
that in a similar way the day will come when people will be
ignorant of what we once were, what our Europe and empires
have been; that we have no right to erect with arrogant precision any system, nor to proclaim the infallibility of any traditions, or the positive truths of narratives, definitions, analogies,
memories, all those modern impostures received as gospels
on which we thrive. Who knows if, at an immense distance from
now when I write, Louis XIV will not be confused by a far
remote posterity with this Louis XVI in whose reign the sceptre
of sixty-three kings was broken—until even more distant generations arise who will never hear of either king.

Worms that we are.

And will the earth perish? "The great globe itself shall dissolve." Who told you so, dear friend?

I sometimes think likewise . . . sometimes think otherwise.

"The earth is cooling down, the sun is waning; these are symptoms of decay."

Who disclosed to you, dear friend, that glowing heat is a necessity for the continuance of this globe, as a warm climate is assumed to be a remedy for consumptive people? Who said to you that a waning sun will not be replaced by thousands of years of another more brilliant and glowing sun? Who proved to you that the whole system is not but a blending of apportioned contrasts, a well-contrived recurrence of decadence and regeneration? Who told you that the earth had not thus several times declined before regaining a new splendour, a new youth, which your eyes have not seen and will never see?

So, believe me, let us speak of what we see, of what we touch and what surrounds us. Let us speak of it modestly as is fitting to blind people and visionaries such as we are, since we live in an inexplicable dream from birth to death, and possess no mathematical data about anything. Since we can judge sanely neither what is round us, nor what makes us, nor what each man is in himself, let us limit ourselves to some short estimates, honoured by many doubts, of the spectacle offering itself to us during the little spark that is our life. Let us hand down to our sons some of the facts that appeared to us indisputable because we happened at the time to be actors or spectators. Let us write, since a craze for tachygraphy has gone to the head of everybody; but let us abstain from abstractions, decrees, verdicts, irrevocable decisions, rigid theories, unanswerable proofs, historical certitudes, the study of the universe, the calculations of chronology, and all the lavish cant of our chimerical presumptions, which we ought to christen the history [1] of our doubts, our blindness, and, above all, our errors. Let us write, I repeat, with the conviction that our written words and assertions will be altered, that only a mutilation of our narratives will reach distant generations, themselves obliterated by others who will know nothing of these facts, no more than we have any knowledge of most of the highly interesting incidents that preceded us in ancient days.

This one solemn and terrible occurrence which to me appears plain, but which will certainly be disfigured and opened to question for some of my successors, and perhaps entirely unknown to others following them, is to-day happening under my frightened eyes, while my heart is frozen with horror and my reason staggers. If anything great or terrible has ever been performed

amongst the children of man, it is the work of this day. . . .
All you living spectres, my companions during this journey
through this valley of gloom, all you future spectres due to be
born and soon to die, you may believe me. . . . I have been
an eye-witness, I have seen. . . . Listen to me!

The palace of our kings is in flames, the hand of Heaven
stirs up the fire. The oldest established throne in the world is
cast down; its occupant, the descendant of the glorious rulers
of glorious France, is dragged unresisting towards disgrace and
death, across a palace strewn with the dead. He tries to escape
with his family in the glare of his blazing palace, which is col-
lapsing; he goes to beg life and freedom; the gifts of those
whom he implores are a prisoner's bonds, their treaty of peace
is signed in the grave. In the midst of the huge crowd clamouring for his deposition and execution, do you not recognise the
gangs of foreign murderers? Do you not hear their jargon?
Do you not see by their features that they were not born among
you, that they lead a credulous and unruly mob, an army of
proletarians, and that they are in short but foreign bandits
let loose in this realm by the enemies of France? They are supported and maintained by some of your misguided compatriots,
by others to whom any deed is good, even the destruction of
France, provided they are paid for it.

Fellow countrymen, renowned for fidelity to your rulers, you
who always took pride in your love and respect for the man
who had the honour of governing such a great people as you
are, look at this king hemmed in by the floods of a mob who
once were his subjects, reviled by threats and insults during the
journey which takes him to the hall where the legislative body [2]
holds its meetings. Ah! do not any longer trample under foot
greatness reduced to dust, let your hearts of steel be softened
in the presence of defenceless misfortune! But if the path of
this unhappy prince is strewn with so many thorns, at least he
will find, when he reaches the sanctuary of the law, the inviolable
regard which in all ages has been shown to the misfortunes of
imploring women and frightened children. Alas, no, no, no!
Some well-meaning fanatics, others who are systematic schemers
of crimes, and still others paid by foreign gold, make him taste
every drop of the cup of bitterness through the utmost mortifi-
cation, and further extend the boundaries of his misfortune.

The man who had been king of a nation famous for its
devotion to its rulers hears all the projects of his doom debated

to his very face. A fate which ten years previously it would have been a sacrilege to think of for him is now discussed before him and his family with impudent ferocity. . . . His deposition and captivity are debated, and, if he but knows how to hear, sentence of death is there passed upon him. He is present at the discussion by which is decreed his imprisonment; the last servants who had remained faithful to him are torn from his side; they are reproached for their tears, which for many of them will prove a death-warrant.

August and pitiful family, do not grieve. Preserve a serene brow as you walk towards this tower where the last transaction in your calamities will be settled. Since you will soon escape from men, rejoice that you came to dwell within these gloomy walls. Your greatness belonged to a better world. Could you ever regret this one? Could you ever regret anything pertaining to life? Men can only snatch it away, it is the furthest extent of their power, and it is the favour your enemies reserve for you. Beg them only not to defer it too long; you will leave behind tormentors more to be pitied than the victims.

Vergniaud, whom I have already mentioned, and who was the most eloquent orator in the Assemblies (if eloquence means the power of moving the heart and of lending warmth to debates), Vergniaud, I repeat, viewed with supreme scorn all factions, and perhaps the one to which he belonged even more than any other; but his indifference, his vanity, and his taste for oratory strengthened the bonds that tied him to his party. He would have liked to find some honest means (as if there were need of an honest excuse to forsake what was not honest) to free himself. He would have preferred rest and an income of twenty thousand livres to all this noise and this blood.[3] He used to say so, and perhaps meant it, yet he never agreed to abandon a career he pursued with so much dislike.

He had often said to me: "I feel sure the King is an honest man, but he cannot be saved. Let him abdicate and retire where he likes with the Queen, leaving us his son. There is still time for this. I have taken it upon myself to ask for the decree for the suspension of his power. Warn him, if you like, that he runs the greatest danger, that by one act alone can he escape it, and that he has but one moment to parry the blow."

On the eleventh of August I reminded him of this conversation which I had had with him less than a week previously. I begged him to see that this measure of abdication be adopted,

as well as a decree granting their Majesties permission to retire
with a pension outside the kingdom, etc. . . . *"It is no longer
in my power to do so,"* he replied. *"The moment has passed."*

When such people as the Abbé de M——, the Chevalier de
P——, and other envious ones, declared in London that the
letter I had addressed to the King on July 27, 1792, was well
thought out and well written, but that they did not recognise
my right to write it, these honest folks were saying a stupid and
sorry thing.[4] In circumstances so solemn it was the duty of every
Frenchman to write to the King to inform him of useful truths;
above all is this true of men who, on account of their connections, their acknowledged devotion, and their eagerness to preserve the social structure, could not be suspected in their inten-
tions, nor accused of irreverence even if their zeal expressed
itself somewhat austerely. But envious people, often men who
have no grounds for envy, assume the parts of thinkers and
orators if they have some little gift that way; the thinkers
try to do harm, the orators manage to be an inconvenience;
they do not know that the great and outstanding merit consists
in thinking only sound thoughts and speaking only at the right
moment.

However this may be, that letter which has been often
quoted, even in foreign newspapers, and translated into several
languages, proved of prophetic daring. It contained the whole
truth; it was a warning of death with a statement as to effective
means of warding it off. His Majesty did not judge it as did
MM. de M——, P——, and their likes; he sent me his thanks
by M. de La Porte, and the letter which the King eventually
managed to have handed to me, and which I have deposited in
a safe place,[5] would be sufficient to confound jealous and wicked
people. It suffices at any rate for my conscience and is a full
reward for my fidelity and the fulfillments of my duties, which
I *then* religiously looked upon as binding.

While the ashes of the palace were still smouldering, I wandered about the streets of Paris in the garb of poverty and dirt,
the only means of safety in such a place, and I mixed with this
redoubtable mob from which I could not tear myself. I asked
questions, the answers to which were often heinous, often full
of good sense, but which always showed a predominant thirst
for slaughter and destruction. Not one of these men, drunk with
carnage, remembered that he had been born under a king whom
he had revered as equal to God upon earth; not one recalled the

innate respect his class had felt for the privileged orders. All had shaken off the invisible but sacred chain that unites the whole citizens of a kingdom into one family; the wildest tribes of savages would have been more ready to submit to law. That of destruction which they had taken unto themselves, that of the tiger which slaughters without provocation and without purpose—such was their new law, the only one they obeyed.

I swear that no fear for my own safety ever entered my heart; but I was seized by unconquerable horror at the sight of these torrents of blood shed with the savagery of cannibals and with the sanction of the government, the only government which then ruled over France and which could protect a disarmed majority. Heaven, what an ægis! what a protection! This thought, and the helplessness coupled with it, afforded me a torment others perhaps may not have felt as acutely as I did.

And think of an Assembly debating matters that steel and the flames had judged beforehand; resolving problems whose solutions were murders; and being victorious over the royal family already then captive and marked for the axe!

One can contemn life yet find oneself weak when confronted with widespread destruction, with an array of horrors that freeze the imagination through despair and helplessness.

Arrests increased steadily, all fears seemed justified, all excesses went unpunished. Consternation or daring, hopeless fear or unbridled license, distorted all faces. The henchmen of murder and anarchy had several times entered my rooms, either by force or cunning. I kept away from home for twenty-four hours, but was yet hesitating, for it is so hard to flee from one's country even if she has become a harsh mother who disinherits her children or slaughters them!

The Abbé d'Espagnac,[6] whom I met at the house of some friends, advised me to see Danton, and offered to take me to him. I was civilly received by him, and he showed himself interested, though he told me from the first that he knew my principles and my views, of which my behaviour was the consequence. He preferred them, he added, to the sham Jacobinism prevalent amongst my caste, and he would prove to me that he held my frankness in higher esteem than the hypocrisy of a false patriotism or the cowardly zeal certain men displayed for a revolution that they really hated and ought to abhor. In fact he promised me my life; he spoke in good faith.

But triumvirs at all times have always disputed, conceded,

snatched, or handed over victims to each other. I learned on the next day, through Manuel, and I feel sure it was Danton who had me warned, that he had forsaken me against his will at the importunities of Fabre d'Eglantine, and that my head had been the subject of a wrangle between them! . . . Evil tongues will say that it was scarcely worth the trouble of a dispute; I willingly agree with them; but men whose heads were worth even less than mine did all they could to preserve them.

It became also impossible to entertain doubts as to Condorcet's sinister plotting against me, a vengeance he had been brewing for a long time. Some very suspicious emissaries were seen in the neighbourhood. Questions they asked about me so alarmed a valet that he followed them, joined them, adroitly questioned them, and learned for a certainty at whose bidding they came. On my arrival in London, six weeks later, I published a statement which attracted enough attention to perpetuate both my scorn and the shame of this academician and geometer [7] turned conspirator. A famous doctor whose vanity I had hurt, and who had acquired some influence, also pursued me unmercifully; he wanted to treat me as he did his patients.

With so many inducements and such good reasons, it was quite permissible not to hesitate any more. I no longer opposed the earnest entreaties of one of my woman friends, who did more to bring me to leave France than mere advice, reflections, and dangers. She procured me a passport, which I filled myself with an assumed name after I had more or less clumsily counterfeited the signatures of the two municipal officers Da—— and Ta——. This passport, which ought to have given me away a thousand times, helped me to cross the whole kingdom and—just as happens to Fame—acquired more substance on the way than it had at Saint-Denis where I proudly exhibited it for the first time. It is there that it began to be adorned with the signatures of both civil and military authorities; it was only looked upon unfavourably at Abbeville, where I made the mistake of being seen in broad daylight in a sort of post-chaise which I had hired at the previous relay.

I was taken to the town-hall to the officials of the place, who were the most arrant demagogues that a provincial town could have vomited for its administration. They were five or six fanatics quite in keeping with their functions and their epoch. They wanted to write to their brothers of the Paris municipality. I represented myself as sent on a secret mission, and held them responsible for any delay to which their patriotism might compel me. My face and some vestige of elegance and decency did not please them, though I entertained them in the best style on the measures *we* had taken in Paris after the fall of the late "tyrant." At last the least ferocious of the gang decided in favour of "Let him go," and his opinion prevailed; so it is at Abbeville that I finally found my papers in perfect order, since I had the satisfaction of seeing my rag of a passport endorsed: "After submission to the permanent council, at a sitting of our assembly, the present passport, duly examined and verified, and to each of its clauses having affixed our signatures, etc, etc. . . ."

Before leaving Paris I had handed over to Champcenetz the key of a desk, and had begged him earnestly to go to my rooms after my departure, as soon as he could do so in safety, and burn two packets of letters labelled No. 5 and bearing green seals. I had also enjoined that he should try all means in his power to see if he could not send me a portrait which I greatly treasured. Most likely he was unable to comply with my wishes, for not only did I never receive the portrait, but I have learned since from a man who held quite against his will some official posts at that period that the letters had been read by the municipal council, and had hugely amused its esteemed members. This was fortunate! But what was less so was that a society lady, whose regard I most highly valued, was compromised in the eyes of the man it was most to her interest to spare. If these pages come to her hands, she will no doubt regret the letter which reached me in Hamburg in 1797; she will acknowledge that I was guilty only in having too long delayed in destroying tokens of an affection she so much forgot, and of which I have made no mention in these memoirs, where no indication of it, however minute, will ever be recorded.

As for this unlucky Champcenetz, I had done all I could to snatch him away from the murderers who slaughtered him. It was not difficult to foresee that the man who had jested about everything would be marked for death when those who distributed it made of it a joke. I demonstrated to him only too easily that no miracle could happen in his favour, and that it would be truly one if he were to avoid the exile now so general a rule. For the only possible way of saving oneself was by obscurity and silence. A man whose life was spent in showing himself and creating a sensation, in seeing his joke of to-day quoted on the morrow, in making others laugh and in himself bursting with laughter on their behalf and his, such a man could scarcely be suspected of conspiracy, but would become a too conspicuous target ever to be missed in days when the victims were sent to the scaffold in the order in which they attracted attention, and when the sole means of keeping alive was to pass for dead. His mind heard me, but his laziness did not understand me. So that I might myself fall a victim the more certainly, he not only did everything to induce me not to leave the kingdom, but even offered me a bed in his rooms and one half of his flat. He predicted that in the state of affairs then prevalent, with the gates of Paris closed and suspicion everywhere armed and on the watch, I would be arrested in the country as so many others had been, would be identified and reserved for a more frightful death.

It was not my fate to believe him; I said my last farewell to him in this world. In subsequent months, I watched for long and with anxiety, and found his name much later than I expected on those fatal lists which Europe read with terror and indignation, while despairing of saving a population of frightened lambs whom tigers crammed into caves, before glutting themselves on their blood.

The woman friend who had brought me to leave France, had also secured me a man whom she could rely on as much as on herself. I left Champcenetz and found my escort awaiting me at my friend's rooms. He dressed me up in a braided hat and a coachman's long coat, and made me climb up in this garb at the back of his cabriolet. We arrived near Saint-Denis at an out-of-the-way house, where I spent the night in a room that could hardly be honoured by the name of loft. On the next day I took leave of my guide, and made my way towards a seaport, sometimes on foot, sometimes in hired vehicles, most often hidden by day and travelling by night, recognised three times on the road by men who could have betrayed me, but arriving at Boulogne on August 25, 1792, at ten o'clock at night.

The description of my appearance had reached there before me. I had, however, previously decided to trust myself with the Englishwoman who kept the Hôtel d'Angleterre. I had often put up there, but in a very different state from that which I was now about to offer to her gaze. I looked in through the windows in the courtyard, where I noticed a light, to discover if I could see Mistress Knouth. Having recognised her, I walked into the parlour where to my great satisfaction I found her alone. My dirty clothes, my face already somewhat lean, and the secrecy I enjoined on her, made her welcome me with a kind of dread. She perhaps mistook me for one of those ghosts which her countrywoman, Mistress Radcliffe, scatters with such profusion in her novels, conceived and written most likely in church-yards. I gave her my name, and it took some time to convince her that I was still an inhabitant of this worst of all possible worlds. At last I asked her if she would justify my trust, or inform against me; I only urged her not to keep me waiting long. She did not hesitate, and taking me herself to a room where she locked me in, she soon after brought me some supper. I slept fifteen hours, forgetful of the Revolution, municipal officers, murderers, and tyrants. Even my dreams were as peaceful as my sleep.

When I woke up, the Sieur Parker, the business partner of that honest woman, came to offer to get me on board a ship which was taking Lord Gower's servants and horses to England. He brought me the captain, who undertook to provide me with a strawbed on his ship for the sum of twenty-five louis. I should have agreed if he had been equally eloquent to convince me that I could elude the customs officers and other public officials who would visit his ship. But as this attempt seemed to me too dangerous I offered the captain a present to make sure of a silence which he kept. At last Parker appeared in my hiding place with a companion of most crabbed and sorry countenance. The fellow was, said Parker, the most honest of smugglers, who answered on his life to get me to Dover safe and sound. The services of this man were dearer: he demanded forty louis.

Who could guarantee that such a man would not betray me, or have me drowned at sea to shorten matters? . . . But there was no time to consider such miserable details, I trusted myself to him straightway. He slung a game-bag over my shoulders, he made me take a gun. We walked the short distance to the sea, and were soon in the water knee-deep and following the coast. My companion kept on using his gun, and obliged me to do the same, to shoot I do not know what birds which often were beyond our reach, and which I took no care to hit. At last, after two hours of going thus, we had to get into the water up to our breasts to reach a boat that seemed to have a wretched bed sheet for a sail and was under the care of two seamen whose language and whole appearance could scarcely inspire confidence. My companion said a few words I did not understand, and, catching hold of me by the waist, threw me into the boat as one would a man whose money one has received and whose legs and arms are not to be reckoned with.

My position was neither brilliant nor pleasant. I did not take long to size it up, and quickly decided to remedy it. I took a seat at one end of the boat. "Be sure," I told them as I drew two pistols from my pocket and loaded them, "that I shall kill the first man who attempts to approach me. On the other hand you will receive the ten louis I have on me, if we reach Dover before nine o'clock this evening, or any other port in England." My speech seemed to surprise them, but without more being said that I can recall, and after a crossing of ten hours, we arrived in the evening before seven at Stockport, drenched like the hero in an opera who reaches shore by swimming.

The clergyman and the magistrate of the place came at once to me with the most obliging and hospitable proposals. Their kind-heartedness and patriotic ardour were mingled with an inquisitiveness and a longing to know the real state of affairs in France. I satisfied their curiosity in a few words, and as soon as horses were harnessed I gratefully bade them good-bye. Then, getting into the post-chaise, I set out on the road to Dover where I arrived two hours later.

There I at last breathed freely. I thanked God for my escape from my enemies, and for my arrival in a safe country. But the comforting sight of this land could not make me forget my own, from which I found myself exiled against my will. I remained two days at Dover, wandering at random on the beach; and in the agitation and disquiet of my mind I asked the waves the purpose of these sudden changes which swing us from storms to peace and back again from peace to storms; I asked them how they could so swiftly raise up their crests towards heaven and as swiftly again appear perfectly smooth; my questions went up to Him whose all-powerful hand raises the waves to hurl them back again into the depths of the abyss; a mournful and clamouring voice seemed to answer: "The God of storms is also the God of revolutions." Everything on land and sea implies change and inconsistency; yet nothing happens but through an immutable order, and in accordance with the designs and the wisdom of the Almighty; everything in the universe follows a fixed plan and imperishable principles.

I glanced with regret at the land and the sea, and, buried in deep thoughts, then looked towards the sky; my hope was in Heaven, which is the last and sole refuge for hope, where man is neither betrayed nor forsaken.

At Dover I found Lord Cholmondeley with his charming wife. I had made his acquaintance in France. They were on the beach looking at the sea, but for reasons other than those which moved me. They were happy; they had a country; they possessed all that lends it value and renders it pleasant; they lived amidst the enjoyments of a huge fortune. Lady Cholmondeley was fond of society, not in the manner generally displayed by her sex, for women are less bound to it and value it less when they are under the sway of a passionate love-attachment, but as a happy woman who has become indifferent to it in her happiness. She was about to embark for Naples, hastening to go to her mother the Duchesse de Ru——, who was dying; and she had come to the beach, trembling and undecided, to find out whether the sea would carry her quietly to the shores of Italy. She seemed engaged in exorcising the waves, which she did not find peaceful enough; but her husband was endeavouring to give her courage, though he shared her anxiety, and tried to postpone as long as possible the hour of their parting. They neither of them considered that the sea is never more dangerous than when it conceals its storms, and that its anger often immediately follows peaceful and cloudless moments. France also had thus once been peaceful and her sky serene!

I had some bills of exchange on the firm Minet and Factor, and after settling this business I started on my way to London, where I arrived before night. For the sake of truth I must say that in England I found all classes disturbed and depressed over the unrest, trouble, and prospects in France. The fate of my fatherland excited general interest from the highest to the lowest classes. The man who held the reins of English politics and extended his leadership over all Europe, the man whom France could justly name as the originator and instrument of her fall and her griefs, this man, Pitt, surely must have abhorred as a man the principles which as a British minister he followed. I trust that before the judgement seat of the Almighty he will be able to show adequate grounds for having kindled the flames that were to consume France, until a salving hand extinguished them. To his own country he left a future of unhappiness which on his death-bed he foresaw when he cried: "Oh, the times! Oh, my country!" These last words of the son of the great Chatham are also mine.[8]

But here I stop, I throw down the pen, and I shall wait to publish, or at least to write, the second and most interesting part of this story (more than fifteen years of wandering without aim or rest in the chief states of Europe and the New World) until I have submitted this work to a tribunal that never deceives if self-conceit is kept in check and the mind is sincere: I mean the tribunal of Time and Reflection. I shall, above all, wait until without risk of danger, bitterness, and evil results this work, which is at all events unusual, may do no harm either to its author or the actors I have placed on the stage; and the best means of attaining this useful and moral aim is to arrange that the book appears only after the death of both author and actors.

NOTES

INTRODUCTION

[1] Charles-Joseph, Prince de Ligne—born in 1735 in Hainault, the son of Prince Claude Lamoral and the Princess of Salm and the Holy Empire—belonged to one of the most ancient and distinguished houses in the Netherlands, then in the possession of Austria. The family was allied to various royal houses and occupied the highest rank in the Austrian viceregal court at Brussels, where, as well as at Belœil, the Princes de Ligne had palatial residences. Our Prince de Ligne served in the Austrian army, but was always imbued with the French spirit which predominated in Brussels. He was at home in all the courts of Europe and is considered the last great figure in the European world before it was broken up by the French Revolution and the Napoleonic wars. He died in Vienna in 1814, where, at the famous Congress, he had been surrounded by the young aristocrats of all nations, eager to hear his stories of the ancient world, and he retained to the last the courage of his characteristic gaiety. Much is still written about him; see for instance L. Dumont-Wilden, *La Vie de Charles-Joseph de Ligne* (1927). Both the German and early French editors of Tilly give the Prince de Ligne the title of "Comte de la Tour-d'Auvergne"; it is not easy to understand why, for he had no claim to that title, and the mistake could hardly have been made by Tilly. *Trans.*

CHAPTER I

[1] The original German translation (the first published edition of the Memoirs) gives no date. The German translator adds in a footnote: 1764 or 1765. *Trans.* [2] Mademoiselle Guéroult de Boisclairaux, daughter of M. Guéroult de Saint-Loup. *Trans.* [3] In these Memoirs many names are indicated only by their first letters. The German translator tells us that Tilly added the marginal note: "I set down only the first letters, often only three stars, for I would rather be accused of writing romance than of writing libels." Mme de C—— was Suzanne Esnault, born at Le Mans on July 22, 1711, and married to François-Louis le Bourdais de Chassillé. She died in 1785. *Trans.* [4] Who since . . . (qui depuis . . .): an allusion to a line in Voltaire's *Henriade:* "Qui depuis . . . mais alors il était vertueux." *Trans.* [5] Apparently the Marquis de Vennevelle. *Trans.*

CHAPTER II

[1] Marie Antoinette was then twenty-three years of age. *Trans.* [2] This is a line of Corneille: "Et le voilà connu, ce secret plein d'horreur."

Trans. ³ The Prince d'Hénin traced back his ancestors to the Comtes d'Alsace, one of the most ancient families of Europe, regarding itself the equal of the Bourbons. It had a common trunk with the Hapsburgs. The Prince d'Hénin mentioned here was sentenced to death by the Revolutionary tribunal in 1794. *Trans.* ⁴ François Bertholet Campan, husband of the well-known Madame Campan (née Jeanne-Louise Genet), who wrote the *Mémoires sur la vie de Marie-Antoinette.* Madame Campan was at first reader to Mesdames, Louis XV's sisters, then for many years first lady-in-waiting to the queen; as she had, as she puts it herself, "spent half her life at court either by the side of Mesdames or near Marie Antoinette," she was well placed to "gather many curious facts whose publication may prove interesting." These Memoirs, however, were not published until 1823, the year after her death. Born in Paris in 1752, she died in 1822. *Trans.* ⁵ Master of the queen's pages. *Trans.* ⁶ This refers to Tilly's open liaison with the actress Adeline. *Trans.* ⁷ Monsieur de Nancré. *Trans.* ⁸ The mistake was that Mlle Allard was the dancer and Mlle Sophie Arnould the actress. *Trans.* ⁹ A line from Voltaire: "Où l'honneur outragé devait verser du sang." *Trans.*

CHAPTER III

¹ This lady was attached to the household of Madame Adélaïde, great-aunt to Louis XVI. There were fourteen such ladies of whom seven were countesses. *Trans.*

² Bellevue, on the Seine, between Versailles and Paris, was the seat of Mesdames, the king's great-aunts, sisters of Louis XVth. *Trans.* ³ *Zémire and Azor:* a light opera very popular at that period; *Andromaque,* by Racine; *Zaïre,* by Voltaire. *Trans.* ⁴ Perhaps in 1804 [the German translator states that in the original manuscript 1804 had first been written 1803] when I write this, the habits of high society have somewhat changed, and perhaps the school for manners, which polite circles were, is for ever closed. Well! it will be the easier for writers to be more correct in their portraitures and truer in their pictures. . . . If out-of-date customs are mentioned in their presence, or things marked with the stamp of this good taste reputed the best, they will say as the Maréchal de Termes at eighty years of age, when someone mentioned a woman in childbirth: "Do they still make love nowadays?" *Author.*

CHAPTER IV

¹ That is to say the living bound to the dead, body to body and face to face, as described by Virgil in the Eighth Book of the *Æneid. Trans.*

CHAPTER V

¹ Claude Joseph Dorat left behind him fables, much verse of a fugitive kind, and many tragedies. He was a typical representative of what was considered the effeminate elegance of the eighteenth century. *Trans.*

[2] The *Cours de littérature. Trans.* [3] French grammarian and critic, of great authority in his own day, who had spoken very contemptuously of Dorat's *Célibataire. Trans.* [4] Once prime minister under Louis XV, M. de Maurepas was recalled to this post by the young Louis XVI at his advent to the throne, and upon the recommendation of the king's great-aunt, Mme Adélaïde. Although almost eighty years of age at this time, M. de Maurepas still retained the light-heartedness which had caused him to lose his post under Louis XV on account of some frivolous verses he had written about Mme de Pompadour. *Trans.* [5] Parfaite Thais, daughter of Louis Mailly Comte de Rubempré and highly connected. She had been married at 13 to the count, afterwards Prince de Montbarrey and minister of war, and was noted for her charm, her wit and independence of character, which last trait made her residence at court rather disagreeable to her. *Trans.* [6] I apologise for the faithfulness of this narrative, which is not in the best of taste, but I wanted to preserve the energy of the wording; the count thought that, speaking to an Englishman, he might depart from strict propriety. General Clerfayt was present during the conversation and I have the account from him. *Author.* [7] Philippe-Égalité. *Trans.* [8] I express myself thus in agreement with current and popular belief, but it is evident to me (I shall perhaps speak of this later) that M. le Duc d'Orléans has never sincerely aspired to the throne; he would have been much embarrassed by it. The ringleaders have not even thought of it for him, except that, for a few weeks, Mirabeau perhaps had such views, but quickly abandoned them since he had too much tact to look upon their fulfilment as possible when he considered his hero. *Author.* [9] I show those monsters Robespierre and his assistants, who are a disgrace to the French name and to humanity, too much honour when I compare them to Marius and Sulla. These Romans had great qualities and great talent, though they stained them with a thirst for blood. That is why I mention them here, and also because the men of blood in France invoked their example which they did not follow but outdid. A second Augustus, Bonaparte, has arisen who has not, like him of old, stained his fame with proscriptions, but though great and victorious in the field is still greater by his restoration of political order in France, laying afresh the shattered foundations of social life. *Author.* [10] From Racine's *Bérénice: Dans l'orient désert quel devint mon ennui!" Trans.* [11] From. Racine's *Phèdre: Ainsi que la vertu, le crime a ses degrés Trans.* [12] A parody on lines from the *Misanthrope* of Molière. *Trans.* [13] This conversation, a sequence to events I do not try to justify, was at any rate in French and carried on tête-à-tête; it would be impossible to imagine, like our new-fangled novelists, that it took place in a salon or during a dinner. *Author.* [14] *Lupa sum, et lupa permanere volo.*

CHAPTER VI

[1] Gabrielle Yolande Martine de Polastron, born in 1749, died in Vienna in 1793. She was already a little over thirty when she became the Queen's favourite. *Trans.* [2] He was the King's chaplain, whose tastes for hunting and gambling were much opposed to his calling but did not prevent him from fulfilling his duties. After spending most of the night at

the gambling table, he never went to bed without reading his breviary. *Trans.* ⁸ He was a minister of state, but not well thought of. An epitaph written for him runs: "Here lies a common little man, Who bore three names and left none." Mme de Maurepas was his sister. *Trans.* ⁴ The famous Princess de Lamballe who died on the scaffold through her devotion to the queen, having returned from England to be at her side in the hour of danger. She was the superintendent of the Queen's household, but when the Duchesse de Polignac became the Queen's favourite she was less in demand, although she retained her official position. She was noted for her charm, good heart, and cheerfulness, but was not highly intelligent. She had a very sensitive nervous system and was liable to faint at the smell of violets or the sight of a lobster. It appears that her doctor was inclined to attribute such nervous attacks, which were then common amongst women of high society, to solitary vice engendered by the rigid rules of court life. *Trans.* ⁵ From Racine's *Britannicus*. The translation of these lines is borrowed from Mary Duclaux's *Life of Racine*. *Trans.* ⁶ I am convinced that I know every trait of Mlle de la Vallière, whom of course I never saw. There are two women I have been in love with from early youth, whose portraits I bear in my heart and in my pocket book and believe that I know far better than any of the people I have associated with in real life. One is the Duchesse de la Vallière whom I know, so to speak, by heart, having so thoroughly absorbed the descriptions of Petitot, Mme de Sévigné and the memoirs of the time. The other is Rousseau's Julie whom, however, I left off loving when she became Mme de Volmar; of the latter it was all the easier to make an imaginary picture since she never existed. Campana made an exact picture of her from my indications. I kept it a long time and then sacrificed it to the caprice of a second Mme de Merteuil, who told me I was too sensible to be so foolish as to keep the portrait of an imaginary person, and that it must represent a real woman I had loved; in short she must have it and destroy it. I was weak enough to give it to her. As regards Mme de Tourvel, her I actually knew in real life as I will tell later. *Author.* Mme de Merteuil and Mme de Tourvel are characters in Laclos's *Liaisons dangereuses*. *Trans.* ⁷ He was of creole origin, born in Santo Domingo, of which his father was governor. He became lieutenant-general and was appointed grand falconer of France. He was the best friend of the Comte d'Artois (second brother of Louis XVI and later on Charles X). He was extremely popular at court and successful with women, although he became a very good husband and father, and Mme de Genlis quotes a saying to the effect that "there are only two men who knew how to talk to women, Lekain on the stage and Vaudreuil in society." A letter of his to Tilly is given in the introduction. *Trans.* ⁸ This Abbé de Vermond was French tutor to Marie Antoinette, first at the court of Vienna, and later at Versailles, where he followed her previous to her marriage to the Dauphin at the age of fifteen. Of humble origin, Vermond is supposed to have become the confidant and the sole adviser of his young pupil, whom he guided and dominated. He retained his ascendency over Marie Antoinette even after she became Queen, although Louis XVI did not show great liking for him. Mme Campan refers to him as Marie Antoinette's "evil star," and reproaches him, amongst other things, with having given his pupil a strong dislike for court etiquette, so necessary a part of the duties of a queen of France. When the Duchesse de Polignac had left France, popular hatred fixed itself on the Abbé de Vermond, and the Queen, fearing for his life, facilitated his escape to Vienna. *Trans.* [9] This incident of the clock is not to be found in the German translation, and was perhaps introduced by the first French editor from Mme Campan's *Mémoires sur la vie de Marie-Antoinette,* though the wording is different, and Mme Campan gives eleven instead of ten as the hour at which the king used to retire. *Trans.* [10] Staff officer and lieutenant in the king's body-guard; he has since shown great fidelity to the unfortunate Louis XVI, and has been esteemed and loved by the king as he was worthy to be. *Author.*

CHAPTER VII

[1] He, nevertheless, died in hospital where, as a special favour, he had been transferred, on account of illness, from the prison in which the terrorists were detaining him. His son, a man of great promise, was shot dead by a gendarme, in these days of freedom, and in the same country-house. [Here ends Tilly's note. This uncle must have been René-Louis de la Molnière who defended the palace of the Tuileries against the mob on August 10, 1792, the day when Louis XVI, Marie Antoinette, and the royal family sought refuge near the Assemblée Nationale to be, two days later, put in the Temple prison. Tilly de la Molnière was there wounded. One of his sons was killed in Maine, during the Vendée Rebellion. He must be the one referred to by Tilly. *Trans.*] [2] Belesme and Alençon, in Maine. *Trans.* [3] Tilly added later: "She is dead." *Trans.* [4] The poem not bearing on the story, it seems best to give it in French as a sample of Tilly's verse. *Trans.* [5] Auguste Henri Marie Picot de Dampierre, born in Paris in 1756, had early in youth shown a strong liking for the life of a soldier and daredevil. Having obtained an officer's commission in the Guards, he secretly went off to the siege of Gibraltar, but was arrested at Barcelona by the King's orders and brought back to his regiment. He sought further adventures by being amongst the first to ascend in one of Montgolfier's balloons, and by going to Berlin to study the military displays which Frederick the Great organised. Louis XVI one day, while reviewing the Guards, noticed Dampierre wearing a long-tail wig and remarked: "Look at that madman with his Prussian ways!" This remark, added to other unpleasantness, caused Dampierre to leave the Guards. He later became an associate of the Duc d'Orléans (Philippe Égalité), and sided with the Revolution as did this Prince. However, having been defeated during a battle while in chief command of the *Armée du Nord,* he deliberately sought death. It is well known that the Convention was merciless to defeated generals; one defeat was sufficient to result in recall and even indeed the scaffold. *Trans.* [6] This is a reference to the Chevalier de Boufflers' tale, *La Reine de Golconde. Trans.* [7] "Listen," he said to me one day, "to *my* definition of Luxury; it is the best which was ever given." "Keep it to yourself," I replied, "for me it is *superfluity." Author.* This Gabriel Senac de Meilhan, politician and author, son of Senac, doctor to Louis XV, was in turn governor of Aunis, Provence, and Hainault. He was indeed devoured by ambition, and put forward the most ridiculous pretentions. The Revolution brought his political career

to an end. He took refuge in Germany, Poland, and finally Russia, where he became an intimate friend of Catherine II. However, the Empress, being less satisfied with the man than with the author, and fearing the whims of Paul I, granted Meilhan a pension and sent him away. He settled in Austria and died in Vienna in 1803. *Trans.* [8] The word *roué* has a double meaning: *roué,* a criminal broken on the wheel (*roue*), and *roué,* a libertine, a profligate. This second meaning originated in the early part of the 18th century, during the Regency, to designate a gallows-bird, a man without morals or principles, one worthy of the wheel. Mercier, in his *Tableau de Paris,* wondered how the expression could ever have come to be used lightly. "People even speak of an *amiable roué,"* he exclaimed, "meaning a man of the world who is a libertine, but adorns vice with seductive charm and wit." *Trans.*

CHAPTER VIII

[1] I know a man, who occupies a very distinguished position in a northern court, of whom it is only fair to say that he became a complete idiot after he had killed a man in a duel, this almost against his will. As he is absent-minded and by nature rather impolite, people kindly bear in mind that he is obsessed by a ruling idea which has upset what brains he had. For the last twenty years this poor devil can scarcely take in what he is told; he hardly knows what he does or what he says. All this is a credit to him. Such and such a Frenchman who has killed several men sleeps twelve hours out of twenty-four. Is this *for* or *against* France? I answer in all seriousness: against! *Author.* [2] "This assumption of being the first lover is so deceitful," says M. de Buffon, "that men ought to grow easy of mind on this point, instead of giving vent, as is usual, to either unfair suspicions or false rejoicing, according to what they imagine they have found." *Author.*

CHAPTER IX

[1] Perhaps Tilly had in mind the Margravine of Anspach whom he is said to have struck with a whip. See Introduction. *Trans.* [2] The German editor remarks that this was a woman loved by Tilly, who sought and found her death by drowning. See the Introduction to the present translation. *Trans.* [3] If all of Homer's verses were in beauty equal to these, he would entirely deserve his reputation as a classic, and if *La Motte* had always written such poetry, he would rank amongst the greatest French poets. *Author.* In view of this remark, the translator thinks it best to give these lines from Homer in La Motte's version so much admired by Tilly. *Trans.* [4] Parody of a line of Molière in *The Misanthrope:* *"Voilà de vos arrêts, messieurs les gens d'esprit."* *Trans.* [5] Monseigneur Duplessis d'Argentré. *Trans.*

CHAPTER X

[1] Allusion to Pimbêche, the lady who enjoyed going to law, as portrayed in Racine's *Les Plaideurs*. *Trans.* [2] Paris convents in which
illicit operations were often carried out. *Trans.* [3] The Palais Royal was
the residence of the Orléans family, and this Duc Louis-Philippe
d'Orléans, known as *Le Gros,* is the father of Philippe Égalité so often
mentioned by Tilly. The Marquise de Montesson had for many years
been his mistress, and she had married him in his old age, though the
marriage was secret as the King refused to grant the Marquise the title of
Princesse. The Duc de Lévis tells us that, notwithstanding her awkward
position, Mme de Montesson was universally well thought of, both as a
model wife and a perfect hostess. Her house was famous for society gatherings, and the plays acted there were most often of her own composition.
Trans. [4] In particular the great comedian Molé who, although so much
gifted and such a man of parts for his art, yet had many defects and committed great mistakes. He never in his life recited a line of verse without
spoiling it with a *but,* or an *if,* or a *for;* also he always stuttered! *Author.*
[5] Moralists will say that he always had a mistress, that in old age he still
retained all the weaknesses of youth: and what of it? He was a most civil
man, with a pleasant wit and a mind well adorned through a fine memory.
He had been closely acquainted with Monsieur de Choiseul who usually
did not choose fools nor bores for friends. The French court never did
anything for him, but when he was over sixty Spain bestowed on him the
Order of the Golden Fleece, most likely through sheer habit, since the
men of his name had received it for seven or eight generations back.
Author. [6] This Prince de Monaco gave himself the airs of a king in his
little principality, and held a real court modelled on that of Louis XV.
He was notorious for his numerous mistresses, and for the duel he had
fought with the Prince de Condé with whom his wife had fallen in love.
The Princesse de Monaco obtained a separation and settled with Condé,
later marrying him when she became a widow. The end of the Prince's
dissipated life was brought about by the Revolution. He died on the scaffold in 1794. *Trans.* [7] Walking one day at Vincennes he saw a certain
man beating a woman, probably his mistress. He jumped on the fellow
and knocked him down, calling out all the while: "On your knees before
madame!" Author. [8] It ought to be Henri IV. His body-cook was
Vardes, who also carried love letters for the King's sister, so that Henri
used to say: "He gains more by carrying my sister's *poulets,* than by
spitting mine." A word-play on *poulet* which means *billet doux* as well
as chicken. Vardes was finally exiled. *Trans.* [9] Henri III founded the
Order of the Saint-Esprit in 1578. *Trans.* [10] At the end of 1791. *Trans.*
[11] The Prince de Ligne, to whom the Comte de Tilly dedicated these
Memoirs. *Trans.* [12] 1782. *Trans.* [13] Philippe de Noailles, Duc de
Mouchy, born in 1715, had a long military career, and later became Governor of Guienne. All through life his kindly and peaceful disposition
made him beloved by all. His great devotion to Louis XVI brought him
back to Paris in his old age, forsaking a life of retirement to stand by his
king during the memorable days of June 20 and August 10, 1792, when

the mob broke into the palace of the Tuileries. Looked upon as one of the outstanding aristocrats, he was sent to the scaffold at the age of 79.

CHAPTER XI

[1] This scheme was abandoned at the peace of Versailles in 1784. Tilly happened to write this, in 1804, when Napoleon was taking up the plan again. *Trans.* [2] This important paragraph was omitted by the French editors. *Trans.* [3] The first French editor of the Memoirs mentions that this must have been Lacroix, member for Eure et Loir at the Convention, and sentenced to death in 1794 with his friend Danton. *Trans.* [4] Some readers will object that this sentence is not clear, and will ask whether I slept in Versailles or in the palace gallery; it is not worth the trouble to reply. *Author.* [5] Some sorry jesters called this duchess the *white mare*. *Author.* She was generally called the second dowager; she belonged to Mme Adélaide's household. *Trans.* [6] Unhappy princess! you reached the same end as his. *Author.* [7] Such as in a very bulky volume by a M. or Abbé Soulavie, all the more disgusting since it contains a few plausible pages, and offers now and again a semblance of good work. *Author.* [8] Hotel at Versailles. *Trans.* [9] It would be unfair to men holding offices, who cannot see to everything with their own eyes, to attribute to them the negligence with which their orders are carried out. I have read somewhere, and I am ready to believe the story, that the Cardinal de Richelieu, having been taken across the Rhone, ordered his servants to give fifty louis to the ferrymen. "Make it twenty-five, your Holiness, but let your Highness give them to us yourself." How sharp of the fellow! *Author.* [10] The Duc de Biron, in his youth known as Duc de Lauzun, was an officer and above all a man of fashion, a Lovelace, who could display wit, elegance, valour and courtesy, which qualities, coupled to a handsome face, made him a favourite with women. He has, like Tilly, left memoirs in which, however, his contemporaries, like the Duc de Lévis and Mme Campan trace "anecdotes more scandalous than true, particularly those in which he pictures himself as the hero." He sided with Philippe Égalité (Duc d'Orléans) during the revolution and died on the scaffold in 1794. *Trans.* [11] This descent of the French on Jersey was made in January, 1781. Rulecourt with eight hundred men (mostly deserters and adventurers he had himself recruited) landed on the island, pushed back the English troops marching against him, and reaching Saint-Hélier made the governor of the island sign an act of surrender. It was rumoured that he was followed by five thousand men. But with the dawn, the governor and the inhabitants of the island seeing no traces of the French fleet with which they believed themselves threatened, easily repulsed the French. Rulecourt lost his life in the fight as did the English Major Pierson, who defended the island. *Trans.* [12] Berlin. *Trans.*

CHAPTER XII

[1] The Comte Champcenetz de Riquebourg lived a life that corresponded closely to Tilly's, as a soldier, a roué, a lover of *belles-lettres,* a writer of

verse, and a wit whose sallies sometimes led to imprisonment. Like Tilly he was an active collaborator to the royalist paper *Les Actes des Apôtres,* but he was saved from the massacres of the Abbaye, and would have escaped the scaffold had he not returned to Paris. *Trans.* [2] Rivarol was an attractive personality, a noted conversationalist and a brilliant wit whose writings do not correspond to the reputation he gained in his lifetime. Sébastien-Roch-Nicolas, known as Chamfort, was a moralist who wrote famous Maxims a translation of which has in recent years been made into English. *Trans.* [3] Condemned to death by the horrible Fouquier-Tinville, he asked him if it were not as at the Assembly where one could find a substitute. "Why?" replied the monster.—"Because I should choose you to fill my place." This is wit, a fine sally which indicates a courageous soul. *Author.* [4] Tilly is here referring to an earlier writing of his, an open letter to Condorcet, the distinguished philosopher who was prominent as an orator in the then prevailing Convention. In this letter, dated from London, Nov. 5, 1792, Tilly wrote: "He [Condorcet], the Sieur Fabre d'Églantine and others who are now with the Devil had tried to have me murdered on the 13th of August, 1792, to put an end to the little war these gentlemen had waged against me during the last two years. It had become necessary to leave a country where these gentlemen were masters. . . . I escaped from them with the greatest difficulties, hiding in the day-time, and travelling by night. I took almost three weeks to reach a port; I left behind my best wishes with these gentlemen and took away with me the presentiment that their good fortune would not last long." This presentiment was fulfilled. Condorcet took poison on March 27, 1794, the day before he had to appear before the revolutionary tribunal; Fabre d'Églantine, actor and playwright, was condemned to death a few days later. *Trans.* [5] A man of wit, a most original mind, though rather cynical. The fact was not correct; but it is all one, there is no need to be so particular. The truth is I was reciting in front of him the passage about the death of Germanicus in a rather bombastic fashion, and Champcenetz, at whose rooms this was taking place, could not easily hide his vexation at not being able to take in a single word; Martin merely stopped me at the word *praebere* to say, for no reason clear to me, since I scarcely knew him: "There is no need to emphasise this word which, as you know, is very simple for it means to give." There are several repartees of his, much in the style of Diogenes. He used often to go to a café which many men of letters frequented. The manageress of the establishment, always much decked up, was a coquette but not pretty. M. Martin one day asked for a cup of chocolate, and finding it detestable he complained. "Sir," retorted the lady, "many *gentlemen from the court* who come here find it very good." And he, taking up a piece of glass he used to call his eye-glass, remarked: *"They most likely also told you, you were pretty."* People quote another of his bon-mots, though I believe it to be M. Favier's, a man far more witty than Martin, whom I had met only on a few occasions. Someone was one day staring at him rudely at the Opéra, between the acts. "Do you know me? And why do you stare at me thus?"—*"A dog may look at a bishop." "And who told you that I was a bishop?"* *Author.* [6] A line from Destouches's *Le Philosophe Marié. Trans.* [7] A court journal of the time. *Trans.* [8] Brissot de Warville was the famous leader of the Girondins in the Convention; a friend of Mme Roland and her husband, he shared their fate and died on the scaffold in 1793. *Trans.* [9] Not that I wish to encourage those unwearied *quotators* who blab out borrowed knowledge as one would a lesson. "Est modus in rebus." One might say to them, with Lord Chesterfield: "Wear your learning, like your watch, in a private pocket, and don't pull it out to show that you have one; but if you are asked what o'clock it is, tell it." *Author*. The quotation from Chesterfield is given in English by Tilly. *Trans.* [10] Under the title "Mes relations avec M. de Rivarol" (included in Tilly's *Œuvres mêlées*). After highly praising him Tilly continues: "That is how I depreciated the man to whom I had been attached during sixteen years, and who had for me many of the feelings that I had for him, until some persons who admired him without having any scales in which to weigh him, and who indeed hardly knew him, brought about a quarrel between us in the last four years of his life. Oh, insanity of coteries! Oh, emptiness of drawing-rooms! Oh, the stupidity of uncalled-for jealousy!" Rivarol died in Berlin in 1801. *Trans.*

CHAPTER XIII

[1] *Le Cercle* (The Club), as we are informed by the German editor, was a little comedy by Poinsinet in which a young marquis and colonel, finding himself in the company of people engaged in gaming, talking, singing, and reading, sits down at some embroidery work. The author of this dramatic satire wished to throw ridicule on certain society gatherings. *Trans.* [2] This quotation from Lord Chesterfield is given in English by Tilly. *Trans.* [3] Claude Victor, Prince de Broglie, like La Fayette and another friend of Tilly, the Vicomte de Noailles, had fought on Washington's side in the War of Independence, and had come back from America full of ideas of freedom and enthusiasm for the new era in France. Having been elected member for the nobles at the States-General of 1789, he joined the popular cause and became member of the Tiers-État. Refusing, however, to recognise the decrees of August 10, 1792, which prepared the abolition of the monarchy, he had to resign, then later was arrested and condemned to death on June 27, 1794, at the age of thirty-seven. *Trans.* [4] The first time he was arrested during the Terror, a woman came to see Danton to ask for the release of the Prince de Broglie. "I shall give him back to you," said the champion of democracy, "but please tell him, madame, that we trust neither himself nor his relatives; let him go to sleep, let him keep quiet and leave to us the painful task of the demagogues, the dirty work of the sans-culettes." That is honesty! That is speaking to the point! It shows the will of a strong man who works to assert his position, and who points out the weakness of him who is doing his best to lose his. I knew both Danton and Broglie. What an abyss nature placed between the energy of the first and the colourless ingratitude of the other! The former was in the first rank of the men who made the revolution and were made by it; the latter was one of the worst weaklings whom the court produced and who brought the court to grief. I spoke to Danton twelve hours before leaving Paris; I placed my hand in his bloody hand without shuddering. I heard his

terrible voice, but there was also something human in it; there was nothing terrifying in the tones with which he promised me his protection. Danton had much evil to make good; he wished to do so. The Prince de Broglie only found means to do a little evil, but his repentance even for that little amounted to nothing. *Author.* ⁵ This Louis-Marie, vicomte de Noailles, is the friend of Tilly so often referred to in the Introduction to this translation. He was the second son of the famous Maréchal de Mouchy, mentioned previously, a staunch supporter of the monarchy, who died on the scaffold. The family of Noailles gave many men of mark to the army, and Louis-Marie, Vicomte de Noailles, was as distinguished for his bravery as most men of the name. But, as was the case with many young aristocrats who thereby opposed their own fathers, he fought on the side of the Revolution, having brought back from the War of Independence in America a warm enthusiasm for the new ideas. Many of these young men, however, were never able to forsake entirely the old traditions of ancient France, and led a life of unrest, fitting nowhere. Noailles knew days of exile, but was recalled to France under the Consulate and joined the army once more. He was killed on January 19, 1804, fighting against the English in the West Indies. *Trans.* ⁶ This Noailles's brother-in-law was the famous La Fayette. His character is well illustrated in his correspondence with Jefferson. See *Letters of Lafayette to Jefferson,* edited by Gilbert Chenard, 1930. *Trans.*

CHAPTER XIV

¹ The German editor suggests that this is the Marquis de Senecterre. *Trans.* ² Belœil was the name of the famous gardens designed by the Prince de Ligne and his father on the ancestral estate in Belgium. Ligne wrote a book about it, *Coup d'œil sur Belœil,* which has in modern times (1922) been carefully edited by the Comte de Ganay. *Trans.* ³ The three towns of Metz, Toul, and Verdun formed then a little principality of their own, though under French control, known as *les Trois-Évêchés* (the Three Bishoprics). *Trans.* ⁴ Joseph-Alexandre, Vicomte de Ségur, second son of the Maréchal de Ségur, was a distinguished officer at the outbreak of the Revolution. He refused to be mixed up with political events, and devoted his time to writing, his book *Sur les Femmes* being still appreciated. He also edited and published the *Mémoires du Baron de Bezenval,* who was very devoted to him, and by some believed to be really his father. He must not be confused with his better-known brother, Louis-Philippe Comte de Ségur, the historian. *Trans.* ⁵ The German editor designates here the Prince Karl of Hesse Rheinfeld Rotenburg, who during the Revolution had himself called *le Citoyen Hesse,* and served in the revolutionary army as brigadier-general in command of Perpignan. He was later discharged, and the Jacobins refused to admit him in their midst because he was a prince. Remaining, however, a revolutionist, he went on denouncing suspects at random. During the governments subsequent to the revolution (directoire and consulate), his bitter hatred made him objectionable to most parties and led to his imprisonment. Being later implicated in a plot against the consulate, he was deported to the island of Oléron, then finally sent back to Germany to be under the control of his

family. *Trans.* ⁶ This is the name which had been given to Fénelon, the famous preacher and author, while he was Bishop of Cambrai. It may be remembered that he was tutor to the Duc de Bourgogne who later was to become Louis XVI. *Trans.* ⁷ Pierre-Ambroise-François-Choderlos de Laclos was born at Amiens of a recently ennobled family coming from Paris; his mother probably belonged to Picardy. He received a careful and excellent education, and entered the artillery, a branch of the service which had at that time attained a high degree of technical perfection and which appealed to his scientific tastes. He reached the rank of general, and his professional abilities were high, though he was in many respects unfortunate for he became attracted to the party of Philippe-Égalité, duc d'Orléans, and when the duke was executed Laclos was imprisoned and narrowly escaped the guillotine. Later he fought under Bonaparte, then first consul, and died serving in the Army of Italy. His fame rests on *Les Liaisons Dangereuses* published in 1782. A book has seldom produced so powerful a sensation. Its cool penetrating analysis of seduction fell like a bomb amid the frivolous and superficial but yet rather simple-minded society of his time. It was regarded as an outrage on morality, and Laclos became "the infernal author of *Les Liaisons Dangereuses*," for it seemed that in painting Valmont he could be describing only himself. In reality he had nothing in common with Valmont, and it is amusing, if not pathetic, to find Tilly, who has so much better a claim to be the typical roué, sharing the opinions of his epoch about a book that is to-day recognised as one of the great classics of French literature. Laclos was from first to last a man of the highest character, reserved and taciturn in temperament if not actually austere, a most devoted husband and father. His beautiful letters in late life to his wife ("an adorable mistress, excellent wife, tender mother," as he called her) were published in 1913, and his essay on *L'Éducation des Filles,* somewhat on the lines of Rousseau, in 1903. *Trans.* ⁸ These rather oratorical words, which I remember as if it were yesterday, struck me at the time all the more since his cool and methodical conversation was not usually in that tone. *Author.* ⁹ It has been suggested that this is either the celebrated Monge, or Meusnier who collaborated with Lavoisier; both were great friends of Laclos. *Trans.* ¹⁰ These initials correspond, Melchior-Bonnet points out, to those of a Mme de la Tour-du-Pin de Montmort whom Stendhal in his *Vie d'Henri Brulard* tells us that he knew when he was a child at Grenoble; she used to give him sweetmeats. Stendhal once met Laclos at a theatre in Milan, and relates how the latter would be "moved" when speaking of Grenoble, which he certainly knew. *Trans.* ¹¹ High seneschal and grand-bailli d'épée are synonymous terms. Though the post was antiquated, it conferred very imposing rights, amongst others that of convoking in national difficulties the nobility of the province, from the highest to the lowest, and of leading them to the seat of war; in ordinary times, the right of promenading about the town under a canopy adorned with gilt fringes and plumes, and followed by men in livery, some of them even gentlemen, who were obliged to accompany the seneschal. It is true that officer looked very much like a guy with his feathers, his gold chain, his long sword, his cloak, etc., etc. It would have required a fortune to induce me to become the actor in such a farce. *Author.* ¹² As Tilly here remarks, the most distinguished member of this family is the Comtesse de Genlis (1746-

1830) wife of the Chancellor de Sillery. In the society of artists, authors, and learned men in which she was reared, her beauty and wit made her shine. She married the Comte de Genlis in 1762, and ten years later became the mistress of Philippe-Égalité, Duc d'Orléans, whom she greatly influenced. In 1777 she accepted the post of governess to his daughter, and caused a sensation when in 1781 she was appointed "tutor" to his three sons. She thus educated the future king, Louis-Philippe, and was still alive when he ascended the throne. Of her numerous writings her Memoirs still deserve notice. *Trans.* [13] Jacques Necker was a financier and banker born at Geneva. He was twice called by Louis XVI to become chancellor of the exchequer, as he had in Paris a great reputation for skill and probity. His wife, Suzanne Necker, was known for her wit and kind heart. His daughter was Madame de Staël. *Trans.* [14] This Philippe-Louis de Noailles, Prince de Poix, was a son of the Maréchal de Noailles, and therefore a brother of Tilly's friend, the Vicomte de Noailles. He showed the usual military brilliance of his family and in the Revolution escaped to London, where we hear of him with Tilly at the Margravine of Anspach's house. *Trans.* [15] In a duel with the Comte de Lambertye, who was severely wounded. *Trans.* [16] Tilly means the Viscount Mountmorres, an Irish peer who was regarded as a clever and well-informed, but eccentric man. He was amiable, upright, and extremely polite, but fond of talking. It is said of him that he once published a speech he intended to deliver in the Irish House of Lords, duly furnished with "cheers" at the appropriate spots, but was prevented from delivering it. *Trans.* [17] This expression is given in English by Tilly. *Trans.* [18] Virgil, *Æneid*, VII, 129. *Trans.* [19] That is to say in 1783. *Trans.*

CHAPTER XV

[1] In spite of the different spelling, lovers of Sterne will here recognise the "Mons. Dessein" immortalised in the *Sentimental Journey*. Sterne, however, arrived at this hostelry—which, it has been said, he "made famous for all time"—in 1765, some eighteen years before Tilly put up there. *Trans.* [2] A ridiculous character and bore in Destouches's comedy, *La Fausse Agnès*. *Trans.* [3] The Comte de Valbelle; he had been the lover of the famous actress, Mlle Clairon, specially associated with Voltaire's plays. *Trans.* [4] The famous Marquis François Claude de Bouillé (1739-1800), French general, who is well known in England as a gallant and brilliant opponent in the West Indies. An ardent royalist, he helped to prepare the flight of Louis XVI from France. Obliged to emigrate during the Revolution he lived in England where he was extremely popular, and died in London. He left memoirs which were later published by his son. *Trans.* [5] One of their leading statesmen once said to me: "Burke's oratory is rather turgid." *Author*. The quotation is given in English by Tilly. *Trans.* [6] Colin d'Harville and Picard were writers of comedies popular at the time. Picard has remained the better known; he showed great skill in delineating the manners of his days, and all the gaiety of the *ancien régime;* he was termed "the Teniers of Comedy." His plays lost popularity in the new order of things, but they are still held in esteem. *Trans.* [7] All the English expressions found in italics in the course of this

chapter are given in this language by Tilly. *Trans.* ⁸ Virgil, *Æneid,* II, 390. *Trans.* ⁹ The most virulent part of this diatribe against England has never been published in France. The French edition of the Memoirs appeared shortly before the Revolution of 1830 when (as various witnesses testify) it was enough for Englishwomen merely to appear in the streets of Paris to be greeted with cries of "Vive les belles Anglaises!" and to be invited to assist in building up the revolutionary barricades, which they sometimes did. The German editor, whom I here follow, excused himself for translating the passage in full on the ground that it illustrates a section of French opinion at the time (1804) when it was written. *Trans.* ¹⁰ This refers to Monceau, property of the Duc d'Orléans, Philippe-Égalité. In his youth, when Duc de Chartres, he had there his gay quarters, often nicknamed "La Folie de Chartres" (The Bedlam of Chartres). The present Parc Monceau occupies only a portion of the ancient gardens. *Trans.*

CHAPTER XVI

¹ The French edition gives the name of this uncle as M. de Ch——; the German edition gives it in full. *Trans.* ² The chevalier has left no name behind, but that of the "famous brother" indicates Sylvain Gratet de Dolomieu, a celebrated geologist. *Trans.* ³ We know that she had an income of 16,000 livres. *Trans.* ⁴ But Turin, which became French in 1798, ceased to be so even during Tilly's lifetime, in 1814, when Piedmont was restored to the house of Savoy. *Trans.* ⁵ This is a positive misstatement, and the question must be left open as to whether it was due to error of memory or unwillingness to admit his position at the time. We know from Canon de la Manouillère's unimpeachable record at that time (see Introduction) that when Tilly's grandmother, Madame de Chassillé, died on April 3, 1785, Tilly was in prison for debt. *Trans.* ⁶ Mme de Broc seems to have belonged to the Savonnières family, and the marquis to have been her brother. He was a colonel in the dragoons, later became an officer in the body-guard of Louis XVI, and was killed when the Parisian mob attacked the palace of Versailles in October 1789. *Trans.* ⁷ She was sixty-five at that time and died in the following year, 1787. We find her referred to from time to time in the chronicle of Canon de la Manouillère, who confirms Tilly's high opinion of her. It is not clear how she was related to Tilly. *Trans.* ⁸ Canon de la Manouillère, who knew her, says: "She was a very gentle and very good young woman mourned by everyone." The canon's editor, Father Esnault, adds: "After a century the memory of Madame de Broc still persists in Le Mans. Her grace and beauty are recalled, as well, we must add, as her frivolity, then general in society." He adds the story that had been handed down, that after a drink given to her at a ball by Tilly "she expired in a few minutes and was laid out on her bed in her ball-dress where all Le Mans came to bid her a last farewell." The canon, however, writing at the time, says that while "she suddenly fell down unconscious on the Tuesday, she recovered temporarily, saw her confessor, and died on Wednesday at midday; a post-mortem examination showed hæmorrhage in the lower part of the abdomen and much clotted blood." She died on the 5th of April, 1786. *Trans.* ⁹ The name of Dolomieu comes strangely in this place. All this

chapter appears to have been written under the stress of great emotion, and, while very important as bearing on Tilly's life, it shows him at his worst as to style. *Trans.* [10] These lines furnish a good sample of Tilly's verse, but as they merely repeat what he has just said in the preceding paragraph, it has not seemed necessary to translate them. *Trans.*

CHAPTER XVII

[1] These four lines are, I believe, by Mme de Staël. *Author.* [2] This refers to the well-known Trappist abbey of Grace-Dieu in Normandy, founded in 1140. In 1662, the famous abbot, Armand de Rancé, known as the Thundering Abbot, caused a great sensation by introducing drastic reforms. Driven to religion on account of the death of his mistress, the Duchesse de Montbazon, Rancé instituted in his community severe rules of silence, manual labour, fasting, and other austerities. The Abbé Henri Brémond has lately published a life of the Thundering Abbot, which has been translated into English. *Trans.* [3] Tilly's account of Joseph's visit to Paris is confirmed by other contemporary descriptions. The emperor would sometimes refuse to dine with the royal family, returning to the inn to dine alone very simply, saying (apparently as a reflexion on his sister's life) that monarchs should not play with the wealth of their subjects. Joseph II was shocked by the French court and the kind of society the queen admitted to her presence. When he overheard Mme de Guémené reproached for cheating at faro, he spoke severely to his sister and said the place was a gambling den; and the Queen, who was attached to her brother, promised to reform the court, for a time did take steps in that direction, and was more careful in bestowing her favours. (See, for instance, Pierre de Nolhac, *Marie-Antoinette the Queen.*) But with the birth of her first child (1778) she really entered a new life. *Trans.* [4] It is now well known that there is no truth in these suppositions, but that the sums received by Joseph II through his sister were given him by Louis XVI in accordance with secret treaties with the court of Vienna. *Trans.* [5] The German editor tells us that this was Elizabeth Württemberg, sister to the dowager empress (Maria of Russia). *Trans.* [6] Archduke Charles of Austria. *Trans.* [7] I could make a whole chapter of all the miserable tales which have been gravely reported to me concerning this unfortunate victim of both men and Fate. And from whom these tales? From the most important people in the countries which I have visited. *Author.* [8] This refers to the Vicomte de Noailles and the Duc de Lauzun. Of the former, Tilly has spoken at length in earlier chapters. As regards the latter, we must beware of the account he himself gives of his favour near the queen. Madame Campan, in her *Mémoires sur la vie de Marie-Antoinette,* mentions the passage in Lauzun's *Memoirs* as "an insult on the queen's character," and shows that "self-conceit" had caused the duke to exaggerate and to imagine things which were not, so as "to render himself unworthy of an honour granted to his name and his rank." *Trans.* [9] François-Henri de Franquetot, duc de Coigny, was for a time first equerry to the king, and later became a lieutenant-general. Mme Campan refers to him as "being honoured by the queen's regard," but adds, "in truth, he was thought a great deal of at court, as much by

the king as by the queen." *Trans.* [10] This was the third duke of Dorset. He was ambassador extraordinary and plenipotentiary at the court of France from 1783 to 1789. He is described as a man of fine manners and good sense matured by a wide knowledge of the world. *Trans.* [11] Mme Campan gives most of these names, and even adds a few others, such as the Comte d'Artois (later Charles X) and the Baron de Besenval, and agrees with Tilly that all these stories were "foolish accusations and calumnies." *Trans.* [12] Axel de Fersen. Thanks to documents only lately accessible, such as the diary of Fersen published by Mme Söderhjelm, the Memoirs of the Comte de Saint-Priest, some letters of the Queen to Fersen, and a few other letters, more light is thrown upon this attachment of Marie Antoinette to the Swedish count. Notwithstanding the fact that Fersen destroyed the greatest part of his diary dealing with his stay at the French court, these documents now before us leave no doubt that Tilly has here given a true picture of the tender affection which most likely united these two hearts. There is, in *Autour de la Reine* by Pierre de Nolhac, an admirable chapter devoted to the Comte de Fersen. *Trans.* [13] More often known as the flight to Varennes, June, 1791. *Trans.* [14] The Duc de Fleury, the French editor states. *Trans.* [15] This Mme d'Angivillers held at Versailles a sort of salon. The Duc de Lévis, in his *Souvenirs and Portraits,* gives a delightful picture of this old lady and "her grotesque way of dressing; her only beauty was her hair which reached the ground, though this was easy as she was so small; she decorated it with feathers and flowers which made her face appear all the more wrinkled. . . . But under this ridiculous appearance was a superior mind, judgement as prompt as it was sound, warmth without exaggeration, piquancy without bitterness, learning without pedantry, and finally always a serene amiability." He further adds that "she did not meddle with politics, and her one pleasure was the conversation of the interesting people who met at her house, all most distinguished *gens d'esprit." Trans.*

CHAPTER XVIII

[1] Mlle Adeline's real name was Maria Madeleine Colombe; she adopted another name to avoid confusion with her two elder sisters, who were notable actresses. They were the daughters of a wandering Venetian musician. Adeline was born in 1760 and first appeared as a child at Audinot's Theatre. She was a less distinguished actress than her sisters, but her life, it has been said, was itself a novel. All three sisters, indeed, had lives that were full of strange adventures (see Lyonnet, *Les Comédiennes,* 1930). She left the stage in 1809 to retire to Versailles, and lived until 1841, so that she had ample time to read the *Memoirs* of Tilly. We do not hear that she disputed the authenticity of the narrative. *Trans.* [2] He was the controller of the posting-houses of the kingdom, and one of the richest men of France; he gave Adeline 10,000 francs a month. Tilly mentions him again in Chapter XXII, where he relates his tragic death. *Trans.* [3] The virtuous heroine of Laclos's *Les Liaisons Dangereuses. Trans.* [4] The German editor states that all this paragraph, though still legible, had been struck out by Tilly. *Trans.* [5] Paul Jones, the famous naval adventurer, was of Scottish origin, his real name being Paul. Most

of his exploits were carried out under the American flag, but he was received with enthusiasm in France on account of his activities against England. He died in obscurity in Paris. *Trans.* ⁶ This Sartine (son of Antoine de Sartine, who was long head of the police and later naval minister in France) became immensely rich, and as he failed to emigrate at the Revolution he was executed in 1794, with his wife and mother-in-law, Madame de Sainte-Amaranthe, both of whom Tilly introduces in a later chapter. *Trans.* ⁷ This is an allusion to the well-known story about Ninon de Lenclos's lover La Châtre, who having to leave Paris obtained from her a letter solemnly promising to be faithful in his absence. A little later, in the arms of another lover, she suddenly remembered her promise and exclaimed: "Oh! le beau billet qu'a La Châtre!" *Trans.* ⁸ Louis-Marie-François, Prince de Saint-Mauris, was the only son of the Prince de Montbarrey, once minister of war and previously mentioned by Tilly. *Trans.* ⁹ The Œil-de-Bœuf (the "Ox's Eye" so named on account of a round window called by that name in French) was in the palace of Versailles, the anteroom to the King's private apartments, where the courtiers awaited the King's presence. According to Pierre de Nolhac in *Autour de la Reine,* when Louis XVI once a week honoured special courtiers with an invitation to supper in his private rooms, it was in the Œil-de-Bœuf that the usher called out the list of the guests so invited. The lady here referred to by Mlle Rosalie having eyes like an ox, the joke is obvious. *Trans.* ¹⁰ Youngest son of the Prince de Monaco mentioned in the first volume. *Trans.* ¹¹ Jean Antoine Marie de Cazalès. His claims to fame are based on his speeches in the Constituent Assembly in defence of the monarchy. After the flight of the royal family to Varennes, he went into exile. At the time of Louis's trial he asked leave to come back to France to defend his king, but this was not allowed. He published his *Défense de Louis XVI* and never mixed again with politics. *Trans.* ¹² A well known Jesuit of that period and eloquent preacher whose sermons were published in seven volumes. *Trans.*

CHAPTER XIX

¹ Yves-Marie Desmarets, Comte de Maillebois, lieutenant-general and son of the Maréchal de Maillebois, had through his intrigues incurred disfavour at court. He was later restored to his former functions and sent on a mission to Holland. With the advent of the Revolution he settled in that country where Tilly saw him again. *Trans.* ² Madame de Cassini, sister to the Marquis de Pézay mentioned in the previous volume. *Trans.* ³ Tilly is here probably referring to the gauzy and transparent costumes fashionable during the Directoire period. *Trans.* ⁴ This is on the contrary easily explained since this Comte de Maillebois was a grandson of Nicolas Desmarets, a nephew of Colbert and minister of finance under Louis XIV. A manuscript of Louis XIV may quite possibly have come to the hands of Nicolas Desmarets, who was much in favour at the court of Louis le Grand. *Trans.* ⁵ Etienne-François Duc de Choiseul, foreign minister under Louis XV, showed great ability and foresight in this capacity. Marie Antoinette partly owed him the throne of France, for he influenced Louis XV in this matter, and skillfully carried out the neces-

sary negotiations with the court of Vienna. Very ambitious, and claiming warm partisans, he later became the leader of a cabal at the court of Louis XVI, and was accused, no doubt absurdly, of having poisoned the Dauphin Louis, father to Louis XVI. Under this latter king, he fell into disfavour. *Trans.* ⁶ A reference to Aline, the country-girl, heroine of Boufflers's story, *The Queen of Colconda. Trans.* ⁷ Ovid, *Metamorph.* III, 9. *Author.* ⁸ The bodies of Roman criminals, after being strangled in prison, were dragged down the Gemonian steps to be thrown into the Tiber. *Trans.* ⁹ This passage is a reference to the lady in Berlin who drowned herself after a love-affair with Tilly. See Introduction. *Trans.*

CHAPTER XX

¹ Frédéric de Salm-Krybourg, born at Limbourg, served in the French army. He seems to have had a predilection for revolutions; he helped the Dutch rebels at Utrecht, and at the outbreak of the Revolution obtained a commission in the national guard. He nevertheless died on the scaffold. *Trans.* ² In Destouches's *Le Glorieux. Trans.* ³ In Molière's *Don Juan.* Poor M. Dimanche was the type of the shy and slow-witted creditor who could always be pacified by a few adroit words of flattery. *Trans.* ⁴ The wedding of Camacho the Rich, in *Don Quixote,* when a whole ox was roasted on a mountain of faggots. "In the capacious belly of the ox were a dozen soft little sucking-pigs, which, sewn up there, served to give it tenderness and flavour." *Trans.* ⁵ Nicolas Restif de la Bretonne, a noted and prolific writer, was in many respects a literary pioneer, and revealed many social aspects of French life in his time, especially among the lower classes. His most famous work, *Monsieur Nicolas, or the Human Heart Unveiled,* has lately been for the first time translated into English in six volumes (John Rodker, 1930). Tilly's account of his meeting with Restif is perhaps the most interesting personal sketch of him we possess. *Trans.* ⁶ Fanny, Comtesse de Beauharnais, was married at fifteen, becoming the aunt of Empress Josephine. She separated amicably from the Count and settled in Paris, surrounded by men of letters and maintaining what was considered the last famous salon of the century. She possessed social grace and much benevolence and could be a devoted friend. *Trans.* ⁷ He left behind a portion of this inheritance to a few men, and specially bequeathed it to M. de Fontanes, his friend, his disciple, and his rival, though, for the glory of letters, it is perhaps to be deplored that the latter should spend most of his days at other occupations. *Author.* ⁸ I believe that the men who built the pyramids would be somewhat disappointed if they came back on earth to find that their names are scarcely known; a rather disheartening fact for amateurs of immortality. . . . And where would the difference be if these names were known? . . . *Author.*

CHAPTER XXI

¹ The Marquis de Fénelon. *Trans.* ² Auguste Vestris was the son of the famous Italian dancer, Gaetano Vestris, and was himself renowned for his marvellous springs in mid-air and his acrobatic feats. *Trans.*

³ The Duc de Fitz-James, who has so nobly redeemed himself during the revolution, showed more wit than this. As he one day found at Contat's rooms this same attractive and nimble rival, he said to him with great kindness: "I shall show consideration for your legs, but if you ever put your foot here again, I will break your arms." *Author.* Louise Contat was a comedian who excelled in the parts of coquettes in Molière's and Marivaux's plays. *Trans.* ⁴ In Egypt, whither he had accompanied Louis IX. *Trans.* ⁵ Anne Pierre, Marquis de Montesquiou-Fezensac, was brought up at court and became attached to the princes of the royal blood as gentleman companion. He was later appointed first equerry to Monsieur, and rose to be a field marshal. *Trans.* ⁶ The Lake of Bienne. *Trans.* ⁷ Where he might be invited to share the King's dinner. *Trans.* ⁸ Frédéric Melchior, Baron de Grimm, friend of Diderot, d'Alembert, Holbach, etc., who, as a gifted letter-writer, kept a correspondence with many crowned heads of Europe—the empress of Russia, the queen of Sweden, the king of Poland, etc.—in which he expounded the ideas of the Encyclopedists. Most of these letters, under the title of *Correspondance littéraire, philosophique et critique,* were published a few years after his death and remain his chief title to fame. *Trans.* ⁹ The Grand Château de Chantilly was levelled by the mob at the Revolution, leaving the more ancient Petit Château; the whole was slowly restored by the Duc d'Aumale during the nineteenth century and finally presented to the Institut de France as a museum. *Trans.* ¹⁰ Sophie Arnould, the famous operatic actress who for twenty years held Paris spellbound by her rendering of tragic parts in the operas of Rameau, Gluck, etc. *Trans.* ¹¹ Louis Félicité, Duc de Brancas, Comte de Lauraguais, left the army to devote himself to letters and art; he is, however, mostly known for his witty repartees, his queer disposition, his fondness for a gay easy life, and his liaison with Sophie Arnould which proved the most lasting of her life and out of which was born a son. *Trans.* ¹² M. Fleury and still some others are great artists, but everyone must die, and I am almost certain they will not leave behind pupils able to display the kind of taste I describe; written parts are not enough to provide this; we are in need of general types of humanity which will stand as models and which even from afar will be unconsciously sought after and copied. *Author.* ¹³ This is no doubt Mrs. Bingham, the mother of Tilly's ex-wife. See Introduction. *Trans.* ¹⁴ A reference to the female villain of *Les Liaisons Dangereuses. Trans.* ¹⁵ Philippe-Henri, Marquis de Ségur, father of Joseph Alexandre, Vicomte de Ségur, previously mentioned by Tilly, and of Louis Philippe de Ségur, the historian. *Trans.* ¹⁶ I have not written for the present time (1804-1805); I shall satisfy no party and have no longing to do so; all I have is a conscience; if it misleads me, it is in good faith. I would always follow Truth as much as it is given to any man to do so whenever he makes this his purpose. My sole activity, as regards politics, has been never to cease being a Frenchman; to live amidst foreigners without becoming one, though paying due homage to what is honourable and estimable amongst them; to disapprove of my country's excesses, yet to love her and to form more wishes for her happiness than her most deadly enemies ever did her harm. *Author.* ¹⁷ Mention has often been made of a M. de Pontavice, a post captain belonging to a good family of Brittany, who came to make his début when he was fifty, and displayed the taste prevailing at Brest and

Toulon, the full elegance of one of Neptune's courtiers, which has no striking likeness to that of Versailles. This honest sailor was as resplendent as a gilt chalice, and for long waited in vain in the Œil-de-Bœuf, each day appearing with more embroidery. He was thus being bored while courting ruin, when the naval minister at last asked him what he was doing there. "I came," he replied, "to take a snack with the master, and I shall not go back before it is an accomplished thing." The king heard of this; they took pity on the poor man, his name was called out once, and he felt as if he had won a naval victory. *Author.* [18] I was saying to a man of my acquaintance: "I no longer see you with M. de B——, your relative and a man from the same province as yourself, with whom you have been brought up."—"We see one another in the country," he replied gravely, "but here, *he does not belong,* he has not been presented, *he is a nobody,* we never meet." I much doubt whether M. de B—— entertains in his countryside a very sincere affection for his friend of the summer months. *Author.* [19] Which does not alter the fact that during the emigration (stupid word!) it would have been absurd for the grandson of one of the king's secretaries to find fault with the Duc de Coigny's genealogy, or to hesitate as regards the respect he owed to the Maréchal de Castres. A Babel confusion from which sprang many evils. *Author.* [20] These had to go back two hundred years without traces of ennoblement at the outset. With the exception of a few chapters such as those of Strasburg, Lyons, Saint-Claude, Remiremont, they were about the most thorough one might have to produce in these days. The proofs required for the Ecole Militaire, for that of Saint-Cyr, or even of Malta, were only of four generations. *Author.* [21] The Maréchal Duc de Lévis had in fact been for twenty-five years an infantry captain, and had been in command of a company of grenadiers. *Author.* This is François-Gaston, Duc de Lévis, Marshal of France, father of Gaston Duc de Lévis who left behind interesting *Souvenirs et Portraits* of the period. *Trans.* [22] Normandy and Maine. *Trans.* [23] People in Germany constantly refer to Wittekind whenever they wish to say something very striking against the house of Bourbon, which it is quite natural not to like since it once was so powerful and is now so unfortunate. You are gravely told that such or such a house which descends from Wittekind is much more ancient than that of France. This is charming! heavenly! But it offers one little inconvenience, namely that the house of France and that of Wittekind are one and the same. Wittekind II (son of the one whom Charlemagne conquered and had baptized) was called Robert and was the father of Robert le Fort, Marquis de France, the great-grandfather of Hugh Capet! *Author.* [24] It was not Candide but Dr. Pangloss who made the remark. Candide found it hard to believe. *Trans.* [25] The Hosiers had been from father to son famous genealogists. The name is usually spelt Hozier. *Trans.* [26] It will be seen later why I dwell so much over the peculiarities of an embarrassing event which had no foundation, but which evil-minded people believed they could turn to account. I will not seek justification for spinning out my narrative at great length, as this is necessary. "People complain," says Diderot, "at the slowness of such or such a narrative, yet nothing can be well understood which is not given in full details. Does not the least business transaction in our society take time and cost endless trouble? Yet the reader would do away with the *details* so indispensable to the achievement of a work of art!" *Author.* [27] The Tilly family arms, states the German editor, show a white lily on a golden field with the motto: *Sic tinctum sanguine nostro. Trans.* [28] M. d'Hosier had said to me: "They will have as much trouble to prove you are not their relative as you, on your side, to prove that you are." *Author.* [29] Genealogists mention a branch issued from a Bishop of Bayeux, Harcourt by name, and a female Tilly whose son was acknowledged and made legitimate by means of the secularisation and marriage of the father, for which Pope Paul III (Alexandre Farnèse) gave authorisation by a bull; and the King of France, Francis I, by a royal command ratified in 1535. If this stock had been mine, I should not have been in the least embarrassed to acknowledge it, even at a time when so much importance was attached to such discoveries; it would be a birth as good as others. But it is clear from the patents of nobility of my branch, which for so long were in the hands of MM. d'Hosier and Chérin, that this is not our stock, though people have wished to reproach us with it. The last man issued of that branch, which produced distinguished men, died young and childless in 1733, in the mousquetaires. Moreover, my pen only relates these details as memory would retrace a dream. *Author.* [30] The German editor states: "Vicomte Charles de Tilly-Blaru was, during the emigration, often under great obligation to Comte Alexandre de Tilly, whom he had at one time been unwilling to acknowledge as his relative. He has recorded the gratitude which he has since felt in a written statement worded as follows: 'The Comte de Tilly has obliged me in such a gracious and noble way as to win my everlasting gratitude as well as that of my family.'" *Trans.* [31] I have not forgotten your generous tears and brotherly affection, oh, my worthy friends, not even the anxious and tender interest displayed by this unfortunate Prince d'Hénin, sometimes so ridiculous, but fundamentally always so kind-hearted. *Author.* [32] Such was the appellation and the title given to the marshals of France when sitting as a court. *Trans.*

CHAPTER XXII

[1] He had been first-gentleman-of-the-bedchamber. *Trans.* [2] This case did as little credit to the tribunal as that of M. d'Harambure, and, above all, that of the Vicomte de Noé, which made it most unpopular amongst the aristocracy. *Author.* [3] One of his colleagues, who had behaved just as abominably on this occasion, excused himself from seeing me; he sent me word that he was in bed with some fever. I never called at his door again to ask how he was. *Author.* [4] The first French editor states: "There has only been one Tilly employed by the revolutionary government in the sense here implied by the writer of these memoirs, a man who was chargé d'affaires at Genoa in 1783 and 1794; he was later on arrested and transferred to a prison in Paris, out of which he was only set free after the Terror. As the memoirs of the period refer to him only with great disfavour, it seems evident he could not have been the general Comte de Tilly, issued from an aristocratic family of Normandy, though not that of Tilly-Blaru and the other Tillys, who after a distinguished military career during the wars of the revolution, died in Paris as a lieutenant-general and grand-cordon de la Légion d'Honneur, in January, 1822."

Trans. [5] This brings back to my mind a repartee of the Comte d'Estaing
to whom the Chevalier d'Oraison was saying: "We want the death of
abuses."—"Then you must be weary of life, for you are an abuse in yourself." Which was true. *Author.* [6] The famous *cahiers de doléances*
(memorials of grievances) of the revolution are too well known to use
here another word. However, the *cahiers* Tilly mentions here in connection with the Orleanese party were most likely political pamphlets. The
"parti d'Orléans," or "Fronde du Prince," met at the Palais Royal, the
home of the Prince, and besides including such people as the Vicomte de
Noailles, the Vicomte de Ségur, the Duc de Lauzun, the Comte de Sillery-
Genlis, Mme de Genlis, and Laclos—*"l'âme du parti d'Orléans"*—there
could also be seen there men who were later to play a great part in the
assemblies of revolution: Sieyès, Bailly, Barère, Mirabeau, Talleyrand,
etc. *Trans.* [7] The Duke had recently been refused permission to travel to
England. *Trans.* [8] The Comte de Vaudreuil, states the French editor.
Trans. [9] Favier, whom I met a great deal, and often listened to from
the time of my presentation to the King. Author. Jean-Louis Favier,
political writer, often displayed great insight. *Trans.* [10] François
Joseph Foullon (as the name is more usually spelt) became minister of
finance after the withdrawal of Necker. He, and his son-in-law, Berthier
de Sauvigny, were most likely the first victims of the revolution. Arrested
on the 12th of July, 1789, he was hanged from a lamp-post on the 15th,
the day following the fall of the Bastille. *Trans.* [11] In 1794, in the Rue
de Chartres. *Trans.* [12] Joseph Barnave, a lawyer and brilliant orator,
was the youngest deputy to set out for Versailles as member of the Third
Estate in the States General. The nickname here given to him of Néronet
(Néron né: a born Nero) is a reference to his well-known saying, at
the time of the protest against the murders of the first victims of the
revolution: "Was the blood of Foullon and Berthier then so pure?" "That
unpremeditated phrase stuck to him until his death," writes J. Mills
Whitham in his *A Biographical History of the French Revolution,* "so
that he met people who were astonished to find that he had neither the
face nor the voice nor the manners of a ferocious man." For indeed
Barnave was a sincere idealist, "who had loved men and expected too
much of them." He died on the scaffold at thirty-two in punishment for
this. *Trans.* [13] The Salon was then held at the Louvre. *Trans.* [14] A
Mme C—— who made her début at the Comédie Française. *Author.*
[15] Françoise Raucourt was a well-known tragic actress of the time. *Trans.*
[16] Basile, in Beaumarchais's *Barbier de Séville:* "Cast slander abroad,
always slander, that is the main thing! Some of it is sure to stick." *Trans.*
[17] Philosophy, in the worthy sense of the word, has made as great progress
amongst us, and has had as many distinguished spokesmen, as with the
English; but they were our predecessors in this branch of human knowledge; they took the initiative . . . above all they had a Newton! *Author.*
[18] Against Mirabeau's advice, the duke, obeying the king's orders, went
over to England on Oct. 14, 1789. *Trans.*

CHAPTER XXIII

[1] Agnès de Bouvier de Cepoy had married the Comte de Buffon, a
colonel, and son of the famous Buffon, the naturalist. At the time men-

tioned here she was the mistress of the Duc d'Orléans, showing herself openly as such, having followed him to England. She was soon to lose both her husband and her lover on the scaffold. *Trans.* [2] This is the Prince of Wales, who later became George IV. *Trans.* [3] The Duke had begun to realise that this supposed mission to England had been devised to get him out of the way, on account of his views and popularity. At the time here mentioned he wanted to go back to France, and La Fayette had sent to London M. de Boinville, one of his aides-de-camp, with orders to prevent this return. The Duke, however, arrived in Paris on the 11th of July, 1790, with the faithful Laclos and Mme de Buffon, and henceforth began the career of Philippe-Egalité. *Trans.* [4] This saying of the Duke was an allusion to a sharp quarrel I had had at Versailles, at M. de Sillery's house, with the Duc d'Aiguillon, who had spoken of the Queen with virulent indecence. I was not paid to defend her, but there are duties which are all the more precious to fulfill if one appears under no obligation to do so. I brought to the matter all the fire of youth and of fervent partisanship. Sillery, very much disturbed, contrived so that the affair went no further. Shortly afterward the Duc d'Orléans said to me: "I heard fine news about you, why be such a Don Quixote?"—"I cannot prevent M. d'Aiguillon," I replied, "being a dishonest man; but I do not wish his confidential talk to make me appear a party to his views." *Author.* [5] This was written in 1805, and refers to Napoleon. *Trans.* [6] In all the French national assemblies there were no men who could be placed for patriotism and virtue beside an Algernon Sidney or a Hampden; and yet both of them in reforming their governments were exposed to the severest reproaches and have not found grace before the judgement seat of history. The former was guilty of ingratitude after his first attempts had received royal forgiveness, and came to grief in the course of new intrigues against the court. It is not enough to say: "I am at heart a good republican." The answer is: "If you want to be a republican, abandon a monarchial state and go to Ragusa." Hampden, not less guilty and more highly gifted, with all those qualities which deserve to bring him personal esteem and admiration, can likewise make no claim to the name and reputation of a good subject. *Author.* [This note was omitted by the first French editor of Tilly. *Trans.*] [7] This does not seem an English name, but Tilly may have meant "Povey." *Trans.* [8] The famous pastoral novel of Honoré d'Urfé, still popular in Tilly's early days. *Trans.* [9] Louis XV is said to have asked an Englishman if he came to Paris to make love. "No, sire," was the reply, "I buy it ready made." *Trans.* [10] Mrs. Elizabeth Montagu (née Robinson) became a leader in the London world of letters and fashion. She is described as "handsome, fat, and merry," a vivacious woman with great social gifts, who has been termed "the English Mme du Deffand." Having heard Voltaire deliver "an invective against Shakespeare" at the French Academy, on her return to England she published an essay on the genius of Shakespeare, which was highly thought of and translated into French. The members of her circle were called "blue-stockings," though whether on account of the unconventional blue stockings of some men of intellect who came to her house, or as a mark of distinction by the ladies themselves, has been disputed. Numerous books have been written about Mrs. Montagu. *Trans.* [11] The German editor also says that the respect due to this high personage prevents his being named; it is probably the Prince of Wales, afterwards George IV, who was still on the throne at the time the Memoirs were first published. *Trans.* [12] The Marquis de Saint-Helens. *Author.* Baron Saint-Helens, whom Tilly wrongly styles here "marquis," had been created an Irish peer, and was English ambassador and envoy in various lands. He is described as a man of fine manners and consummate prudence. *Trans.* [13] I have underlined all I remember word for word. *Author.* [14] The Marquis du Guesclin, the last person of the name, since one cannot count the Duchesse de Gesvre, was already dead when the Marquis de Saint-Helens asked this question; but seven or eight years earlier it would have had some foundation as well as the answer. *Author.* [15] There are left no direct descendants to M. de Turenne, but people of his house (La Tour-d'Auvergne) have borne his name right on to the revolution. There may even now be someone bearing this burden. *Author.* [16] There was then no revolution in France, and would never had been any, especially against the nobility, if peace had not lasted so long. *Author.* [17] Nowadays in France, public opinion selects first and foremost victorious officers for promotion to the highest ranks. In the course of time they will constitute the nobility, just as a high grade in the army already lends consideration. *Author.* [18] This way of reasoning, which was good at the time I speak of, is still so to-day, for there will always be a nobility, or a class taking its place, as well as distinctions (above all military ones) which will have this end in view. Besides (and I was the first to write it at the time of the decree for the abolition of hereditary aristocracy) nobility is only what lives in the memory. The historical names of the monarchy will survive all the insulting measures that are taken to guard against them. To pass decrees to suppress the nobility means only not keeping word with the king's secretaries. If Marshal Berthier leaves children, can anyone prevent his descendants from boasting that they spring from one of Napoleon's companions in victory, a man whom he raised to the highest military honours? On the other hand, who can prevent the name of Montmorency from being found on every page of the history of France? *Author.* [19] A play of Molière's, where the ghost of a commander appears. *Trans.* [20] He was slowly murdered with bayonet thrusts, in a baker's oven where he had hid himself. *Author.*

CHAPTER XXIV

[1] I am not joking. *Author.* [2] The Baron de Batz, general and politician, was much occupied with finance. During the Revolution he was the main agent of vast conspiracies with the object of saving the King and Royal Family. His life, related by G. Lenôtre in *A Gascon Royalist in Revolutionary Paris* (translator Mrs. Rudolph Stawell) makes fascinating reading. *Trans.* [3] The German editor states that part of this history was published in London in 1795, and that not all of it was burnt. *Trans.* [4] This refers to Mme de Cassini, already mentioned in connection with her brother the marquis de Pézay. *Trans.* [5] In the *Annales de la vertu* of Mme de Genlis, a lady as noted to-day for her religion and devotion as she was in former days for her rather profane charms, one finds in chronological summaries about such and such a king who was a hero and

won many battles, that she only mentions him on account of a chapel he had built or a convent he founded. Mme de Genlis used to have better sight than this in former days. Her spectacles are not as good as her eyes . . . but she believes that this sort of thing fascinates ours. *Author*. [6] The respectable Mme de Genlis says in one of her novels or one of her stories (it matters little which) that Mme de Maintenon died (this is certainly a fact) leaving a name worthy of the highest praise *in several respects,* and a reputation of true piety and a keen mind. . . . This piety was akin to that of Mme de Genlis herself in her early life. As for *keenness* of mind, that of Mme de Maintenon was the keener of the two, for she puzzled her contemporaries, while those of Mme de Genlis easily appraised her virtues. *Author*. Tilly's dislike of Mme de Maintenon seems to be based on her responsibility for Louis XIV's revocation of the edict of Nantes, the direct result of her Catholic fanaticism, though she was a descendant of the famous Protestant family of Agrippa d'Aubigné and had been brought up in his faith. *Trans*.

[7] Here lies the famous Chamillard,
 The King's protonotary,
 Who was a hero at billiards
 And a cipher in the ministry.

Such was the man, as well as others like Villeroy, Tallard, Marsin, whom Mme de Maintenon constantly protected, while she had sent away from the King's council and command in the army such men as Vendôme, Catinat, etc. . . . with the excuse that with their lack of religion they could bring only misfortune to our troops. *Author*. [8] Brigadier-general, a brave officer of aristocratic birth, and what is more, a man of honour. *Author*. [9] I was not obliged to take him at his word; neither is the reader. *Author*. [10] This is literally true. *Author*. [11] A vulgar expression generally used by all ill-mannered subalterns. *Author*. [12] This refers to the *cordon bleu,* belonging to the insignia of the chevalier de l'ordre du Saint-Esprit. *Trans*. [13] This is quite true. The Noailles are men of fine tradition both by family and as soldiers; that a Noailles should have been an officer in the service of the house of Bouillon, then ruling princes at Sedan, does not alter the essential facts. *Author*. [14] "Elle avait de beaux yeux pour des yeux de province." Gresset's *Le Méchant,* Act III. *Trans*. [15] Virgil has been reproached with having made his hero lachrymose: *Sic fatur lacrymans Lacrymis affatur obortis.* I will not maintain that tears are the best vehicle for epopee, but they are certainly the soul of the dramas of love. I do not know what can be refused to a woman made more beautiful by her tears. *Author*. [16] Florimond, Comte de Mercy-Argenteau, a Belgian nobleman, was the Austrian ambassador in France when the revolution broke out; he did his best to try to help the royal family. Compelled to leave France, he retired to Brabant, and there, as governor of the Netherlands, worked for the maintenance of the Austrian rule in Belgium. Finally, when Austria abandoned Belgium, he was appointed ambassador in England where he died in 1794. *Trans*. [17] Tilly means Andrew Plimer, a fashionable London miniature painter whose work is highly valued by collectors. *Trans*. [18] Young Duras, first gentleman of the bedchamber. The mob (in April 1791) snatched him from the steps of the royal carriage, but the King held him back by the hand and begged them to spare him. *Trans*.

CHAPTER XXV

[1] The flight to Varennes (June, 1791). *Trans.* [2] On the day of the King's departure, I met at the Tuileries a deputy of some standing in his own party, who has since held rather important posts which he filled with credit. "Well, Sir," he exclaimed, "victory is yours, but let us wait a bit. At all events, if the trumps remain yours, and we are not all hanged, I shall go to end my life in New England."—"Fear nothing," I replied laughing, "I shall see to your safety; we aristocrats have an inexhaustible reserve of generosity." The fatal news of the King's arrest reached Paris, and I saw this man again. How different his features and bearing! "Come," he said to me, "do not be dejected; I promise you your life." He laughed; I had no wish to do so. We never saw each other again. *Author.* [3] Jean Sylvain Bailly, well-known astronomer and academician, was the first president of the Constituent Assembly, and later became mayor of Paris. He was extremely popular at first, but lost this popularity during the demonstrations against the King referred to in this passage (the Champ de Mars riots July, 1791) when he declared martial law and was held responsible for the massacres. *Trans.* [4] The Deuxième Sénatus-consulte organique du 6 Floréal an X (April 26, 1802) allowed the émigrés to return to France, with a few exceptions among which was Tilly. He attributed this not to Bonaparte, but to court intrigues. He received permission to return a few years later. *Trans.* [5] Mme de Sainte-Amaranthe (Tilly spells it "Saint") and her family were victims of the revolution through the false declarations of informers. She was of good family, but had led a rather loose life. The beauty and high spirit of her daughter, whose name is usually spelt Émilie, has become a tradition, and her romantically tragic life has been written by d'Alméras and other authors. The episode with Tilly occurred when Émilie was quite young; soon after she fell in love with a popular singer, Elleviou, and remained attached to him till the end in spite of her marriage to Sartine. *Trans.* [6] The 20th of June, 1792, when the people broke into the palace of the Tuileries where the royal family then resided. Tilly always refers to it as the 21st. *Trans.* [7] How could journalists and compilers water down this striking saying? *"Do not undeceive them."* "Do not tell them who I am, let them think I am the queen. My death will prevent a greater crime." This is what is read everywhere, but what composed scorn and virtue, which are given to few words, never said. *Author.* [8] This praise will seem exaggerated to those who have not known her. She was the most handsome woman in Paris of her time. A painter, a sculptor would have commended the whole of her, not finding one blemish. I have in no country met any woman to approach her, none to make me forget her, none to be so absolutely perfect. My heart has loved other women more deeply, but has never admired any more completely. *Author.* [9] She was guillotined in 1794, together with her mother, brother, and husband, altogether a procession of fifty-four persons, largely innocent of any offence whatever; they were, by order of Fouquier-Tinville, all draped in red; on the way to the scaffold Émilie tried to console her distracted mother and said: "See, mother, how pretty the red cloaks are! We look like cardinals!" Her composure was only disturbed when she saw her lover Elleviou (for

whom she had just cut off her beautiful hair as a souvenir) madly making his way through the crowd. Tilly's "Ode Funèbre à la Mémoire de Mme de Sartine, née Emilie de Saint-Amaranthe" in fourteen stanzas, written in 1797, is not in his *Œuvres Mêlées*, but was known to his German editor. See chapter on "The Red Mass" in Lenôtre's *A Gascon Royalist*. *Trans.*

CHAPTER XXVI

[1] *Historia, testis temporum, lux veritatis, vita memoriæ, magistra vitæ, nuntia vetustatis.* (Cicero.) Could not this passage be translated as follows: History, the false witness of Time, the glitter of lies, a deception of memory, a school of errors, a fable about antiquity. This translation does not quite correspond to the text, but the sense is perhaps nearer to truth. *Author.* [2] That is to say a body which promulgates benevolent laws approved of by justice and generous hearts! *Author.* [3] I was authorized by M. de La Porte to make him a better offer than this. *Author.* [4] As I have elsewhere asked, were the scoundrels who daily insulted the King the only men allowed to send him their insolent diatribes? *Author.* This letter to the King appears in Tilly's *Œuvres mêlées*. It was translated and published in English in Tilly's lifetime. The main purport of it was to warn the King of his probable doom and to advise him to rally the nobility of the kingdom to his side in an armed force against rebellion. *Trans.* [5] The German editor states that this letter was not found among the papers Tilly left in Berlin. *Trans.* [6] Marie-Raymond Sahuguet d'Espagnac, was a canon in Paris before the revolution, but had little vocation for the ecclesiastical state. He became mixed in politics as an agent of the minister Calonne, and later joined the revolution, acting as army contractor. Being accused of fraudulent dealing, he was sentenced to death on the 5th of April 1794. *Trans.* [7] He certainly displayed great gifts as a geometer, though far less as a man of letters; judged as a writer, it might be said he had no talent. His twisted style, fashioned with such painful art as must be felt even by the least experienced reader, is often unintelligible. When he was in charge of the editing of the *Journal de Paris,* the proprietors hastened to take it away from him, not only on account of the guilty use he made of it, but because it was disgustingly written. *Author.* [8] This paragraph, like others in Tilly's Memoirs that are hostile to England, was omitted by the French editor, French relations with England being very friendly at that period. Tilly gives the words of Pitt in English. There has been much controversy concerning Pitt's last words, and the subject was debated in the Times during the last fortnight of April and the first week of May, 1930. According to one version they were, "I think I could eat one of Bellamy's veal pies," but that version is dismissed. Pitt's nephew, Stanhope, who was present, states that the words were, "My country, how I leave my country!"—expressing grief at the seemingly hopeless isolation of England—and that is the version now accepted by the best authorities. *Trans.*

SUPPLEMENTARY NOTES

After leaving the translator's hands, but before being placed in the hands of the actual publisher, the translator's notes, which were planned to appear as footnotes, were considerably mutilated and many deleted. This was only discovered after the work had been made up into pages. The more serious of these omissions have here been restored. Trans.

CHAPTER I

Following note 2, text, page 62—The French word *"Mousquetaire"* does not correspond to the English word *"Musketeer."* The mousquetaires were chosen from the nobility to form a special royal troop. *Trans.*

CHAPTER II

Following note 9, text, page 75—Cardinal de Bernis is well known to the readers of Casanova. M. de Boufflers was a prominent and attractive figure of the age and is now probably best known as the author of *La Reine de Golconde.* The Comte de Guibert was a prominent officer in the army and also an author; he is well remembered as the lover of Mlle de Lespinasse. *Trans.*

CHAPTER V

Following note 4, text, page 103—M. de Pezay, born in 1741, was not of noble birth, but by intrigue succeeded in becoming a marquis, a mousquetaire, and also confidential correspondent to Louis XVI. It was his business to inform the King concerning the state of public opinion, the misdeeds of his ministers, and secrets which were hidden from him. Such correspondents sometimes acquired great influence. But Pezay was finally exiled to Blois and died at Pezay in 1777. *Trans.*

CHAPTER V

Note 7. *This note should read:* The famous prince of royal blood, Louis-Philippe-Joseph d'Orléans, born in 1741, who became known in history under the name of Philippe-Egalité. He was a cousin of Louis XVI through a collateral line of Bourbons, issued from a brother to Louis XIV, to which belonged the other famous Duc d'Orléans, regent to Louis XV. The two branches of the royal family were at feud with one another, so Philippe-Egalité was unpopular at the court of Louis XVI, and much disliked by Marie-Antoinette. He joined the Revolution at the outset, and feeling himself wronged by the throne, was even among those members of the Convention who voted the King's death. The word *crimes* which Tilly uses in speaking of the duke can only be accepted as applied equally to all leaders of political parties who in times of revolution may prove the means of changing the fate of a nation. Whether or not Philippe-Egalité ever seriously aspired to the throne, he was certainly made a tool of by party leaders (such as Danton and Marat) and those who wished to give France a new monarchy in preference to a republic. The part he played in the events of the Revolution did not save Philippe-Egalité from the scaffold, where he died on Nov. 7th, 1793. Memoirs of the time are full of anecdotes about him; he appears to have been the perfect type of a prince as man of the world. His tastes and activities were extremely versatile; he was the first French prince to fight at sea; and he made English ways fashionable in France. *Trans.*

CHAPTER V

Note 12—*This note should read:* A pastiche of these lines from the *Misanthrope* of Molière.

> *Ce style figuré dont on fait vanité,*
> *Sort du bon caractère et de la vérité;*
> *Ce n'est que jeux de mots, qu'affectation pure,*
> *Et ce n'est point ainsi que parle la nature.*
> > *Trans.*

CHAPTER VI

Note 5—*This note should read:* Racine's Britannicus
> *. . . Dans le simple appareil*
> *D'une beauté qu'on vient d'arracher au sommeil.*

The translation of these lines is borrowed from Mary Duclaux's *Life of Racine. Trans.*

CHAPTER X

Following note 3, text, page 161—This formal right of entry (*ordre de début*) and the coach rights (*preuves pour les carrosses*) is here a reference to the custom, established by Louis XVI, of requiring from any aristocrat who was presented to the King (a ceremony called *débuter*) and thereafter allowed to enter the King's carriages, proofs that his patents of nobility dates as far back as 1400, and in direct descent. Tilly devotes a later chapter to this point, relating difficulties he himself encountered over bringing forth such proofs. *Trans.*

CHAPTER XII

Note 2—The translation referred to is that by Mr. Powys Mathers. *Trans.*

CHAPTER XII

Note 6—The line from Destouches is
> *Bravo,*
> *Appuyez, mon neveu:vous faites des merveilles!*
> > *Trans.*

CHAPTER XV

Following note 10, text, page 243, at the words *sponging-house*—Tilly uses the English term. This institution, often referred to in the novels of the eighteenth century, was the house, frequently the private dwelling of the bailiff, in which a well-to-do debtor was confined for 24 hours after arrest, to give his friends an opportunity to settle the debt and save him from being put in prison. *Trans.*

CHAPTER XVII

Following note 4, text, page 275, at the word *Luciennes*—Louveciennes. Tilly spells the name wrongly. It may not be here out of place to mention that Mme du Barry was far from deserving the hatred meted out to her, Mistress to Louis XV, known as the *roué*, "we must pity her," writes Pierre de Nolhac in his *Autour de la Reine* (1929) "to have been at the school of so terrible a master." But it remains true, nevertheless, that judging from documents of the time, "moralists and lords, men at court and revolutionaries, all have agreed to trace a sympathetic figure in Mme du Barry," whose distinctive quality appears to have been "goodness of heart." The fine chapter of Pierre de Nolhac in *Autour de la Reine* goes a long way towards rehabilitating a much maligned woman. *Trans.*

INDEX OF NAMES